ABOUT THE AUTHOR

BARNABY ROGERSON was conceived upon a yacht and born in Dunfermline. He shares a birthday with the Ayatollah Khomeini and first visited Morocco when he was sixteen, on an errand to buy fresh vegetables for his mother from the market at Tetouan. He has been going back ever since but otherwise uses his time to restore temples and lay pebble floors in grottos.

CADOGAN GUIDES

Other titles in the Cadogan Guide series:

AUSTRALIA
BALI
THE CARIBBEAN
GREEK ISLANDS
INDIA
IRELAND
ITALIAN ISLANDS
ITALY
ROME
SCOTLAND
SPAIN
TURKEY
THAILAND & BURMA
TUSCANY & UMBRIA

Forthcoming:

COLOMBIA,
   ECUADOR &
   THE
   GALAPAGOS
NEW YORK
NEW ORLEANS
MEXICO
PORTUGAL
TUNISIA
VENICE

Dear Readers,
        Please keep writing as each letter helps towards a better book. The best letter
writers will receive a free guide of their choice.

The Publisher

CADOGAN GUIDES

MOROCCO

BARNABY ROGERSON

Illustrations by Pauline Pears

CADOGAN BOOKS

LONDON

Cadogan Books Ltd
(Holding Company – Metal Bulletin PLC)
16 Lower Marsh, London SE1

Cover design Keith Pointing
Cover illustration Povl Webb
Maps Copyright © Cadogan Books Ltd,
Thames Cartographic Services Ltd

Series Editors: Rachel Fielding and Paula Levey

First published in 1989

British Library Cataloguing in Publication Data

Rogerson, Barnaby Hugh, *1960–*
  Morocco.
  Morocco—Visitors' guides
  I. Title
  916.4′045

  ISBN 0–946313–84–9

Photoset in Ehrhardt on a Linotron 202
Printed and bound in Great Britain by Redwood Burn Ltd,
Trowbridge, Wiltshire

First edition 1989

CONTENTS

Introduction

Part I: General Information *Pages 1–31*

Part II: Moroccan Culture *Pages 32–86*

LIST OF MAPS

PLEASE NOTE

Every effort has been made to ensure the accuracy of the information in this book at the time of going to press. However, practical details such as opening hours, travel information, standards in hotels and restaurants and, in particular, prices are liable to change.

We intend to keep this book as up-to-date as possible in the coming years. Please write to us if there is anything you feel should be included in future editions.

ix

ACKNOWLEDGEMENTS

I would like to thank Michael Scott for the loan of a house in Tangier and for freely sharing the secrets of an extensive library and his long experience of Morocco. His friends in Tangier, David Herbert, Gordon and Eleanor Brown and Bruce Conde were no less generous with their knowledge and hospitality. I am particularly indebted to Bruce Conde for lending his unpublished manuscript on the Andalucian influence on Tetouan, Chechaouen and Martil. To Paula for giving me the job, Rachel for maintaining high tolerance levels within days of giving birth, Becky for speeding things up and Michael Brett of SOAS for his incisive comments on Moroccan history.

Others who have kindly talked or walked Morocco with me are Nellie Piggot, James Graham Stewart, Hannah Rothschild, Laura Keene, Sebastian Crewe, Milly Dunne, Saville Ryan, Christopher Gibbs, Mary Clow, Melissa North, Araminta Aldington, Eddie Beezley, Richard Jackson, Captain Zoomba, Mohammed from Tangier, Ezzireg Mustapha from Sefrou, Hatim Lahcen from Boujad, Bouhambi Hassan from Midelt, Colonel Abdesalam Bouziane from Rabat, Mr Hajouji of the Moroccan Tourist Board and Madame Fatima from Al Hoceima.

I am indebted to my parents for many years of shared enthusiasm for Moroccan adventures, a word processor and research on bird and plant life. To Rose Baring for the language section, for bringing out a back axle to Agadir, for reading, advising and for over a year sharing her life with me.

INTRODUCTION

If travel is a search for lost paradise, the Muslim Kingdom of Morocco is large and mysterious enough to infinitely prolong the quest. It has an exoticism all of its own, created by the conflicting influences that have washed against this northwestern corner of Africa. Whatever your experience of the latin temper of southern Europeans, the heady lifestyle of Morocco is more dramatic. From the moment you land adventure assails you. In simple transactions, like buying a kilo of oranges, there is unexpected drama, humour and competitive gamesmanship.

The sun is always shining somewhere in Morocco, and from March to October it is difficult to avoid. Travelling from the cool peaks of the Atlas mountains to the baking heat of a Saharan oasis, or from the city of Marrakesh to a beach, is cheap and easy. You can fly, drive, take the train, or share the tempo of native life by packing into a communal taxi or bus.

It is not only the sites of Morocco—the Roman ruins, the ancient cities, mountain kasbahs and elegant Islamic monuments—but also the everyday way of life that lingers in the memory. A concert of scents will haunt you: the pungent fragrance of the spice market; breakfast of fresh coffee and croissants; the heavy odour of virgin olive oil; and the pyramids of fruit, vegetables and nuts which are so fresh and pure they seem like a new species altogether.

Moroccan life, landscape and culture is extraordinarily diverse, but ultimately it is the people that prove most fascinating. In any one Moroccan there may lurk a turbulent and diverse ancestry: of slaves brought across the Saharan wastes to serve as concubines or warriors; of Andalucian refugees who came from the ancient Muslim and Jewish cities of southern Spain, and of Bedouin Arabs from the tribes which fought their way along the North African shore. All these peoples have mingled with the indigenous Berbers, who have continuously occupied the land since the Stone Age. The ruler of Morocco, King Hassan II, shares these influences as well as being a direct descendent of the prophet Mohammed. He explains the peculiar temperament of his country by likening it to the desert palm: rooted in Africa, watered by Islam, and rustled by the winds of Europe.

The frenetic energy, noisy animation, odours and ceaseless babble of the streets initially threaten to overwhelm a visitor. In Morocco, however do as the Moroccans do. A certain wry but friendly sense of humour is all that is needed to cope with the anarchic but addictive lifestyle.

MOROCCO

N

0   200km

Madeira (Port)

ATLANTIC

OCEAN

Canary Isles (Sp)

Tarfa

Laayoune

Bou Craa

Ad-Dakhla

Fderik

Lagouiria Nouadhibou

Land over 1000m

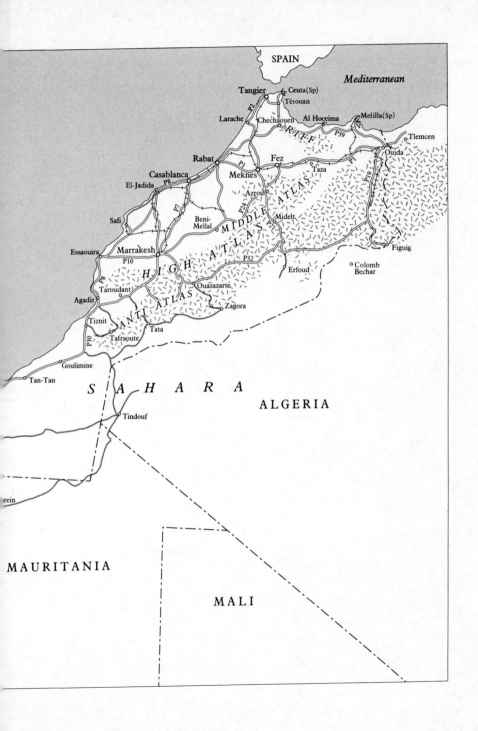

Part I

GENERAL INFORMATION

Fantasia rider

Getting to Morocco

By Air

From Britain

Gibraltar Airways started a service in March 1989 flying from Gatwick to Casablanca, via Gibraltar on Tuesdays, and via Tangier on Fridays. Royal Air Maroc fly from Terminal 2, Heathrow, five times a week to Agadir, four a week to Casablanca, five a week to Marrakesh and twice weekly to Tangier. The flights depart between 16.15 to 17.30 and take between three and five hours. By booking a fortnight in advance and by naming your return date you can get a flight to Tangier for £145 or Marrakesh for £185. Tickets from 174, Regent Street, London W1, tel 01–439–8854. Flight times are given in local time which throughout the winter is the same in both Britain and Morocco.

Charter flights are generally cheaper, less comfortable and for stays of exactly one or two weeks. They fly from Gatwick or provincial airports principally to Tangier or Agadir. Over Christmas, Easter and other peak periods they can cost more than a regular Royal

Air Maroc flight. Off-season last minute tickets have been picked up for £40 but usually expect to pay around £110 for a return to Tangier. Check prices and availability from any travel agent or look in the bucket shop ads in the back pages of *Time Out*, *Private Eye*, *The Sunday Times* and *The Observer*.

An alternative is to catch one of the regular British/GB Airways flights to Gibraltar. A late booked ticket, bought the day before the flight, costs £72 for a single or £59 for a standby, whilst an apex return can be £134. There are often special deals available or charter seats. A useful specialist in this field is Gibraltar Travel at 24, New Broadway, London W5, tel 01–579–0307. Gibraltar is connected by two flights a day to Tangier on Monday, Tuesday, Wednesday and Friday. It is a memorable but short flight with 'instant saver' returns for £32 or single standbys for £19. For up to date GibAir information telephone London, 01–897–4000, Gibraltar 79200/79852 or Tangier 35211.

From France

Paris has the best air connections with Morocco. The routes are shared equally between Air France and Royal Air Maroc. There are 30 flights a week to Casablanca, 12 to Marrakesh and half a dozen each to Agadir, Oujda, Tangier, Fez and Rabat. From provincial cities like Toulouse, Strasbourg, Nice, Marseille, Lyon and Bordeaux there are at least twice weekly flights direct to Casablanca.

Air France offices can be found at 119 Av. des Champs Elysées, 75384 Paris, tel 42–99–23–64, or in the Latin quarter at 62, Rue Monsieur le Prince, 75006 Paris, tel 43–23–81–40. Royal Air Maroc at 34, Av. de l'Opera, 75002 Paris, tel 47–42–10–36/42–66–10–30.

From North America

It is cheaper to fly across the Atlantic and pick up a regular flight from Paris or London. If cost is not your primary concern there are frequent direct flights from New York to Casablanca, Rabat and Tangier. Montreal has weekly Royal Air Maroc flights to Agadir, Casablanca, Fez and Marrakesh. The fares are currently around $3,356 first class, $1414 economy. In high season an apex flight booked a week in advance is $680, low season $580.

The Royal Air Maroc office is at 666, 5th Av., New York, NY 10019, tel 212–974–3845 and in Montreal is found at 1001, De Maisonneuve West, tel 285–16–87. Students can get a 20% reduction by buying directly from these offices.

By Ferry

There are no ferries from Britain or Northern Europe to Morocco.

From France

The car ferry *Marrakesh* sails from Sète, near Marseille, three times a week in summer and once a week over the winter, taking 36 hours to arrive in Tangier. This is a popular

French passage but an odd route from Britain. You need to book in advance at the SNCM office at 4, Quai d'Alger, Sète, tel 67–74–70–55.

From Spain

Almeria
The 10-hour trip from Almeria to Melilla is covered by five sailings a week in the summer and three in the winter. Tickets from Intercona at Parque Jose Antonio 26, tel Almeria 23–63–56.

Malaga
Ferries run daily throughout the summer for the 8-hour trip to Melilla and in the winter there are sailings every day apart from Sunday. Two boats a week travel to Tangier, a 5-hour sail, throughout the year. Tickets from Limadet, Muelle Heredia 8, tel 22–33–05 or Trasmediterranea, Calle Juan Diaz 4, tel 22–43–93.

Algeciras
This is by far the quickest, cheapest and most popular connection to Morocco. Of the two choices of destination—Tangier and Ceuta—the sailing to Ceuta is temptingly cheaper and quicker, but the lack of public transport and delays at the border crossing can make this a false economy. Unless you want to visit Ceuta it is easier, even with a car, to go to Tangier. All ferry tickets can be bought at the port gates, Recinto del Puerto, tel 66–52–00.

In high season there are 12 one and a half hour crossings to Ceuta a day, and 8 in the winter. Prices in 1988 were 1100ptas for a single passenger, 4380ptas for a small car and 1090ptas for a 250cc motorbike.

In high season there are three or four crossings to Tangier, down to one or two in the winter. 2550ptas for a single passenger, 7500ptas for a car and 2400ptas for a motorbike. The journey takes two and a half hours.

Transtour run daily, passenger only, hour-long hydrofoil services to Tangier for about £8.00. They will not run in rough weather or on Sundays. In summer a service also runs to M'diq.

Tarifa
From here, for about £8.00 as well, you can catch the half-hour hydrofoil to Tangier.

Gibraltar
The celebrated steamer SS *Mons Calpe* no longer connects Tangier to Gibraltar. Transtour run a daily hour-long passenger service for £12.00.

By Train

From Britain
Leave from Victoria Station, London, for the Folkestone or Dover crossing and then south to Paris.

3

From France

The night train leaves the Gare de Lyon, Paris, at 22.00 and arrives at Algeciras 36 hours later. Alternatively there is an Intercity Express service between Paris and Madrid, where you can change for Algeciras. Information from L'Office d'Informations des Chemins de Fer Espagnols, 3, Av. Marceau, 75016 Paris, tel 47–23–52–01 or SNCF information (France), tel 45–82–50–50.

Discount tickets

Transalpino/Eurotrain is available from any European city for the journey to Morocco. Inclusive of the Algeciras ferry crossing it works out at 35% below the normal price, i.e. about £80 single and £160 return. The London Transalpino office is at 71 Buckingham Palace Road, SW1, tel 01–834–9656.

InterRail. This gives an under-26-year-old free rail travel in Europe and Morocco for a month at £140 and half price on ferry crossings. Remember that express trains and sleepers will require a supplement and that British Rail will charge a half-fare to the channel ferry port. Available from British Rail travel centres.

Eurail. Non-Europeans are not supposed to be able to buy InterRail, and the Eurail youth pass, for those under 26, costs $310 for a month or $400 for two months. It has all the disadvantages of InterRail and is also invalid for Morocco.

By Bus

From Britain

Between April and September four buses a week leave Victoria coach station for the two-day drive south to Algeciras. A single ticket from Eurolines, tel 01–430–0202, is £64.00, a return £104.00. Reduced services run over the winter and students can get a 10% reduction.

From France

Eurolines leave Paris from La Porte de la Villette station on Monday, Wednesday, Friday and Saturday for Casablanca. Depart 10.30, arrive two days later in Tiznit at 15.00, having stopped at Tangier, Rabat, Casablanca, Marrakesh and Agadir. Single to Tangier 845FF, return 1410FF, to Tiznit single 1075FF, return 1780FF. Another bus departs on Wednesday and Saturday at 10.30 arriving at Nador two days later at 11.00, having stopped at Tangier, Meknes, Fez, Taza and Oujda. A single to Fez, 955FF, return 1590FF, to Oujda or Nador, single 1020FF, return 1695FF. For reservations tel Eurolines at Port de la Villette on (1) 40–38–93–93 or (1) 42–05–12–10.

By Car

It is possible with two drivers and very little rest to get from England to Tangier in two days, although four or five days would allow you to enjoy something other than fast driving.

There is a full range of Brittany and P&O ferries connecting the various channel ports of France and England. The most useful is the Portsmouth–Le Havre night crossing. The ferries pass close by the naval base with the rigging of HMS *Victory* and HMS *Warrior* floodlit in contrast to the sinister black of berthed submarines or the silent grey of type 22 destroyers in active service. Arriving at Cherbourg or Le Havre in the early morning you can cross France that day to camp or stay in the Pyrenean foothills that night. Crossing Spain can be taken more leisurely, perhaps stopping at Segovia before concentrating on the splendours of Moorish Andalucia at Granada, Cordoba and Seville.

There is a twice-weekly ferry from Plymouth to Santander, no sailings in January, but it is an expensive and tedious voyage. Ferry cafés compare badly in expense, entertainment and quality with the roadside inns of France and Spain.

Travel Agents

There are four Moroccan specialists who give good advice on hotels for an itinerary, book rooms and can arrange flights and car hire: **Creative Leisure**, suite 25–30, 12/13 Henrietta Street, London WC2, tel 01–836–2916; **Morocco Bound**, suite 603, Triumph House, 189 Regent Street, London W1, tel 01–734–5307; **Moroccan Travel Bureau**, 304 Old Brompton Road, London SW5, tel 01–373–4411; **Morocco Made to Measure**, 4a, William Street, London SW1, tel 01–235–2110.

'Adventure' Tours

You will get more adventure and satisfaction by travelling on normal buses in Morocco than with a group of tourists tucked into a truck and shepherded by a guide. By hiring a landrover or even a Renault 4 you will be able to travel anywhere that an adventure tour goes. This adventure touring is however a growing business, and their brochures full of maps and pictures make harmless browsing.

Topdeck run a 5- or 7-week tour through Spain, Portugal, Morocco, Algeria, Tunisia and Italy, a whistle-stop cultural skirmish that is popular with foreign students and Australians: 64–65, Kenway Road, London SW5, tel 01–373–5095.

Encounter Overland run a 15-day tour of Morocco (between May and September) which starts from Malaga and costs around £355 from 267, Old Brompton Road, London SW5, tel 01–370–6845. **Guerba**, 101 Eden Vale Rd, Westbury, Wiltshire, tel 0373–826–611, **Explore Worldwide**, 7 High Street, Aldershot, Hampshire, tel 0252 319–448, and **Exodus**, 1st floor, 27/31, Jerdan Place, Fulham, London SW6 1BE, tel 01–385–0176, also run similar trips.

Package Tours

The **Moroccan Tourist Office**, 174 Regent Street, London W1R 6HB, tel 01–437–0073, collate all the available package tours and distribute a tempting photocopied sheet of the prices. If you already know where you want to go, these companies can be a useful way of getting reduced prices from some of the most elegant and expensive hotels, like Tangier's **El Minzah**, Fez's **Palais Jamai**, Marrakesh's **Mamounia** or Taroudant's **Gazelle D'Or** or **Palais Salaam**. Telephone the agents direct for their current brochure; **Horizon**—tel 021–632 6282, **Wings**—tel 021–632–6282, **Cosmos**—tel 01–464–4300, **Thomson**—tel 01–387–8484, **Cadogan Travel**—tel 0703–332551, **Creative Leisure**—tel 01–235–0123, **Enterprise**—tel 0293–560777, **Sovereign**—tel 0293–517866, **Martin Rooks**—tel 01–730–0808, **Morocco Bound**—tel 01–734–5307, **The best of Morocco**—tel 0622–46678, **Standard**—tel 01–254–6444, **Kouni**—tel 0306–740500, **Hayes and Jarvis**—tel 01–245–1051, **Club Mediterranie**—tel 01–581–1161, **Longshot Golf Holidays**—tel 0730–66561, **Moroccan Sun**—tel 01–437–3968, **Just Morocco**—tel 01–372–6161, **Abercrombie and Kent**—tel 01–730–9600.

Passports and Visas

A valid Australian, British, Canadian, New Zealand and United States passport allows you to enter Morocco for 90 days. Temporary passports are not accepted. Long hair, Israeli and South African entry stamps are all official reasons for refusing entry to Morocco, but if you are stopped for any of these reasons there is nothing to stop you trying a different boat, port or immigration officer on another day.

For extending a visit beyond 90 days you are officially required to report to a gendarmerie headquarters. In practice even these officials recommend a day trip across to Ceuta, Gibraltar or Melilla for a fresh stamp and visa.

As a retaliation for Benelux restrictions on Moroccan migrant workers, Dutch and Belgian passports now require a visa which is valid for only a month.

Customs

You are allowed to bring a litre of spirits into the country. The customs are very alert on the import of cars to Morocco. Do not sell your car, however tempting the offer. Even if it irrevocably breaks down you will be required to tow it out of Morocco before you can leave.

Moroccan National Tourist Board

The Tourist Board, the ONMT and French-styled Syndicats D'Initiatives are found in every city and even in most small towns of Morocco. They are useful as a source of official guides, glossy handouts, hotels, the dates of local festivals, the location of rural souks and the odd local map. They are seldom informative about local history but very keen on the regular run of tourist sites, bazaars and large hotels.

Before you depart for Morocco one visit to the office of the Tourist Board can stock you up with the full range of handouts. There is a useful green booklet of all the classified hotels, a collection of package tour prices, a sheet of this year's maximum hotel prices and half a dozen coloured regional leaflets. In London look in at 174, Regent Street, W1, tel 01–437–0073/74, in Paris at 161, Rue Saint Honore, Place du Théâtre Français, tel 260–64–78, New York at 20, East 46th Street, 5th floor, Suite 503, NY 10017 and in Toronto at 2, Carlton Street, suite 1803, Toronto, M5B 1K2.

Where and When to go

The Tourist Board claim 350 days of sunshine a year, and as hotels and restaurants remain open throughout the year, any month is a good time to visit Morocco. There are however seasonal variations to take into account when planning the shape of your holiday.

From November to March there is the possibility of rain, and except for Tangier you will find the northern beach resorts distinctly off season. The flowers, temperate climate and lack of tourists make it a good time to tour central Morocco providing you are not interested in a tan. This is the prime period to visit the oasis valleys of the Sahara, Agadir, Taroudant and the Western Sahara, which are all bearably hot and comparatively green in these months. February sees Tafraoute and the Anti Atlas at its best, although weather may include rain.

March, April and May are reliably but not crippling hot and the countryside with its fast ripening harvest and busy rural souks is at its most interesting. It is a good period for a general tour of the country.

June, July and August are the hottest and busiest tourist months, with little activity in evidence during the heat of the day. The farmland is baked dry and most schools, offices and industries have stopped work. The nation is on holiday, if not at the beach. These months however witness most of the moussems and festivals. The High and Middle Atlas mountains are at their most accessible and attractive in these months.

September and October witness a slight but welcome reduction in temperature and in the crowds. Olives and dates are ripening and these two months make another fine period for a general exploration of the country.

The temperature chart below may be of some use, though these are monthly averages which hide an often dramatic range in daily temperature. Even in the mid-summer months a sweater may be useful against evening coastal breezes, the cool of the high mountain peaks and the desert nights. At the very least it can be moulded into a pillow for long bus journeys.

Chart to show average temperatures in Fahrenheit

	Jan	Feb	Mar	Apr	May	June	July	Aug	Sept	Oct	Nov	Dec
Agadir	69	70	72	75	76	78	80	79	79	78	76	69
Hoceima	61	62	65	67	72	78	83	85	81	74	69	63
Casablanca	63	63	66	68	72	75	81	81	80	77	68	64
Essaouira	64	64	64	66	68	68	72	70	70	70	68	66
Fez	61	63	66	72	79	88	97	97	90	81	66	61
Marrakesh	66	66	73	79	84	91	102	101	91	82	66	61
Meknes	59	61	64	70	74	84	93	93	86	79	66	61
Ouazazarte	63	67	73	80	86	96	102	100	91	80	70	62
Rabat	63	64	66	70	73	77	82	82	81	77	68	64
Tangier	59	61	62	66	72	77	80	82	79	73	64	61
Taroudant	72	73	79	81	86	90	99	100	96	90	77	72
Safi	64	66	68	72	77	81	86	86	82	79	70	66
Zagora	69	73	78	86	93	102	108	106	97	86	78	70

A Traveller's Checklist

A photocopy of the first four pages of your passport may come in handy if you mislay it for any reason. Visit the Tourist Office for leaflets, and look at the Book List (pp. 544–47) before buying your holiday reading. Each Eurocheque can cash up to a maximum of 2000dh; check that you have more than enough. A corkscrew and knife for picnics, a good lighter, a torch, a spare bath plug, one roll of soft loo paper and a packet of Immodium and Nurofen provides a useful holiday survival pack.

To ease your passage around the country, as presents buy a stock of amusing decorated pens and anything with a football or Bob Marley motif. Printed tee-shirts and Bob Marley cassettes are immensely popular and can be useful trading items.

Getting Around

Distance chart (in kms) between principal cities, by road

	Agadir	Casa	Fez	G'mine	M'kesh	Oujda	Rabat	Tangier
Agadir		490	739	199	256	1082	608	860
Casablanca	490		290	689	234	633	92	370
Fez	739	290		938	483	343	198	307
Goulimine	199	689	938		465	1281	807	1059
Marrakesh	256	234	483	465		826	541	604
Oujda	1082	633	343	1281	826		541	604
Rabat	608	92	198	807	326	541		278
Tangier	860	370	307	1059	604	604	278	

By Air

There are plenty of internal flights between the principal cities of Morocco, though the timetables shift constantly. Contact the nearest Royal Air Maroc office for details—and to give you a rough idea of prices, it currently costs about £55 to fly from Tangier to Agadir.

Additional connections

As well as flights between the obvious cities, you can fly from Casablanca to Laayoune, Hoceima from Agadir to Laayoune, Ad-Dakhla and Tantan, from Marrakesh to Ouazazarte and from Laayoune to Smara.

By Train

The Moroccan state railway service, the SNCF, runs over 1700 km of line on two axes, from Tangier to Marrakesh and Casablanca to Oujda. Both these long routes have a sleeper service but otherwise daytime travel is divided between 1st, 2nd and 3rd class. A second-class ticket is not much more than the bus fare, though the air conditioning and limited seating of 1st class makes this especially attractive in the summer. A bar and restaurant operates on the major connections. For details of prices and daily departures, look under 'Getting Around' in the relevant sections of the guide.

Under-26-year-olds can, of course, travel with their InterRail cards in Morocco.

By Bus

Morocco is well served by buses, which apart from being a quick, cheap and convenient way across the country are a pleasure in themselves. Musicians, beggars and vendors collect around bus stops throughout the country and often wander down the aisle before departure. There is an undoubted camaraderie of travel, and buses are one of the best places in which to meet some of the vast majority of unhustling Moroccans, a relaxing place to gather unbiased information, exchange oranges or cigarettes, enjoy unusually frank discussions and perhaps collect an invitation to tea.

There is a barrage of bus companies that all enjoy some level of state or provincial funding. CTM (or SATAS in the south) is the efficient national network. Local firms tend to run older, slower buses that stop more frequently and only leave when they are full. Above CTM in speed and comfort is ONCF, the state railway, which runs inter-city express coaches connecting cities like Agadir, Tetouan, Nador, Beni Mellal and Laayoune to the railway system. Tickets are up to 50% more, but as buses are so cheap anyway these are well worth buying.

Increasingly in each town, all bus companies are being brought together in one terminal. This makes buying tickets in advance for popular inter-city routes an easy and effortless procedure. Even if companies still run separate depots, check out the travel situation yourself as soon as you have deposited your bags. Hotel porters, guides and Tourist Offices cannot ultimately be relied upon. It is customary to pay 1 or 2dh for each item of baggage stored on the roof but not for the use of the side lockers.

By Taxi

Travelling by 'place' in a **grand taxi** should work out only a few dirhams more than a bus ride. At specific collection spots, which are mentioned throughout the guide, taxi drivers shout out their destination and if there is none going in your direction ask around. However, as six passengers are packed into a white diesel Mercedes before the taxi will leave, this method of travel has the advantage of speed but not always of comfort.

Grands taxis only travel on routes where they can be sure of picking up a full load. For more individual destinations you will have to bargain a price for the journey or employ the taxi for the whole day. Though much more than a 'place', when compared to hiring a car it appears reasonable enough.

Petit taxis are limited to three passengers and the city limits. Outside of Fez, Casablanca and Rabat the meters seldom seem to function. The going rate for locals is around 1 to 2dh per person but as a tourist expect to pay around 10dh a journey.

By Car

A British or EEC driving licence is valid in Morocco and a car may remain in the country for 6 months duty free. You will need to bring your Vehicle Registration document and the International Green Card will have to be extended to give you third party insurance in Morocco. Fire and theft insurance can be arranged with the Norwich Union for a month but no company is yet prepared to give comprehensive cover for any longer period. If you are bringing a caravan you will need an International Customs Carnet.

Petrol is roughly the same price as in Britain and stations are reasonably well distributed. Moroccan mechanics are among some of the more resourceful and innovative in the world. I witnessed a clutch plate carved from an old Bedford truck in Er-Rachidia being fitted into an Alfa Romeo, though if you are driving a Renault, Peugeot or Landrover there should be no lack of orthodox spare parts.

Driving on the near empty Moroccan country roads is a treat in itself. Remember to drive on the righthand side. Watch out for lorries on narrow roads, as they will expect you to move out of the way. Vehicles coming from the righthand side have priority, so give way to cars coming on to a roundabout. Driving in cities becomes especially confusing with streams of mopeds and cyclists weaving through the traffic. It is often better to find a hotel, park and then forget your car. Beware of patches of gravel on the hairpin bends of mountain roads which can have the same effect as ice. Though comparatively empty of cars, the roads seldom lack wayside fruit stalls, dogs, drifting livestock, cyclists and children.

I saw two children killed in the confused light of dusk by a careless lorry driver. The road was quickly filled with ululating women. Angry farmers rushed in from the fields armed with hoes and forks to demand instant justice from the police who were, fortunately, at hand. Be careful.

Car Hire

Buses, though admirably friendly, keep you on well-established routes. In practice, despite the best of intentions, you often end up whizzing from one tourist feature to another. By hiring a car you can explore empty sites and the magnificent and hospitable countryside of Morocco.

In each city section of the guide, full list of car hire firms is given. Even the big agencies are often prepared to drop prices or do deals in tune with the season and demand. The various offices are usually found in close proximity to each other on the major avenue of the new town. It is worth shopping around and finding out whether you can return the car to another depot.

As a basic indication, a Renault 4 can be hired for 135dh a day plus a charge of about 1.5dh a km with a 12% tax on top. Mileages can be high and you might opt for a blanket charge of something under 2000dh (£140.00) for the week. At the top end of the rentals, a landrover can be hired for around 6000dh a week, but book in advance to be certain.

Conditions: Minimum rental for one day, a driving licence held for a year by someone over 21, usually 25 for landrovers. A deposit between 2000 and 2500dh, accepted by most agencies through credit cards. Hire includes third party, fire and theft insurance. There are often optional personal insurance policies and you might check the spare tyres and accident coverage if you are planning on any piste driving.

Bicycle, Mopeds and Donkeys

Moroccan enthusiasm for any sport extends to bicyclists who can expect a welcome and consistent interest wherever they go. Ask about bicycle, moped or donkey hire from hotel porters who usually know much more about this shifting pattern of trade than the Tourist Office. A day's bicycle hire is around 50dh, you can buy a donkey for 600dh but rental works out at about 10dh an hour.

Maps

Despite the great care spent over city maps in this guide the Medinas often remain a maze for the first few visits. It is however a great advantage to know the general street pattern. The free coloured Tourist leaflets and the beautifully produced *Editions Gauthey*, 23dh, to Tangier, Rabat–Salé, Casablanca, Agadir, Marrakesh and Meknes certainly help in this.

There are a large number of national road maps to choose from. Bear in mind that any map that marks a border or even a difference in scale between Morocco and the Western Sahara is liable to be confiscated. Road conditions change and most maps seem to contain one or two inaccuracies. Kummerley and Frey (1:100,000), Michelin sheet 169 (1:100,000), Hildebrand (1:900,000) and Reise und Verkehrsverlag (1:800,000) all publish maps which can be used in conjunction with the 'Maroc, Carte Routière, Editions Marcus, Paris' (1:400,000), which is the most accurate and is freely available throughout Morocco for 30dh.

Moroccan survey sheets of the High Atlas (1:50,000) can be obtained from Stanfords Map Centre, Covent Garden, WC2 or McCarta, 122, Kings Cross Road, WC1, tel 01–278–8278. The relevant sheets are also readily sold in Imlil, the centre of the Toubkal National Park, and the central base for High Atlas climbing. For specialist information for walking, 'Guide Collomb: Atlas Mountains' is available from West Col Productions, Goring, Reading, Berks. The Royal Geographical Society have an Expeditionary Advisory Service which runs weekend courses and can point you towards old reports and maps.

Tourist Information

Money

The Moroccan currency is the Dirham which currently fluctuates at about 14dh to the £, 9dh to the US$. It is divided into 100 units, which are officially called centimes but are occasionally and confusingly referred to as francs, pesetas or reales. The denominations of notes are 100, 50 and 10. There are silver-coloured 5, 2 and 1 dirham coins and brass 50, 20, 10 and 5 centime coins.

There are active restrictions against exporting dirhams from the country although you can usually buy dirhams in Malaga, Algeciras or Gibraltar. There are no black-market rates though shop keepers will often be happy enough to accept dollars and European currencies. Keep your currency change slips, for at the departing border you will only be able to change back half what you can prove to have changed in the first place.

Banks, Post Offices, Museums and Opening hours

All of these are efficient, reliable and well distributed around the country. Bank charges, if any at all, are only 5dh a transaction. Banks and Post Offices are open from 8.30–11.30, 15.00–18.00 on Mondays and Fridays and 8.30–14.00 during the month of Ramadan. In the larger cities most banks cash Eurocheques and one can often be found open on Saturday mornings. In towns there will usually be one bank that cashes Eurocheques whilst travellers' cheques can be cashed at all the larger hotels.

Post Office hours are usually 8.30–14.00. They can cash International Giro Cheques, sell stamps (letters 2dh, postcards 1.25dh) and receive Poste Restante mail, although a large hotel is a safer and more accessible address. The central office will normally have a separate international telephone room. These have longer opening hours and, though generally filled with a long long queue, are much cheaper than hotels. Estimate on 10dh a minute to Europe and 30dh a minute across the Atlantic.

Museums decide their own opening hours and can extend the lunch break over most of the afternoon. As a rough guide, think in terms of 9.00–12.00, 15.00–18.00 with a 1–5dh admission ticket plus departing tip to the custodian. They are generally open throughout the week but closed on Tuesday. Medersas will be closed on Friday morning and often fail to reopen until Saturday.

Embassies and Consulates

The British Embassy is in Rabat. There is a consul and his assistant in Tangier and a commercial consul in Casablanca. These and a number of European and American consuls are listed in the body of the guide.

Police and Other Uniforms

The Moroccan police force is modelled on the French, and is divided into two forces—Gendarmerie and Sûreté. The Gendarmerie live under a semi-military discipline, wear serge khaki and green berets and carry batons. They cover both cities and the country-side with a regular grid of barracks, and could be compared to a mixture between a county constabulary and a reserve regiment. The Surété are the grey uniformed and armed police who patrol the roads and the cities. They are more directly concerned with crime and law enforcement and are considered, as in France, more street-wise, sophisti-cated and corrupt. Commonly referred to as 'Ali Baba and the . . .'.

Grey customs officers may be seen, particularly on the northern coast, trying to control the flow of electrical goods smuggled in from Ceuta and Melilla, and kiff being smuggled out. Prison officers wear blue. Firemen wear blue with red piping and might be seen trying to sell their calendars to unwary motorists, particularly on the road south from Tangier. The army, by comparison, look rather underdressed in their plain lovat green uniform.

Tipping

Service charges and tax are added on to most restaurant and hotel bills but a waiter will be happy with another 5dh a head. For parking a car and having it watched, 1dh is accepted throughout Morocco. 1–5dh is the going rate for photographs of camels, water carriers, etc. Museum curators like the odd dirham extra, as do barmen, hairdressers, porters and petrol pump attendants. Taxi drivers are not customarily tipped.

Alms and Beggars

Keep and collect all loose change from cafés for alms and tips. A dirham is considered generous, any more than that and you will be presumed not to recognize the value of money and possibly be asked for more. On the giving of alms the prophet Mohammed says: 'What shall we bestow in alms? Say, "what you can spare." Thus God instructs that you might think more deeply', and 'but if you turn away from them, while you yourself hope for help from God, at least speak to them in a kindly manner.'

Official and Unofficial Guides

These can be hired from the Tourist Office for 30dh for a half-day and 50dh for a whole day. They are well trained in history, fluent in most languages and trustworthy. If you arrive in the evening, want a more varied dialogue, a less stereotyped itinerary or have not yet found the Tourist Office, you will not find it difficult to find yourself an unofficial guide.

Dealing with the attention of unwanted urban guides is one of the recurring problems of travelling in Morocco. The discordant cries of hustlers just as you arrive fresh at a town or the Medina gates can be irritating. Accept this as a facet of Moroccan life. There is certainly no easy way to avoid it short of jumping in a taxi and hiding in a hotel.

A little humility is useful. On your first visit to a large or strange town would some help in finding your hotel or a taxi not be useful? The aggression with which many visitors cold-shoulder themselves through potential helpers then later bemusedly consult their imported maps and guides is a faintly ridiculous, but curious and revealing, insight into European attitudes.

Meet the problem in a Moroccan manner and use qualities of charm and enthusiasm. Enjoy the human skills required in choosing the friendliest character from a group. Greet him with a salaam and a handshake, praise the weather and his town and tell him how delighted you are at last to be here and if need be check out your character judgement over a cup of tea. Tell him exactly where you want to go and what you intend to give, which however rich you are should never be over 10dh.

A guide's natural interest lies in directing you to the Medina. For in the confusing labyrinth of Medina avenues you become more dependent on the guide and here bazaars lurk, and bazaars can earn commissions and kudos for your guide. Be aware of this, and if need be hold out a visit to a bazaar as a carrot at the end of the day.

You will soon find out that the habitat of the hustling guide is almost entirely at bus stops and Medina gates. Marrakesh, Fez, Tangier and particularly Tetouan have hustling reputations. But in all these cities when you know your way around (and show a lack of interest in bazaars) you will find yourself increasingly left alone. As a corollary to this, try not to pack too many large cities into a short itinerary.

When you feel annoyed run over a few relevant facts. An unskilled labouring wage is 3dh an hour. The chances of getting even that in a country of 25% employment is low, whilst with over half the population under 21 years old competition is heavy. Even the British unemployment dole of £30 a week converts into an enviable quantity of dirhams. Under those conditions might you not try your luck at skimming a few dirhams off often arrogant and unfriendly foreigners? A wise old woman told me that the street kids of Tangier reminded her of nothing so much as her youth in Edinburgh.

Kif

In 1840 Hooker and Ball remarked that 'the use of tobacco for smoking appears to be unknown in Morocco while kif, prepared from the chopped leaves of common hemp is almost universally employed for that purpose both by Moors and Berbers.'

The Riff mountains grow some of the best common hemp, *Cannabis indica*, in the world. In the Ketama region its cultivation is legal until another crop can be found that will grow as well on these denuded hills. The hemp is planted in February and harvested in June. The pollen-rich plants are shaken in a gauze-lined hut and the sticky mass kneaded into cakes. This resin is sold by farmers to the gangs who deal in the riskier but profitable smuggling trade to Europe. The cut leaves and flowers are preferred by locals for its gentler aromatic smoke which is inhaled from a thin pipe with a disposable pottery head. Or the flowers and seeds can made into *majoun*, an edible fudge.

In the north of the country discreet possession and use is, in practice, tolerated, and the police concentrate their activities on monitoring the big traders. The law framed in 1954 is, however, quite explicit. Possession, purchase and transportation is illegal, the minimum penalty is three months imprisonment and a 2400dh fine, the maximum, five years and a 240,000dh fine with the confiscation of any camouflage and transport involved.

Visitors who wish to smoke Moroccan kif can reduce the risk of receiving these penalties by buying small quantities for their own use, preferably not in Tangier or Tetouan, and not travelling with any in their possession. For as in all cultures the dealers also double as police informers. It would be foolish and quite misguided to attempt to smuggle kif. Smuggling is an extremely intricate big business which does not tolerate amateurs. Whilst possession of small quantities of kif in Spain is now legal, in Algeria you can be imprisoned for life for this offence.

About a dozen British and twenty Americans are arrested for drug-related offences a year in Morocco. Consuls are unsympathetic but professional, and try to visit within a week of imprisonment, every three months whilst on remand and twice a year during imprisonment. The current penalties run on a rough quantity tariff, a girl hitching from Ketama to Chechaouen with half a kilo strapped to her thigh was given a month in prison and fined. A New Zealand pilot caught loading a light aeroplane got five years and the full fine.

On a note of caution, most of the shake downs and heavy hassles seem to involve kif. Never smoke with someone or somewhere that makes you the slightest bit uneasy.

Lavatories

Most classified hotels and large restaurants are equipped with Anglo-Saxon flush bowls, though water supplies and efficient drainage can be variable, particularly in the summer. It is a wasteful system for a nation grappling with the recurring problems of drought, and has been established largely for the benefit of tourists. Urban cafés and houses have a crouch hole, no paper but a tap for washing your left hand and an old tin for sluicing. There are no public lavatories, though in tanneries you will see urinals that collect urine for use later in curing the hides.

Electricity and Gas

220 volts AC has now largely replaced the 110 volt AC system. On or off the grid cooking, heating and lighting is largely dependent on charcoal or gas. The ubiquitous blue gas bottles are subsidized by the government as one of the principal dependencies of the poor.

Cameras

'Destroying the present for an unsatisfactory image of the past in the future.' Films can be developed and bought from most large towns. Excluding anything remotely military, you are free to photograph anything architectural. Do not photograph anybody, least of all a rural woman, without permission. Be prepared to tip for photographing animals or people.

Health, Chemists and Medicines

No inoculations are officially required to enter Morocco. For peace of mind, you should be up to date on your typhoid, cholera, tetanus and polio immunization and you might talk to your doctor about the pros and cons of a hepatitis jab. In the far south anti-malarial pills are sometimes advised during the summer, though these can cause various side-effects. Bilharzia worms lurk in some of the oasis streams and still pools south of the High Atlas though I have swum and waded through many with no ill effects—yet. Tap water is quite safe north of Marrakesh though you may prefer to drink from the ubiquitous bottles of Sidi Ali and Sidi Harazem mineral water. It is considered by connoisseurs to be amongst the best mineral water in the world.

Travel insurance can be brought in Britain from travel agents, banks and airports for less than £15 for a month's cover. The chemists are usually knowledgeable, sympathetic and well stocked throughout Morocco and can often recommend a French-speaking doctor. They sell contraceptives, including the pill, but tampons, soap, shampoo and toilet paper are often easier to find in a general store. Even the most basic travel kit should include a good supply of painkillers and Immodium for rapid relief of diarrhoea. For most big cities, medical addresses have been given in the guide. The larger package-tour hotels often have a medical specialist. In an emergency, dial 19 for the police or 15 for an ambulance.

Sexual Attitudes

'In the towns and among the Arabic speaking mountaineers of Northern Morocco, where pederasty is exceedingly prevalent it is practically regarded with indifference' (Westermark).

'Abd as Slam, Malika's husband is young and handsome. Like most young Moroccan men in Tangier he dreams of finding a rich Christian woman who will take him to Europe or the States and make him a rich man.'

Moroccans traditionally have an uncomplicated attitude to sex but a great respect for outward forms and standards of dress. Homosexuality is neither scandalous nor unusual and is socially treated not so much as a condition but as a mere matter of personal taste. The Koran cautions against celibacy, 'as to the monastic life they invented it themselves . . . many of them were perverse'. To the confusion of Jewish and Christian sexual guilt, the Koran freely acknowledges sexual appetite, 'your wives are your field, go in therefore to your field as you will but do first some act for your soul's good', and is only mildly disapproving of homosexuality—'come ye to men, instead of women lustfully? Ye are indeed a people given up to excess.'

Islam has been in advance of Western sexual attitudes for centuries. However in Sura 414 the Koran declares, 'God desireth to make your [women's] burden light, for men have been created wiser . . . Men are superior to women' and elsewhere, 'Blessed art thou O Lord God who hath not made me a woman.' These can be interpreted gnostically, but male Arab attitudes remain harder to dismiss. 'The conception of the woman as a lust-driven animal that must be kept under lock and key is one of the sickest and most disgusting aspects of Arab culture.' For the woman traveller these attitudes entail some extra consideration, although little more alteration in dress or attitude than is required in any Mediterranean country. The easiest way for women to cope is to play one of the stereotyped but recognizeable 'unavailable' roles: the wife, the mother, the intellectual, etc., though travelling with a companion or a man would be more relaxing. If you do travel with a man, the most irritating thing will be the way in which any decision will be instantly referred to him by the Moroccans.

In 1987 there were only six cases of Aids acknowledged though one would have presumed many more. The Health Ministry plans to screen all blood stocks by the end of 1988. Public education on the spread of the virus has been low key. As yet only the king has managed to break through the general reluctance to air these matters publicly, and given a few general talks on television.

Public Holidays

National Holidays on the Gregorian Calendar
  1 January, New Year's Day
  3 March, Feast of the Throne
  1 May, Labour Day
  14 August, Allegiance Day
  6 November, Day of the Green March
  18 November, Independence Day

Muslim Holidays are based on a lunar calendar which looses 11 days a year (or 12 in a leap year) against the Gregorian Calendar. The great events of the Islamic year are the fast month of Ramadan and the feast of Aid es Seghir which celebrates its end. Aid el Kebir commemorates Abraham's sacrifice of a lamb instead of his son and is a great excuse for family reunions. Moharran is the feast of the Muslim New Year and Mouloud the prophet's birthday.

In 1989 Ramadan starts on 8 April and finishes with the feast of Aid es Seghir on 8 May. Aid el Kebir is on 15 July, Moharran on 4 August and Mouloud on 14 October.

For 1990, subtract 11 days to find that Ramadam starts on 29 March, Aid es Seghir on 28 April, Aid el Kebir on 5 July, Moharran on 24 July and Mouloud on 3 October.

For 1991, subtract 11 days; . . . etc.

Ramadan

This is the Muslim equivalent of Lent. The fast has remained a great institution in Islam and is cherished as an act that binds the whole nation, if not the entire Muslim community, together in a month of asceticism. Apart from the sick, travellers, children and pregnant women, Ramadan involves abstaining from food, sex, drink and cigarettes during the hours of daylight.

Non-Muslims are not involveu, but you will find many cafés, bars and licensed grocers firmly closed. It is insensitive to smoke, eat or drink in public during Ramadan. It can be more rewarding to join Ramadan quietly as a volunteer, sharing the exuberance at dusk when the daily fast ends with a bowl of harira soup and the grill cafés fill up with customers and music. A spirit of relief breaks out across the nation and continues deep into the night.

Festivals

As well as the national and Islamic calendar there are numerous local festivals, of which only the more prominent have been listed below. They celebrate a saint or a harvest with a vivid week- or day-long fair mixed with food, dance and religious music. A number of tourist-oriented moussems have been added, most successful of which is the magnificent **Folklore Festival** held at the end of June in Marrakesh.

The dates are impossible to predict accurately, and you will have to ask a local Tourist Office for information nearer the event. Over Mouloud there is a moussem at **Moulay Brahim**, a candle procession at **Salé** and the Aissawa moussem at **Meknes**.

Date	Place	Celebration
February	Tafraoute	Festival of Almond blossom
March	Casablanca	Festival of Theatre
End of April	Fez	Student fête of Sidi Harazem
May	Essaouira	El Katania
May	Immouzer Ida Ouatane	Honey fête
May	El Kelaa Mgouna	Rose festival
June	Sidi Ifni	Moussem
End of June	Marrakesh	Folklore Festival & Fantasia
June	Oulad Teima	Sidi Bou Moussa
June	Sefrou	Cherry fête
June	Asni	Moulay Ibrahim
End of June?	Tantan	Moussem
June	Goulimine	Moussem at Asrir
June	Larache	Abdelkader Jilali
July	Asni	El Aounia
July	Immouzer du Kandahar	Apple harvest
July	Marrakesh	Sidi ben Yasmin
July	Martil	Water festival
August	Moussem of zaouia of Sidi Ahmed ou Moussa	
August	Mehdia	Sidi Boughaba
August	Moulay Idriss	Moussem
August	Ourika	Setti Fatima
August	Rabat	Dar Zhirou
August	Sefrou	Sidi Lahcen Lyoussi
August	Azzemour	Moussem
9 August	Chechaouen	Sidi Allal el Haj
August	Moulay Abdullah	Moussem
August	Tiznit	Sidi Abder Rahman
September	Agadir	Fête of African music
September	Fez	Moulay Idriss & El Bernoussi
September	Skhirat	Moussem
September	Tangier	Dar Zhirou & Musical fête
September	Taza	Sidi Ahmed Zerrouk
September	Moulay Bousselham	Sidi Ahmed ben Mansour
September	Ouazazarte	Moussem
September	Oujda	Sidi Yahia
September	Boujad	Sidi Mohammed ech Chergi
September	Meknes	Fantasia

September	Imilchil	Marriage fête
October, 1st week	Tissa	Horse fête
October	Fez	Driss El Azhar
October	Essaouiria	Music fête
October	Erfoud	Date harvest
November	Goulmima	Sidi Bou Yacoub
December	Ghafsai	Olive harvest

Media

Papers

English newspapers are available throughout the year in Tangier and Agadir, and less reliably in Marrakesh for under 10dh. French newspapers are more widespread and cost about 5dh. The daily official French language paper, *Le Matin du Sahara*, is worth buying for 1dh though its coverage and certainly its opinion seldom changes. Morocco remains a good place to shed your paper habit and pick up tuning into the World Service direct from Bush House on 9.41 and 5.975 mhz—31.88 and 50.21m.

Cinema and Television

There is little temptation outside of a rain storm to visit a cinema in Morocco. If you do find yourself inside, tickets for under 10dh, you could become more fascinated with the audience than the film. The different cultural attitudes to humour, violence and romance always make fascinating study. The films fall into two divisions, American violence or Indian/Egyptian romance. This alternation between heroic deeds of male violence and cloyingly rich romantic melodramas will come as no surprise to those who have read any traditional Arabic poems or tales.

Despite an enormous and enthusiastic audience there are no indigenous Moroccan films, although a soap opera has recently been produced in Casablanca for television. Television is mostly filled with sport plus cartoons and American and Egyptian films. This is interrupted by glamorous news and weather reports which concentrate on the activities of King Hassan II and the Crown Prince.

The Moroccan south is a favourite location for foreign films. Amongst the more memorable are:

Le Grand Jeu, J. Freyder, 1934
The Man Who Knew Too Much, A. Hitchcock, 1934 and 1956
La Bandera, J. Duvivier, 1935
Courrier Sud, P. Billon, 1937
A Night in Casablanca, A. Mayo, 1946, with the Marx brothers
Ali Baba, Jacques Beker, 1955
Othello, Orson Welles, 1952
Oasis, Yves Allegret, 1954
Lawrence of Arabia, David Lean, 1962 with Peter O'Toole

Tartarin de Tarascon, F. Blanche, 1962
100,000 Dollars au Soleil, H. Verneuil, 1963
The Man Who Wanted To Be King, John Houston, 1975
Jesus of Narareth, F. Zeffirelli, 1978
The Return of the Black Claw, F. Ford Coppola, 1982
Le Vol de Shinx, L. Ferrier, 1984
Harem, A. Joffe 1984, with Nastassia Kinski and Ben Kingsley
Ishtar, 1986
The Living Daylights (James Bond), 1987
The Last Temptation of Christ, Martin Scorcese 1986

Sports

As a conversational ploy, athletics and football hardly ever fail to attract an enthusiastic response. Next to seducing a rich European, the quick fame and wealth earned by playing football is every poor boy's favourite daydream. All over Morocco football matches are arranged that kick off on Sunday at about 13.00. For a visitor, the chief sports are fishing, shooting, skiing, golf, tennis, hill walking, rock climbing and swimming.

Fly Fishing

You will need to bring your own rod and tackle. The streams and lakes of the Middle and High Atlas provide some tremendous opportunities for trout. Staying at Khenifra you could fish the deserted upper streams of the Oum er Rbia or from Ourigane the upper waters of the Nfis. Permits are available from Administration des Eaux et Forêts, 11, Rue Revoil, Rabat, tel 25335.

Coarse Fishing

This is a more popular sport. The natural lakes around Ifrane and the Bine el Ouidane, Moulay Youssef (east of Marrakesh), Idriss (east of Fez), Ouel el Makhazine (east of Ksar el Kebir), el Kansera (west of Meknes) dams are stocked with bass, perch and pike. Permits, official seasons, lists of approved dams and lakes can be found from the address above.

Sea Fishing

No permit is required to fish anywhere from Morocco's enormous coast line where mackerel, bream, sea bass, rouge, or loup de mer can be caught from boat or line.

Shooting

Sochatour at 72 Blvd Zerktouni, Casablanca, tel 277513, organizes shooting holidays for foreigners on behalf of the Administration des Eaux et Forêts. They run sporting estates, organize suitable hotels, provide dogs and keepers, and arrange for a temporary shooting licence and the import of your guns.

On offer are snipe, turtle doves, duck, pheasant, pigeon, quail and wild boar from forests near Tangier, Agadir, Marrakesh and particularly the 120,000 hectare preserve around Arbaoua.

The snipe, duck and pheasant season is from October to March, turtle doves from May to June, partridge October to January and driven wild boar from October to mid February.

Skiing

Mischlieffen, between Ifrane and Azrou in the Middle Atlas and Oukmaiden in the High Atlas are the principal resorts. Snow can be found between November and March—see these two areas of the guide for details.

Golf and Tennis

Tangier has an 18-hole golf course 3 km from the city. Rabat has a 45-hole golf course at Dar es Salaam, closed on Mondays, green fee 120dh, 14 km south of the city. Moham-media has an 18-hole golf course beside the sea. Marrakesh has an 18-hole golf course 4 km from the city. Agadir is extending its 9-hole course to 18. The Casablanca golf course has 9 holes and is found in the middle of the race track. Tennis courts and instructors are available at most large hotels.

Mountain climbing

The established centres for the major mountains are Imlil for the High Atlas, El Kelaa des Mgouna for Djebel Saghro, Talioune for Djebel Siroua and Midelt for the Middle Atlas. Look these up in the index for details. There is nothing to stop you hill-walking throughout the country and a number of less visited peaks are suggested in the text.

Swimming and water sports

The major resort beaches for summer water sports are Agadir, Tangier, Mdiq-Cabo Negro, Azilah, Mohammedia and El Jadida where donkey rides, water skiing, sailboard-ing, pedaloes, or paragliding can be found. When swimming on the Atlantic coast do constantly be aware of the powerful undertow.

Shopping

Souks

Arab cities were designed with the souk or market at the centre of the community. Islam has none of the Christian anxiety about mixing trade and worship. The streets around a grand mosque are usually the busiest and the richest and are known as the Kissaria. The outer walls of mosques are commonly obscured by workshops and stalls whose rent helps pay for the upkeep of the building. A new zaouia or mosque was often the initial impetus that coalesced a trading community into existence. On Friday morning you will notice a marked reduction in trade as the merchants shut shop for the noon prayers.

Rural souks

The endless pattern of tribal feuds mitigated against any one tribe being happy at either attending a market deep in the territory of their rival or hosting a market full of potential enemies in their central village. Souks were established on tribal borders, usually beside some distinctive feature, a spring, cult tree or koubba. The most successful were naturally placed on the divison between a pastoral and agrarian culture which allowed the two separate communities to trade surpluses of grain, oil and fruit for milk, wool and meat. The site of a souk was often completely deserted apart for the actual day of the market. It would be named after the day of trading which might be combined with the name of the region, a local saint or dominant tribe to distinguish it from others. Souk el Had is 'the first or Sunday market', Souk el Tnine, 'the second, i.e. Monday', el Tleta, 'the third—Tuesday', el Arba, 'the fourth on Wednesday', el Khemis 'the fifth on Thursday'. There are no rural souks held on Friday, though the village that had a mosque licensed for Friday prayers might be known as el Jemaa, 'the assembly'. Es Sebt, 'the seven' is the Saturday market.

In these more settled times souks have become a natural focus for local administration and the first permanent traders, though rural souks that exist for only the day of trading can still be found throughout Morocco.

Crafts

Moroccan crafts remain active and have recovered from the exodus of over 250,000 Moroccan Jews who were amongst the most skilled artisans in the country. The Jews were particularly prominent in jewelry, tailoring, weaving and non-ferrous metal work. All large towns maintain an **artisanal centre** where traditional trades are taught and products exhibited for sale. Tourism greatly assists the craft economy and it has been assessed that 20% of any visitor's expenditure is spent on crafts.

A visit to a typical contemporary Moroccan home reveals a subtle difference in taste. Rich embroidered cloth covers the cushions and day beds which with blankets and masses of deep carved wood are dominant. Ceramics tend not to be Islamic in decoration but plain glazed earthenware or a Chinese pattern for grand occasions. The radio, television or tape recorder will be conspicuous and you notice the complete absence of any pictures (other than an obligatory photo of the Moroccan football team and the king) and the tiled floors are rarely covered by carpets. It is chiefly in the traditional female embroidered kaftans, low tables and all the impedimenta of a tea ceremony that the tourist bazaar taste and the domestic economy coincide.

Wood

The skilled carvers and joiners of Essaouira create some of the most attractive and durable items that you can acquire in Morocco. Inlaid chess boards, backgammon sets, polished cedar boxes and carved jars can be bought directly from the craftsmen.

Clothing

The city souks are full of the distinctive clothing of the Maghreb: gandoras, burnous, kaftans and djellabas. Though vital for dressing up at home, a European usually looks awkward and foolish in these clothes. Straw hats are useful in the summer but no one should encourage any further manufacture by buying a hateful nylon Fez. There are felt ones to be found, or lambs wool, 'Nehru' hats.

Leatherwork

The distinctive Moroccan slipper, the pointed and trodden heeled yellow babouche are more immediately useful. You can also hunt for a softer chamois leather version though the heavily embroidered and gilded tend to have little flexibility or use out of a dinner party.

Gilt-embroidered belts can be easily absorbed into western dress. They look better and more amusingly ostentatious the shabbier the trousers they support. Check that the leather isn't cardboard and that the buckle is strong enough.

The stamped and gilded large red or ochre wallets are generally made of fine leather and make admirable cases for letters or detachable bindings for books. The desk sets are also usually of a high quality. If you have time ask for a favourite book to be Morocco bound.

Ceramics

Pottery plates or large open fruit bowls, particularly the traditional geometric design of blue on white—plain glazed or green—translate well and seldom look out of place in Britain. The ceramic centres of Morocco are Fez, Meknes, Tetouan and Safi. Good rural Berber pots are also found for sale in Oued Laou, Amizmiz and Tamegroute.

Jewelry

Jewelry, although more portable than pottery, is seldom as successful a buy unless you know someone who adores bangles. The filigree, heavy stones and enamel of brooches and necklaces, though fascinating, can look just too ethnic and souvenirish in Britain. Aunts and nieces become the surprised beneficiaries of Berber pieces that the buyer found impossible to wear.

Metalware

There is a mass of decorated brass plates and implements in every bazaar. Candlesticks, mirrors, trays, pestels and incense burners can be acquired before you even realized you had a need. The distinctive Moroccan teapot is the most attractive single item. The weak hinge of the lid and the failure of the insulating handle seem to be universal faults. Handkerchiefs are used for pouring and bent nails secure the lid throughout Morocco.

Minerals

Fossils and minerals are initially less tempting and suffer from over-salesmanship. But for under a pound you can pick up superb pieces of Sahara rose, amethyst and goniatites from the High Atlas and the Ziz valley.

Spices

Moroccan spices, principally cumin, harissa (hot pepper), paprika, ginger, saffron (4dh for a red thread), cinnamon and bunches of fresh mint, coriander and parsley create the most colourful displays in the souk. The intriguing displays of the apothecary and cosmetic stalls are often found close by. Blocks of silvery antimony, Kohl—ground antimony for the eyes, henna—in leaf or powder, ghassol—a brown mud for washing, snib at 5dh a kilo (for stopping shaving cuts), cochineal, porcupine quills, teeth cleaning twigs, incense and dried Dades roses can be bought.

Carpets

The oldest surviving carpet is a two thousand five hundred year old Scythian carpet which is now preserved in ice in the Hermitage. Tools of this nomad race have been excavated and found to be startlingly similar to those in use today. It is fitting that Persia, a nation whose history is a catalogue of successive nomadic invasions, brought the art to its apogee. One of the most beautiful Persian carpets, the 'Chelsea', can be seen hanging in the Victoria and Albert Museum. Persian techniques and styles were imitated in Muslim Andalucia and were brought to Morocco by Andalucian refugees. (Just as Persian techniques were copied by the French in the 17th century and then Huguenot exiles brought these skills to Wilton and Axminster in England.) The last wave of Andalucian exiles settled in Rabat and Salé and created the basis of the urban Moroccan carpet industry. The 'Rabat' carpet is a development from the garden, geometric and prayer mat designs of Persia. These traditions have been combined and now often depict a single decorated mihrab arch with a decorative floral or geometric band on a general muted or wash background of light blue or pink. They generally have little appeal to western taste.

Killims

Of much greater interest are the traditional carpets and killims produced in the Middle or High Atlas. These borrow little from any textile tradition and appear strikingly in tune with traditional Berber ceramic decoration and ancient mosaic and tile designs. Killims have a shorter life than carpets for they are woven, not knotted, though a rich pattern of embroidery can sometimes confuse this distinction. Tribal killims and carpets feature strong broad horizontal lines of colour broken by diamond and triangular lozenges.

There are good examples of these in the craft museums of Rabat, Marrakesh, Fez and Meknes. Tribes favoured certain designs and colours. Traditionally the bolder contrast in colours and the more harshly defined geometric forms were produced by tribes who lived in the high mountains. The more detailed patterns of lozenges and shapes were produced by tribes in the lower richer pastures. The 'message rugs' as seen in the souks are largely a 20th-century innovation. Some of the figurative and animal forms are based on traditional themes but most are just copied straight out of a pattern book and are too often embroidered without attention to overall design on a bright woven background. Carpet-making is a well established craft industry and as much performed in bidonvilles, workshops and artisan centres as in the rural hinterland, though it is a common enough sight to see merchants selling bolts of brightly died wool to women in rural souks or dealers distributing woollen stock in advance of collecting the finished work.

Middle Atlas
Traditional killims of the Middle Atlas nomadic tribes have narrow strips of detailed geometric on a traditional red background. They are as likely to be found woven for a practical purpose, as saddlebags, belts, waistcoats, sacks, cushions than as convenient lengths of carpet. For Beni M'guid work try Azrou, Mrirt, Itzer or Ain Leuh. For Beni M'Tir try El Hajeb. For Zaiane, Zair or Zemmour try any of the towns that ring these three tribal zones: Khenifra, Mrirt, Boujad, Oued Zem, Rabat–Salé, Rommani as well as looking at the rural souks detailed in the text.

At Taza look out the work of the nearby Ait Yacoub and the southern tribes, particularly Beni Ouarrim. The most comprehensive selections held in stock are to be found at Midelt and from the well-established merchants of Meknes who, more so than Fez, pay attention to Middle Atlas produce.

High Atlas
Marrakesh is the great souk of the south that stocks Ait Ouaouzguit, Tensift and Glaoua carpets as well as supporting its own workshops. Look also at Tazenakht, Ouazazarte and Agdz for Glaoua and Ait Ouaouzguit work and the rarer Ait Haddidou killims. The Glaoua were fond of the use of stripes of black pile broken by strips of flat weave. The Ait Ouaouzguit used black pile as well but traditionally overlay with a red and white trellis adding broad displays of yellow and madder red.

The Arab tribes who grazed the plains around Marrakesh kept to their own traditions. In particular a basic red pile with aprons of blue, black, yellow, white and chestnut. Chichaoua is the centre for this work and has an artisanal ensemble where the designs of the Oulad Bou S'baa, Rehamna and Chiadma are maintained.

Buying

Only buy for your pleasure. Moroccan carpets are not an investment and you can only expect a fraction of the price by selling back to a British dealer. London is still the centre of the international bulk importing and auction sales. **Eastern Kayam OCM**, the largest dealers who have been trading in Chinese and Persian goods for 150 years, are frankly not interested in Moroccan products. A Persian carpet may have between 150 and 1200 knots a square inch, Moroccan ones rarely exceed 40 to 50. Their ability to age, and increase in value, is therefore correspondingly reduced. The quality of thread is often drastically inferior and occasionally is found to be partly synthetic. The dyes used in Morocco are almost all aniline now, and produce harsh single colours with few tones though some tribes have kept their integrity and still make their own dyes. Carpets are aged to produce more muted colours by being exposed to the sun and are sometimes even painted with weak solutions of bleach. The colours admired in a strong African light can often look too harsh in England. A claim to have used silk in the embroidery can easily be tested, pluck a strand and if it smoulders into a grey ash when burnt it is silk, if it flares up and produces an acrid smell and black ash it is likely to be mercerized cotton.

Do not however be discouraged from visiting the great carpet bazaars in Tetouan, Fez, Meknes, Rabat and Marrakesh which are often housed in magnificent interiors and offer tea whilst they display their still tempting wares.

Blankets

Striped blankets that form a traditional internal tent band or the pure brown and black 'hanbels' that are sewn together to create a nomadic tent are a useful alternative to buying a carpet. Even the poorest itinerant can be seen with his blanket and they remain part of the normal local economy in a way that carpets no longer do. They are found throughout Morocco in a great variety of colours, sizes and designs.

It is perhaps indicative that the north, not an area of carpet production, weaves the finest woollen cloth. Tetouan, Ouezzane, Ksar el Kebir and Chechaouen have the finest looms. They produce the short distinctive Riff blankets of red stripes, though you find some with blue and black, which are worn as pinafores by the mountain women. They also weave various grades and tones of brown, black and ochre cloth for the ubiquitous djellabas. In central Morocco, Boujad used to enjoy a reputation for creating bright coloured blankets and preparing the delicate orange and white cotton used for turbans. The souk of Marrakesh is well stocked with the looser woven large brown and white blankets that make excellent bed covers. In the souks of the far south you come across brilliant patterns of tie-died cotton for the women's haiks and the enormous, many-coloured thick blankets of the Saharan region. Two of these can completely line a nomad tent and provide excellent protection against the bitter nights.

Bargaining

It is an art that is fully enjoyed and understood in Morocco. But without a firm idea of the price you should pay you are helpless. A visit to a museum to remind yourself of what quality you are aspiring for and the state run **artisanal ensemble** for the maximum price is a good start.

It is good tactics and in the highest order of gamesmanship to greet the shopkeeper, shake his hand and praise his colouful display of goods before he does. Look at some items other than what you actually are interested in first and have a friend act out the negative, mean and unenthusiastic role. Delay for as long as possible the mentioning of your first price, praising the goods but looking sad, wistful and tearful in turn at the impossible prices. Once you have named your price be obstinate and watch out for the skilful rachet ploy by which he gradually drops the price in exchange for a gradual rise in yours.

There are three rules. Never bargain for something you don't want, don't hurry, and even if you think you have just made a great financial coup praise your opponent for his ruthless hard bargaining and great skill.

Where to Stay

Hotels

The Moroccan National Tourist Board keeps a close eye on the standard of hotels in the country. It routinely inspects and classifies hotels into ten standards from *B to *****Luxe and each year decrees the maximum prices for all but the ***** hotels. In 1989 the maximum price for a double room in a *B is 86dh, 98dh for a *A, 112dh for a **B, 138dh for a **A, 186dh for a ***B, 212dh for a ***A, 292dh for a ****B and 358dh for a ****A. It is not easy to recognize the difference between As and Bs and this division has been dropped from the guide though star rating and prices are everywhere listed.

Below this efficient bureaucratic grid are a large number of small pensions and rougher café hotels. In the old cities these are often found at the entrance to the Medina quarter. These 'Medina' hotels do not have their prices controlled and can increase their charges in the peak summer months beyond the customary 25dh for a single bed.

It is rare to find any Moroccan hotel, of whatever standard, without clean bedrooms. The beds are made up with freshly laundered cotton sheets and never nylon. Reliable supplies of bath water can be more problematical, and even the grandest hotels have their off days, but three-star hotels and above can usually be relied upon. In the body of the guide there is a complete price range of hotels to choose from in each city. A large number of addresses have been listed for the small and popular towns but a deliberate selection from the larger choice in the bigger cities. In general hotels of age, with character and gardens have been chosen over those of scrupulous efficiency and sanitation.

Campsites

The best campsites in Morocco tend to be on the coast. The beach camps at Asilah, Moulay Bousselham, Ec-Chiania, Oualidia, Souria Kedima, Taghazoute, Sidi R'bat and Kalah Iris are all delightful. Going inland the campsites at Meknes, Zerhoun/Volubilis, Ifrane, Tinerhir, Zagora and Meski all have some special charm though there are many others that are perfectly adequate. Be prepared, particularly in Fez, Rabat and Marrakesh to sacrifice scruples and spend one or two nights in a hotel. Sleeping on a hotel roof can be almost as cheap and romantic as camping. Prices vary but if you plan in terms of 5dh per person, 5dh per tent, 5dh per vehicle with 15dh for a caravan or camper you will not be far out.

Youth Hostels

There are youth hostels at Asni—40 beds, Azrou—40 beds, Casablanca—80 beds, Fez—60 beds, Meknes—50 beds, Chechaouen—30 beds and Marrakesh—89 beds. They are uniformly clean, spartan and charge 10dh a night.

Eating out

Eating, for all but the rich, French-influenced merchant class is a home-based family affair. In a country of high unemployment the shared family meal of couscous enlivened by a few chunks of steamed meat and vegetables is the one great source of sustenance for the day. All the more conspicuous cafés are male social centres that might serve a cake or croissant with mint tea or coffee, but seldom anything more substantial. Rural cafés serve tagines (spicy stews) on market days but can usually run up an omelette and salad at any time. Restaurants have, for convenience, been divided into four categories in this guide: grill cafés, New Town restaurants, Moorish palaces and the 'best'.

The best

If you want fresh seafood or excellent traditional cooking but less tourist-inspired razmataz, you don't always have to pay the earth. Tafraoute, Oualidia, Taroudant, Ourika valley and Ouirigane have restaurants where you can eat extremely well for under 100dh. However, to eat and drink at some of the top restaurants in cities like Marrakesh, Casablanca and Fez costs between 100–250dh.

Moorish palaces

A number of old merchant palaces in the Medinas of Fez, Meknes, Tangier and Marrakesh have been converted into restaurants. Traditional Moorish cooking is served in a typical Moorish interior and music and dancing entertainments arranged. Some are licensed but you should not be surprised to see that they are almost entirely filled by tour groups.

New Town

For dinner that you can spin out over an evening you must usually go to the French-built new town or port. The menus combine French, Moroccan and international dishes. The food is rarely as fresh, as cheap or as good as the grill cafés, though there are honourable exceptions, particularly in Tangier and Casablanca. But here you will dine in a calm environment with waiters, table cloths, mineral water, glasses and wine.

Grill cafés

These serve delicious spiced salads, bread with fried or grilled meat, fish and vegetables. They are invariably found clustered around the bus station. Their clients are principally travellers and workers away from home who are deprived of their customary meal. They are easy to sniff out and perched on a shared bench are excellent for a quickly consumed lunch or supper.

Traditional Moroccan cooking

Morocco has a distinctive national cuisine. Whatever your budget, try to eat at least once during your holiday in a good restaurant and accept any genuine invitation to a share a family meal. One of the most striking features of the cooking is the quality and freshness of the ingredients. Produce comes from a land without pesticides, fattening sheds, chemicals, hormones and preservatives. Animals are slaughtered hours before they are eaten and not even goats hooves or heads are left to waste. Meat will generally be mutton not lamb. Market vegetables will have been gathered that morning. Spices, herbs, fresh fruit, nuts and dried fruit have an invigorating relevance and a freshness that seems completely removed from the packaged and imported products available in the west.

For details of Arab and French pronunciation, see the language section at the back of the book, but here are the some descriptions to encourage you:

Harira: a thick soup of chick peas, lentils, haricot beans often flavoured with mutton or chicken, lemon and tarragon.
Brochettes: grilled kebabs of mutton, liver and fat.
Kefta: spicey meatballs made of minced mutton and offal, often served piping hot in a rich sauce with an egg.
Pastilla/Bastilla: a pie of layers of flaky pastry filled with pigeon meat, eggs, almonds and spices. Chicken or fish is sometimes used instead of pigeon meat.
Tagine: slowly simmered stew, cooked in its own juices in an earthenware bowl. A tagine is a framework for a whole galaxy of ingredients, spices and styles. The most popular are: *tagine de viande*, mutton stew with vegetables or served alone with prunes. *Tagine de poisson* is usually bream or sardines, cooked with tomatoes and herbs. *Tagine de lapin* is rabbit stew. *Tagine de poulet aux olives et citron* is delicious, chicken cooked with lemon and olives.
Mechoui: a lamb roasted whole on a spit or baked in a special oven. This delicate and fragrant meat, far removed from the usual mutton, is eaten with bread. It is, however, an elaborate luxury which is often only available if ordered well in advance.
Couscous: Flour is half baked and ground to form semolina-like grains. A perfectly prepared couscous is laboriously cooked in a succession of steamings and oilings that allow each grain to cook while retaining a distinct granular texture. Couscous served outside of a home or a good restaurant is unlikely to be found at its best. It is usually accompanied with the 'sept legumes', seven steamed vegetables with the odd lump of mutton. It can also be served as a pudding with sugar, cinnamon and rich warmed goat's milk.
Cornes de gazelle: Croissant-like pastries filled with honey and almonds.

Drinking

The Koran has this to say of alcohol: 'They shall ask you concerning wine and games of chance. Say in both is a great sin and an advantage also to man, but their sin is greater than their advantage', and 'O Ye true believers, come not to prayer when you are drunken but wait till ye can understand what ye utter.'

Morocco is a Muslim nation. There is a law that prohibits Moroccan Muslims from buying bottles of alcohol—though this is not strictly enforced outside of Ramadan. This ban does not apply to visitors and it is in any case legal for Muslim Moroccans to drink at bars which are found discreetly tucked behind closed doors in the New Towns. Outside of hotels there are seldom any bars in a Medina and away from cities or major tourist towns drinking is confined to a few hotels.

Wine is grown in Morocco in three regions: Berkane, Meknes and Boualoune. The white is seldom much good but a chilled rosé is fine. You might find the reds rather strong and heavy to drink without a meal and are much better at accompanying a rich spiced meat tagine. The principal reds are Toulal, Rabbi Jacob, Beni Snassen, Père Antoine, Le Chatelain, Valpierre, Les Trois Domaines, Amazir Beni M'Tir and Cabernet President. If you have a choice you might try the last two first. The best of the whites is Special Coquillages and after that Valpierre Blanc de Blanc which is dry and not too astringent. The two best rosé wines are Gris de Boulaouane and Oustalet. If you want an advance tasting you can now order Moroccan wine from Ricketts Exports, 3 Daleside Road, Epsom, Surrey, tel 01–394–1252. A case of Gris de Boulaoune costs just under £35.00.

The principal drink of Morocco is mint tea. This is green or gunpowder tea (first imported to Morocco by British merchants in the 19th century), flavoured with a few sprigs of mint and saturated with sugar. It is almost repulsively sweet when you first taste it. You will however be offered glasses of mint tea in every house or shop you visit. It is expected that a guest drinks at least three glasses of tea before departing. Enjoying mint tea becomes a vital social grace and before long you might begin to enjoy this invigorating and thirst quenching drink. Before tea was brought to Morocco, hot infusions of sweet mint, verbena, absinthe and atron were popular. These are still occasionally added to normal tea.

Freshly squeezed orange juice enlivened with a little grapefruit or lemon is available in most cities.

Itineraries

It is a mistake to move too quickly around Morocco. Too many people visit a city, suffer all the initial hassle and leave before they are relaxed enough to explore beyond the major tourist sites. If you are coming to Morocco for a week or ten days it is often more rewarding to choose a city and explore the surrounding hinterland. Travel agents advertise a number of classic routes. 'The Imperial cities' is the most popular, a whistle-stop tour from Casablanca to Rabat, then on to Meknes with a visit to Volubilis before moving to Fez and then down to Marrakesh before returning to Casablanca. A variation on the theme is to nip across the High Atlas after Fez, visit the Erg Chebbi, the Todra gorge and Ouazazarte before approaching Marrakesh from the south.

An ideal introduction to Morocco would begin with a cheap flight to Agadir which you would quickly leave to stay at the Immouzer Ida Outane Hotel before travelling north to Essaouira. Then inland to Marrakesh for a few days before staying at Ourigane and crossing the Tiz-n-Test pass to reach Taroudant. From Taroudant on to Tafraoute for a couple of days walking in the mountains. Then down to Tiznit with a trip to Sidi Ifni and some lesser known beaches before returning to Agadir for the flight home.

The Best of Morocco

Unexploited beaches: Plage Blanche, Oued Laou, Moulay Bousselham, Kalah Iris, Sidi R'bat.

Deservedly popular towns: Essaouira, Chechaouen and Tafraoute.

Undervisited towns: Larache, Tetouan, Salé, Safi, Taza, Sefrou.

Remote: Tata, Figuig, Smara, Ad Dakhla, Oulmes les Thermes.

Natural landscape: Cascade D'Ouzoud, Erg Chebbi, Todra Gorge, Source of Oum er Rbia, Tafraoute, Dades Gorge, Ouzoud Gorge, Imi n Ifri.

Souks: Fez, Meknes, Marrakesh.

Night clubs: Casablanca, Tangier, Agadir, Meknes, Mehdiya.

Hot mineral baths: Camel cave at Beni Snassen, Abaino, Figuig, Gouttitir, Moulay Yacoub.

Mountain roads: Tiz-n-Test, Route D'Unitie.

Roman ruins: Volubilis, Lixus, Banassa.

Mountains: Djebel Toubkal, Lalla Outka, Djebel Siroua, Djebel Ayachi.

Memorable ruins: The Chellah, Telouet, El Badi, Kasbah Boulaoune, Mzorah.

Museums: Archaeological Museum of Rabat, Oudaia kasbah, Dar el Makhzen at Tangier, Dar Jamai at Meknes, Dar Batha at Fez.

Islamic architecture: Koubba el Baradouiyn, Ben Youssef Medersa, Bou Inania Medersa, Medersa es Seffarin, Medersa el Attarin, Oudaia gate, el Hassan tower.

Hotels: Grand Hôtel de Villa de France and The Continental at Tangier, Palais Jamai at Fez, Palais Salaam at Taroudant, CTM in Marrakesh, Immouzer Ida Outane, La Fibule du Draa in Zagora.

MOROCCAN CULTURE

Orange Harvest

A History of Morocco

Introduction to Moroccan history

Morocco is a nation with a long and distinguished history. The Berber tribes of the Riff mountains have occupied the same land since the Neolithic revolution. Tangier is older than the eternal city of Rome and, when Oxford was a muddy unlettered village, Aristotle was being translated in the court of the Sultans. Though the British monarchy is considered long established it cannot compete with the ruling Alouite dynasty of Morocco who are descendants of the prophet Mohammed.

Moroccan history, whatever its antiquity, is essentially the tale of a conservative society. Four great mountain ranges run across the breadth of the land, breaking up the geographical unity of the area and providing a secure refuge for the indigenous Berber people against any central power. Beyond the difficulties of a nation broken into regions by mountain ranges is the position of Morocco itself, isolated on the north western corner of Africa by the Sahara desert and the Atlantic Ocean.

Through this geographical barrier three great revolutionary changes have intruded to transform Moroccan society. The first great change was from 1,000 BC when Phoenician traders brought achievements of settled agriculture and urban civilization to Morocco. The second revolution was religious. Arab armies conquered the entire North African seaboard and forcibly brought Islam to Morocco in the eighth century. Arab military rule lasted only a few decades but the spiritual and social message took deep root. All subsequent rulers of Morocco were only legitimate for as long as they championed Islam, either as reformers or as military protectors. The third great revolution was in the twentieth century when the French, albeit for the selfish motives of a colonial power, implanted the industrial revolution in Morocco. The industrial revolution, with its accelerated population growth, is still incomplete, whilst the gifts of the Phoenicians are too far in the past to be of general interest.

The central and most consistent influence on Moroccan history is Islam. Idriss, the great grandson of the Prophet, was the first to establish a Muslim kingdom. This achievement was overshadowed by the Almoravides, a reform movement from the Sahara, which under the leadership of Youssef ben Tachfine created an Islamic Empire which stretched from the Pyrenees to the river Niger.

The Almoravides were supplanted in the mid 11th century by the Almohads, an even more militant reform movement founded in the High Atlas by the theologian Ibn Tumert. Abdel Moumen, his chosen successor, established an equally extensive Empire which reached east to modern Libya.

By the mid 13th century the Merenids had replaced the Almohads as rulers of Morocco. They championed no religious revival but proved themselves worthy by fighting Spanish Christians and founding numerous religious colleges. The last two Merenid princes, however, were found wanting in zeal and were lynched for failing to defeat the Christian Portuguese invaders. Their heirs, the Wattasids, presided over a disintegrating and discredited state.

They were brushed aside by the Saadians who earned their legitimacy by leading the holy war against the Portuguese in the far south. Saadian rule reached its golden apogee under Ahmad el Mansour, but glorious though his reign had been, his son lost all power when he sold two Moroccan ports to Christian Spain.

A half century of feuding by petty states led to the rule of the Alouite dynasty. The fifty year reign of Moulay Ishmael was the peak period of Alouite authority. Though few of his successors achieved a fraction of his power, none could be accused of lacking the Islamic virtues of militancy and orthodoxy. Throughout the 19th century Morocco, despite the heroic attempts of a number of Sultans, fell increasingly under European influence. In 1912 France established a protectorate and delegated the extreme north and south to the administration of Spain. A new society had been formed by the time Mohammed V led the struggle for Independence which was granted in 1956. Despite the great social and demographic transformation the role of Islam remains central to the national consciousness.

Africa, the origins of man

About 5 million years ago a species of ape, Australopithecus turned to scavenging in the highlands of East Africa. From these creatures a bipedal, stone-using ape man, Homo Habilis, evolved who was in turn replaced by Homo Erectus, a new sub-species with a brain half as big again. Homo Erectus crossed the Sahara into Morocco and spread thinly across the world (except for America and the Pacific). Some of the most important finds of Homo Erectus remains, dating back about a million years, have been made in Morocco, at Rabat and Casablanca.

The various ice ages of the last million years worked as an enviromental rachet on Homo Erectus. Eras of hardship diminished the race and allowed only the fittest specimens to survive.

At the beginning of the last major ice age, about 70,000 years ago he had become 'Neanderthal man'. In Morocco important finds of Neanderthal bones have occurred at Tangier, Temara and Djebel Irhoud and there is more frequent evidence of his existence in stone tools, which are known as products of the Mousterian culture.

When the last ice age retreated in 10,000 BC the Mediterranean coast of Africa was occupied by a white race while the Sahara to the south was occupied by black peoples.

North African prehistory

From about 6000 to 4000 BC the Sahara enjoyed a brief wet period. Cave paintings and rock carvings in the Moroccan Sahara record an era when elephants, hippopotamus and crocodiles were hunted far to the north of their present habitat.

The new stone age—the neolithic or food producing revolution, did not reach Africa until around 5000 BC. Specialized agricultural and herding skills replaced the drifting families of hunters. This social revolution was spectacularly successful in Egypt where the world's first nation state had arisen by 3000 BC but progress in Morocco was tempered by the country's geographical isolation, by the desert to the southeast and the Atlantic to the west but not from the Megalithic culture of western Europe. At least two Megalithic stone circles in northern Morocco have been dated to around 1800 BC, and the quality of chattels found in the tombs of the time around Tangier suggests a very early trade in ivory with Europe.

By 1500 BC the population of North Africa had become Berber, speaking a language of the Hamitic family related to ancient Egyptian. The men were devoted to war, were polygamous and allowed their women to perform most of the agricultural labour. The horse, which was first bred in Africa in this period, and the donkey were greatly prized, whilst in the savannah plains the war chariot was dominant. The Berber tribes expanded into the Sahara, an event which is recorded in cave paintings as the cattle herders are replaced by conquering charioteers, and carvings of the distinctive Libyo–Berber 'script' appear.

Phoenician Influences

The Berbers of Morocco enter the history of the Mediterranean world through the influence of the trading cities of Phoenicia, chief of which was Tyre. The mines of southern Spain were an important source of metals and the Phoenicians established permanent settlements on both sides of the Straits of Gibraltar before 1000 BC. These trading colonies were responsible for the diffusion of new skills to the tribes of the North African coast. The pottery wheel, an alphabet, improved weaving, dressed stone, new crops, arboriculture, iron and metal work were all Phoenician gifts to the Berbers.

Leadership of the Phoenician colonies had passed in the 5th century BC to Carthage. By this period a string of settlements existed on the Moroccan coast at Rusadir (Melilla), Tingis (Tangier), Lixus (Larache), Sala (Rabat) and Mogador (Essaouira) which traded in corn, oil, fish, dyes and ivory. Hanno, a Carthaginian admiral, is recorded in a temple inscription to have sailed down the Atlantic coast of Morocco in an attempt to open direct trade with West Africa. All the coastal cities of North Africa accepted the protection of the Carthaginian navy and her direction in foreign affairs. They never attempted to rule the tribal hinterland, though the Punic temple of Melkart at Volubilis demonstrates the heightened culture introduced to the interior.

The Mauretanian Kings, 200 BC–AD 44

The final destruction of Carthage by the **Romans** in 146 BC brought a new power to the North African shore. The Roman province of Africa was formed from the ruins of Carthage and the independent Berber kingdoms to its west were gradually absorbed. The principal coastal towns of Morocco had already fallen under Roman suzerainty when Juba II, who had been educated in Emperor Augustus's court, was made the client King of Mauretania in 25 BC. Mauretania in this period covered both Morocco and eastern Algeria and was ruled from the two capitals of Volubilis and Caesarea (Cherchel, west of Algiers).

Juba II's reign saw a further advance in Roman influence in Morocco which was coupled to growing tribal resentment. By the time of his death in AD 19 Juba's authority was upheld by Roman troops and a Roman official even administered his capital of Volubilis. In a clumsy political act that contradicted the successful policy of gradual absorption, the Emperor Caligula had Ptolemy, Juba II's son and heir assassinated in AD 42. This visible act of despotism threw Morocco into revolt against Rome. The tribes and even a number of coastal cities rose under the leadership of Aedemeon, an official from Ptolemy's court. The revolt took an army of four legions over three years to subdue.

A Roman Province

In AD 44, the Emperor Claudius officially annexed the area but the fierce resistance of the tribes left the new province of Mauretania Tingitania substantially smaller than the original kingdom. The frontier extended south to Salé and just east of Volubilis but there was no permanent land link to the Roman province of Mauretania Caesariensis, whose western frontier reached the river Moulouya.

Roman authority was continuously challenged by the Berber tribes throughout the two hundred years of direct rule, but the Romans further developed the trade and settlement patterns established in the Phoenician period to create a prosperous and civilized province. During the reign of the Emperor Diocletian, 285–305, the Romans withdrew to a defensive line stretching from Tetouan to Larache, protecting their two useful ports, Tangier and Ceuta, which remained under Roman authority until 429, when an army of Vandals crossed from Spain to Tangier. Their leader, Genseric, marched his people east, meeting no opposition until they arrived at the rich grain lands of Tunisia. Vandal rule lasted a century in North Africa until their defeat in 535 by the Byzantine general Belisarius. He reestablished garrisons along the North African coast and appointed a count to govern Ceuta and Tangier. Byzantine governors remained dominant figures in local politics until the Arab invasion two centuries later.

Berber tribalism

The cities of Tingis, Lixus, Sala Colonia and Volubilis had risen centuries before the Romans, Vandals or Byzantines arrived and survived their departure. In the early stages of the 8th-century Arab invasion of Morocco many of the cities continued as trading centres, governed by councils of leading merchants and local chiefs. These urban centres contained strong Jewish and Christian communities which as 'peoples of the Book' were respected by the Arab invaders.

It was the largely pagan Berber tribes of the countryside who bore the brunt of Arab hostility. Their lack of religion, under Muslim codes, made them legally enslavable. The Berbers formed a patchwork of tribes whose internal and external feuds were a social function designed to check the advancement of an individual or a tribe over its neighbour. Tribal unity was maintained by belief, not necessarily factual, in a common ancestor. Tribes were customarily divided into fifths. Each fifth elected an annual president from a council who supervised customary law. For warfare a general, an 'Amghar n tuga', was elected from one fifth but held in check by the natural jealousy of the other four fifths. To signify his role a sprig of basil, the royal herb, was inserted into the fillet which bound his hair. To add to the natural divisiveness of the Berber political system there were three separate groups loosely associated by their distinct dialects: the desert Sanhaja, the Chleuh of the southwest and the Zenata of the Riff and eastern plains. Creating a central political authority for a country whose whole social structure was designed to frustrate this required more than mere tribal allegiance.

The Arab Conquest, 704–740

The Arab conquest brought Islam to Morocco: a religion, a social code and a system of law that was to provide the central identity of all future Moroccan states. Its introduction was not by peaceful missionaries but by armies despatched by the caliphs, the political heirs of the Prophet. Within 25 years of the Prophet's death the first three caliphs had conquered an Empire covering Syria, Mesopotamia, Persia, Egypt and Libya.

Muslim advance along the North African coast was delayed by a succession dispute, but in 682 Uqba ben Nafi made his famous raid on Morocco. The raid is a cherished episode in Moroccan history but is almost certainly a legend. According to this myth Uqba defeated a joint Berber and Byzantine army, was welcomed by Count Julian into Tangier, accepted the submission of Volubilis and went on to conquer the Haouz, the Draa valley and the Souss. Arriving at the Atlantic he rode deep into the surf declaring, 'O God, I take you to witness that there is no ford here. If there was I would cross it.' This was all to no avail, for on his return east Uqba was ambushed and killed by an old Berber adversary.

The Arab conquest of Morocco did not begin in earnest until 705 when Musa ben Nasser arrived at Kairouan in Tunisia to take up his appointment as commander of the western Arab army. Between 705 and 710 he advanced rapidly westward, content to accept the nominal conversion of towns and tribes which he enforced by establishing garrisons, notably at Tangier, Tlemcen and Sigilmassa. His aim was to secure Morocco in order to be able to proceed with the conquest of Spain.

Letting this be known proved wise policy, for Berber warriors flocked to the banners of the Arabs once they understood that this would entail the invasion of the rich provinces of Spain. In 711 an advance guard of 7000 Berber warriors under the command of **Tariq**, the governor of Tangier, crossed the straits, first landing at what came to be known as Djebel Tariq or Gibraltar. Tariq was welcomed by the Christian and Jewish population of Spain as a deliverer from the rule of the German Visigoths. In one day's work at the battle of Barbate River, Tariq destroyed the Visigothic army. Muslim armies quickly occupied Spain and the Arab advance north into Western Europe was not checked until Charles Martel stood firm at Poitiers in 732.

The Berber Khajarite Revolt of 740

After the conquest of Spain, Morocco returned to the periphery of the Arab world. The Berber tribes had accepted the new religion with enthusiasm but soon sought to separate it from the less attractive aspects of Arab conquest.

The Governors appointed by the Omayyad Caliphs treated the Berbers with contempt and saw Morocco merely as a source of slaves and tax. A succession of rapacious governors were assassinated before the first Khajarite revolt erupted amongst the Berber garrison of Tangier in 740. The Khajarite heresy, which stated that the Caliph should be elected from all active believers whatever their race, was naturally appealing to the Berbers. From Tangier the revolt spread east to Algeria and Tunisia where two Arab armies were defeated by a coalition of Berber Khajarite tribes. Arab governors eventually regained Tunisia but Morocco, the Maghreb el Aksa, 'the land of the furthest west', remained quite beyond their control.

Idrissids

It is a testament to the enthusiasm that the Berber tribes felt for Islam that only a few years after ridding themselves of the despotic Arab governors they welcomed Moulay Idriss, an Arab refugee, and elected him their leader.

Moulay Idriss, the great-grandson of the Prophet, was one of the few members of his family after their failed revolt against the Abbasid caliphs in Arabia in 786. In the company of his faithful slave Rachid he fled to Morocco which was one of the few Muslim countries safely beyond the reach of any Abbasid revenge.

Arriving at the principal city of Volubilis in 789 he was enthusiastically welcomed as the great-grandson of the Prophet and elected leader of the local Auraba Berber tribe. Supported by the central Berber tribes he was able to conquer a sizeable state in northern Morocco but he was poisoned by an agent of the Abbasid Caliph in 791. He left a pregnant Berber concubine who gave birth to a boy which allowed his old slave Rachid to maintain the tribes' loyalty and rule as regent. Rachid was himself poisoned in 802 but two years later the eleven-year-old Idriss II was recognized as Imam.

Idriss II's reign had a more distinctively Arab character than his father's. He appointed an Arab as his grand vizier and equipped himself with an Arab bodyguard of 500 men. His most enduring achievement was the development of his father's foundation of Fez. The city, swelled by Arab refugees who fled from a civil war in Cordoba in 818 and from revolution in Kairouan in 826, became a centre of Arabic language, religious knowledge and technical achievement that gradually fertilized the cultural life of Morocco. Idriss II enlarged his father's dominions, which by his death exceeded the size of the old Roman province. The mountainous Riff and Middle and High Atlas regions remained outside his authority as did the southern coastal provinces of the heretical Berghawata Berber tribe. The region south of the High Atlas was also beyond Idrissid rule but orthodox Islam permeated the oasis valleys from the strong Arab trading settlement of Sigilmassa in the Tafilalet oasis. Idriss II died in 828 and his inheritance was divided amongst nine of his sons. Though the Idrissid state immediately lost its cohesion, the various princes pursued the conversion of Berber tribes in their petty states, a period that is remembered in dozens of local folk tales.

Fatimid (917–970) and Omayyad (920–1031) influence

After the disintegration of the Idrissid state the country returned to the familiar pattern of feuding Berber tribes. Fortunately the urban centres survived this disruptive period by falling under the protection of first the Fatimid and then the Omayyad Empire.

The Fatimid Empire was originally based on Tunisia. In 917 an army sent by the Fatimid Mahdi occupied the northern coast of Morocco and deposed the last Idrissid prince of Fez, Yahya IV, four years later. Ignoring the Berber heartland they seized the other Arab power centre, Sigilmassa in 960. The extension of the Fatimid Empire over the trading towns on the Atlantic coast was only halted by their seizure of Egypt in 969 which shifted their ambitions dramatically to the east. The governors they left behind in Tunisia, the Zirids, proved unequal to the task of controlling Morocco.

When Fatimid interests moved east, the Omayyad caliphate of Cordoba naturally filled the political vacuum and appointed governors over northern Morocco. The foundation of an Omayyad state in Spain repeats the extraordinary story of Moulay Idriss. In 750 after the death of the last Omayyad Caliph of the Muslim Empire one of his heirs managed to escape the general slaughter. He fled to a maternal uncle at Ceuta and from there seized control of Muslim Spain. His descendants had been alarmed by the growth of Fatimid power in Morocco and occupied Melilla in 927, Ceuta in 931 and Asilah and Tangier in 974 to forestall any Fatimid plans for an invasion of Spain. From these bases it was a simple matter to expand south when the Fatimids lost interest in Morocco from 970. The Omayyad state was formally dissolved in 1031 after a long civil war but the petty Andalucian successor states maintained control over the northern ports of Morocco until the Almoravide, Youssef ben Tachfine, demanded their surrender in 1080.

The Almoravide achievement

The Almoravides created Morocco. Their brief Empire wedded the civilized northwest of the country to a vast hinterland. From the 11th century, whatever the physical extent of later states there is an awareness of a common identity in Morocco. An identity that was all the more powerful for having been created by a Muslim reform movement from one of the Berber Sanhajan tribes of the Sahara and not by some technically advanced Imperial power.

Almoravide rule had a revolutionary quality. The ruling class of princes and tribal Emirs were deposed, and all taxes not sanctioned in the Koran were abolished. Islamic law according to the Malekite tradition was imposed upon society. It is a law which was, and still is, believed to be a code for the perfect management of society, as composed by God. Almoravide generals subdued even the remotest hill tribes, built stone castles to enforce their authority and encircled cities in protective walls. After the conquest of Spain, skilled craftsmen were brought over to build and decorate mosques, fountains and baths for public use. Talented Andalucian secretaries, employed in the court, brought increased literacy and the Maghrebi script to the country.

The Almoravide Sultans also made a practice of consulting the doctors of Islamic law in order to seek their approval before making any major decision, even in matters of war. This council, the *ulemaa*, remained a central feature of the Moroccan state. They sought recognition from the caliphs of Baghdad for their title, 'Amir al Muslimin'—commander of the Muslims, which aptly expresses their championship of orthodox Islam.

But there was a darker side to their rule. The great flowering of Andalucian poetry was suppressed and they halted any form of intellectual inquiry other than that directly concerned with Malekite law. Their insistence on collecting only Koranic taxes left them short of revenue which they made up by extortions from the Jewish community in Spain. Their narrow puritanism also led to the persecution of the Jewish and Christian communities in Andalucia.

Almoravide origins and rule from 1071–1147

The core of the Almoravide reform movement was the Berber Lamtuna tribe. They first dominated the other Sanhajan tribes of the Sahara which once united formed a potent military force. Unity amongst a single Berber tribe was rare enough but amongst a group of tribes it was exceptional. This unity was formed by the shared ideal of creating a true Islamic state. There are also convincing political and economic reasons for unity amongst the Berber tribes of the Sanhaja in this period.

In the 8th century the Sanhajan Berbers had begun to exploit a route across the Sahara, exchanging desert-mined salt for gold. This highly profitable trade was only possible as the camel had recently become acclimatized to the Western Sahara. Their dominance waned with the opening of new routes to the east and the arrival of competitors, not least the kingdom of Ghana. By the 11th century they were in need of a unifying force to return them to prosperity.

This came in the form of a religious scholar from the Souss valley, Ibn Yasin. Supported by the chief of one of the Sanhaja tribes, the Lamtuna, he established his own community or r'bat for warriors of the faith. It was in 1042 that this disciplined band of holy warriors, the Almoravides, emerged. They were recognizably different from the usual tribal raiding force in that they neither raped or pillaged a defeated community. They first enforced their authority over the other Sanhajan tribes and then advanced north into Morocco and south to the river Niger.

Ibn Yasin died fighting the Berghawata heretics in 1059 and the leadership was assumed by a Lamtuna noble, Abu Bekr, who established an advance base north of the Atlas at Marrakesh in 1070. He appointed his cousin Youssef ben Tachfine to its command when he headed south to suppress a revolt by a dissident Sanhajan tribe in the desert. On his return to the north Youssef presented him with sumptuous gifts, 'so that he would lack for nothing in the desert'. Abu Bekr took the gifts which implicitly accepted a division of power with his cousin and returned to rule the Sahara where he died in 1087.

It was Youssef ben Tachfine who established Almoravide rule in central Morocco. By the 1080s he had crushed all opposing tribes and at last held the city of Fez securely. Thirteen years later his authority extended far over the eastern plains to Algiers.

In 1086 the Muslim prince El Mutamid of Seville appealed for aid against the Spanish Christians but when Youssef ben Tachfine landed on the Spanish shore he came as a master not an ally. The Christians were promptly defeated and then the 26 petty Muslim states of Spain were gradually absorbed into the Almoravide Empire. El Mutamid ended his day a prisoner at Aghmat, just south of Marrakesh.

Ali ben Youssef, 'Ali son of Youssef', succeeded in 1107. He completed the conquest of Muslim Spain four years later and his generals further advanced the frontier by adding Lisbon and the Balearics to the Empire. Ali reigned for 37 years and was responsible for the great building projects of the Almoravides: the Great Mosque of Tlemcen, the Qaraouyine in Fez and the Ben Youssef in Marrakesh. His personal piety restricted his political response to the Almohads, a Muslim reform movement which from 1125 became an increasing threat to the Sultan's authority. Nothing is more indicative of this than the construction of city walls for Marrakesh in 1129.

By Ali's death in 1144 it was already too late, though his two sons, Tachfine and Ishaq, struggled valiantly for their inheritance. When Tachfine died fighting the Almohads near Oran, Andalucia broke into open revolt. Two years later Ishaq perished when his Christian mercenaries betrayed the gates of Marrakesh to the Almohads.

The Almohad Empire, 1147–1248

The Almohad reform movement which was created by Ibn Tumert and led to victory by Abdel Moumen destroyed the Almoravide Empire after twenty years of war. Though they were implacable enemies the two Empires had much in common. Their combined period of two centuries of authority was for the Berber people of North Africa a unique age of strength and independence. They were both founded by charismatic Muslim reformers whose zeal created a movement that transcended tribal loyalties. The actual military conquest was achieved by their successors, practical and longlived military men who founded the ruling dynasties.

The Almohads brought the period to its zenith of confidence and achievement. They did not even nominally recognize the authority of the caliphs of Baghdad and instead assumed the caliph's own title, 'The commander of the faithful'. Whilst the Almoravides had been content to enforce the Malekite code of Islamic law as it had been defined in Arabia the Almohads enforced their own distinctive teachings. Ibn Tumert represented an indigenous source of Berber spiritual legitimacy, one that recognized no greater theological authority after the prophet. His identification as the Mahdi meant that he was the divinely appointed guide to the truths of religion.

Though the Almohads held Muslim Spain they never succeeded in subduing the Almoravide heartland of the Sahara. They more than compensated for this by the conquest of the North African seaboard. The Empire was composed of the modern states of Morocco, Algeria, Tunisia and western Libya, protected by a powerful navy which gave Islam a brief dominance over the Western Mediterranean. Regional capitals were established at the old cities of Taza, Tlemcen, Tunis and Seville while Marrakesh remained the centre of the Empire, and a new port city was built at Rabat.

However, like all rulers of Morocco they ultimately failed to create a national army. Viewed at its most basic level the Almohad Empire was the rule of a coalition of High Atlas tribes. It was an aristocracy of seven tribes that imposed its authority by conquest. Whilst victorious and successful in war they could recruit and command great armies, but after their first major reverse, the crushing defeat in 1213 at the battle of Las Navas de Tolosa, the internal unity of the aristocracy of tribes dissolved and the Empire fragmented.

Ibn Tumert and the Foundation of the Almohads, 1121–30

Ibn Tumert was a Berber theologian who returned from his studies in Arabia to create a disciplined army from the tribes of his homeland. His religious authority and reforming zeal provided the cohesive force that bound six Berber Chleuh tribes into a single strong force.

He was born at Igilliz, a Chleuh Berber village on the northern slopes of the Anti Atlas. The Chleuh, also known as the Masmuda, were mountain peasants hostile to the Almoravide Empire which had been created by their ancient enemies, the nomadic Sanhajan Berbers. He travelled east to Mecca and studied at all the great Islamic universities, like Baghdad, Jerusalem, Damascus and Cairo where he was taught by the great Islamic philosopher and mystic Al Ghazzali for three years.

By 1117 his long search for knowledge was complete. He rejected all four of the established juridical traditions of Sunni Islam. He preached the need to return to the true source of faith, the Koran, which should not be compromised by commentaries partly based on reason, compassion and humanity. He fiercely rejected attempts to represent God in human terms, and taught that a true Muslim has a duty to enforce religious truth on society. His militant opinions were respected but remained unheeded and so with a handful of followers he returned home to Morocco announcing that he would 'reprove what is disapproved and enjoin what is good'. This was the starting point for his campaign to establish his own theocratic government. Ibn Tumert reached Marrakesh in 1121 and after a series of court debates decided on a public break with Almoravide authority. This, due to the sultan's respect for Ibn Tumert's teaching, was more difficult than he imagined but even the pious Ali could not ignore Ibn Tumert when he knocked his sister off her horse for riding unveiled. Chased by government troops, Ibn Tumert retired south to the safety of his tribal homeland.

Three years later, with the active support of Chleuh tribal leaders he established a secure base at Tinmal in the High Atlas. His movement became known as the Muwahhidun, the Almohads or unitarians, and in four years he extended his control over the Chleuh mountain tribes with a mixture of inspirational teaching and ruthless political skills. He lectured the Atlas tribesmen, who until then were largely ignorant of even the most basic understanding of Islam, in their native dialects whilst he taught them the Arabic of the Koran. The veil for women was enforced and music, dance and decoration were forbidden to this growing community who considered Ibn Tumert as the Mahdi, the prophesied successor of Mohammed. In 1128 total obedience was enforced in a forty-day purge of all suspected dissidents. The movement retained its strong tribal structure. Every follower was by birth or adoption placed in one of the six High Atlas tribes which formed the community of the Almohads. Ibn Tumert ruled with a council of ten which was composed of tribal chiefs and a few of his early disciples. This was joined by a representative body of 40 for great sessions.

By 1129 the growing Almohad threat had finally forced Ali, the Almoravide sultan, into action. Marrakesh was encased in strong walls and from the fortresses of Taroudant, Tasseghmout and Aghmat a three-pronged attack was launched against the Almohad citadel of Tinmal. All three columns were defeated in the mountains and flushed with these victories, Ibn Tumert ordered an assault on Marrakesh. He underestimated the Almoravide army which in its turn inflicted a crippling defeat on the besieging Almohads. Ibn Tumert died the next year and his death was kept secret for three years whilst his chosen successor, Abdel Moumen, made sure of his position.

Abdel Moumen, 1130–62

Abdel Moumen succeeded Ibn Tumert when he was 36 years old and ruled until his death 33 years later. Under his leadership the Almohads changed from a reforming movement to a military aristocracy that governed a North African Empire. In the process he established his own family as its ruling dynasty.

His position was however initially precarious for he was from the Kumia tribe from the region of Tlemcen and although he had been adopted into the Hargha, Ibn Tumert's own tribe, he could not rely on the personal support of any of the Almohad tribes. He proved to be a brilliant general and learning from the defeat of 1129 he organized a classic guerrilla campaign, avoiding any direct battle in order to concentrate on piecemeal actions that won him control of the mountains. From a new military base established at Taza he slowly tightened his grip on the major cities of the Almoravide Empire: Tlemcen, Fez and Marrakesh. In 1147 after an epic siege of eleven months the Almoravide capital of Marrakesh finally fell. The Almoravides were massacred, their palaces destroyed and even their mosques and tombs despoiled. The next year the chief cities of Muslim Spain had all fallen to Almohad commanders. Though much of Muslim Spain remained outside his control Abdel Moumen then turned his attention east.

A century earlier (in 1050) an invasion of bedouin Arab tribes had destroyed central government in Libya, Tunisia and Algeria. A scattering of coastal city-states struggled to survive the continued depredations of the bedouin Arab tribes who had turned once prosperous and populous agricultural countries into a pastoral plain for their flocks. In 1152 Abdel Moumen won the great victory of Sitif against the bedouin Arab tribes. The Algerian cities greeted him as their saviour but Abdel Moumen did not press the war against the Arabs or advance further east. He recognized the military worth of the bedouin tribes and began a policy of recruiting individual tribes into government service, where they were particularly useful in suppressing obstinate Berber tribes. The Berber Berghawata of the Atlantic coast, who had successfully resisted the Idrissids and Almoravides, were finally destroyed in this way. All succeeding Sultans continued this policy which over the centuries led to large areas of Morocco being occupied by Arab tribes.

The military situation secured, Abdel Moumen from 1152 to 1159 concentrated on the Almohad internal structure and succeeded in turning a religious movement into a dynasty. This was begun in 1154 with a second great purge which removed all of Ibn Tumert's descendants and envious Almohad tribal chiefs. He then appointed one son as his heir and made his other sons provincial governors. To distract attention from the debatable legitimacy of this new dynasty he publicly strengthened the cult of Ibn Tumert and built a great sanctuary mosque at Tinmal whilst throughout the Empire prayers continued to be called in the name of Ibn Tumert. The privileged position of the Almohad tribes was firmly established. They were given preferential tax treatment and the remaining loyal tribal chiefs were awarded with prestigious posts. Religious officials from the Tinmal tribes were revered as 'Almohad scholars' whilst everyone else whatever their ability had the lower status of a 'Town scholar'. As each governor was advised by an Almohad scholar this tied the interest of the new dynasty and the Tinmal tribes together.

In 1159 Abdel Moumen felt secure enough to continue with the conquest of the east. An army of 200,000 men, supported by a strong navy, incorporated Tunisia and western Libya into the Almohad Empire. Abdel Moumen arrived more as a deliverer from the twin threats of the bedouin Arab tribes and the Normans in Sicily than a conqueror.

In 1162 at the height of his powers the sultan was able to bring his own tribe, from the region around Tlemcen, into the aristocracy of the original six Almohad tribes. That achieved he gathered together an enormous army at Rabat for the complete conquest of Spain but he died just before giving the orders for its embarkation.

Abu Yaacoub Yussef, 1162–84

He was succeeded by a son whose 22-year reign was in the words of the chroniclers, 'that of a true King'. He was famed for his word, his generosity, singleness of purpose, intelligence and statesmanship. He presided over a period of prosperity and organized a fair system of taxation which produced abundant revenues. These were spent on public works, the defence of the Empire, the patronage of scholars and the encouragement of religion. It was the sultan's personal interest and protection that encouraged the work of two of Islam's greatest scholars: Abu Bakr and Ibn Rushd. Ibn Rushd is known in Europe as Averroes, his translation and commentary of Aristotle can be considered the starting block of the European Renaissance.

The sultan meanwhile completed the formation of the Almohad Empire. His first years were consumed in suppressing the Riff tribes of northern Morocco who had risen in revolt. This was achieved when he crushed the Ghomara tribe, the core of the revolt, in 1166. From this time he was able to direct his attention to Muslim Spain whose eastern provinces were finally incorporated in 1172. Even the cynical, squabbling Andalucian princes were impressed by the chivalry of the sultan and they rallied to his service. The sultan died of wounds that he received leading an attack on a Portuguese castle in 1183.

Abu Youssef Yaacoub, 'Yaacoub el Mansour', 1184–99

The two previous sultans had sifted the doctrines of Ibn Tumert in the interests of good and efficient government. Abu Youssef Yaacoub came into conflict with the Almohad scholars who claimed to represent the authority of Ibn Tumert. The sultan determined to outflank the claims of the Almohad scholars by returning directly to the source of faith, the Koran, just as Ibn Tumert had preached. In the process he put aside the writings of

Ibn Tumert and unleashed a rigid puritanism. Ibn Rushd was forced into disgrace and his books were publicly burnt which brought an early end to rational Islamic philosophy. More immediately the political conflict among the Almohads resulted in growing disorder in the administration of justice and tax collection.

The sultan moved from these internal problems to face dangerous enemies on two quite separate fronts. In Tunisia a surviving Almoravide prince had allied with the bedouin Arab tribes whilst in Spain the Christian kings formed a coalition. On both fronts he was successful, the victory over the Christian kings at Alarcos in 1195 won the sultan the title, El Mansour, 'the victorious'. The great Almohad building works of this reign were crowned by the construction at Rabat of the Great Mosque of el Hassan though work stopped in 1199 on the day the sultan died. His reign, so outwardly impressive, hid the weakening internal structure of the Almohad Empire.

Mohammed en Nasir, 1199–1213

Three years after his succession Mohammed en Nasir had conquered the Balearic islands and five years later suppressed a new Tunisian revolt with a swift campaign by land and sea. These achievements were eclipsed in 1213 by the defeat at Las Navas de Tolosa in Spain. The Almohad army was destroyed and with it the authority of an Empire which rested squarely on an impressive military record. The sultan escaped the battlefield to die in Marrakesh the next year.

The collapse of the Almohad Empire, 1213–48

The disaster of Las Navas de Tolosa was magnified by the accession of a child sultan, Youssef al Mustansir, upon whose death in 1223 the Empire dissolved into civil war. The Almohad tribes refused obedience to the quarrelling dynasty and plundered the countryside in league with Arab tribes. Provincial governors established petty states. In Muslim Spain these rapidly fell to Ferdinand III of Castile who captured Cordoba in 1235 and Seville in 1248, to leave only the mountainous kingdom of Granada independent. In Tunisia an Almohad governor established the Hafsid dynasty whilst western Algeria fell to a Berber tribe, the Ziyanids who ruled from Tlemcen. Only in Morocco did the dynasty survive, albeit precariously, for 40 more years.

A determined revival was attempted by Sultan Abu Said who in 1244 set out to regain Tlemcen from the Ziyanids. His early death and the destruction of his leaderless army at the river Moulouya in 1248 destroyed this last Almohad hope, though princes ruled Marrakesh until 1269 and Tinmal, the first and last Almohad, bastion lasted out for another seven years.

The Merenids, 1248–1465

The Merenids could not claim descent from the prophet nor did they champion any religious sect or reform movement. They seized control of Morocco from the ruin of the Almohad Empire due to the political skill of their chiefs and the military strength of their tribe, the Beni Merin. The Beni Merin were the largest of the tribes that occupied the eastern desert plain and like every pastoral tribe were trained from birth for war. It is interesting that the second most numerous tribe of these eastern plains, the Beni Ziyin, also succeeded in creating a state for themselves—the Ziyanid kingdom of Tlemcen.

The Beni Merin were first brought into the political arena by the Almohad sultans. They were recruited into the Almohad army as cavalry and served in a number of Spanish campaigns which whetted their appetite for the rewards of political power. After the defeat of the Almohad army in 1212 at Las Navas de Tolosa, the Beni Merin enthusiastically entered the civil war. Despite a number of victories, between 1216 and 1244 they lacked strong direction and their campaigns had more in common with plundering raids than a determined bid for power.

Abou Yahya, 1248–58

In 1245 the Beni Merin came under the control of Abou Yahya, a brilliant and ruthless tribal warrior. He sent a token force of 500 men to join the army of the Almohad Sultan Abu Said in 1248. After Abu Said's death near Tlemcen this force guided the Almohad army into an ambush laid by Abou Yahya at the river Moulouya. At a single stroke the entire Almohad army was destroyed and those who could, like the Christian mercenaries, defected to Abou Yahya. Within two months he held Fez and Meknes and contained the Almohads in Marrakesh to dominate central Morocco for ten years. He selected Fez for his capital but by massacring the populace after a rebellion he permanently alienated the civilized Fassis. Right from the start the Merenid dynasty was faced with its central dilemma. They wanted and needed to be recognized as civilized, worthy successors to the throne but their most civilized subjects refused recognition. Though the undoubted political master of Morocco, Abou Yahya was a mere tribal chief and lacked national prestige.

Abou Yusuf Yacqub, 1259–86

Abou Yusuf Yacqub succeeded to the leadership on the death of his brother Abou Yahya in 1259. During his 27 year reign he completed the establishment of Merenid power.

In 1260 on the night of the feast of Aid el Kebir a Castilian fleet sacked Salé and enslaved the population. In a celebrated journey Abou Yusuf Yacqub arrived to assume the leadership of the counterattack having ridden from Taza in a day. He followed this prestigious display of concern with another nationalist gesture. He sent his sons and nephews, who were a troublesome lot anyway, to fight the Christians in Spain, publicly instructing them to obediently serve the Muslim king of Granada for no reward.

The final destruction of the Almohads was delayed by continuous trouble on the eastern plains. A series of victories at Moulouya, Isly and Tlemcen secured this frontier and allowed Abu Yusuf Yacqub to direct his attention south. Marrakesh was stormed and Ishaq, the last Almohad prince, died defending Tinmal in 1276.

Once secure of the throne, Abou Yusuf Yacqub led an army into Spain and won a victory against the Castilians which proved that as successful leaders of the jihad, the dynasty were worthy possessors of the throne. The reverses of Salé and Las Navas de Tolosa were revenged and Abou Yusuf Yacqub took the old Almoravide title, 'Commander of the Muslims', and founded New Fez to celebrate the victory.

Merenid policy

New Fez was a quite separate and defensible Royal city to the west of old Fez. Its strong walls, moats and barracks for mercenary guards were symbolic of the Merenids' continued distrust of the population. Although Fez enjoyed a golden age under Merenid rule the city always remained hostile to the sultans.

One way that the Merenids could prove themselves civilized monarchs was in architectural patronage, and the dynasty have left eloquent testimonials to their taste. The Chellah at Rabat, the medersas of Fez and numerous mosques, fountains and fondouqs scattered throughout the provincial towns of Morocco bear witness to this elegant policy.

Abou Yusuf Yacqub built the first Medersa, the es Seffarin, in Fez in 1280. Having no religious authority of their own the Merenid sultans determined on a strict orthodoxy that would eradicate the cult of Ibn Tumert. The medersas also served as a university where the Merenids could train a new generation of officials for loyal service to the dynasty. Their patronage of intellectuals was chiefly motivated by a demand for chronicles, histories, biographies that praised their rule, though in fairness Ibn Khaldoun and particularly Ibn Battuta received disinterested help and encouragement from the Merenid court.

The Merenids continued to involve themselves in Spanish campaigns although no major effort was made to reconquer the lost Muslim territories. They did however devote great energy to controlling Spanish ports like Algeciras that both protected the Moroccan coast from invasion and allowed for quick Merenid interference in Spain. Most of the Merenid interventions were to maintain the balance of power between the Castilians and the Muslim Nasrid kingdom of Granada.

In contrast to this enlightened policy of minimum force the eastern frontier was a continous war zone. Merenid sultans commonly devoted the major part of their reign in attempting to conquer Tunisia and Algeria. Possession of the North African ports also gave complete control over the lucrative Saharan trade which in the 14th century attracted fleets of European merchant ships to Moroccan ports like Ceuta, Asilah and Bades.

There is also the dynamic of authority to consider in explaining this succession of eastern wars. Like previous rulers the Merenids were ultimately dependent on the strength, cohesion and loyalty of their army. Obedience and assured control of these forces could be only maintained by a near constant state of war. Excluding Fez, there was no administrative structure of government independent of the army. Merenid society was clearly divided between the privileged tribes of the government—the army—who collected taxes and the subject tribes who produced them. The recruitment of bedouin Arab tribes into the government proceeded throughout the centuries of Merenid rule. The more civilized Arab tribes were rewarded with land in central Morocco whilst potentially dangerous groups, like the Maqil, were directed south into the sub-Sahara.

The details of eastern wars and dynastic intrigue amongst the Merenids are fabulously confusing. The two centuries of Merenid rule, 1248 to 1465, divide into two roughly equal periods. The first hundred years of rule leads up to the peak decades of achievement under the reign of Abou Hassan, 1331–1351 and his son Abou Inan, 1351–1358.

Merenid armies were poised at the brink of the complete conquest of Tunisia and Algeria and architectural and intellectual patronage was at its zenith.

After Abou Inan's death in 1358 (he was strangled in his sick bed by his chief vizier when only 33 years old) there is a hundred years of decline. The power of viziers, financiers and the army generals grew unchecked and the government was consumed by its own vicious internal intrigues. One sultan, Abou Said Uthmann, 1398–1420, emerged from this unhappy period and attempted to reverse the disintegration of the state. He was assassinated by an infuriated Fassi mob after he failed to recapture Ceuta from the Portuguese in 1419. He was succeeded by Abdul Haqq, who was elevated by a Wattasid vizier to the throne as a mere one-year-old child. In 1465 a popular revolution finally exploded against the corrupt regime. The continuing failure against the Portuguese invaders was in sharp contrast with the harsh and efficient exactions of the army and Jewish financiers. The citizens of Fez dethroned Sultan Abdul Haqq and dragged the last of the Merenids through the streets to his execution.

The failure of the Wattasids, 1472–1554

The eighty years of Wattasid rule almost destroyed Morocco as an independent nation. By the mid 16th century Portugal controlled the Atlantic coast and the Wattasid Sultans ruled only in Fez which they could only hold with the assistance of the Ottoman Turks.

The revolution against the Merenids had been led by the city's Idrissid Sherifs. They controlled Fez for seven years before a powerful ex-vizier of the Merenids, the Wattasid Mohammed al Sheikh, took the city. He had surrendered Asilah to the Portuguese in exchange for support against independent Fez. The initial disgrace of this act remained to tarnish the reputation of the new dynasty. It was new only in name for as cousins and hereditary viziers of the Merenid Sultans the Wattasids had been the power behind the throne for decades.

Once installed in Fez the Wattasids proved incapable of defending Morocco. The Portuguese seized Tangier in 1471, Larache in 1473, Safi in 1508, Azzemour in 1486 and Essaouira in 1506. They also built a string of new forts down the Atlantic coast; at El Jadida in 1502, Souria Kedima in 1521, Mehdiya, Massa and Agadir in 1505. In the far south Spanish colonists from the Canary Islands built slave-raiding towers on the Western Saharan coast and captured the important Moroccan Mediterranean trading posts of Melilla in 1497 and Badis in 1508.

Spanish interest in a full Crusade into the Moroccan hinterland ended with the death of Isabella, the 'Catholic Queen', in 1503. They were however heavily involved in Algeria and Tunisia as part of the larger conflict against the Ottoman Empire. The victories of Barbarossa, a pirate turned Ottoman admiral, brought an additional threat to Morocco. A Turkish garrison was established in Tlemcen in 1545 which was soon enmeshed in intrigues to bring Morocco into the Ottoman Empire. The Wattasid Sultans had since 1536 been dependent on Turkish military support and seemed content to drift into a client relationship.

The Christian Portuguese remained the greatest threat. The Crusade against Morocco was a natural continuation of the long war for Portuguese independence and was insolubly wrapped up in their national ethos. The seizure of Ceuta in 1415 had been the first step in the creation of the Portuguese maritime Empire. From their coastal forts

Portuguese cavalry penetrated deep into the interior and attempts were made to capture Marrakesh and Ksar el Kebir long before King Sebastian's invasion of 1578.

As the Wattasids failed to organize national resistance to the invaders the leadership of the struggle fell to local chiefs. Tribal jealousies and racial antagonism between Arab and Berber usually required that leadership fell to a holy dynasty who they could both trust. In the north an Idrissid marabout, Moulay Rachid, who was also descended from the master of Djebel Alam, a celebrated 12th century mystic, established the Emirate of Chechaouen, Tetouan and Targa. This state led the resistance to Portugal in the north from 1471 and reinforced by Muslim refugees from Spain continued the holy war until it was conquered by a rival maraboutic dynasty from the south, the Saadians.

The Saadians, 1510–1668

The Saadians' greatest achievement was the preservation of independence from the triple threat of the Portuguese, Ottoman and Spanish Empires. Mohammed ech Cheikh expelled the Portuguese from Agadir in 1541 and Ahmed el Mansour's victory against the invasion of King Sebastian in 1578 is still commemorated each year in Morocco. They reversed the 150 year old decay in government, reuniting the regions and expanding the state to create a golden age of prosperity from 1554 to 1603. The death of Sultan Ahmed el Mansour in 1603 brought these promising achievements to a sudden close. The dynasty discredited itself by selling two towns to the Portuguese and destroyed itself in a succession dispute. It was only the rivalry between various emergent petty states that preserved the dynasty for another 65 years.

The origins of Saadian power, 1510–40

The Portuguese had seized control of the southern coastal trade by constructing forts at Agadir and Massa. The tribes were incapable of an effective unified resistance and so in 1510 agreed to accept the leadership of the Saadians, a holy Arab family from the village of Tamegroute in the Draa valley.

Control of the Souss valley and the possession of the one free port of the region allowed the Saadians to trade gold and sugar for war munitions with the Genoese. They also assumed leadership of the Jazuliya Sufi brotherhood, which had since 1465 pursued a fierce vendetta against the Merenid–Wattasid dynasty. By strongly associating themselves with this brotherhood the Saadians indicated the full extent of their ambitions.

Although Agadir was still held by the Portuguese by 1517 the Saadians felt confident of their control of the south. They advanced north to occupy Marrakesh in 1524 which was confirmed when they destroyed a Wattasid army on the Tadla plain, half way between Fez and Marrakesh, in 1536. The leadership of the Saadians had been divided, since 1517 between two brothers. A peace agreement in 1540 with the Wattasids allowed the more militant brother, Mohammed ech Cheikh, to depose his brother and assume sole leadership.

Mohammed ech Cheikh, 1540–57

In his 17 year reign Mohammed ech Cheikh completed the conquest of Morocco, humbled the Portuguese and checked the growing Turkish influence. The year after he deposed his brother the capture of Agadir greatly raised his national prestige which was further enhanced by the Portuguese evacuation of Azemmour and Safi in 1542.

The Wattasids since their defeat on the Tadla plain in 1536 had become totally dependent on the support of the Turks, who in effect were Mohammed ech Cheikh's main opponents. In 1545 he defeated the Turkish–Wattasid army in two engagements and in the latter took the Wattasid Sultan Ahmed prisoner. The remaining Wattasid princes in Fez appealed for more aid from the Turks and, insulted by a letter from the Ottoman Sultan, Mohammed ech Cheikh decided on a final assault on Fez which he seized in 1549.

Two years later he sent his son with an army of 30,000 against the Turks in Tlemcen. This attack failed and allowed the last Wattasid prince briefly to reoccupy Fez in 1553 with the aid of Turkish troops. The Saadians were never popular with the leaders of Fez who produced evidence that they were not in fact descendants of the prophet but just run of the mill Arab tribesmen. This may have confirmed the Saadians in their choice of Marrakesh as the capital, and forts were built above the city walls of Fez to control the population.

The danger from the Turks was still strong. Taza was turned into a fortress and an alliance was made with Spain. But before Mohammed ech Cheikh could organize a joint attack with Phillip II on the Turks he was assassinated. A squad of Turks succeeded in carrying the severed head of Mohammed ech Cheikh from the High Atlas to the Ottoman pasha in Tlemcen.

Abdullah el Ghalib, 1557–74

When the news of the sultan's death reached Marrakesh the Caid of the city ordered the execution of six Saadian princes to clear the succession for Abdullah el Ghalib. It was a harsh but politically effective act for the twenty year reign of Abdullah el Ghalib was an enlightened era of peace and prosperity. The sultan directed a public building programme, but was criticized for not giving active support to a Muslim rebellion in Andalucia—the heroic two-year Morisco resistance of 1568 to 1570. He could not however afford to alienate the Spanish who were vital in keeping the Turks in Algeria at bay. Abdullah died whilst still young, having wrecked his health on the sensual pleasures of his court life.

'The Battle of the Three Kings'

Abdullah el Ghalib was succeeded by his son, Mohammed el Mutawakkil who appears to have been a bigoted and treacherous monarch. He lasted two years before he was deposed by Abdel Malik, one of the two surviving brothers of Abdullah el Ghalib who had spent most of his life in exile. Abdel Malik was an educated and enlightened man who spoke Arabic, Turkish, Italian and Spanish and revealed his cosmopolitan taste by employing English musicians four hundred years before they became fashionable.

The deposed Mohammed el Mutawakkil retaliated by surrendering Asilah to the Portuguese in exchange for military support. Sebastian, the idealistic boy King of Portugal, landed at Larache in 1578 with grand schemes of being crowned Emperor of Morocco at Fez by the end of the year. An army of 26,000, encumbered by priests, carriages and courtiers advanced slowly but magnificently inland towards Ksar el Kebir. Beside the river Loukkos the entire Portuguese army was destroyed in a fierce engagement that is known as Ksar el Kebir or the battle of Three Kings. All three of the major contestants died that day: Sebastian's corpse was discovered covered by the bodies of Moorish warriors that he had slain, Mohammed el Mutawakkil drowned in a river whilst attempting to escape and Abdel Malik died of poison in the hour of his victory.

Ahmed el Mansour, 1578–1603

This left Ahmed, the younger brother of Abdel Malik as the survivor who was acclaimed 'El Mansour', 'the victorious'. A fitting inauguration to his long and glorious reign.

The booty from the defeated army and the ransoms received from the captured Portuguese nobility brought the sultan a vast fortune. He also continued the Saadian policy of encouraging external trade and enforced a national collection of taxes. Morocco in the 16th century produced a healthy customs revenue for as well as acting as a conduit for the rich Saharan trade it produced refined sugar, silks and saltpetre, a component of gunpowder.

The Saadians had never been identified with any specific tribal interest and from the abundant state revenues Ahmed el Mansour was able to create a professional army. The sultan recruited Andalucian exiles, Christian renegades and Turks to forge a technically competent army unaffected by any distracting tribal loyalties.

The Sultan borrowed the customs and manners of the Ottoman court to enhance further his absolute rule. He gave audiences behind a screen and introduced the scarlet parasol which is still a distinguishing mark of a Moroccan sultan's sovereignty. He built at Marrakesh the palace of El Badi to be the magnificent ceremonial heart of his court. Through entertainments and patronage he drew the secular and religious leaders away from provincial politics to the glittering life of the capital. His rule was that of an enlightened despot, in the words of the chroniclers, 'he sweetened his absolute power with much clemency'.

The foreign policy of Ahmed el Mansour, 1578–1603

Ahmed el Mansour and his brother conducted a skilful and light-footed foreign policy through the rapidly changing requirements of this period. During the years of the Portuguese threat, the previous Saadian policy was reversed and they allied themselves heavily with the Turks. For a brief period prayers were even said in the name of the Ottoman Caliph. After the battle of Ksar el Kebir the Portuguese threat disappeared and the Ottoman Turks were again perceived as the principal threat. The Turkish alliance was hastily dropped and a rapprochement was made with Phillip II of Spain.

By 1580 a new policy was required. The Ottoman Empire, already weakened by the naval defeat of Lepanto, had become heavily involved in a Persian war. Spain, who that year absorbed the entire Portuguese Empire, was now considered as the major threat. An alliance was then contrived with Protestant England, then locked in war with Catholic Spain. In exchange for saltpetre England was persuaded to defy a general European ban on trading munitions with Muslims. Cannon, ships, timber, ammunition and even galleys were provided from 1585 by the English Barbary Company. Ahmed el Mansour and Elizabeth of England even dabbled with plans for a joint Moroccan/English attack on Portugal. It is also clear that the Moroccan Ambassador in London was engaged in technical and commercial espionage for his master.

The sultan by 1591 felt sufficiently secure to indulge in schemes of African conquest. Pasha Judar, a Spanish renegade in the Sultan's service, led an army across the Sahara in a 135 day march and then with his superior firepower destroyed the negro kingdom of Songhai. By 1594 the key Saharan posts of Gao, Taghaza, Tuat and Timbuktu were all held by Moroccan governors, and the sultan received his first tribute from Timbuktu of 30 mules laden with gold. By the end of his reign 10 tons of gold had been delivered to the sultan's treasury.

Fall of the Saadians, 1603–26

In 1603 Ahmed el Mansour died and his sons, Zaidan and Mohammed ech Cheikh II fought over the glittering inheritance. The promising diplomatic developments, the sugar and saltpetre trade and the recently acquired Saharan Empire were all neglected in the fury of a succession war. Tunis and Algiers acquired the bulk of the Saharan trade, and the French and Dutch found it easier to trade directly with West Africa.

In 1610 Mohammed ech Cheikh II surrendered Badis and Larache to the Spanish in exchange for military aid against his brother Zaidan. This national treachery completely discredited the Saadian dynasty. Even Zaidan at Marrakesh shared the disgrace and became dependent on the protection of a Sufi brotherhood in the High Atlas. When Al Halis, the sheikh of this brotherhood, died in 1626, Zaidan's remaining authority disintegrated.

Sufi brotherhoods

Morocco has never been affected by the great division in the Islamic world between Sunni and Shiite. Sufi brotherhoods have however played an important role in Moroccan political life. Sufism is not a separate branch of Islam but a mystical discipline which could be compared to a Christian monastic community. They have generally been the the champions of a regional identity and the central government has always been concerned to reduce their influence. The Saadians during their struggle for power allied themselves with the Jazuliya brotherhood but once in power neutralized the Jazuliya and attempted to destroy the influence of other brotherhoods. After the collapse of Saadian power two brotherhoods, Djila and Tazeroualt seemed poised to rule Morocco but they were too closely identified with the interest of one region to be accepted by the whole nation. Sufi brotherhoods always grew in influence during periods of weak government. The head of the brotherhood, the sheikh, gave religious instruction and the blessing of baraka which can be translated as divine luck or favour. A sheikh on this voluntary basis of respect was able to provide all the services of a government. His word could guarantee the security of a traveller, his zaouia was a refuge from feuds and tribal fighting, dispensed tribal justice, ran schools and provided charity to the ill and poor. The brotherhoods provided more than the central government was ever capable of and attracted veneration and loyalty. The zaouia of a brotherhood could easily develop from a regional centre into an independent state and defended by a loyal army could play an influential role in national politics.

Bou Regreg, Tazeroualt and Djila, 1626–66

From the confusion of the Saadian civil war half a dozen petty states emerged. By 1650 a dynasty of sheikhs from the Middle Atlas brotherhood of Djila had cleared the field of rivals but final victory evaded their grasp. It was the Alouites, an Arab holy family from the oasis of Tafilalet, who succeeded in seizing the throne in 1666, which they still hold to this day.

One of the more colourful and richest of these petty states was the Republic of Bou Regreg though it was never a serious contender for the leadership of Morocco. The republic was the creation of Andalucian refugees, for in 1610 King Phillip III expelled all his citizens of Moorish descent from Spain. The refugees settled on both banks of the Bou Regreg river at Rabat and Salé. The community took to piracy as a profitable way to extract their revenge from Christendom. Their ships ranged far out into the Atlantic trade routes and the Salée Rovers, who raided coastal settlements as far away as Iceland and Cornwall, achieved a desired notoriety. A council of elders elected an annual president but by 1631 the pirate republic had lost its independence to Al-Ayyashi, an Arab chief.

In 1626 the sheikhs of the Tazeroualt brotherhood ruled the mountains of the Anti Atlas. Five years later they had complete control of the Souss and the oasis valleys which gave them command of the lucrative Saharan sugar and saltpetre trade. Tazeroualt enjoyed good commercial relations with European traders and seemed set to repeat the Saadian road to power. However their expansion north of the Atlas was checked in 1636 by the Djila sheikhs. Tazeroualt remained a regional power that continued a shadowy existence until the late 19th century when it was suppressed by Sultan Moulay Hassan. The distinctive local codes of law were retained and the zaouia still exists although it is now known as the zaouia of Sidi Ahmed ou Moussa.

Djila was founded just south of Khenifra in 1560 by Abu Bekr, a pious Sufi mystic who established a lodge to feed the poor and propagate doctrine. It quickly established itself as a regional power but it was the third sheikh of the dynasty, Mohammed al Hajj who began an assertive extension of power. Having established the High Atlas as the boundary with Tazeroualt he turned his attention south, defeating a Saadian force from Marrakesh in 1636 and capturing Meknes two years later. He then allied with the republic of Bou Regreg for a joint attack on the dominant figure of central Morocco. This was al Ayyashi, chief of the Arab Beni Malik tribe who had gained great prestige by leading the attacks on Portuguese coastal forts like El Jadida and Mehdiya. Al Ayyashi was defeated on the banks of the Sebou river and Salé, Fez and Tetouan then passed under the control of Djila. From 1650 to 1662 Morocco was in the control of the sheikhs of the Djilan brotherhood. A series of rebellions weakened their power just as the Alouites emerged as a militant new rival.

The Alouites

The Alouites came to the Tafilalet oasis with the great influx of Arab tribes in the 13th century. The oasis had since the 8th century been an influential centre of Arab and Islamic culture whose merchants dominated the Saharan trade routes. The Alouites, respected because of their descent from the prophet Mohammed, were an influential local family of merchants, warriors and marabouts. In 1636 Tafilalet was at the centre of the struggle between the armies of Djila and Tazeroualt. The inhabitants chose an Alouite, Moulay Ali Sherif to lead them against this twin threat. Early in the struggle Moulay Ali Sherif was captured and sent into honourable exile into the Souss valley. There he was presented with a negro slave girl who subsequently gave birth to two sons who were destined to be Sultans, Moulay Rachid and Moulay Ishmael.

Mohammed, a son from an earlier marriage, had succeeded to his father's leadership of Tafilalet oasis. Blocked by the power of Djila and Tazeroualt, Mohammed expanded his realm into the eastern desert region and won the support of its Arab tribes.

Moulay Rachid, 1666–72

In 1664 Mohammed was killed by his ambitious half brother, Moulay Rachid. The new Alouite leader revealed astonishing energy and ruthless military leadership. Establishing himself at Taza he had mastered the country by July 1668. The Djila zaouia, where as a youth he had taken refuge and been educated was left in a smoking ruin and the last Saadian princes were beheaded in Marrakesh.

The speed of his victory requires some explanation. The Djila zaouia's success had been coupled with a generous magnanimity in victory. This, though admirable, allowed its defeated rivals to unite in revenge around the Alouite challenge. The Djila zaouia was an identifiably Berber Middle Atlas movement. The untamed nature of the Middle Atlas tribes alarmed the sophisticated Andalucian culture of the towns. The Arab tribes were even more reluctant to accept a Berber sultan. The Alouites however appealed to both of these influential groups. The tribes respected their distinguished Arabic ancestry whilst the towns could not help but identify with rulers who had risen to eminence as defenders of the urban civilization and merchants of the Tafilalet.

Moulay Rachid enjoyed the fruits of victory for four years but was killed in a midnight riding accident in the Aguedal gardens at Marrakesh. He was succeeded by his brother Moulay Ishmael who had served as governor of Meknes.

Moulay Ishmael, 1672–1727

The 54 year reign of Moulay Ishmael is one of the great periods of Moroccan history. Like the Saadian Sultan Ahmed el Mansour who had reigned 70 years before him he created a despotism which was independent of tribal support, firmly upheld by an obedient foreign army and controlled from a magnificent new administrative and ceremonial capital. Both sultans used Europeans captured in war as a skilled slave labour force and viewed with hostility the independent and critical spirit of the citizens of Fez. They presided over long periods of internal peace but it was a personal achievement, and the order of their reign was followed by decades of anarchy.

The important difference between the two was that the Saadian ruled through a paid mercenary army whilst Moulay Ishmael ruled through an army of negro slaves. Whilst the Saadian skilfully masked the true nature of his despotism with a reputation for mercy and patronage, Moulay Ishmael stressed the full nature of his power with frequent arbitrary executions. Legends of his madness and cruelty increase every year but behind the fables there is a consistent policy. Terror was the instrument that kept his provincial governors, the Berber mountain tribes, the Arabs of the plain, his negro army and battalions of slaves at work and obedient.

Throughout Morocco you will find evidence of the constructive nature of his reign. He founded towns, built bridges, ports, forts and secured the safety of roads. He encouraged trade, reformed religious life, purged unorthodox cults but restored approved shrines and mosques. He enlarged and secured the conquests of his brother, recaptured the ports of Mehdiya, Larache and Tangier and strengthened the eastern border against the Turks in Algeria.

It would be hazardous to distinguish the sultan morally from his contemporaries in Europe. Was the sultan's justice less merciful than English law? Do the wars and religious persecution of Louis XIV's France provide an uplifting comparison? Or the slave traders of Liverpool, Boston and Amsterdam?

Securing the frontiers

Moulay Ishmael expelled the Christians from their fortresses on the Moroccan coast, crushed internal dissidence, and pushed back the principal threat—the Turks in the east—to establish the present national frontiers.

The first years of his reign were consumed in suppressing the revolts that broke out on the death of his brother, Moulay Rachid. The Turks supported two candidates, Ghailan, a warlord in the north, and a new Sheikh of Djila whose army was destroyed at the great battle of Oued el Abid in 1678. Though deprived of the leadership of the Djilan Sheikhs the Berber Middle Atlas tribes consistently rebelled against Alouite sultans. Moulay Ishmael placed garrisons at Sefrou and Taza and founded Azrou, Tadla and Khenifra to contain their dissidence. He even contemplated connecting this line of forts with a walled frontier that would stretch from Fez to Marrakesh.

He was then free to direct his energy against the Turks on the Algerian frontier. Fortifications at Oujda, Taourirt, Guercif, Msoun and Taza provided a defence in depth whilst offensive campaigns in 1679, 1682 and 1695 confirmed his control of the frontier.

It was paradoxically the south, the Alouite homeland, that was the greatest problem for the sultan. His nephew, Ahmad ibn Mahriz, continually undermined and threatened the sultan's rule from his base in the Souss. Uncle and nephew fought each other in fourteen years of intrigue and war. In 1686 Moulay Ishmael finally defeated his nephew and in a calculated act of terror slaughtered the entire population of Taroudant, the chief city of the Souss.

His authority in the south was also diminished by the Ait Atta, a Berber tribal confederacy. The Ait Atta were not commanded by any dynasty or Sufi brotherhood and proudly retained their loose democratic constitution. They were subsequently an elusive enemy and succeeded in defeating the sultan's army when it penetrated their mountain home of Djebel Saghro in 1679. Moulay Ishmael made no further attempt to subdue the Ait Atta but strengthened his alliance with their principal enemy, the Ma'qil Arabs. The Ma'qil Arabs were doubly useful as they organized annual slaving expeditions across the Sahara which provided new recruits for the sultan's black army.

The sultan's most prestigious victories were those that could be seen as the jihad—the holy war—to clear the Christian invaders from the soil of Morocco. He forced the Spanish out of their strong fort of Mehdiya in 1681 and from 1674 the English in Tangier were placed under a guerrilla siege. This prevented any trade or expansion into the hinterland and successfully forced Charles II to abandon the town in 1684. In 1689 a direct three-month siege regained Larache and boosted the sultan's slave gangs with thousands of skilled Spanish prisoners which were replenished with the fall of Asilah in 1691. In the north the sultan's governors organized sieges against four remaining Spanish coastal positions. This though unsuccessful at least kept the troublesome Riff tribes occupied. The war against the Christians at sea, led by the Andalucian refugees of Tetouan and Salé, was encouraged by the sultan who assumed a 60% share in every pirate enterprise. Curiously these two towns were also the centres of European commercial activity and a lively speculative trade in ransoming. The sultan corresponded frequently with European monarchs but his attempt to forge an alliance with France against Spain foundered over his refusal to limit the activities of his pirate fleet.

The slave army of the sultan

Moulay Ishmael's mother and favourite wife were both negroes. The negro army was a source of obsessive interest to the sultan and he may have been attempting to create a separate military class. Negroes were brought fresh from the slave caravans, from existing owners, whilst even free citizens of negro blood were recruited into the Abid regiments. The sultan personally chose wives for his Abid soldiers and made himself responsible for their children. Boys from the age of ten to thirteen were taught practical crafts, followed by five years of military training before they joined an Abid regiment. Girls were trained in domestic work before being presented to their Abid husband.

By the end of his reign the sultan had one out of every twenty men in Morocco in his army. The Abid force alone numbered 150,000. Half were dispersed amongst the various garrisons and the rest concentrated as a rapid strike force on Salé and the capital of Meknes. The sultan also recruited Berbers from the Riff and employed Arab tribes to create an army divided between three races and united only in their loyalty to the sultan. Fez and Marrakesh were neglected and Meknes was created as the new administrative, ceremonial and military centre of the nation. Vast store houses, stables, barracks and compounds were built to supply the army which maintained the sultan's peace. The historian al Nasiri noted that during the sultan's reign there was an abundance of cheap food, an active internal trade and that the roads were so safe that a woman or a Jew could travel across the length of the country without being molested.

Anarchy of the Seven Heirs 1727–45

Moulay Ishmael had ruled as an absolute monarch for fifty years. After the rebellion of his most competent son, Mohammed el Alim, in 1703, he became even more reluctant to delegate authority. By his death in 1727 the nation had become accustomed to all political decisions originating from the Imperial city of Meknes. The sultan's failure to train or even designate an heir is characteristic of a harem court with its tempestuous factions of wives and concubines. This weakness served to wreck his life's achievement.

Without a master the enormous army was quick to feel the extent of its power. Rival viziers bought their support on behalf of any of the many legitimate heirs in an escalating rate of bribes and bounties. The viziers for their part selected the most easily dominated and disordered princes.

From 1727 to 1745 at least seven different sons were elevated and deposed. The vicious court politics of Meknes were soon extended to the provincial garrisons and the country was exposed to thirty years of anarchic pillage and retribution. It is estimated that in one of the peaks of disorder 80,000 perished in just one month.

Moulay Abdullah, 1745–57

Moulay Abdullah had been a contender for the throne since 1729. By 1743 the double threat of the pillaging army and an invasion of Riff tribes allowed Moulay Abdullah to forge a new army from threatened Arab and Berber tribes. In a series of decisive campaigns he destroyed the Riff army, disciplined the Abid and imposed his authority over the coastal towns and the three cities of Meknes, Fez and Marrakesh.

The military alliance of rival tribes deteriorated after they had destroyed their common threat but the sultan, though he hardly ruled the nation, was at least secure in Fez.

The wise reign of Sidi Mohammed, 1757–90

As a boy of nine Sidi Mohammed had escorted his grandmother to Mecca. His father, Sultan Moulay Abdullah, appointed him pasha of Marrakesh but a rebellion forced him from the city. He took his talents to Safi and proved such a capable ruler that a delegation of the citizens of Marrakesh humbly pleaded for his return. From Marrakesh he was forced to march to Meknes to suppress another rebellion of the Abid who had risen in his name against his father. His firmness in refusing their support left a lasting impression and in 1750, at the age of thirty, his father entrusted him with the rule of the country.

Sidi Mohammed renewed the siege of the Spanish enclaves of Ceuta and Melilla and in 1769 succeeded in expelling the Portuguese from their fortified port at El Jadida. A rebellion in Agadir revealed how precarious his control of the south and its valuable Saharan trade had become. He determined to create a port firmly under the control of the government and started in 1760 to rebuild the harbour and defences of Essaouira. Jews were settled in the town, exports banned from all other ports and rebellious Agadir was closed down. Custom tariffs were set at a uniform rate of 2%. By 1780 12 European firms were buying a million pounds worth of goods a year.

During his regency Sidi Mohammed had signed a commercial arrangement with Denmark that had given the Danes virtual control over Agadir and Safi. In the latter part of his reign he displayed a confident awareness of European politics and came to profitable agreements with Britain, her rebellious American colonies in 1786, Naples, Venice, Spain, France and Sweden. His long reign was a renaissance in trade and government, but a series of natural disasters at the end of the 18th century, prolonged drought, bubonic plague and a cholera epidemic drastically reduced the population.

His one failing—and it was a great one—was in the choice of a successor. For his favourite son, Yazid, was brave but cruel to the edge of madness. His (1790–1792) short but violent reign was dominated by another abortive siege of Ceuta, tribal dissidence and the rebellion of both Fez and Marrakesh. The two cities championed rival sons of Sidi Mohammed, Sliman and Hisham, for the throne. Yazid died of blood poisoning while subduing Marrakesh, and at his own wishes he was buried in the Saadian necropolis. A bitter struggle amongst the sons of Sidi Mohammed continued for four more years. By

1796 Moulay Sliman had achieved a dominant position but only became undisputed ruler when his brothers all died during the cholera epidemic of 1799.

The orthodox rule of Moulay Sliman, 1792–1822

Moulay Sliman was the last sultan to try and rule a purely Islamic nation. He devoted the greater part of his energies in supressing Sufi brotherhoods and dissident tribes and attempted to seal Morocco from any contact with Europe. It was a misguided reign that ended disastrously.

He was passionately orthodox and strongly influenced by puritan Wahabi preachers from Arabia he determined to destroy the unorthodox Sufi brotherhoods. The Sufi brotherhoods provided religious instruction, education, served as tribal mediators and centres for charity. They provided the tribes with all the facets of government they required, based on voluntary respect. The sultan underestimated the degree of tribal support for the brotherhoods. Moulay Sliman had already destroyed the zaouia of Boujad on the Tadla plain when in 1818 he turned his attention to the Middle Atlas. A confederacy of Berber tribes united under the Derkawi brotherhood carried out a night attack which destroyed the sultan's army. Moulay Sliman was captured, entertained for the customary three days and then escorted back to the Royal Palace at Meknes.

From this defeat the sultan accepted the impossibility of enforcing rule in the Berber highlands, the Bled es Siba, the land of dissidence. He and his successors followed a policy of ruling, if at all, in these areas by influence and diplomacy with a regional chief, like the Sherif of Ouezzane. The towns and the agricultural plains remained under the direct authority of the sultan, the Bled es Makhzen, the land of the government.

Moulay Sliman's foreign policy was dominated by suspicion of all Europe and a particular loathing for the French revolution. Despite being offered Ceuta and Melilla he refused to recognize the upstart Bonaparte as king of Spain. All exports were banned, a 50% duty imposed on imports and European consuls were confined to Tangier in an attempt to keep outside influence firmly at bay. In some matters the sultan inherited his father's wise outlook. In the 1811 treaty with the United States he extracted $10,000, essentially protection money, which bought immunity for US merchants from Moroccan pirates. The sting in the tail was that there were no longer any Moroccan pirates. In 1716 there had been a fleet of ten corsairs but by 1764 this had dropped to two frigates. Moulay Sliman had made Algiers a present of his last and hardly seaworthy ship in 1818, after he had freed all remaining Christian captives and banned piracy.

Abder Rahman and the growth of European influence, 1822–59

Moulay Sliman ignored the claims of his inadequate sons and nominated his nephew Abder Rahman to succeed. The new sultan abandoned his uncle's unpopular religious reforms, opened Morocco to European trade and without a strong army managed to achieve a measure of internal stability by skilful use of patronage and diplomatic manipulation.

During his reign the political, commercial and military supremacy of Europe became apparent. The sultan's assistance to the Algerian tribes after the French invasion of Algeria was halted by crude threats in 1832. In 1843 the Algerian resistance leader, the

Emir Abdul Kebir, took refuge in Morocco. The Moroccan army despatched to Oujda to protect this Muslim hero was crushingly defeated by the French at the battle of Isly, a defeat which was followed by separate naval bombardments of Tangier and Essaouira. The tribes' reaction to these humiliating defeats was widespread revolt against the sultan.

Suddenly aware of his nation's vulnerability, the sultan played on the strong and traditional Anglo–French rivalry. He associated with the British who were interested in opening up Morocco to their traders and keeping the straits of Gibraltar open for their shipping. As a corollary of British dipomatic support against the French, the 1856 Treaty of Tangier removed all the sultan's restrictions on trade except his monopoly on tobacco and arms. It instituted a flat 10% customs rate and introduced consular courts and privileges which soon deprived the sultan of any control over his nation's trade.

Spain became envious of British influence. In 1859, as the sultan lay dying, a Spanish army advanced from Ceuta to defeat a tribal army and occupy the city of Tetouan. The tribes rose again in revolt against their defeated government and British protection was revealed to be a false and illusory hope.

Sidi Mohammed ben Abder Rahman and the reduction of sovereignty, 1859–73

Abder Rahman's son was faced with a chequered inheritance. The Spanish demanded a crippling indemnity of 100 million pesetas before they would leave Tetouan, a pretender to the throne appeared in the Riff and the Rehamna tribe pillaged Marrakesh. Internal dissidence was subdued by 1864 and the Spanish left Tetouan in 1862, paid off by a British loan which required the surrender of customs revenue and its administration by the British and Spanish.

The unhappy start to the reign was followed by the remorseless growth in European influence. By 1900 there were over 10,000 European residents in the country. Foreign consuls in the ports of Tangier and Casablanca organized lighthouses, port works, sanitary services and a national postal service, increasingly replacing the sultan's sovereignty. The consular privileges of the trade treaty of 1856 put European merchants and their numerous Moroccan agents beyond the law of the sultan. As a graphic illustration of this trend, between 1844 and 1873 the national currency lost 90% of its value. Trade was conducted in the French five franc coin.

Moulay Hassan 1873–94

Moulay Hassan was an exceptional monarch. He attempted the almost impossible task of modernizing Morocco whilst keeping the nation's independence. He had experience of the difficulties as he had served his father as pasha of Marrakesh.

On his accession in 1873, he began a programme of reform to revitalize Morocco in order to stand up to European expansionism. Whilst instituting his reforms, however, he still had to maintain central authority through the traditional system of annual military campaigns. The students he dispatched to Europe to learn the latest medical and engineering skills returned unable to cope with the political realities of their homeland.

The sultan attempted to stabilize the currency by minting the Koranically approved

Riyal in Paris. It was of such quality that it was hoarded or smuggled abroad. At the Conference of Madrid in 1880 he attempted to limit the ruinous extent of consular protections, and a limit was set of two agents per country in each port. No European power except Britain respected these terms. The sultan also instituted a tax reform clearing away all the previous exemptions enjoyed by foreign merchants, caids, shereefs and Sufi sheikhs. However these previously exempt classes conspired to ruin the reform.

Moulay Hassan attempted to use Muslim instructors from Turkey and Egypt to reform his army. When the European powers blocked this scheme he wisely balanced their influence; there was a French military mission, a British chief of staff (Caid Mclean), the German Krupp firm were given contracts for coastal defence and the Italians built and ran a munitions factory at Fez. The sultan also attempted to check French incursions on his eastern and southern borders, building kasbahs at Tiznit, Selouane and Saidia. He diplomatically consolidated his position by recognizing caids in the outlying oases of Figuig, Salah and Tuat, and supplying those in the Middle Atlas and Smara with building materials and troops. He exhausted himself in the service of his country, reasserting order and personally dispensing justice in regions that had not seen an official of the sultan for a hundred years. He died on campaign in 1894.

Abdul Aziz 1894–1908

The two sons of Moulay Hassan are like the two sides of his character. Abdul Aziz had the reforming western oriented approach and Moulay Hafid was the patriarchal traditionalist. They both struggled to maintain the independence of Morocco but they had neither the balance, energy or vision of their father. They presided over the last stormy decade of Moroccan independence.

On Moulay Hassan's death his chief vizier, Bou Ahmed, appointed the child Abdul Aziz to rule and with the support of the young sultan's mother deposed his ministerial rivals. Until the vizier's death in 1900, the country remained under control but thereafter the attempt of the young sultan to push ahead with Moulay Hassan's policy resulted in a grotesque parody of the modernization programme.

Useless western products were enthusiastically acquired, their purchase financed through ruinous foreign loans. Abdul Aziz, surrounded by a court composed of European adventurers, unscrupulous salesmen and doctors, became alienated from his traditional advisers and political realities. Meanwhile the tribal chiefs and caids appointed by Moulay Hassan, notably in the High Atlas, expanded their power in the vacuum created by the disordered central government. In the Riff and the eastern plains the 1904–1909 revolt led by a pretender, the 'Rogui' Bou Hamara, threatened the dynasty itself.

It is doubtful however whether any ruler could have successfully resisted the anarchy created by the advance of French power in Morocco at this time. In exchange for a free hand in Morocco the French had begun to negotiate a series of bargains with the other colonial powers. Spain was offered territory in northern and southern Morocco, Italy a free hand over Libya while the French agreed to recognize Britain's rule over Cyprus and the Sudan, with the additional promise that Tangier would remain a demilitarized zone. The only power the French hadn't settled with was Germany, who refused to be ignored. The Kaiser William II upheld Moroccan independence in a speech in Tangier in 1905, and a German gunboat was anchored off Agadir which formented the crisis of 1911. After the latter exercise in brinkmanship they were paid off with a generous slice of the French Congo.

French control was tightened in 1904 when Abdul Aziz accepted a loan of 50 million francs from a consortium of French banks. In 1906 the Conference of Algeciras ratified the various secret negotiations that had been taking place between the Europeans over the future of Morocco. The French army had slowly been occupying oases on the eastern frontier since 1900 but in 1907 the lynching of a few Europeans in Marrakesh and Casablanca gave them the excuse for direct intervention. Oujda was occupied in the east and 3000 French troops were promptly landed at Casablanca.

Moulay Hafid and the Treaty of Fez, 1908–12

Moulay Hafid replaced his brother on a wave of popular nationalism but he proved equally incapable of resisting the steady advance of France. After the French had landed unopposed at Casablanca Moulay Hafid declared himself sultan with the support of Madani el Glaoui, an influential High Atlas caid. Moulay Hafid, a traditionalist to the core and a recognized Koranic scholar, received the enthusiastic support of the tribes and his brother abdicated.

Once established as sultan, Moulay Hafid failed to lead the tribes in open war against either the French or the Spanish who were advancing inland. Instead he concentrated on strengthening his own internal position. The pretender, Bou Hamara, was captured and executed in 1909 and using the forces of Madani el Glaoui, the new sultan hoped to gather enough tax to recruit his own loyal army. His failure to battle against the Christians had however discredited him with the tribes. They soon rebelled against his heavy taxes and sponsored their own sultans who would lead them to war.

By 1912 Moulay Hafid had isolated himself from his original supporters and failed to create a new army. For over a year he had been dependent on French military protection from tribal dissidence. In March he accepted the inevitable and signed the Treaty of Fez which established French rule over Morocco. An elaborate fiction was invented that the French Resident General was a mere agent of the sultan commissioned to reform and unite the country. This did not stop Moulay Hafid being replaced the next year by a more compliant younger brother, Sultan Moulay Youssef.

Tribal resistance to the French protectorate, 1912–34

Though the central government had capitulated to France resistance continued from the cities and tribes of Morocco.

Two weeks after the Treaty of Fez was signed revolution broke out in the Fez el Bali. Eighty resident Europeans were lynched and the walls were manned, but the next day the city was shelled and occupied by the French.

In the south El Hiba, the blue sultan, was proclaimed ruler in Tiznit. His tribal army of 12,000 warriors advanced swiftly, leaving Tiznit in July to reach Marrakesh four weeks later. In September El Hiba moved towards Fez but his tribal force was destroyed by the cannon and machine guns of Colonel Mangin waiting at Sidi Bou Othman. The French were able to master Marrakesh the same day. The caids of the High Atlas, the Glaoui, the M'touggi and the Goundaffi were confirmed in their power and sent south across the Atlas to chase El Hiba out of the Souss. Taroudant was taken in May 1913 without the use of a single French soldier.

The French alliance with the High Atlas caids was vital during the First World War when France needed every available soldier for the war against Germany. Under Lyautey, the first French Resident General, a skeleton military presence held the subdued lowland areas and garrisoned the traditional strongholds on the edge of the Middle Atlas: Taza, Azrou, Khenifra and Tadla, while the immense expanse of the High Atlas was kept in order. The Riff, Middle Atlas and south of the High Atlas remained beyond French control until reinforcements in 1921 allowed the conquest to proceed. This conquest was slowed down by the Riff rebellion and by the obstinate resistance of the Berber mountain tribes. The Ait Haddidou held out on the Koucer Massif until 1933 and the Ait Atta were not subdued in their stronghold of Bou Gaffer until 1934. By 1936 the last nomadic tribes of the Sahara had sued for peace. 'No tribe came to us spontaneously', described General Guillaume. 'None gave in without fighting and some of them not until they had exhausted every means of resistance.'

The Riff Rising, 1921–26 and Djeballa resistance, 1911–19 against the Spanish Protectorate

By previous agreement with the French the Spanish were to administer the far north and the far south of Morocco. The sultan was represented in the Spanish protectorate by a khalifa who was mere figurehead for the ruling authority of the Spanish High Commissioner in Tetouan. The Spanish protectorate consisted of Sidi Ifni (an enclave in the Anti Atlas), a stretch of desert south of the Oued Draa and the mountainous northern coast of Morocco—'the bone of the Djeballa and the spine of the Riff'. The northern coast, a mountainous and determinedly independent zone was divided between the antagonistic Arabic-speaking tribes of the western hills, the Djeballa, and the Berber speaking tribes of the eastern hills.

The Spanish occupied the Djeballa in 1911 with the assistance of Raisuni, a rebel sherif who had used his military strength to become the recognized ruler of the region. The Spanish military governors found it impossible to share power with the rapacious Raisuni, who ruled from his palace 'the House of Tears' in Asilah. After two bouts of guerrilla war Raisuni was in 1919 at last forced to sue for peace. In exchange the Spanish restored his mountain top palace of Tazerout where he agreed to retire in internal exile supported by a generous pension.

Such was Raisuni's pride and the strength of the traditional rivalry between the Riff and the Djeballa tribes that he refused to break his peace with the Spanish and support Abdel Krim's Riff rebellion in 1921. Raisuni was seized by Riff commandos in 1925 and died a few weeks later.

In the eastern Riff the dominant position of the Beni Ouriaghel tribe was acknowledged in a common Riff proverb, 'the rest of the tribes dance to the sound of the Ouriaghel drums'. For a period the Spanish attempted to control this tribe but by 1919 the experiment was over and both sides prepared for war. Abdul Krim assumed the leadership of the Beni Ouriaghel on his father's death in 1920. He launched a surprise attack, 'the rout of Annoual', against the extended Spanish positions in July 1921 which annihilated the Spanish army.

Apart from Melilla the entire eastern Riff fell under Abdel Krim's control. In February 1922 an Islamic Republic of the Riff was declared, the presidency of Abdul Krim and his descent from the prophet announced and various ministries all under the control of the Beni Ouriaghel tribe established. Arms were obtained from German and English speculators and by May 1924 an army of 120,000 had pushed the Spanish out of the Djeballa and even shelled Tetouan. In 1925 Abdul Krim launched his army south against the French protectorate which fought to within 25 km of Fez. The next year enormous French and Spanish armies were assembled for a joint assault under Marshal Pétain, and by the end of 1926 they had subdued the entire region.

From 1926 to 1956 the 69 tribes of the mountains were governed by appointed caids who were placed under the supervision of a Spanish district commissioner. It remained a quasi military rule, and Spaniards were not encouraged to move to the Protectorate. 500 km of surfaced road and an iron mine outside Melilla were the limits of its commercial development. In July 1936 a large proportion of the army supported by regiments raised from the Riff tribes left Morocco and played a crucial part in the victory of General Franco in the Spanish Civil War.

Meanwhile the French honoured their agreement with the British and Tangier remained a demilitarized zone. A constitution in 1923 provided the international city of Tangier with a ruling council of consuls, a small house of representatives and the mendoub, the representative of the sultan. In practice French and Spanish officials dominated the administration, the Italians gave the best parties and the British kept the best gardens.

The French Protectorate, 1912–56

The French Resident General held all civil and military power in Morocco. The sultan's only role was to approve new decrees and administer the religious endowments through the ministry of the 'habous'. Caids and pashas continued to govern and cadis to dispense justice in the sultan's name but at every level they were placed under the supervision of French civil or military officers. Marshal Lyautey, learning from the mistakes of Algeria, made certain that the traditional pattern of life was left completely undisturbed and in particular that no offence should be given to either Islam or the sultan. The French managed to win the support of some of the most conservative elements of society, like the Berber caids of the Atlas and influential sheikhs of Sufi brotherhoods.

Despite this apparent conservatism a great but slow alteration in social life was caused by the pacification of Morocco. Peace, the end of tribal pillage and administrative extortion, led to a rapid growth in population and trade. In 1921 Morocco had a population of 3 million. After only thirty years of French rule this had risen to 8 million.

Apart from military conquest and administration the Protectorate's chief concern was to develop Morocco's agricultural and mineral wealth. French banks financed major public works, ports, dams, roads and railways, and the government attracted capitalist investment into mining and agriculture by a tempting package of low taxes, cheap labour and land.

The confiscation of government estates from the losing political leaders and outright purchase produced enough prime land for France's immediate colonizing needs. A second tranche was assembled by the registration of tribal land. 15 hectares were assessed for each tent or family and the substantial residue, usually the more accessible and fertile areas, became available for colonial use. Outright purchase and manipulation of the vital water rights also produced a slowly increasing acreage. By 1953 1 million hectares, concentrated on the fertile coastal zones, the Haouz (by Marrakesh) and the Sais plain (by Meknes) was under French ownership. In 1951 there were 325,000 Europeans in the country, including a rich controlling minority of 5000 and a sub-class of 80,000 'poor whites'. An impressive infrastructure of road, railroads, ports, administrative centres and dams was developed to provide water and electricity for the settlers. Hospitals, schools and hotels were also built, for the use of settlers and a tiny minority of the traditional Moroccan ruling class of caids, merchants and sheikhs. Even by Independence in 1956 less than 15% of the Moroccan population had received any sort of education.

French rule over Morocco was based on military force allied to skilful manipulation of local leadership. They won on the support of a number of Sufi brotherhoods which for varying reasons of ambition or revenge were often prepared to work against the sultan and his family. More practical military assistance had been secured by the early alliance with the tribal caids of the High Atlas. The Glaouai brothers Madani and Thami had outmanoeuvred their rivals the M'touggi and Gondaffi caids and by 1934 Thami, as pasha of Marrakesh, controlled an extensive empire within an empire, a feudal domain that stretched from the foothills of the Atlas south to Algeria. In the 1950s he was of vital political use in orchestrating the spectacular tribal demonstrations against the sultan.

This 'great caid' policy paid spectacular dividends and encouraged by its success the French attempted as early as 1914 to consolidate its effect by separating the Berber-speaking mountain areas, about 40% of the population, from the Arabic-speaking community. In these Berber areas customary law was recognized, and from 1923 a number of French schools were established. Arabic was forbidden and a college of higher education founded at Azrou which aimed to create a clique of Berber officers and administrators loyal to France.

Second World War

Morocco was involved in the events of the Second World War as a protectorate of France. After the defeat of France by Nazi Germany in 1940 the British launched a world wide attack on units of the French fleet. The new government of Vichy France, which controlled the colonial Empire, broke off all relations with Britain.

Fortunately the Casablanca landings of November 1942 were a primarily American affair and the North African Vichy high commmand had secretly agreed to surrender after token resistance. General Patton sailed directly across the Atlantic to land 35,000 with great confusion on three beaches, at Fedala, 15 km north of Casablanca, Mehdiya and Safi. Two months later, in January 1943, Roosevelt and Churchill held a conference at Casablanca. In a suburban villa in Anfa the invasion of Sicily was planned and Roosevelt announced that the war should be fought until Germany was completely defeated. In a meeting with Sultan Mohammed V the American president gave private encouragement that the post-war era would bring a return of sovereignty to Morocco.

The Free French managed to muster a force of 110,000 French, Moroccans and Algerians for the invasion of Sicily. By the end of the war there were 300,000 Moroccans under arms. The Moroccan 4th Mountain Division distinguished itself in May 1944 by storming Monte Casino to penetrate the Gustav line. The opposing German general, Kesselring, had a particularly high opinion of their fighting quality: their 'tempestuous and skilfully commanded breakthrough . . . had really won the battle for the allies'. The Moroccan 2nd Division captured Monte Pantano in 1943 and also won great respect for crossing the Rhine under heavy fire on 31 March 1945 to establish a bridgehead on the east bank of the river.

Though there was no immediate political evidence, the Second World War saw a transformation in the power relationship between France and Morocco. Republican and then Vichy France had been visibly defeated first by the Nazis and then by the allies, whilst Moroccan forces had contributed to the liberation of Europe. The European colonial powers had been replaced by the anti-colonial world leadership of America and Russia. India and Egypt, who had both rapidly achieved independence at the end of the war, pointed the way for Morocco.

Mohammed V and the struggle for independence, 1927–1956

Mohammed V had been chosen by the French in 1927 to succeed his father for his apparent docility. He proved to have an unexpectedly strong character and enjoyed the moral high ground against a series of unimaginative generals who served as Residents. The sultan resisted all of Vichy France's anti-semitic measures and refused to receive a single German officer. While 200,000 French Jews died in Nazi concentration camps the sultan protected all 300,000 of his Jewish subjects. Ironically the post-war period saw an influx of Nazi collaborators expelled from France who settled in north Africa.

The independence movement can be traced back to the intellectual Salafi movement for orthodox Islamic reform. It gathered strength during the successful protest against the French attempt to separate Arabs and Berbers in 1930 and from the labour and water riots of 1936 and 1937. But in the post-war period the demand for independence was an issue that no longer required the support of an aggrieved class or populist issue. By 1947 the new independence party, 'Istaqlal', had 15,000 members and in Mohammed V's speech of 10 April 1947 at Tangier the nation learnt that their sultan was working towards the same end.

Joint opposition by the sultan and Istaqlal was concentrated against the partisan, 'settler's tax budget' of 1951. The Resident General, Juin, called on the support of Thami el Glaoui and the sherif of Ouezzane to stage a massive demonstration that would prove that the sultan's alliance with Istaqlal was unpopular, that, in Thami el Glaoui's words, 'he was the sultan of Istaqlal and not of Morocco'. Rabat and Fez were surrounded by threatening Berber tribesmen and the sultan was forced to distance himself publicly from the independence movement.

The following spring, in March 1952, the sultan took the offensive by writing a public letter to the French President requesting a return to full sovereignty. This led directly to an orchestrated plot for his deposition.

In April 1953 the sultan was condemned by a council of Sufi sheikhs whilst in August Thami el Glaoui obediently organized another march of Berber tribesmen on Rabat and

Fez. The sultan was again forced to back down to avoid civil strife. This satisfied the French but the Sufi sheikhs and Thami el Glaoui felt that they had committed themselves too deeply and that they would loose influence if the sultan stayed on the throne. The French fully realized the importance of keeping their political allies strong. By the end of 1953 the sultan had been exiled to Madagascar and a compliant cousin, Mohammed ben Arafa, placed on the throne.

It was a disastrous move, for the sultan's exile united the modern nationalism of Istaqlal to the much wider tribal veneration of the sultan as the religious leader of the nation. Individual acts of terrorism escalated throughout the country and by June 1955 even the supposed allies of France, the Sufi brotherhoods and Berber hinterland, threatened the administration with armed revolution. The Liberation Army had been formed and was rapidly winning control of the Riffs, the Middle Atlas and the Sahara. The Moroccan people were again prepared to fight for their independence at the very moment the French lost the will and confidence to commit themselves to wholescale repression.

By October 1955 the French cabinet had determined to give Morocco and Tunisia independence in order to concentrate resources on the war in Algeria. In November 1955 the sultan returned to Morocco and by March 1956 the French had formally recognized Moroccan independence.

Post independence, 1956–61

Upon Independence the sultan restyled himself as King Mohammed V to emphasize his position as a modern constitutional monarch removed from the practices of the pre-1912 regime. In the euphoric first years of independence a national government established schools, universities, newspapers and elected regional assemblies. The Sufi brotherhoods were reformed, orthodoxy and public morality reaffirmed and massive public work schemes launched. Labour battalions absorbed unemployment and created lasting monuments, like the Route d'Unité which joined the road systems of the separate French and Spanish protectorates.

Mohammed V was quietly determined that the monarchy should remain the controlling force of national politics. Istaqlal as the sole national party posed a potential threat. It dominated the first cabinet though Mohammed V insisted on control over the army and the ministry of the interior. By 1959 the left wing of Istaqlal under Ben Barka broke away to form the UNFP and ranged themselves for a socialist alliance with the UMT labour union. The centrist rump of Istaqlal then established their own labour union, the UGTM the same year. The rural Berber hinterland remained suspicious of the urban Istaqlal party and with discreet support from the king, a new and conservative party, the Mouvement Populaire was formed.

Crown Prince Hassan was given the task of creating a royal army. Units of the Liberation Army were absorbed within this new force which by recruiting experienced veterans of French service soon rose to 30,000 men. In 1958 and 1959 rebellions in the Riff, Saharan oases and the Middle Atlas tested the army's discipline and efficiency. The more radical and militant members of the Liberation Army were meanwhile directed south to the unofficial siege of the Spanish enclave of Sidi Ifni and the liberation struggle for the Western Sahara.

In February 1961, at the height of his powers, King Mohammed V died and was succeeded by his son.

Hassan II, 1961–

The new king excluded the socalist UNFP party from government by forming a cabinet from the Mouvement Populaire and Istaqlal in June 1961. In December 1962 a referendum was held to give popular approval to Morocco's first democratic constitution. The UNFP called for a boycott, but unsupported by the labour unions this failed. The new king, having won the referendum, no longer felt the need for Istaqlal support and sacked its members from his cabinet.

In March 1963 the first parliamentary election was held with the ministries of Agriculture and Interior assisting the electoral victory of the FDIC, a royal coalition with the Mouvement Populaire which took a majority of the vote. Istaqlal was strongest in the older cities and successful farming areas like Tadla, Doukkala and the Gharb, UNFP in the new cities of the coast, Rabat, Casablanca and Agadir and throughout the Souss valley. The Mouvement Populaire's greatest support came from Marrakesh and the Berber hinterland as well as Oujda, Taza and Nador.

The socialist UNFP increasingly identified itself with the Arab Republics of Egypt and Algeria which they publicly cited as role models for Morocco. The local elections of July 1963, and the conspicuous but fixed FDIC victory of an 85% vote encouraged the UNFP to think in terms of revolutionary change. The king responded by arresting over 130 UNFP militants on treason charges later in the month. Ben Barka, the leader of the UNFP, fled to Paris and widened the political breach by calling on the Moroccan army not to resist Algeria in the border war fought in the Sahara during the winter of 1963.

The first parliament was a failure. A three-year plan drawn up in 1964 was aborted as the planners had failed to consult the Finance Ministry. In 2 years of existence, it passed only three minor bills, and a liberal party formed around disgruntled technocrats appalled by the jobbery and factional intrigue that occupied the parliament.

The student and worker riots of Casablanca in March 1965 encouraged the king to dissolve parliament in June and rule directly though he retained the bulk of the parliamentary cabinet. Ben Barka was assassinated in Paris that August in a plot that was traced back to the Moroccan Ministry of Interior. The king, in an adroit political move, borrowed a popular UNFP issue and initiated the nationalization of foreign businesses and farms.

By August 1970 a new constitution was prepared and approved in a national referendum that gave the king increased influence over parliament. Istaqlal and the UNFP boycotted the elections which left the parliament filled with loyalist place men. As a result of this narrowing of the field of power there were two coup d'états. A group of senior army officers had grown disgusted at the scale of corruption in government and the extent of patronage and client networks. In the coup of Skhirat in July 1971 they attempted to purge the royal court and replace it with a puritanical reforming military council. In 1972 there was another failed coup when the king's aeroplane was ambushed by air force jets but saved by a quick talking pilot. Investigations traced the plot back to General Oufkir, the widely feared Minister of the Interior. The king was shaken but continued in his skilful manipulation of the ruling cliques.

The Green March of 1975 buried the political problems of the past in a surge of nationalism. The king orchestrated a march of 350,000 civilians south to reintegrate the Spanish colony of Rio de Oro, the Western Sahara, into greater Morocco. It was a brilliantly timed political gamble which caught the Spanish government paralysed by the lingering death of General Franco. The resulting war against a group of the Saharan tribes, united under the Polisario movement, prolonged the spell of national unity. Libya and Algeria supported the Polisario but this 'revolutionary' alliance led to firm backing for Morocco from both Saudi Arabia and the United States. Militarily the war has now been won (see the chapter on the Western Sahara for details) and the enhanced pay, equipment and prestige afforded to the army has kept it loyal to the king.

The enormous cost of the fighting, an estimated $1000 million a year, has added to Morocco's grave economic problems. Union-organized strikes in 1979 led to the arrest of activists but wages were increased to keep abreast of the annual 10% inflation rate. The political temper had been heated by the strikes and later that year teachers and students demonstrated against the presence of the ex-Shah of Persia who had sought refuge with the king.

By June 1981, the situation had been aggravated by a succession of bad harvests that increased basic food prices just when the IMF insisted that the state subsidy of them must be reduced. An organized day-long demonstration against the IMF cuts degenerated into looting and rioting. The police restored order after many casualties and some of the organizers of the original demonstration were prosecuted.

Local elections were held in June 1983 but the scale of the royalist victory suggested heavy-handed electoral influence. Parliamentary elections were subsequently cancelled and the king assumed constitutional emergency powers in October, though again he skilfully checked criticism by assembling a cabinet from a broad spectrum of political parties. In January 1984 the events of 1981 were repeated as the IMF insisted on further heavy cuts in subsidies in exchange for vital government loans. Riots broke out throughout Morocco, the king withdrew the cuts but at the same time heavy police action against rioters and political dissidents put 2000 men behind bars.

The state of emergency lasted only six months and by the summer of 1984 a new parliament, which produced a moderate government committed to economic reform, had been elected. Today, political parties are free to address social and economic issues but criticism of the king, the constitution and the desert war are effectively forbidden. The press operates within the same parameters but despite these limitations remains one of the liveliest of any Arab or African nation.

No one can be certain of the future. From the past you learn that Islam, anarchy, regional loyalties and a confident nationalism are consistent if contradictory features of Moroccan history. But you can be confident that only a strong man can rule a nation of such triumphant individualists.

Morocco today

The economy

Over-ambitious central planning and 14 years of desert war have pushed the load of foreign debt perilously high. In recent years the annual budget deficit has been reduced to 6% of revenue but this, though commendable, still results in annual additions to the estimated total debt of $17 billion. This is equal to the entire annual domestic economy and without international relief would require over 60% of exports just to service the debt. The situation has recently been improved by the collapse in oil prices, the fall in the value of the dollar which has reduced interest rates, and a succession of better harvests.

In the domestic economy farming remains of paramount importance. The industrial sector is based on the Casablanca–Rabat–Kenitra axis but remains hampered by monolithic public holding companies riddled by corrupt vested interests and inefficient administration. The IMF have given Morocco a $240m loan to restructure its industry and create something approaching a free market to encourage local enterprise and foreign investment.

Custom duties, as throughout most of Morocco's history, provide the bulk of state revenue. The internal tax situation remains in an anarchic state. Incredibly the big earners, tourism, agriculture and property speculation, enjoy an official tax holiday. At present most state industries run at a 'loss', while a flourishing black market, covering much the same ground, turns over an estimated $5 billion a year. Current reforms aim to introduce an open stock exchange, statutory accounting for businesses, VAT, cuts in the top-heavy civil service and some accountability in the state phosphate monopoly.

Foreign exchange comes from three major sources: receipts from over a million migrant workers, $1000m, tourism, $610m and phosphates, $480m. The export of fruit, vegetables and fish to Europe is a lesser earner and this market is severely threatened by the entry of the similar agricultural economies of Spain, Portugal and Greece to the EEC. An unlikely but valuable national resource is King Hassan's friendship with the royal families of Saudi Arabia and the Gulf states. Generous loans, help in rescheduling debts and outright gifts have propped up the Moroccan economy on numerous occasions. In 1985, for instance, $250m suddenly appeared in the ledgers of the foreign currency reserves when all other sources were known to be exhausted.

Foreign affairs

Since independence, relations with the old colonial powers of **France** and **Spain** have been dominant. Over 40% of Morocco's imports come from France and Spain and both countries have proved generous suppliers of government loans and arms. Despite the nationalization of foreign-owned businesses, both France and Spain still have a substantial stake in the Moroccan economy, for French and Spanish banks hold influential shareholdings in Morocco's own chain of commercial banks.

Relations with Spain are currently acrimonious, with disputes over the EEC, transport and fishing rights. The Spanish territories of Ceuta and Melilla are not yet a major issue, but in a future period of popular unrest they could provide a tempting nationalist diversion.

France has a much stronger, less contentious, influence and thousands of skilled French technicians, teachers and governmental experts are still employed by the government of Morocco. French and Moroccan troops have even performed joint operations like the 'policing' of Zaire in 1979.

The other central diplomatic theme is rivalry with the neighbouring state of **Algeria**. Plots, border wars, skirmishes, the long running **Polisario war**, different styles of government and Moroccan claims over much of the Algerian Sahara fuel this affair. Relations have however greatly improved in recent years as both nations share common economic difficulties. In June 1988 full diplomatic ties were restored with Algeria. This was followed by a truce in the Western Sahara and the first and amicable meeting between the king and the Polisario leadership. In the spring of 1989 all the countries of north west Africa—Libya, Tunisia, Algeria, Morocco and Mauritania—signed the **Maghrebi Union Treaty**. This is not likely to have any dramatic consequences but may allow an easing of border relations, which will allow Morocco and Tunisia to sell food to net importers like Libya and Algeria. It may also allow a stronger hand to be played against the EEC.

US support and aid throughout the desert war has drawn Morocco quite firmly into the western camp. Bases have been put at the disposal of American rapid deployment forces and *Voice of America* relay stations have been established.

Hassan II has toyed, like many Arab leaders, with Middle East peace plans. Moroccan forces fought bravely on the Golan heights in 1973 but the PLO has never received direct aid from Morocco. The king has hosted a series of Arab summits and an almost equal number of discreet meetings with Israeli leaders, many of whom, like Moshe Dayan, are descended from Moroccan Jews. It is to the king's lasting credit that he has repeatedly committed himself to the unpopular role of the protector of the Moroccan Jewish community.

Problems

The virtual tax-free economy of the influential merchants and industrialists in Morocco has perpetuated unpalatable extremes of wealth. Revenue raised by taxing this small prosperous class could be spent on much needed social and educational aid for the 60% of the nation who live below the poverty line. The fast growing population—from 8 million in 1952 it is now over 20 million—puts a continuous strain on the slow-growing economy. Over half the population of Morocco is under 20 the majority of this age group are unemployed and 60% are illiterate. This is combined with a shift from the conservative society of the land to the radical identity of the shanty towns which house over 20% of any urban population. Which ever way you look at things this augurs future political stress.

Muslim fundamentalism does not seem to have emerged as a difficulty in Morocco, though typically **the Riff** may yet prove to be an exception. The chief fundamentalist newspaper *al Jamaa* has a print run of 3000 which compares badly with the 70,000 copies of the establishment *Le Matin du Sahara* or the 50,000 copies of *Al Alam*, the Istaqlal paper, or the 17,000 daily sale of the left-wing USFP paper, *Al Muharmir*.

A single authoritarian figure has been necessary throughout Morocco's history to check the strong regional loyalties, though the king or his successor could only strengthen the state by allowing the increasing number of educated middle class and officials an effective role in the national political life.

Key dates

146 BC	Fall of Carthage
42	Aedemeon's revolt against Roman rule
622	Mohammed's flight from the persecution of Mecca to Medina
681	Uqba's first raid into Morocco
711	Tariq's invasion of Spain
732	Charles Martel halts Arab advance at Poitiers
789	Foundation of Fez
1062	Almoravides found Marrakesh
1147	Almohads capture Marrakesh
1213	The battle of Las Navas de Tolosa
1451	Portuguese leave Agadir
1485	Fall of Granada to Ferdinand and Isabella
1578	The battle of Three Kings/Ksar el Kebir
1591	Ahmed el Mansour's conquest of Timbucktu
1844	Battle of Oued Isly
1859	Battle of Tetouan
1907	French land troops at Casablanca
1912	Treaty of Fez, El Hiba defeated at battle of Bou Othman
1942	Casablanca landings by Anglo–American forces
1947	Sultan Mohammed V's Independence speech in Tangier
1953	Sultan Mohammed V sent in exile to Madagascar
1956	Independence
1961	Accession of Hassan II
1975	Green March into Western Sahara

The Moroccan dynasties

Mauretanian kings

106– BC	Bocchus
–46 BC	Juba I
46–33 BC	Bocchus II
24 BC–AD 19	Juba II
AD 19–42	Ptolemy

Rome

44–253	Central Morocco ruled as province of Roman Empire
253–429	Tangier and Ceuta remain under Roman rule
429	Genseric the Vandal raids Tangier
535	Belisaurius recaptures Ceuta for Byzantine Empire

Arab conquest

682	Uqba ben Nafi raids Morocco from Kairouan, Tunisia
705–711	Musa ben Nasser completes conquest and invades Spain
739–742	Berber Khajarite revolts

Idrissids

788–791	Moulay Idriss
791–804	Rule of regent Rachid
804–828	Idriss II
828–836	Mohammed ben Idriss
836–848	Ali I
848–1050	Various Idrissid principalities
917	Yahya IV accepts Fatimid suzerainity
917–970	Fatimid governors in Fez, Alhumecas and Sigilmassa
980–1061	Ommayyad or Andalucian governors in Tangier, Asilah, Ceuta and Fez

Almoravides

1052–1059	Abdullah Yacin establishes the 'Almoravides'
1059–1071	Abu Bekr delegates rule of north in 1071 to Youssef
1071–1107	Youssef ben Tachfine
1107–1144	Ali ben Youssef
1144–1145	Tachfine ben Ali
1145–1147	Ishaq ben Ali

Almohads

1121–1130	Ibn Tumert establishes 'Almohads' at Tinmal
1130–1162	Abdel Moumen (Fez taken in 1145, Marrakesh in 1147)
1163–1184	Abu Yaacoub Youssef
1184–1199	Abu Youssef Yaacoub, 'Yaacoub el Mansour'
1199–1213	Mohammed en Nasir
1213–1223	Youssef al Mustansir
1223–1248	Abu Said and other sons of Youssef
1248–1266	El Mutarda rules Marrakesh
1266–1269	Abou Dabbus rules Marrakesh

Merinids

1248–1258	Abou Yahya
1258–1286	Abou Yusuf Yacqub
1286–1307	Abou Yacqub Yusuf
1307–1308	Abou Rabia
1308–1331	Uthman
1331–1351	Abou Hassan
1351–1358	Abou Inan

1358–1396	sons and grandsons of Abou Inan
1396–1398	Abd Allah
1398–1420	Abou Said Uthmann
1420–1465	Abdul Haqq

Wattasids

1472–1505	Mohammed al Sheikh
1505–1526	Mohammed al Burtughali
1526–1548	Ahmed

Saadians

1554–1557	Mohammed ech Cheikh
1557–1574	Abdullah el Ghalib
1574–1576	Mohammed el Mutawakkil
1576–1578	Abdul Malik
1578–1603	Ahmed el Mansour
1603–1628	Zaidan
1628–1631	Abdel Malik II
1631–1637	El Walid
1637–1655	Mohammed ech Cheikh III
1655–1660	Ahmed el Abbas

Alouites

1666–1672	Moulay Rachid
1672–1727	Moulay Ishmael
1727–1745	anarchic succession of seven princes
1745–1757	Moulay Abdullah
1757–1790	Sidi Mohammed
1790–1792	Yazid
1792–1822	Moulay Sliman
1822–1859	Abder Rahman
1859–1873	Sidi Mohammed ben Abder Rahman
1873–1894	Moulay Hassan
1894–1908	Abdul Aziz
1908–1912	Moulay Hafid
(1912–1956 French and Spanish Protectorate)	
1912–1927	Moulay Youssef
1927–1961	Mohammed V, king of independent Morocco from 1956
1961–	Hassan II

Islam

Allah is a noun which can be translated as 'the divinity' or 'the only and true God'. Islam literally means 'submission' or obedience to the divinity. The **Koran** means 'the recitation'—the announcement of the word of God to **Mohammed** via the archangel Gabriel. This at its simplest is the Muslim religion; recognition and obedience to the single divinity whose will is clearly stated in the Koran.

The prophet Mohammed is not considered divine but a mere human mouthpiece for divine will. There is no veneration for a single historical act in the life of Mohammed, unlike Christianity where the moral teaching of Christ tends to get obscured by attention to his birth, crucifixion and resurrection. Nor does Islam encourage any hopeless if heroic attempt to imitate the perfect life of Christ. Instead it establishes a moral code that is possible for the entire community to follow and which assures salvation for those who honestly attempt to obey and damnation for those who ignore it or fail. It is a legal code rather than a heroic example.

Islam is not considered a new religion but a reformation of the ancient monotheistic worship of Abraham. The teachings of Mohammed presented an opportunity for the squabbling Christian and Jewish sects to unite on the common basics of belief. Moses, St John the Baptist and Christ are honoured in the Koran as great prophets, but Christ is not considered to be the son of God or to have died on the cross. Towards the end of his life Mohammed realized the impossibility of converting all the Christians and Jews. The direction of prayer was changed from Jerusalem to Mecca and whilst he instructed his followers to respect the **'peoples of the book'** his views hardened. From the tolerant words of his early teaching, 'Will you dispute with us about God? When he is our Lord and your Lord! We have our words and you have your words but we are sincerely his', the Prophet progresses to 'O believers! Take not the Jews or Christians as friends.'

The Prophet Mohammed

Born in 570 the young Mohammed was left an orphan and was brought up by a succession of his relatives from the influential Koreisch clan. As a young man he served as the agent for Chadjilla, a wealthy widow fifteen years his senior, whom he later married. Mecca was the centre of pagan Arab spiritual life and Mohammed and his wife joined the circle of **Hanyfs**, the puritan seekers after enlightenment. The Hanyf venerated the religion of Abraham and were familiar with Jewish, Christian and Persian doctrines. These influences are repeatedly acknowledged in the Koran, 'nothing has been said to thee which has not been said of old by apostles before' and 'every people has had its own apostle'. He received the first revelation in 610, fifteen years after his marriage, when his was forty years old. The archangel Gabriel appeared to Mohammed in a cave outside Mecca that he frequently used for prayer and meditation. He was at first doubtful about these revelations but, encouraged by his wife, he risked ridicule and shared the word of God. His ardent monotheism and criticism of the pagan worship that was centred on Mecca won over some followers but even more enemies. Eventually the protection of his Koreisch clan proved inadequate and to avoid assassination he **fled to the city of Medina** on 15 June 622, which is taken as the start of the **Hegira**, the Muslim era. Mohammed was welcomed to Medina and invited to become its ruler. There he established a theocratic state and ironed out practical moral and legal codes for his community. From Medina he waged war on the Meccans and gradually subdued the surrounding Jewish and pagan tribes. By 630, two years before his death, his authority extended over all Arabia. The divisions that still exist within the Muslim world originated over the succession to the leadership of the prophet. The **Shiites** believe in the claims of Ali to have succeeded Mohammed whilst the **Sunni** accept the legitimacy of the first three caliphs. Lesser sects like the **Ismailis**, **Druze** and **Khajarites** maintain their own beliefs in the rightful succession of the caliphs.

The Koran

'The recitation' was dictated to the illiterate Mohammed by the archangel Gabriel who first appeared in a cave above Mecca. More verses were revealed to the prophet in successive years and memorized and written down by his followers in both Mecca and Medina. The Caliph Othman established the first written version 18 years after the death of Mohammed in 650. 114 unequal chapters, the **suras**, containing 6211 inspired verses, were carefully assembled but were arranged by order of length which has given the Koran a chronologically haphazard order. The suras are labelled, but their names, the cow, the bee, the ant, etc., have no significance other than as a memory aid. In content the Koran can be divided under four headings: the worship of Allah, the day of judgement with the division between heaven and hell, stories of earlier prophets and lastly proclamations and social laws. A collection of the prophet's sayings and traditions remembered by his companions was also assembled but despite great efforts there is no definitive edition of the **Hadith**. From the Koran and the Hadith a system of civil law was created—the **charia** which is administered by a cadi who in Morocco follows the **Malekite tradition** of jurisprudence.

The religious life

The prophet codified the religious life of his community into the **five pillars of Islam**, which are prayer five times a day, the pilgrimage to Mecca, the fast of Ramadan, alms and acceptance that there is no other divinity but God.

The first prayer is known as **Moghreb** and is held four minutes after sunset; **Eshe** is held when it is quite dark, **Soobh Fegr** at dawn, **Dooh** at noon just after the sun has passed its zenith and **Asr** midway between noon and sunset. At each mosque a muezzin announces prayers by calling, 'God is great. I testify that there is no God but God. I testify that Mohammed is his prophet. Come to prayer, come to security. God is great.' For Soobh Fegr, the morning prayer, an extra inducement, 'prayer is better than sleep', is added.

Alone or in a mosque the believer ritually **purifies himself** by washing with water or sand. Then turning to Mecca the believer stands with hands held up and open to proclaim that Allah is great. He then lowers his hands and recites the **fatiha prayer** still standing, 'Praise be to God, Lord of the worlds, the compassionate, the merciful, king of the day of judgement, thee do we worship and your aid do we seek. Guide us on the straight path, the path of those on whom you have bestowed your grace, not the path of those who incur thy anger nor of those who have gone astray.' The believer bows with his hands on knees and completes a full prostration. Kneeling up again he recites the **chahada**, a prayer for the prophet. The **three positions of prayer** have a symbolic interpretation, standing distinguishes the rational man from an animal, bowing repre- sents the act of a servant to his master and the prostration represents abandonment to the will of God. On Fridays the noonday prayer is only recited in the Grand or licensed Mosque. This is followed by a sermon, the **khutba**, announced from the steps of the pulpit-like minbar though the throne and higher steps are left symbolically empty.

The **pilgrimage to Mecca** was an annual monthly event centuries before the Islamic era. Mohammed acknowledged the **Kaaba stone** as the altar of Abraham and a specific Islamic calendar of events was imposed in 630. For a poor man it may be the journey of a lifetime and he will return to his community with the proud title of 'Hadj'. The distance increased the attraction of local Moroccan shrines which like Moulay Idriss claimed that five local pilgrimages equalled the trip to Mecca. The **fast of Ramadan**, over the daylight hours of the ninth month of the Muslim year, commemorates Mohammed's spiritual practices before the Koran was first revealed to him. It was specifically based on existing Christian and Jewish spiritual practices. The **giving of alms** is a continual duty for the Muslim and the **zahir**, 'the fortieth', was a tax that originated out of this obligation.

Sufism

Ali, the cousin and son-in-law of the prophet, was the first **Sufi**, the originator of the mystical approach to Islam. The word comes from 'suf', the coarse woollen cloth used by penitents. A Sufi attempts to go beyond mere obedience to Islamic law and reach for experience of God in this life. **Sufi brotherhoods** arose as followers gathered around a celebrated mystic who naturally evolved into the master, the sheikh, of the community. The mystical discipline was passed down through the generations, in a human chain of masters each of whom trained his disciples to succeed him. New brotherhoods were all proud to be a link in this chain of spiritual succession.

Two great scholars of the 12th century are central to the Maghrebi brotherhoods: **Abu Medyan of Tlemcen**, who died in 1198, and **Abdessalam ben Mchich** (the master of Djebel Alam, the patron saint of the Djeballa region of Morocco) who died in 1228. They united the teaching of **Sidi Harazem of Fez** (familiar as a brand name of mineral water) and the great eastern masters, **Al Jilani of Baghdad** and **Al Ghazzali** (1059–1111). The Almoravide Sultan Ali burnt all Al Ghazzali's books, *The deliverer from error*, *The revivification of the religious sciences* and *Incoherence of the philosophers*, and sentenced to death any Muslim found reading them. Their spiritual heir was **Abou el Hassan Ali ech Chadhili of Tunisia** who died in 1258 and from whose teachings 15 separate Sufi brotherhoods arose. **Al Jazuli**, who taught and wrote in Fez *The manifest proofs of piety*, was a continuation of this tradition. After his death in 1465, there was another explosion of brotherhoods who all considered themselves his heirs.

The Sufi brotherhoods, whatever the exact pattern of their spiritual regime, all owed total obedience to a sheikh, their master. Asceticism, charity and teaching were some of the outward features of the search for *wajd*—for ecstatic experience of the divinity. To that end *hizb*—recitation, *dikr*—prolonged recitation, *sama*—music, *raqs* and *hadra*—dancing, and *tamzig*—the tearing of clothes, were some of the spiritual tools used by the initiate. For an outsider the most common Sufi trait was indifference to the concerns of the world. This trend was developed by the **Aissoua** and **Hamadasha brotherhoods** into self-mutilation to show indifference to pain, whilst the more off-beat practised the

75

prolonged contemplation of a beautiful young man, an ephebus, who was believed to embody the divine.

Sufi brotherhoods influential in Morocco

The **Chadhilia** were founded by Abou el Hassan Ali ech Chadhili who was a native from the Riff coast of the Ghomara. Before his death in 1258 he established a college near Chechaouen from where the brotherhood spread.

The **Jazuliya** was founded by Sidi Mohammed ben Sliman el Jazouli, a respected Sufi teacher in Fez who was poisoned in 1465. His body was transported by Al Shawyal as a centre for dissidence before being buried in Afughal in Haha province before it was exhumed 62 years later and taken to Marrakesh.

The **Aissoua** were founded in the 16th century by Sidi Mohammed ben Aissa, who despite numerous legends died before the rule of Moulay Ishmael but was buried at Meknes. Similar to the excesses of the Aissoua were the **Hamadasha** who were founded in the 18th century by Sidi Ali ben Hamdasha, who is buried in the village of Beni Rachid in the Djebel Zerhoun. Also based on Djebel Zerhoun are the **Dghuglia** who were founded by Sidi Ahmed Dghughli, a disciple of the above, who is also buried in the neighbouring village of Beni Ouared.

Derkawa/Derkaoua was founded by al Arbi al Darkawi (1760–1820) who was born north of Fez. It remains strong in rural areas, central Morocco and the Sahara. Its gentle chanting rituals and theological discussions are open to women.

Tijaniyya was founded by Ahmed al Tijani (1737–1815) who first founded a college in Algeria in 1781, but whose descendants later set up headquarters in Fez to avoid foreign rule. Its original influence came from the teachings of the 14th-century Ottoman Khalwatiya brotherhood. The sheikhs claimed to enjoy ecstatic communication with the prophet but remained strongly orthodox and loyal to the sultans. It was a brotherhood for courtiers and intellectuals.

The **Naciri** revitalized the zaouia of Tamegroute in the Draa valley and laid great emphasis on education and orthodox knowledge of the Koran.

The **Taibia** were an influential brotherhood amongst the northern tribes of Morocco and Algeria in the 19th century; their sherif ruled from Ouezzane.

The **Kittania** were founded by an Idrissid shorfa, Sidi Mohammed bel Kheir el Kittani. The sect grew in influence throughout the 19th century. A Kittani sherif claimed the throne in 1911 but his defeat and execution by Moulay Hafid led the brotherhood to side strongly with the French in order to pursue a vendetta against the Alouites.

Of lesser orthodoxy was the **Rma brotherhood** for soldiers and the **Gnaoua**, a spiritual community of negroes and slaves from west Africa that is widely admired for its music but feared for its occult powers.

Music

You are just as likely to hear reggae or contemporary Egyptian singers as modern Moroccan bands on the ubiquitous radios and cassette players. Traditional Moroccan music however is alive and well, developing under new influences in the modern cities of the coast whilst remaining true to its origins in the countryside.

The indigenous music of the Berber tribes is best heard in the Riff or the Atlases. The Atlas tribes specialize in great circles of women dancing and singing to music produced by men. In the Riff the women singers tend to be fewer and more circumspect. Beyond these regions the music brought up from west Africa by negro slaves, generically known as **Gnaoua/Gnawa** and the formal music produced by the sophisticated Arab courts of Andalucia, the classical **nubas**, are dominant influences. The Andalucian-influenced cities of northern Morocco, Tetouan, Chechouan, Rabat, Fez and Larache, are the major repositories of classical music. The Djeballa region has developed 'Toqtoqa' music from Andalucian strains for the lascivious boy dancers of the northwestern hills. Marrakesh is the centre of Gnaoua music but centuries of the slave trade have brought west African influences to most corners of the nation. The erotic swaying dance of the Sahara, the **Guedra**, performed by women on their knees, shares many of the influences of Gnaoua spirit music.

Borrowing from Berber tribal, Andalucian and negro influences the **Sufi brotherhoods** have produced the most specific musical repertoire. The musical accompaniment to chanting rituals and ecstatic dances has a spiritual goal that necessarily extends over hours. Anybody interested in discovering more should look at the list of recordings in the bibliography at the back of the guide.

Islamic art in Morocco

Throughout the Muslim world the two dominant art forms are **architecture** and **calligraphy**. Titus Burkhardt has defined Islamic art as the way to ennoble matter by means of geometric and floral patterns which, united by calligraphic forms, embody the word of God as revealed in the Koran. Of these forms of decoration only calligraphic can be considered an Islamic invention though in their manner of combination a distinctive Islamic style was born. The decorative themes from architecture and calligraphy provide the motifs and inspiration for the lesser arts of **ceramics** and **carpet making**.

Architecture

As Islam and Christendom approach books from different ends, so do they architecture. This is less of a philosophical division and more to do with a difference in climate. Islamic architecture aims to enclose space, to create a sheltered garden from a wilderness. Architectural decoration, of pavilions, fountains, raised paths and pools is reserved for the interior of this enclosure. European traditions are the complete reverse. Gardens or parks emanate from outside the house, decoration is reserved for the exterior of a structure and the interior has more to do with a collection of rooms sealed from the environment than any feeling of a defined space.

In the architectural details both Christendom and Islam share the same classical influences, though it is interesting that Islam has more fully identified itself with the domes and arches of Christian Byzantium whilst Europe continually reaches back for its references to the earliest pagan temples of Greece. From the early centuries Muslim architects in North Africa rejected horizontal beams and began experimenting with **horseshoe arches**. They also moved away from using columns as a central structure and developed rectangular piers to support their arches. **Columns** that freely borrowed their capitals from Classical, Egyptian and Persian styles were increasingly used as mere decoration. Often combined in pairs, they flank a window frame, the side of a pier, define the edge of a horseshoe arch or appear so ornate and thin to be almost free standing beside a load-bearing pier of an arch. In short the column becomes vestigial, and in Andalucia and its artistic colony of North Africa all attention is focused on the horseshoe arch. It is developed into an all-pervading, almost obsessive regional theme. The interlocking arch inspires the ubiquitous **entrelac decoration**, intercrossing arches rise from walls to support domes, serried ranks support the roofs of every major mosque and define the lowest tier of every interior courtyard. The **squinch**, the awkward corners left by a dome, are filled by **muqurnas** which can appear like disordered dripping stalactites, though in their origin they are highly ordered tiers of arches. The surface of the arch itself is next adorned, with circular half lobes, with entrelac and muqurnas. By the 19th century the style had become debased; to see it with its true virility, confidence and elegance you must visit the **koubba el Baroudiyn** in Marrakesh.

Geometric decoration

Islamic art draws attention away from the real world to one of pure form. **Geometric decoration** presents a direct analogy to spiritual truths, for both direct attention away from the confusing patterns of the world to find hidden cores of meaning. From the muddled three dimensions of the physical world geometry creates a clearly defined two-dimensional order. But beyond the soothing ordered geometric patterns a single hidden point rules the kaleidoscopic images of the surface. Thus does all relate to the one, just as at the day of judgement all that has been created will return to the single entity of the creator. Time, space, angles, planes, lines will collapse in on themselves and the physical universe will return to the one. There is no God but the one God.

Islam also inherited earlier semitic religious traditions that saw sacred art as having an essentially geometrical and mathematical nature. Many of the familiar Islamic geometrical patterns were borrowed from Egypt and Syria. Representational art was a dangerous distraction that could all too often degenerate into graven images and paganism. Numbers and figures however were seen as symbols that defined a perfect world, of that created by the single creator. Islam also absorbed the Platonic and Pythagorean respect for the divine harmony of **geometry and mathematics**. Numbers and shapes in the Pythagorean and Kabbalistic tradition were connected to mystical properties. For instance a pyramid with its six sides represented fire, a tetrahedron air, earth was represented by a cube and water by an icosahedron. This was the basis of a detailed symbolic vocabulary which allowed hidden abstractions to be built into a pattern.

The infinite repeating geometrical patterns, the lattices, interlaces, compounds, overlays and borders are also the perfect aesthetic accompaniment to the human ritual of Islam, to the endless chanting of single phrases, the recurring ritual of daily prayer and the repetitious nature of the Koranic verses themselves.

Floral decoration

According to the Koran every artist on the day of judgement will be challenged to breathe life into his work and on failing will be condemned. The **floral art** of Persia and Rome was not considered to fall under this interdict and was eagerly borrowed by the first Muslim conquerors. Floral motifs, acanthus, peonies, tulips, roses, pinecones, vine leaves, pomegranates and palmettes are also a constant reminder to the faithful of the **rewards of paradise** for the Koran is full of references to the over-hanging trees and fruits in heaven. The symmetry of flowers and seed pods also revealed the geometrical hand of the creator.

Calligraphic decoration

It is believed by many Muslims that **Arabic** is the divine language and that their language did not exist before the prophet Mohammed received the first verses of the Koran.

Arabic grew from the Nabato–Aramaic script which was itself a successor to Phoenician. The earliest Arabic inscription was found near Aleppo and has been dated to AD 512, though there appear to have been four distinct Arabic scripts before the Islamic era. A reform by the Caliph Abdel Malik (685–705) established the **two schools of calligraphy** that exist today. These are **Kufic**, an angular, solid hieratic script suitable for carving and ornamental texts, and **Cursive**, a rounded flowing script (sometimes referred to as Nashki) suitable for everyday use.

This reform did not check the continual development of scripts which were codified in the 9th century but continued evolving until the spread of printing. Among the more characteristic is the graceful Persian **Taliq**, the variant cursive of **Rihani**, **Tughra** the cryptic Tartar lettering, the thick stout **Riqa** script of the Turks, **Sayaquit** the secret script of the Seljuk clerks or the opulent **Diwani** of the Ottoman court. **Ghober** allowed for letters to be carried by pigeon post and it could only be read with a magnifying glass whilst the different tones of **Manachir** could indicate reprimand or satisfaction before even the first letter had been read.

Up to the 12th century Morocco remained dominated by the old **Cursive** script of Kairouan, in Tunisia. This was replaced by the distinctive **Maghrebi script** which had been developed in Andalucia. This preserved an ancient synthesis of Kufic and Cursive and is described as 'virile and generous with angular outlines, both horizontal and vertical well emphasized and accompanied by large cursives open at the top'. Maghrebi script was written in black with ink prepared from scorched wool taken from a sheep's stomach. The official standard pen was composed of 24 donkey hairs, though dried reed was a common substitute. A red copper pen was used for marriage documents, a silver or stork beak pen for a special friend and a pomegranate sliver was used for an enemy.

In architectural decoration Cursive and Maghrebi can be found, though a plain Kufic or floral Kufic is much more common. Beyond its own attraction, horizontal bands of script are often used to bind different sections of materials and decoration together as the Koran binds the community of Islam, for by the common but widespread belief Arabic came to earth as a a subsidiary gift from heaven, the precious language of the revelation.

Mosques

All mosques in Morocco are closed to non-Muslims though you are free to admire the exterior details like gates and minaret towers. A mosque literally means the place of prostration. At its simplest it can be an open air space with a small niche, the **mihrab**, that indicates the direction of prayer towards Mecca. These are known as **msalla** and can be seen outside the walls of Marrakesh and Fez where they are used during festivals. In the poorer rural areas the next stage in the development of the mosque can still be seen in use where a wall has been built to enclose the prayer area and the mihrab extrudes, to appear like a white sugar loaf. It was only a small further development to roof the **prayer hall**, leaving an open air court, the **sahn**, exposed at the opposite end to the prayer niche. The sahn or an adjoining building could be equipped with basins or a fountain for the **ritual washing** enjoined in the Koran.

In the construction of the cathedrals of Islam, the first **grand mosques**, Byzantine influence from Syria was strong. The tendency to embellish the central aisle of the mosque which leads up to the mihrab with arches, pillars and domes strongly echoes the nave of a church. That characteristic Islamic feature, the **minaret**, was initially developed from the short towers that used to define a Byzantine churchyard. The first Muslim architects also borrowed from previous religious practice and elaborated the mihrab into a cave-like half dome, upon which the two declarations of faith were carved, whilst the exterior of the niche was covered by an arch and flanked by two columns. The walls and floors of Moroccan mosques are kept free of architectural decoration. The white **pillars and arches** may carry some simple carving but there is seldom any colour introduced beyond the hip-height reed matting that is pinned along the walls or the carpets on the floor. Decoration was reserved for elaborate **chandeliers** and the pulpit-like minbar. The original minbar, used by the prophet for his readings and lectures at Medina, had six steps. He used a lower step in order to leave the throne symbolically empty. More steps were added by his successors which allowed them to sit further from the throne, in order to distinguish their lesser spiritual authority.

The only substantial mosque that a non-Muslim may enter in Morocco is also one of the oldest. The half-ruined **Grand Mosque of Tinmal** in the High Atlas was built by the Almohads in the 12th century. It is a contemporary with the great achievements of Moroccan architecture, the **Koutoubia of Marrakesh**, the **Grand Mosque of Taza** and the **Hassan tower of Rabat**. The minarets of the Koutoubia and Hassan led to the creation of a characteristic style. Moroccan mosques all echo these two tall, **square towers** that should be capped with a lantern that is exactly a fifth the size of the tower. The new Syrian mosque in Tangier shows a different development, whilst Tunisian mosques tend to sport a low dome.

Medersas

The earliest specific residential, religious college was built in Persia in the 9th century. **Medersas** were not built in Morocco until the 13th century under the patronage of the Merenid sultans. Until then **teaching** was performed in the courts of a mosque or in the houses of the lecturers. The earliest surviving medersa, the **Seffarin** in Fez from 1280, clearly shows the origin of this religious college in the town house of a lecturer. Later medersas drew more heavily on Andalucian decoration and the architectural developments of Cairo, though the basic plan of open-air court surrounded by an upper storey of student lodgings and leading to a prayer hall remains consistent. Marrakesh, Salé and Meknes each have a medersa that is open to the public and Fez has half a dozen.

Palaces

The oldest accessible palace in Morocco is the ruined 16th-century **El Badi in Marrakesh**. Of the palaces built in the 17th century by Sultan Moulay Ishmael, the **Dar el Makhzen in Tangier** and the **Oudaia in Rabat** are well preserved and open to the public as they now house museums. Meknes for all its past glory gives little insight into palace architecture. Of the royal palaces built in the 19th century, only the **Dar Batha in Fez** is accessible as it has also been turned into a museum. There are however a number of lesser viziers' palaces that have survived from this period and are open to the public: the **Palais Jamai Hôtel** in Fez, the **Jamai Museum** in Meknes, the **Bahia** and the **Dar Si Said** in Marrakesh.

The Roman ruins of **Volubilis** contain a number of palatial houses that correspond in design with the lesser palaces of Muslim rulers. They both have an inconspicuous exterior and a covered hall that leads to a central open-air court. Around the walls of this court are arranged four public reception rooms or **pavilions**. The **women's quarters** are secluded from this male preserve and were known as the forbidden, the **'harem' court**. This arrangement of courts could be endlessly repeated or expanded in scale. The entire complex was known as the **'Dar'** and a suite of rooms around a court a **'Bayt'**. The **'Mechouar'** was a space outside the immediate palace confines but within the outer walls where a ruler could review military parades or receive selected portions of the populace.

Ksar (plural—ksour)

The pre-Saharan region and the oasis valleys are studded with **ksour**, fortified villages of cultivators. A **ksar** was administered by a council of headmen who strove to remain independent from the influence of the surrounding nomadic tribes. Ksour are constructed out of stone or pise (packed and baked mud), with the internal timbers and wattling largely constructed from date palm. The use of palm trunks set a natural limit to the internal dimensions. The rooms and passages of a ksar subsequently have harmonious proportions but were often dark, infested and airless. Their attraction is chiefly found in brick or pise **decorated towers** but as the interior could be the product of any culture in the last two or three thousand years, they have an ageless sense of stimulating mystery. Each oasis system has its own distinctive style which gives off flickering references to Egypt, Mesopotamia, Tyre, Mycenae or Gothic Christendom. They may last for a few generations, but it is rare for a pise ksar to survive for more than two hundred years. The disintegrating pise reveals little to archaeologists and, though widely spread throughout Saharan Africa, their origins and architectural inspiration is unknown.

Agadirs

The Berber hill tribes were more capable of defending themselves than oasis or valley dwellers. They could afford to live in smaller family units but stored their corn in communal stone-built hill-top fortresses which are known as **agadirs** or **igherms**. These are well distributed south of the High Atlas and there are some fine examples in the Anti Atlas.

Kasbah

Whilst a ksar can be defined as a fortified village, a **kasbah** has a looser definition. It can be a fortified farm, the citadel of a city, an isolated government garrison or a tribal fort. In the pre-Saharan region the difference between a kasbah and a ksar is slight. **Tiznit**, for instance, was a group of kasbahs that was protected by a common wall to create a fortified community, a ksar which was embellished by a kasbah for the royal governor.

The rise in power of the High Atlas caids and particularly the **Glaoui** has left the southern region of Morocco studded with decaying kasbahs from which they administered their feudal domain. Glaoui kasbahs can still be seen at Telouet, Tazzerte, Tioute, Talioune, Tinerhir, Tiffoultoute, Tamdaght and Anemiter. At their best these fuse the dazzling variety of traditional Berber battlemented exteriors with finely proportioned interiors that drew on Andalucian palaces for their inspiration.

Most of the ancient cities of Morocco retain a large portion of their outer walls, but the kasbah citadel has too often decayed beyond recognition. Tangier, Safi, Rabat and Chechaouen provide honourable and accessible exceptions. The finest government kasbahs were built by **Moulay Ishmael** in the 17th century and can be seen at Tadla, Boulaoune, Mehdiya and Agourai. The walls of Essaouira are in even better condition, for they were built on the best European principles in the 18th century. Other towns on the Atlantic coast have older defences that date from the Portuguese occupation. Ksar es Seghir, Asilah, Azzemour, El Jadida and Safi are the best preserved.

The land

It is a land fit for the gods, full of extremes to reflect the changing whims and petulant egotism of divinities—high mountain chains, desert plains, long rivers, lush reclusive valleys, broken wooded hills and undulating farmland.

The **Riff mountains** run along the northern, the Mediterranean coast of Morocco. They reach their peak at **Djebel Tidirhine** above Ketama and decline as they approach the Algerian border. To their south fertile **plains** surround Fez and Meknes and a thin strip of low land to the east—the Taza gap—separates the Riffs from the Middle Atlas. Beyond Taza the brief gap in the mountains opens out into the wide eastern desert, the plain of Jel and that of the Rekkam.

The **Middle Atlas** is an amorphous mountainous mass, a vast irregular limestone plateau that occupies much of central Morocco. The three great rivers, the Sebou, the Moulouya and the Oum er Rbia drain its forested slopes. The **High Atlas** extend east from the Atlantic coast for 700 km and exceed 4000 m at the summit of **Djebel Toubkal**. The northern face shelters numerous streams, mountain valleys and wooded heights. Its southern slopes face the Sahara and though dramatically denuded collect whatever rain falls and direct it south to create for 100 km the **oasis valleys** of the Dades, the Draa, the Rheris and the Ziz.

The **Anti Atlas** at the Atlantic coast is 100 km south of the High Atlas, divided by the verdant Souss valley. But at the eastern extension of the Anti Atlas, the massifs of Siroua and Saghro merge their twisted barren slopes with those of the High Atlas. Beyond the Anti Atlas the flat wasteland of the **Western Sahara** stretches immutably south. A harsh landscape that shows a 1000 km face of savage cliffs to the Atlantic broken by beaches at Tarfaya, Laayoune and Dakhla.

The **northern Atlantic coast** shows the same alternation of cliff and beach but in a gentler fertile aspect. Just north of the High Atlas the wooded coastal belt extends less than 50 km from the sea which is replaced to the east by an open denuded plain, the **plateau of phosphates**. The streams from the High Atlas create a basin of fertility, the **oasis of Haouz**, near the city of Marrakesh. Following the coast line north you pass through the rich but flat and largely treeless agricultural provinces of Doukkala, Chaouia and the Gharb punctuated by the cities of El Jadida, Casablanca, Rabat and Kenitra before reaching Tangier on the western edge of the Riffs.

Flora

The progression from Mediterranean to a Saharan flora occurs in a diagonal belt across the country. To the east the desert virtually reaches the Mediterranean whilst in the south, around Marrakesh and Beni Mellal, irrigation allows groves of olive, orange and cypress to flourish. Water supply rather than latitude is the key to identification. Plant growth ceases from June to August but begins with the rains in October. Some species flower throughout the winter but most perennials peak in March and April.

The mountain valleys of the western High Atlas, Haha province and the Souss have their own distinctive and equitable climate. This was identified as early as 1840 by a botanical expedition from Kew Gardens as an area rich in hundreds of endemic specimens. **Acacia Gummifera** is distinct to the Rehammna plain and the Souss valley. Its seeds are ground to create the distinctive red dye used by the tanners.

The **argan tree** will only grow in a radius of 100 km from the Souss valley and is found nowhere else in the world. Its nearest relation is the tropical ironwood tree (sider oxylon) which is an equally slow-growing thorny tree whose wood is indestructible to insects. Argan leaves are like the olive but fuller in shape. Flowers appear in June and the green fruit ripens in March. Goats climb the branches for the fruit which can also be consumed by sheep, camels and cows but is invariably refused by horses and mules. A hard nut is recovered from the dung and is cracked, parched, ground, worked into paste and separated out with water to extract the oil which is used for cooking, lamp fuel or turned into soap.

The fierce-looking dark green cactus, **euphorbium**, is another native of southwest Morocco. It is named after King Juba II's doctor and the king himself wrote a learned article on the various uses of opium and euphorbium. To extract the gum the plant was bled every four years by masked men, for its pollen causes chronic sneezing. The gum was used as an emetic and purgative.

Thuja is only to be found in the Atlas mountains of Morocco although a similar tree is indigenous to Madagascar. Thuja wood was held in the highest esteem and is praised by numerous classical writers, from Homer to St John who knew it as citrus wood, adrar and alerce. The most prized wood comes from the thick root of the trunk. The convoluted patterns of knots, spirals and veins were identified as tiger, panther and peacock eye by the cognescenti who preferred wood the colour of wine mixed with honey to all others. Cicero paid a million sesterces for a thuja table whilst King Juba II sold a fine four-and-a-half-foot wide specimen for 1,200,000 sesterces a few years later. Its resin, known as sandrac, was a prized medicine but has now fallen from favour.

The **cedar**, **date palm** and **almond** are dominant in different regions. The almond is described in the section on Tafraoute, the cedar in the section on Ifrane and Azrou and the date palm in the introduction to the oasis valleys. In the summer **mint** and **oleander** are alone found healthy and flowering in an otherwise parched landscape. Fresh mint is in demand the whole year throughout Morocco. That produced outside Meknes is most esteemed. Oleander produces a blast of colour on the dry river beds. Traditionally the first plant was created from Fatima's tears when she discovered that her husband Ali had taken a second wife. The leaves are still unbearably bitter.

Traditional enclosed **Moorish gardens** aim to create a harmony of audible flowing water and shade thrown from elegant trees, typically laurel, cypress and olive. Roses, violets, jasmin, hollyhocks and blossoming fruit trees were planted chiefly for their scent. Modern gardens borrow some of these themes but are often dominated by recent imports like mimosa from Australia, bougainvillea from Brazil in 1829 and the 'boulevard palm' from the Canary Isles. Another very noticeable import is the **prickly pear** which with maize, potatoes, tobacco and tomatoes came from America in the 16th century. The Arabs were responsible for bringing oranges and lemons from Asia. The Phoenicians introduced arboriculture to the Berbers and specifically imported the **olive**, fig, vine and pomegranate.

Distribution Summary

Mountain forests: Cedar (above 1000 m), kermes oak (below 800 m), holm oak, juniper, thuja, aleppo pine (up to 1000 m), walnut and almond. Flowers in the Atlas mountains may include crocus sieberi, narcissus bulbcadium, orchis laxiflora, asphodelus fistolus/albus/microcarpus and lutea, matthiola, Jacob's ladder, echium diffusum, genista and ononis speciosa and orchids in lush places.

Lower slopes: Fig, carob, olive (not above 6–800 m or anywhere where the temperature averages less than 3°C in the coldest month of the year), cypress, almond, prickly pear (from America) trefoils, medicagos, vetches, dwarf prickly oak, gum ammoniacum.

Maquis or shrubland: pink or white cistus or rock rose (C. ladaniferus), two sorts of broom (Cystisus tridentatis and battandieri), mastick, lavender, wormwood, rosemary, lentisk, acacia, mimosa.

Spring meadows: Chrysanthemum, lupens, crimson adonis, deep orange marigold, blue pimpernel, dwarf palm, iris, squill, asphodels, blue-tinted daisy, esparto, saffron, convolvulus, orchids, lotus tree, jujube, mugwort, echinops ritro.

Sahara: Acacia, tamarisk, date palm, eucalyptus, sea lavender, cladathus arabicus.

Atlantic coast: Cork, poplar, willow, eucalyptus.

Southwest/Souss: Argan, euphorbia, banana, sugar cane, bamboo.

Animals

Even the most distant and desolate landscape of wilderness is likely to be a seasonal grazing ground of a village or nomadic herd. You are more likely to find herds of goat, sheep and camel than wild beasts but it is possible, even without entering the guarded sporting and forestry reserves of the Administration des Eaux et Forêts, to spot wild boar, Barbary apes, a range of mountain cats, snakes and foxes.

Dominant tribes sometimes maintained sacred herds that acted as their standard or totem. The **horse** came to Morocco in about 1600 BC, the **Arabian camel** was not successfuly bred in the Moroccan Sahara until about AD 600. Whether or not there was a specific sacred herd, most nomads recognized the ancient sacred animals of a herd like the **Saiba**—the chief mother, the **Bahira**—the eleventh calf and the **Hami**—the senior stallion. In a widespread custom that extends throughout Africa and Arabia, a sacrificial calf is designated from birth and left free to graze over any field or boundary. Dedicated to a saint or spirit, it was sacrificed at the shrine and then consumed at the communal feast.

Birds

The birds are easily the most impressive aspect of Morocco's wildlife. There are a large number of residents and dazzling concentrations of migrant flocks that gather on the north coast for the seasonal migrations. The migrants are generally in Africa for the mild winter from October to March and fly across the Mediterranean for the European summer. Lakes and coastal estuaries are the best spotting places, and even if you have never shown any interest before, a bird book may soon become vital.

The **swift, swallow** and **crag martin** are respected as birds inspired by Allah to protect the harvest and remove noxious insects and reptiles. The **stork** is Morocco's other great holy bird and there are numerous legends to explain their constant attitude of prayer and their symbolic prostration whenever they rest. Hospitals were established in Fez and Marrakesh for the care of injured birds where they could recover or die peacefully in protected enclosures.

The small heron-like **little egret** is another popular bird. It is white with yellow feet and is often seen stalking in marshes or picking vermin off the backs of cattle. The **crested lark**, which is often seen pecking at dung heaps, is known as the kubaa or hooded one in Morocco and has a lower status. Foot-long **bee-eaters** travel in great flights and attract notice from their cries. They have a useful function, feeding on wasps and bees but have a tragic life, wearing away their bills in the construction of tunnel nests and then often falling prey to snakes. The **roller bee-eater** has a brilliant electric blue plumage, a little like a crow-sized English jay. The **great grey shrike** is a more aggressive bird that impales its prey on a larder of thorn spikes. The striped **hoopoe** is conspicuous during its migration but is trapped, for its heart and feathers are powerful charms against evil spirits. The **barn owl**, a permanent resident of Morocco, is recognized to be the clairvoyant ally of the devil. The owl cries out the name of a fore-doomed individual who can only escape by cursing the owl with its own hidden name. Even a normal owl cry has the power to kill a child unless there is someone to spit and curse as they fly overhead. The **short eared owl**, the **marsh owl** and **scops owl** that live in cork woods have lesser powers. The **Tangier raven** is also viewed with suspicion and always lays its eggs on 21 April. Killing a raven soothes the evil eye whilst a raven's liver, tongue, brain and heart are made into useful antidotes.

The most spectacular of all migrants are the **birds of prey**. Ospreys, marsh harriers, Montagu's harriers, buzzards, rufous buzzards—the Khabbas or great hunters, golden eagles, Bonelli's eagles (with a white patch on their back), the small booted eagle, the short-toed or snake eagle, goshawks, sparrowhawks, red and black kites, honey buzzards, merlins and kestrels can be seen in large numbers every year. A March morning with an east wind blowing over a hill outside Tangier would be the ideal time and place. You could also look out for the rare **griffon vulture** and the more common **Egyptian vulture** which is one of the foulest feeding birds that lives, its 'nests decorated with dog's heads, boars' tusks, dead kittens, rotten hedgehogs, snake skeletons, mummified lizards, rotten fish and excrement of both man and beast.'

Part III

A DICTIONARY OF ISLAMIC AND MOROCCAN TERMS

Camel Market

ABASSIDS. The 2nd dynasty of CALIPHS who ruled the Muslim world from their capital of Baghdad from AD 750–1258.

ABD—sing., ABID—plural. A slave. By inference a negro, and used to distinguish the negro regiments from the tribal ones in the SULTAN's army. Also widely used to create names in conjunction with one of the 99 names of God, as in Abd-Allah.

ACANTHUS. Low plant with a broad serrated green leaf found throughout the Mediterranean. The leaf was a familiar classical motif that was retained and developed by Muslim carvers.

AGADIR. Principal city and port of southwestern Morocco. Literally the fortified communal hilltop granaries of the Berber tribes, also known as IGHREM.

AGDAL. Enclosed garden or park that contains a water tank, as in the 'Aguedal' in Marrakesh.

AID. The feast, as in Aid es Seghir at the end of RAMADAN and Aid el Kebir that commemorates the sacrifice of Abraham.

AIN. Spring or water hole. Plural AIOUN.

AISSOUA. A SUFI religious brotherhood.

AIT. Child of, as used in the creation of a tribal identity, such as AIT ATTA.

AIT ATTA. Berber tribe from DJEBEL Saghro who dominated the south from the 16th century to 1934.

87

AKBAR. 'The Great'—as in Allah Akbar.

ALI. Cousin and son in law of the PROPHET through his marriage to FATIMA, and father of Hassan and Hussein. ALI succeeded Othmann as 4th CALIPH in AD 656 but his reign was punctuated by disputes which split Islam into the SUNNI, SHIITE and KHAJARITE camps. He is considered a great Islamic hero and warrior, the founder of SUFI mystical practices but was assassinated in the mosque of Kufa and succeeded by Muawiyya, the OMAYYAD governor of Syria.

ALMOHAD. The unitarians. An Islamic reform movement founded by Ibn Tumert in the High Atlas which replaced ALMORAVIDE rule over Morocco. The ALMOHAD Empire, AD 1147–1248 was a peak period of Moroccan history, an era of great military power, burgeoning architecture, civilization and indigenous religious authority.

ALMORAVIDE. The warrior monks. An Islamic reform movement founded by Ibn Yacin in the Sahara which under his successors Abu Bekr and Youssef ben Tachfine controlled an Empire that stretched from Spain to West Africa AD 1060–1147.

ALOUITE. The present ruling dynasty of Morocco who from their base of the Tafilalet oasis replaced the Saadian sultans in 1666. They are also known as the FILALI and considered to be descendants of the PROPHET through his son-in-law ALI.

AMGHAR. The war leader of a Berber tribe.

AMIN. Tax collector.

ANDALUCIA. The Muslim principalities of southern Spain which were conquered by the ALMORAVIDE and then the ALMOHAD Empires. The flow of Andalucian refugees and craftsmen from the cities of Seville, Cordoba and Granada from the 10th to the 17th centuries greatly contributed to the development of cultured urban life in Morocco.

ARABESQUE. General adjective describing the architecture and the calligraphic, floral and geometrical decoration of Islam.

ARGAN. Hard oil-producing thorn tree that only grows in southwestern Morocco.

ASIF. River that flows throughout the year.

ATRIUM. Central court or hall of a Roman house.

AVERROES/IBN RUSHD. Muslim scholar born in Cordoba in 1126 who originally enjoyed the patronage of the ALMOHAD sultans. His translation of Aristotle and philosophical works was of great long-term influence to the Christian universities, though the orthodox of both Islam and Christendom condemned his rationalism.

AZROU. Rock, and the name of a town in the Middle Atlas.

BAB. Gate.

BARAKA. Blessing or holy luck. A gift passed down through saintly dynasties and obtained from pilgrimages to the shrines of saints.

BASTILLA. Traditional pigeon pie made with flaky pastry.

BENI. The sons of, often used in the description of a tribe, like the Beni Merin.

BERGHAWATA/BERGHOUATA. Heretical Berber tribal group who occupied the coastal region from Salé to Casablanca until conquered in the 12th century by the ALMOHADS.

BIT. Room.

BLED. The land or countryside, as in the division between the Bled es Makhzen, the land of the government and the Bles es Siba, the land of dissidence.

CADI. Judge of Muslim law.

CAFTAN/KAFTAN. Formal outer garment though it is increasingly used to describe an embroidered cotton robe.

CAID. Magistrate who in the lawless areas was often a tribal chief recognized by the sultan. Now the chief magistrate of a commune.

CALIPH. The successor of the PROPHET to the rule of the Muslim community. The ALMOHADS in the 12th century were the first Moroccan rulers to assume the title, which implies a claim to the sole leadership of the original Muslim Empire.

CALLIGRAPHY. The art of writing with different styles of script which in Arabic are divided between the rounded CURSIVE and the angular KUFIC.

CARAVANSERAI. Defensive lodgings on a caravan route.

CHAHADA. The profession of faith: 'La illaha illa ilah. Mohammed rasul illah.— There is no divinity but God. Mohammed is the messenger of God.'

CHARIA. The Islamic code of law derived from the KORAN and HADITH.

CHIKHA. Professional female dancer.

CHLEUH. One of the three Berber tribal groupings who occupy the western High Atlas, the Souss and the Anti Atlas. They are also known as Soussi or Masmuda and speak a dialect known as Tachelhait.

CURSIVE. The familiar style of flowing rounded Arabic script.

DAKHLA. An entrance to a gorge and the name of a town of the Western Sahara which was known as Villa Cisneros until 1976.

DAMASCENE. A decorative inlay, principally of silver or copper on to iron or brass.

DAR. House, building or palace. City quarters are often named after the most distinctive house of the quarter, like Dar Sejene in Meknes. The Dar el Makhzen is the house of government, a royal palace or administrative settlement.

DAYA. Lake.

DIRHAM. The Ommayad Caliphs based the first Muslim silver coinage on the Byzantine Drachmae. The name and style was in turn copied by Moroccan mints.

DJEBEL/JEBEL. Mountain. The DJEBALLA are a specific group of Arabic-speaking tribes that occupy the western Riff. It is also a city dweller's label of contempt for the unsophisticated, the hill-billies.

DJEDID/JEDID. New. As in Fez el Jedid, new Fez, the 14th-century royal extension to the city.

DJELLABA. Large cotton or wool outer garment with sleeves and a hood.

DJENAN. Garden, green space and a metaphor for paradise.

DOUAR. Thorn hedge or stockade of thorns arranged as a wall for a marching army.

DRAA. Arm. The river Draa flows south from Ouazazarte into the Sahara.

EMIR. He who commands. Originally the military deputies of the CALIPH, and transformed into a title of sovereignty. Their leadership of the JIHAD won or lost these commanders of the faithful their right to rule.

ERG. Dunes or region of dunes in a desert. The Erg Chebbi east of Erfoud is the largest accessible sand desert in Morocco.

FANTASIA. A display of horsemanship featuring small charges, dramatic halts and the firing of muskets. Performed at national holidays, at the festival of folklore in Marrakesh and at the Meknes FANTASIA festival. FANTASIA displays can be seen all the year round at Agadir and Marrakesh.

FAQIH. Lawyer of religious law.

FARADIS. Persian word meaning walled garden, used by MOHAMMED to describe paradise.

FASSI. An inhabitant of Fez. It can also refer to the rich merchant class in Morocco.

FATIMA. Only surviving daughter of the PROPHET, wife of ALI and mother of Hassan and Hussein. The central female cult figure of Islam who absorbed many earlier beliefs. Hence the Tunisian/Egyptian Fatimid dynasty which claims descent from her. The Hand of Fatima is an ancient good luck talisman.

FILALI. Red leather goat skin made in the Draa valley and the Tafilalet. Family name for the ruling ALOUITE dynasty.

FIQH. The Islamic legal code. There are four traditional codes acknowledged by the orthodox Muslim: the Malekite, Hanefite, Chafiite and Hanbalite. The MALEKITE is favoured in Morocco.

FOGGARA/KHETTARA. Underground irrigation canal.

FONDOUQ/FONDOUK. A courtyard surrounded by rooms which takes on a great range of functions. Stabling, hotels, artisan and trading centres, auctions, markets, and brothels are all arranged around a central courtyard.

GANDOURA. Mostly worn by men, a simple cotton tunic with sleeves and plain collar.

GARUM. Peculiar fish paste, made of salt and mashed tuna intestines beloved by the ancient Romans and manufactured on the Moroccan Atlantic coast.

GHARB. West. The GHARB is the fertile coastal region between Larache and Kenitra.

GNAOUA/GNAWA/GNAIWAYA. Negro religious brotherhood from West Africa and also the name of their spirit music.

GUICH. Tribal troops in the sultan's service, excused from taxes and often rewarded with gifts of land.

HABOUS. Religious foundations. Gifts of property to the faith whose rents are spent on the construction of mosques, fountains, hospitals and schools. In Morocco, the HABOUS is controlled by a government minister appointed by the king.

HADITH. The collected sayings of the PROPHET remembered by his companions.

HADJ. A pilgrimage to MECCA. The honorific title for those who have made the journey is HADJI.

HAIK. Large cloth used by women to cover themselves in the street.

HAMMADA. Flat pebbly plateau of the Sahara.

HAMMAM. Steam or Turkish baths. The direct continuation of the classical public baths with underfloor heating. Washing is typically done from buckets, while the more sophisticated hammama contain a series of chambers each one hotter than the last, cold pools, showers and masseurs.

HARATINE. Black serf caste in the south, having no tribal loyalties but often attached in a share cropping arrangement to a nomadic warrior group.

HARKA. The burning. An apt description of the progress of royal armies through rebellious provinces.

HARMATTAN. Hot dry winds which blow from the Sahara.

HASSAN II. King of Morocco, succeeded his father Mohammed V to the throne in 1961. Born in 1929, he was educated in Rabat and Bordeaux where he read law. He accompanied his father into exile from 1953 to 1955 and on Independence was put in command of the new royal army. Married Lalla Latifa of Fez in 1960, with whom he has four children.

HEGIRA. The Islamic era which began with the flight of the PROPHET from MECCA to MEDINA in July AD 622. The Muslim calendar is based on a lunar rather than a solar year and is therefore 11 days shorter than each Gregorian year.

HENNA. A red dye made from the leaves of the henna tree. Used on the hair and for creating intricate and temporary patterns on hands and feet.

HILALI. A nomadic bedouin tribe that with the Sulaym left the Arabian peninsula in the 11th century to advance west along the North African coast. They destroyed cities and agricultural communities, reversing the achievement of centuries of civilization in a furious and bloody migration.

IBN BATTUTA. Travel writer who was born in Tangier in 1304 and died at Fez in 1377. Trained as a CADI, he travelled, worked and married throughout the Muslim world from Timbuktu to China.

IBN KHALDOUN. Celebrated historian and sociologist who was born in Tunis in 1332, his parents having fled from Andalucia. He obtained positions in a number of Muslim courts and lived at Fez before settling in Egypt as the Melekite Mufti of Cairo. He met Tamerlane on a mission to save Damascus before he died in 1406.

IDRISS I/MOULAY IDRISS. Great-grandson of the PROPHET and founder of the first Muslim kingdom of Morocco in AD 788. His tomb at Moulay Idriss is the preeminent national shrine.

IDRISS II. Posthumous son of IDRISS I by a Berber concubine. Creator of the city of Fez where his tomb is venerated. His descendants, the Idrissids, have been a numerous and influential clan throughout Moroccan history.

IGHREM. See AGADIR.

IMAM. Leader of prayers and by implication also a political leader.

ISLAM. Submission to God. MOHAMMED is the best-known and the last of a long line of prophets who taught submission to God, giving rules for the conduct of life and threatening unbelievers with divine punishment.

ISTAQLAL. Independence party founded by Allal al Fasi in 1934, which took a leading role in the civil resistance to the French PROTECTORATE. It held a strong position in post-Independence government from 1956 to 1962.

JIHAD. Holy war against the enemies of Islam.

KAABA. A meteorite venerated from antiquity in Mecca and situated on the spot where Abraham traditionally erected his altar. Muslims pray towards the Kaaba and circle it seven times before kissing it as the culmination of the HADJ.

KASBAH. The citadel of a town or a rural fortress. The meaning of the word has been extended to describe any defensive building.

KEBILA. An extended patriarchal family housed in one or two tents which is the basic unit of a tribe.

KHAIMA. Grand tent of a tribal leader now much reproduced for use at fêtes and as restaurants.

KHAJARITES. An early schismatic sect in the Muslim world which considered that the CALIPH should be elected from the minority of the true community of believers. This belief was particularly attractive to the Berbers of North Africa in their struggle against the tyranny of their Arab governors.

KHATIB. Preacher who delivers the KHUTBA, the sermon after the noon prayers on Friday.

KHETTARA. See FOGGARA.

KHUMS. Arabic for a fifth, as in a fifth of a tribe. Plural—Akhmas.

KILLIM. A woven carpet.

KOHL. Ground powder of the metallic-looking sulphur of antimony. Applied to the eyes, it stimulates an attractive watery sheen that is useful protection against soot and dust.

KORAN. The word of God dictated to the PROPHET Mohammed by the archangel Gabriel in Arabic.

KOUBA. Women's room.

KOUBBA. Dome. By extension a koubba is the shrine of a saint's tomb which is usually covered by a small white cupola. They often form the object of a pilgrimage and are at the centre of much female spiritual activity.

KSAR, pl. KSOUR. An Arabic noun derived from Caesar that describes a fortified village.

KUFIC. Angular style of Arabic script, named after the city of Kufa in Iraq, which is chiefly used in stone and plaster carving.

LABES. OK, no harm.

LALLA. Lady, a title of respect used for a female saint or woman of dignity.

LAMTUNA. Dominant SANHAJAN Berber tribe of the Almoravide movement.

LEO AFRICANUS. Born in Granada in 1483, El Hassan ibn Mohammed el Fasi was enslaved by Christians and on recognition as an intellectual was presented to the Pope. He was freed, baptized and awarded a pension by Pope Leo who encouraged him to write his famous description of North Africa. Having completed the great work he died a Muslim in Tunis in 1554.

LITHAM. Veil.

LYAUTEY, HUBERT. An officer of the French Colonial Army, he served in campaigns in Madagascar and Indo-China before directing the absorption of eastern Morocco from the Algerian frontier. As RESIDENT GENERAL from 1912 to 1926 he directed the shape and objectives of the French PROTECTORATE. His policy of ruling through the existing power structures kept the cost of running this empire low during the crucial years of the First World War. Promoted a Marshal of France in 1921, he was summarily removed four years later during the alarming height of the Riff rebellion. A flamboyant but inspiring figure, he was a romantic and a homosexual who surrounded himself with a glittering court of aristocratic young officers and a personal negro guard. His work developing and pacifying the country is respected by many Moroccans. His statue remains in Casablanca.

MAGHREB. The land of the furthest west, containing the three nations of Tunisia, Algeria and Morocco.

MAKHZEN. Government.

MAKSOURA/MAQSARA. Wooden screens in a MOSQUE that protect rulers from assassination.

MALEKITE. The most widely practised school of judicial practice and Koranic interpretation in North Africa. It was formulated by Malik ibn Anas, a judge from Medina who died in AD 795.

MARABOUT. Holy warrior, ascetic or the chief of a religious brotherhood who has won the respect of the people. His tomb may be covered by a dome and kept in repair and veneration for as long as he retains devotees.

MAURETANIA. The two Roman provinces of Mauretania Caesariensis and Mauretania Tingitana, whose boundaries approximate those of modern Morocco and Algeria, were created by the Emperor Claudius out of the Kingdom of Mauretania. It now refers to the Saharan country south of Morocco on the Atlantic coast.

MECCA. Sacred town of the Muslims, 8 km inland from the Red Sea, on the old caravan route from Syria to Yemen. MOSQUES are all oriented towards MECCA, 35° east and 11° south from Fez. In practice, the older MOSQUES tend to be pointing too far south.

MECHOUAR. A place adjoining a palace in which the population can assemble to pay homage to the ruler.

MEDERSA. Residential schools for the study of the KORAN and religious law. They were introduced into Morocco in the 12th century, though the earliest surviving buildings date from the 14th. The MERENID dynasty were the most enthusiastic builders, anxious to restore orthodoxy into the confused religious life of Morocco. Their design follows a common plan, supposedly based on the house of MOHAMMED. A hall leads into a central courtyard with a fountain. Three chambers lead off from the courtyard—one used as a prayer hall, one as a library and the other as a school room. Two storeys of student bedrooms are positioned above the courtyard. The MEDERSA courtyard is usually richly decorated with panels of faience, carved plaster and cedar surrounding marble floors and carved fountains.

MEDINA. Walled city or old city in distinction to the new European-style quarter. Named after the city that MOHAMMED fled to to avoid persecution in MECCA.

MELLAH. The Jewish quarter. The name derives from the word Melh, meaning salt, as the Jews used to perform the task of salting the severed heads of the sultan's enemies in order to preserve them.

MENDOUB. Agent or representative of the SULTAN, as found in Tangier from 1927–1956.

MERENIDS. Dynasty who originated from the Beni Merin nomadic tribe who dominated the eastern plains of Morocco. They replaced the ALMOHADS in 1248 and built a series of fine MEDERSAS throughout Morocco and particularly in Fez.

MERLONS. Decorative battlements.

MIDHA. Fountain for ritual washing before prayer.

MIHRAB. A niche in a place of prayer which indicates the direction of MECCA.

MINARET. The tower of a MOSQUE used for calling the faithful to prayer. The pinnacle is crowned with domes representing the daily prayers, and a blue or green flag flying indicates Friday, the Muslim sabbath.

MINBAR. A pulpit-like staircase in MOSQUES used for the noonday Friday sermon, the KHUTBA, given by the KHATIB.

MINZAH. In a palace, a garden pavilion, especially one enjoying a fine view.

MOHAMMED. The PROPHET, the last in the succession of Abraham, Noah, Moses and Jesus who have called man to worship the one God.

MOHAMMED V. The popular monarch whose portrait is seen throughout the land. He led the struggle for Moroccan Independence and was exiled by the French. He had since the death of his father, Sultan Moulay Youssef, in 1927 been the titular ruler, but after Independence in 1956 he initiated a new era by ruling as King Mohammed V. He died in 1961.

MOKHAZENES. Gendarmes, men of the MAKHZEN, the government.

MORISCOS. Muslim refugees from Spain, arriving in Morocco throughout 10th–17th centuries, but particularly after the fall of Granada in 1493.

MOSQUE. The place of prostration, the place of reunion, the place of prayer. At its most basic a defined space for prayer with a MIHRAB, indicating which way to pray.

MOUKARNAS. Stalactite-like decorations chiefly of carved wood, stone or plaster. A frequent component of Moorish ceilings.

MOULAY. Honorific title, approximately 'lord'. Used in Morocco by the descendants of the PROPHET.

MOULOUD. The great feast day celebrating MOHAMMED'S birthday on the 12th day of the Muslim month of Rabi at-Tani.

MOUSSEM. Originally an annual popular pilgrimage to the tomb of a saint, but now by inference any festival or outdoor entertainment.

MSALLA. Prayer area.

MUEZZIN. The call to prayer, also the prayer caller.

NASRANI. Nazarene, Christian.

OASIS. An island of life in the desert supported by a water gathering system. Were it not for man these would revert back to desert.

OMAYYADS. The first dynasty of CALIPHS who ruled the Islamic world from AD 660–750. After the death of ALI, the prophet's cousin and son-in-law, Muawiya, the governor of Syria, was proclaimed CALIPH. The Omayyads inherited the organization and architecture of Byzantine Syria and introduced a standard coinage. They faced the schismatic rebellions of the SHIITES and the KHAJARITES, and were replaced in 750 by the ABASSIDS.

OUED. River.

PASHA. Provincial governor, or the governor of a city.

PISE. Packed wet clay, naturally baked by the sun. Widely used throughout Morocco for the construction of walls, KASBAHS and roads.

PROPHET, see MOHAMMED.

PROTECTORATE. Period of French colonial rule of Morocco from 1912–1956. Conducted by the RESIDENT GENERAL under the pretence that the SULTAN had contracted his authority to France by the 1912 Treaty of Fez for the efficient modernization of the country.

RABAT/R'BAT. A R'bat is a fortified monastery. Rabat is a city founded by the Almohads on the site of an old R'bat which has been the capital of Morocco since 1912.

RAMADAN. Muslim month of fasting in the ninth lunar month of the year. No food, drink or sex is allowed during the hours of daylight. Travellers, the sick, the old, the pregnant and pre-pubescent children are exempt.

RAZZIA. Desert raid.

REGUIBAT, a desert Berber tribe, see the Western Sahara section.

REHAMNA, an Arab tribe that dominated the arid plains north of Marrakesh from the 16th century.

RESIDENT GENERAL. The French rulers of Morocco from 1912–1956: Lyautey, Steeg, Saint, Ponsot, Peyrouton, Nogues, Puaux, Labonne, Juin, Lacoste, Grandval, Boyer de la Tour and Dubois.

RIAD. An ANDALUCIAN garden with sunken beds and paths.

ROGUI. A pretender to the SULTANATE, and a derisive label used against Bou Hamara who proclaimed himself Sultan at Taza in 1912.

ROUMI. Roman, Christian, foreigner.

SAADIAN. Moroccan dynasty who replaced the Wattasid sultans in the 15th century and repulsed the Portuguese. They originated as SHEIKHS from the the Draa valley and established their first capital at Taroudant.

SABIL. Public drinking fountain.

SANHAJA. One of the three great groupings of the Berber people occupying the Sahara and parts of the Middle and High Atlas. Their dialect is known as Tamazight.

SEBKA. Decorative repetition of interlaced arches, as were often used on the stone gates and walls of the ALMOHADS.

SEBKHA. Lake or lagoon.

SEGUIA. Irrigation canal.

SHABAN. The month before RAMADAN.

SHEIKH. Leader of a religious brotherhood.

SHERIF/SHORFA. Descendant of the PROPHET.

SIDI. Male honorific title, always used to denote a saint but also more widely used.

SOUK. Market.

SUFI. General description for mystical Islamic brotherhoods, who cultivate techniques of chanting and dancing to free the spirit from the body.

SULTAN. Ruler. A word of Turkish origin which implies a single, paramount ruler.

SUNNA. Orthodox Islamic dogma, the body of law followed by the SUNNI.

SUNNI. The orthodox Muslims, and the prevalent Moroccan form of Islam. The dispute between the schismatic Shiites and Sunni which embroiled other Muslim nations has never been of importance in Morocco. Perhaps because IDRISS I, the accepted fount of SUNNI orthodoxy, was of the highest SHIITE descent.

SURA. A verse of the KORAN.

TABIA. Mud or clay used for building.

TAIBIA. Brotherhood.

TAGINE. Traditional Moroccan stew.

TARGUI, pl. TUAREG. The Sanhajan Berber tribe that occupy the central Sahara and dominated the caravan routes. They alone have retained a Berber alphabet, known as Tifinagh and speak a Berber dialect known as Temajegh.

TIZI. A mountain pass.

TOLBA. Koranic reciters.

ULEMA. The council of professors of Islamic law who since the 12th century have been consulted by sultans for the approval of new laws. They must also formally approve the accession of each new ruler.

VIZIER. Chief minister of an Islamic ruler.

WADI. Dry river bed.

WAHABBI. Puritanical reforming Muslim sect from Arabia who were active from the 18th century.

WALI. Friend. WALI-ALLAH, a friend of God, a saint.

WATTASID. Cousins of the MERENID sultans who first became hereditary VIZIERS and from 1472 ruled directly until replaced in 1554 by the SAADIANS.

ZAOUIA/ZAWIYA, pl. ZOUAWI. The sanctuary or college of students that often collects around the tomb or sanctuary of a MARABOUT. A ZAOUIA is a seminary for the cult-influenced Islamic life of the countryside which contrasts with the urban orthodoxy inculcated at the MEDERSA.

ZEKKAT. A land tax sanctioned by the KORAN, the basis of the old Islamic taxation system.

ZELLIG. Geometrical mosaic pattern usually seen on the lower portion of a wall made from chipped glazed tiles.

ZENATA. One of the three great divisions of the Berber people, whose homeland is the northeast, the Riff and the eastern plains. Their dialect is known as Riffi or Tarifit.

Part IV

TANGIER, THE RIFF & THE MEDITERRANEAN COAST

Tangier market ladies

The Riff mountains rise immediately south of the Mediterranean coast of Morocco and run parallel to the shore. They are the dominant physical feature of the region, and have either reduced the coast to a narrow fringe of land or overawed its beaches by lines of menacing cliffs. The Riffs are central to national history for they have protected and isolated the distinctive culture of Central Morocco from mainstream Mediterranean civilization. The coast is littered with the history of failed colonial settlements and the fortresses of maritime powers from every age. Spain still maintains five sovereign settlements on the Riff coast: the two accessible ports of Ceuta and Melilla and the inaccessible islets of Penon de Velez de la Gomera and Penon de Alhumecas and the empty Chaffarine islands.

The barrier formed by the Riffs against the Mediterranean is not just physical. The mountains are inhabited by some of the most independent and intransigent of all the peoples of North Africa. These tribes have occupied the mountains since Neolithic times, they had their own Berber dialect, known as Tarifcht or Zenata and a rich body of traditional music and beliefs. There is an ancient division between the people of the eastern and western mountains. The latter, known as the Djeballa, are distinguished from the eastern tribes by their acceptance of homosexuality and common use of the Arabic language.

Only the strongest sultans have been able to conquer either of these mountainous regions, where it was a deadly insult to assert 'that your father died in his bed'. This bellicose tradition was immortalized in the Riff rising of 1921 to 1926. The tribes of the

99

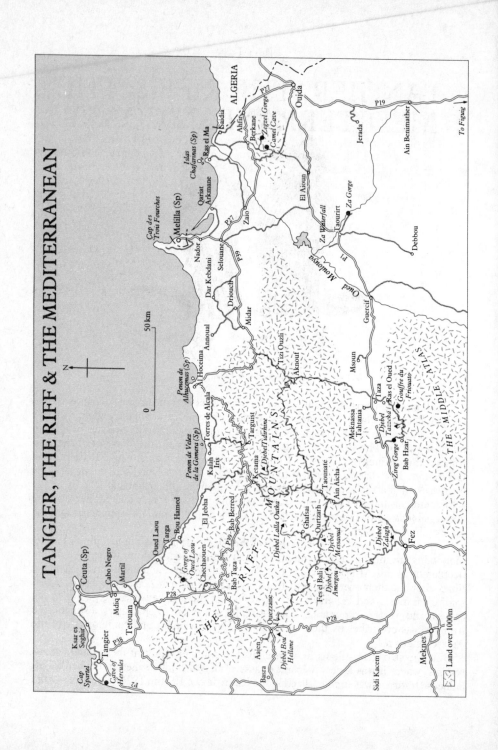

TANGIER, THE RIFF & THE MEDITERRANEAN

eastern mountains, under the command of Abdel Krim, almost succeeded in driving both France and Spain completely out of Morocco. The peculiar dissident nature of the region is still strong. On Independence, when the rest of the country would have happily died for the national hero, King Mohammed V, the women of Tizi Ouli refused to even come out of their houses to sing a welcome. It is still one of the poorest and most troublesome regions in the country and the eastern mountains, due to 'business'—the semi-tolerated drug traffic in marijuana—are close to being a no-go area.

In the heart of the Djeballa mountain region are the two old, compact and beautiful towns of Chechaouen and Ouezzane. They are the customary goal for travel in the region, friendly and accessible stops on your way south. The two northern cities of Tangier and Tetouan, despite their sophistication and equable climate, share an evil reputation with travellers. Countless first-time visitors to Morocco, fleeced or hassled by 'guides' the minute they get off the bus or ferry, leave before they have become accustomed to the initial shock of the street culture. The high quality of their sights, the surrounding countryside and beaches are often easier to appreciate at the end of a holiday. The city of Oujda on the Algerian border, and its neighbouring attractions Saidia beach and the Beni Snassen mountains, are easier and safer to approach from Fez. The road across the eastern Riff is the preserve of kif bandits and is exciting, but not recommended for first-time travellers in Morocco.

TANGIER

'That African perdition called Tangier'
—Mark Twain

Tangier is the oldest continually inhabited city in Morocco. It is a bustling port which squats on the North African shore of one of the most important waterways in the world.

Crossing the straits from Gibraltar the stained outer walls of the old city are the first element to emerge from a background of low hills. Drawing closer, the city begins to earn its accolade of 'Tangier the white' as the houses of the Medina and the new town rise above the docks. A skyline of Christian spires and Muslim minarets bears witness to its confused past.

Tangier's position on the straits of Gibraltar has always made it prized, and the town has been controlled by a continuous succession of empires. For most of this century it was too controversial a possession for any one power, so until 1956 it was an international city ruled and misruled by a council of mostly foreign consuls.

It was during this period that Tangier earned its reputation for sexual and commercial licence, the shadow of which still haunts its streets. However it is now, less glamorously, a mass passenger port and an international tourist resort where, in the unmistakably African streets, the cultures continue to mix but never completely blend.

History

6000-year-old tombs rich in ivory goods have been found outside Tangier. Such discoveries add to the city's long history, which begins with a suitably convoluted mythology to explain the origins of its name, originally Tingi under the Phoenicians and Tingis under the Romans.

In the region of Tangier, Poseidon mated Gaia, the Goddess of the Earth, who gave birth to the giant Anteus. He was married to the beautiful nymph Tingis. Anteus challenged all strangers to wrestle with him, since he was invulnerable whilst his feet remained in contact with his mother—the earth. Despite this considerable advantage, he was still foolish to have challenged Hercules, who lifted the giant from the ground in order to crush his spine. He was buried under the Charf hill which remains a popular cemetery to the southeast of Tangier. His widow, Tingis, was made pregnant by the victorious Hercules, who returned after the birth of the boy, Sophix, to pull Africa and Spain apart so that his son could rule a city protected by the sea. King Sophix named his city Tingis, after his mother.

The two great mountains on either side of the straits of Gibraltar, Gibraltar itself and Djebel Musa, are known as the Pillars of Hercules. Two classical historians, Pliny and Strabo, claim to have seen sand banks in the straits up to the first century BC, remnants of land left behind by Hercules.

Phoenician and Roman rule

Tangier was under the control of strong Mediterranean empires for the first thousand years of her history. The city, from earliest times, showed its ability to bend with the prevailing wind, and pursued a course independent from the rest of the country inland.

The first identifiable settlement is that of the 8th-century BC Phoenician port of Tingi, though Phoenician traders from Gades, modern Cadiz, must have used the site centuries before they established a permanent colony. Like all Phoenician settlements it accepted the leadership of Carthage in foreign policy. After the destruction of Carthage in 146 BC it rapidly fell under the influence of Rome, when it became known as Tingis.

The city was fortunate in supporting Octavian long before he emerged supreme as the Emperor Augustus. He rewarded Tingis with the privileged status of 'colonia', which left the growing city under the rule of its own elected magistrates. This political independence continued even after the Roman province of Mauretania Tingitana was established over central Morocco in AD 44 with a governor ruling from Volubilis. In AD 285 the Emperor Diocletian abandoned central Morocco, but retained control of the northern coast which was ruled from Tingis. In 429 the city briefly fell to Genseric, King of the Vandals, but in 533 was regained for the Byzantine Empire.

Arab Conquest

In the 7th century a succession of Arab armies were sent by the Caliphs to conquer North Africa. Tangier was a key objective in the planned advance into Europe through southern Spain. Count Julian, the last Byzantine governor of Tangier and Ceuta, found it expedient to welcome the first Arab expedition into Tangier in 682, but closed the city gates to the much greater threat posed by the arrival of Musa ben Nasser in 706. Musa stormed the city and massacred the Christian population, appointing one of his ex-slaves, the Berber Tariq, as Governor. In 711 Tariq led an expedition of 7000 Berber warriors across the straits to conquer Spain. He landed at what became known as Tariq's mountain, 'djebel Tariq'—Gibraltar.

Tangier's importance was confirmed by the rapid conquest of Spain. Arab governors ruled Morocco from the city, but in 740 their rapacious attitude triggered off the successful Berber Khajarite revolt which smouldered on in northern Morocco for centuries. Despite this, when the orthodox Idriss I established his kingdom at Volubilis in 788, Tangier was quick to recognize his authority. The list of subsequent rulers of Tangier reads like a catalogue of the great Islamic dynasties of the Maghreb.

A Portuguese and English Fortress

From 1415 to 1685 Tangier was a European fortress, completely isolated from the interior. It was a destructive period for the city. Before 1415, the bay of Tangier had been a busy trading centre, open to the shipping of the world, but by 1685 the city was a deserted and smoking ruin.

The Portuguese, after an initial failure in 1437, succeeded in seizing Tangier in 1471. The city remained in their hands until the 17th century. Then a new Portuguese dynasty, anxious to be fully accepted by the courts of Europe, gave it as part of a generous dowry, including Bombay and £40,000, when Catherine of Braganza married Charles II of England in 1661.

The first English governor destroyed all the Muslim and Catholic religious buildings on his arrival. His garrison in the Montagne was besieged by a Moroccan force. They succeeded in massacring two English expeditions which dared to advance beyond the protection of the garrison walls.

Beyond the mere cost in lives, Tangier was consuming 13% of the Crown's annual income. The diarist, Samuel Pepys, who as Treasurer to the Tangier Commission had added his own substantial cut of corruption to the costs, pressed for the abandonment of the town. A Portuguese offer to buy back Tangier was spurned. The Kasbah, called York Castle for those few years, was blown up, the city burnt and the harbour mole laboriously demolished. To add to these cultural achievements, the English had expelled all Jews from the town in 1677.

In 1685, after the English had left, Sultan Moulay Ishmael ordered the reconstruction of the desolate town. He rebuilt the city walls, the Kasbah, the Grand Mosque, encouraged the Jews to return to their Mellah quarter and settled Riff regiments that had been involved in the siege of Tangier in the Medina and on the surrounding farm land. Ali ben Abdallah er Rif was appointed Pasha, 'the Caesar of the north', and waged continual war against the Spanish in Ceuta. Ahmed succeeded his father as Pasha but died making an attempt on the Moroccan throne. Political anarchy followed this period of strong rule and by 1810 Tangier had shrunk to a small town of 5000 inhabitants.

International Tangier

In the 19th century the city reemerged as a centre for European mercantile and diplomatic activity. The first bank in Tangier was founded by Moses Pariente, who had lent Nelson much needed cash for munitions on the eve of the Battle of Trafalgar. Perceptibly, the influence of the European consuls and their trading concessionaries turned into controlling power. Fifty years later in 1923, this was codified into the Statute of Tangier, which established an international authority for the city and 140 square miles of the surrounding country. Spanish and French political influence was predominant, the Italians gave the best parties and the British occupied themselves with gardens and a rigid social hierarchy.

The lack of regulations attracted a variety of otherwise illegal financial services, but it was the brothels, bars, spies, smugglers, artists, eccentrics and exiles which gave the city its peculiar reputation. The Arabic-speaking hill tribes around Tangier have a respect for homosexuality that has proved a powerful attraction for Europeans, who for over a century, from Oscar Wilde to Ronnie Kray, have been drawn to the tolerance and licence of Tangier.

Reunification

Tangier was reunited to Morocco on 29 October 1956. The boy brothels were closed and the international banks moved elsewhere. Parientes now run their affairs from an office in Geneva. The 'Moroccanization' of business in the sixties intensified this natural depression. The city's population has now grown to 300,000 and the local economy is based on the twin pillars of migrant work in Europe and tourism. Four times more passengers pass through the city's airport and docks than live here.

GETTING AROUND

By Air

Tangier's airport, Boukhalf-Souahel, is 15 km southwest of the town off the P2 coast road to Rabat. As well as a large range of international flights, it offers internal flights to Agadir, Casablanca, Marrakesh, Oujda and Rabat. There are also two useful connecting flights to Gibraltar on Mondays, Tuesdays, Wednesdays and Fridays, currently leaving at 9.35 and 17.35 for the 1 hr 20 min journey.

The Royal Air Maroc office is on the Pl de la France, tel 34722; Air France at 7, Rue Mexique, tel 36477; British Airways at 83, Rue de la Liberté, tel 35211; Iberia, 35, Bd Pasteur, tel 33747 and Lufthansa at 47, Rue du Mexique, tel 32994. A taxi ride to the airport should cost 50dh.

Ferries

Until the turn of the century passengers were carried ashore on the naked shoulders of a native stevedore. Now alas tickets can be brought at any of the travel agents or the official office just to the left of the port gates, and gang planks are always used. Do however still allow an hour or more for boarding; the near anarchy of immigration departure forms, passport and customs control does however eventually sort itself out. A passenger ticket to Algeciras costs 170dh, the journey takes over 2 hrs, and boats leave at 7.30, 10.00, 12.30, 14.00, 15.30 and 16.30 in the summer. Hydrofoil sevices run daily to Tarifa at 14.30, passengers only, tickets 170dh for the hour and a half journey. The hydrofoil to Gibraltar runs twice daily on Mondays, Tuesdays and Fridays at 9.00 and 16.00, 140dh.

Train

The station is just 50 m beyond the port gates. Trains are the obvious, efficient and easy way to travel further south. For Casablanca and Rabat, tickets are 78dh and 60dh, trains leave at 7.22, 8.12, 14.15, 16.22, 23.30 and 24.00. For Marrakesh change at Casablanca, Gare des Voyageurs, or catch the direct midnight Express sleeper that should leave at 20.15. For Meknes and Fez, 53dh and 64dh, trains leave at 7.22, 8.12, 14.15, 16.22 and 24.00. The left luggage office at the station can only accept bags with a secure lock, 3dh a bag.

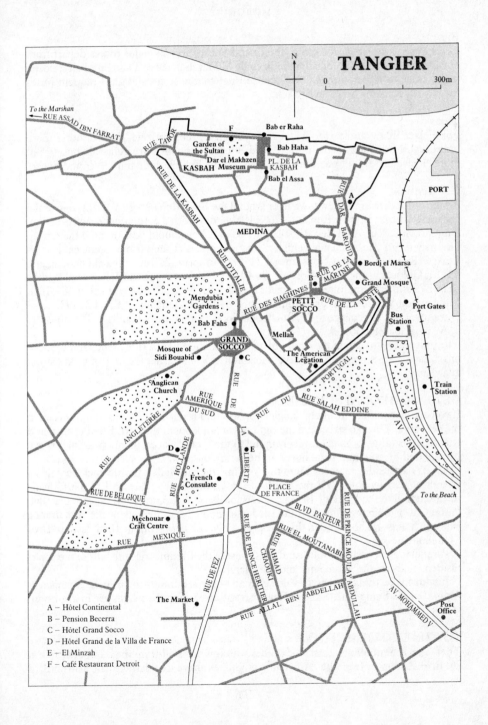

TANGIER

0 — 300m

N

To the Marshan
← RUE ASSAD IBN FARRAT

RUE TABOR

F Bab er Raha

Garden of
the Sultan Bab Haha

Dar el Makhzen
KASBAH Museum PL. DE LA
KASBAH

Bab el Assa

RUE DE LA KASBAH

RUE DAR BAROUD

A

PORT

MEDINA

RUE D'ITALIE

Mendubia
Gardens RUE DE LA
MARINE Bordj el Marsa

B Grand Mosque

RUE DES SIAGHINES PETIT
SOCCO RUE DE LA POSTE

Bab Fahs Port Gates

GRAND
SOCCO Bus
Station

Mosque of
Sidi Bouabid C Mellah

The American
Legation

Anglican
Church RUE DE
AMERIQUE
DU SUD RUE DU RUE SALAH EDDINE Train
Station

RUE PORTUGAL

RUE D'ANGLETERRE

RUE DE LA LIBERTE

D E

French
Consulate PLACE
DE FRANCE

RUE DE BELGIQUE To the Beach

BLVD PASTEUR

Mechouar
Craft Centre RUE DE PRINCE MOULAY ABDULLAH

RUE MEXIQUE RUE EL MOUTANABI

RUE AHMAD CHAOUKI

RUE DE FEZ RUE DE PRINCE HERITIER

AV MOHAMMED V

The Market RUE ALLAL BEN ABDELLAH Post
Office

A – Hôtel Continental
B – Pension Becerra
C – Hôtel Grand Socco
D – Hôtel Grand de la Villa de France
E – El Minzah
F – Café Restaurant Detroit

Bus

Local buses leave from the top of the Grand Socco, and all major routes depart from outside the port gates, officially the Place de la Marché-Verte. There are half a dozen buses a day to Rabat, a tiring 6–7 hour journey that only costs 50dh. Frequent buses leave for Tetouan when they are full.

Taxis

For a place in a grand taxi to Tetouan or Asilah try the port gates, but for other more individual destinations start in the Grand Socco. Petits taxis are generally busier and more elusive but are found at the port gates, on the Blvd Pasteur and the Grand Socco.

Car Rentals

All the offices are in the new town in or around the Blvd Mohammed V. Cady, one of the cheapest offices, offers a Renault 4 for 110dh a day, with a 1.1dh charge for each km. They are at 3, Rue Allal Ben Abdallah, tel 34151. You should bear in mind that cheap hire may mean a less reliable vehicle. Compare prices at the various agencies: Dany's Cars, 7, Rue Moussa Ibn Noussair, tel 31778; Europcar, 2, Rue Jabha al Ouatania, tel 33113; Goldcar at the Hotel Solazur, tel 40164; Hertz at 36, Blvd Mohammed V (they charge 2156dh for unlimited mileage for a week), tel 33322; Marloc/InterRent, 87, Blvd Mohammed V, tel 38271; and Tourist Cars, 84, Blvd Mohammed V, tel 35493.

Garages: For Peugeots go to 37, Rue Quevedo, tel 35093; for Renaults to Tanjah Auto, 2, Av de Rabat, tel 36938.

The best places to park in the centre of town are on the Medina side of the Grand Socco or on any of the streets off the Blvd Mohammed V. Pay a flat fee of 1dh to the street guardian.

GETTING AROUND TANGIER

If you are just passing through Tangier you will find taxis, buses, boats and trains all in the port area. The two streets on the right as you walk out of the port, Rue Portugal and Rue Salah Eddine, both lead steeply uphill to the Grand Socco, an open circular space surrounded by taxis and local buses at the centre of town.

On its north side, gates lead into the Medina, the old walled town, which contains a warren of narrow lanes. To the south of the Grand Socco, Rue de la Liberté leads further uphill to the Place de la France. East of Place de la France, on the left, the Blvd Pasteur turns imperceptibly into the Blvd Mohammed V. The bulk of the restaurants, bars and hotels will be found in this, the New Town, on or just off the Blvd Pasteur/Blvd Mohammed V.

Parallel to the coastline, south and southwest of the Medina, rise the hills of the smart residential areas, the Montagne and the Marshan.

Just to make things more confusing, road signs are found in French, Spanish or Arabic, a road being Rue, Calle or Zankat respectively, and the names are in a constant state of change.

TOURIST INFORMATION

There are 115 multilingual trained guides who can be hired from the Tourist Office at 29, Blvd Pasteur or from the Association of Guides above Le Claridge café also on Blvd

Pasteur, tel 31372. A full day costs only 50dh, a small price to pay for some assistance in the confused pattern of Tangier streets. Locals can physically show you what they could not hope to describe or locate on a map.

HASSLE AND UNWANTED GUIDES

Tangier has a reputation as an aggressive city for travellers. The chorus of prospective guides at the port gates does come as a shock after the indifference of Europe. As a newcomer do not expect to be left alone to explore the town. Accept this fact in advance, hire a taxi, an official guide or select a pleasant unofficial 'student guide'. Do not rush things, have a cup of coffee and settle a price and your destination firmly in advance.

Think of Moroccan unofficial guides as cats, independent souls who stick around as long as there is something in it for them, entertaining but totally unreliable and very susceptible to your mood. They will spit and shout if you are rude but love politeness and mannered charm, which is indeed a rare commodity amongst the bulk of tourists.

Try to enjoy them as in every large city you will find them difficult to ignore. Morocco has 80% male unemployment, over half the population is under 21 and the basic labouring wage is 3dh an hour. Are you sure that under those conditions you might not be tempted to try your luck with comparatively rich and often arrogant visitors?

USEFUL ADDRESSES

The central Post Office is at 33, Blvd Mohammed V in front of which are sold European, Arabic and American newspapers. The Banque Populaire and Banque du Maroc are found at 76 and 78, Blvd Mohammed V.

For the police tel 19, Ambulance tel 15. There is a 24-hour chemist at 22, Rue de Fes, and if you need a hospital head for either the Hospital Kortobi, Rue Garibaldi, tel 31073 or the Spanish Hospital, tel 31018. The emergency number for the latter is tel 34242. The British Consulate has recently moved to an office at 9, Rue Amerique du Sud, tel 35895, and the US consulate is on Rue Achouak, tel 35904.

The Grand Socco

At the heart of Tangier, just outside the walls of the old town but by no means part of the new, sits the large open circular space of the Grand Socco. Blue buses noisily park beneath the cinema, taxis queue by the central patch of grass and cars attempt to push their way through the chattering crowds. Grill kitchens, stalls and cafés ring the space. Storms of angry shouts or laughter break out from the cafés, usually over nothing more substantial than the loss of a few bottle-top game counters. A slender minaret to the southwest of the Grand Socco is entirely decorated with rich coloured mosaic. This is the Mosque of Sidi Bouabid, a valuable landmark by which to find the souks that ring the Grand Socco.

Tangier still follows the ancient plan of the Roman city. The Grand Socco has always been an open market space outside the walls, surrounded now as then by cemetries and markets. Its official name is the Place du 9 Avril 1947, celebrating a speech made here by King Mohammed V which marked the beginning of a ten-year struggle for independence.

On 31 March 1905, Kaiser William II, with considerably less sincerity, also made a speech here in favour of Morocco's independence. A series of secret agreements had just been completed amongst the European powers that put Morocco under the French and Spanish sphere of influence. Germany had been excluded from the bargaining but demonstrated her determination to be involved with this impromptu gesture. However the Moroccan crowd reacted so enthusiastically that William II decided to return to his cruiser *Hohenzollern* before the celebratory party was even half way through.

Grand Socco Souks

The country surrounding Tangier uses the city as a permanent souk. The market ladies with distinctive broad hats, red striped cloth and folded blankets around their waist come into town to trade throughout the week and are especially busy on Thursdays and Sundays. The Rue Salah Edine on the way down to the port is lined with stalls and entrances to internal covered markets. The clothing market is on the right opposite 41, Rue Salah Edine, which is Ahmed Oughar's good Moorish pottery shop. It is 'fixed price' so you need not worry about the prospect of bargaining. The smarter covered food market is found in the Medina itself, first right through an archway once you've gone through the Medina gate from the Grand Socco. A chaotic covered souk exists below the minaret of Sidi Bouabid where old clothes, chickens, car radios and herbs are for sale.

The Mendoubia Park

Behind the minaret of Sidi Bouabid, to the west, stretch large overgrown cemeteries and below it the old offices of the Mendoubia are set in their own park. The mendoub was the representative of the sultan in the independent city of Tangier, a job that was held by two generations of royal cousins. A low green door is usually open and no one seems to mind you entering to admire an enormous 800-year-old banyan tree. Beyond the empty and desolate residence is a terrace lined with a fine collection of bronze European cannons. The Ministry of Justice have taken over some of the buildings but have left this garden, right in the centre of town, deliciously overgrown and neglected. The steady thud of rubber stamps can be heard from the legal offices.

The English Church

Looking at the minaret of Sidi Bouabid from the centre of the Grand Socco, the cross of St George can be seen flying from the English church to its left. The church and its graveyard are entered from the Rue d'Angleterre. The caretaker Mustapha Cherqui will open the church and point out the Lord's prayer, carved in Arabic above the chancel.

The graveyard is full of stones that commemorate a past era of British influence in Tangier and Morocco. Look out for a stone that commemorates Walter Harris, the flamboyant journalist, adventurous travel writer and intimate of the bandit Raisuni who had a house both in the Kasbah and out towards Cape Malabata. Sir John Hay, the British consul in the 19th century, was a close friend of Sultan Moulay Hassan and worked throughout his life to maintain the independence of Morocco. Sir John secured the appointment of Harry Mclean in 1877 to train a modern army for the sultan and his son. Caid Mclean's tombstone can be found here and his portrait still hangs in the bar of the El Minzah Hotel.

Most romantic is the story behind the tomb of Emily, the Sherifa of Wazzan. She came out to Tangier as the companion of Mrs Perdicaris. The powerful hereditary saint, the Sherif of Wazzan (or Ouezzane), fell in love with her whilst she was singing and combing her hair on a seaside balcony. They were married by Sir John Hay in a Christian service, had children and perhaps just as inevitably separated. Emily, however, stayed on in Tangier, running a free inoculation clinic and dispensing vast quantities of sweets to children until her death.

Across from the church are a number of stalls that sell striped Berber cloth and Islamic red or black embroidered scarves.

The New Town

A covered fountain, decorated in the full Moorish taste, can be seen by walking up the Rue d'Angleterre from the church. This was raised in memory of John Hay's successor and son-in-law, William Kirby-Green.

If you continue up this road you reach the Rue Belgique. Turn left and opposite you will see the Artisanal Ensemble, where traditional crafts are taught and in which you can compare prices with those offered in the souk. The chipping of coloured tiles to create shaped pieces for faience mosaics is a fascinating process. Another stall embosses leather, and books can be Morocco bound here quite reasonably, given a few days notice.

Walk down the Rue Belgique to the Place de la France for coffee at one of the tables of the Café de Paris, a prime observation post for watching the absorbing and diverse stream of Tangier life: holidaying homosexuals, turbanned Berber farmers, students, beggars, burned package tourists, elegant European residents, portly businessmen who could be Jewish, Soussi, Fassi or Spanish, veiled women and young street Arabs who like your sugar lumps. The tables have witnessed a legendary parade of resident intellectuals, political exiles, spies and smugglers. Captain Zoondab may be seen quietly smoking at

Waterseller

one of the tables in his fez and white burnous. Now an experienced tourist guide, as a young boy he ran messages between Golden Curney, the British gun runner, and Abdul Krim, the leader of the Riff rebellion.

Returning to the Grand Socco down the Rue de la Liberté, the imposing French consulate is on the left. Below it on the street is the **Gallerie Delacroix**, one of the best places in Morocco to find exhibitions of contemporary art. The Gallerie, in which most of the exhibits are for sale, is run by Georges Bousqet, tel 41054, and also holds lectures, film shows, readings and promotes visiting drama.

The Medina

Tangier's Medina follows the ancient Roman city plan. The Medina walls mark the line of the Roman defences, the Kasbah is on the old capitol, the Grand Mosque rises on the exact site of a Temple to Neptune and the Petit Socco covers the area of the forum.

Rue es Siaghin

From the Grand Socco if you pass through the right-hand of the two Medina arches you will find yourself on the busiest and widest market street of the Medina, thickly lined with the major tourist bazaars. This is the Rue es Siaghin, the silversmith's street, though there is little to support that name today. Off to the right, two alleyways lead into the Mellah, the old Jewish quarter, where there are over ten synagogues, the most impressive of which are the old Nahom Temple and the Ribby Tahya Temple. Back on Rue es Siaghin you pass a locked **Spanish Catholic church** complete with a bronze dome on your right. It was supposedly established on the site of the old Franciscan mission, where five of the brethren were slaughtered by the Muslims in the course of their preaching ministry. St Francis on hearing their fate cursed the city, 'O Tingis! Tingis, O dementia Tingis, illusa civitas.' ('Oh Tangier! Tangier, oh demented Tangier, foolish citizens . . .')

Petit Socco

At the end of the Rue es Siaghin lies the Petit Socco. In the days of the international city this was the centre for male prostitution, boy brothels, and pornographic film shows where rooms in the adjacent streets could be rented by the half hour. It still retains a furtive, slightly conspiratorial air, a place where you can readily imagine the shadowy figures of Camille, Saint Saens, Burroughs, Jean Genet, Jack Kerrouac, Alan Ginsberg. The central café remains open throughout the night, and is a delightful place to play backgammon or ludo, sipping glasses of café au lait after a tour of the night clubs and bars.

The Petit Socco is a convenient and recognizable place from which to explore the rest of the Medina. The first narrow left turning, the Rue des Chrétiens, leads up towards the Kasbah quarter, which contains the old palace, the Dar el Makhzen, now a museum. The alleys opposite skirt past the Grand Mosque and lead through the old tanneries to the port gate.

The Kasbah Quarter

Taking the Rue des Chrétiens, a shop-lined alley which joins a climbing street, Rue ben

Raisuli, you will pass an ornamental fountain on your left before climbing through the **Bab el Assa**, the gate of watchfulness, to enter the pebble paved Mechouar, the courtyard beside the Dar el Makhzen.

More generally, this whole area, the highest part of the Medina, has been the preserve of palaces and castles for thousands of years. Roman governors, Byzantine counts, Arab princes and Portuguese crusaders all succeeded in possessing the citadel. When they left Tangier in 1685, the English destroyed the existing ancient medieval fortress with fire, gunpowder and pick axe. What you see now was largely built by Sultan Moulay Ishmael and his Pasha in the 17th century.

In the late 19th century British remittance men, like the writers Walter Harris and Richard Hughes, built oriental palaces for themselves here behind innocuous pise walls. A continuous gallery of exquisites have settled, danced, dined and debauched here ever since. One such decadent fed his cats from tins of caviar and bankrupted himself entertaining the sister of the king. Barbara Hutton gave her silk underwear away to the people in the street after a day of use, employed Saharan nomads as doormen and in moments of boredom distributed money to her guests in order to persuade them to leave.

The Mechouar—Place de la Kasbah

In the Mechouar, also known as the Place de la Kasbah, the area immediately around the Bab el Assa was the site of the punishment and execution of criminals. The closest corner of the Dar el Makhzen palace contained the old law courts, the Dar ech Chera. In the past its colonnaded arches would have been packed by many an anxious litigant, petitioner and chained defendant. Beside it to the left rises the octagonal minaret of the kasbah Mosque, while the rest of the crenellated, white Dar el Makhzen stretches away to the right. Notice, to the right of the Dar ech Chera, the triple bayed pavilion that gave entrance to the treasury, **Bit el Mal**.

On the seaward length of outer wall a gate, the **Bab er Raha**, leads to a terrace with a fine view over the straits. A rough path allows you to follow the sea walls of the Medina from the outside. A cascade of rubbish flows from the houses of the Medina down the sea cliffs to create the perfect odour for a full impression of a walled medieval city. The port compound is securely fenced so that ultimately you have to retrace your steps.

Dar el Makhzen

The 17th-century palace built by Moulay Ishmael and embellished by his Pasha and successors now houses a museum. It was last used as a palace in 1912 by Moulay Hafid, his four wives and sixty concubines, who stayed here whilst a larger palace was built to the west of the city. Accommodation was cramped and the ex-Sultan was forced to use the gate house, where he played cards with his European friends and carried on with his scholarly research into the Sufi Tijaniyya brotherhood.

Like most museums in Morocco, the actual palace vies with the exhibits for your attention. Architecture has always been the highest art form in Islam. It is closed on Tuesdays, open the rest of the week from 9.00–12.00, 15.00–18.00 in winter and 9.00–15.30 in the summer.

The private apartments of the palace are fully embellished with the customary architectural decoration for a Muslim prince. Deep carved floral motifs on dark stained cedar doors, geometrical mosaic tile work, plaster carved with rich calligraphic forms of Koranic verses and delicate traceries of plants all compete for attention.

The portable arts of Morocco are triumphantly displayed in salons off a large colonnaded interior court. Each room displays a different collection: musical instruments, swords and rifles, leather work, fine embroidery, wrought iron, the more delicate incised and damascened metal ware, killims and carpets. The pottery collection illustrates the different styles of the artisans of Meknes, Safi, Tamegroute and Fez. The hues of green, blue and yellow in the tradition of floral ceramic decoration contrast with the obsessive blue and white of the geometric tradition. The room devoted to the products of Fez is the natural climax of the exhibition, where the illuminated and beautifully bound Korans deserve special attention. The Muslim passion for calligraphy is naturally inaccessible to most Europeans. But in a culture with little or no figurative work, it is central to their artistic expression.

The **Archaeological Halls** are to be found down a passage off the inner courtyard. The mosaic of Venus and the copies of the bronze busts recovered from Roman Volibuilis are the most striking exhibits—the originals can be seen in Rabat. There are also a number of objects recovered from the classical sites of Lixus, Banassa, Thamsuda, Tamuda, Cotta, Sala and Ad Abilem and a map illustrating the extent of the Roman province. Upstairs there are four rooms devoted to Morocco's prehistory, with displays of coins, ceramic shards, flintwork and a number of excavated funerary remains.

The Sultan's Garden

The walls of the Dar el Makhzen enclose a beautiful, mature Andalucian garden, a formal shrubbery with constant delightful changes of light, odour and colour which contrast strongly with the monochrome details of Phoenician graves. Orange, canary palm and lemon trees provide shade whilst at dusk datura and jacaranda fill the garden with a rich heady perfume. On the northern face of the garden artisan halls are sometimes busily demonstrating the art of carpet making. As you leave the garden you pass the entrance to the Detroit restaurant, which has a fine collection of Moorish pastries, and the tea room, though reminiscent of a cross channel ferry, has a good view over the straits of Gibraltar.

To return to the Grand Socco avoiding the Medina, take Rue Riad Sultan out of the Mechouar, turn right into the Place du Tabor and continue out through the gate straight ahead. A right turn takes you down the steps of the broad Rue d'Italie, passing beneath aged old balconies, past street stalls, the outer Medina walls and the Café des Colonnes.

Grand Mosque

Opposite the entrance to Rue des Chrétiens on the Petit Socco, the two alleys, the Rue de la Marine and Rue de la Poste, both skirt the Grand Mosque, forbidden to non-Muslims, and then descend through the old area of the tanneries back to the port gates below the Medina.

Take the left of these two, the Rue de la Marine, which passes a fountain in front of the Grand Mosque. The bulk of the Mosque is hidden by shop fronts but the impressive gates, green and white minaret and its acreage of green tiled roof can be seen. It was built by Moulay Ishmael over the ruins of a Portuguese cathedral, itself raised on the foundations of an earlier mosque built over a Roman temple. Opposite the Mosque you can see the gates of a **Medersa** founded by the Merenids in the 14th century. Inevitably, it was destroyed by the English, but rebuilt in the 18th century by Sultan Sidi Mohammed.

After the Mosque you reach a terrace overlooking the port, built on top of the Bordj el Marsa, the port battery, which contains two cannons and was constructed on the orders of Sultan Moulay Hassan in 1882.

Coming off the terrace, turn right along the Rue dar el Baroud which takes you past the Hotel Continental where you can have mint tea in the tranquil faded grandeur of its hall. Another reward for the inquisitive explorer is the Café Makima, a reclusive Moroccan local tearoom which overlooks the sea walls. Just follow Rue dar el Baroud to the little Place de l'Arsenal, then follow the Rue Zaitouna and Rue Bouhacin to the end.

The American Legation

There is an enormous and innocent fascination in blindly exploring a Moroccan Medina. Its confusing landscape of dark tunnels, endless worn staircases, twisting narrowing alleys, old secretive closed doorways, veiled women and aggressive youths is like some dream or nightmare sequence from adolescence. To sate the fascination to find out what happens behind one of these firmly closed gates, head for the American Legation, at 8, Rue America.

The Legation is open everyday from 9.30–12.30, 16.00–18.30, admission free. You can approach it by striking south from the Petit Socco, but it is much easier to find from the Rue du Portugal where a gate passes through the Medina outer walls. The gate of the Legation is on the left a few metres further, under a covered arch.

The Legation was established here in 1821, on both sides of the Medina alley, connected by an overhead arch. There are a number of elegantly furnished 19th-century New England rooms and a series of delightful courtyards. The library is open and there is a interesting collection of old engravings and maps of Tangier. Exhibitions of Moroccan art are organized here and the Legation has been lent some fine Moroccan portraits, executed by the self-taught Aberdonian artist James McBey. The correspondence between the sultans and George Washington, for the Sheriffian court was the first to recognize the independence of the USA, deserves a closer study. The subject they primarily debate is the amount of gold and silver America is to pay in order to buy immunity from Moroccan corsairs.

The Marshan

From the Mehouar you can walk west, parallel to the coast along the Rue Assad Ibn Farrat towards the Marshan, once a smart residential quarter on the sea cliff plateau but now gently ageing. You will pass the football stadium on your left, the centre of Tangier life for the one o'clock Sunday match and surrounded the rest of week with informal games played in the dusty shade of eucalyptus trees. Opposite, on the right, Rue Haffa leads to an open green space overlooking the sea. Here there are a number of superbly sited **Phoenician rock cut tombs**, which point due east through the Pillars of Hercules. A reclusive and entirely Moroccan rush-matted tea house can be found off to the left.

Palais Mendoub

On the corner of Marshan square is the Palais Mendoub, where the American publisher Malcolm Forbes has created the slightly bizarre **Museum of Military Miniatures**. His enormous collection is open every day from 10.00–17.00, admission free, tips accepted.

The battles of Leuthen, the Somme, Waterloo and Dien Bien Phu have been recreated. Of more immediate relevance to Moroccan history is the arrangement for the Battle of Tankodibo against the negro kingdom of Songhai, in 1591, when the Saadian Sultan El Mansour ordered an army to cross the Sahara and capture the gold mines. There is also a tableau of the Battle of the Three Kings in 1578 when the Portuguese invasion of King Sebastian was defeated, and the Green March of 1975 when the present King Hassan II recovered the Spanish held Western Sahara. The gardens, immaculately maintained terraces descending towards the sea, offer spectacular views.

The road to the left of the Museum, the Rue Shakespeare, passes two large 19th-century mansions before it eventually deteriorates into a track that takes you to the healing sands of the Jew's beach.

Almost opposite the Museum is the **Palais Marshan**, now a conference hall but originally planned to hold the parliament of International Tangier.

A **monument to the great traveller Ibn Battuta** (1304–1377) is being constructed behind the football stadium. A trained Islamic jurist, he travelled all over the Islamic world from China to Timbuktu but was born a citizen of Tangier. Av. Hassan II will take you back to the central Rue Belgique, passing on your left the sanctuary **tomb of Tangier's patron saint**, Sidi Bou Araquiza, and then the **Cathedral** with its inverted minaret spire. Beyond can be seen the massive, high and inelegant minaret of the Kuwaiti Mosque.

The Port

At midday the port and the baking expanse of heated tarmac and docksheds is not much of an attraction. At dusk or dawn it can be interesting to wander through the port gates and watch the fishing fleet preparing to sail or landing their catch. Just inside the port gates on the right is the **Tangier Yacht Club**, which is usually quite welcoming to any reasonably dressed and affable visitor.

The Beach

The Tangier beach stretches west of the port bordered by the railway line and an ugly silhouette of large modern beach hotels. Though it provides sheltered and safe swimming it is usually worth the effort of travelling to any of the less crowded beaches to the east and west of Tangier; see Cape Spartel and Cape Malabata below.

Swimming or playing football on the Tangier beach is free for all, though a local law forbids changing or heavy clothing on the beach. This is thought to have been designed to exclude traditionally dressed Muslim women from the seafront. Walking east beyond the line of bars, clubs, restaurants and changing rooms you enter a soliciting ground made famous in the diaries of Joe Orton, though the Miami Beach, Macumba and Windmill Club bars might be just as efficient. The Windmill has a nightly cabaret in the summer, and the beach after dark can have some unusual human tableaux, but by day an efficient police and first aid post opposite the Almohads Hotel discourages this.

SHOPPING
The intriguing interior of the antique shop **El Tindouf** and the **Bazaar Tindouf**, two doors down, is one of the more restful and interesting places in which to browse. They

have a stock of old postcards and are found directly opposite the El Minzah Hotel on the Rue de la Liberté.

The **Librairie des Colonnes** on 54, Blvd Pasteur has an excellent range of relevant English and French literature, Moroccan history and books on various Islamic topics.

On the Grand Socco, as you approach the entrance to the Medina you will see a corner shop selling raffia suitcases and picnic baskets, one of the best selections in Morocco where a reasonable first price is offered.

The perfumerie **Madini** at 14, Rue Sebou in the Medina, accessible from Rue d'Italie or the Petit Socco, is a great treat, a shop rich in coloured liquids on shelves laden down by heavy bottles where over 60 scents are assembled, some to recipes held secret by generations of the Madini family.

The **Epicerie Marhaba** at 45, Blvd Mohammed V, just west of Hotel Rembrandt, or the **Spanish grocery** at 63, Rue Hollande are two of a fair number of grocers in the new town that sell wine, spirits and beer.

Three streets down Rue de Fez going south from the Place de la France, the **central courtyard market**, nicknamed the **bourgeois market**, is an ideal place in which to assemble a picnic.

SPORTS
There is an 18-hole **golf course**, the Country Club de Boubanah, **riding** at Club de L'Etrier at Boubanah and **tennis** available on Rue de Belgique.

FESTIVALS
The Palais de Marshan is the seat of many national and international conferences. A **musical festival** is held in Tangier in July, and an **International week** in September, when the **Moussem of Dar Zhirou** also takes place.

WHERE TO STAY
There are at least 50 hotels and pensions scattered throughout Tangier, but telephone booking in high season is still advisable.

El Minzah on the Rue de la Liberté is one of the most celebrated 5-star hotels in Morocco, a massive cool solid building arranged around numerous courts. It has in recent years lost some of its cachet by filling empty rooms with Thomson package tours from Britain. There are 100 rooms, a swimming pool, tennis court. A single bed here costs 400dh, 500dh for a double, breakfast 36dh. Lunch and dinner costs 180dh at either **El Erz**, the international restaurant, or **El Korsan**, the Moroccan restaurant, tel 35885.

Of the beach-front hotels, the ***** **Riff** is by far the most tranquil, on the Av. Far, tel 35810, with a good pool, garden, night club and a hammam.

The **Grand Hôtel Villa de France** at 143, Rue de Hollande, tel 31475, retains a delightful air of gracious if slightly shabby ease. Poised just above the Grand Socco and entirely surrounded by a mature garden, do stay here if you can afford it, 138dh for a single and 168dh for a double. There are fine views from many bedrooms, especially nos 15 and 35. Lunch and dinner from a set menu costs about 70dh, and there is a popular bar by the pool.

The **Continental** is another exceptional hotel. It has no bar or restaurant but gives you the welcome feel of staying in a well-furnished house, and has a splendid view over the harbour from the terrace. It is a reclusive private place on the walls of the Medina. The entrance can be found at 36, Rue Dar Baroud, the Medina. A single for 63dh, a double for 80dh, tel 31024/31143.

Down market from these but well placed in the heart of the city is **Hôtel Grand Socco**, where a single costs 30dh, a double 40dh. The entrance is at 32, Rue Casa Biera, tel 33126. In the heart of the Medina, at no 8, Petit Socco is the **Pension Becerra**, a secure comfortable place with 35 rooms, balconies and showers, tel 32369.

Camping
There are two campsites, the **Miramonte** on the Marshan, a plateau 3 km to the west of the port, and the **Tingis**, 3 km to the east at the far end of the beach beside the coast road out to Cape Malabata. The Tingis, tel 40212, is open all the year and in summer fills its pool and runs a shop. 9dh a night, 5dh for a car.

EATING OUT
There are a number of fine restaurants off the Blvd Mohammed V that serve French, Italian and Spanish menus. The licensed restaurants serving Moroccan dishes tend to include tourist-oriented floor shows that can vary from appetite-destroying belly dancing to the soothing repetitive melodies of Moroccan traditional music.

European food
La Grenouille is a French restaurant on the Rue Rembrandt, off Blvd Pasteur, which serves a good value three-course meal with wine by the carafe, but is closed on Mondays. **San Remo** at 15, Rue Ahmed Chaouki, tel 38451, is a clean, simple, reasonably cheap and popular Italian restaurant. Try the house speciality of dressed crab or the lasagne followed by their chocolate gateau, or the menu for 45dh. **Nautilius**, up from Velasquez Hotel at 9, Rue Ibn Oualid has a good menu—try the peanut soup, steaks, duck, chicken or fish. A main course and a bottle of wine together come to around 50dh, and it is a small and deservedly popular restaurant run by Rachid Temsamani. **Negresco**, 20, Rue Mexique with a tapas bar next door, specializes in seafood and paellas. **Le Provençal**, Rue Fernando de Portugal, is another place to find good French cooking, tel 37471. **Romero**, for those who need Spanish cooking and seafood dishes is at 12, Rue du Prince Moulay Abdullah, tel 32277. Or there is **Guitta's** at 110, Sidi Bouabid, tel 37333, one of Tangier's delightful surviving institutions from the international era, soup for 12dh, a salad niçoise for 26dh.

Moroccan Cooking
Damascus, in Rue Prince Moulay Abdullah, tel 34730, includes floor shows. Here bastilla is 30dh, tajine 25dh, salad 8dh and a bottle of wine 40dh. In the Medina there is **Le Detroit** which was founded by Brion Gysin in the sixties above the exit from the Dar el Makhzen Museum. Don't be put off by the grim interior, the food and the view are excellent, tel 38080. In and around the Medina you can also try **Hammadi**, Rue de la Kasbah, tel 34514 or the **Ibn Batouta**, Rue es Siaghin, tel 34527. **Marhaba**, 67 Palace Ahannar, can be found down an alley to the left of the Rue de la Kasbah. A wonderfully over-decorated hall contains a collection of junk antiques. The restaurant serves menus

at 60 or 70dh, and a bottle of wine for 50dh. The **El Minzah Hotel's** Moroccan restaurant is worth considering. They have a floor show on Tuesdays and Fridays.

Cheap Grill cafés

In many ways the most entertaining place to eat is in one of the eight cafés that line the Medina side of the Grand Socco, at tables behind the grills or up steep staircases that lead to secretive dining rooms above. Salads, grilled or fried vegetables, meat and fish are available at about 10dh ahead. Up from the Grand Socco just below the El Minzah to the left off the Av. de la Liberté is **El Idrissi** café and **Restaurant Chaabi**. Otherwise the square outside the port gates is lined with grill restaurants. The **Wasteel**, the first café on your left out of the port, sells beer as well. A number of bars and restaurants run along beside the railway line behind the beach. If you want to eat rather than just mix, the restaurant **Nautilius** is probably the best.

Cafés

The internationally celebrated **Madame Porte's** has sadly been closed but may yet reopen under Moroccan management. **La Colombe**, opposite the Rembrandt Hotel on Blvd Mohammed V, has a good selection of cakes including the gazelle horn of pastry stuffed with honey and almonds, the most famous Moroccan speciality patisserie. The **Café de Paris,,** Place de la France, or on the opposite side of the road the **Café de France** and the **Semiramis** are excellent places in which to while away part of the midday heat. The best shoe shine in Tangier is received from Laarbi Ouezzani who now works from the Café de Paris, having run a bar in Aberdeen for three years.

BARS

The bar by the pool at the **Hôtel de Villa de France** has recently become a popular meeting place for young Moroccan men and women. The **Caids Bar** in the El Minzah Hotel is a well recognized international gathering point and is good for a look with its deep leathery atmosphere. Opposite the El Minzah down a market passage you will find the friendly and occasionally musical **Segovia Bar**.

Considerably down market from these is the **Tapas Bar**, Juano de Arco, on the Rue Allal ben Abdellah, something of a meeting place for Tangier's Moroccan literary and artistic community. **Dean's Bar**, the watering place of Hemingway and Eroll Flynn still functions, though socially it plummeted after Dean died from a cocaine overdose in 1963. Opposite the British Consulate at 2, Rue Amérique du Sud and now run by Brahim, it retains its secretive air, photographs of the famous and polished brass bars.

The Pub on 4, Rue Soroya, tel 34789, opposite the Ritz Hotel despite or perhaps because of its name and English decoration is a popular place with Moroccans and visitors. Barry and Nigel serve bangers and mash and cottage pies, Pimms, champagne and lager to all.

The **Tanger Inn** bar which opens at 21.00 is run by John Sutcliffe whose book *The Unknown Pilgrim* is on sale at the bar. The hotel above, the El Muniria, housed William Burroughs in room 9 whilst he wrote *The Naked Lunch*.

NIGHT CLUBS

The Hotels **Solazur, Almohades, Rif, Sherezade, Tanger, Africa** and **Tanjah Flandria** run disco/night clubs. Along the Rue el Moutarabi are a string of disco clubs, the **Churchill**, the **Rancho Bar** and at no 13 the **Gospel** night club. All have free entrance and sell beer for around 15dh. The **Koutoubia Palace** charges 30dh. Cabaret turns of belly dancers and fire eaters mix with dance turns and bands in this capacious hall with ugly plastic seats and two busy bars.

La Palace Disco, entrance on Rue Ibn Rochd, is run by the Hotel Tanjah Flandrine. The entrance price of 25dh gives you a free drink and then you can dance under purple lights and rotating globes. On the Rue Prince Moulay Abdullah are three further clubs, the small **Pic Nic**, the **Borsalino** guarded by a bouncer dressed as a Chicago gangster. This is the 'smartest' of the clubs with its white interior designed to contrast well with a blazer.

Next door is the **Radio Club**, a wonderfully seedy place, where the bouncer has a double role as a lead singer in the band. It is one of the few places in Tangier where you can be sure of listening to Moroccan music. The club is full of bar flies promoting generosity and quick drinking in wonderfully stereotyped roles, whilst the elegant dark lady behind the bar consumes gin in a flash and tidies the ashtrays by spilling their contents on the floor. Prices and entertainment endlessly variable.

There is also **Scotts**, on Rue Moutanabi, where the walls are decorated with Stuart Church's pictures of young Moroccan boys in Highland uniform, setting the mood for this club, which embraces a friendly mix of homosexual and heterosexual couples.

Fahs di Tanja

The Fahs di Tanja, the environs of Tangier, is the description for the tribal lands that surround the city. Unlike other areas of Morocco the 17th-century social system was left undisturbed for the region was under the nominal authority of the international city of Tangier.

Over 50 villages are hidden in the folds of the surrounding hills where agriculture is combined with animal husbandry. The village of **Midyuna**, near Cape Spartel, alone indulges in industry by carving mill stones from the schist hills. The houses, called *nwala*, form a square courtyard of rooms that enclose the animals at night, a prickly-pear hedge typically surrounds the house on three sides, often decorated with drying washing. The fields are ploughed after the spring and summer rains by odd pairs combining ox, horse, mule or donkey that pull a single wooden plough.

The tribal lands are inalienable for they belong to the government by right of conquest and may only be acquired through inheritance, though the smaller pieces of property known as *mulk* may be sold. Men inherit the land; daughters must be provided with money for their dowry which they recover from their husbands should they divorce.

The Sultan Moulay Ishmael after the reoccupation of Tangier from the departing English in 1684 peopled the devastated land and city from an army that had been recruited from the Berber Riff tribes. Though Arabic is spoken in a Fahs village many of the inhabitants can recite their lineage back through eight generations to a particular tribe in the Riff. As a form of auxiliary militia they had no tribal Caid but remained directly responsible to their commander in chief, the Pasha of Tangier. The Cadi, the Islamic judge, in Tangier settled all other civil disputes, for there are no intermediary families of Shorfa in these hills. The region was intimately tied to the city at another level.

There are no rural souks in the Fahs, for the souks of Tangier attract all the trading, taxes were paid directly to the Pasha and the men travelled into town on Friday for the social noonday prayers and sermon at the Great Mosque.

Out from Tangier

The Fahs can be explored in four directions. The closest and most travelled route is on a loop road west that takes you past Cape Spartel, the caves of Hercules and Roman Cotta. South of Tangier, off the P2 road to Asilah are the more discreet charms of the **Chez Abdou beach** and the **Zaouia of Sidi Kacem**. The road to Ceuta takes you past the ruined Portuguese **castle of Ksar es Seghir** and the beaches grow steadily more dramatic and empty as you travel east. To the southwest the major attraction is the hill of Charf which provides a memorable panorama over Tangier. The few minor Roman ruins are unlikely to delay a journey to Tetouan.

West of Tangier

The Montagne

Leave the city centre and follow the Rue de Belgique for the road west to Cape Spartel. The Oued el Ihoud, the Jews' river, after 3 km divides the city outskirts from the garden suburb of the Montagne. The central tree-shaded space at the foot of the Montagne hill becomes an animated vegetable and clothes market on Sunday morning. A dirt track to the right of this rustic forum passes below the Miramonte campsite to lead down to the small **Jews' Beach** where there is a café restaurant run by Sidi Mustapha. The beach was named after the first landing place of the Jewish refugees who had been expelled from Spain due to the harsh religious and racial laws of the Catholic monarchs. The hot sands in the summer are a recognized cure against gout and rheumatism. The beach was invaded in 1930 by a large army of lobsters who have not since returned.

A road leads up the hill of the Montagne past the villas lived in by such British painters as Sir John Lavery and James McBey. Where the tarmac ends, a stone-paved cliff walk continues the 11 km to the lighthouse at **Cape Spartel**. This is a fine position from which to watch the flocks of migrating birds that travel to Europe from late March to April and return south to Africa in October.

The Montagne used to be dense scrubland, a refuge from where Mujhadeen, holy warriors, harassed the infidel Portuguese and English, who held the port of Tangier from the 15th to the 17th century. It was transformed into an exclusive English expatriate community from the turn of this century and now lot by lot is slowly returning to affluent Moroccans.

Cape Spartel

The road to Cape Spartel skirts below the Montagne to pass the English-inspired People's Dispensary for Sick Animals which has a farm, a clinic and an expanding animal graveyard. The road then climbs up past heavily guarded and meticulously maintained villa-palaces of the king where his deposed great uncles, the Sultans Abdul Aziz and Moulay Hafid, retired. Ravenscraig, the old villa of the British consul, Sir John Hay, is now the property of King Hassan II. The last wild lion of the region was seen from a terrace here in 1859. Stubbs, the celebrated English artist, painted over 50 pictures of a lion attacking a horse. He is supposed to have received his obsession with this subject by witnessing an actual scene on the north Moroccan coast. The last immense palace on the right is that which was recently built for King Fahd of Saudi Arabia.

Continuing through these wooded hills you pass a number of tracks that lead to fine views over the straits of Gibraltar. The **Belvedere de Perdicaris** is the most popular. This is where the Greek American millionaire built a villa from where he was kidnapped by Raisuni. The **Spartel lighthouse**, 14 km from Central Tangier is built on the far northwestern corner of Africa, known to the ancients as the cape of vines. The lighthouse is not open to the public but you can sometimes catch a glimpse of its interior Moorish courtyard—a delightful space of worn brick paving with a central schist menhir which supports a giant conch of cascading flowers and a little fountain. The nearby café is however open all the year.

Caves of Hercules

Travelling south from the lighthouse you pass three sandy bays separated by rock outcrops before you reach the tourist village that has developed around the caves of Hercules. From the car park, concrete steps lead down to a ticket booth, 1dh entrance, and the opportunity to buy a woolly hat and employ a multilingual guide.

Schist millstones have been quarried from the cave for centuries and the incised lines high up in the cavern roof gives the fanciful impression of a giant scallop shell. The sea picturesquely thunders into a turbulent cleft carved into a lower cave whilst on the cliff edge a number of blow holes produce dramatic blasts of water during a heavy swell.

The caves were until independence the haunt of prostitutes who practised their trade in the dark recesses. Customers were escorted by a guide with a lantern who discreetly extinguished the light once a choice had been made. This is no longer a feature of a tour of the caves though prostitution may have been a very ancient tradition here. In the 1920s a pre-Neolithic gallery of hundreds of ritual phalluses was discovered in one of the more secluded sea caves.

Ancient Cotta

A short 5 minute walk south from the caves takes you to the site of the 2nd-century Roman Cotta, a small area of stone ruins just above the beach. A guide will appear from a shed and show you the temple arch, an altar stone and a small tiled courtyard. The olive press and storage tanks are easily recognizable. Cotta specialized like many of the Moroccan coastal classical sites in the manufacture of the rancid sauce made from fish guts, Garum, that was so beloved of the Romans.

WHERE TO STAY AND EAT
The largest bay south of the Cape Spartel lighthouse is bordered by the **Café Restaurant Sol**, tel 31548, that provides a plate of fish for 30dh; it has a full bar but serves

unpleasant coffee. **Camp Robinson** just before the Caves of Hercules has 114 spaces for tents and a few bungalows for rent at 80dh a night. Opposite is the **Hôtel Les Grottes d'Hercule** which has its own pool, Arabian nights disco, kiddies corner and is only fully running from March to September. A single terraced room that opens out directly on to the sea costs 138dh. A licensed café restaurant, the **Robinson**, with sea-view terraces and caged Barbary apes is further along, beside the caves of Hercules. Here you can hire a **horse** for an hour ride along the long beach to the south for 50dh. You can also take a brief **camel ride** or rent a **fishing rod** from the shop.

South of Tangier

Sidi Kacem

Just south of Tangier airport, to the west of the main P2 coast road to Asilah, is Daya Sidi Kacem, a brackish estuary near to the coastal shrine of Sidi Kacem. The blue dome and white outbuildings are surrounded by a grove of wind-blown trees. Kacem, the fourth son of Idriss II, retired to a life of piety and poverty in a hermitage on the coast in disgust that his brothers should fight each other over their ample royal inheritance. An important yearly pilgrimage is held here at the time of the summer solstice festival of the Ansra which should be held on 24 June but often strays into early August. For three days feasting, dancing, and ritual bathing, popular for young brides to ensure their fertility, is held in an encampment city beside the shrine. Until recently the traditional Berber solstice sacrifice of bulls was performed. A nearby hill, the megalithic necropolis of **El Mries**, has been found to contain 30 sacrificial pits amongst numerous graves. Perhaps the burnt dead from these pits also danced and sang on the same beach to celebrate the longest day of the year.

Chez Abdou

The coast road south from Sidi Kacem runs past the Diplomatic forest, an area used by the European consuls for their pig sticking parties. A turning 17 km out of Tangier takes you through these woods to Chez Abdou, an entertaining beach restaurant with a Moroccan dining room, generous plates of seafood and a delicious hot fish and vegetable tagine. There is space for tents beside the restaurant under a screen of firs. A famous English actress once entertained the entire Tangier football team here.

Southwest from Tangier

Hill of Charf

Leave Tangier from the circular Place de la Ligue Arabe, decorated with the conspicuous new **Syrian Mosque** whose thin minaret lights up to cast a green glow at the times of prayer. The **Spanish bull ring** beside the road was built during the Second World War when Franco assumed control of Tangier from 1940 to 1945. Rumours of a hoarded Nazi art collection still persist from that extraordinary era when Tangier was the favourite neutral ground for espionage deals and misinformation campaigns. Beyond the bull ring a number of roads on the left lead up the Charf hill. This is the traditional burial site of the giant Anteus and a cemetery has spread out on the southern slopes of this hill. The **Koubba** on the summit is not a saint's shrine but an elegant folly built by the Spanish. A café here serves snacks and coffee during the summer; the view of the port, Medina and new town of Tangier gives one of the best perspectives of the city. At dusk the lights start up all over the town, the call for prayer whispers over the bay as the sun declines over the Montagne hills to the west. It is a perfect prospect for a visitor wishing to understand the geography and extent of this fast growing city.

The P38 road for Tetouan

4 km out of Tangier just to the east of the road on the rocky summit of a hill are the traces of a small Roman hill fort and 10 km further, again to the east, are the ruins of a larger Roman camp, known as **El Benian**. 8 km beyond the Larache turning you climb the Haouz hills and pass a prominent Spanish-built barracks on the site of the strategic **El-Fondouq**, a necessary fortified staging post for mechants trading between Tangier and Tetouan who wished to preserve property or life from the Anjara and Djeballa hill raiders. From the Fondouq, **Tetouan** is only 22 km, through rough wooded hills, its mass of tight-packed white houses bursting suddenly into view before you catch sight of the Mediterranean. See page 130 for Tetouan.

East of Tangier

Cape Malabata

Pass along the bay of Tangier and avoid the new tourist developments. The Club Mediterranée now occupies the grounds of the **Villa Harris**, which was a gift to the people of Tangier but is now alas inaccessible. Walter Harris, *The Times* correspondent for Morocco, designed an elegant garden here which, with his homosexual affairs, occupied so much of his time that his wife left him, though she only cited the gardening as grounds for divorce in the London law courts.

Where the Oued Melaleh estuary emerges by the sea are the ruined walls of an outlying **Portuguese settlement**. 8 km out of Tangier a turning to the left leads to the clean and tranquil **Murissat beach** which has a few grill cafés in the high summer. One km on, a curious Gothic folly, the **Chateau Malabata** appears on the skyline. It is now inhabited by a hospitable Moroccan farmer and his family and the track leads down to the deserted lighthouse on Cape Malabata with an excellent view of Tangier and the straits.

The S704 coast road passes by many attractive and deserted beaches rarely without a complement of beached fishing boats. If you examine the coast carefully you can spot customs men on look-out from ex-Spanish pill boxes. They were first built to halt the smuggling of arms to the Riff army of Abdel Krim in the 1920s.

Ksar es Seghir

Ksar es Seghir is 37 km east of Tangier where a ruined Portuguese fortified town sits in a bay encroached by dunes and bordered to the west by the estuary of Oued el Ksar. A wharf erected on this estuary provides a base for a few fishing boats and a popular fish restaurant can be found beside the road whose terraced dining room overlooks the ruins.

It was an important crossing point to Spain, and held the name Ksar Masmuda during the period of Almohad rule. This was tactful as the Masmuda from the High Atlas were the aristocracy of the Almohad Empire and fancied themselves, with little supporting evidence, to have been the allies of Tariq in his 8th-century conquest of Visigothic Spain.

The Merenid Sultans renamed it Ksar al Majaz, the 'castle of the crossing' and due to the rising power of Christian Spain they strengthened the castle with massive gates and walls in 1287. Alfonso V of Portugal advanced from Ceuta to seize the town in 1458, as part of a long-term campaign to conquer all of northern Morocco. He expelled the Muslim inhabitants and turned the Mosque into a church.

Excavations of the castle have revealed mass graves outside the walls and a pit full of dismembered bodies in the churchyard. It is not known for certain what episode these grim remains represent though it is thought that an outbreak of virulent plague encouraged John III in 1550 to order the evacuation of the town, a sudden reversal of his decision the previous year to extend the defences.

The walls of the town were circular with two strongly fortified gates. The paved flooring of the **Hammam** and old **Mosque** can be seen amongst the ruins. The citadel which guards a double wall still stretches right down to the beach, its sea gate arch still complete.

Djebel Moussa

The road continues another 12 km along the coast, with a turning to the little-visited lighthouse and beach at **Cape Cires** marking the beginning of the ascent up the flanks of Djebel Moussa. This mountain is a conspicuous feature on the eastern horizon from Tangier, its peak 842 m high is often obscured in a wreath of clouds. It is the northerly extension of the line of mountains, the Haouz, that runs along the coast between Ceuta and Tetouan. Djebel Moussa is one of the two pillars of Hercules that guards the entrance to the Mediterranean. There is an old belief that a natural tunnel travels under the sea to connect Gibraltar to Djebel Moussa. They do indeed have certain connections; geologically Gibraltar is a piece of Africa and Barbary apes and partridges are curiously found to breed nowhere else in Europe. Both mountains also possess caves high up on their flanks where Mesolithic remains have been discovered; migrating birds of prey also use the thermal winds from both peaks to climb to a sufficient height to make a safe crossing of the straits.

At the foot of the mountain is the old Arab port of **Balyounesh**. It was one of the ports used for the invasion of Spain by the Arab and Berber army in the 8th century. The tarmac road that snakes down to the village has become dangerously eroded.

There is a splendid view over Ceuta from the main road as you come from these invigorating heights. The dusty frontier town of **Fnideq**, 60 km from Tangier, is beside the Ceuta to Tetouan coast road.

CEUTA/SEBTA

Ceuta is one of the five Spanish enclaves in Morocco and has been held against an almost continuous siege since 1580. It occupies the narrow spit of land lying to the east of Djebel Moussa, a fiercely contested bridge that guards the shortest crossing between Africa and Europe. For six centuries the cross and the sword have been dominant in Ceuta, symbolized by massive stone-dressed walls protected by a sea moat and the gloomy baroque interior of the cathedral. The present is represented by serried rows of ugly apartment blocks to the west and a town full of duty free Indian shops selling cigarettes, alcohol, electrical goods and gaudy knicknacks to be smuggled across the border into Morocco.

Like Melilla, Ceuta only really makes sense as an arrival or departure point, the deliberate delays at the border crossing make a day visit a frustrating and largely bureaucratic experience, testing to one's patience. For all its seediness it is a curious historical survivor that can easily consume half a day. Its Baroque churches appear particularly striking after a couple of weeks peering at the exteriors of Moroccan mosques.

History

The town's name is derived from *septem*, a reference to the ancient and widespread myth of the seven sleepers. Local variations connect it with Calypso's enchantment of Odysseus's crew for seven years or point out with relish a random selection of seven neighbouring hills as the secret lairs of giants or sleepers.

Ceuta's vital strategic position has influenced its entire history. It was used by the Phoenicians and held by Rome until the Vandals seized the port on their way east to conquer the corn lands of Tunisia. Belisaurius reconquered it for the Byzantine Empire in the 6th century.

Count Julian was the last Byzantine governor of Ceuta. He became a figure of legendary duplicity in the traditional account of the Arab conquest. He welcomed Uqba ben Nafi in 681 yet encouraged Tangier to resist Musa ben Nasser in 705, but prudently abandoned the city before it was sacked. He is even credited with initiating the Muslim invasion of Spain in 711 in order to avenge himself on Roderic, the Visigothic king who had seduced his daughter.

The Muslim sovereigns of Ceuta in the following centuries changed with dazzling frequency. It passed like a symbolic orb to the strongest power of the day: Idrissids, Omayyads, Almoravides, Almohads and Merenids succeeded each other. In the 13th century it became the centre of a mesh of shifting alliances that involved the Christian kingdoms of Castile, Aragon, Portugal and the Muslim kingdom of Nasrid Granada and Merenid Morocco. To add to the diplomatic complexity it was the favourite refuge for exiled princes and emigré courtiers. The high political intrigue seems to have had little adverse effect on the town, which throughout this period was a leading commercial and intellectual centre. El Idrissi, the Muslim geographer, was born here in 1099 and Sidi bel Abbes, the great missionary to Marrakesh, was born in Ceuta in 1130. Recent excavations in the neighbouring towns of Ksar es Seghir and Benzu attest to the domestic prosperity and achievements of the period. The port was full of Mediterranean traders and the town decorated with fine Mosques, town houses, baths and colleges.

Nemesis struck in 1415 when King John of Portugal descended on Ceuta with a fleet of 200 ships and army of 50,000 men. He was able to knight his four young sons amidst the carnage and ruins of a once great city. The eldest son, the Infante Ferdinand, was fated to end his life imprisoned above a gate in Fez. On his death he was skinned, stuffed with straw and hung by his heels like a butchered goat. He had been captured in 1437 during a failed attempt to take Tangier and the price of his release was the surrender of Ceuta, to which his brothers would not agree.

The Spanish took the fortress when Phillip II inherited Portugal in 1580. It was the object of many raids over the centuries. Many a sultan won the affection of his people by attacking Ceuta and in the absence of a formal siege the Anjera hill tribes sniped and raided away at will. It was one such raid that provided the formal excuse for the Spanish invasion of Tetouan in 1860, when Spain returned to the offensive which was eventually to lead to the Spanish protectorate over northern Morocco. Ceuta was also a springboard for Franco's nationalist army to enter the Civil War in 1936, but since Moroccan independence, time has hung heavily on the fortress. It is still heavily garrisoned by bored Spanish conscripts.

GETTING AROUND

The customs are very thorough, and confiscate all maps of Morocco that do not show the Western Sahara as an integral portion of the nation and to the same scale. Currently all books, even guides, are examined with great suspicion and can be confiscated. I recently lost an old copy of a Mohammed Mrabet, one of Morocco's leading novelists and a book on Sufi mysticism whose title, *Islam, the way of submission*, caused great consternation.

Ferry

You can buy tickets for Algeciras or Melilla along Muelle Canonero Dato, the port road that leads to the ferry pier. From the Transmediterranea office, tel 515476 or directly from the port from the Islena office, tel 518340. A passenger ticket is currently 1100 pesetas, a dozen boats leave Mon–Fri between 8.30–22.30, on Sundays five boats depart from 8.30–21.00.

Buses and Taxis

Spanish buses and taxis can take you to and from the border but Moroccan taxis stop short of the frontier and leave you with a half kilometre walk along the coast road to the village of Fnideq. At Fnideq the 38 km ride south to Tetouan in a grand taxi, shared how you like, should cost 70dh, though heavy demand can push the price up. Local buses in Ceuta leave from the Placa de la Constitution, the no 7 costs 33 pesetas for the 3 km ride south to the frontier at Fnideq. The long distance Spanish bus station is on the southern coast road just west of the San Felipe moat and has periodic coaches for Al Hoceima, Casablanca and Nador. It is usually quicker and more reliable to taxi down to the Tetouan bus station.

Car

To cross by car into Morocco you will need a green insurance card, a vehicle registration document and passport and to fill in an immigration form. Crossing from Morocco into Ceuta you will also have to attest that you are travelling with no Dirhams. There is a

Citroen garage on the Muelle Canonero Dato, a Fiat garage at 2, Marina Espanola and a Peugeot at no 20, Marina Espanola; fill up with petrol which is cheaper in Ceuta than Morocco.

TOURIST INFORMATION

The Tourist Office is on the Muelle Canonero Dato, by the ferry pier, and can provide a complete list of pensions. The Banco De Espana is found on the Placa de Espana and Banco Popular Espanol is on the Pasco del Revellin 1. The American and British do not keep a Consul here but the French and Belgians have a joint office at 47, Muelle Canonero Dato, tel 515741.

The Port

After the Portuguese conquest of 1415 the port changed from a great entrepôt which had connected Mediterranean merchants with the Saharan trade to a moribund military base. It is now enlivened by the fishing and smuggling boats and a terminal dealing with 2,000,000 passengers a year.

Museum of Antiquities

Directly in front of the port is the small Museum of Antiquities surrounded by an Argentinian garden with the door protected by two 17th-century bronze cannon bearing the arms of Henry IV. Inside is a collection of Neolithic, Punic, classical and medieval pottery shards. The star of the collection is a decorated Roman white marble sarcophagus whilst outside is the entrance to the tunnels built in the 16th and 17th centuries in which to shelter from bombardments and store fresh water and provisions. It is open from Monday to Saturday, 9.00–13.00, 16.00–18.00 and on Sundays and holidays from 10.00–14.00.

The Ramparts

The massive inner walls with their angular battlements draped in bougainvillea look at their best as you cross the moat of San Felipe. Built in 1530 with the aid of Portuguese crusading orders, the battlements and twin towers guard a number of tranquil shaded gardens.

The Old Town

The **Placa de Africa**, the formal centre of the town, is immediately behind these defences. This in the 15th century was the central souk for the Muslim city and was lined with medersas and palaces. The **church of Our Lady of Africa** to the north occupies the site of a mosque. She is Ceuta's patron saint who in 1744 was given authority over the town by the despairing Governor Pedro de Vargas when the town was ravaged by the plague, which she promptly dispelled. King John I of Portugal had invested his first governor with an olive branch and this in an annual ceremony is now presented by the ruling governor to the 16th-century image of the Virgin. The church is a Baroque extravaganza of the early 18th century. Unexceptionable if you have just arrived by ferry from Spain but has a strong impact if you have spent some time in Muslim Morocco.

In the middle of the Placa is a **monument to the Spanish invasion** of 1859 when General O'Donnel led an army of 25,000 to do battle in the heights above Tetouan. 1300 Spanish soldiers died that day but a victory mass was sung in the Grand Mosque of Tetouan the next day.

The **Cathedral** is directly opposite. It was built over the Grand Mosque in the 15th century, but was refurbished in the Baroque taste in 1729, decorated with the heraldry of the bishops of Ceuta and immense gloomy oil paintings from the life of Christ.

The **Gran Via** with its central gardens leads east past the **Town Hall** on the corner. The hall inside is decorated with panels exonerating the grave duties of colonialism, painted by Mariano Bertuchi, which you can take a peak at.

Continue along the Gran Via to the **Placa de la Constitucion**, ex General Galera, and on east through different names, Camoens and Revellin to begin with, to the foot of Mount Hacho. This is the most animated street with shops, cafés and bars. At the Placa Ramos is the **church of San Francisco** where rests the body of the young King Sebastian. His body was returned to Phillip II of Spain free of charge by the Saadian Sultan Ahmed el Mansour. Sebastian became the focus of a 16th- and 17th-century quasi-nationalist cult which believed he would be reborn to lead Portugal to greater glory. Even further east, on the left, you can visit another church, **Nuestra Señora de Los Remedios** built in 1716 and housing a memorial to the Spanish struggle against Napoleon.

Monte Hacho

By car or taxi you could in half an hour follow the coastal roads around Mount Hacho with fine views of Gibraltar to the north and the Riff coast and mountains to the east.

The southern road, Recinto Sur, leads past an old Portuguese fort on the far eastern edge of the island, **Pointe Almina**, where there is also a lighthouse. Before you pass these monuments a turning to the left allows you to travel up to the **hermitage of San Antonio**, whose chapel was built in 1593. A festival with dancing and picnics takes place here on the saint's day, 13 June.

The fortress that crowns Mount Hacho, **El Desnarigado**, has recently opened a **military museum** that is open on the weekend from 11.00–14.00 and 16.00–18.00 with five rooms packed with military memorabilia of varying interest.

Returning back to the coast road you look over a cemetery that faces some offshore islands which are quite often obscured by the smoke from burning rubbish. A stone nationalist monument commemorates the departure of Nationalist troops from Morocco to Spain on 17 July 1938; it was removed from Ketama and placed here in 1956. You then pass a formal Andalucian garden with an open air theatre and a possibility of a swim at the **plage de San Amaro** before returning to the port.

FESTIVALS
There is a carnival in February, processions on Holy Week, a fete at San Antonio's hermitage on 13 July, a procession of fishing boats on 16 July for Our Lady of Mount Carmel and the festival of Our Lady of Africa on 5 August.

WHERE TO STAY

Unless you have forged an unusual love for Ceuta there is no need to stay a night; Tangier is only 75 km away and Tetouan 38 km. The **** **La Muralla** on the Placa de Africa is the grandest hotel of Ceuta with 83 bedrooms, a bar, restaurant and a night club held on Saturday nights, tel 514940. On the cheaper end there are two small ** hotels at no 23 and no 6, Av. Reyes Catholicos, the **Miramar**, tel 514146 and the **Skol**, tel 514148, or try the **Pension Oriente**, Teniente Arrabel 3, tel 511115, 1600 pesetas for a double bed. For the card-carrying Youth Hostel user, the **Posada de Juventud**, offers bargain dormitory beds at 27, Placa Viejo, tel 515148.

EATING OUT

La Torre at no 15 Placa de Africa is considered the best restaurant in town. The **Delphin Verde** is easy to find, just opposite the ferry pier on Muelle Canonero Dato. **Meson de Serafin** is a good place to stop on your way around Mont Hacho, tel 514003, or you could try **La Campana** at 15 Paseo del Revellin. The **Casa Fernando** on the northwestern corner of Ceuta, the **Benitez beach**, tel 514082, is an exclusively Spanish affair untouched by tourists, with a good reputation for fresh seafood.

Ceuta to Tetouan

The line of the Haouz mountains follows the Mediterranean shore, a fierce horizon which graphically represents the old predatory power of the Anjera hill tribe.

Superb Mediterranean beaches continue for 40 km in an almost unbroken line from the Moroccan border at Findeq to **Martil**, the old corsair port of Tetouan. Moroccan families return to camp along sections of this beach every summer to escape from the heat of the cities. Large hotels have recently been built but unlike the controlled development at Agadir they have been allowed to sprawl along the length of the coast, ugly but convenient bases for packaged beach holidays.

The exclusive sporting beach club image of these hotels is exemplified by the **Club Mediterranée**. But by staying at Tetouan you can travel every day to a different beach on the 3dh shuttle buses and return in the evening to the fascination of a Moroccan city.

Fnideq

Fnideq is on the edge of the military *cordon sanitaire* that encircles the Ceuta border; it is a rough frontier village full of mechanics shops and cafés, though there is one emergency pension. The heavily draped market ladies smuggle vegetables under their clothes, forcing their way past the officials in a numbing war of persistence.

A right turn takes you on the S704 road up the slopes of Djebel Moussa. You immediately enter the wild hill country of the Anjera tribe. There are a succession of memorable views over the machiolated round Spanish towers that surround Ceuta.

Beyond Fnideq on the main P28 coast road are the crumbling ruins of an immense baroque **Spanish Palace**. It is guarded by pyramidical gate towers that reveal an intriguing vista of a central dome which is shedding its ornamental roof and wall tiles. If you walk up to explore, an unarmed soldier may appear and tell you politely to go away.

Smir Restinga

Smir Restinga is not a village but merely a number of seasonal roadside hotels like the **Boustane, Karabo**, apartments and holiday villas of **Club Med** and **Maroc Tourist**, built beside the estuary of the Oued Smir and the camping **Freja**, tel 7722. The latter is at least cheap; they charge 7dh for a car, 7dh for a person and 5dh for a tent.

Mdiq

The fishing village of Mdiq is 23 km south from Ceuta and is now at least half way in the process of becoming a resort. There is a growing collection of roadside café restaurants like the **Chico** and **Hotel-Bar Playa**. A clean double room at the Hotel Playa should cost only 30dh, tel 7510. There are also two holiday villages, the **Kabila** and the **Golden Beach Hotel** established along the beach.

The fishing harbour built out from the Ras Tarf hill is lined with wooden fishing boats which can be seen in every stage of construction along the carpenters' quay. Peregrine falcons nest in the cliffs above. The fish grill café in the harbour provides the most interesting place for lunch.

Cabo Negro

The other side of the hill from Mdiq, 2 km by road is the Cabo Negro beach. It has the finest stretch of sand and is dominated but fortunately not yet owned by the **Club Med Yasmina** and the neighbouring and ugly **Hotel Petit Merou**. Just off the beach there is the restaurant **Al Khayma** which serves Moroccan meals in its Moorish interior. **La Ferma** is more expensive, an old house admirably converted into a restaurant but a little overcrowded in the evening. You can hire horses for a ride along the surf from the nearby **Horse Club**.

The hillside as you approach Tetouan begins to become speckled with villas, by the roadside are some entrancing displays of pottery, wicker-work chairs, baskets and piles of fruit for sale. The melons in summer are particularly delicious with a fresh honeydew flavour that can quite spoil your appetite for anything less. There are also great piles of oranges, grapes, water melons and children offering to peel prickly pears. One km before Tetouan is a turning to the left for Martil.

Martil

Martil is the town beach and old corsair port of Tetouan, a friendly relaxed place with wide streets and unpretentious, almost shack-like, houses. The tempo is far removed from the pressure and salesmanship of the Tetouan Medina though it would be as well to keep a firm look-out over your more portable possessions. The estuary served as the riverine port for Tetouan but has silted up considerably in the last few centuries. The broken pattern of tidal islands provided an excellent refuge for the corsair fleets that operated here from the 15th to the 18th centuries despite a number of ineffectual Spanish blockades.

The estuary of Martil held a number of rough forts built on islands to protect the corsair craft. The present **Kasbah** was built on the foundations of a fort from the reign of

Moulay Ishmael. It was finished in 1759 and protected by a moat. In 1775 a small squadron of ten 30-oared light corsair vessels was back in commission. The Kasbah is still in a reasonable state of preservation and with a little persistence you can enter and climb up to the roof where one rusting cannon still commands a fine view, through its portal, of the estuary.

The whitewashed **Spanish church** survives, an inflated Koubba with the extending cruciform wings decorated with Baroque arches. As there is only one Spanish family left in Martil this amusing building is now usefully employed as a home for disabled children. Martil now has a correspondingly **Grand Mosque** which was built in 1984 with the help of skilled stonemasons from Salé.

FESTIVALS

The **Water Moussem of the Ansara** used to be held the other side of the estuary below the tell of Sidi Abdussalam al bahr on 13 August. It has now been transferred to Martil and is held in July in a more secular vein.

WHERE TO STAY AND EAT

The **Hotel Rabat** or the **Pension Rif** by the bus station charge 40dh for a room, they are both pleasantly social places. On the corner formed by the beach and the estuary is the **Camping Martil**, tel 9339, a friendly though not desperately secure place despite a Spanish-built pill box at the entrance. It charges under 10dh for car, tent and a person. Almost directly opposite on the Rue Miramar you will find the **Nuzha** or **Pension Merhaba**, both usually charge 20dh ahead. Following the beach north you will meet the fish restaurant **Rio Martil** on the beach front Plaza at the end of the Rue Moulay Hassan. Opposite, on the Rue Moulay Hassan is the slightly upmarket **Etoile de la Mer** with its own café restaurant and reliable water supply, a double room costs 97dh.

TETOUAN

Tetouan, a city with a population of over 350,000, has a dramatic visual impact. The densely packed white city falls from the slopes of Djebel Dersa to dominate the green valley of the Oued Martil, overlooked by improbably folded and majestic mountains to both the north and south.

Tetouanis claim that they are the true heirs of the Andalucian civilization and affectionately call their city 'the daughter of Granada'. Architecturally the Hispanic influence is dominant for it was built by Muslim refugees from Spain in the 15th century, and enlarged by the Spanish government in the 20th century to create the formal capital of their protectorate of Northern Morocco. Its Medina is one of the most fascinating and absorbing in the country, a delightful warren of detail not always free from a tinge of alarm for the newcomer. The Spanish new town complements the old Andalucian Medina. The ostentatious grandeur of the high and formal official buildings, constructed on a grid of regular streets contrasts well with the eclectic individual disorder of the Medina.

Beneath this civilized veneer Tetouan is also very much part of the Berber hinterland.

Tetouan is a Berber word which can variously be translated as: 'the eyes', 'the springs', 'the edges of water' or 'the female wild boar'. The last has a certain ironic appeal for a Muslim city and as a warning to visitors. Tetouan shares the dissident mentality of the Riff tribes and has a reputation for harbouring the most assertive and aggressive tourist hustlers. It can subsequently make a frustrating start to a holiday but is also a rewarding city once you become adapted to Moroccan street life.

History

Tetouan has a cyclical history of destruction and renewal. It has been the vortex around which the two dominant influences of the region have struggled for mastery. On the one hand a series of sophisticated cultures have continually attempted to settle the coast, and on the other they have just as continually been opposed by the Riff tribes of the mountains. It is a dynamic of opposing forces that is still far from settled today.

Phoenician-influenced Berbers established Tamuda, the first major settlement here, in the 3rd century BC. They strongly opposed the Roman annexation of Morocco, and as a result Tamuda was totally destroyed in AD 42 by the legions of the Emperor Claudius as a horrific example to the rest of the nation. No settlement was attempted again until the 2nd century, and this somewhat indicatively remained more of a fortified legionary camp than a civil city and was abandoned the moment the Roman garrison left in the 5th century.

In 1306 a Merenid Sultan built a Kasbah on the present site of the city in order to check the influence of a cousin who had established himself as ruler of Ceuta. The new community rapidly prospered but in the winter of 1399 Henry III of Castile landed at the mouth of the river, sank the Merenid fleet, sacked the town and enslaved the entire population. The city lay neglected and empty for a century. It functioned as a graveyard and a battleground between the Portuguese knights riding out from Ceuta and the hill tribes.

The Medina of Tetouan as we might recognize it was established in 1484. A few years before the fall of Muslim Granada a number of its citizens, led by a nobleman, al Mandari, left the doomed city and settled on the ruins of Tetouan. The new community was supported by a local Moroccan dynasty, the Idrissid Emirs of Chechaouen. Tetouan dedicated itself to a corsair war of revenge against the Christians who had conquered their mother city, Granada.

Tetouan's greatest era of prosperity was under the rule of al-Mandari's young wife who began by assisting her increasingly blind husband in the town's administration. In 1512 after the death of her husband, the twenty-year-old Fatima bint Ali Rashid was the feared Hakima, the governess of the corsairs. She could count on the support of her brother Ibrahim, the Emir of Chechaouen, and her new husband Ahmed, the Wattasid Sultan of Fez. Fatima was also an enthusiastic ally of the Ottoman Turks and sailed to their forward base, Velez de la Gomera, in order to offer supplies to the fleet of Barbarossa. Nor did she allow the military struggle against Catholic Spain to betray the intellectual traditions of Granada. The Dutch savant Nicholas Kleinatz fled from Christian persecution and received protection and patronage at her court. This extraordinary and talented woman ruled Tetouan for 33 years before her son-in-law, Hamad al Hassan, expelled her in a palace coup in 1542. She was escorted to her home town of Chechaouen where she lived a life of piety and scholarship for another twenty years.

Tetouan, despite its corsair fleet, developed good trading relations and by 1712 the French had placed a consul here, who was soon followed by a British rival. However the British office had to be closed down in 1772 after an English sportsman walking the hills for barbary partridges shot a Moorish woman by mistake.

Under the cloak of religious unity the Muslim Andalucians had been able to establish a civilized community amongst the Berber Riff tribes. However the tribes took advantage of the political disorders of the 18th and 19th centuries to raid this rich city of merchants and corsairs. Thenceforth the walls and gates of Tetouan had to be constantly manned against the double threat from Riff tribes and the Spanish. In 1859 a Spanish army marched out from Ceuta, fought a bloody battle in the hills above the town and occupied Tetouan for a year. They left only after they had extracted a fortune 'in reparations' from the Sultan.

They returned in 1913 to establish the capital of the Spanish protectorate at Tetouan. They arrived on a comparative wave of popularity for the city had just endured the rapacious rule of a tribal warlord, the celebrated bandit Raisuni. Throughout the Riff rebellion Tetouan remained firmly under the control of the Spanish, though in a spectacular propaganda coup Abdel Krim succeeded in shelling the town for a day from a hidden cannon in the mountains. The 45-year rule of the Spanish protectorate created little of economic value for Tetouan, apart from the odd cement and ceramic works, but their relatively liberal rule did further enhance the city's strong cultural position. Tetouan has a respected university, a conservatoire of music, a dominant position in the visual arts and its intellectuals were at the forefront of the early Independence movements.

GETTING AROUND
Travelling by bus or grand taxi to Tetouan is quick and convenient.

Bus
Buses arrive in the central covered station and the ticket booths are in the hall up the stairs. There are hourly services for Tangier and the Ceuta border post of Fnideq, 8dh and about an hour's ride. Chechaouen is a 2 hr trip, 4 departures a day at 10dh. For Fez, Marrakesh and Rabat you might consider travelling to Tangier to catch the train, although there are two daily departures for both Rabat and Fez; both coach trips take 8 hrs and cost around 35dh. The beaches to the north, in the summer, are served by a very efficient 3dh shuttle service that leaves just down hill from the Av. Hassan II. To the more tempting beaches of the east coast there are three buses a day to Oued Laou.

Taxis
The petits taxis collect customers just to the left of the bus station. The grands taxis depart from Moulay Abbas, the street to your far left that runs above but parallel to the Av. Hassan II circuit road. A place to Tangier costs 20dh or under, a ride to Ceuta about 15dh.

TOURIST INFORMATION
The Tourist Office is at 30, Av Mohammed V, tel 7009, and shares the same office hours as the Post Office. The Post Office is on the Place Moulay el Mehdi and is open from

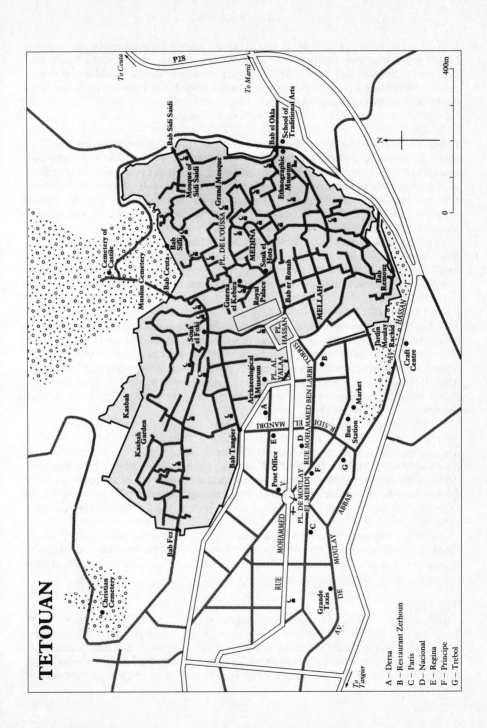

TETOUAN

To Ceuta

P28

To Martil

Bab Sidi Saidi

School of
Traditional Arts

Bab el Okla

Mosque of
Sidi Saidi

Ethnographic
Museum

Grand Mosque

PL. DE L'OUSSA

Cemetery of
Castle

MEDINA

Cemetery of
Castle

Bab
Sifli

Bab Ceuta

Muslim Cemetery

Souk el
Hots

Bab er Rouah

Bab
Remouz

Guersa
el Kebira

Royal
Palace

MELLAH

Souk
el Fok

Jardin
Moulay
A/c Rachid

AV. HASSAN

PL.
HASSAN

Craft
Centre

Kasbah

Archaeological
Museum

Kasbah
Garden

PL. AL
YALAA

R. SIDI EL MEHDI

RUE MOHAMMED BEN LARBI

B

Bab Tangier

A

C/ TORRIS

EL MANDRI

Market

Bab Fez

Post Office

E

D

F

Bus
Station

Christian
Cemetery

RUE   MOHAMMED

PL. DE MOULAY
EL MEHDI

G

C

MOULAY

ABBAS

Grande
Taxis

DE

To Tangier

AV.

N

400m

0

A – Dersa
B – Restaurant Zerhoun
C – Paris
D – Nacional
E – Regina
F – Principe
G – Trebol

8.00–15.00 Monday to Friday and 8.30–12.00 on Saturdays. In high summer it closes at 12.00 but reopens from 14.30–18.30. There is a telephone kiosk behind the Post Office in operation from 8.00 to 20.00, Monday to Saturday. The Banque du Maroc is at no 7 and the BMCI at no 18, Rue Sidi Mandri and an after-hours currency exchange from the BMCE on Place Moulay el Mehdi.

THE SITES
Tetouan has a reputation for being a difficult city to visit in the high summer. The university is closed, the beaches open and the student hostels taken over with more than enough eager young men persistently pushing their claims to be your guide. New arrivals will be met at the bus station and at the edge of the Medina. It is in the nature of the country, and rather than indignantly resist, spend your energies trying to choose someone that you can vaguely trust, or for your first visit to the Medina you could swallow your pride and employ an official guide from the Tourist Office.

This only applies for the bazaar-strewn Medina; a walk around the Ramparts, the New Town or a visit to the Archaeological or Ethnographic Museum is easily made and trouble-free. The exertion and absence of any commercial possibilities of such a tour will in any case discourage all but the youngest and keenest of your new friends.

Place Hassan II
This has always been the centre of urban life, the focal market and place of assembly contained in the past within the old circuit of walled Medina. Its character was drastically altered in 1988 when the formal Spanish central Andalucian garden was swept away and replaced by the present wide sweep of paved Islamic design, incidentally built by Italians. The north face is occupied by the Ministry of Justice, the dominant east face is the new Palace built for the King on what used to be both the residence of the Spanish High Commissioner and the Khalifa's palace.

Few chambers of the **Khalifate's Palace** have survived the transformation. It was built by Moulay Ishmael's Pashas Ahmed and his son Ali er Riffi. It was later occupied by the Khalifa (the Sultan's representative) Moulay el Mehdi during the protectorate and returned to King Mohammed V after Independence in 1956. The neighbouring residence of the High Commissioner was turned into the Spanish consulate upon Independence. A chapel was built here in 1860 by a leading Muslim family in return for an agreement that the Spanish army would no longer use the Grand Mosque for their services.

The Place is now dominated by four towering, self-supporting minarets with floodlights. It is still too early to see what effect this will have on the cafés and pension balconies that surround the square. It is likely that the kif smoke and the cries of boys selling smuggled cigarettes will remain.

The Mellah
To the south of the Place Hassan II there are two entrances to the Mellah, the Rue de la Lunetta or the Rue al Qods which is just to the right of the Bab er Rouah. This quarter, the **Kouds**, has tall square buildings, a regular grid street pattern and dark painted iron balconies with ornate window grills that distinguish it from the Muslim Medina. The original 15th-century **Jewish quarter** is less easy to distinguish; it is in the cramped

streets that surround the Grand Mosque. The community exchanged this in 1807, during the reign of Moulay Sliman, for the present larger site to the south. Three synagogues can be found, one at no 12 Florida street, the Ben Dayan Temple and the Grand Synagogue on Benguali street. A fountain installed in 1908 in honour of Israel has had its inscription obscured by whitewash and can be found on the right of the Rue al Qods. The Arab–Israeli wars forced the majority of Jews to leave Morocco for Israel or South America. Moshe Dayan, the distinguished general and archaeologist is from a prominent old Tetouan family and the ex chief minister of Gibraltar, Sir Joshua Hassan, comes from another family of the Mellah. Franco and his wife were befriended by Jews when they lived in the Tetouan Medina; the Caudillo in thanks was supposed to have issued Spanish passports to Sephardic Jews during the war to save them from his Nazi allies. Sephardic Jews were socially much in demand during the protectorate as they had retained the language of 15th-century Spain, the Labino, which was much appreciated by the Spanish conquerors of the 20th century.

For the skilled street navigator it is possible to follow the Rue de la Luneta to its end and then turn right for the **Mosque** by the Bab Remouz. Walking out through the gate from the narrow shady streets of the Mellah to the glaring view of the coast around Martil is a fine dramatic contrast. A ramp leads down from the walls to descend to the ornamental rampart gardens known as **Parc Cajigas** or Jardin Moulay Rachid.

The Medina

The old city contains over 50 mosques of which only eleven are licensed to hold Friday prayers. The meanest looking doors can give entrance to delightful high courtyard houses with each floor holding four elegant traditional rooms. The centuries of occupation are reflected on the worn paving cooled with buckets of fresh water drawn from private wells.

The eastern corner of the Place Hassan II gives entrance to the Medina through the **Bab er Rouah**, the gate of winds. By keeping to this main thoroughfare, the Rue Ach Ahmed Torres, you can pass across the Medina to the east gate, the **Bab El Okla** and the **Ethnographic Museum** and the school of traditional arts. This route will take you over the hidden mazmoras, the underground slave pens that in 1648 still housed 690 Christians who were allowed by day to visit their wives who lived in huts on the surface. A Spanish priest excavated the chambers this century to find a well, a chapel and an oratory for the resident priest.

Souk el Hots

Pass through the Bab er Rouah and take the first left, opposite a mosque to reach this delightful tree-planted intimate square. The Souk el Hots is lined with stalls selling terracotta pots and glazed ceramics but also passes as a fish market in the early morning and a butcher's shop by day. Behind the square are the 15th-century walls of the **Alcazaba**, a small brick and stone fortress; the tower of homage is in the northwest corner. It is now partly occupied by a weaving cooperative that produces fine black woollen cloth for jillabas. The entrance into the Alcazaba is through a modern passageway beside the octagonal minaret of the mosque and its associated baths.

Guersa el Kebir

The left passage from the Souk el Hots takes you in 25 m to the Guersa. The right passage takes you on a more absorbing tortuous route passing under a number of arches before the left turning, the Rue El Sattain throws you into the Guersa.

It is an irregular clearing that was once a great garden but is now a dusty open-air market. In the centre are the cloth stalls of the market ladies from the mountains, displaying piles of the distinctive striped blankets, predominantly red and white but also with black and blue lines. This fouta is worn as an outer skirt over a folded brown blanket worn around the waist that gives the women of the Riff such a stout profile. In this sunbaked court the slumped sleeping figures of the women can blend imperceptibly with their wares.

Place de l'Oussa

Behind the Guersa is a pretty little area, more of a thoroughfare than a square, ringed with whitewashed houses and heavy decorated doors. An ornamental tiled fountain provides welcome cool water to wash your face, vines provide shade and a café allows you to pause and examine the procession of Medina life. Stubble-faced hill farmers in thick jillabas, women from the mountains in their broad pomelled hats, street kids hiding alert eyes behind dark glasses and graceful aged figures in clean white linen crowned with a fez, perhaps the last of a long line of scholars from Andalucia.

The Place is easily reached from the right-hand corner of the Guersa, the Rue Sattain again, take the first left turn.

Souk el Foki

The central commercial area of the Medina is north from these small squares. The wood carvers, coppersmiths, leather workers and cobblers are found along or in fondouqs off the Rue El Jazzarin which leads up to the Bab Ceuta. This naturally leads you into the Souk el Foki, a recognizable area bordered to the north by two mosques, the first of which is the **sanctuary of Sidi Ali** where snack shops, spice stalls and wood carvers collect.

From the Souk el Foki a left turn opposite the fountain leads down the twisting Rue el Mechouar and takes you under arches and buttresses to pass the richer stalls; the tailors, embroiderers, jewellers and arrays of decorated babouches, to take you back to the Place Hassan II.

Alternatively continue along the Rue de Fez, a bustling straight alley that passes through the Trancats and Ayun quarter out through the Bab Fez. Vegetables and kitchen equipment predominate with intriguing low dark alleys disappearing off to left and right. You pass a number of mosques, that of **Sidi Ben Messaoud** with its carved stalactite portal, the **Ayun Mosque** by the fountain and the tiled **sanctuary of Sidi Ahmed en Naji**. The stalls sell little to attract the tourist and it is subsequently a pleasant carefree street busy with local trade.

A Tour of the Ramparts

The present extent of the walls contains fragments of 15th-century Andalucian work that followed the Merenid foundations. The ramparts largely date from the 17th century when the corsairs were in full operation and the war against the Spanish in Ceuta was being waged by Moulay Ishmael's Pasha Ahmed er Riffi from Tetouan.

Along the Rue Mohammed V, before the Place Hassan II, is the triangular **Plaza of Al**

Yalaa where a cannon captured by the corsairs, dated 1607, has been placed below a fragment of wall. The zaouai of Abdul Qader Jilen can be seen opposite.

The line of city wall can next be admired by walking down to the ring road, the Av. Hassan II, which is just below the bus station. On the right is the **craft centre** with a well displayed collection of traditional and modern designs in two halls. You should be able to reach lower prices in the bazaars.

Opposite are the **gardens of Moulay Rachid** running beneath the walls, their formal seats offering a splendid view of Djebel Ghorgez. A ramp leads up to the Bab Remouz and the Mellah. Continuing along the road and below the walls, you pass the Suika quarter to reach the Bab el Okhla.

School of Traditional Arts
Opposite the gates is the school of traditional arts, open from 9.00–12.00, 15.00–17.00, closed on Sundays and holidays. Here some of the techniques of Moorish decoration are revealed and you can witness the creation of damascened metalware, wood and plaster carved stalactites and verse. The mosaic wall tiles, the zellij, provides the most fascinating demonstration. In Tetouan the wet clay is cut to shape and then fired and glazed before being fitted face down into the pattern and sealed in portable segments with mortar. The Fez style used elsewhere in Morocco is to cut the mosaic pieces after firing from plain square tiles.

Ethnographic Museum
Within the crenellated gates just on the left is the entrance to the Ethnographic Museum where an Arabic plaque proclaims, 'in the name of God the merciful and compassionate, the triumph, the consolidator . . .'. Open 8.30–12.00, 14.30–18.00, closed on Tuesdays, no photographs.

A beautiful collection in the upstairs rooms of Andalucian Jewish and Islamic embroidery. A dazzling display of skilled design and technique concentrated on the sumptuous trousseaus with rooms prepared for the rich traditional marriage ceremonies. The exhibition of a countryman's house downstairs with its simple loom producing striped cloth illustrates the large gulf between the rural tribal culture and that of the sophisticated urban merchants. There is also a Moroccan kitchen and a display of armaments and embroidered saddles. One of the most dramatic features is when the curator theatrically throws open a door to the sunbaked terrace: the darkened interior full of rich secretive female clothing suddenly gives way to a panorama of sunlight and mountains.

Of less interest is the **Brishka Palace**, a well signposted 19th-century Muslim merchant's house which now sells carpets.

Bab Saidia
A short distance inside the gate is the elegant **Mosque of Sidi as Saidi**. A fountain plays opposite and water also flows below the elaborate entrelac decoration of the minaret. The entrance to the Mosque, forbidden to non-Muslims, is from the decorated covered arch to the side. It was built in 1738 by the Pasha Ahmed er Riffi but incorporating the 13th-century shrine of the saint who lived from 1227–1254. This saint's main claim to fame was that he killed the assassin of Moulay Abdessalam of Djebel Alam. On his death he was buried in Tetouan and a Koubba raised during the Merenid foundation of the city some thirty years later.

Bab Sfli/Bab el Jiaf

The gate of evil odours which may have referred to the tanning vats which used to be just inside the town walls here. It reearned its name in the 19th century when rotting bodies piled up against the gate in a failed siege of the town by mountain tribesmen.

Cemetery of Castile

The walls are clearly defined here as a cemetery extends to cover the rising ground above the town. To the northwest is the cemetery of Castile, one of the largest Sephardic burial grounds in the world. The upper area houses tombs from the 15th century with the sex of the dead symbolically indicated on the stone carvings. Holy men can be distinguished by an urn decorated with books and the tomb of Jacob Benmalka, the cabalist, is still visited, and a meteorite that protected a Cohen grave from desecration is still whitewashed and spotted with wax from votive candles. In the Muslim cemetery beside the walls the large modern tomb honours both the 15th-century Andalucian founder of Tetouan and Abdul Khaleq al Torres who established an early nationalist cell here in 1932.

Bab Ceuta

Just inside this gate, also known as the Bab Maqr, the cemetery gate are the elaborate portals of the Harraquiza zaouia of the Derkaoua Sufis which was built in 1828 over the tomb of a celebrated Sheikh. Walking by on a Friday you may overhear the arm-linked ritual chanting or a faint whisper of the theological discussions held within.

Kasbah garden

You can clamber up past the walls of the Kasbah which is still garrisoned by the FAR and subsequently inaccessible. Immediately to the left after the Kasbah and up a dirt track are the ruined ornamental gardens below the military whitewashed walls with their flaking Andalucian tiles and monuments framed by palm trees. It provides a superb view over the city roofs of white Tetouan down to the river and the surrounding mountains. Youths play football in the dust and old friends puff on a tranquil pipe in the shade amongst the elaborate ruins of the formal promenade of the Spanish garrison. Steep steps can take you down into the Rue de Fez of the Medina or you can retrace your steps to pass around the Catholic cemeteries with their despoiled tombs surrounded by a wall of elegant dark cypress.

Bab Fez and Bab Tangier

This will bring you to the Bab Fez also known as Bab Noider, the threshing gate. It is guarded on the right by the hexagonal **Shorfa's tower** while to the left is the town's electrical **souk**. A long extent of recently repaired wall alongside the Rue Al Jazaer brings you to the Bab Tangier/Bab Tiout, the old mulberry gate. Until the 20th century Tetouan was a walled city ringed to the south and the east by a patchwork of orange groves and mulberry trees for the local silk industry. Then the tightly packed Medina deserved the nickname Hamari il Baidha, the white dove. Just to the right of the Tangier gate is an ornamental fountain built by the 18th-century Lucas governor who reestablished the full extent of city walls levelled by the tyrannical er Riffi Pasha after Tetouan had rebelled against his rule.

Archaeological Museum

This small museum, on the left as you walk from Bab Tangier to the Place Hassan II is an ideal cool and tranquil finish to a tour of Tetouan. It is open from 9.00–12.00, 14.00–18.00 but closed on Tuesdays and holidays.

The shaded, well-kept mature garden with two classical mosaics from Lixus and littered with amphorae, Punic stellae, carved Libyan script and Jewish and Iberian grave stones is the greatest attraction.

The Museum rooms have a very dusty antique smell. In the entrance hall there are two further mosaics, the three Graces with the four seasons in corner medallions and the more animated scene of Bacchus being led in triumph on his mule by two naked supporters. In the first room there is a fine prehistoric rock carving of a bison taken from Smara in the Western Sahara. The model of the **Mzoura stone circle** before the desecration of the excavation may prompt your interest. It is found off the Tetouan to Larache road. The second room has a fine head of Oceanus amongst the bronzes and four further mosaics, two of which star Venus discovering Adonis on your left and being discovered asleep by Mars in her turn. The upstairs has bits and bobs from excavations at Ksar es Seghir, Tamuda and Ad Mercuri and various Punic graves. The large tribal and antiquities map is really more absorbing.

SHOPS
The enclosed fish and vegetable market is right beside the bus station. A fine library is maintained by the Ministry of Culture on Av. Mohammed V. The main bookshop has a good stock of Spanish and French books including Robert Aspinon's initiation into the Berber dialects, written when he was a Lt-Col. des Affaires Musulmans.

WHERE TO STAY
There are a large number of pensions scattered through the town and in particular around the Place Hassan II. Unclassified by the government, their prices and security, though normally reasonable, can be variable. On a first visit to Tetouan the ordered refuge offered by a central and listed hotel can be well worth the extra dirhams.

The ** **Hotel Dersa** is on Rue de Prince Sidi Mohammed, ex Rue General Franco. It is a massive and attractive hotel with an elegant hall beside the large sitting room with a subterranean room decorated in the Imperial opera style which serves as a popular late night bar. The **Dersa** has 74 spacious rooms and a restaurant, the faded grandeur is well worth 99dh for a double room, tel 6721. The * **Hotel National** at 8, Rue Mohammed ben Larbi Torres, tel 3290 is another distinguished and ageing hotel arranged around a cool tiled central courtyard where there is a calm café. A single for 77dh and a double for 89dh, 64 rooms with a bar and restaurant.

If both of these are booked up there are a number of other perfectly adequate places. Try the ** **Omaina** on Av. du 10 Mai which has 37 bedrooms and a restaurant. There is also the ** **Paris** at 11, Rue Chkil Arsalane, tel 6750 and the * **Ragina** at 5, Rue Sidi Mandri, tel 2113 which has 58 rooms and restaurant, a single for 49dh and a double for 72dh. The * **Trebol** at 3, Rue Yacoub el Mansour, tel 2093, is a small, simple and comfortable hotel just above the bus station, a single for 38dh and a double 52dh. The **Hôtel Principe**, which has a downstairs café, is just beyond the Trebol on Av. de la Résistance, a single for 35dh and a double for 48dh.

EATING OUT

The **Zerhoun**, 7 Av Mohammed ben Larbi Torres, tel 6661, is the smartest restaurant in Tetouan with a darkened dining room, green embroidered cushions and low Moorish tables. A complete menu for only 35dh, or you can peck at tapas dishes at the small back bar. Licensed with friendly efficient service and open from 12.00–22.00.

Or try the **Italiano** at 8 Av. Mohammed ben Larbi Torres or the **Saigon** on Rue Mohammed V which has despite its name has a Spanish or Moroccan menu with quick, cheap and largely unexciting food like salads, fish, paella and omelettes. The restaurant **Granada**, a little-known attractively lit place on the triangular Place Al Jala, has a certain charm.

There is also the **Café Moderne** on 1 Pasaje Achaach, between Av. Mohammed V and Av. Mohammed Torres, a busy cheerful cheap local place that serves tagines for 18dh.

The Riff Coast, La Côte des Ghomara

The S606 road from Tetouan to El Jebha is now completed, a thrilling 125 km journey on an exhilarating twisting coastal hill track that passes above desolate cliff-fringed sandy beaches, pebbled bays with beached fishing boats and across the beds of five mountain streams. The farmers and fishermen of the coast are generally welcoming and easy going. 'Business', the kif industry, is much in evidence and smugglers' tales can be heard in every café, though there is none of the hard sell to visitors and outright banditry of the Ketama highlands.

As you first approach the sea, a piste track on your left provides a 20-minute walk to the **Koubba of Sidi Absullam al Bahr**. The tomb has been established on the site of an old trading post and the ruined tell mound contains the foundations of a Punic temple which is still used as a cemetery. A salt marsh estuary extends inland and the white houses of **Martil** can be seen on the opposite bank. A pillbox is now used as an observation post by the customs below the Koubba.

On 13 August, the herds of the Beni Madan tribe used to receive their ritual washing in the sea, surrounded by boats of musicians and dense crowds singing from the shore. The siren Lamna was appealed to for the fertility and protection of the herd. At night the music around the fires was zazuka, an ancient Punic relic now almost completely forgotten.

This pagan ritual was closed down in the early reforming years after Independence and the funds established to preserve the Moussem directed to the founding of a **Koranic school** where shaded with bamboos you can hear children chanting lines of the Koran as the waves break on the beach.

Oued Laou

The road to Oued Laou passes a scattering of villas and the camping Alanana before climbing around a number of small fishing bays and toiling up the surrounding cliffs to provide a dramatic and fascinating 44 km journey to the long beach and fertile open valley of Oued Laou. This village is strung along part of the beach that follows a delightful, wide and empty bay. Fishing boats are beached on the shingle and in summer half a dozen café restaurants open directly on to the beach. The café **Restaurant Hotel Layyoune** is open throughout the year where you can stay for 20dh a night eating fresh fish tagine, vegetables, salads and fruit. **Camping Laou** is open over the summer; the site is a little inland from the beach beside the road.

The octagonal **mosque** has each face encased in different ceramic tiles and vies for your attention with the false castellated **barracks** of the Spanish, which now house the gendarmerie. A feature of the Ghomara coast are the rival twin villages that flank each fertile valley. The eastern Oued Laou has a smart new café and a number of stalls selling well stewed and spiced fish tagines.

2 km beyond the first village a right turn can take you up along a tarmac road to Chechaouen past the **Gorges of Laou**. As you approach the gorge the road follows along a continuous land slip of gravel which falls down to the banks of the cool muddy water of the oued which has polished smooth great grey and white boulders on its river bed. On the other bank an immense golden cliff decorated with occasional remnants of stalactites looms up and hints at a past existence as a subterranean gorge. A hydro scheme further upstream restrains the seasonal excesses of the oued and forms the lake which you pass before joining the P28 some 10 km north of Chechaouen.

Targa

59 km from Tetouan along the coast road is Targa, a striking village of traditional old houses set in the folds of the hills and facing two conspicuous outcrops of venerated black stone. The nearest rock is crowned by a stone fort and both contain whitewashed caves and are associated with some of the lively saint cults of Targa. The old low brick-built **Mosque** was built in the 5th century of Islam and has witnessed frequent reversals of fortune. Andalucian refugees reinforced this port in the 15th century. It was then a large enough corsair base for Diego Copez de Siquira to attack with 70 galleons in 1495, having already raided Targa the previous year when he had captured 300 slaves and sunk 25 small ships.

Now Targa has only one café and a food store to tempt the visitor. The fortifications on the hill are largely the work of the Spanish protectorate and are now used by the Beni Ziat tribe for sorting out the kif harvest. The big Moussem is well worth witnessing if you are staying nearby on 15 July.

Steha and Bou Hamed

Beyond Targa travelling east are a number of cliff-fringed beaches of black sand, tranquil exquisite wastelands. 18 km beyond is the valley of the Oued Bouhia with the two villages of Steha and Bou Hamed, **souk** on Tuesday. Steha is the new administrative centre with an efficient seasonal campsite, a vet and the gendarmerie. Bou Hamed is the old village of the Beni Bouzra tribe with charming fragments of paving and architectural detail from a grander past. **Dar M'Tir** is on the oued of that name from which you get tantalizing views of El Jebha.

El Jebha

Just before El Jebha, which is also known as La pointe des Pecheurs, you cross the Oued Ouringa where it is possible to camp in the summer. The town is a striking blue and white creation of the Spanish, neatly arranged on a grid plan and overlooked by the surrounding forested mountains. The bleak hill to the east is decorated with Spanish defences and the **Koubba of Sidi Yahia el Uardani** which overlooks the harbour, and a charming cliff-fringed turquoise bay on the other side. By negotiating with a fishing boat it is possible to be taken to the bays of **Teknint**, **Si Mektor** or on to **Hamed Saidi**, the central village of the Mestassa tribe. El Jebha is still off the beaten track and it will be presumed that you have come here on business. The gendarmerie faces the harbour, there are a number of cafés, some basic provision shops, a decaying Spanish square, a few fish grills and a garage. Even the bandits, easily recognizable by their leather jackets and large fast cars, are reasonably friendly.

In summer some of the cafés may let roof space or the odd room but otherwise it is the **Petit** or the **Grand Hotel**. The Grand is opposite the harbour to the right of the police station, a first-floor selection of three adjoining rooms packed with beds equipped with some grey blankets and sometimes a bottle of water. The **Petit Hotel** is less comfortable. The **fish souk** is on Tuesday morning, a good day for taxis or lifts in lorries to Tetouan, and a reliable bus leaves at about noon for the 7-hour ride to Tetouan; a less dependable service connects with Chechaouen and Tetouan on alternate days. It is a memorable journey, goats travel with the baggage and farmers clasp baskets of lightly salted fish destined for the hills. The moment the bus has departed sweet smelling smoke from a dozen pipes calm the passengers. The drivers always stop for a refreshing drink at a mountain spring and a snack at Oued Laou.

South of El Jebha

A badly pot-holed tarmac track, the 8500, does at a small risk take you up through a splendid panorama of Riff mountains. The track is narrow and its intense coils, holes and hidden bends demand careful driving on the 61 km climb from sea level to 1500 metres on the Ketama road. On Saturday a **souk** is held at **Es Sebt** and a Monday market at **Souk Tnine d' Uxgan**; both these hamlets are directly along the road.

There are two other piste mountain tracks for the adventurous, one follows the west bank of the Oued Ouringa to reach the Sunday **souk** of **El Had** 8 km before the Ketama road. The other piste route passes through a separate **Es Sebt**, Saturday **souk**, about 10 km from El Jebha and the turning for Tleta Asifane before reemerging at Bab Berred.

Tetouan to Chechaouen

The approach road to Chechaouen from Tetouan is through a growing splendour of mountain scenery. The view over this 60 km journey is the main attraction. Some of the distinctive history of the Ghomara region can be absorbed at a number of minor sites; Tamuda, Zinat, Djebel Alam and the souk of the Beni Hassan.

Tamuda

Leaving west from Tetouan in 4 km you pass the turning for Tangier. Crossing the Oued Martil on the road to Chechaouen the ruins of Tamuda are immediately to your left.

This was a Berber city that was founded under Punic influence in the 3rd century BC but was totally destroyed by the army of the Emperor Claudius during Aedemeon's revolt against Roman rule in 42 BC. The visible walls are not from this period but are the remains of a Roman legionary camp that grew into a town between the 2nd and 5th centuries AD. It was abandoned when the Emperor Honorius withdrew these last forces in the last desperate years of the Western Empire, and the exact site has never been reoccupied.

Zinat

12 km out of Tetouan on your left is the village of **Beni Krich**, the chief market of the Beni Hozmar tribe which is perched below the Gorgue mountain range. The village of Zinat is 5 km further on hanging on the slopes of the mountain to the left of the road. Raisuni was born the son of the village Sherif here in 1871. His family house, which he enlarged into a palace, was built around a cult tree whose health was supposed to relate directly to the strength of this mountain dynasty.

A turning to the west, opposite Zinat, on to the S602 takes you into the reclusive spiritual heartland of the Djeballa.

The Master of Djebel Alam

17 km along the S602 is the Tuesday market of **Tleta des Beni Yder**. The deteriorating road can be followed another 16 km to approach the famous **Koubba of Moulay Abdessalam ben Mchich**. This saint who died in 1188 is venerated throughout Morocco but held in particular regard by the Djeballa tribes. An important Moussem collects here during the summer solstice in July to celebrate. The Sidi taught the chadilisme doctrine, one of the four theological pillars of Islam. Every bridegroom of the Djeballa turns on his marriage day to the mountain and declares, 'I am under the protection of Allah and of thee, O blessed Abd es Salaam Moulay Abdessalam.' He is also known as the master of the Djebel Alam and his descendants, of which there were 16,000 in 1930, are known as the Alamines. He left strict instructions for his burial on the mountain top of Alam, 'for the place where I am buried shall be flat like the earth around, for I am of no greater value than the earth'. To this day no one dares cover his actual grave with a roof. Raisuni, a descendant of the Sidi, swore the tribes of the Djeballa in loyalty to his leadership at a mass oath taken on the mountain top on the night of a full moon.

The Beni Hassan

Back on the main road, the P28, you pass a mountain lake that has been formed by damming the Oued Hajera. The Wednesday market of the Beni Hassan is reached on a 3 km piste track that loops off to the right; the turning is 37 km out of Tetouan on your right.

The tribe of the Beni Hassan still speak the Tamazight Berber dialect unlike the other surrounding Arabic-speaking tribes. They were for long the most powerful and militant tribe of the Ghomara region. They were quick to convert to Islam and served under the

Medaka Street, Chechaouen

first Arab governors of Morocco. They were also quick to revolt and from 740 to 1163 the Beni Hassan were the unconquered champions of the Khajarite heresy. They were finally subdued in a four-year campaign commanded by the Almohad Sultan Abu Yaacoub Youssef.

5 km before Chechaouen there is a turning just before another dammed lake. This is the road that in 44 km takes you down past the Laou Gorge and the Talemboute Hydro dam to the beach of Oued Laou.

Chechaouen/Chaouen/Xaouen

Chechaouen, 'the horns', is one of the most beautiful towns of Morocco and hangs like a crescent from high twin mountains. The Medina, a mass of red tiled roofs, crisp whitewashed walls and elegant architectural details, is a precious 15th-century relic from the Muslim civilization of Andalucia. The cemetery immediately above the town creates a fine contrast between the wilderness of graves and the tightly packed Medina, and surrounded on all points of the compass by the Djeballa mountains this compact town is a popular but still friendly destination.

HISTORY
Chechaouen was founded in 1471 by Sherif Moulay Ali bin Rachid, a descendant of both Idriss II and the patron saint of the Djeballa. He established it as a fortress for the faith, a secure mountain citadel from which to assault the growing power of Portugal which was established in numerous fortresses along the Moroccan coast. Andalucian refugees from the Muslim Kingdom of Granada, which had fallen in 1489, were welcomed and were responsible for the rapid and elegant growth of the town. Strengthened by this skilled influx, Rachid and his heirs were able to extend their rule over the north of Morocco for almost a century. The dynasty, known as the Emirate of Xaouen,

144

Tetouan and Targa was recognized and allied to the Wattasid Sultans of Fez but fell to the new power from the south, the Saadians who conquered the emirate in 1562. The last Emir escaped from the Saadian siege of Chechaouen and died a pilgrim in the holy city of Medina.

After the fall of the Emirate the sense of common purpose forged between the surrounding Berber hill tribes and the skilled Andalucian population of the town was destroyed. The feud between the town and country was started in earnest during a Saadian succession dispute in 1576. From that time the gates of Chechaouen were locked each night, the souk which attracted the local tribes was held below the town walls and the population, isolated in the Djeballa mountains, interbred and brooded in upon itself for centuries. Before the Spanish arrival in 1920 only three Christians had even seen the town, the intrepid French ascetic Charles De Foucauld saw the walls for an hour disguised as a rabbi in 1883, Walter Harris, the flamboyant Tangier-based reporter for *The Times* saw the town in 1889, whilst William Summers, an American missionary, died of poison here in 1892.

On 15 October 1920 Chechaouen was occupied by a Spanish column after token resistance from the town which was then under the command of Raisuni's sixth cousin, thrice removed. The Chechaouen Jews, with little regard for the history of their town, welcomed the Spanish troops as liberators. To the amazement of their conquerors they spoke in the pure accent of 15th-century Andalucia and shouted to the bemused Spanish, 'Viva Isabella', the Castilian queen who had expelled their ancestors from Spain. Three days later another aspect of Spanish civilization arrived—the army whores. They were just in time to witness an attack from the hill tribes who much to the delight of the town were repulsed with heavy casualties by the Spanish.

The advance of Abdel Krim's army during the Riff rising forced the Spanish to withdraw from the town in 1924, in a long bitterly fought retreat to Tetouan that left a trail of 14,000 dead. The Riff soldiers reverently entered the gates of Chechaouen and showed their respect by marching in bare feet. The Spanish army returned in 1926 and finally left in 1956 upon Independence. The Andalucian garden at the centre of Place Mohammed V, the Catholic church and Pepe's bar are their finest memorials. The 500th anniversary of the founding of Chechaouen was celebrated in 1971 with a concert of traditional Andalucian music.

GETTING AROUND
Half a dozen daily buses from Tetouan provide the easiest connection. The coaches for Fez or Meknes which currently leave at 6.30, 11.30 and 12.00, a 6–7 hr ride, are usually fully booked up and it is worth buying tickets well in advance. There are two buses a day for Al Hoceima, an 8 hr ride, which would take you through Ketama, though an equally exhilarating journey is the 7 hr twice weekly bus to El Jebha.

TOURIST INFORMATION
The Tourist Office is just off Place Mohammed V, open sometimes in the summer but of little to no use. The Post Office is on the Av. Hassan II with an English-speaking clerk on the telephone switchboard, and the Banque Populaire is on Av. Hassan II.

The New Town
The circular Andalucian garden, the **Place Mohammed V**, is at the heart of the

Spanish-built new town to the west of the Medina. From the Place the elaborately decorated Av. Hassan II leads to the foot of the Medina. To the left, hidden by the ornate wall, is a cemetery whilst to your right, below the Hotel Magou is the souk area and bus station. You can enter the Medina through the arched gate to the left, the **Bab el Ain**, which will allow you to climb up through the busiest street to arrive at the centre of the Medina, the Place Uta al Hammam. Just before the Bab el Ain you pass on the left the elaborate portal and grotto that guards the richly carved 16th-century **tomb** of one the town's patron saints, **Sidi Ali bin Rashid**.

The Medina

On a first visit or by car and taxi it is easier to reach the Place Uta al Hammam by the Rue Chari Tariq Ibnou Ziad, the continuation of Av. Hassan II that climbs uphill around the Medina walls.

Pl El Makhzen

The Place El Makhzen is the small open area in front of the Chaouen-Parador Hotel where taxis and cars can park. From here the tower of the **Kasbah** can be seen to your left and the central square at the heart of the Medina, the Uta al Hammam opens out before you. Pass a couple of stalls selling minerals and fossils to enter this delightful cobbled area surrounded by cafés and the cheaper pensions.

Uta al Hammam

The cafés that line the Uta al Hammam, the 'flat place of the baths', are equipped with perforated tin cones to protect the sweet mint tea from the local vociferous and determined bees. The various types of honey from the mountains provide an almost complete pharmacy, the honey produced from bees feeding on a red button berry is a cure for diabetes. Franco throughout his life was constantly supplied with marjoram honey from Chechaouen. The upper rooms of the cafés are frequented by kif smokers, the odd hippy and students studying in the shade. A few boys sell cannabis resin to visitors but the locals prefer to smoke the cut and dried leaves. The experienced kif smoker dips his long wooden pipe into a leather pouch, packs the herb tightly into the small clay head and takes three puffs before blowing the glowing residue out on to the floor with accustomed skill and ease. On the Uta al Hammam square, at no 34 is a fondouq used on souk days by farmers for their donkeys and mules, whilst the first floor is reserved for men. Behind Lehsen's café and in front of the Castellane pension is the 15th century **Hammam**, a Moorish bath which male tourists are welcome to use.

Slave boys were still being openly sold in the Medina markets of Chechouan until 1937 and the hill tribes of the Djeballa have always been open about their sexual affairs. E. Westermark, who collected local proverbs from these hills from 1910 to 1930, records that intercourse for three days in succession with an ass was then considered a cure for gonorrhea, with a black dog as a permanent safeguard against imprisonment, whilst boys abused she asses in order to make their penis grow. The nearest one can get to a moral comment is, 'Nakeh z-zwamel kaiwarrat d-damel', 'Intercourse with boy prostitutes produces boils.'

Grand Mosque

Opposite the cafés is the Grand Mosque, easily recognizable with its octagonal minaret.

This was one of the first buildings erected by the Sherif Ali bin Rashid though it has since been restored in the 17th and 18th centuries. Next door you can notice the smaller portal of a 16th-century **medersa** which was founded by the last Emir of Chechaouen, but is currently not open to visitors.

The alley that separates the Mosque from the Kasbah leads down to a zaouia and school where the Sitt al Hamra is buried, the Emir's daughter who ruled the corsairs of Tetouan for 33 years.

The Kasbah
The conspicuous **Tower of Homage** was restored by Moulay Ishmael. The interior contains a pleasant pattern of cobbles and gardens, certain chambers are being restored, the dungeons can be visited. In the northwest corner a 15th-century tunnel used to lead out of the walls to the site of the present Parador Hotel. The last Emir used this route to escape from the Saadian siege in 1562.

The Medina
The Medina is small and friendly enough for you to explore leisurely at your own pace from the Uta al Hammam. It provides an endless range of fascinating vistas with a high accent on individual decoration. The high pitched red tile roofs are an architectural memory of Granada where the roofs had to be capable of supporting a heavy fall of snow. The houses also retain the Andalucian motif of horseshoe double windows, shielded by eyebrows of ceramic tiles and protected and decorated by twisted metal grilles. The walls of the houses are painted with contrasting shades of electric blue and pure whitewash which flows out to demarcate part of the alley.

Elaborate fountains play, the smell of fresh bread wafts from a local bakery, artisans ask you in for a smoke and to admire their work, whilst areas of pebble and stone mosaic reflect and complement the traditional and intricately carved wooden window frames.

The Walls
The walls are best appreciated by walking in the cemetery, above the town. Here the bodies of two Riffi officers, Mohammed M'Kram and Sherif Wafi Quera were buried on the night of Aid el Kebir; they were part of the junta of 72 officers who had attempted a coup against the king.

With the aid of a guide it is easy to identify the **Bab Mamluk**, the mountain gate, surrounded by 500-year-old olive trees. The **Bab es Souk** is the only gate that retains its architectural decoration, and through it General Berenguer formally entered the town; he was then made Count of Chaouen by Alfonso XIII.

MARKETS AND FESTIVALS
The town has two market days, on Monday and Thursday with extended groups of vegetable stalls in the courtyards below the Hotel Magou. The main shopping thorough-fare for woollen cloth, carpets and worked leather is the street that leads downhill from the Uta el Hammam to Av. Hassan II. Chechaouen is nationally famous for its looms which weave from mountain wool the striped Riff cloth, jillabas and blankets. Threads spun by the tailors' apprentices crisscross the narrow streets in an endless game of cat's cradle.

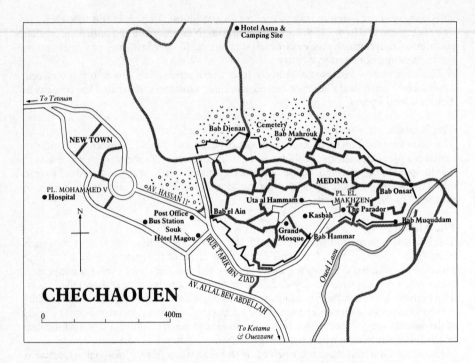

CHECHAOUEN

0   400m

Chechaouen nurtures a long memory and a number of saints' tombs. The biggest and most accessible Moussem is that of Sidi Alla el Hadj held on 9 August.

WHERE TO STAY

Chechaouen is a small but popular destination and as beds can be in short supply, most of the town's hotels are listed below. The **** **Asmah Hotel** looks an unforgivable intrusion on the historic skyline of the town. The architect and the interior designer should certainly feel ashamed, but the hotel does in fact occupy the exact site of the old Husu Abdul Hamid fort. It has a pool, efficient plumbing and a magnificent view of the town. A double costs 168dh.

*** **Hôtel de Chaouen**, tel 6136, is the old Spanish parador with a pool, bar, restaurant, 37 bedrooms and the best position in town. The Mosque on the hill opposite is a folly built by the Spaniards to add a final touch to the view. The one two-star hotel in town is the **Magou** at 23 Rue Moulay Idriss, tel 6275. Just above the souk and below the Medina, it is a comfortable but unexceptional place; 68dh for a single room, a double for 85dh.

* **Hôtel Rif**, 29 Rue Tarik Ibn Ziad, is run by the genial Ihaddouchin Mustapha who covers the furniture of his hotel with his own painted floral designs. A very hospitable relaxed place, a double for 46dh, a single for 25dh, a three-course dinner for 30dh, breakfast 8dh, 22 bedrooms. * **Hôtel Hibiza**, tel 6323, and * **Hôtel Salam**, 39, Rue Tarik Ibn Ziad, tel 6239, single 35dh, double 46dh are fine if everywhere else is full up.

148

The Medina pensions are intimate popular places to stay throughout the year, much beloved by backpacking European students. They are all easily found in the streets around the Uta al Hammam and in the rare event of no helping guide at hand they are well signposted. You may have to try them all before finding a room; ask for **Pension Rachidia, Pension Barouta. Pension Mauritania** is at 20 Rue Kadi Alami, tel 6184, 10dh a bed in communal dormitories awash with music and international camaraderie. **Pension Andaluz** at 1, Rue Sidi Salem, tel 6034, has clean individual rooms for 15dh a bed. **Pension Castelliana**, 4 Rue Sidi Ahmed Bouhali, tel 6295, just off the square charges 10dh a bed and is next door to the male Hammam.

EATING OUT
For a formal meal you will have to go to either the **Hôtel Asma, Parador** or **Magou**. The **Restaurant Kasba** is perhaps the best of the number of grill cafés on the Uta al Hammam. **Restaurant-Bar Omo Rabi**, tel 6180, next door to the travel agent on Rue Tarik Ibn Ziad, is licensed to sell beer and wine and a complete menu here comes for 30dh. There is also the **Restaurant Azkhar** by the Post Office on Av. Hassan II which has music, disorder and tagines for only 10dh.

SWIMMING AND WALKING
The stream that supplies the town with excellent cool clear water, the Ras al Ma, flows down from the high valley between the Djebel Meggou, 1616 m and Djebel Tisouka, 2050 m, the two horns of Chechaouen.

A spacious shaded café with crumbling terraces sits beside a collecting pool which can be reached by walking uphill through Medina streets from the righthand corner of the Place el Makhzen. Nearby is the **tomb of Sidi Abdallh Habti** who died in 1555.

A scrambling walk allows you to follow the stream uphill for 3 km to its source, where it emerges through the rocks. This has been traced back through numerous caves and reportedly snakes some 4 km underground to the east. The horizon of mountains from the source is fringed with cedars. Walks up the surrounding mountains may allow you to see or meet hyenas, wild boars, red cobras, golden eagles, kites, buzzards, Barbary apes and partridges. Alternatively you can join the piste track that leads back to the town via the Asma Hotel, providing you with excellent birds-eye views of the Medina.

The **Oued Laou** has a number of swimable pools and running beside the main P28 road it is easily accessible by taxi or car. Alternatively take the road to the coast, a 42 km drive that passes the Oued Laou gorge before reaching the coastal fishing village of Oued Laou, see page 140.

Chechaouen to Ouezzane

A journey of 60 km on a twisting mountain road, the P28 takes you through the heart of the Djeballa hill country. The crossing of the Oued Loukkos provides a good excuse for a stop. The old Franco-Spanish frontier post just by the bridge has been converted into a covered roadside **souk** busy with grill cafés, and a waterfall on the right provides a pleasant cool picnic site. Beside the road are a number of decorated fountains, originally established for mule trains but are now occasionally used for overnight parking by camper vans. On Saturday morning there is a **souk** just to the west of the road at **Es Sebt** which could be worth a visit.

Ouezzane

The view from the Medina of Ouezzane, particularly in the morning light, is of lines of receding wooded hills which seem to grow in strength towards the ascending horizon to the north. Their olive green slopes are gradually transmuted to blue and the final crest of mountains tipped white by snow from December to March.

The town has kept its aura of a highland sanctuary, it has expanded on either side of the old Medina to retain its form, that of a half moon that hugs the slopes of Djebel Bou Hellal. There are delightfully few concessions to the tourist in Ouezzane, it remains a calmly prosperous provincial town famous for its olive oil and its holy dynasty of Sherifs. If you can arrive here on Thursday morning you will find Ouezzane full of mountain farmers drawn to the busy **souk** and the artisan shops in the Medina at their busiest and most accessible.

History

Ouezzane for all its venerable attitude is entirely a creation of the 18th century. The distinguished Idrissid Sherif Moulay Abdullah ben Brahim settled here in 1727 and established a Taibia Sufi brotherhood. Before his arrival Ouezzane was known as Dechra Djebel er-Rihan, the village on the mountain of myrtles. The Sherif gave moral direction to the tribes and instructed them in the Sufi mysticism of the Taibia. His prestige as the heir of one of the senior lines of descent from Idriss II and hence from the Prophet, the spread of the Taibia brotherhood throughout the whole of North Africa and the lack of a strong government in this period catapulted the Sherif and his heirs into a position of great influence.

By the early 19th century the Sherifs of Ouezzane enjoyed the respect of all the tribes of the Riff and the Djebala. Typically it was the family of the Sherif, not the Sultan, that led the hill tribes to the defence of Tetouan during the Spanish invasion of 1859. In the maze of bitter tribal rivalries their impartial arbitration and declarations of peace were of great value. Many tribes voluntarily contributed a tithe in order to share the Baraka, the blessing or holy luck of the Sherifs. The Sherifs used these gifts to feed travellers, protect widows and orphans and act as a patron to craftsmen, students and scholars. The Sultan in Fez governed through requests to the Sherifs and employed members of his family in high positions at their court. The proud boast of Ouezzane was, 'No Sultan for us, without us no Sultan.'

This strong position of sanctity and authority also encouraged a streak of hereditary madness. One Sherif often mistook pilgrims for hares and shot at the new arrivals from the terrace of the sanctuary. This was considered a great honour but guards were discreetly posted to discourage the devout who imagined that death at the hands of the Sherif would guarantee a place in heaven.

Sherif Si Absellam caused great scandal at the end of the 19th century by divorcing his three wives to marry an English girl, Emily Keene, who he had met riding outside Tangier. His wife, far from converting to Islam, insisted on an Anglican marriage. The Sherif explained his wife's difficult religious attitude to his relations with a parable. He would pour sugar on the floor and watch ants arrive from each corner. All have attained the mountain and achieved sweetness. Such is the case with Muslims, Jews and Christians in their search for the one God.

This kind tolerant man eventually fell victim to his family's madness; he developed a paranoid fear of assassination and a craving for alcohol (good Muslims claimed that champagne turned to milk in his mouth), but also fell under the damaging influence of the French consul Ordega. He used the Sherif as a front to acquire vast land holdings and mineral rights for the French Companie Maroccaine. Within a few decades the Ouezzane family had lost most of its power and influence though they retained great status throughout the French protectorate. The present line of Sherifs are descended from the children of Emily and Si.

GETTING AROUND

The large triangular space at the foot of the Medina, the Place de L'Indépendance is the heart of the town, where the Thursday **souk** assembles. All three roads to Ouezzane naturally lead to the Place, where you find hotels, cafés and a Bank Populaire. To the east of the Place is the small stalled square, the Place du Marché, whilst the Av. Mohammed V leads out to the west. The bus station is just below the Place on the Rue de la Marché Verte.

Ouezzane is 60 km south of Chechaouen and 135 km north of Meknes. There are half a dozen daily buses that stop at Ouezzane on the regular Chechaouen to Fez and Meknes runs. On Thursdays in particular there are any number of places available in grands taxis for Chechaouen, Meknes, Fez and west to Souk el Arba.

WHAT TO SEE

The old **Medina** climbs uphill from the Place de l'Indépendence. An enchanting intriguing network of cobbled streets, shop fronts, arched buttresses and aged town houses decorated with tiled eaves which it is easy and entertaining to explore.

Ouezzane is a provincial town and remains a craft and marketing centre for the hinterland of surrounding mountain villages. It has few tourist-oriented bazaars, and retains a profusion of artisan stalls—all the usual crafts, weavers' looms, tailors, cobblers and smiths but with a local speciality in painted furniture.

From the Place turn left past the Grand Hotel café to climb up the Rue Abdellah ben Lamlih which leads to the centre of the souks, the triangular Place Bir Inzarane. Take the left turn, the Rue Haddadine, to turn under the Mosque of Moulay Abdullah Cherif opposite which is the covered **souk of smiths**. Here you can find the Café Bellevue, its stone pillars now enlivened by an unmissable layer of gay new paint. It has a wonderful uncommercial atmosphere and a fine view of the folding landscape of mountains from its high terrace. Immediately below the café the blacksmiths create a soothing pattern of hammer blows.

Continue on, keeping right and passing through an arch you walk into the broad Rue de la Zaouia. This internal space is dominated by the octagonal minaret of the **Mosque of the Taibia brotherhood**, built by Moulay Ali Sherif; it has a wistful appeal, the fading green faience tiles enclosed by a bas relief of intricate stone arches is graceful even in decay. The surrounding buildings, old pilgrim lodgings and apartments, are deteriorating at a faster rate, the formal gates to the Sherifian palace look particularly precarious. The towers of the old sanctuary palace are often used by nesting hawks who teach their young to kill above the confused roof tops of the Medina.

The town's reputation for skilled craft work is reflected in two state-run **Artisanal Houses**, open from 8.00–19.00. One faces the Place de L'Indépendence and the other is on the Av. Hassan II, the Fez road, just before the Lalla Amina square. The municipal **swimming pool**, open in the summer months, is in the corner of the sports area also on the right of Av. Hassan II.

Out of Ouezzane

Djebel Bou Hammal provides a fabulous view of the town and the mountainous country from its summit of 609 m. You can walk up through the Medina alleys and out through the olive groves or drive. Travelling in your own vehicle or taxi, take the road for Fez and turn right 50 m after the public gardens and modern church for the climb up the mountain slope. A viewing platform is found about 400 m on from the end of the tarmac.

To the east of Ouezzane, on the P23, a turning to the right, the 2365, will take you 9 km to the village of **Azjen**. Here is buried the celebrated 18th-century Jewish rabbi, Amrane, famous for his arcane knowledge and magical powers.

WHERE TO STAY AND EAT
There are no officially classified hotels in Ouezzane but it is easy to find a bed in one of the half dozen small unpretentious places that are grouped below the conspicuous square clock tower on the Place de L'Indépendence. The **Marhaba**, the **Horloge** and **El Elam** all have one or two rooms with balconies over the Place for 30–40dh a single, 50–60dh a double. If these are full there is also the **Grand Hotel**, in name only, and the **Hôtel de Poste**, just off the Place on Av. Mohammed V. Opposite the Poste is a Hammam associated with the Mosque which travellers are welcome to use.

The Place holds practically all the café-restaurants in town which offer the ubiquitous menu of fresh salads, kebabs and brochettes. Eat early as most of the cafés close early in a town ungeared to tourist requirements.

West from Ouezzane

The Tangier–Rabat road is 45 km west from Ouezzane, a pleasant if unexceptional drive through undulating hill country. 33 km along this road, the P23, a small village of corrugated iron roofed farms enveloped in their individual hedges of prickly pear is encircled by an extent of standing stone and towered walls.

These once enclosed the great city of **Basra** founded at the same time as Fez, at the end of the 9th century by Idriss II. It alternated like most Moroccan cities in contrasting cycles of prosperity and disaster. The walls were acquired in the 10th century though they failed in the 16th century to preserve Basra, already in decline, from final destruction from the alternating evils of the Portuguese cavalry and aggressive hill tribes.

South from Ouezzane

There are two routes south. The P28 road is the quicker direct route, favoured by buses and taxis travelling to Fez or Meknes. The P26 is longer and slower but potentially much more interesting but is badly served by public transport.

To Fez or Meknes on the P28

The first 30 km south to Meknes is through the steadily decreasing grandeur of the hills of the Djeballa. The small market town of **Ain Defali**, which has a **souk** on Wednesday, marks the end of the lawless highlands and the beginning of the easily ruled flat fertile river plains. Bridges cross the slow flowing Oued Ouerrha and then the Oued Sebou. For the tireless souk watcher there is a right turning to the agricultural market of **Khenichet**, a 15 km drive on the S223, 51 km from Ouezzane, or a right turn on a 6 km piste track to **souk el Had des Tekna**, **souk** on Sunday, 3 km after the bridge over the Oued Sebou. 84 km from Ouezzane you reach a major road junction; the P3 leads directly to Fez whilst a route to Meknes, the P28, takes you past the classical ruins of Volublis and the holy city of Moulay Idriss (see page 289).

To Fez on the P26

This route passes through the dramatic scenery of a highland border zone to descend due north of the city of Fez. There are isolated village souks to visit and a selection of mountains to climb with a series of wonderfully rewarding views. There are no hotels in this area, so it is most easily explored by car or taxi from Fez or Ouezzane.

The turning 3 km out of Ouezzane on to the P26 spins off into a twisting series of descents and climbs. The 6 km piste track to the Koubba and Saturday **souk of Sidi Redouane** are some 24 km later on the right. Just past this turning the road swings around a mountain of only 335 m which does however enjoy a fine view north to the looming peak of Djebel Issoua in the land of the Riff Beni Zeroual tribe. The Tuesday **souk of the Beni Mezguilda** tribe is 48 km from Ouezzane just off the road to the left.

Djebel Ouriaghel

In order to climb the heights of Djebel Ouriaghel some preparation is required. Take the left turn on the 4207 and at the village of El Khemis hire a mule for the three-hour ride, about 15 km, through the remote settlement of Kissane to the foot of the mountain. Its summit is crowned by an old French frontier fort, known as **El Bibane**, which was over run in 1925 when Abdel Krim launched his Riff battalions against the French protectorate; his attack got within 25 km of liberating Fez.

Fes el Bali

Just after this turning, on a hill to the right, beside the main road about 70 km from Ouezzane is the sprawling farming settlement of **Fes el Bali**, Fes the old. This was an 11th-century Almoravide foundation which established an urban centre for the Beni Taouda and a military post for the war being fought further north against the Khajarite heretics on the Ghomara coast. Sections of the red pise walls can still be traced amongst the village paddocks and one of the farm boys may show you the surviving Almoravide **Hammam**, a remarkably Roman-looking rectangular building decorated with marble and a fountain. The proud city of the Taouda tribe did not survive long after their Almoravide patrons fell from power. Their old tribal enemies on the Ghomara coast fell upon the town and slaughtered all the inhabitants.

Lalla Outka

5 km east a turning to the left, the S304 takes you twice across the Oued Ourreha in a 18 km drive to the village of **Ourtzarh** positioned by the junction of two rivers and overlooked by the heights of **Djebel Messaoud**, 835 m. This mountain is accessible for climbing by following the piste track a few km towards **El Kelaa des Sles**, a right turn just after the second bridge.

The view from the summit of Lalla Outka, 1595 m, about 40 km north is even finer, offering perhaps the most extensive and famous view of the Riff mountains. Just before the bridge across to Ourtzah a tarmac road leads 14 km north to **Rafsai**, a centre for olive cultivation that celebrates the harvest every year with an olive Moussem in December. From Rafsai, also known as Ghafsai, a good piste track climbs 37 km past the Sunday **souk of El Had** and the village of **Tamesnite**. From Tamesnite the track, passable only in summer, gets considerably more exciting but the prospect from the summit is considerably more breathtaking than the drive.

The view northwest from the summit partly overlooks the reclusive territory of the Beni Ahmed tribe. They were believed by many, including Raisuni, 'to have a secret city, so hidden that none may ever see it, and marvellous parchments written in a strange language . . . it may be that there is something, for there are Ulema among the Beni Ahmed who did not learn their wisdom at the schools.' A linguist investigated these persistent rumours after the war, but he cut short his work after his female informant quickly died in a shooting accident.

Djebel Amergou

81 km from Ouezzane on the road to Fez is the small roadside village of **Et Tnine**, a minor **souk** of the Fichtala tribe. The **shrine and zaouia of Moulay Bouchta** is only 1 km away up a track to the right of the road. This saint and his equally venerated daughter Aicha are appealed to for rain in the frequent periods of drought. This genial intercessor with Allah is also the patron for local singers and musicians who assemble here in late September to honour their saint in the lively Moussem of Moulay Bouchta.

Overlooking the shrine is the outcrop of Djebel Amergou, a mountain 681 m high whose summit is crowned with a rare surviving Almoravide fortress. On the hour and a half walk to the peak you pass through a secluded mountain top village, an idyllic thatched cluster of houses with a mosque and a mountain spring. The **Kasbah of Amergou** is in surprisingly good condition, the stone perimeter wall studded with a dozen towers is complete and even the arched entrance gate still survives. The interior is divided by a central keep into two extensive courts, the eastern half retains its plastered water tanks. The extent of this great ancient fortress is made doubly memorable by its position on the peak of a mountain that overlooks the Ouerrha valley far below to the north. The Kasbah of Amergou was built in the 11th century, as the military citadel for Fes el Bali. Its solid uncompromising structure recalls the other Almoravide fortress ruin far to the south on the edge of the Sahara at Zagora.

On the climb back from the deserted Kasbah you may notice a cave. Recalling Leonardo da Vinci's analysis of the conflicting emotions, 'and after having remained at the entry some time, two contrary emotions arose in me, fear and desire—fear of the threatening dark grotto, desire to see whether there were any marvellous thing within it', some years ago I entered this fly filled cave to quickly smell and then see the blood stained clothes that surrounded a pair of fast decaying corpses. Not more than fifty yards from the cave entrance a limping mountain shepherd offered to share his meal with me. This was finished with a glass of mint tea that was fetched by his infant daughter on a fine engraved tray from a distant hut. The noble hospitality of Morocco contrasted strongly against evidence of some recent act of violence, as if some goddess had offered two aspects of true self to a bewildered worshipper.

A further 16 km to the south the hills give way to the fields of the Sebou valley. The Tuesday **souk of Karia Ba Mohammed**, 7 km along a tarmac road on your right attracts a number of hill tribes, the Ouled Aissa, the Cheraga and the Ouled Hajoua to its market. Another souk is also held on Saturday at **souk es Sebt**, 17 km south of the bridge over the Oued Sebou. The land rises again after this market into the rounded hillscape of Lemta, which in the green of spring is like some immense improved version of the Downs. It is these calciferous hills that surround the northern walls of the city of Fez. 10 km before you reach Fez a piste turning to the left leads 4 km to the foot of **Djebel Zalagh**, 902 m high, that offers a splendid introductory panorama of the city. 4 km before this turning you will have passed the 19th century **Koubba of Sidi Ahmed el Bernoussi**, who was a disciple of Sidi Harazem in the 12th century. Sidi Ahmed retired to live a hermit's life of poverty and contemplation in these hills. He is counted among the host of saints who protect Fez, and his Moussem in September is a popular event.

The Riff Mountains; Chechaouen to Ketama

Bab Taza

8 km south of Chechaouen the road crosses the Oued Laou and there are turnings for Tetouan, Ouezzane and Ketama. This crossroad is a favourite police check point for those returning from Ketama. The road east to Ketama climbs through scrubby wood-land for the 15 km to the col de Bab Taza at 1675 m. The village of Bab Taza which has a ruined Spanish fort and a café restaurant marks the edge of the Ketama region. After the village the road follows the mountain crests and exposes you to an intermittent line of kif salesmen. Small boys will hiss 'Shit' and perform a crumbling mime with their thumb and fingers or a smoker's drag anywhere along the next 135 km of road.

Cheferat

Cheferat, 15 km east of Bab Taza, has for half the year a spectacular cleft spring. Cold mountain water rushes spouting out from the cliff as if Moses had just tapped the rock with his staff. The water is channelled into fast-flowing channels and spun around an intriguing central corkscrew whirlpool to draw the water under itself and pass onto another level. To the right of the road are two cafés which serve good snack lunches.

Bab Berred

Before the town of Bab Berred you pass below the disturbed foothills, scree slopes and cavern-strewn face of **Djebel Tisserine**. There is a basic **café Hotel** at Bab Berred which you might conceivably need to stay at for it is not until you enter the cedar forests beyond the Bab Besen pass that you enter the area of really aggressive salesmanship. Cars are frequently sandwiched by vans on this exhilarating mountain top drive to enable great lumps of marijuana resin to be offered for sale. Headlights flash from woodland clearings and urgent hand signals insist that you stop. Do not be tempted to dawdle in admiration of the mountains and the cedar forests. Stop for no one, however innocent the situation appears to be; travellers' tales of extortion, theft and enforced sales of kilos of marijuana are true and common enough.

Ketama

After the thrill of the mountain scenery and the heady aroma of bandit country the little roadside junction village of Ketama is slightly disappointing. Large gendarmerie barracks line the approaches and pine woods enclose the few buildings. The cone shaped mass of **Djebel Tidirhine**, 2,448 m high to the east dominates the horizon, its peak capped in snow throughout much of the year. It is the sacred mountain of the Riff where bulls were and may still be sacrificed on the summer and winter solstices. Noah by local tradition landed the Ark on this peak.

Ketama was a popular hill walking and langlauffing station during the protectorate. It is no longer a resort but an internationally recognized market place for marijuana. This grows naturally throughout Morocco but the hill farmers of the Riff specialize in the cultivation of this cash crop in their high isolated valleys. The terrain and the tradition of tribal dissidence are remarkably similar to the other great marijuana producing areas: Lebanon, Afghanistan and Mexico. Harvested in the summer, the pollen is extracted by beating the plants in gauze-lined huts. The sticky residue is hand compacted into the resin blocks for the export trade. The flower heads and leaves are too bulky for smuggling and are the preferred local smoking material in the ubiquitous kif pipes of northern Morocco.

The distribution, sales and smuggling to Europe are handled by rival gangs whose activities are broadly tolerated by a government fully aware of the region's poverty and explosive history. It is so influential and rewarding a trade that the word 'business' is now in the Riff synonymous for kif. An outsider attempting to enter into this competitive market will inevitably be sold by the dealers to their friends in the customs, police or gendarmerie. Despite this, about a dozen British a year try schemes involving light planes, frogmen, yachts and crosscountry marches. The jail sentences, served in Morocco, follow a rough tariff on quantity, currently ranging from 6 months for a kilo to 5 years for a plane load.

This all gives a certain prurient vicarious excitement to the first hour in Ketama. It is unadventurous but wise to refuse politely any invitations to visit a neighbouring farm. Throughout your stay you will be ceaselessly offered enormous quantities at bargain prices, a strict no smoking policy will allow you to keep your judgement unimpaired.

If Ketama sounds undesirable it remains useful as a bus connection and has the one efficient hotel between Chechaouen and Hoceima.

WHERE TO STAY
The Maroc-Tourist run the **** **Hotel Tidighine**, the one sanctuary from business in Ketama. This has a tennis court, swimming pool, a bar and restaurant with 68 largely

empty and unused bedrooms. A single is 166dh and a double 210dh. The porter will nod his head in sadness at your innocence if you ask for a mountain guide.

Otherwise the unclassified **Café-Hotel Saada** or the **California** on the road to Fez can offer a room for 50dh a night.

The Route de L'Unité

The road south to Fez, the S302 or the route de L'Unité, is one of the most exhaustingly dramatic and thrilling mountain roads in Morocco. It was cut out of the mountains in the first heady years of Independence, linking the Spanish protectorate of the northern coast to central Morocco. Voluntary labour battalions mixed the hill tribes and city dwellers in units that absorbed potential dissidents and allowed education in the new nationalism and Islamic reform.

9 km out of Ketama is **Tleta Ketama**, a hamlet with a few cafés and a small **souk** on Tuesday. The piste track that runs around the slopes of Djebel Tidirhine is 500 metres south of Tleta on the left. This will still leave the intrepid with a good climb for the magnificent views from the summit. The track continues on to Zerkat on the S606 to Targuist.

Passing through wooded hills, forested slopes and pretty waterfalls you receive the first of a succession of magnificent mountain panoramas 10 km south of Tleta Ketama. Possibly the most dramatic portion of the trip is after the Sunday market, the **Souk el Had**, of the Iknaouen tribe, though the drama extends for the 40 km down to Taounate, a large new town built at 600 m above a fertile valley watered by the Oued Sra. **Taounate** has a souk on Friday and a Moussem in September if you care to stop.

From Taounate to Fez, 90 km, the rolling hills inevitably suffer in comparison to the Riffs. A possible detour half way would be the left turn to **Tissa** on the S318, where there is a large Moussem in August to the tomb of the 15th-century saint Sidi Mohammed ben Lahcen. In October there is a horse fair, a perfect time to see fantasias performed away from tourist tents.

50 km south of Tissa is the village of **Ain Kansara** one of the ring of springs that surround Fez. The remains of a medieval caravanserai can be seen, 26 km from Fez, the first staging post on the road to the port of Badis. Just before joining the P1, the Taza road, you cross over the Oued Sebou on Moulay Rachid's bridge, an eight-arched affair built on the first Alouite Sultan's orders in 1670. Fez now beckons less than 9 km away.

East of Ketama

After the cedar forests of Ketama the land grows barren. The eastern hills of the Riff are stark rounded slopes stained with shades of red. The soil looks dangerously leached and the slopes are bare of any woods. The houses are square blocks set alone without any benefit of garden or shade-providing trees in the hard-worked ground. Even in the brief spring the land does not seem to bloom as in the rest of Morocco. The Riff breeds heroes not flowers. The fields are constantly being cleared of stones and feuds in this landscape begin to look like a form of relaxation.

12 km east of Ketama is the left turn that can take you down a rough tarmac road, the 8500, 60 km to El Jebha. It is an exhilarating twisting drive which you take at some risk to your sump. There is a mechanic at El Jebha, the nearest tow trucks are in Tetouan.

Torres de Alcala

37 km east of Ketama a left turn, the 8501, takes you 30 km down to the coast through the territory of the Beni Bu Frah tribe. The village of **Beni Boufrah**, 5 km inland from the sea, has two shops and a Post Office with a telephone. Torres de Alcala is a small whitewashed village beside a river a few 100 m inland from the coast. A track leads to a pebble beach with its three fishermen's huts, beached boats and a single basic café. On a hill above the remaining towers of a fortress survey the emptiness and serenity.

Badis and Penon de Velez de la Gomera

From Torres de Alcala a bad piste road travels east to the site of the old Muslim port of Badis which faces Penon de Velez de la Gomera, a tiny island still in the possession of Spain. The Penon is just visible without travelling along this road. It can be recognized by a white tower that crowns this improbably steep island. It is so overshadowed by the surrounding folds of the mainland mountain of Boklayas that it takes time to separate it out from the background. It appears so hopelessly quixotic, so outrageously useless a possession that it hardly figures as an insult to Moroccan sovereignty but more of a glorious Spanish absurdity.

Badis was in the Middle Ages one of the principal trading ports for Fez. The installation of the Spanish in the island in 1508 began a rapid decline in trade. Velez was recaptured from the Spanish in 1522 by an alliance of local tribes and Turks led by Bou Hassoun, a Wattasid prince. Bou Hassoun invited his Turkish allies to use Badis as a corsair port from where a number of raids were launched on the Spanish coast. Encouraged by his success, Bou Hassoun led an army from Badis in an attempt to reclaim the Wattasid throne from the Saadians in 1554. He was welcomed into the city of Fez but having reestablished a Wattasid court he died shortly afterwards in battle against the Saadians.

The victorious Saadian Sultan Moulay Abdullah was then more alarmed at the Turkish corsair fleet in Badis than at the power of Spain. He secretly betrayed Badis to Phillip II who destroyed the port for ever in 1564. The Spanish still garrison the Penon opposite, and during the protectorate used it as a secure prison.

Kalah Iris

Kalah Iris is 4 km to the west of Torres de Alcala. It is a stunningly beautiful length of beach broken by a central spit that connects an island to the shore where the fishermen moor their boats. Another island sits offshore and the whole area is sealed from the hinterland by enclosing cliffs. A charming campsite is run by Ahmed Hmeddach, planted with mimosas and open throughout the year. A fish restaurant functions during part of the summer and a café throughout the year, providing the generator is in action. Each year there seem to be fewer visitors to this picturesque tranquil beach; a bungalow can be rented for 80dh, camping costs 15dh a night.

Targuist

42 km east of Ketama on the P39 road a turning leads down to the town of Targuist. The chief attraction of the town is that it is just beyond the influence of the kif bandits of

Ketama and makes the first satisfactory stop for a quiet exploration of Riff mountain life. The surrounding plateau of Ghis is over 1000 m and is cultivated with groves of olives, almonds and walnuts. Targuist has a **souk** on Saturday, though the café restaurants are open and busy throughout the week. It is a strong regular featured town which is proud to be have been the last refuge of Abdel Krim before he surrendered to the French forces in 1926. There are a number of cheap basic hotels in the centre. The cheapest, providing you don't mind sharing your washing water with other guests from an old oil barrel, is the **Hotel Chaab** at 14, Calle Hassan II, which charges 5dh a night. A Hammam for washing can be found just off the central roundabout, the Calle Sahat Rifal.

Al Hoceima

65 km from Targuist is **Youssef ou Ali**, the old chief village of the Beni Ouriaghel tribe and home of Abdel Krim. From here a road leads straight down to the coastal town of Al Hoceima.

White houses cascade down the hill with few architectural embellishments to form neat long avenues that reach down but never manage to overlook the bay. The small attractive but well-populated area of beach is confined by two surrounding massive sea cliffs and the **Maroc Tourist Hotel** takes up the area of falling ground that connects town to beach. The Place du Riff is the main centre of town life, lined with cheap cafés and hotels. A small fishing port is to the west and a camping beach to the east. The massive central block of the old Spanish residency has now usefully been transformed into a school and cultural centre.

Al Hoceima was built by the Spanish in 1926 immediately after they had suppressed the Riff rebellion. It was known for the first thirty years of its existence, until Independence, as Villa Sanjurjo. It was deliberately sited in the midst of the Beni Ouriaghel lands so that the Spanish garrison and administrators could keep a strong hold over the leading tribe of the Riff rebellion. It is now a confident, leisured city, housing a military garrison but has little immediate reference to the harsh mountain hinterland. The people have however a charm and social ease that makes Al Hoceima a pleasant stop; it is a hospitable town, even the mosque doors are set wide open and the streets are largely hassle free.

TOURIST INFORMATION
The helpful Tourist Office, ready with leaflets, a town map and lists of pensions and local souks is now on Tario Ibn Zeyyad, open 8.30–12.00, 14.00–18.00. There is a Banque Populaire at 47, Av. Mohammed V. The town **souk** is held on Tuesday. Buses leave from Place du Riff, west for Tetouan via Chechaouen at 13.30 and 21.00, a 10-hour trip for 37dh, and east to Nador at 13.00, a 5-hour trip for 19dh.

The beaches and the Penon

To the east of Hoceima is the relatively fertile bay of **Alhumecas** fed by the Oued Rhis and Nekor. The beach stretches along most of the bay, a tranquil calm area in delightful contrast to the crowded town beach. The **Penon de Alhumecas**, an offshore island in the possession of Spain, is capped with a church and tower. At night dressed by lights it looks like some visiting liner at anchor in the bay.

It was briefly coveted and possessed by England and France before the Spanish took it in 1673. The Beni Ouriaghel tribe kept the Spanish under a continual sniping siege for two hundred and fifty years and took the fortress under their chief Abdel Krim during the Riff rising. Now the Club Mediterranée keep guard from their private beach directly opposite, used from May to September.

WHERE TO STAY
The three big hotels, **Maghreb el Jadid**, **Mohammed V** and **Quemado** are all run by Maroc Tourist as an interchangeable beach front unit for the packaged tours that fly into the local airport. This leaves the **National** at 23 Rue de Tetouan, tel 2431, and the much larger **Hotel Karim** at 27 Av. Hassan II, tel 2184, as the two comfortable, efficient but unexceptional two-star hotels in town. They both have a bar and restaurant and charge 85dh for a double room. All the cheaper unclassified hotels are clustered around the Place du Riff where the CTM buses arrive, and can be relied upon to have clean beds but dubious water supplies. The café **Hôtel Florido** is the most immediately obvious of these, decorated with the truncated star of David, the emblem of Abdel Krim's Republic of the Riff. If full there is also the **Riff Hotel** on Rue Sultan Moulay Youssef, the **Essada** on 15, Rue Al Alaoyouin and the **Hotel Saada** which is opposite a Sufi lodge and hires a bed for 20dh, which though a little rough is run by the delightful Madame Fatima. A seasonal camping site, **El Jamil**, tel 2009, is a 500 m walk east down from the town to a pleasant little bay directly opening on to its own beach with fine views looking over the Riff mountains. The **Cala Iris** is larger, more popular and further along.

WHERE TO EAT
The three Maroc Tourist hotels, the **Karim** and **National** all have bars and restaurants. Near to the National is the café **Tamsamaon** on Calle Al Amir Moulay Abdulah, which can feed you on salads and brochettes for 15dh. The café **Marhaba** on the Place du Riff is the busiest and serves grilled chickens, meat and salads, cheap and cheerful.

East of Al Hoceima to Nador

Nokour

2 km after the Al Hoceima airport a turning could take you to **Im Zouren** which has a busy **souk** on Saturday morning. 7 km further along the P39 road is the village of **Beni Bou Ayach** beside the Oued Nokour.

This modern looking settlement was once the capital of the Emirate of Nokour. The Emirate was founded in 709 by one of the earliest Arab conquerors and remained a centre of Islamic orthodoxy and Arab culture amongst the Berber traditions and heresies of the Riff. Nokour, safely isolated by the Riff mountains from the major conflicts, received a steady flow of Arab exiles and managed to maintain a precarious independence for 350 years. This was ended in the 11th century by the Almoravide Sultan Youssef ben Tachfine who descended like a desert wind to destroy the town and incorporate it into his Empire.

Nokour could have revived as an urban centre when the French established by negotiation a trading station on this coast in the 17th century. Their commercial rivals, the English and Dutch, were however quick to destroy this promising venture during the Spanish War of Independence. After the Spanish built a fortress on the Penon de Alhumecas in 1673 a continuing state of petty war sealed the area from any useful development until the 20th century. The post-Independence achievements like the new **Ibn Abdel Krim Khattabi dam**, 3 km to the south but closed to visitors, may yet herald a new Nokour.

Taourirt

42 km east from Hoceima as you cross the Oued Nokour a tarmac route on the right, the 8505, leads in 5 km to the **Kasbah of Taourirt**, one of the few surviving monuments in these hills, a dark magenta red fort on a dramatic outcrop of land above the Oued Nokour. Though a modern Spanish building the Kasbah is an ancient seat of power and served as a secure Beni Merin fortress in the long battle to succeed to the Almohad throne in the 13th century. Beyond the Kasbah the track deteriorates but leads up to **Djebel Hammane**, 1944 m, where the Beni Ouriaghel made their last stand against the Spanish at the end of the Riff rising in 1926.

The village of **Talamight**, just before the S312 mountain road for Taza, has a few snack cafés in its roadside row of arcaded shops and the **Taza café Hôtel**. 13 km past this turning you should watch out for the piste track on the left for the hot springs of **Ain Chiffa**.

Midar, 102 km east of Hoceima, is another middle-sized Riff town, its square unforgiving architecture is set in the equally unforgiving landscape. It has an old Spanish fort, provision shops, petrol and the **Café Central** for rooms and a meal (there are also basic hotels at both Driouch and Mont Aroui). Wednesday is a more entertaining day to pass through when the town is full of farmers come in for the **souk**.

Annoual

Both Midar and Driouch 15 km east have tarmac turnings to the north. This was the area that saw the original dramatic success of the Riff rising. It was not a set battle but a confusion of individual engagements. Abdel Krim in a series of preparatory raids established that the Spanish forces were of poor calibre and their supply lines over-stretched. By 17 July he had organized all the tribes to launch a simultaneous mass attack on the Spanish posts which, individually overwhelmed, were unable to support each other. By 9 August **Mont Aroui**, the last Spanish held fort outside Melilla, had fallen. An army of 18,000 had been destroyed in what became known as the route of Annoual, the few prisoners that survived tribal vengeance were sold back to Spain in the next year.

There is not much of positive interest to draw you on to this undulating arid plain but a detour inland off a main road always has its own stimulus. Travelling northeast from Midar on the 8112 you reach in 8 km the village of **Tafersite**, 9 km further is the turning to **Annoual**, a comparatively fertile and unalarming place with a small riverine gorge. It is fortunately difficult to imagine the appalling massacres that took place here, where young Spanish conscripts were impaled on barbed wire posts and raped with bayonets. A piste track from Annoual leads to the coastal shrine of **Amar ou Moussa**. Returning back to the 8112 you can proceed through the long settlement of **Ben Tieb** which has a line of mosques crowning the escarpment to the north. 18 km on, you reach **Dar Kebdani** where the Beni Said have a **souk** on Thursday. The parked Mercedes with Dutch and Belgian number plates are not visiting tourists—this surely will never be a tourist trail, but witness to the success of Riffi migrant workers in Europe. The **Kasbah of Kebdani**, once a regional power centre, is now an unexciting part occupied, part ruined 20th-century Spanish fort. Travelling south, back to the main road, on the 8105 you cross three river beds and on your right a remaining Spanish block house can be seen on a hill half way along the 11 km between Dar Kebdani and Kandoussi. The block house of three floors demonstrates many crucial weaknesses, classically exposed, surrounded by dead ground which could conceal an attacker and removed from water supplies.

The villages of **Tiztoutine** and **Mont Aroui** bestride the main P39 are distinguished by the enormous width of their central avenue. Tiztoutine, 140 km east of Hoceima, has a conical shaped mystical mountain on its horizon but Aroui has a better range of café restaurants for a stop—try the **Café du Nord**—and holds a **souk** on Sunday. 4 km out of Mont Aroui a righthand turn, the S605, can take you almost due south to Taourirt where the crossing of the the Oued Moulouya is the single striking feature. The river has been dammed to create a striking lake and a water-filled gorge which fuel a number of irrigation canals and a hydro works. The bridge, the old boundary between the French and Spanish protectorates, is still guarded by armed soldiers and there is a café open most of the year from where you can view all this activity in the midst of an otherwise desert landscape.

Selouane

This village on the Oujda–Hoceima–Melilla road junction has been enthusiastically written up as the iron town. The skyline is indeed ugly with pylons but so far there are only two lonely looking factories to be run by Sonisad, the state metal industry. One of them was recently built by a British firm to process cheap imported iron and steel into the rods used everywhere in Morocco for running up ferro-concrete houses. The lone **Café Central** on the Selouane crossroads has a grocery store and by turning left here you will shortly see an old iron bridge. A stream occasionally flows by almost to form a moat on two sides of the **Kasbah** of Selouane. This was built by Moulay Ishmael on an old site in the 17th century and was reinforced in 1859 as it was feared that the Spanish might invade from both Ceuta and Melilla. It was used for seven years, from 1902 to 1909, as a military base by a pretender to the throne, the 'Rogui Bou Hamara' who was supposed to have buried his treasure here but never revealed the location despite the tortures of Sultan Moulay Hafid. The large castellated compound is partly occupied by some friendly squatter families and is also used as a secure store for great loads of agricultural produce. As you leave Selouane and travel north to Nador you enter an efficiently irrigated coastal plain with broad acres of corn, sugar cane and olive groves.

Nador

Nador is not a tourist destination but as the border into Spanish Melilla can be unpredictable you may find yourself needing to stay a night here.

It is the creation of post-Independence planners and now houses 120,000 citizens. Though Melilla is only 15 km north, the newly independent Morocco wished to create a Mediterranean port free from Spanish control. A new urban centre would also attract industry to the north and absorb the surplus and potentially dissident population of the Riff. These calculations were based on the assumed mineral wealth of the Riff mountains which has since proved to be something of an illusion. There is only a little low grade iron ore outside Selouane, coal from Oujda and local agricultural produce to export through the port. Nor has Nador fulfilled its industrial expectations and in common with most of the north increasingly feels neglected by the central government. There is a long tradition of Riff dissidence to which Nador has added its own footnote of occasional political violence in the last few decades.

The town is designed on a grid plan and falls off from the low hills to face east across the salt water lagoon, the Sebka Bou Arg. The whitewashed houses with their details picked out in blue and green look pleasant enough and the central avenues are elegantly lined with palms. The Av. Mohammed V runs along the shore line and in its centre is the conspicuous **Club Café** set out on stilts in the lagoon where you can while away an hour or two over coffee and cakes. The lagoon's water does not look either very inviting or safe to swim in. The vegetable and fish markets on the way into town provide a better distraction and there is a nearby beach at **Qariat Arkmane**.

Above the new town as you leave on the main road to Melilla is a ruined **Spanish fortress barracks**. Guarded by a charming sentry box with tiled benches, the walled compound contains barrack blocks still wearing their decorated corniches and areas of glazed tile work. The friendly squatters give a picturesque rather bizarre scene with turkeys, goats and chickens milling around the military debris where once only majors and colonels ruled.

TOURIST INFORMATION
There is a Banque Populaire on Rue de la Ligue Arabe and the BMCE on the corner of Av. Ibn Rochd and Youssef ben Tachfine. All buses arrive in the main station, 4 departures for Al Hoceima, 2 for Fez, Taza and Casablanca and 4 for Tetouan and a dozen for Oujda.

WHERE TO STAY AND EAT
Nador is not a thrilling town and if you decide to stay a night it might be worthwhile taking a reasonably comfortable hotel.

The *** **Hôtel Rif** on the Av. Youssef Ibn Tachfine, tel 3637, partly overhangs the lagoon; a double room here costs 150dh, the restaurant closes early, do arrive before 20.00. Or there is the **Mansour Ed Dahab** on 101, Rue de Marrakesh, tel 2409, also with a restaurant and bar. Opposite from the Rif is the **Hôtel Mediterranean**, tel 2611, who charge 147dh for a double and 65dh for dinner. There is also the new **Hôtel Khalid** at 129, Av. des F.A.R. where a double room costs 113dh and breakfast 13dh.

163

Qariat Arkmane

20 km east of Nador, on the 8101 through the coastal agricultural plain are the beach, campsite and restaurants of Qariat Arkmane. This faces out on to the Mediterranean avoiding the mud and dubious water of the lagoon. The restaurants have a deserved reputation for fish and scallops and are well patronized by the Spanish from Melilla. The campsite, **Karia Plage**, charges under 10dh for a tent, person and car. The long spit of sand dunes that encloses the lagoon can only be approached from here and its wilderness of reeds and birds explored on foot.

North of Nador you pass a turning on the left, before you reach the port installations of **Beni Enzar**, which can take you above Melilla to explore the peninsula. The **Cap des Trois Fourches** is 38 km north, half of the route is tarmaced, with fine views but no sandy beaches.

Melilla

The North African port of Melilla has been in the possession of Spain since 1497 and is considered by Madrid, at least, to be sovereign Spanish territory. The border is open and Melilla makes an unusual point of entry into Morocco. It is linked by government-subsidized ferries to three other Spanish ports, Ceuta, Malaga and Almeria, but it is still an expensive way to bring a car or motorcycle to Morocco.

As part of an itinerary it is less of a success, the Moroccan customs and immigration officers deliberately discourage visitors from crossing the border with a masterful demonstration of bureaucratic delay. Waiting in the midday sun for your passport, green card, registration document, immigration form, currency form to be approved and reemerge is possible but deeply frustrating.

HISTORY

The sheltered bay to the south of the citadel promontory has always proved attractive to merchants. The Phoenicians first established the city of Rusadir here and a full catalogue of invaders have in turn despoiled and revived the port; Romans, Vandals, Byzantines, Visigoths, Arabs, Omayyads, Idrissids, Almoravides, Almohads and Mere-nids. During Merenid rule traders from the city states of Europe berthed at Melilla to acquire the fruits of the Saharan caravan trade. Melilla or Mlilya means the white in Arabic, which the Berber tribes translated into their own dialect as 'Tamlit'.

In 1494 the Berber hill tribes rebelled against the Wattasid Caid of Melilla and expelled him. Two Castilian captains who were trading off the coast found Melilla temporarily undefended and returned quickly to alert their king. In 1497 Juan de Guzman, the Duke of Medina Sidonia, despatched Pedro Estopinon with part of Columbus's second fleet to seize Melilla. After a few years of Spanish rule the Muslim inhabitants were forcibly converted to Christianity. The Inquisition arrived to monitor the new converts which led to an exodus of the original inhabitants who mostly took refuge in Muslim Tetouan.

The Riff tribes, periodically assisted by a Sultan, were never able to recapture the fortress but nor were the Spanish capable of extending their rule beyond the city walls. As a result a desultory border war flickered on for centuries. This intensified when

Spanish engineers, extending the walls, demolished the holy tomb of Sidi Auriach in 1893. The most famous casualty of this border war was General Margallo who was shot by one of his own lieutenants for being too conciliatory. The peace negotiations in Madrid were also complicated when the Moroccan Ambassador was assaulted at court by General Fuentes. The cycle of ambushes and raids continued to escalate and the Riff rebellion of 1921 to 1926 can be seen as the last and greatest stage of the Melilla border war. Abdel Krim acknowledged that his one great regret was in not seizing Melilla in the aftermath of the rout of Annoual. During the Spanish protectorate Melilla enjoyed a brief relevance and prosperity that united it with the hinterland for the first time since 1497 but after Moroccan Independence in 1957 it returned to its isolated fortress mentality. Despite its proud walls Melilla is now less of a bastion of Imperial Spain and more of a supermarket of gadgetary for smugglers. The colony's population has in recent years almost halved to 60,000.

GETTING AROUND
By Air & Sea: Iberia flights connect Melilla to Malaga, tickets can be bought at their office at 2, Candido Lobera, tel 681507. Ferry tickets from Compania Transmediterranea, Plaza de Espana. Boats leave for Malaga and Almeria, a single passenger ticket costs 2040 pts. Almeria departures are on Monday, Wenesday and Friday at 11.30, Malaga departures on Tuesday, Thursday and Saturday also at 11.30.
Buses leave from the Moroccan frontier to Nador at least every hour and cost 10dh. See Nador for further connections.

TOURIST INFORMATION
The Spanish Tourist Office is at 20, Calle del General Aizpura, tel 684204 and is open from Monday to Friday 9.00–14.00, 16.00–18.00 and on Saturday from 10.00–12.00. The Post Office is on Calle de Pablo Vallesca, the Banco Central at 1 Calle del Ejercito Espanol and Banco de Espana on the Place de Espana, tel 682190.

The Town

The circular central garden **Plaza de Espana** above the port divides the regular avenues of the new town from the old citadel, the Ciudad Antigua. The Av. Generalissimo Franco is the most animated of these broad streets all named after military commanders who have fought against Morocco. The Hernandez Park leads west from the Plaza and at its far end a left turn leads to the bull ring.

The Citadel

The citadel, a rocky acropolis still enclosed within 16th-century walls and almost entirely surrounded by the sea, is of much greater interest. Enter through the Marine gate at the end of the Av. General Macias and twist through to the interior Plaza de la Maestranza. The **chapel of Santiago** is ahead whilst a tunnel to your left passes below the walls to the court of the Guards. Ahead is the monumental **gate of Santiago** decorated with the arms of the Emperor Charles V. It gives entrance to the Plaza de Armas, the military barracks. Return back to the Plaza de la Maestranza and pass around the chapel for a walk beside the battlements. This leads to the **bastion of Concepcion** where there is the **Municipal Museum** which is open from 9.00–13.00, 16.00–18.00 but closed on Monday and Friday, entrance 5 pts. It houses old weapons and a selection of archaeological finds and some prehistoric carved stones from the Western Sahara.

The view from the Museum battlements is perhaps the finest, taking in a broad sweep of old city, new town and the Moroccan Cap des Trois Fourches to the north. Continue on around the battlements, darting up any of the narrow climbing alleys that take your fancy on the right to eventually leave through the Tunnel de Florentina which leaves you south of the walls above the port.

FESTIVALS

There is a procession of penitents during Holy Week, the festival of Spain in July and our Lady of Victory at the end of September.

WHERE TO STAY AND EAT

A tour of Melilla with a meal can occupy three hours and few visitors find they need to stay a night. Compared to Morocco the hotels are expensive and rooms can be surprisingly hard to find. The best hotel is undoubtedly **Don Pedro de Estopinian**, tel 684940, to the north of the Post Office across the Lober park with a garden, the only pool in Melilla and a bar and restaurant. Next in comfort is the **Anfora**, 8, Calle Pablo Valesca, tel 683340, the Avenida, 24 Av. del Generalissimo Franco or the Rusadir San Miguel, 5, Calle Pablo Vallesca.

At the cheaper end you can take your pick from half a dozen clean one-star hotels, the **Cazaza** at 6, Primo de Rivera, tel 684648, **Espana** 10, General Chacel, tel 684645, **Miramar** on the portfront Av. General Macias, **Nacional** at 10 Primo de Rivera, tel 684540, **Parque**, 15, General Marina, tel 682143 and the small **Hotel Rioja** at 6, Ejercito Espanol, tel 682709. Prices for these last six should be around 1600 pts a night.

The **Metropol** on the Plaza de Espana, tel 683514, is the traditional busy restaurant to see and be seen, and the **Victoria** on Calle del General Pareja has also been recommended, tel 682226.

Ras el Ma and the Moulouya estuary

The Oued Moulouya is born near Kenifra in the mountainous centre of Morocco and then flows northeast to drain all the southern slopes of the vast range of the Middle Atlas before emptying out into the Mediterranean. It brings to the arid plain of the Gareb and Jel a narrow fertile valley, a natural boundary continually fought over by rival empires and preyed upon by surrounding nomadic tribes.

Zaio, 25 km east from Selouane, is now on the edge of this rich irrigated zone. It appears strikingly rich and green in comparison to the scorched treeless landscape of the eastern Riff. A thin tarmac road travels north from Zaio, the 8100, winding beside the river and overlooked to the west by the harsh contours of the Kebdana mountains. 49 km from Zaio is the Mediterranean coastal village of **Ras el Ma**. On this isolated stretch of coast is a fine sandy beach. The **Moulouya estuary** teems with bird life and in the summer there is a scattering of tents camped happily along the shore looking out towards the **Isles Chafarines**. These islands were seized in 1848 and comprise the most eastern of the five Presedios of Spain on the North African coast. Their threatened tourist development has fortunately not yet occurred, they are inaccessible from Morocco and only used by a handful of visiting Spanish fishing crews.

Saidia

On the eastern side of the Oued Moulouya estuary stretches the 10 km long sandy beach of Saidia. The town of Saidia is a seasonal beach resort, a motley collection of chalets, sports areas, three camp sites and four hotels. It has however the relaxed raffish air of all Moroccan holiday towns, the hotel bars are busy, music and laughter are almost continuous and here there is no 'business' or bazaar touts.

For those who prefer solitude the long beach, easily accessible from the 5013 coast road, fringed by a natural bird preserve of marsh and broken woodland is an enticing sanctuary, a paradise for bird watching or sunbathing.

To the east of the town is the closed Algerian frontier, well guarded by both nations with manned pillboxes and watch towers. The **Kasbah**, a recently restored large square enceinte was built by Sultan Moulay Hassan in the late 19th century to deter further erosion of his borders by the French. The interior is occupied by villagers and in summer is enlivened by cafés and musicians. A pleasant area of mature trees surrounds the walls to provide welcome mid-day shade, a popular place for family picnics.

GETTING AROUND
Buses and grands taxis leave regularly from Oujda for Saidia. Sunday is the busiest day because of the **souk**. The 60 km trip costs only 7dh, the buses arrive beside the Kasbah. Driving to Saidia from the west take any of the two roads north from Berkane, a rapidly expanding and prosperous agricultural centre, where the wines of Beni Snassen are grown.

WHERE TO STAY AND EAT
The ** **Hotel Hannour**, Place du 20 Août, tel 5115, is more conspicuous as a nightclub with a bar and restaurant. The nine rooms are usually well booked in advance. The * **Al Kalaa**, tel 5123, just inland from the conspicuous corner **Blue bar** which faces the sports square and sea front is a safer bet. It also has a bar, a restaurant throughout the summer and 33 bedrooms; a double with a bathroom costs 82dh. The * **Select**, Blvd de la Moulouya, tel 5110, has 18 rooms and a bar. These are the cheapest rooms in town, a single with a shower costs 38dh, a double 50dh. There is also the **Hotel Sherif**, behind the Kasbah, a boisterous place with a bar and cabaret.

There are three official campsites, the **Camping du Sit** is reserved for families. Just east is the **Camping Caravaaning Al Mansour** and the less fussy **Camping Tours** is found behind the sports arena.

Beni Snassen

Between Saidia and Berkane stretches a fertile coastal plain, fed by water from the river Moulouya which passes along the Triffa irrigation canal. South of Berkane, away from this industrious tractor-strewn landscape is the more striking scenery of the mountains of Beni Snassen. The Beni Snassen are a sedentary Berber tribe, related to the Riff hill tribes who successfully defended themselves from destructive Arab nomadic invasions in their mountains. These mountains are accessible by car or taxi and make an interesting day's exploration from either Berkane, Oujda or Saidia. There are seven roads that enter the region, providing a number of possible mountain track drives.

Along the Oujda to Berkane road, the S403, is the high mountain village of **Taforalt**, a small faded hill resort which does however still have a café and a traditional **souk** on Wednesday. 1 km to the south of Taforalt there is a fine view extending on clear days over the Moulouya valley to the sea. A tarmac road turns east from here into the mountains. 1 km on your right are the **Grotte des Pigeons** where three small streams trickle down a hillside leaving a number of calciferous deposits. The actual cave system has been wired off due to the apparently endless excavations amongst the Palaeolithic remains. The last report was published at Casablanca in 1962 by D. Ferembach, *La necropole epipaleolithique de Taforalt, étude des squelettes humains.*

Camel Cave/Grotte de Chameau

The Grotte de Chameau is a further 8 km east along a pleasant wooded twisting mountain tarmaced road. An unobtrusive turning to the right takes you to a mountain face where there are two entrances to the cave system across a small stream.

You will need a strong torch for each person. The long entrance passage is easily navigated but the great stalagmite halls, multiple paths and potentially dangerous holes require a certain caution. Narrowing tunnels lead deeper underground and grow noticeably hotter. It is quite easy to briefly lose oneself for the caves are wonderfully free of any organization, tickets or lighting systems. A hot water stream flows out from the depths and a camel-shaped stalagmite near the entrance enjoys a reputation for curing sterility. Boys bicycle up to the caves for picnics and it is not unusual to hear discordant strains of Moroccan music coming up at you from the echoing passages. Candle and torch lights throw weird shadows and silhouettes of gyratic dancers against the powerful looming stalactite walls.

Out from the caves the hot stream flows into a number of deep smooth rocked pools where you can bathe.

Zegzel Gorge

The entrance to the Zegzel Gorge is a 1 km beyond the Grotte turning. The cultivated orchards and terraces of the valley floor contrast admirably against the violent bare cliff faces dotted with intriguing caves. A difficult mountain track can be attempted that follows the gorges east allowing you in 50 km to rejoin the main Oujda to Saidia road. The safer and equally interesting road, a left turn at the Gorge entrance, follows the Oued Zegzel 12 km down to Berkane.

Oujda

'The City of Fear', the eastern-most city of Morocco, is in fact a calm and easy place in which to arrive and stay. It is despite its long history a preeminently modern town, a

20th-century city of half a million, quietly prosperous from agriculture and the coal mines of Jerada. The Medina is still at the centre of the city and, partly enclosed by 12th-century Almohad walls, can be explored in an hour.

Whatever direction you have travelled from, Algeria, Figuig, Hoceima or Taza, the long hot journey can be comfortably broken at Oujda from where trips to the beach at Saidia or the Beni Snassen mountains can be planned.

HISTORY

Before the Arab invasions of the 7th century this area was a settled agricultural community. The Roman town of Marnia, part of the province of Mauretania Caesariensis—modern Algeria—has been discovered nearby. Roman rule was an isolated era of peace for a region that has since been dominated by border wars and rivalry between the nomadic tribes of the eastern plains.

Oujda was founded in 994 by Ziri Ibn Attia, who was the leader of an aggressive nomadic Berber tribe, to be the commanding citadel for his rule of the eastern plains. Ziri, who prided himself on his Islamic orthodoxy and Arab speech, was succeeded by a different but like-minded dynasty of Berber nomad chiefs. The Emirs of the Magrawa nomads ruled the east from Oujda for 80 years, their authority extending far south to Sigilmassa before the Almoravide Youssef ben Tachfine destroyed their rule in 1070. The Almohads captured Oujda in 1206 from its Almoravide governor and ordered the construction of the present extent of the city walls. The Almohad Empire extended far to the east to modern Libya, and Oujda was for once in its existence removed from any disputed frontier.

The decay of the Almohad dynasty ushered in centuries of wars where a fast changing cast of conquerors aptly earnt Oujda the title of the 'City of Fear'. The 14th and 15th centuries saw this shifting pattern of allegiances at its most unstable, bloody and unpredictable, for the ruling dynasties of Morocco and Algeria had both originated from nomadic Berber tribes from the eastern plains around Oujda. The bitter rivalry between the Merenids of Morocco and the Ziyanids of Algeria was reflected in a continuous struggle for possession of Oujda, Tlemcen and Sigilmassa. This pattern of border war has continued ever since though there have been changes in the cast. The Turks advancing from Algeria were opposed by virtually every active Sultan of the Saadian and Alouite dynasties. The French replaced the Turks in Algeria from 1830 but continued the history of this smouldering frontier. There were border wars in 1844 and 1857 before the conquest of Oujda in 1907, the same year that the French landed at Casablanca. During the Algerian struggle for Independence this border zone was a key area of activity but after the French left the border saga continued with rivalry between the newly independent states of Algeria and Morocco. Fortunately the armed clashes of the sixties have been replaced in recent years by a slowly improving understanding which has culminated in the Maghrebi Unity Treaty of 1989.

GETTING AROUND

Air

The airport is 15 km north of Oujda, off the P27 road to Saidia, has flights to Casablanca for 390dh, 290dh if you are under 21. The Air France and RAM offices are in the Oujda

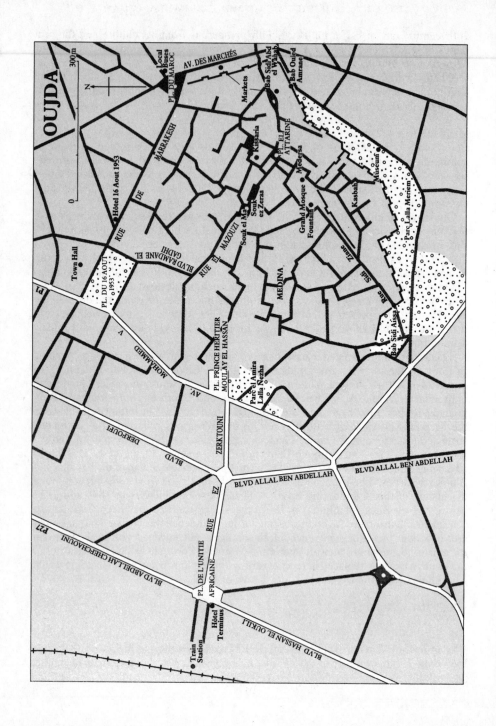

Hotel on Av. Mohammed V, tel 4072. From Casablanca you can connect with flights over Algeria to Tunisia for 1400dh.

Rail
The railway station is conspicuously aligned on the city's central avenue, the Rue Ez Zerktouni which leads directly east to the Medina. There are three daily trains to Taza for 38dh, from where you can continue to Casablanca, Fez or Tangier. Once a week, over Saturday night, a train departs on the 8-hr journey to Bouarfa from where buses can be found for Figuig or Er-Rachidia.

Bus
The CTM and other bus companies increasingly depart from the Oued Nachef depot—a 10-minute walk from the railway station, right along Blvd Hassan al Oukil, right at the junction to cross the bridge over the Oued Nachef. The old CTM departure point was at Rue Sidi Brahim behind the central Post Office and from the Place du Maroc. Until the situation stabilizes you might check first at the Tourist Office.

There are six buses to Saidia, an 80-minute journey, 7dh a ticket, six to Berkane, an hour's ride, three for Casablanca currently leaving at 5.00, 6.00 and 18.00 for around 70dh, two for Fez, 5.00 and 11.00, and four for Nador, 16dh a ticket. The most epic bus ride is the 7-hr, 370 km journey south across the desert plateau of the Rekkam to Figuig oasis for 33dh.

Grands taxis can be found at the station or by the Hôtel de Ville, 2 hours to Taza or Nador, under an hour to Saidia.

Car hire from Hertz at 20 Blvd Fetouaki, tel 2838, or Avis on 110, Av. Allal ben Abdellah, tel 3993.

TOURIST INFORMATION
The Tourist Office on Place du 16 Aout is unusually helpful and hands out a city map in addition to the usual glossy leaflet.

The Post Office is on Av. Mohammed V just north of the Hotel de Ville, the BMCE bank at 93, Av. Mohammed V and the Banque Populaire at 34, Blvd Derfoui. Though noticeably low on hasslers, visitors to Oujda will inevitably be offered black market Algerian currency. Beware of the 500 Algerian dinar notes which because of skilled forgeries have been completely withdrawn from circulation. The conspicuous **Catholic Church**, on the Place El Amira Lala Nezha, off the Av. Mohammed V celebrates Mass in a side chapel at 18.30 on Saturday and 9.00 on Sunday morning. The French priest, though fond of drink, draws skilfully upon the Koran, perhaps inspired by the ecumenical influence of the local shrine to Sidi Yahia/John the Baptist.

THE BORDER CROSSING
There are no direct flights or trains to Algeria though it is hoped that the Maghrebi Unity Treaty of February 1989 may soon alter this. Moroccan trains stop at Oujda, Algerian trains start at Tlemcen, 62 km east from the frontier, though crossing by car, motorcycle and even bicycle is legal and straightforward. Crossing the Oujda border by foot, by taking a bus or taxi 25 km to the frontier, is still theoretically illegal but by tidy dressing and relying on patience, persistence or charm it is often possible to cross. Conditions at

the frontier directly reflect the political wind blowing between Algiers and Rabat which is for the moment set fair. Every traveller has to buy at the border point 1000 Algerian dinars. This you can consider as a transit tax for elsewhere in Algeria the widespread black market rates offer dramatically more favourable rates. Students used to be exempt from this condition but are no longer; French francs used to be required (they still are useful for the Figuig border), but now dollars, about $260 worth, or even pounds are accepted. British citizens do not require a visa to enter Algeria but Americans, Canadians, Australians and New Zealanders do. These can, in Morocco, only be obtained from Rabat. The Algerian Consulate is to reopen in Rabat, until it does the United Arab Emirate Consulate has an Algerian interest department at 12, Rue D'Azrou, tel 24287. Open from Monday to Friday, 9.00–13.00, you will need $15 US, four passport photographs and allow a couple of days for the visa request to be processed.

How on foot can you cross to Algeria? Travel 370 km south to Figuig, making certain that you have a visa and have already enough French francs to buy 1000 Algerian dinars.

The border crossing back from Algeria to Morocco is an easy, comparatively joyful event.

The Almohad walls of the Medina

Leave the central Place du 16 Août 1953 off the Av. Mohammed V and follow the broad Rue de Marrakesh to the Place du Maroc. Surrounded by stalls, it is an animated twinkling area of gas lights in the evening, busy with departing local blue buses. Half way along the Rue de Marrakesh you will have noticed the **Bab Ouled Amrane**, the gateway that gives access to the old **Jewish Mellah quarter** of the Medina. South of the Place du Maroc runs the Av. des Marches where there is a long covered area of vegetable and dry good **souks** on your right below the city walls. The **Bab Sidi Abd el Wahab** is the best preserved of the Medina's gates, a high imposing battlemented entrance flanked by towers. This 'the gate of the heads' was where the grim relics of decapitated criminals and rebels were displayed transfixed on poles until the early 20th century. Even without this display it remains the most bustling active area of the city, best appreciated at dusk when the grill cafés come to life and musicians and acrobats often entertain the crowds.

Immediately within the gates in a wide central space are three covered markets, dusty frenetic areas overlooked by the battlemented walls and tombs of local saints.

Continuing outside the walls again a pleasant shaded wooded and flowering park faces the entire and most impressive extent of walls on the southern face of the Medina. The entrance to this **Parc Lalla Meriem** is along the Rue Maghribi el Arabi where there is also housed a local **ethnographic collection**, a familiar display of clothes and crafts. It is open from 8.30–12.00, 14.30–18.00.

The gateway at the end of the park leads directly towards the **Grand Mosque** whilst the next gate, **Bab Sidi Aissa**, would allow you to wind along the Rue el Ouahda passing below the high towers of the conspicuous and still functioning **Catholic church** to rejoin the Av. Mohammed V.

The Medina

The Medina can be entered half way along your circuitous walk around the walls at the **Bab Sidi Abd el Wahab** or from the Place du 16 Août. Starting from the Place take the corner street from the square, the Blvd Ramadane el Gadhi and turn right on to the Rue El Mazouzi that takes you straight into the **souk el Ma**, the water market dominated by the minaret of the **Mosque of Sidi Oqba**. Here is the fountain of **Tlat Skaki**, its three niches covered in mosaic tile work. The water from the fountain is free, what is sold in the souk el Ma are the rights to so many hours of water from the irrigation canals, a commodity whose price is affected by the wildest caprices of climate, season and speculation. Pass naturally into the **souk ez Zeraa** and then turn left to enter a chain of small interlocking market spaces; the **kissaria** with its arcades enclosing the more expensive shops rich in gold embroidery, its associated fountain court and then the place of the Khattayine zaouia full of cloth merchants before taking a right turn to reach the Place El Attarine, the tree shaded centre of the souks decorated with a central fountain and Koubba. From the Place El Attarine the Rue Chadli leads east past innumerable artisan stalls to the large space of covered market just inside the **Bab Sidi Abd el Wahab**. Prominent gates on the southern face of the Place El Attarine lead to the **Grande Mosque** with its associated **Medersa**. The Mosque and Medersa, both closed to non-Muslims, were built by the Merenid Sultan, Abou Yacqub at the end of the 13th century. A passage allows you patiently to trace the outer walls, diving under occasional arches to face the main entrance where a fountain plays in this dusty square. On your right is the old **Kasbah quarter**, the residence of the Pashas and the machinery of government.

Sidi Yahia

The shrine of Sidi Yahia was venerated by all three Peoples of the Book, for it is considered to be the tomb of St John the Baptist, where the actual body, or Salome's dancing prize of his head, is buried, the traditions do not relate which. The enticing grove of baobab and palm trees watered from sacred springs was once approached by a 6 km long ceremonial road east from the Oujda Medina. The expansion of the town has not dealt too kindly with this retreat; the approach is now through twisting suburban roads and some municipal planner has been let free to add a profusion of pavements, paths and parking zones around the sanctuary.

The stream still snakes through the groves of trees and there is seldom a shortage of pilgrims visiting the various Koubba, lighting candles or praying at the tombs, washing in the water (a cure for rheumatism) or tying fragments of cloth to the trees or sanctuary grilles.

The grove in the past attracted hermits, Jewish, Christian and Muslim holy men who camped in poverty under the trees hoping to be possessed by the same spirit that animated St John. One of the **hermitages**, once occupied by **Sidi bel Abbes**, one of the seven patron saints of Marrakesh, is still preserved and venerated. Another cave has been named **Ghar el Houriyat**, the grotto of the Houris, those handmaidens that wait in paradise beside cool shaded streams for the believers but who look disappointingly Scandinavian in contemporary Islamic popular prints.

The true origins of the shrine are likely to lie in pre-Islamic beliefs that venerated sacred springs and groves. Sanctuaries for poetry, prophecies and worship such as Mecca was when Mohammed first received his inspiration but remained not after his vision was imposed on the tribes of Arabia.

You can camp or picnic here in the shade, wash in the stream, buy candles and holy trinkets or snacks from the stalls. The Moussem held here in summer and September, a riot of colour and celebrations, should not be missed. A taxi from Oujda can run you out for a few dirhams, the walk or drive is not inspiring.

MARKETS AND FESTIVALS

A walk through the Medina will naturally expose you to the full range of Moroccan crafts. Local crafts are also displayed for sale at the **Ensemble Artisanal** on the Place Dar el Makhzen and the **maison de l'Artisanat** on Blvd Alla ben Abdellah. The city is large enough to maintain an almost continuous level of market activity throughout the week, though Sunday and Wednesday are the traditional **souk** days, with extra vegetable, cloth and flea markets springing up in the suburbs.

Sidi Yahia is the pre-eminent saint of Oujda and has two Moussems, one in the high summer, usually August, and another in September.

WHERE TO STAY

In Oujda stay at the **** **Terminus Hotel** if you can possibly afford to. Near the station on the Place de L'Unité Africaine, it is the ideal reward after a hot journey, it has a fine pool, a mature garden, efficient plumbing and a good restaurant. The pre-eminent hotel in Morocco east of Fez, the bar is a natural rendezvous for all species of travellers.

Otherwise there are four good clean hotels with comfortable bedrooms and reliable water supplies. The **Lutetia**, 44, Blvd Hasan el Oukil, tel 3365, which also has a bar, charges 48dh for a single, a double costs 65dh; the **Royal** on Blvd Zerktouni, tel 2284, offers a single for 49dh and a double without bathroom for 63dh; there is also the **Simon**, Blvd Tarik Ibn Ziad, tel 5826, or the **Ziri** on Blvd Mohammed V, tel 4305, where a single can be found for 43dh and a double with shower for 51dh.

For the Medina enthusiast, the new **Hotel of 16 Août** on a crossroads on the Rue Marrakesh has scrupulously clean rooms and showers. A room with a view of the street life costs only 32dh, tel 4197.

EATING OUT

Outside the Terminus Hotel there are a few good restaurants to choose from, you could try the **El Bahia**, Blvd Zerktouni, tel 3731, the **De France**, 87–89 Blvd Mohammed V, tel 3801, or **La Mamounia**, Rue Medina el Mounara, tel 4072 which specializes in traditional Moroccan cooking.

East to Algeria, South to Figuig

Tlemcen

Across the border in Algeria is the walled city of Tlemcen bristling with minarets; there you are free to enter the great 11th-century **Almoravide Mosque**. The **Antiquities Museum** on Place Abdelkeder is also excellent; it is open from 8.00–12.00, 14.00–16.00. **Mansourah**, 11 km south of Tlemcen, has Roman and Merenid ruins and two fine mosques.

South to Figuig oasis

The 292 km journey south to **Bouarfa**, on the junction of the Figuig road is across the barren plain of the Rekkam. Apart from the thrill of a desert crossing there is very little of interest, the heat and direct sunlight, even in winter can be quite exhausting. The earliest possible departure by bus is advisable and if you are going by car a night drive through the astonishingly cool clear sky with the desert lit by the moon and stars is an attractive alternative. There are basic café hotels at Ain Beni Mathar, Tendrara and Bouarfa. **Guenfouda** is 28 km south of Oujda where a **souk** is held on Saturday. Beyond is the Jerada mountain pass, 1150 m high, which is just before the mine crossroads. To the west a road leads to the coal mines of **Jerada-Hassi Blal** which have been in production since 1952 and which now send 700,000 tonnes a year north to port Nador. To the east are the mines of **Bou Beker**, the reserves of lead and silver have been almost worked out but large deposits of zinc yet await extraction.

Ain Beni Mathar is 83 km from Oujda, the ancient central market of the Mathar nomads. Their **souk** is held on Monday and a number of old **Kasbahs** survive in the village, two date from before the 19th century, a venerable age for buildings that seldom long outlive their creator. 4 km to the west, along the S330 to Moulouya is the oasis of **Rass el Ain**, a palm-shaded water source beside the Oued Za water course. 18 km down stream, though seldom flowing, is a waterfall with a larger fall another 10 km beyond that.

It was this settlement that Lyautey, then commander of Algeria's western frontier, captured in 1904 as part of his aggressive forward policy. His political masters had forbidden such an advance but by renaming Ain Beni Mathar as Berguent he successfully fooled his superiors in Paris who searched their maps in vain for such a town.

Tendrara, 198 km from Oujda, is an isolated desert administrative post, the **souk** of the nomadic Beni Guil tribe is held here on Thursday. 62 km on, you descend through a cleft in black hills to arrive at **Bouarfa**, the P19 goes east to Figuig, the P32 west to Er-Rachidia.

Part V

THE ATLANTIC COAST
BETWEEN TANGIER & AGADIR

Tower of Almohad, 12th-century Rabat

The Atlantic coast was known by the French as 'Maroc Utile'—useful Morocco. It is the industrial, commercial and political heartland of the country concentrated on the three neighbouring coastal cities of Kenitra, Rabat and Casablanca. Furthermore the fertile coastal provinces of the Gharb, Chaouia and Doukkala have long been prized as the grain bowl of the nation.

The Atlantic has also served as the frontier of Morocco. Phoenician traders first brought the higher arts of agriculture and civilization to the country through a chain of colonies established on this coast. The Roman province of Mauretania Tingitana had no eastward land connection to Algeria and at its most extensive barely extended 100 km inland from the line of Atlantic ports.

The long destructive relationship with Europe was fought out on the Atlantic shore. Centuries of raids, invasions and occupation increasingly deprived Morocco of the full use of its most important asset, the Atlantic coast. This started in earnest with Viking raids in the 10th century and continued with the Normans whose destructive crusading impulse was inherited by Spain and Portugal in the 15th century. Over the 17th and 18th centuries the European fortresses on the coast were recaptured and Muslim pirates brought the war into enemy territory, raiding coasts and plundering the sealanes of Europe. Just as the cycle of aggression seemed to be playing itself out history was preparing to repeat itself. An enormous revival of trade in the 19th century rekindled European ambitions, though this time France replaced Portugal as the major predatory power. The Atlantic coast was invaded in 1907 and from 1912, under French direction,

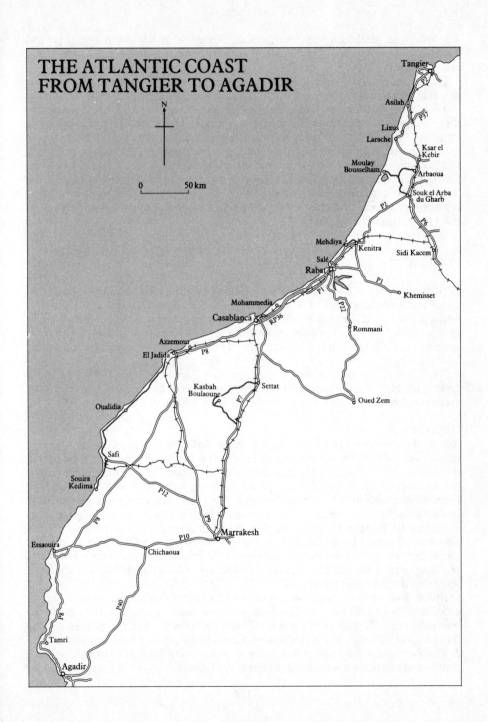

THE ATLANTIC COAST
FROM TANGIER TO AGADIR

the industrial revolution was implanted in Morocco. It has taken firm root and Casablanca is now one of the corners of African commerce along with Cairo, Lagos and Nairobi.

For the tourist the comparatively prosperous and western-influenced Atlantic coast serves as an excellent bridge to the more striking and aggressive culture of the interior. No visitor should avoid witnessing the realities of contemporary Morocco expressed by the metropolis of Casablanca, but the older smaller towns are likely to prove more attractive. The perfect blend of architecture, beach, night life, fine cooking and historical monuments is a highly personal choice. Journeying south along the coast you can afford to be selective, picking a route that might include picturesque Asilah, ruined Lixus and Spanish Larache, the beach of Moulay Bousselham, the monuments of Rabat, the Medina of Salé, the seafood of Oualidia, the coast by Safi and concluding with the finest town of all, Essaouira. All share the same sea which has throughout the year a strong and potentially dangerous undertow.

Asilah

Portuguese defences enclose the dazzling blue and white washed houses of the pictur-esque and well photographed Asilah Medina. The sea laps at battlements to the west whilst at the foot of the eastern walls a souk attracts farmers who ride in from the hills each morning. Asilah is a seaside resort that prides itself on treating visitors with more sympathy than Tangier. It is a pleasant restful place, but suffers from a corresponding lack of energy.

If this is your first taste of swimming on the Atlantic coast beware. The breakers give great sport but the undertow is strong; ten years ago my brother and I, much to our excitement, rescued a drowning man who never said thank you.

HISTORY
Asilah, the first harbour off the Atlantic coast, has a history of continuous foreign interference. The town was founded by Phoenicians in the 8th century BC who named the settlement Zili. It was sophisticated enough to be minting coins in the 2nd century BC for the kings of Mauretania but supported the losing side in a Roman civil war. The Emperor Augustus deported the entire population and filled the town with more reliable Iberian colonists. The new foundation governed itself and in the succeeding centuries weathered the political storms of the Roman withdrawl and the Arab conquest. It was absorbed into the Idrissid kingdom in the 9th century after which Arab chroniclers record that it was destroyed by repeated raids of the English, a blanket term for the fleets of Vikings and Normans. The Ommayad Caliph of Cordoba rebuilt Asilah in 966 but it was again destroyed by Vikings.

By the 14th century, Asilah had revived and Christian merchants berthed here in order to trade with the interior. The Portuguese so valued the port that they seized it for themselves in 1471 with an Armada of 477 vessels. This was bitterly resented and the fortified port of Asilah was for the next two centuries a constant battleground.

The Portuguese governor of Asilah in the 16th century, Joao de Continho, waged a continuous but curious war against Ibrahim, the Emir of Xaouen. In courtly behaviour that exceeded the chivalry of Saladin and Richard I, the governor and the Emir exchanged presents and prisoners, and when there was a lull in the fighting organized jousts on neutral ground. When the Emir and his wife fell ill with fever the governor sent his doctor to Chechaouen to cure the couple. This was capped by a treaty in 1530 that agreed on the conduct of cavalry raids. These could carry off herds but were forbidden to despoil gardens, burn standing crops or orchards. Throughout this period of war a Portuguese trader, Sebastiao de Vargas, made frequent trips to Fez and Meknes and dealt freely in diamonds, spices and Moroccan wheat.

By 1589 the temper of war had changed and the boy king of Portugal disembarked his crusading army of 20,000 at Asilah, set on deposing the reigning Sultan. After the total destruction of the Portuguese, the victorious Saadian Sultan Ahmed el Mansour recaptured the port of Asilah but in a notorious act was betrayed to the Spanish by a later Saadian prince in exchange for aid in a civil war. The Spanish held the town for eighty years before Sultan Moulay Ishmael stormed the defences in 1691. He sent the captured Spanish garrison in chains to join the slave army that was building the Imperial city of Meknes. The Sultan encouraged settlement of the new town which he made the capital of the unruly Djeballa mountain district.

Raisuni is the most famous Caid of Asilah who won this position from Sultan Abdul Aziz as part of his terms for the release of the American millionaire Perdicaris in 1904. Raisuni was a remarkable man, born a Sherif and trained in Islamic law, he was both a bandit, freedom fighter, saint, philosopher and a tyrant. He built a palace at Asilah at the height of his powers in 1906 when he was the virtually independent ruler of the north. In the confused diplomatic period before the Protectorate, Raisuni played a bewildering political game, intriguing with all the colonial powers and the Sultan's court. As the acknowledged leader of the northern tribes he at first welcomed the Spanish in 1911 but then fought two bitter guerrilla wars with them before making a final peace which he refused to break even at the height of the Riff rebellion. His neutrality was vital to the Spanish in maintaining their hold over the eastern mountains, and Abdel Krim's Riff commandos kidnapped him from his mountain palace of Tazrut in January 1925 and he died a few weeks later.

GETTING AROUND

By Train: The train station is 2 km to the north of the town where the half dozen beachside camp sites are clustered. It is the first stop from Tangier, 9dh for the hour and a half ride and half a dozen trains a day.

By Bus: The bus takes an hour from Tangier with hourly departures from 7.00 to 19.00, and drops you near the CTM office on the Av. Mohammed V with connecting services for the south.

By Taxi: Taxis to the station from the town centre should charge 5dh, a place in a grand taxi to or from Tangier is 20dh and on to Larache 10dh.

By Car: Asilah is 46 km south of Tangier off the main P2 road running south to Rabat.

The Spanish built a harmonious new town beside the Medina below which stretch the beaches that extend along the northern coast. The main avenue of the new town, Av. Mohammed V houses the bank, the police and a pharmacy. It leads past corner cafés and the tower of the closed church for 200 m to the garden-fringed Place Zelaka that is bordered by the ramparts of the Medina.

WHAT TO SEE

The 16th-century **Portuguese ramparts** of Asilah are of an attractive worn yellow stone. They were built in two years by the great military architect Botacca after a prolonged Moroccan siege had virtually breached the earlier defences.

Botacca punctured the walls with three gates. The **Bab Homar** is the central land port gate and is decorated with the faded royal arms of Alfonso V of Portugal. The **souk** is clustered here below the outer walls in the welcome partial shade of ramparts and gardens. Across the road, opposite the battlements, are gateways leading to two large courtyards where masses of donkeys are tethered by the farmers riding in from the hills to sell their vegetables. The **Bab el Bhar**, the old sea gate, or the **gate of the Kasbah** are the easiest through which to enter the **Medina**. Both take you naturally into the small continuous courtyard of Sidi ben Hamdouch and Ibn Khaldoum overlooked by the small central keep, the **red tower, 'el Hamra'** in Arabic. The children of Asilah are usually kicking a football here or employed in twisting long lines of thread for the fine embroidery of the town's tailors. A right turning will take you down to the sea wall ramparts where fishing boats bob on their buoys. Until 1987 the old Portuguese breakwater provided partial but picturesque protection for the Medina port against the Atlantic. The harbour has now been reinforced and enlarged by a monstrous breakwater composed of a jigsaw of three-dimensional concrete tetrahedrons.

The **Palace of Raisuni** is also known as the House of Tears, for it was built with forced labour and an extra burden of taxation, but it was beautiful and built within a year. Raisuni himself declared, 'In my life I have been little loved and much hated, but above all I have been feared.' The palace partly hangs over the sea walls and has an upper gallery of arches from where Cape Spartel can be seen on a clear day. You approach the main block along a covered way. On the left side was a row of prisons and on the right a long shaded seat for petitioners. This roofed passage leads into an interior courtyard with the house on one side and an audience chamber on the other.

The house and audience chamber are theoretically open to visitors but in practice the custodian and his keys are difficult to find. The fame of Raisuni is the palace's chief attraction. The two stages of rooms built around a great court with a fountain from Italy, a floor of black and white marble and walls decorated in the familiar Moorish style with faience mosaic, sculpted plaster and carved wood are cool and attractive enough. Raisuni has been described in the books of Walter Harris whom he kidnapped and in a biography by Rosita Forbes, a journalist whom he merely charmed.

The **Intellectual festival** in August is held at the palace with poetry, music and painting competitions. Asilah is fortunate for its parliamentary representative is also Minister of Culture who has also recently created a **Horse festival** at Asilah to follow the two weeks of art.

Beyond the palace you continue with the sea view obscured towards a charming **cemetery**. A small worn pier of stone extends below the corner bastion to give a beautiful view of the town's sea walls and over the small cemetery courtyard immediately below. The **Koubba and small prayer hall of Sidi Mamsur**, attached to the cemetery, have been painted a bruised bluish white wash and the interior court is covered in aligned and tiled tombs.

As you return through the Medina you will notice one of the many striking **murals** that decorate its walls. These have been made as a free gift to the town by artists grateful for the August festival. Each year new works are painted, often over previous designs, giving an interesting contrast between these modernist geometrical forms and the Medina's traditional pattern of life. A walk from the cemetery to the Bab Homar takes you past many of the murals and two communal bakery ovens.

There are a few tourist bazaars which will be part of the itinerary of any guide but the Medina is an easy place in which to walk and well used to visitors.

MARKETS
Everyday the **vegetable souk** can be found beneath the eastern battlements. The **Thursday souk** extends the activity with baskets and wicker work piled up for sale near the **Koubba of Sidi Al Arbi of Azilah**. The saint had a reputation for healing the mentally ill who were chained to a tree near the saint's tomb with an iron collar fettered around their necks. Prolonged exposure to the saint's baraka was thought to drive away the djinn who had possessed the victim.

Old coins and belt buckles are sold opposite the Bab Homar with the Av. Hassan II leading up to a long line of artisan shops making goods for the local Moroccan market. The fish market is held in the morning by the old Spanish church.

WHERE TO STAY
The ** **Hôtel Oued El Makhazine** on Av. de Melilla, tel 7090, is the most comfortable in Asilah with efficient baths, 29 well decorated rooms, a bar and a view over the sea. A double for 113dh. The **Hôtel Asilah** at 79, Av. Hassan II has rooms on the second floor that overlook the battlements and the souk below. The rooms are basic but clean with showers available; a double is 44dh. The **Marhaba** at 9, Rue Zallakah (on the right as you walk down the Mohammed V towards the ramparts), has a calm friendly atmosphere with cool tiles and a good central position.

Asilah is better known for its seaside camp sites that are spread out along the beach to the north of the town. The camp **Club Solitaire**, the **Atlantic Safari**, the **Ocean**, the **Sahara** and the **Atlas** are just north of the railway station and **Camp Africa** and **Eguidal** are just south. The atmosphere can be a little intense and over-organized with discos, barbecues and displays. Camping Sahara is the cheapest and most basic and generally less crowded.

WHERE TO EAT
La Alcazaba is a long established and famous licensed fish restaurant, run by Lord Churchill for many years, and nestling beneath the ramparts at the sea end of the Place Zallach. The corner opposite contains the kitchens and a cooler interior dining room suitable for lunching. Lobsters available but cheaper plates of prawn pil-pil or squid for 23dh. Open for lunch and dinner Monday–Saturday, tel 7012.

There are a number of good snack cafés in the souk stalls below the ramparts but in the evening the pavement cafés along the Mohammed V are better. The neighbouring restaurant cafés **Fez** and **Lixus** can give you soup, salad, tagine and yoghurt for under 30dh. Impromptu musical sessions can spring up in the evening and supplant the interminable games of bottle top draughts.

Ad Mercuri

10 kms inland from Asilah are the ruined walls of Ad Mercuri. Though the remains are all Roman it was first established by the Mauretanian kings inland of the semi-independent Phoenician port of Zilla.

Mzoura

'For in these stones is a mystery, and a healing virtue against many ailments. Giants of old did carry them from the furthest ends of Africa and did set them up in Ireland what time they did inhabit therein', Merlin in Geoffrey of Monmouth's *History of Britain*.

15 km south of Asilah on the road to Rabat is the inland road for Tetouan. On this road you take the first left after crossing the railway line to find yourself on a 4 km loop road to the village of **Souk Tnine de Sidi el Yemeni**. Here you can ask for a guide to show you the way to the hamlet of **Chouahed** and the **stone circle of Mzoura** which is 5 km northeast over a confusion of dirt tracks.

Mzoura in Arabic means 'The Holy Place', and here, partly obscured by rampant hedgerow growths of prickly pear, is one of the most impressive pre-Islamic sites in North Africa. Before the excavations of 1935 Mzoura there was a large and untouched tumulus surrounded by a complete low wall of worked and squared rectangular stone blocks. This tumulus, now severely scarred by the unfilled excavation work, is thought to be the tomb of an early Mauretanian king that was inserted in the centre of a much older stone circle.

The conspicuous thin tall upright stone to the north of the circle is known as **El Uted**, which was in local tradition considered to be the peg for a Pharaoh's horse, and beneath which King Sebastian picnicked the day before his death.

The circle was originally composed of 167 stones, of no uniformity but all hammered and polished by hand. They were arranged in a perfect ellipse which has made frequent use of the Pythagorean right-angle and shows conformity with Thorn's megalithic yard of 0.830 metres in its construction. Of the 400 stone circles in Brittany and the British Isles there are only 30 with a perfect ellipse and there are no other elliptical stone circles anywhere else in the world. This curious conformity hints at an ancient cultural link for stone circles comparable to Mzoura in Britain are dated between 1600–2000 BC. To the north and northwest of the circle are at least three separate outer groups of stones as well as an artificially filled level earth platform. With so many stones and outlying circles all sorts of stellar, lunar and solar alignments are possible. The most striking alignment at Mzoura is that the major axis of the ellipse aims at the summit of Djebel Si Habib, the largest mountain on the horizon, and the east–west alignment of the ellipse marks the path of the setting equinoctial (the spring or autumn) sun very closely.

The 1935 excavation which has severely scarred the central earth filled tumulus has only added further mystery to Mzoura. The archaeologist Cesar Luis de Montalban cleaned everything out of the centre of the tumulus and disappeared leaving only some stone slabs set into the ground that could have been the remains of a royal sepulchre. No reports or findings have ever been published, though a well known Egyptologist, Marthe de Chambrun Ruspoli, saw a photograph of an altar supported by sphinxes that was supposed to have been excavated from Mzoura, and two brief handwritten notes turned up in Tangier referring to strange flints from the centre of the tumulus and a grave to the west of el Uted.

The Ruins of Lixus

The ruins of this ancient town are scattered on a coastal escarpment that overlooks the meandering estuary of the Oued Loukkos as it reaches the sea. Less than 5 km north of Larache beside the main road to Tangier this site is easily explored as part of a visit to that town. The dock-side garum factory, the amphitheatre, the baths with a mosaic of Oceanus and the Acropolis, the hilltop temple quarter, are the chief attractions.

Lixus was one of the Phoenicians' first and most successful settlements in Morocco. They landed here before 1000 BC and some surviving foundations have been dated to 600 BC. Makom Shemesh, city of the sun as it was known by the Phoenician settlers, was influential enough to mint its own coins. The fall of Carthage in 146 BC merely allowed the Mauretanian kings to emerge as overlords who wisely respected the liberties of the city. Makom Shemesh joined the general revolt against Rome but its walls fell before the legions of Claudius in AD 44. It was lucky not to share the fate of Tamuda which was totally destroyed and the emperor even presented it with the privileged status of a Colonia.

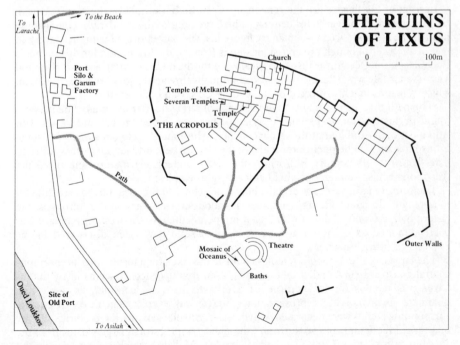

THE RUINS OF LIXUS

To Larache

To the Beach

Port Silo & Garum Factory

Church

0   100m

Temple of Melkarth

Severan Temples

Temple

THE ACROPOLIS

Path

Mosaic of Oceanus

Theatre

Baths

Outer Walls

Oued Loukkos

Site of Old Port

To Asilah

Practically all the visible remains are from this Roman period when the town, now named Lixus, entered a great period of prosperity as a centre for the export of wild animals for the circus, olives and corn, whilst salt, then as now, was extracted from pans in the estuary and fish gathered from the sea. Garum, a peculiar highly spiced, almost rancid, fish sauce was manufactured here. It was a profitable export and the tuna fish from which it was made appeared on the Lixus coinage. Diocletian withdrew the Imperial administration at the end of the 3rd century AD but Lixus continued some form of existence in the following centuries as Arabic coins found in excavations attest.

The Ruins of Lixus

The **port buildings** would have been to the east of the road; Pliny mentions that Lixus was an island, a forgivable error when the sea penetrated much deeper inland up the Loukkos estuary almost to surround the city. The vats of the garum factory and port store houses are beside the road, on the right just before the signposted turning for Plage Rasmanal—the Larache beach. The guardian of the site who lives with his family and chickens on the hillside will appear and lead you up the broad path to the theatre.

It had one of the largest **orchestras** known; at 33 m in diameter it is even wider than the theatre at Athens. Tastes changed and it was later converted into an **amphitheatre**, the orchestra was converted into an arena for fighting wild beasts by building a 13-foot-high wall to protect the audience.

In front of the theatre are the remains of a **public bath**, built by the North African Severi dynasty in the early 3rd century. The large floor of the tepidarium contains the head of the sea god Oceanus, an angry figure his wild hair entwined with the claws and feet of a lobster. Though the craftsmanship is Roman, the inspiration for this theme is Phoenician, for Oceanus is just a classical label for the ancient Syrian sea and river god Yam-Nahar. He was a hostile deity who continually threatened to overwhelm the earth, which was fortunately protected by the god of the sky and rain, Baal.

The path then climbs up through the ruins of a rich quarter of **villas**. The mosaics found in this quarter: of Helios, Mars and Rhea, the Three Graces and Venus with Adonis, are all exhibited at the Archaeological Museum of Tetouan along with some bronze statuettes. The **perimeter walls** of the city can be traced far out to the south and date from the 4th century BC, whilst the walls immediately to your left guard the **Acropolis** whose summit once held at least eight temples.

The **temple ruins** are now at waist height or below, and the scant traces are difficult to untangle. Religious life has continued for thousands of years on the Acropolis, the cistern hall, the only building with a roof on, perched above the western ramparts has been identified as a church and traces of a mosque have been discovered in the excavations of M. Euzennat.

The largest of the Acropolis temples could be mistaken for a forum with its enormous central courtyard surrounded by the ruins of an Ionic portico. It seems likely that as Lixus was famous for its **Temple of Melkarth** that this conspicuous, large and dominant sanctuary is it. A representation of the divinity was placed in the centre and the surrounding niches were decorated with mosaics. Smaller sanctuaries, oratories and the quarters of the temple priests surround the great complex which largely dates from the 1st century BC. Gades (Cadiz) also had a Temple to Melkarth which was served in the 1st century AD by barefooted priests clad in linen who maintained a simple, ever burning fire without human images or animal sacrifices. It seems likely that a similar pattern of worship established itself in Lixus. Far removed from the exotic cult of the Phoenician goddess Tanit, whose temple servitors included boy and girl prostitutes and whose sacrifices involved ritual shaving and the incineration of two-year-old children.

To the southeast of this landmark there are three buildings built on the orders of the Severi dynasty in the 3rd century, **two temples** which sandwich a public office. Directly east another **Phoenician temple** can be recognized from the skilled and massive stonework of the walls.

Mythology

Lixus is wrapped in a confusing but intriguing riddle of myths that may be all that remains of a past era of forgotten achievement. The Phoenicians, who originated from the ancient coastal cities of Lebanon, shared many beliefs with Greece and Egypt, the mother of knowledge. The most obvious example is the Phoenician god Melkarth who is Hercules but under a different name. It is fitting that there is a Temple to Melkarth/Hercules at Lixus for this was an area of some of his greatest exploits. The valley of the Loukkos was considered to be the garden of the Hesperides where the Golden Apples were guarded by a dragon and the daughters of the giant Atlas.

As his eleventh labour Hercules had to steal these apples. On his way he erected the pillars of Hercules, drove off the flesh-eating flocks of Geryon, king of Cadiz, and landing at Tangier he was forced to wrestle and kill Antaeus, the giant son of Poseidon. In return for rescuing his daughters, the grateful Atlas presented Hercules with the golden apples and taught him the secrets of astronomy. For Atlas knew so much that he carried the globe on his shoulders, as it were. In the mythical record Hercules takes the globe from the giant's shoulders, which can be interpreted allegorically as sharing the secrets of astronomy which would ultimately lead to him becoming Lord of the Zodiac.

Atlas had the consolation of having the great Western Ocean, the Atlantic, bear his name but the mountains that guard its approaches, Gibraltar and Djebel Moussa have always been known as the pillars of Hercules. The great sanctuary of Melkarth at Tyre (upon which the Temple of Solomon was modelled) was decorated with two great columns, one encrusted with gold and the other with emeralds, that represented the pillars of Hercules.

These achievements of Hercules are thought to derive from some memory of a pre-Phoenician incursion to the furthest West, possibly by Egyptians, who brought back some astronomical knowledge and details of solar worship to the middle east. The stone circle at Mzoura, inland from Asilah, has been tentatively identified as an ancient astrological device which provides a tempting solution to the riddle. What does seem certain is that far from discovering the Moroccan Atlantic the Phoenicians were returning to a land described in some of the oldest and most enduring myths.

The Phoenicians believed in El as the supreme beneficent god, the sun and King of the West, who was married to Asherat, mother of the earth and Queen of the Sea. Watching the sun set into the western sea from the surrounding ruins of the Acropolis of Temples you can follow the benign El as he sinks into his wife Asherat.

El Araiche/Larache

El Araiche, which is also known as Larache, is poised on the embankment above the estuary of the Loukkos which meanders out reluctantly to meet the sea over a sand bar. Sea cliffs seal the town to the west, and it spreads out to the south into the surrounding orange and tangerine groves. The strongest architectural influence is that from the Spanish Protectorate, a relatively prosperous period from 1911–56, that has left Larache with a dignified collection of Hispano-Moorish official buildings and hotels. The new post-Independence housing has maintained the town's colour scheme of blue and white, whilst the old Medina quarter survives in good repair overlooking the river wharfs. A boat taxi takes passengers across the Loukkos estuary to the beach.

Larache is comparatively neglected by tourists to the benefit of those who stay a few days here. It is remarkably easy to be accepted into the life of the town. Watching the sun set into the Atlantic from the ruins of the Punic temple at Lixus is reason enough to stay a night at neighbouring Larache.

HISTORY

Larache is a continuation of the ancient mythological narrative of Lixus. It was founded during the Arab conquest of Morocco in the early years of the 8th century and named after 'El Araich' Beni Arous as a pure Muslim city on the opposite bank from infidel Lixus. These twin cities existed on their opposite banks for centuries, but by the 11th century the Andalucian geographer El Bekri describes El Araiche as the great town of the region. It was acknowledged to be the principal port on the entire Atlantic coast before a Spanish fleet destroyed the town in 1471.

Juan II of Portugal fortified the deserted ruins in 1489 but only held Larache for a year before a Saadian army swept away the puny Christian fort. The Saadians decided to push the war forward into enemy territory by establishing a naval base at Larache for raiding the Portuguese and Spanish coast. A Kasbah was built in 1491 and skilled Turkish and Andalucian refugees were recruited to man the corsair fleet. It was an excellent base, as the estuary sandbar sealed the Oued Loukkos from the deep-keeled Christian warships whilst the shallow draught of the corsair galleys had an almost invulnerable sanctuary. The Portuguese surprised the corsairs with a land attack from Asilah in 1504 when they were able to burn four ships. Repeated naval bombardments, by Spain in 1546, France in 1765 and the Austrians in 1829, indicate that the meandering banks of the Loukkos remained for long a safe harbour for the sleek prows of the corsair craft.

Larache's history as a corsair base was interrupted by a seventy-year period of Spanish rule. In exchange for military support for Prince el Mamoun in a civil war, King Phillip III of Spain received the port of Larache in 1610. This was but one of a number of treacherous acts by this Saadian prince that discredited the entire dynasty. In the anarchy of this period the Spanish had no difficulty in holding on to their new fort but once central authority had been restored in Morocco, Larache was recaptured by Sultan Moulay Ishmael in 1689. Sultan Sidi Mohammed ben Abdallah reinforced the defences in 1780 as part of his campaign to revive the corsair fleet which survived in reduced and illegal form until 1830.

The Spanish returned to Larache in 1911, with Raisuni's assistance peacefully occupying the town, where they set up one of the three provincial capitals of the Spanish Protectorate of Northern Morocco.

GETTING AROUND

Buses and grands taxis leave frequently for Tangier or Rabat and several travel inland to Fez. The bus station is just 300 m in from the Place de la Libération on the Rue Mohammed ben Abdellah. The no 4 bus leaves from the port every 20 minutes for the 7 km land route to the beach opposite, which passes the Lixus ruins. The boat taxi from the fishermen's wharf is a more romantic crossing to the beach which has cabins, summer camping and cafés grilling fish. The Bank Populaire and the Post Office are both found on the Av. Mohammed V and a residual Spanish consulate at 1, Apartado de Correros.

WHAT TO SEE

Place de la Libération

The **Avenue Mohammed V** leads off from the Tangier–Rabat road to the heart of the town. This graceful avenue, decorated with gardens, leads to the **Place de la Libération** surrounded by cafés and hotels that congregate in an elegant and very Spanish plaza around a central tiled fountain. The Place opens out towards the coast which is capped by the **Esplanade Moulay Ishmael**, a long garden balcony that overlooks the surf and cliffs. The esplanade leads to the south up to a lighthouse, whilst to the right it sweeps below the **fortress of Kebibat** in a curve down to the fishermen's wharf where you can catch the boat taxi for 1dh across to the beach. The beach offers the best view of the Kasbah Kebibat which is now a gaunt ruin. It was refurbished by the Spanish as a military hospital to deal with some of the casualties of the Riff rising, but now the tile and plaster decoration mixes with mounds of waste that cascade down from the high terrace to the gardens below.

The Medina

Returning to the Place de la Libération, pass through the **Bab el Khemis**, an impressive arch of aged bricks and tiles lined with swallows' nests, to enter the **souk** and the old pre-Spanish town. The atmosphere immediately changes as you step from the leisurely café life of the Place to the souk in the heart of the Medina. The souk is a long cobbled courtyard lined with aged galleries. Small artisan stalls compete with Berber market ladies for attention and although the souk is most active on Thursday it is an area of perpetual animation. Just past the Bab Khemis you'll find the greatest density of cafés selling mint tea and brochettes. An old fountain at the far end of the souk flows beneath the long arch of the **Bab Kasbah**.

Kasbah de la Cigogne

The Rue Moulay el Mehdi runs from here to take you twisting and turning out of the Medina to an esplanade created on top of the old battlements that offers a fine view over the sinuous Loukkos river. Behind and partly covered by a sprawling garden are the higher ramparts of the Kasbah de la Cigogne, a Moorish fort built by the Saadian Sultan el Mansour to hold the Portuguese prisoners after the battle of three kings in 1578, whilst he arranged profitable ransoms from their families.

Archaeological Museum

The smaller stone-built bastion nearer the estuary looks and is a Christian **fort**. It was so thoroughly restored at the beginning of this century that it is best seen as a monument to the Iberian occupations of 1489–1491, 1610–1689, 1911–57 than as surviving from any particular period. It is decorated with the arms of Charles V that the Spanish brought to Larache to give the place a better look.

It now houses the Archaeological Museum which is open every day but Tuesday from 9.00–12.00, 15.00–17.30, admission free. It is a slightly uninspiring collection of cast copies and lesser items from the digs at Lixus but with some figures of Zeus, Bacchus and some pleasant geometrical mosaics.

Opposite is a whimsical **Andalucian palace** built in 1915, a fitting exterior for the **national conservatoire of music** which maintains uncorrupted the musical heritage of the Andalucian princely courts and teaches the modern guitar.

Walk down past the Kasbah de la Cigogne to rejoin the Av. Mohammed V. The town **market**, a splendid turreted affair, can be reached by following the third turning to your left on the Place de la Libération as you enter from the Av. Mohammed V. The cliff walk up to the lighthouse will lead you past the ruins of the **Spanish jail** and the active Moroccan one with daily queues of women bringing parcels of food to their relations. This vaguely disturbing walk past shanties and savage cliff faces dotted with long bamboo fishing lines is a fitting start for the pilgrimage to the grave of **Jean Genet**, the great French post-war novelist and playwriter, in the Spanish graveyard to the south of Larache. A constant resident of both Larache and Tangier, both towns enhanced by compounds of imprisoned men, his last boyfriend Mohammed accidentally killed himself with Genet's gift of a fast car days after the author died.

FESTIVALS

There are three local Moussems but like most genuine Muslim celebrations they do not correspond to any fixed date in the Christian calendar. The festival of **Moulay Abdelkader Jilali** and that of **Lalla Menama** are held in June and that of **Sidi Allal ben Ahmed** sometime during the spring.

WHERE TO STAY

There is rarely a problem finding a bed in Larache. There are a scattering of pensions and hotels around the Place de la Libération and the Av. Mohammed V.

The **Hôtel Riad** is on the left of the Rue Mohammed ben Abdallah a street leading off the Place. It is the old house of the Duchess of Guise set in a mature and delightful garden. It has a calm atmosphere with dignified attentative uniformed staff, a pool, a bar, a restaurant and only 24 rooms. A double costs 125dh, a single 98dh, tel 2626.

The * **Hôtel Espana** is on the corner of the Place and the Av. Hassan II. It is a large, cool, echoing and rather grandly shabby place where a double will cost 52dh and a single 38dh. The **Hotel Cervantes** has immaculately clean rooms on the second floor with views of the sea or overlooking the Place. Prices generally vary with demand, and range from 13–60dh for a room. The cheapest rooms are in the **Hôtel Atlas** just in the Medina through the Bab Khemis. The bar restaurant **Flora** runs a camp site in summer, 1 km out of Larache on the road south to Rabat. In summer a semi-official Moroccan camp is established on the beach.

WHERE TO EAT

The **Café Central**, also known as **El Pozo**, is the most resolutely Spanish of the café bars around the Place and is run as a delightful rearguard of the Protectorate with its polished bar and tapas. The **Café Koutoubia** or the **Café Lixus**, also on the Place can give a three-course dinner with fresh fish for 35dh. The **Café Restaurant Oscare**, on the corner of the Place and Av. Mohammed V produces a good three-course dinner for 20dh. There are some conspiratorial grill cafés just inside the Medina through the Bab Khemis situated in holes in the wall. They serve a delightful range of salads and fish for a few dirhams.

Larache to Ksar el Kebir

Ksar el Kebir is only 36 km south from Larache. The road passes beside the fertile Loukkos valley whose upper slopes are covered by great orange, tangerine and lemon groves. Until the 20th century a sacred forest was left undisturbed by plough or herdsmen in the midst of this prosperous region. Raisuni remembered that sick men were cured of illness under the branches of the sacred wood and many lepers used to go there hoping to lose their sores.

Ksar el Kebir

Ksar el Kebir is bypassed by the main Tangier to Rabat highway and the modern town has gravitated towards the railway station where the huge Sunday market is held. This prosperous and growing agricultural town, set above the steep alluvial banks of the river Loukkos, is ignored by most visitors and a first glance at the neat new boulevards, breeze-block construction sites and tall sugar and flour mills may reinforce this decision. However behind this modern façade the old Medina does contain evidence of a dignified urban past fuelled by centuries of cultured Andalucian refugees, though the external walls of the mosques and sanctuaries are all that a non-Muslim may see. A guide, necessarily an amateur in this non-tourist town, will be able to show you around the old buildings of Ksar el Kebir that are all the more fascinating for being discovered in such an outwardly unpromising town.

GETTING AROUND

The railway, bus and grand taxi stations are all up by the Sunday market above the town to the east. If you are not travelling by car this is an obvious day to arrive with travel in every direction easy to organize. Just off the main Rabat to Tangier highway, the P2, Ksar el Kebir is 36 km southeast of Larache and 37km north of Souk el Arba du Rharb.

Walk down from the station to the Place Granada and the gate on your left, the Bab el Oued, gives entrance to the Medina.

HISTORY

Ksar el Kebir means 'the great enclosure', a name which was awarded after the Almohad Sultan Yaacoub el-Mansour enclosed an earlier 11th-century foundation with massive walls. Stones from the old Roman town of Oppidum Novum are still being found deep in the banks of silt during recent building works.

The city was embellished by the Merenids and survived as an unconquered bastion against the spreading power of Portugal throughout the 15th and 16th centuries. Ksar el Kebir attracted large numbers of Andalucian refugees as well as Moroccans forced out from the coastal ports. The Battle of the Three Kings, also known as the battle of Ksar el Kebir, brought to an end the Portuguese threat and the town's great period.

Ghailaine, a Moroccan general with political ambitions, who had made his name by besieging English-held Tangier, made Ksar his capital in 1652 before the Alouite Moulay er Rachid asserted himself as Sultan in 1666. Moulay Ishmael's recapture of the ports of the northern seaboard, Mehdiya, Tangier, Asilah and Larache, from European powers in the late 17th century inevitably reduced the importance of this citadel of Islam. A local revolt led by Ghailaine encouraged the Sultan to raze the Almohad walls of the city and in the long struggle for the succession throughout the 18th century the now defenceless town was ravaged by opposing armies. The many mosques and shrines were respected, and provide the core from which the post-Protectorate town has grown.

WHAT TO SEE

On Sunday the streams of donkeys, mule carts and farmers draws you to the twin compounds of the market above the town to the east. The **Souk of Sidi Bouhamed** is the largest on the left of the Place Moulay el Mehdi and the **souk of Sidi Merzouk** is on the right a little further into the town.

The **Medina** is entered through the **Bab el Oued**, the river gate where the local artisans and manufactories still operate. The older houses of the Medina have been constructed from elegant courses of narrow brick. It is an unusually calm and tranquil place and you might well have to drink a few cups of tea at a café outside the gate in order to find a guide to the Medina.

Passing through the gate leads you to the **Souk el Attarin** and the stalls of the spice merchants. The benevolent Alouite Sultan Sidi Mohammed founded a new market courtyard, the Fondouq es Soltan, at the end of the ruinous 18th-century succession wars, as a secure place where the more expensive imported wares were sold. The **Mosque of Sidi Mohammed ech Cherif** nearby can be recognized by its octagonal minaret.

Further into the Medina past the souk es Seghir, ask to see the old **fondouq of the weavers**, a most impressive place with a double layer of busy looms existing in baffling proximity. They produce bolts of thick brown and black woollen cloth which is sold at auction.

The **Grand Mosque** was erected in the 12th century by the same Almohad sultan, Yaacoub el Mansour, who built the walls. The twin windows of the minaret were taken from Roman ruins. The mosque is currently being carefully restored. The crypt of the sanctuary has been found to have been built over an ancient church. A souterrain was discovered leading down to a spring of fresh water which may account for the local tradition that a tunnel led from the mosque to a secret escape cave on the banks of the river. A 14th-century Merenid **Medersa**, a college for orthodox Islamic instruction, erected next to the Grand Mosque by Sultan Abou Hassan, is currently closed to visitors but worth enquiring about.

The Medina is littered with maraboutic shrines, zaouia and mosques. In the same quarter as the Great Mosque is the **shrine of Sidi Dais**, the ex-Sultan of Cadiz who left the troubled politics of Andalucia for a devout life in Ksar.

You can wander happily ignorant through the Medina or ask to be shown the 15th-century gate of the **Mosque of Sidi el Haj Zmiri**, the zaouia of the Hamadasha sect, the **sanctuary of Lalla Fatima** (another exile from Andalucia), the **Mosque Souqia** and the **Mosque Saidia** with an old abandoned medersa at the end of the road. The western quarter near the Place de L'Amitié has the **Mosque of ed Drizi**, and the **koubba of Sidi Yaacoub** is the most attractive of the many found here, most of which are tombs of Mujhadeen, holy warriors killed in the fighting against the Portuguese and Spanish on the coast.

A **tannery** is situated on the edge of the Medina overlooked by the tall modern flour mill. Even in this active courtyard with the distinctive tanning and dyeing vats you cannot escape from memories of the dignified urban Islamic past. Low fragments of the Almohad city wall can be seen, as well as two shrines and a distinctive stone-built minaret. Long removed from its associated mosque, local legends suggest that it was used as a last resort by fathers who imprisoned daughters reluctant to leave home and marry.

Just further south other remnants of the city wall enclose the eight-sided **tower of Sidi ben Abbase**, venerated by Muslims and the now departed Jewish community alike. The three faiths of the Book have their separate burial plots beyond—the Christian graveyard is increasingly desecrated, the Jewish cemetery contains a pleasant central pillared dome and the Muslim graveyard boasts a shrine overwhelmed by a vast and decaying cult olive tree.

Out of the Medina walking on the 'New Road' towards Tangier you will pass a complex of new religious buildings, the **sanctuary and college** that belong to the premier saint of the town, Sidi Boughalebe, who was a 13th-century princely refugee from the wealth and corruption of Andalucia, who sought and found the simple life in Ksar el Kebir.

WHERE TO STAY OR EAT

Opposite the station there are several grill cafés. There are a number of indifferent pensions but stay at the **Andaluz café and Hôtel** on New Street. It has fallen on hard times and you enter through a grand but decaying portico with a lemon tree growing in the courtyard. The ground-floor rooms are scrupulously clean and cost only 15dh a night. Food and soft drinks are available from the adjoining animated café.

The battle of Ksar el Kebir

The battlefield is 12 km due north of Ksar, marked by the railway station of Makhzen, where the victory is commemorated every year on 5 August. A track, the 8201, runs to the west of the railway line and a left turn at Tleta Rissana would lead you back to Larache.

Moroccan independence in the 16th century was threatened by three powerful neighbours, the Ottoman Turks, the Portuguese and the Spanish. The battle of Ksar el Kebir was a decisive victory against the Portuguese which impressed both Spain and Ottoman Turkey.

In 1578 the boy King Sebastian of Portugal landed at Asilah with an army of 20,000 men, supposedly to champion the cause of the ex-Sultan, El Mutawakkil. Sebastian's real motive was the conquest of Morocco and his army moved inland with the immediate objectives of seizing Ksar el Kebir and Larache before marching on Fez.

The Saadian Sultan Abdel Malik positioned his force of 50,000 between the Makhzen and Ouarour streams with his artillery on the high ground and his Andalucian troops to the fore. In a bitterly contested battle the Moroccan forces annihilated the Portuguese, largely due to the resilience of the Andalucian infantry and ferocity of the regiments of tribal cavalry.

Sebastian died surrounded by slain warriors and covered in wounds, his client the ex-Sultan drowned whilst escaping and Sultan Abdel Malik died in the hour of his victory—probably poisoned by an agent of El Mutawakkil. His brother Ahmed al-Mansour, 'the victorious' succeeded him as Sultan and collected a vast fortune from the booty and ransoming captured Portuguese nobles whom he imprisoned at Larache.

King Sebastian had sworn to convert or kill every Jew in Morocco when he became Emperor. The few surviving synagogues of Morocco still celebrate the anniversary of the victory that saved them from such a fate.

The Gharb

The western coastal plain, the Gharb, is one of the most fertile areas of Morocco, well irrigated by the sluggish waters of the Oued Sebou. Though the land is rich and valuable it is not beautiful. The hotel in Arbaoua is the best in the region, there are two minor Roman sites, Banassa and Thamsuda but the beach at Moulay Bousselham is the chief attraction of the region.

Arbaoua, almost exactly halfway between Rabat and Tangier, is a group of French-built lodges, a camping site and a hotel on a wooded hill off the main Tangier to Rabat highway. It is a purpose-built base for hunting in the 35,000 hectare game reserve that stretches west from here to occupy much of the rough coastal land between Larache and Moulay Bousselham. The **Hostellerie Route de France**, tel 18, is a piece of the French Alps transported to Africa and subsequently popular with Moroccans taking a discreet weekend. The hotel is decorated with hunting trophies and massive wooden fittings throughout. The thirteen bedrooms are large and comfortable with efficient baths. The bar is busy and the dining room a gastronomic treat, specializing in the hunting season in game dishes like snipe, duck, partridge and wild boar. A double room costs 96dh. The camp site is open all the year round and is shaded by tall fir trees.

Souk el Arba du Gharb, 27 km down the road, is a local market centre and roadstop complete with a bank, a number of busy licensed restaurants and a couple of hotels. On the junction for the Fez and Meknes road, it is a pleasantly lively place for a meal but makes for a noisy night. A three-course meal with wine at the **Grand Hôtel**, tel 2020, of omelette, salad, steak and fruit costs 50dh. Whilst a single room at the ** **Gharb**, tel 2203, which also has a bar and restaurant, costs 90dh. Buses and grands taxis depart from here for Moulay Bousselham, 36 km to the west, and Ouezzane, 53 km to the east, two interesting and little-visited destinations.

Moulay Bousselham

This is both a small seaside resort and the sanctuary for an important annual pilgrimage. Sandy cliffs ring beaches both sides of this one-street village which is strung above a sea-filled lagoon. A large brackish lake extends inland, the **Merdja ez Zerga**, which is separated from the sea by a spit of settled sand.

The simple avenue of the village is lined with a row of half a dozen unlicensed fish restaurants, all under a continuous arcade which faces the new **mosque**. This mosque partly hides the view of a delightful family of **seven Maraboutic shrines** that dip down the slope towards the sea. On the other side of the lagoon a single shrine looks in danger of being engulfed by the cascading sand of a towering dune.

As a centre for an important Muslim pilgrimage the town shelters some surprising local beliefs. The marabout Moulay Bousselham, literally the saint in a cloak, was the Egyptian Abou Said, a pantheistic Sufi who fled from orthodox persecution to take refuge in Morocco and where he died in 951. He was buried by the sea shore at the then Phoenician trading post of Mulechala.

The **tomb of Joseph, the son of Aristotle**, is venerated in a cave near to that of **Bou el Kornien**, a two-horned man. Bou el Kornien has been interpreted as a wild green man from the woods, a universal figure of male fertility, or Alexander the Great—in his manifestation as the son of Zeus–Baal–Ammon, the ram-horned supreme deity—for Alexander after the siege of Tyre visited the Berber oracle of Ammon at Shiwa in the Sahara, where he was received as the son of the god. Some strength is added to this interpretation in that Alexander's tutor was Aristotle. It remains however a striking cult survival that was possibly brought to this shore by Phoenician traders. It would have appealed to the 10th-century refugee, the syncretic mystic Moulay Bousselham who must have been delighted to find such an oddity in his place of exile. In the cave where Bou el Kornien is venerated, a sacred stalactite secretes a salty milky fluid which is sucked for good luck by devotees, an adoration ritual that a Kleinian will have no difficulty in explaining.

To the north of the town on the rising ground are the traces of an **old fort**. Moulay Bousselham was known to Pliny the Elder and Phoenician Mulechala survived intact at least into the 12th century. It was then fortified to provide a secure port for the inland city of Basra whose fate it apparently shared.

FESTIVALS AND SPORTS

The **pilgrimage to Bousselham** takes place in late June or July with the prepared space by the petrol station transformed into a holiday town. Bulls and sheep are sacrificed and eaten with much general music and festivity. A quieter Moussem occurs in September for **Sidi Ahmed ben Mansour**. Throughout the summer the beach chalets are full of prosperous Moroccan families on holiday. The lake is full of boats as it has a great reputation for **fishing**, whilst the coastal platform is one of the most celebrated places for **scuba diving** and **spear gun fishing** in Atlantic Morocco. On the lake **boats** can be hired and there is a 40dh flamingo trip regularly touted. As everywhere on the coast the sea provides exhilarating but dangerous surf and warning flags and lifeguards are employed here in the summer.

WHERE TO SLEEP AND EAT

The only hotel in Moulay Bousselham is the *** **Lagona**, tel 25, a comfortable new hotel that overlooks the lagoon. It has the only bar, licensed restaurant and swimming pool in town. Downstairs there is a disco club with a television/video room off the open plan central lounge. A double room costs 150dh. The **campsite** is one of the most delightful in Morocco. It is right down by the edge of the lagoon, with the fishing boats beached up to its perimeter fence. The sites have been carefully arranged so that you are screened and shaded by the many trees.

The few chalets above the beach are individually owned and not generally rented. The restaurant owners live in villages outside Bousselham and if they offer you a bed for the night that is where you'll be going. For those with a car, the **hotel at Arbaoua** has more character and is 45 km away.

Out of Moulay Bousselham

A good road runs 44 km south to **Kenitra** between the coast and an irrigation canal on flat land. Travelling east to Arbaoua or Souk el Arba du Gharb you pass a forest of eucalyptus. Between the villages of **Lalla Mimounia** and **Lalla Rhano** you can distinguish a distinctive outcrop of rock in this basically flat undulating belt of farmland. Only a rough track exists that could provide access for an interesting day's walk in order to scale the ridge and investigate the enormous number of stone-framed **Neolithic and Phoenician burial chambers** that cover its surface.

Back on the main road south from Souk el Arba you pass through the irrigated sugar-cane fields of the Sebou valley to reach in 15 km **Souk et Tleta du Gharb**, which has an agricultural **market** on Tuesday. There are two Roman sites, **Banassa** and **Thamusida**, off the road between here and Kenitra which are best visited with the extra distraction of a picnic.

The Roman ruins of Banassa

3 km south of Souk Tleta du Gharb take a left turn, cross the Oued Sebou and then left again after another 3 km look out for a faded sign on the left indicating the farm track for Banassa.

A cluster of cypress trees on the brow of a hill and a scattering of maraboutic shrines indicate the surrounding ruins of baths, forum and temples of the city of Banassa pleasantly sited above the high earth banks of the Oued Sebou.

The city of Julia Valentina Banassa has been excavated to reveal three distinct pre-Roman layers that date back before the 3rd century BC. The present visible remains and the typical, regular Roman street pattern date from the enlargement of Banassa into a colony by Octavian before he became the Emperor Augustus in 27 BC. A circuit of walls, defended by towers and over five feet thick, was built in the beginning of the 3rd century, and there are traces of an army camp to the west, but Banassa does not appear to have survived Diocletian's withdrawal. The custodian who speaks French lives by the ruins and will show you around the main features.

The **forum**, the public square of the town, is easily recognizable as it retains its 3rd century AD paving stones. To its southern end is the three-chambered state shrine on a high terrace, the **Capitol** dedicated to the triad of Olympian gods, Jupiter, Juno and Minerva that was rebuilt in the 2nd century AD. Opposite the temple is the **basilica** with its vaulted round arch where justice was seen to be dispensed. South of the forum are a number of rooms that were almost certainly municipal offices. Here the **tribunical rostrum** still stands where speeches and declarations would be made.

There are five sets of **public baths** in Banassa. The large western baths are approached by crossing the old principal road of Banassa which would have the major shops, factories and houses ranged along its pavements. A hoard of 457 coins was found by archaeologists hidden in a baker's oven. The central hall of these baths, the under-floor heating system and the cold plunge pool, at the end on your right, are all quite distinctive.

The **Macellum or meat market** was bordered with a colonnade of stalls and held a mosaic of a stylized tree. The little western baths are just to its north. They held a Dionysic scene with a portrait of the god of wine surrounded by grapes and four lovers. The fresco baths are nearby at a lower level, overlooked by a well that is still in active use. The floor is covered in a herringbone grid of worn bricks and the fresco wall paintings are still in position. Details of Oceanus with his court of sea animals are recognizable and the surrounding panels have been painted to imitate marble. The hot rooms have geometrical mosaic fragments where village boys still wash with water drawn from the nearby well: a continuity of use that briefly brings these dry stones sparkling back into life.

Pliny the Elder recorded that the Gharb was infested with elephants. An inscription from the Emperor Caracalla confirms this, thanking the town for a gift of elephants and cancelling any back tax owed to the Imperial chancery. Archaeologists have also discovered an elephant head carved from blue schist with marble tusks and evidence that the Egyptian goddess Isis had a temple here.

Roman ruins of Thamusida

Thamusida is 13 km north of Kenitra and 5 km west of the main P2 road on a farm track that becomes a muddy quagmire at the merest touch of rain. The turning is by the petrol station in the low village of Souk el Khemis, continue until you reach a major junction of three tracks, take the central one and continue down a slope until you see the ruins beside a house on the left surrounded in eucalyptus trees.

Thamusida like Banassa was built beside the banks of the Oued Sebou. The present remains are based on a fortified Roman camp of the 2nd century AD which was abandoned in the third. It was built over the ruins of a settlement of the Mauretanian kings that was probably destroyed by Claudius's legions during Aedemen's rebellion. The camp wall is 5 m thick and measures 165 m by 135 m with the interior divided into quarters by the regular grid of two streets. The **praetorian gate** is fortified with an outer defence work and the old river quays can be traced. Within the ramparts are well preserved **baths**, a **temple** of three chambers surrounded by a sacred **boundary wall**, numerous truncated pillars and a number of mills.

Kenitra

On the south bank of the Oued Sebou is the sprawling modern city of Kenitra. It is entirely a child of the French who in 1913 started the construction of a new town, first known as Port Lyautey, which was intended to be the new industrial heartland of Morocco, and was built on the same latitude as Meknes and Fez. In 1942, as one of the few all-weather bases in North Africa, it was a prime objective of the Casablanca landings. It is now a city of 300,000 though it has long lost the battle for primacy with Casablanca. The airport base of Kenitra was at the centre of the failed military coup against the king in 1972.

A broad central avenue runs straight through the town with the major hotels and bars found to the west of the main administrative square. As representative of new Morocco it does not have much of interest for the visitor apart from a comparatively active bar and disco club lifestyle. If you do find yourself wanting a bed here go for the ** **Hôtel La Rotonde** at 50, Av. Mohammed Diouri, tel 3343, a comfortable, efficient and tranquil hotel. The **Mamora**, Av. Hassan II has two-star prices and a swimming pool, nightclub, restaurant and bar with a busier environment. Banks are at 363 and 365, Av. Mohammed V, the central street where the Post Office and the CTM station are also to be found. The railway station is to the south of the town.

Forest of Mamora

South and east of Kenitra is the extensive Forest of Mamora, a mixture of scrubby wilderness and of plantations of pine, eucalyptus and cork. This can be appreciated by driving to the Maison Forestiére Sidi Chaouri which is at the centre of a number of forest tracks. To get there take the P3 road from Kenitra to the village of Sidi Yahya du Gharb where a right turn takes you southeast through 40 km of woodland to Sidi Chaouri.

From Kenitra to Rabat

South of Kenitra, off the unpromising and busy road to Rabat, are three distinctive attractions. At **Mehdiya** there is a magnificent sprawling Kasbah overlooking the sea with the unusual charms of the Hôtel Atlantique. At **Plage des Nations** a hotel in splendid isolation commands a magnificent beach. The **Jardins Exotiques** at Boukna-del is an earnest French creation that is now imbued with a more tranquil Moroccan tone.

Mehdiya

A turning to the west, 11 km south of Kenitra, takes you through a nature reserve established along the Sebou estuary and around the resort village of **Mehdiya Plage**. The **Lake of Sidi Boughaba** is a wonderful place for bird watching. You can soon become quite blasé about ospreys fishing the waters. The Sidi in his Koubba, alone like St Francis amongst the birds, is visited in a Moussem that occurs in August.

HISTORY
Mehdiya has a typical Atlantic history. It was founded as a Punic colony by the Carthaginian admiral Hannon in the 5th century BC. Known as el Mamora, 'the populous', and surrounded then as now by forests, it was a natural choice for the Almohad sovereign Abdel Moumen as his principal shipbuilding yard, but the scheme never prospered.

The Portuguese managed to build a fort here in 1515 which they were able to hold for only a few years. In the latter half of the 16th century it became the base for Mainwaring, an enterprising pirate who worked by turn for all the major pirate bosses: the Bey of Tunis, the Duke of Tuscany, the Venetian Republic and the Sultan of Morocco. From Mehdiya he preyed on all shipping and according to the religion and the race of his victims sold them at either the slave markets of Villefranche, Fez, Leghorn or Algiers and retired from this profitable enterprise just before the Spanish raided the estuary in 1610.

The Spaniards returned four years later and fortified the Kasbah. There they remained for 50 years until they were expelled by Moulay Ishmael's general, Ali er Riffi, the 'Caesar of the North'. The 17th-century palace, gate and mosque of the Kasbah all date from the rebuilding undertaken after this reconquest.

The Kasbah of Mehdiya last witnessed military action in the American landings of 1942. In the one elegant gesture of this muddled campaign two trim destroyers, the **Bernadou** and **Cole**, swept up the estuary on the morning of 8 November, raked the harbour with machine gunfire and landed dry marines on the quay.

Mehdiya Plage

This is a quite unattractive rectangular grid of beach chalets. It is a very Moroccan resort, bustling with promenade activity in summer but the complexe touristique's pool, bar and restaurant are wistfully empty throughout the rest of the year. The campsite, swimming and beach here are not at all recommended. What is delightful is the ** **Hôtel Atlantique**, a raffish, intriguing place that comes to life after dinner in the evening and buzzes until 3 or 4 in the morning. Throughout the year a Moroccan group performs with heightening intensity as the night progresses. This is far removed from the folk shows of tourist-frequented hotels; the music and musicians flow, change and improvise in a jazz-like style. The singers, of such outstanding character, intensity, size and determination, broaden your appreciation of Moroccan women overnight. Be careful of the bars which tend to sag if you lean too heavily on them, and you may also have to keep a watch on the bar prices. The audience can also be entertaining; I was lucky enough to observe the arrival of the chief of police, an enormous tall negro immaculately covered in a double breasted suit who, having had his hand kissed by anyone who ought to, sat sipping a sticky green cordial for hours and watched the singers with an almost proprietorial interest.

You can have dinner on the hotel verandah looking towards the sea for 65dh or a meal at the **Auberge de la Forêt**, tel 106, or the coast-front **Restaurant café Dauphine**. Do not plan to leave early in the morning, if you can get a room, for the connecting doors between the night club and the bedrooms are locked and no one gets up here very early. A double bedroom costs 110dh.

Mehdiya Kasbah

The Kasbah is further up the estuary. The road cuts through some old ramparts where you'll find the **Café Belle Vue** with its shaded tranquil terrace and balcony where you can get a light lunch of salad, omelette, fish and yoghurt for 35dh. Beyond is the fishermen's wharf where a long stairway climbs the hill up to the Kasbah. The road continues beside the Sebou estuary and the first right turn takes you up to the impressive landport **gates of the Kasbah**.

The gates are protected by two flanking castellated towers that were erected by Sultan Moulay Ishmael. Stairs lead up to the lefthand turret which provide a fine view of the large interior compound of the whole fortress. Walk down to pass close to the 17th-century rustic **mosque** and enter the **Palace of the governor** through the ornate brick arch. Dark subterranean passages give way to sudden pools of light illuminating a brick-paved courtyard flooded with branches of figs. Stairways lead up to bare balconies that provide odd vistas of the pockets of buildings, barracks, cisterns and storehouses that are now deserted and enclosed by weeds but were once occupied by Moulay Ishmael's negro Abid regiments.

As you find your way out walk towards the estuary which is overlooked by a gun platform where seven rusting ships' cannon are still in place.

Plage des Nations

It is 9 km from the Mehdiya turning and a 1 km drive off the Kenitra–Rabat highway to the most attractive and tranquil beach on this area of coast. Named after the favourite haunt of Rabat's diplomatic community, it still retains a certain cachet with the **** **Hôtel Firdaous** sitting perfectly alone on the Atlantic shore and its unchanged fifties interior is beginning to look rather classic. All the hotel rooms face the sea, there are two pools, two restaurants, bars, piano and the staff are friendly to day visitors.

The beach is open to all and a few snack cafés are established here in the summer. Travelling to the beach or the gardens from Salé you can catch the No 28 which leaves about every 20 minutes from the Bab Mrisa and drops you beside the road. A place in a grand taxi will cost 8dh and take you right to the beach.

Bouknadel Garden

Also known as the **Jardins Exotiques**, the gardens with their tattered signpost are on the west side of the road 8 km after the Plage des Nations turning, and 12 km from Rabat. Even if you are not wild on plants, the cool shaded intimate bamboo benches, the flowers, the smells and the tranquillity make it a whimsical and restful place. The gardens are open from 9.00–18.30, admission 9dh.

They were created by the ingenious horticulturist and ecologist M. François in the 1950s and held over 1500 species at their peak. His verse thoughts on ecological principles and his love for Morocco are found at the entrance before a mass of hibiscus and red hot pokers. It originally contained a zoo and aquarium but these cages are thankfully now empty, to leave a delightful profuse series of gardens naturally inhabited by birds, turtles and frogs. It extends in a long thin belt of 4 hectares back from the roadside towards the coastal dunes. There are three sections, an indigenous collection of Moroccan flora, a formal Islamic Andalucian garden and a collection of exotic specimens from all over the world. The lush ecosystems of America, Japan, China, Pacific, Caribbean and southeast Asia have all been skilfully recreated in delightful confusion on this dry sandy coastal plain. The network of bamboo bridges, stone walkways, root passages, ruined temples and pagodas is magnificently eclectic, definitely bizarre and saved from being kitch due to the rapid weathering and luxurious overgrowth. There are special coloured and timed routes of three-quarters or one hour but it is difficult to imagine that anybody would allow themselves to be organized in such a way.

Rabat–Salé

Rabat has been the political capital of Morocco since 1912. It wears the well-ordered urban architecture of the 20th century: broad tree-lined avenues, a central park, apartment blocks and suburban quarters for the Ministries, officialdom and foreign diplomats. The Rabat–Salé conurbation which now has a population of over a million has an impressive air of activity by day. Brisk men armed with briefcases stride to their appointments along the avenues of the city centre, lined with newsagents, book shops, cinemas and cafés, but this familiar core of a modern capital city also contains striking monuments from the past.

The twin cities of Rabat and Salé, which sit on opposing banks of the Oued Bou Regreg estuary, have a long history. All the civilizations of Morocco have been drawn to the estuary's safe harbour which has cut an access to the sea through the forbidding line of Atlantic cliffs. Rabat, the city on the southern bank, has shown greater extremes of fortune whilst the city of the northern bank, Salé, has had a steadier but less glamorous history. Salé, half an hour's walk from the city centre, is now just a suburb of Rabat but it retains its own traditional identity. For Rabat the wheel of fortune has in 2500 years of history turned twice to elevate it as an Imperial capital and twice as a trading maritime power whilst in between these glories it has been reduced to a humble village.

The city walls, gates and tower of Hassan from the 12th-century Almohad empire still

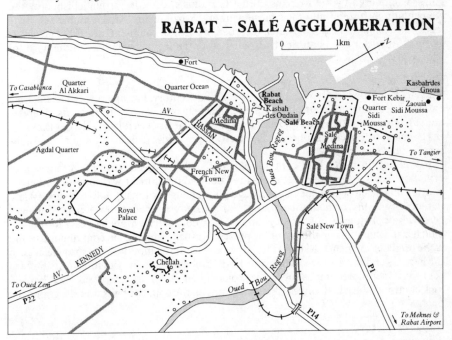

dominate 20th century Rabat. The more intimate achievements from the Merenid dynasty, like the Abou Hassan Medersa can be found in the 13th-century Medina of Salé and in Rabat's royal necropolis—the celebrated walled garden of the Chellah. The Oudaia Kasbah of Rabat, in its strategic position above the sea entrance to the Bou Regreg estuary, has been at the heart of the city's long Islamic history. It has a celebrated Almohad gate, an Andalucian urban interior and a garden palace from the 17th century which has been transformed into a delightful museum. For rarer insights into the Phoenician and classical achievements the Museum of Antiquities and the ruins of Sala Colonia inside the Chellah walls reward you with haunting views and art of the highest order.

RABAT

History

The Phoenician and Roman trading city
The ruins of Sala in the Chellah garden partly cover the site of a Phoenician port established beside the estuary of Bou Regreg. This entrepôt had developed by the 3rd century BC into a sizeable settlement minting Punic lettered coins for the Mauretanian kings. Conquered by the Romans during Claudius's reign, it was embellished by the Roman administration into their most southerly urban centre. Given municipal privileges of a *colonia* by Trajan, it is then recorded in classical commentaries as Sala Colonia and was ruled for two centuries by Rome before the legions withdrew to the north of Morocco.

The R'bat
The city continued to flourish and in the early 8th century, having accepted Islam, Sala enthusiastically identified itself with the Khajarite heresy in order to assert its independence from the orthodox Arab governors. Protected by a powerful local Berber tribe, the Berghouata, who were also heretical, the city successfully resisted a number of armies sent by orthodox rulers.

It was not until the 10th century that Sala Colonia was destroyed. A garrison of orthodox Arabs established a R'bat—a religious community of warriors—on a neighbouring hill from which they could wage continuous legitimate holy war against the heretic city. This orthodox community of pillagers soon destroyed Sala Colonia's centuries of prosperity but the surrounding Berghouata tribe were less easy to subdue. The R'bat, which was on the site of the present Kasbah, remained in continuous use and is the origin of the name 'Rabat'. The Almoravide Empire inherited the struggle against the heretics and the first two Almoravide leaders died fighting the Berghouata in the 11th century. Their more famous successor, Youssef ben Tachfine, refortified the R'bat and took control of the tribal fortress that had grown on the opposite bank, the site of present Salé.

Rabat of Victory
The succeeding Almohad dynasty found this fortress with its history of fanaticism and

war much to their taste. Abdel Moumen built himself a palace within the walls of the R'bat and used it as an assembly point for marshalling the enormous Almohad army which at the start of one campaign numbered quarter of a million men. It was his grandson, Yaacoub el Mansour, who decided to make the old R'bat into an Imperial capital. Marrakesh and Seville were to be mere national centres in comparison to the R'bat el Fath, the Rabat of Victory. He built the enormous and still surviving extent of city walls which were only to be filled and then exceeded in the 20th century. The great mosque of El Hassan was built in scale to the city, but work stopped on the day of the Sultan's death in 1199. The tower of Hassan is in the same unfinished state as the workmen left it 800 years ago. Rabat survived as a city only as long as Morocco's rulers retained an interest in the Atlantic as a route to the Muslim lands in Spain. The crushing Almohad defeat in Spain in 1213, at the battle of Las Navas de Tolosa ended its strategic importance.

In the 14th century the Merenid Sultans with their exquisite taste selected the dwindling city of Rabat to be the backdrop to their royal tombs. They enclosed the neighbouring ruined city of Sala Colonia in walls which were pierced by a magnificent gothic gate. Fine gardens, delicate mosques and sanctuaries were planted within the necropolis sanctuary. Leo Africanus reports on his visit to Rabat in 1500 that it was a mere scattering of a hundred houses. Rabat's future revival was however still curiously linked to the affairs of Spain.

The Republic of Bou Regreg

In 1609 Muslim refugees from the town of Hornachos, near Badajoz, were offered the empty Kasbah of Rabat by Zaidan, a Saadian Sultan, in exchange for support in a succession war against his brother. They were later joined by about 4000 other refugees from Andalucia who settled in the area of the present Medina. For in 1610 an edict of King Phillip III banished from Spain all citizens of Muslim descent, even if they had converted to Catholicism. The Almohad city walls enclosed far too large an area and the Andalucians built the dividing wall that still separates the Medina from the New Town.

The Andalucian refugees had a burning desire for revenge against Christian Europe. Their fierce determination was married with the ability and tactical experience of Christian pirates, outlaws and renegades who found a ready welcome. It was a potent alliance and the pirate fleet known as the Sallée Rovers, ranged far out into the Atlantic and Caribbean to intercept merchant ships returning to Europe.

The bitter civil war between the rival Saadian Sultans allowed the inhabitants to govern their own affairs and from 1627 the two cities had established themselves as the Republic of the Bou Regreg. It was governed by an elected council or Diwan of sixteen members which met in Salé. Each year the Diwan elected a Caid and an Admiral. Jan Jansz, a German renegade who took the name Murad Reis, was the first and most successful Admiral of Salé. In one of his raids he took 237 captives from the village of Baltimore outside Cork in Ireland before proceeding to attack the fishing fleets off Iceland. Five years later, in 1636, he raided the south coast of England and sent his captives across France by land to Marseilles where they were shipped to the slave markets of Algiers. Four years later he was back, and St Michael's Mount in Cornwall lost sixty villagers to the Salé Rovers.

The European renegades were employed in just the navigation and the technical handling of their ships. It was the Andalucian refugees under their captain who acted as the fighting force. They spoke a common dialect called Franco, a mixture of French, Italian, Spanish and Portuguese—a curious forerunner of Esparanto. On return to Salé, 10% of the prize money was awarded to the Diwan which increasingly became an oligarchy of successful captains and merchants. The republic of Bou Regreg was never a homogeneous entity and only constant external pressure from the European powers at sea and rival Muslim warlords by land kept the inhabitants from pursuing faction fights and civil war to their full conclusion. The sand bar across the estuary and the savage cliffs prevented any European fleet from seriously threatening the pirate craft, though a subtle mixture of bombardment, blockade and bribes from the English and Dutch led to the release of some slaves and various protection arrangements.

The golden days of anarchy, profit and adventure ended when Sultan Moulay Rachid took possession in 1666. A brisk trade continued in supplying Moulay Ishmael with European slaves, though as this Sultan assumed a controlling 60% stake in the pirate business, profits were down for other shareholders.

The increased stability of Alouite rule allowed the English Barbary Company to establish a consul here who traded in Manchester cottons, armaments and negotiated Protestant ransoms. Catholic relief was managed by the Trinitarians and between the two over 1500 slaves were ransomed during Moulay Ishmael's long reign. The most famous fictional slave was Robinson Crusoe who was captured by the Sallée Rovers in 1661, sailing a slaver from Hull to West Africa and spent two years a slave at the republic of Bou Regreg.

New Rabat

The period after Sultan Moulay Ishmael's death in 1727 was one of rapid decline in trade and widespread destruction by warring heirs to the throne which was intensified by the traditional rivalry between Rabat and Salé. During the wise rule of Sultan Sidi Mohammed an attempt was made to discourage the remaining pirate activity even before the French bombardment of Rabat in 1765. After the bombardment Sidi Mohammed allowed a French consul to settle in Rabat, established a new administrative palace on its present site—safely out of range of European cannon—and encouraged Rabat to develop its now renowned carpet trade as well as building two new mosques and laying out a park. Unofficial coastal piracy and wrecking continued until the Imperial Austrian navy took a savage revenge for the loss of one ship in 1829 by shelling all the coastal cities of Morocco.

Rabat enjoyed a quiet level of prosperity as one of the towns under the firm control of the government during the 19th century, though without a suitable harbour it was increasingly superseded by Casablanca as a trading centre. Its future was radically altered in 1912 by France who, wary of the old cities of the interior, selected Rabat as the new political centre for the administration of the country. The fiction that the French Resident administered Morocco for the Sultan was vigorously maintained and Sultan Moulay Youssef was installed in the palace of Rabat.

French rule from 1912 to 1957, whilst rapidly developing a glittering New Town, made few changes to the traditional pattern of life in the old city, the Medina. The Protectorate was a colonial régime interested in ruling a conquered Islamic nation with the minimum of expense. This necessarily involved ruling through traditional power structures and avoiding any unnecessary social, moral or political interference. As part of this policy the native quarters were left as sanctums of traditional custom and separate modern quarters for the Europeans built outside. This policy, defensible on aesthetic grounds as well as that of convenient security, was initiated at Rabat by the first French Resident, Lyautey.

After Independence, Mohammed V, and his son, the present King Hassan II, developed the palace of Rabat from a mere symbol into the actual source of national authority.

GETTING AROUND

By Air
Six buses a day leave from outside the Hotel terminus on the Av. Mohammed V direct to Casablanca's Mohammed V International airport. Tickets cost 45dh, departures are at 4.30, 6.00, 8.00, 10.00, 12.30 and 18.00. The Royal Air Maroc ticket office is opposite the train station on the Av. Mohammed V and is open Mon–Sat, 8.00–12.00, 15.00–19.00. Air France is at 281, Av. Mohammed V and Iberia at 104, Av. Mohammed V on the first floor.

By Train
No more expensive than the coaches, punctual, reliable and taking you straight to the city centre, travelling by train to and from Rabat is recommended. The elegant white train station is on the intersection of Av. Mohammed V and Av. Moulay Youssef in the city centre. There are frequent departures for Casablanca, 15 a day for 19dh, 8 daily trains for Fez at 37dh, 5 for Tangier at 47dh, 4 for Oujda and change at Casablanca for trains to Marrakesh. There is a café restaurant and baggage lockers in the station.

By Bus
Local buses can be picked up on the Blvd Hassan II. No 17 heads south for Temara beach, the no 6 or 12 take you to the Bab Fez at Salé. Nos 1, 2 and 4 go south along the Av. Allal ben Abdallah, get off at Bab Zaer where you pass through the outer walls for Chellah. No 30 leaves for the main bus depot at the Place Zerktouni which is otherwise a tedious 2 km walk along the Blvd Hassan II from the Bab Al Had, ticket 3dh or petit taxi for 10dh. At the main bus depot it is well worth getting a CTM ticket at booths 14 or 15. The other services have elastic departure routines and Arabic timetables. CTM departures: Marrakesh and Ouezzane, 3 buses a day, Tangier, Fez and Meknes 4 departures, Tetouan and Azrou 2 departures and there are buses to Casablanca every two hours for 12dh.

By Taxi
Petits taxis are found next to the train station and opposite the Kasbah. Grands taxis for long haul destinations are found along the Av. Hassan II. For a place to Casablanca go to the taxi rank outside the main bus depot at Place Zerktouni, a quicker, more pleasant trip which should cost you only a few dirhams more than the bus ticket.

By Car
Driving in Rabat's one-way system is confusing. It is easier to park your car along Blvd

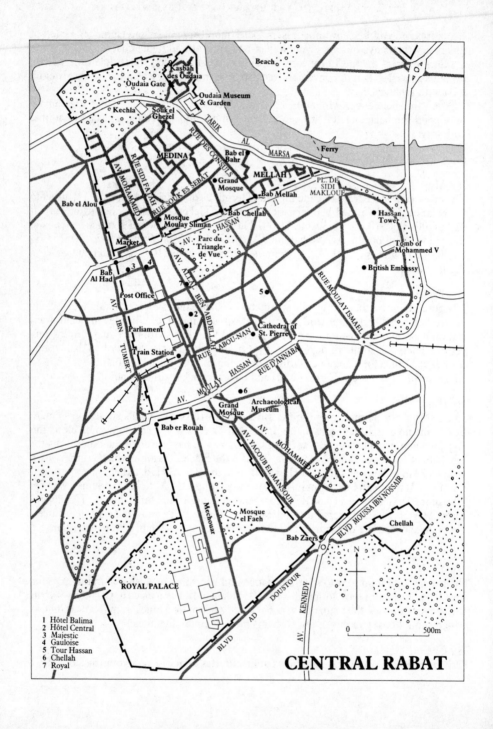

Beach

Kasbah
des Oudaia

Oudaia Gate

Oudaia Museum
& Garden

Kechla

Souk el
Ghezel

TARIK AL

MARSA

Ferry

RUE DES CONSULS

MEDINA

Bab el
Bahr

AV. MOHAMMED V

RUE SIDI FATAH

MELLAH

PL. DE
SIDI
MAKLOUF

Grand
Mosque

RUE SOUK ES SEBAT

Bab Mellah

Bab el Alou

Bab Chellah

Hassan
Tower

Mosque
Moulay Sliman

HASSAN

Market

AV. HASSAN II

Parc du
Triangle
de Vue

Tomb of
Mohammed V

British Embassy

Bab
Al Had

3   4

AV. ALAL BEN ABDELLAH

Post Office

5

RUE MOULAY ISMAEL

AV. IBN TUMERT

2

1

Parliament

Cathedral of
St. Pierre

Train Station

RUE ABOU-NAN

AV. MOULAY HASSAN

RUE D'ANNABA

6

Grand
Mosque

Archaeological
Museum

Bab er Rouah

AV. MOHAMMED

AV. YACOUB EL MANSOUR

Mechouar

Mosque
el Faeh

Chellah

Bab Zaers

BLVD MOUSSA IBN NOSSAIR

N

ROYAL PALACE

BLVD AD DOUSTOUR

AV. KENNEDY

0   500m

1 Hôtel Balima
2 Hôtel Central
3 Majestic
4 Gauloise
5 Tour Hassan
6 Chellah
7 Royal

CENTRAL RABAT

Hassan II and walk. There is a good selection of car-hire firms: Avis, 7, Zankat (Rue) Abou Faris El Marini; Europcar at the Hilton Hotel, tel 71028; Fly Drive, 2, Av. Amir Moulay El Marini; Hertz, 467, Av. Mohammed V; Locoto, 10, Av. Al Yamana; SNA, 1, Rue Patrice Lumumba; InterRent at the Hotel Tour Hassan, Av. Annegai. If you are working out mileage rates the distances from Rabat are: Agadir 608 km, Casablanca 91 km, Fez 198 km, Marrakesh 326 km, Tangier 278 km.

GETTING AROUND THE CITY
Rabat and Salé have spread enormously in recent decades but all the places of interest remain in walking distance from each other. Rabat could hardly be more convenient for the traveller, the Avenue Hassan II divides the Medina from the New City. To the east it leads to the Pont Moulay Hassan, the bridge across the Bou Regreg to Salé and to the west having passed through the Almohad walls it takes you to the main bus station and the road to Casablanca. The Av. Hassan II is crossed by the Av. Mohammed V which leads you north right through the Medina to the Kasbah or south through the Royal Palace to the Chellah.

Its pavement is the heart of the city and here you can find the impressive exteriors of the Post Office, the train station and the major banks. Cinemas, cafés, hotels and restaurants are also all concentrated on the Av. Mohammed V and in the side streets that connect it to the parallel Av. Allal ben Abdallah to the west.

TOURIST INFORMATION
The Syndicat D'Initiative is on Rue Patrice Lumumba, tel 23272, the Tourist Information Office further from the city centre at 22, Av. D'Alger which is marked on some maps as Rue el Jazair, tel 21252. Post Office on Av. Mohammed V and junction with Rue Soekarno. Open Monday to Friday, 8.30–12.00, 14.00–18.45. Central banks: Banque Populaire at 64, Av. Allal Ben Abdallah; BMCE at 260 Av. Mohammed V; Banque du Maroc at 277, Av. Mohammed V. There is a late hour pharmacy on Rue Moulay Sliman and the hospital Avicienne, tel 72871, is on the southern end of Blvd D'Argonne where emergency medical care is available.

EMBASSIES AND CONSULATES
British, Australian, Irish and New Zealand citizens all use the British Embassy on 17, Blvd de la Tour Hassan, tel 20905. The Canadian Embassy is on 13 Joafar Essadik, tel 71315. United States on 2, Av. de Marrakesh, tel 62265, Mauretania on 2, Rue de Normandie, Tunisia on 6, Av. de Fes and Spain on 3, Rue Mohammed El Fatih.

The Medina

The Medina was built by the Moriscos, those inhabitants of Moorish descent who were expelled by Phillip III in 1610. They built the **wall of the Andalucians**, a long rampart reinforced by rectangular towers that was erected to enclose the northerly fortifiable portion from the excessive 5 km perimeter of wall constructed in the Almohad era.

Rue Souiqa–Souk es Sebat
Two gates pierce the Almohad wall from the west, the **Bab el Alou** and the **Bab el Had**,

the gate of the market. As the main entrance to the functioning vegetable market it was this gate, rebuilt by the Sultan Moulay Sliman in 1814, that was decorated with the heads of the executed.

Entering through this gate you proceed along the traditional Medina thoroughfare, the Rue Souiqa which turns imperceptibly into the **souk es Sebat** which leads across to the **Bab el Bahr**, the port gate. The Rue Souiqa is crossed by three north–south streets, Rue Mohammed V, Rue Sidi Fatah and Rue des Consuls, of which the latter leads directly to the Kasbah.

This network of streets are the commercial thoroughfares of the Medina where you will find cubicle artisan's stalls, bazaars and intimate little cafés. Behind these bustling market routes are the tranquil residential quarters of an Andalucian town. Houses of stone are barred by old stained and rivetted doors, walls half plastered and painted with lime with details picked out in azure or ochre yellow. Each quarter contains a local mosque for daily prayers, a communal bakery, a fountain and usually a bath house. The ordered 17th-century Andalucian foundation has given the Medina a regulated European feel with little of the tortuous mystery of an older Arabic street pattern.

At the crossing of the Rue Souiqa and Rue Sidi Fatah is the **Mosque of Sultan Moulay Sliman** which he founded in 1812. Continue on through the intriguing displays of goods, mostly bolts of cloth and kitchen ware, to pass the **Maristan el Azzizi**, an old Merenid hospital that now houses the offices of the habous.

The **Grand Mosque** with its modern minaret was entirely rebuilt in the late 19th century although it was founded by the Merenids. Opposite the Mosque on the right hand side of the road that leads down to the Bab Chellah is a 14th century **fountain**. It is the sole surviving remnant of the Merenid Grand Mosque, the three broken arches with their fading decoration were placed here between 1366–1372. They now provide an impressive façade for an Arabic and Islamic bookshop.

The market area around a Grand Mosque traditionally holds the more expensive merchandise and the Rue Souiqa becomes transformed into the covered **souk es sebat**. This was once a centre for Morocco work, the intricate gold-stamped leatherwork, which can still be found amongst the glittering array of embroidered babouche, filigree belts and ornamental hats. Cross over the Rue des Consuls to reach the **Bab el Bahr**, the port gate out of the Medina. A less conspicuous gate immediately to the right stands opposite the **shrine of Lalla Qadiya** where returning pilgrims from Mecca spend their first night home in prayer within the sanctuary.

Rue des Consuls
The Rue des Consuls is where the larger carpet dealers and bazaars will be found. After the French bombardment of 1765 and before the Protectorate of 1912, all European consuls and merchants were obliged to live on this street. The house of the consul Louis Chenier, father of the celebrated French poet, can be seen on the right at no 62. There are a series of splendid old **fondouqs** on the right, no 109 the Fondouq ben Aicha is the grandest, at no 93 there is the narrow courtyard of Tailleurs, the kissouria de Mouline at no 141 and Fondouq Daouia at no 232 Rue Souiqua.

A righthand turning from the Rue des Consuls takes you to the main road, the Tarik al Marsa. The **National Artisan Museum** which is usually open from 9.00–12.00, 15.00–18.00, with free admission, is on the left and faces over the estuary where there is a display of traditional crafts in two old shops. An **ensemble artisanal** with high but fixed prices is directly opposite where you can do some carpet pricing research.

Souk el Ghezel

The Rue des Consuls leads out to the Souk el Ghezel, now a large tarmaced space in front of the busy road before the Kasbah. This was the wool market for the carpet weavers of Rabat, a space that was also convenient for the auction of Christian captives from the 16th to the 18th centuries, where speculation over the size of the eventual ransom played a large role in the bidding. The square **Kechla, Chateau Neuf**, was built by Sultan Moulay Rachid to keep a check on the Andalucian population of the Kasbah and Medina and has served as a prison, slave pen, arsenal and garrison in its day. An underground tunnel connects the Kechla to the Kasbah but neither this secret entrance or the fortress itself is open.

Blvd el Alou

The Blvd el Alou separates the Medina from this fortress which is surrounded by a large Muslim cemetery. This is enlivened once a year by the **Moussem of Lalla Kasba** where the young girls pray for help in finding a good husband.

Along the Blvd el Alou there are three streets that open, opposite the cemetery, to give access to the cool whitewashed unhurried urban interior of the Medina, a residential place in which it is possible to wander aimlessly in contrast to the busy mercantile thoroughfares.

Returning to Blvd el Alou turn down the Rue Sidi Fatah. 150 m on, near the Mosque el Qoubba is the new baths, **Hammam el Jedid**, a 14th-century Merenid building whose income is partly devoted to the maintenance of the Merenid tombs at Chellah. Walking further down the Rue Sidi Fatah you pass the distinctive overhanging painted wood and plaster porch of the mosque built over the **tomb of el Mekki**, an 18th-century marabout. Its elegant octagonal minaret, decorated with small arches and stalactites under the windows, was last restored in 1908. Continuing on you pass the **zaouia of Sidi ben Aissa**, also on your right before crossing the Rue Souiqa to pass under the Andalucian wall at the Bab al Bouiba to reach Blvd Hassan II.

The Mellah

This quarter of the Medina can be entered through its own gate in the Andalucian wall, opposite the Place Mellah. Then after 50 m turn to your right off the Rue Ouqqasa (the continuation of the Rue des Consuls) to enter the central passage of the Mellah with its many dead-end alleys extending off from both sides.

The Mellah is now very low rent and there are almost continuous street corner flea markets selling old magazines and portions of Singer sewing machines and Primus stoves. The cramped claustrophobic atmosphere is intensified by the street vegetable and meat stalls with their accumulated refuse.

Somewhere within this area are over a dozen synagogues all now closed, some carefully locked and preserved, some the haunt of squatters. It is not however a particularly old Mellah; the Jews of Rabat were constantly being moved around by different Sultans and this cramped but defensible quarter was allocated to the community by Moulay Sliman in 1808. At the far extremity of the Mellah is the **mausoleum** of Sidi Makhlouf, a Jew who converted to Islam. He was venerated in his lifetime for his piety and spectacular miracles, not least of which was parting the waters of the Bou Regreg to enable a student, stranded in Salé, to visit him.

Oudaia Kasbah

The Kasbah of the Oudaias is at the heart of the military history of Rabat. This was the site of the original R'bat from which generations of cavalry have issued out to win the heretic Berber tribes to obedience. It has also been a government bastion against a recurring enemy that came to destroy by sea. Garrisons of Almoravide, Almohad, Merenid, Andalucian and Alouite troops have stood by to repel raiding fleets which from Vikings through to 20th-century France have come from Western Europe.

The Kasbah walls are subsequently ten feet thick and thirty feet high. Built by the Almohads, they have been constantly reinforced, most noticeably by the Andalucian refugees and the Alouite Sultans in the 17th and 18th centuries.

The name Oudaias is a comparatively recent innovation. The Oudaias were one of the bedouin Arab tribes that entered southern Morocco in the 13th century. They became clients of the Alouite Sherifs from the Tafilalet and were an important source of strength in the meteoric rise of Moulay Rachid to the throne. Moulay Ishmael sent part of the tribe to the Kasbah of Rabat to keep an eye on the Andalucians and to campaign against the Zaer, a truculent Berber hill tribe.

The Oudaia Gate

The approach to the Oudaia gate is up the broad stairway from the Souk el Ghezel to the Kasbah. The gate was constructed in the late 12th century by the Almohad Sultan Yaacoub el Mansour. Though capable of defence it has an obvious ceremonial purpose and this side of the Kasbah is not a first line of defence; the city walls screen the land to the west and the coast to the north. The Oudaia gate overlooks the Medina and gave entrance to the original Almohad palace complex in the Kasbah. The Sultan's gate had a role in Moorish society not far removed from a classical forum. Here petitioners would wait, assemblies and meetings take place and justice was seen to be dispensed.

The Oudaia gate is one of the accepted masterpieces of Moorish architecture. The puritanism and self-confidence of the Almohad creed, rather than restricting artistic expression encouraged a triumphant return to first principles. The powerful impression that you receive from the gate is not achieved by either great size, expensive materials or lavish decoration but by an instinctive sense of balance, proportion and inner tension. At one level you have the simple clear strong form of a horseshoe arch cut through a stone wall and flanked by two rectangular towers. At a second level the veneer of exuberant decoration seems to float out from the stone in an abstraction of pure form. The traditional Islamic decorative design has been cut into the same strong ochre rose stone of the gatehouse, the bold cut reliefs casting dark contrasting shadows against the evening glow of burnt gold. Two bands surmount a false circular arch with the corner spaces balanced by two stylized scallop shell palmettes surrounded by bevelled serpentine forms. The false outer arch is decorated with a distinctive band of *darf w ktarf*, that ubiquitous leaf-like profile of interlocking arches. The superior bands each continue the shell motif, one with an escriptive layer and the upper band with a shell-studded relief line of stalactite arches.

The genius of the whole is in the subtle relation of decoration to form. The decorative arch discreetly indicates with its diffuse edge the circumference of a circle whose diameter is exactly half the width of the square formed by the top lintel that includes the two flanking towers. A few minutes spent absorbing this tension, pursuing the clean form as defined by the decorative skin is to enter into a form of meditation.

The **gate house** is composed of two inner halls with the interior face set at a right angle to its more celebrated brother. The doors are quite often closed but an arch to your right gives entrance to the Kasbah. The Oudaia gate is one of the few spots in Rabat where young men opportune to be your guide. This must be a hard task as the Kasbah is small, safe and easy to find your way around in.

Inside the Kasbah

The Kasbah interior is a delightful white-washed Andalucian village built by the refugees from Hornacheros, who also fortified the roof of the gate house in their feud with their fellow Andalucian refugees in the Medina. The central street, the Rue Djemaa, passes the **Kasbah Mosque**, La Jamaa el Atiq, which founded by Abdel Moumen in 1150 is the oldest in Rabat. The minaret was restored in 1700 and the mosque repaired by Ahmed el Inglizi, an English renegade who worked for the Sultan Sidi Mohammed ben Abdallah (1757–1790). Further on is the **semaphore terrace**, a signal station that now provides an intriguing view over the entrance to the Bou Regreg estuary and across to Salé. A storehouse on the right built by the mad Sultan Moulay el Yazid at the end of the 18th century now houses a **carpet school**. Below the platform you can observe further defensive walls and a round tower refortified in 1776 by Sidi Mohammed after the French bombardment. The chief defences of Rabat–Salé remained the estuary sand bar which sealed the harbour from any deep-keeled sailing vessels. The Atlantic swell, the savage cliffs and outlying rocks made naval bombardments in the age of sail a difficult operation.

It is possible to climb down to the batteries where the **Caravelle** restaurant bar discreetly serves fish for lunch or just a cold beer in a shaded dining-room. The beach below is sandy and although it can become quite crowded in summer the Atlantic current keeps the water reasonably clean and provides some gentle surfing.

Museum of Oudaia

The Museum can be entered from inside the Kasbah or from an arch below the Oudaia gate. The Rue Bazzo, the second turning on the right from the central Rue Djamma in the Kasbah, naturally takes you downhill through a delightful twisting path to the Museum. The **Café Maure**, enclosed in a secretive terrace between the Museum garden and the estuary ramparts, is a delightful place to take a restful mint tea and consume plates full of sticky cakes. The Museum is open from 8.30–12.00, 15.00–18.00 for 3dh and is closed on Tuesdays and national holidays.

Sultan Moulay Ishmael built this palace between 1672 and 1694, an intimate pavilion set against the north wall of an Andalucian garden arranged within the bastions of the lower Kasbah. The Palace is a series of cool halls paved in marble with high ceilings that looked over the garden. The tower belongs to a small mosque now used to display carpets whilst the other chambers have a fine collection of blue Fez ware.

The structure and interior of the Museum, the central verdant garden with its charming geometrical arrangement of pebble mosaic paths, vie with the actual exhibits for your attention. It is as well to realize that North Africa never produced very important products in the minor arts and what was done belongs more to the range of folk art rather than fine art. This does not make the large collection of costumes from different regions, tribes and urban periods any less absorbing. There are also interesting supporting collections of armour, jewelry, musical instruments, pottery, killims and carpets. The Muslim and Jewish artisans from Rabat, Salé, Meknes, Fez and Tetouan are credited with distinctive styles. What is more clearly revealed is how much all the cities shared the same Andalucian influences and how little they had in common with the products of the countryside. The geometric pottery of the Berber tribes seems closer to the warrior culture of Greece in 800 BC and the jewelry throws up strong analogies with the torcs and brooches of Celtic Britain.

The Great Mosque of El Hassan

For eight centuries the unfinished tower of Hassan has towered above Rabat. It is the minaret of the Great Almohad Mosque of El Hassan whose truncated pillars stretch out in a great rectangular field below. The mosque had fallen into disrepair and was a bramble covered ruin when Leo Africanus visited Rabat in 1500, but it was not until the great earthquake of 1755, that shattered Lisbon, that the arches and pillars of the El Hassan Mosque were thrown down. On the southern edge of the Great Mosque a white **Mausoleum, Mosque and Library** has been built on a raised terrace to the memory of King Mohammed V.

The Mausoleum and the area of the El Hassan Mosque are open from 8.00 until dusk, admission free, and there is a small guard ceremony which lowers a flag daily at 17.00. The Hassan Tower used to be open to the public but has not been accessible for some years.

The Hassan Tower

Poised on the high escarpment above the river the tower looks particularly magnificent as you approach Rabat by the bridge from Salé. It has great solidity, a lordly purpose and a noble flaw that does not distract from the beauty of its proportions or the decoration of boldly carved entrelacs. It was to be the conclusion of a building programme that raised the Koutoubia in Marrakesh and the Giralda of Seville.

The tower was built between 1195 and 1199 by the Almohad Sultan Yaacoub el Mansour as the centrally aligned northerly pivot to his Great Mosque. Each face of the tower is different, a subtle movement of relief arches and interlaced decoration that is based on two classic designs, the *shabka* and *darj w ktarf* which were brought to Almohad Morocco from the sophisticated culture of Andalucia. A ramp rather than a staircase ascends up through six chambers that become more ornately decorated the further you climb. This ramp deliberately echoes the Samarra Mosque in Iraq which was acknowledged to be the biggest in the world. It was built in AD 850 and allowed the Caliph to ride to the summit on an external ascending ramp and call his army to the Friday prayers.

Behind the tower a staircase leads down to a tomb for the unknown warrior and a small mosque dedicated to the previous ruling dynasties of Morocco.

The El Hassan Mosque

The floor of the mosque was raised and levelled from the surrounding ground so that the tower has two heights; 50 m from the natural level of ground on its north wall and 44 m from the raised mosque floor of the southern wall. The ruins of the El Hassan Mosque and that of Samarra in Iraq are still the two largest in Islam. The Almohad Sultan Yaacoub el Mansour who ruled the Western half of Islam, over an Empire that stretched from Spain to Libya, deliberately attempted to make a mosque that would vie with the finest efforts of the East.

The rectangle of the mosque measures 183 by 139 metres and was crossed by a forest of aisles; 21 longitudinal spans and 28 laterals that multiplie into 312 marble columns and 112 stouter arch bearing pillars. Three arcaded courts open to the sky broke this massive roofline. The open court nearest the tower, the *sahn* or ablution courtyard had rows of fountains that played down on to marble basins and were fed from eleven huge cisterns that were hidden beneath the floor. There were four doors in this north wall and six on the eastern and western sides. The central 'nave' leading up to the mihrab was designed to be significantly wider to draw the worshippers' attention to the direction for prayer. It is difficult now to imagine the splendour of the interior, to ignore the irritating modern paving and transform the truncated remnants into the shifting vistas of columns, flooded with arcaded pools of harsh sunlight and the mass of genuflecting warriors that filled it for just a few years.

The Mausoleum

The tomb has a traditional and distinctive green-tiled pyramidal roof capped with a triplet of golden spheres. It is approached from the old southern face of the El Hassan Mosque up a broad ornate staircase.

Not even the Saadians achieved such a lavish tomb. Royal guards in scarlet with a white burnous patrol the arcade of Italian white marble with its four arches that allow entrance on to the balcony of the Royal Koubba. The sarcophagus is a block of white onyx carved from the mountains of the Hindu Kush and set in a sea of polished black marble whilst a scholar mutters verse from the Koran in one corner or dozes. Heraldic banners from all the provinces and towns of Morocco are suspended in serried ranks from below the balcony and a bronze chandelier of 1 ton hangs from the roof. The decoration of the ascending ceiling must be the last word in gilded ornate. The king's sarcophagus was joined by that of his youngest son, the genial Prince Moulay Abdullah who died in 1983.

The Mausoleum was designed by a Vietnamese architect Vo Toan and finished in 1971, and must aesthetically be considered something of a disaster. It is impressive only in the lavish use of luxurious materials which expresses the Moroccan people's great regard for the king who led them in their struggle for Independence. He has already assumed an almost holy status and the interiors of saints' shrines have traditionally been decorated as richly as the community can afford.

On a lower level of the terrace a mosque has been constructed with its three handsome doors and mihrab arranged on the same axis as the ancient mosque. The colonnade of finely sculpted white marble from Carrara tops a library consecrated to the reigning Alouite Dynasty.

The New Town

The major attraction of the New Town is the small but excellent Archaeological Museum which can be followed with a look at the outside of the Royal Palace and the Bab er Rouah gate in the Almohad wall.

Archaeological Museum

Opposite the Grand Mosque of the New Town, then along Rue Moulay Abdul Al Aziz and first right on to the Rue al Brihi brings you to a low modern building on the corner. This is the Museum which is open from 8.30–12.00, 14.00–18.30, closed on Tuesday, admission 3dh.

The central hall contains a large marble classical statue that was discovered at Sala and has been identified with King Juba II or his son Ptolemy. The handsome marble torso beside it was recovered from Volibulis and considered to be from the 2nd century AD.

Around the walls are the results of the excavations at the microlithic site of Taforalt and Neolithic child burials from Skhirat and Harhoura from about 4000 BC.

PRE-HISTORY IN MOROCCO

Though not on display here there have been some important pre-history finds in Morocco. Homo erectus who replaced the ape man Australopithicus a million years ago crossed the Sahara and colonized all the world except for Oceania and the Americas. His bones have been found in sites at both Casablanca and Rabat. Homo sapiens, Neanderthal man from 40,000 BC, has been found in coastal sites at Sidi Abderrahman, Temara, Tangier, Saidia and Jbel Irhoud south of the Atlas. The Mediterranean was in this period a much smaller barrier and the bones from North Africa show an affinity with European remains rather than with the sub-Saharan and racially distinct Rhodesian man. Evolution removed the heavy brow ridge of Neanderthal and Rhodesian man to create contemporary man, homo sapiens var. sapiens. The Berbers were in possession of North Africa before the dawn of history, their origins a mystery but with obvious similarities to the Semites of Arabia. Linguists have lumped North Africa together under the label Hamites.

The Palaeolithic and Mesolithic eras, the old and middle stone age, are cultural rather than evolutionary labels. Mankind remained a hunting gathering community loosely scattered over the earth. The real revolution is the new stone age, the Neolithic, when man learnt to produce food, either with domesticated flocks or sowing crops. This was associated with a rapid rise in population levels. Egypt was affected in 5000 BC and Morocco by at least 3000 BC. The tombs, monuments like Mzoura and surviving tools, all speak of an immense cultural and intellectual revolution.

The first floor has a chronological collection of artifacts extracted from Sala Colonia in four cases. Bronze fragments of sculptures, a little bust of Juba II, an ivory cylinder with four carved scenes and a representation of Apollo. The second case has ceramic shards and coins from the excavations, the third funerary objects from the classical period and the fourth objects from Islamic Chellah. The next exhibits demonstrate the under-stressed survival of the classical sites into recent history with Christian and Jewish cult objects and evidence of Islamic occupation up to the 14th century.

Recent digs have concentrated on a number of old Islamic sites. The two towns opposite the Spanish coast, Ksar es Seghir and Belyounegh (between Tangier and Ceuta), have revealed the high state of Islamic civilization that these foundations of Ommayad Cordoba enjoyed from the 10th century. Pottery from Sigilmassa, founded in the 8th century and fragments from the medieval sugar mill at Chichaoua (between Marrakesh and Essaouira) can also be seen. Returning to the hall, a small open-air courtyard to the right is lined with a random selection of carved stones from different epochs.

THE HALL OF BRONZES

The treasures of the Museum are contained in a separate and locked hall which you must visit. You pass stones carved with Libyan geometric script arranged outside in the open air. Immediately to your left is a magnificent collection of bronzes. The bust of Cato the younger, of Utica, is from the first century AD and may have been modelled from the death mask of the orator who preferred to die free under the Republic than live under an Emperor. The face is a representation to the full of the Roman virtues of gravitas and civic commitment.

The bust of the young Berber man with his hair bound by a fillet is now firmly associated with King Juba II. It is a hauntingly beautiful and moving portrait. Born in 52 BC he married Cleopatra Selene daughter of Anthony and Cleopatra and was educated in the household of the Emperor Augustus. Fully involved in the intellectual and cultural community of his day he was yet torn by his hereditary obligation as king of a Berber state threatened by Rome. This internal conflict is reflected in the pensive almost prescient awareness of the future. He retreated into a literary world, writing histories and essays on opium and euphorbium whilst Rome increased her hold on his kingdom. He died in AD 24, his son was soon to be murdered and then his kingdom annexed by his childhood friend and fellow historian Claudius. Both Cato and Juba were found buried in sand in the house of Venus at Volubilis. Cato, though he was the last great Republican, was a friend of King Juba and both busts would have been politically inconvenient during the Empire.

The crowned ephebus or the Lustral Dionysius is a superb full-length statue, a Roman copy of the original carved by the Greek master Praxiteles. The fisherman casting his net and the rider with his missing leg are further 1st or 2nd century Roman works. The bronze guard dog from Volubilis was discovered in 1916 and was probably made in the reign of Hadrian at the end of the 2nd century.

In the glass cases further small bronzes can be seen, a horse and rider from Volubilis, a snake discovered in Banassa, a head of Oceanus from Lixus and figurines of Eros and Bacchus. There are some fine marble heads of Diana and a Berber youth. In the extensive collection of classical objects the Military Diploma given by the Emperor Domitian on 9 January to the cavalryman Domitius and found at Banassa gives a striking personal link.

Five Punic stellae are exhibited, their crude symbolic carving looking out of place in this treasure house of humanistic art. They do however convey the Semitic devotion to an abstract divinity which is a much stronger influence in Morocco than these buried remnants of Greece and Rome. One of them was discovered in the ancient tell of the temple the Romans equated with Saturn.

The New Town

The Av. Mohammed V that connects the Royal Palace with the Medina contains the major French-designed public buildings which use Egyptian, Classical and Moorish elements to create an impression of order and stability. The Rue al Mansour ad Uahbi leads to the **Theatre Mohammed V** opposite which is the **Parc du Triangle de Vue**, a pleasant restful urban garden full of paths created in 1920. The northern corner contains the walls of a ruined 18th-century mosque and a number of tombs.

The terracotta-coloured U-shaped **Parliament building** can be seen across from the Balima Hotel. Opposite the station the Rue Abou Nan leads to the Place du Golan and the striking central **Cathedral of Saint Pierre**. Two pallisade-like towers emerge from a totally white nave, the windows and lintels have been decorated with geometric shapes from brick in a deliberately Islamic borrowing. Masses at 19.00 on Saturday and 8.30, 11.00 and 19.00 on Sunday. The PTT ministerial building opposite the Grand Mosque on Av. Mohammed V contains a small **postal museum** dominated by the stamp collection which is open during office hours.

Bab er Rouah

The **Almohad wall** encloses the Kasbah, Medina, Palace and New Town in a surviving 5 km length of wall with five city gates surviving in some form; the **Bab Alou, Bab el Had, Bab er Rouah, Bab Makhzen** and **Bab Zaers**. The section between the Bab el Had and the Bab er Rouah on the Rue Ibn Tumert provides a pleasant 1 km long walk with the ochre battlements decorated with flowering plants and clusters of palm trees. The Bab er Rouah, the gate of the winds, is the only true surviving Almohad structure that is contemporary and comparable to the Oudaia gate. Set above the Place Nasr, isolated from the traffic flow, the two massive surrounding stone bastions still allow you to envisage its central defensive role. The stone carving in this exposed position is still carefully balanced and controlled with a ring of concentric engaged arches rippling out from the gate ringed by an ancient enclosing scroll of the Koran in Kufic script. The interior eastern face has an even lighter cut of stone with a delicate bed of floral and vegetable entrelacs supporting a palmette between arch and the enclosing square. The blend of elegant fantasy, the tension of design and their purpose in defence are reinforced by the interior chambers. Four rooms with elegant cupolas force those who pass into a classic series of vulnerable turns. The rooms are open periodically for exhibitions which is for the moment as close to a national gallery of art as exists. Well worth visiting as much for the pictures as a gathering ground for artists existing in the shadow of palace walls. If open at all it will be between 8.30–12.00, 14.30–20.00.

In from the gate you face the **Grand Mosque, Djemma el-Souna**, which sits above the Av. Mohammed V with its minaret dominating the skyline of the new town. It was built by Sidi Mohammed ben Abdullah in the 18th century and is the victim of frequent restorations.

The Royal Palace

The southeastern corner of the Almohad defences was selected as a site for a new palace in the 18th century and a park was enclosed within the walls that are behind the Grand Mosque. The palace has been constantly altered and improved and has been almost entirely rebuilt by the present king who has also extended the grounds behind the main block to include a private golf course enclosed by a new enceinte of the city walls. Many of the chief offices of state are housed within the walls and it is very much a working palace. Do not walk off the central avenue.

Pass through the ornamental gate, on your left is the **Lycée Moulay Youssef** and a small suburb for past and present employees of the king. On the right you pass the stables, an exercise paddock and the Princes' school before reaching the open Mechouar space. The house for the minister of the Habous is reached before drawing level with the massed roofs of the main block. The outer wings contain the house of the President of the Council and Cabinet offices. A Mosque, the Supreme Court, an oratory and the central **Mausoleum to Moulay Hassan** coexist with the various Royal apartments. The three large windows in the distinctive tower occasionally frame the king in his dressing gown. The Queen Mother has her apartment just to the south next to the kitchen wing with its separate access to the Blvd Ad Doustour. The **Mosque** on the left, **El Faeh**, is used for the official Friday Royal prayers when the King as Imam rides the short distance from the palace in a carriage and returns riding on a horse, his brow shaded from the sun by a crimson parasol of state. This procession, a weekly ritual for past Sultans, is now rarely performed and the 12.30 Friday cavalcade will be advertised well in advance.

Leave the palace compound through gates and turn left along Blvd Ad Doustour to follow the southern Almohad wall to Bab Zaer where you can return to the New Town or take the turning for the Chellah.

Chellah

One of the most beautiful of the many striking historical ruins in Morocco, Chellah is not so much distinguished architecturally but possessed by a wistful, almost tangible atmosphere of antiquity. The walled enclosure has bred strange beliefs, that of the buried treasure of Sultan Yaacoub which is guarded by a prince of the Djinn and a fleeting visit from the prophet Mohammed, though the factual narrative is fanciful enough.

Fresh water springs flow out from this hill less than 500 m from the brackish estuary of the Bou Regreg. Human settlement had probably always clustered on this slope even before the Phoenicians founded Sala. This city after a millennium of existence was reduced to a tell of ruins in the 10th century, but maintained a single continuity of use as a revered burial ground until the Merenid Sultans enclosed it for the use of their own dead in 1320. Now their shrines are also reduced to picturesque ruin and Roman Sala Colonia is under a decade-long excavation. A lush growth of jungle garden is firmly established beside the path that leads down to the Merenid tombs and the sacred spring.

The Merenid Sultan Uthman, 1308–1331, began the walling that was finished by his successor Abou Hassan in 1339 and further embellished by Abou Inan, 1351–1358. The Zippoun Berber tribe were appointed as the hereditary protectors of Chellah, a duty which they continued for centuries after the fall of the dynasty.

The Chellah Gate
The simple arch of the gate is enclosed by half octagonal towers with the conspicuous lean battlements twisted and supported by a delicate tracery of dripping stalactites. The clear square platforms for these outrageous gothic towers use a honeycomb patterned stone for the shift to the octagonal shaft. The Kufic script on the gate reads, 'I take refuge

in Allah, against satan, the stoned one', a useful invocation for the biers of dead Sultans to pass under. The gate enforces a double twist before you enter the Chellah through a more orthodox Islamic horseshoe arch decorated with flanking shell motifs. On your left inside a disused guard house a café operates and vendors and snake charmers sometimes collect. You may be offered tickets or a guide, of which you require neither.

A stairway descends steeply through the well watered and luxuriant gardens, a confused mass of palm, bamboo, banana, hibiscus, fig and datura.

Sala Colonia

To your left are the ruins of Sala which have still not been opened for inspection. They occupy the northern half of the enclosure and border the necropolis. The main thoroughfare, the **Decumanus Maximus**, connects the forum with the Capitol. Foundations of a triple triumphal arch, shops, a terrace, small sanctuaries and a whole range of sumptuous baths are still forbidden of access.

THE SACRED POOL

A group of Koubbas surround a walled pool. Stubs of gutted candles can be found within, the saints venerated, though wrapped in Islamic green shrouds, and familiar whitewashed shrines belong to pre-Islamic cults of great antiquity. The pool is surrounded by old brick chambers and drains out through a gravel stream that runs through an enclosing grove of drooping bananas—in Malaya children are warned from climbing banana trees which are credited with the power to rot genitals. Sacred black eels swim up to lurk in shaded recesses of the pool. Infertile women peel boiled eggs to offer to the eels. Eggs are sold by two boys who sleep on the floor of the shrine above. The scene is so strongly archetypal, such a graphic pagan survival in the shadow of ruined cities and royal tombs that you instinctively check twice to discover if you are dreaming. That barren women should offer eggs, the universal symbol of fertility to be devoured by phallic eels as emissaries of an ancient deity calls any visitor to compose a few lines of verse.

THE MERENID SANCTUARY

The sanctuary is easily recognized with its two minarets, of the mosque and zaouia, invariably topped with a ponderously balanced pair of storks adding to their nest. Enter into the sahn, the small introductory courtyard, and proceed into the ruined **prayer hall** built by Abou Yusuf. The **Mihrab** can be seen straight ahead and the four columns of the pillared **Mosque**. The ruined minaret is conspicuous to your right where there is also a pool. Pass either side of the Mihrab to enter the necropolis.

Leo Africanus counted thirty two Merenid graves here in 1500 which have obviously been reduced in number. The grave of the Black Sultan, Abou Hassan, can be seen to the right lying against the outer wall and within a Koubba decorated with arches and entrelacs. The facing Koubba is that of Sultan Yacoub, the 'Commander of the Djinn'.

The **tomb of Shams ed Douna**, the light of Dawn, can be seen in the southeast corner (bottom left as you stand by the Mihrab) under a recess. Her long tombstone has been carved with verses celebrating the magnificence of her funeral. A Christian convert to Islam, she was a concubine of Abou Hassan and mother of Abou Inan, who eventually deposed his father. Abou Hassan was chased into the High Atlas and died an exile in the winter of 1352 but was buried decently, as you can see, in the Chellah.

The sanctuary also contained a **zaouia**, a religious college, which though damaged is in better state than the Mosque. The minaret is on the left with the wash basins and latrines directly below. The court lined with cells faces a central rectangular pool with two sunken white marble shells producing water jets that drained into the pool. The bases of the thin white marble columns can be seen with some surviving mosaic tilework. A much smaller prayer hall faces the Mihrab with its passage behind that allowed pilgrims to make seven circuits that was believed by some to be equal to the pilgrimage to Mecca.

The beautiful soft red glow of the sanctuary wall shields a tranquil and formal **garden** formed by a double line of orange trees with the plots fed off water from the sacred spring. From here you can look out over the walls to inspect tidy and fertile vegetable plots.

SHOPPING, SOUKS, SPORT AND FESTIVALS
The Medina holds all the traditional Moroccan crafts. Flowers are sold in the market in the Medina and in a square of Av. Moulay Hassan.

Bookshops and Libraries
The new town is conspicuous for its large number of **bookshops**. You will find an English language bookstore at 4, Rue Tanja with a good shelf on Islam and Morocco. It is closed on Sunday and Saturday afternoon. In the same building **American films** are shown on Monday, Wednesday and Friday at 18.30. The train station usually has a good selection of international papers. French–Moroccan phrase books are available from the bookshop at 38, Av. Allal ben Abdallah. The George Washington Library is at 35, Av. al Fahs and the British Council used to have a selection of papers available at 24, Av. Moulay Youssef.

Art Galleries
There are only a handful of places in Morocco that show the works of contemporary artists. The pre-eminent dealer and exhibitor of these is **L'Atelier** run by Madame Demasier who has drawn an impressive range of pan-Arab and Islamic art to her elegant gallery at 16, Rue Annaba, tel 22668.

The **Gallery Marsam** deals purely in prints but it does have a good stock of fine limited editions which enables you to see the work of many of Morocco's leading artists. A print by Hassan El Glouai will cost 1800dh, over £100. At 6, Rue Oskofiah, tel 69257.

Antiquities Lyre on 38, Av. Mohammed V, tel 62432 and **Galerie le Mamoir**, 7, Rue Baitlahm have the same management with one or two good things amongst piles of international junk. The prolific French painter of Moroccan scenes, Henri Pilot, can be seen at work in one or the other gallery. There is also **Galerie la Decouverte** on 11, Rue Soussa and the **Sahara Gallery** opposite the train station on Mohammed V which restricts itself to photographic portraits of the king.

Souks
A brief list of some local souks: on Monday, Souk Tnine, Ain el Aouda and Tiddas. On Tuesday, Souk Tleta du Gharb; Wednesday, Rommani, Tiflet and Souk el Arba du Gharb. Thursday, Sidi Yahya and Salé. Friday at Bouznika. Saturday at Merchouch and

Temara. Sunday at Maaziz, Skhirat, Oued Akrech, Bouknadel and the busiest day for the vegetable market in the Medina.

Festivals
State organized galas and religious festivals like the fête of the throne on 3 March, Mouloud, Aid el Kebir, the Royal birthday on 9 July, the Green March on 6 November and Independence day on 18 November are well organized in Rabat and the hotels will be especially short on beds. In August there is the **Moussem of Dar Zhirou** and the **fête des cires** on Mouloud in Salé. Last year Rabat had a two-week film festival in December below the law courts in the new town which was a great success.

Sport
The Royal Dar es Salaam **golf club**, a quarter of an hour drive from central Rabat, is one of the world's top 50 golf courses. A 45-hole complex was designed by Robert Trent Jones from 1000 acres of woodland. 400 groundsmen maintain three courses, the 9-hole green course, the 18-hole blue and the red, an 18-hole championship course for those with at least a handicap of 18. There are also two **tennis courts**, a **swimming pool** and a luxurious club house where you can eat a three-course lunch with wine for under 140dh.

WHERE TO STAY
Bedrooms fill up quickly throughout the year in Rabat and it is advisable to find a room early in the day or book in advance.

Expensive Hotels
The **** **Chellah** on 2, Rue D'Ifni, tel 64052, is a comfortable but unexceptional hotel near the Grand Mosque and the Archaeological Museum. A double room for 250dh.

There are now three luxurious five-star hotels in Rabat of great use for visiting delegations and international conferences, the **Rabat Hilton**, the **Farah Sofitel** and the **KTH De La Tour Hassan**. The Tour Hassan is the best of these, in the centre of town at 26, Av. Abderrahman-Annegai, with a more calm and dignified atmosphere, though breakfast and a double room will leave little change out of £50.

Hotels in the New Town
The two most comfortable and amusing hotels in the New Town are also the cheapest. The * **Hôtel Majestic** on 121, Blvd Hassan II, tel 22997, has a piano in the foyer, faded furniture and an ageing poster of the Kaaba. A single room costs 60dh.

The **Central Hotel** at 2, Rue Al Basra, tel 22131, fills up slightly later in the day and is run by an efficient but remorseless matron. There are 34 large comfortable rooms in this hotel immediately to the left of the prominent Balima Hotel.

The *** **Balima Hotel**, just off Av. Mohammed V on the Rue de Jakarta used to be the smartest in town. It has now an aged interior but retains all of its exterior dignity and is usually one of the last in Rabat to fill up. The foyer and the café gardens are still at the centre of Rabat social life, looking straight across the Avenue to the Parliament building. A double room with bathroom for 183dh. For twice that, take one of the faded suites on the top floor with balconies that give an alarming view over Rabat. These rooms should be full of the ghosts of Caids, French senators and assorted power politicians who stayed here before petitioning the Resident or his successor the Alouite Kings.

Cheap Medina Hotels

The unclassified Medina hotels can be tempted to up their price with the high demand in summer. The **Hôtel Marrakesh** at 10 Rue Sebbahi, the third turning off the Rue Mohammed V in the Medina has clean rooms with towels, a double room for 35dh, a shower for 2dh and the gaudy **El Alam** and the indifferent **Regina** are nearby if the Marrakesh is full. The second turning, Rue Souk Semara, has another nest of hotels: **The France**, **The Algers** and **du Marche**. The France is preferable for it has a roof terrace but a surprisingly large number of small dank rooms, a well-used double bed costs 38dh. The * **Hôtel Darna** on Blvd Bab el Alou just into the Medina from this gate is the only classified hotel in the Medina and is close to the Kasbah and the Rabat beach.

EATING OUT

Rabat is not a city famed for its food, it has neither Casablanca's reputation for seafood nor Fez's expertise in Moroccan cuisine.

For traditional Moroccan cooking the **Diffa** restaurant in the **Hôtel De la Tour Hassan** is expensive but reliable with a dinner from the menu costing about 130dh. The **Oasis** on 7, Rue Al Osquofiah, old Rue de L'Evêche, is the best value with a menu for 80dh and wine at 45dh a bottle. The **Koutoubia** at 2, Rue Pierre Parent, tel 26125, with its gaily painted interior and separate bar is also good but the food can definitely vary with the temper of the cook. You could also try a meal at the **Palais Kabbaj**, Rue Mokhtar Soussi, tel 34241, or at the dining room of the **Balima Hotel** which provides a filling menu du jour for 55dh.

For French cooking there is **Casabella** at 8, Rue Moulay Abd el Aziz, tel 22600 or the fish-oriented **Relais Pierre Louis** on Zankat Ibn Haoqual, tel 22315. For Italian food there is a pizza specialist—**La Mamma** behind the Balima Hotel at 1, Rue de Tanta, tel 22329.

There are several Oriental restaurants: **Le Hong Kong** at 261, Av. Mohammed V, tel 23594, **Le Mandarin** at 44, Av. Abdel Krim el Khattabi, tel 24699, or **La Pagode**, 5, Rue de Bagdad, tel 32062.

The most rewarding eating is not in these formal restaurants but in the cheaper end of town in stalls in the Medina or in some of the cheaper café restaurants nearby.

The **el Bahia** is built into the walls of the Medina on the right of the Av. Mohammed V entrance. Fixed menu of 22dh for chicken or kefta tagine in an upstairs Moorish dining room above a fountain court.

The **CTM café**, on the corner of Zankat Bayreuth and Av. Hassan II, stays open late serving good cheap Moroccan food on tables around the animated oblong bar. The caged birds when in the mood can produce extraordinary volumes of sound.

The restaurant **Saadi** on 87, Av. Allal ben Abdallah, tel 69903, is in an arcade where you can eat large quantities of mutton couscous for 45dh and wash it down with beer or wine.

BARS AND NIGHTCLUBS

The distinctive feature of Rabat's nightlife is that the city begins to close down at 8 in the evening and is shut by 10. Like other new and earnest political capitals, Ottawa, Canberra and Washington, the demand for sleazey joints and raffish bars does not seem to be strong from amongst the administrators of government. Dancing and floor shows exist at the **Hilton** which has the **Bab Es Samah club**, tel 34141, and the **Tour Hassan Hôtel**, admission 70dh, and there is a distinctively lower market **disco** at the back of the **Balima**.

The conspiratorial **Baghdad nightclub** has belly dancing shows after ten o'clock but they are not as exciting as its exterior black and studded door promises. The nearby **Baghdad bar**, with the same decoration and ownership is on the Zankat Tanto. There are a large number of **cinemas** on the Av. Mohammed V but evening 'people watching' in the café and bar of the Balima Hotel remains the chief entertainment.

SALÉ

Considered old fashioned even in the 16th century, Salé has long maintained a separate identity from Rabat. Its great period of prosperity was under the Merenid Sultans who rebuilt the walls, constructed the Medersa, a medical school, the Mrini Mosque, the Nossak zaouia and an aqueduct. These achievements of the 14th century still seem to possess the spirit of the town. Whilst Rabat had shrunk to a village raided by the Portuguese in the 16th century, Salé according to Leo Africanus had 'all the ornaments, qualities and conditions necessary to make a city civil and this in such perfection that it was visted by several generations of Christian merchants.'

HISTORY
The foundation of Salé is a bit imprecise. There is an enduring tradition that the citizens of Sala Colonia, persecuted by the orthodox inhabitants of the R'bat, moved a few kilometres north and established Salé. Whatever the truth of this, it is known that the petty Berber kingdom of the Beni Ifren had its capital at Salé in the 10th century. This kingdom was conquered by the Almoravides and destroyed in the two year Almohad campaign against local heretical tribes in 1146.

The founder of Merenid rule, the Emir Abou Yahya, established a garrison at the town of Salé in 1249 in order to control Rabat, as part of his life-long campaign to assume the leadership of the Almohad Empire. Salé was destroyed a few years later when Alfonso X of Castile descended on the city during the feast night of Aid es Seghir in 1260. The booty the Spanish captured was immense, the city sacked and most of the citizens killed or enslaved. Abou Yahya's brother Yusuf, in a heroic gesture rode from Taza in one day to come to the rescue of the city. Salé subsequently became a cornerstone of Merenid pride and the sacked city was rebuilt with an energy and elegance which has left such a pervasive identity.

Old Salé maintained a troubled supremacy over the Andalucian settlements in Rabat during the dazzling days of the pirate Republic of Bou Regreg, from 1629 to 1666 but then gently stagnated. The Alouite Sultans always preferred to live and build in Rabat.

GETTING AROUND
A fishing boat for a dirham will take you from the wharf below the Rabat Mellah across the Bou Regreg. The Av de la Plage leads straight up from the Salé wharf to the Medina through the Bab Bou Haja. Walking across the bridge you will arrive at the Bab el Mrisa whilst a taxi or bus will drop you further along at the Bab Fez.

The Medina

The Medina is an under-visited network of twisting and irregular streets. These wind past the white façades of the houses that are little inclined to show any ornamentation other than strongly reinforced doors. Outside the walls Salé has grown greatly in a fairly dismal style to the north and the west since Independence. It is entirely enclosed by walls and roughly rectangular in shape, 800 m wide and 1500 m long, the northern coastal third is occupied by a large cemetery. Three interior streets, the Blvd Touil, Rue la Grande Mosquee and the central Rue Souiqa/Kechachin provide sinuous crossings of the length of the Medina.

Bab el Mrisa

This unmistakeable massive arch is flanked by two elegant towers and decorated with floral entrelacs and sculpted inscriptions. This was built by Sultan Yusuf, between 1260 and 1270, after the sacking of the city, in a similar style to the Almohad gates of Rabat. A reinforced canal led from the estuary through this great water gate into a basin within the city walls. Here the fleet moored in complete safety surrounded by the naval arsenals and dockyards.

The Mellah

The Jews were given this area after the canal had become hopelessly silted. They were moved again, over the road to the north, when Moulay Ishmael required this corner for a garrison of Abids, but they expanded back again before the exodus after Independence. The two neighbouring gates with restored and elegant battlements, the Bab el Mellah allow you to drive through the Mellah into the middle of town.

The Souks

The **Bab Fez** is a natural point of entrance with the taxis, train and bus station clustered outside. Stalls of grilled kebabs, tables full of nuts, sweets and fruit are clustered in and

Stork with young

221

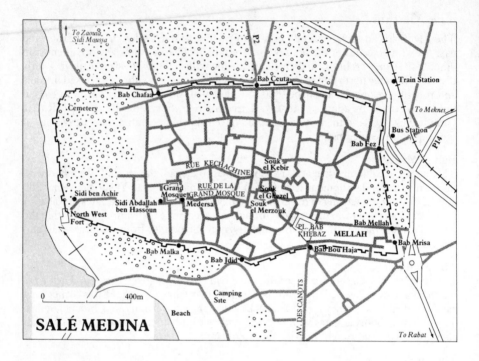

SALÉ MEDINA

around the portals of the gate. Pass the health centre immediately on your left and the second left turning, the Rue Dar Reghai, takes you in a natural flow of pedestrians to the heart of the town.

The stalls are full of products for the local rather than the tourist market, for Salé has remained largely aloof from the world of hassles and quick sales. A number of tempting kitchens exist along this street and its extension, the Rue Souaiqa. Here as well as absorbing the colour and sounds you can also taste the Medina.

On the right you will notice the **tomb and the Mosque of Sidi Ahmed Hadji**, a respected marabout of the 17th century, venerated with gifts of tall green candles.

Souk el Kebir

The triangular souk el Kebir or the grand souk is partly shaded by trees. Piles of secondhand clothes are sorted through at the back whilst carpenters, leather workers and babouche makers create a delightful cacophony of sound and activity.

Christian slaves captured by the Sallée Rovers were often sold here. Despite salacious tales Christian women were generally treated courteously. Any proof of sexual interference from the captors gave automatic liberty to the captive, whilst married women or those who despite beatings refused to embrace Islam were occasionally returned. Barbary piracy was a business activity with a strict code of conduct.

To the left of the Souk el Kebir, just before some gates, a right-hand turning will take you to the Rue Haddadine, the blacksmiths' and tinkers' street that leads directly north to the Bab Sebta. To your left the Rue Kechachine takes you past the workshops of the sculptors in wood and stone, the joiners' shops turning out headboards for beds and footboards for the wall benches that are found in most Moroccan homes.

Kissaria

Taking the left turn from the souk el Kebir takes you to the Kissaria, a small pocket of alleys where the most skilled artisans have their stalls. The **souk el Ghezel**, the wool market, is the open space lined by shops where early in the morning under the protection of canvas and a few trees bales of wool are weighed from tripod stands and gently haggled over.

The adjacent **Souk el Merzouk** is the quarter for the tailors, cloth merchants and embroiderers with their young assistants creating long trails of twisting silk. After the fountain on the right look out for the door of the **Fondouq Askour**, the hospital and school founded by the Merenid Sultan Abou Inan in the 14th century. The courtyard is functional but the door is covered in a cascade of carved stalactites.

Medersa and Grand Mosque

Continue on through the Rue de la Grande Mosque for 300 metres, the tailor shops with their array of kaftans giving way to the larger walled house of the merchants, decorated with their Andalucian and slightly classical proportioned doorways. You arrive at a charming small whitewashed square. Stairs lead up to the great Mosque whilst the Medersa gate is on your left just past an 18th-century fountain. The Mosque was built in the reign of the Almohad Abu Yaacoub Youssef (1163–1184). The clear lines of the doorways and the simple elegance of the carving contrast with the gates of the Merenid Medersa built by the black Sultan, Abou Hassan, in 1341. The rich cedar and plaster carving, the vivid paintwork and overhanging roof over the arch give entrance to a little hall that leads directly into the central court. It is much smaller than the great Medersas of Fez though the details are as lavish and as exciting. A gallery of columns decorated with contrasting designs and coloured zelliges, faience mosaics, leads your eye up to the area of delicately carved cream plaster that gives way to the crowning walls and hanging gallery of the dark sombre carved cedar. The prayer hall has a finely painted ceiling and the **Mihrab** has some fine carved decoration. The courtyard is designed to sit in rather than pace around. A few minutes can be spent spotting the recurring motifs of Islamic decoration drawn entirely from the natural world, flowers, fruit and shells. These are found at every level and worked into each material by bands of the cursive Arabic script of the Koran.

The foundation stone introduces the one distracting secular tone, 'Look at my admirable portal, rejoice in my chosen company, In the remarkable style of my construction and my marvellous interior. The workers here have accomplished an artful creation with the beauty of youth . . .'. Arabic poetry does not always translate well. The courtyard pillars would perhaps present a more serene interior if their distracting decoration was removed. Two galleries of cells can be explored and do not miss the opportunity to get out on the roof with its view over the rooftops of the Salé Medina across the estuary to Rabat.

Zaouia Sidi Abdallah ben Hassoun

Passing under an arcade of the Mosque to the right you face the door of the **zaouia of Sidi Ahmed Tijani** decorated with geometrical mosaics and carved plaster.

At the back of the Mosque you pass the zaouia of Sidi Abdallah ben Hassoun. A window allows you to look into the mausoleum which was rebuilt in the 19th century. Each year a collection of large candles and complicated wax lanterns are escorted through the town in a great procession guarded by the guild of boatmen dressed as Turks or corsairs on the afternoon of Mouloud, the prophet Mohammed's birthday. Followed by the saint's descendants and devotees carrying filigree and silk decorated candles, the retinue deposit these offerings at this shrine where they remain until the new year. Sixteen days later Sidi Abdallah, Salé's patron saint, is venerated by all the religious brotherhoods who sing their chants, psalms and mystical exercises in his honour. Sidi Abdullah came from the south of Morocco but moved to Salé in order to avoid the distractions of tribal politics. He was respected during his lifetime and attracted many pupils before his death in 1604. The Sidi was adopted by sailors and travellers who continue to visit the shrine for auguries to indicate the safety of their voyage.

The Cemetery

The cemetery extends west from this shrine and a dirt track winds out across this large expanse of graves to **Fort northwest**, an 18th-century redoubt containing a number of bronze English and Spanish cannon. At the end of the bastion there is a good view across the estuary to Rabat. The track passes a number of simple whitewashed Koubba, the **shrine** nearest the fort is that of **Sidi Achmed ben Achir**, an Andalucian scholar and mystic who died in 1362. He has a great reputation for curing the sick and the mad and in 1846 Sultan Moulay Abder Rahman built a series of lodgings for pilgrims to stay as they await their cure. The reputation of the Tabib has not diminished, particularly among the women. The old ladies will be upset if you walk too close, perhaps for your own benefit as the saint also has the power to wreck Christian ships along this coast.

Sidi Moussa ed Doukkali

The cliffs along the coast do indeed look evil to shipping; the Rue Circulaire that runs along the edge of the cemetery takes you out through the Bab Chafaa where the road continues above the sea. Patient men with long bamboo fishing poles perch above these high and dangerous cliffs.

A 3 km walk beside the shore will take you to the **Koubba of Sidi Moussa ed-Doukkali**, which Moulay Ishmael carefully restored. The Sidi is greatly beloved by the poor who hold an enormous celebration in August to his honour. He voluntarily chose an ascetic life, grubbing along this shore for edible roots and shifting through driftwood and debris to sell in order to buy fresh bread for the poor. He was also a skilled magician and humbled the arrogant rich by miraculously flying to Mecca each year for the pilgrimage. The shore is lined with refuse and shanty towns extend inland from the road, a fitting environment for the Sidi to continue his work.

Gnaoua Kasbah

Just beyond is the Kasbah of the Gnaoua, a pise fortress built by Moulay Ishmael to house his Abid troops, negroes from the Guinea as the name still proclaims. The wind and the salt spray have etched weird patterns into the walls. Graffiti left by the Abid regiments or renegades with their captives can still be seen etched into the less eroded sculpted walls.

WHERE TO STAY
Above the Salé beach is the **camping municipal** that serves both it and Rabat. It was a pleasant place to be, shaded by the woodland and close to the wharf, but has now been moved a little further north to a bleak open area immediately below the graveyard and surrounded by a 2 m high wall. The beach can be quite littered with detritus.

There is just **L'Hôtel des Saadians** in Salé on the central Place Bab Khebaz which if you are determinedly different you could stay at; the few visitors who do explore Salé are usually content to travel by boat or walk 1 km from a Rabat hotel.

Chaouia, between Rabat and Casablanca

Chaouia is the low coastal plain that stretches between Rabat and Casablanca. Partly covered in belts of woodland, the land rises slowly inland broken by a number of river valleys, farmed by smallholders. It is not a beautiful region and the immediate inland landscape has been scarred by the three big road connections, gravel pits and a railway line. There are however a number of coastal turnings that lead to beaches with some fine campsites, restaurants and hotels useful for a relaxing beach holiday.

GETTING AROUND
The beach areas until recently were useless desert and are frequently named after the nearest inland village. Bear in mind that all trains, most buses and places in a grand taxi will take you to the inland towns leaving you with a 4 km walk on tarmac road to the beach. Temara beach can be reached directly from Rabat on the no 7 bus, the no 17 takes you to Temara town. Mohammedia is well served by train, the station is just inland of the Kasbah, or by bus from Casablanca. Otherwise the other beaches and sites are more conveniently reached by car or grand taxi.

Temara

The Beach

Only 16 km south of Rabat on the S222 coast road, this strip of beach and rocky coves is an obvious popular escape from the city. A moussem is held in August at the coastal shrine of Sidi Lahcene. The holiday atmosphere keeps the bar and nightclub life going, compared to Rabat, late into the night. This is concentrated at the central asphalted area with restaurant **La Baraka**, tel 41346, the **Casino Temara** and the restaurant **Al Khaima** as the hubs of activity. The casino, in name only, has a few basic rooms.

The beach front is lined with several streets of holiday villas for Rabat's more prosperous citizens. The ****** Hôtel la Feloque** appeals to this more affluent community with its 'country club'-like tone for the businessmen of Morocco. It has its own beach front and pool. A double room here costs 241dh. The restaurant provides an excellent seafood meal but a good dinner here will not leave much change out of 250dh a head. A disco-night club operates in the summer.

Temara Zoo

11 km out of Rabat on the P1 and 5 km short of Temera town are signs for the zoo. The zoo opened in 1973 and there are plans to fill up the 50-hectare site with 1800 caged animals. It is with definite feelings of a failure as a tourist that you join the small number of Rabat matrons who escort their delighted squealing children to the zoo. Indeed without the company of children the caged animals give little pleasure. The unnatural mass of caged eagles is a sad sight, though the budgies and mallards are enjoying something of a population explosion and some storks have even voluntarily nested on a suitable tower within the zoo garden. The chief attraction is the half circle of caged great cats and bears. Insane looking beasts lie either asleep in the corner or restlessly pace against the bars. Only one lion seems to have resigned himself to a life of prisoned ease and imitates the zoo keepers by sunbathing on his back.

The Royal tradition of the Menagerie is eradicated in this very European entertainment park for the convenience of the urban bourgeoisie with slides, rides and photo opportunities. Admission 4dh, car parking 1dh. Open from 10.00 to dusk.

Temara Forest

This is a circuit of over a hundred miles, setting out from Rabat by car or taxi in the morning with a picnic and passing through the finest scenery of the area, little frequented forest roads, rural souks and saints' shrines; ideally finished with a swim and a meal in Temara. For another route taking you further inland into the Middle Atlas see Oulmes les Thermes on page 000.

Leave Rabat through the Bab Zaer gate and continue on the P22 road to Rommani. After 12 km a turning to the right takes you to the Royal Golf club Dar es Salaam which has been built next door to the palace created by Mohammed V.

The banks of the Oued Akrechon to the east have scoured the first of a number of gorges. The crossings of the Oued Korifla and Oued el Mechra provide the most dramatic scenery of the route. An attractive route to your right, the S218, takes you in 5 km to the bridge over the Korifal where you can see the **Koubba of Abdullah Ibn Yasin,** the founder of the Almoravide movement, who died here in 1059 leading an army against the heretical Berghouata tribe. Returning to the P22, as you emerge out from the drama of the gorge crossing, is the village of **Nkheila** which has a **souk** on Monday used by the Ouled Mimoun tribe.

Rommani 33 km further inland has the busiest market of the region, the Wednesday **souk** of the Ouled Khalifa. A 15th-century Andalucian saint, Sidi Bou Amar, is the patron of Rommani and a Moussem is held by his tomb in September.

A righthand turn takes you over the Oued Mechra again and past the **Koubba of Sidi Ktab.** Passing through **Merchouch,** with its **souk** on Saturday, and staying on the S208, a canyon has been cut into the landscape by the Oued Korifal. A track to your right before the riverbed crossing can take you into the gorge.

15 km on is **Sidi Bettache,** a village with a marabout's tomb that grew around the old

Almohad Imperial highway from Rabat to Marrakesh. A detour 4 km beyond the town gives a very fine view over the mountains of the Zaer country and the valley of the Oued el Bagra. Otherwise the righthand turning at Sidi Bettache, the S208, takes you for 33 km through sections of the forest of Temara. Perched above the crossing of the river bed of the Oued Yquem is one of the major **souks** of the Zaer tribe, **Sidi Yahya des Zaer**. The souk is held on Tuesday, the tomb of Sidi Yahya is surrounded in a grove of aloes. From here it is 11 km through more of the Temara forest to Temara town.

Temara town

This is 16 km out of Rabat on the P1 road. The old **Kasbah** was restored by Moulay Ishmael to house a branch of his dynasty's major Guich tribe, the Oudaia. This Arab tribe in the pay of the government formed a major portion of the cavalry and was posted in small sections, here and at the Oudaia Kasbah of Rabat, to subdue the rebellious Berber tribes of the Zaer region. It appropriately now houses the **Royal cavalry school** and the small **mosque of Sidi Lahcen** built by Sultan Abdul Aziz in 1900.

Le Provençal restaurant has the best French cooking and fish menu on this coast. A notice proclaims that the virtue of a gourmet is patience and in this case supplies of cash as the menu starts with meals at around 200dh. Le Provençal is on the main road just south of Temara, tel 41111. **La Pergola** used to be a restaurant but now concentrates on selling just beer or wine in its cool interior to off-duty police and soldiers. Beer for 6dh, fish grills operate in summer evenings.

Ain Attig

22 km south of Rabat (6 km beyond Temara), a dirt track leads 2 km south for the source of the Oued Gheboula where a 12th-century **aqueduct** was built to bring pure water to Rabat. The Almohad Sultan Abdel Moumen also built the massive stone **Kasbah of Dchira**, a rectangular fortress studded with 16 towers. The principal gate, the western gate, is now ruinous but the two flanking towers must have presented a strong defence in their day. Inside the ground plan of a **mosque** can be made out, with a central keep for the governor. Several tanks for storing grain or water can be seen cut out of the rock in the northwest corner. A fortress of this strength seems unlikely for just guarding the water supply which could be cut anywhere between Ain Attig and Rabat. It was most likely thrown up as a legacy of the final campaign against the Berghouata in 1149. In spirit it does not feel far removed from the fortresses erected by Edward I to maintain his conquest of Wales.

Ech-Chianha/Rose Marie Plage

23 km from Rabat is ech-Chianha, a coastal resort with a much finer beach than Temara. It is a favourite stopping place for European travellers rather than the Rabati's favourite haunt of Temara. Between the road and the sea is the **Club Hôtel La Kasbah**, tel 41633, which offers a lot of facilities, pool, hammam, solarium, with riding and all manner of ball games arranged and largely filled by the French Fram tour agency. A double for 491dh, single for 325dh.

The neighbouring camping **Rose Marie** is run by the hotel and subsequently well-organized with 75 places, tel 42307.

On the other side of the road from the beach is the cheap **Auberge Gambusia** and a larger slightly chaotic campsite, where you cannot hear the waves or the harsh guttural cries of competitive holiday tennis tournaments.

Skhirat

31 km from Rabat and reached by turnings off the P36, the P1 or the motorway RP 36. At the inland town there is a **souk** on Sunday, a train station and a students' Moussem in September.

Skhirat beach is distinctly upmarket and is almost entirely occupied by the outer walls of the king's summer palace. Villas of officials exist along the shore to the north and army compounds for the many guards are scattered around.

The **Skhirat palace** was the scene of the events of July 1971. The beach palace was full of guests celebrating the king's birthday when a coup was launched by General Mohammed Medbuh, who used the impressionable and mostly Berber cadets under his command. A number of the guests were massacred before this strangely misdirected and anarchic assault consumed itself. Medbuh was shot by his own cadets and the king, once recognized, was able to restore order among the cadets.

Curious rock formations stretch inland from the road. A turning at the southern end of the palace takes you to the **Amphitrite Hôtel**, the most tranquil elegant place to stay along this stretch of coast. The Amphitrite, tel 42236, has 36 rooms, bar, restaurant, beach front and pools with strongly painted murals running along the walls. Full pension for two is 780dh, a double room with breakfast costs 300dh, the same price that you would pay for a full dinner from the menu.

Dahomey/Bouznika beach

41 km south from Rabat is Dahomey, a little string of bungalows where a very simple campsite has just been established. The trees for shade are still growing, the gaily painted reception hut looks precarious but it is different and above a quite sparsely populated beach. Tent, person, car all cost 6dh a head. There is the four square **Bouznika Kasbah** on a hill above the beach occupied by a friendly family squatting with their chickens amongst old ruined cars inside the compound.

Essanoubar beach

Again this down-market resort has no hotel but a campsite at the end of a short drive to a few shabby bungalows clustered beside a small stream. Surrounded by a forest well populated with birds, it is a friendly rather reclusive place.

Itilal/Mansouria beach

No hotels but two good campsites just above what could be considered the far north end of Mohammedia's long beach. Stay at either **Camping Mimosa** or the **Oubaha** which is open all year, tel 13.

Mohammedia

Mohammedia, a town of 46,000 inhabitants, does a surprising seasonal double act. It is on one hand a refinery and oil terminal and on the other hand it is a summer beach resort with a 3 km shore-front promenade, a casino, a race course and a golf course.

The yellow sands of the beach have so far remained untouched by oil pollution and from June to September the town is full of families on holiday from Casablanca. The beach gets emptier and more enticing the further north you travel, though the proximity of the refinery has kept most foreign visitors away.

Mohammedia was visited by Mediterranean trading nations in the 14th century when it was known as Port Fedala. The Portuguese occupied it briefly at the turn of the 15th century but abandoned the site even before their general withdrawal after the fall of Agadir in 1541. The **Kasbah**, though it looks indigenous, was built by the Portuguese. It has been restored and contains a pretty quarter, well paved with gardens and flower boxes, not a particularly Moroccan Medina scene.

GETTING AROUND

Mohammedia is 28 km north of Casablanca on the S111 coast road. The railway station and the main road bring you into town behind the Kasbah whilst buses drop you in front of the restored Kasbah walls. The vegetable market shelters along the beach side wall of the Kasbah. The Banque Populaire is on Blvd Hassan II and cars can be rented from Autoc-location Firdaous on Rue Ferhat Hached, tel 2086. Locally made cane furniture is for sale the other side of the Christian cemetery on the coast road north of town.

WHERE TO STAY

The ***** **Miramar Hôtel** on the Rue de Fes is a large luxurious complex with 300 rooms, pool, bar, casino, night club, golf, riding and water sports but at the unattractive south end of the town where you also find the luxurious but badly sited **** **Samir Hôtel** at 34, Blvd Moulay Youssef. Near to these two hotels are the night clubs, the **Casino de Fedala**, the disco **le Sphinx** and Mohammedia's premier fish restaurant, **Chez Irene** by the port, tel 2466.

There are also a couple of unclassified hotels by the Kasbah. **Hôtel Ennasr** is well run with moderate prices; if it is full try the **Hôtel des Voyageurs** or the **Hôtel Castel** or the camping **Loran**. This is on the coast road 2 km out of town, open all the year and in a good position above the sea. There are a few bungalows available which in summer might be preferable to a hotel room in town, tel 2957.

The **Motel Restaurant Les Sablettes** is at the far end of the coast road with a beach caught between two rocky outcrops that provide good snorkeling and a lagoon for bird spotting at dusk.

Inland from Mohammedia

Ben Slimane, a town of 40,000, is the centre for this interior region of forests and farmers; the big **souk** is held on Wednesday and the Moussem of Sidi Ben Sliman in September. **Souk Jemaa des Feddalate** has its market on Friday, travel on the S1007 from Mohammedia via Ain Tekki on the P1.

Tit Mellil on the S106 has a **souk** on Friday whilst further east on this road are the **phosphate mines of Sidi Hajjaj**.

About 10 km due south of Mohammedia, along the 1008 road off the main P1 highway is the **waterfall of Mizab**. The flow of water is slight but the overgrown terraces, paths and a secluded licensed restaurant in the midst of unspoilt farmland make the 'Casacade Mizab' a welcome diversion.

CASABLANCA

The city is a surprise for those who have been fed with the picturesque images of Marrakesh and Fez. For here is a modern city with a skyline dominated by towering office blocks and sprawling suburbs ringed in the approved metropolitan style by a motorway ringroad. The streets are jammed with cars and the Mediterranean apartment block is the dominant housing motif.

Casablanca dominates the national economy: it is the chief port, the financial, industrial, commercial and manufacturing centre of the Kingdom. It has all been achieved within this century, from a town of 20,000 in 1900 the Casablanca conurbation is now home to 3,500,000. In North Africa only Cairo can compete with Casa in growth, verve and vibrancy whilst this city facing out to the Atlantic seems more fully oriented to the international pattern of trade and sympathetic to Western influences.

The French administration must be credited for much of this achievement. They carefully planned the new Atlantic face of Morocco which they schemed to make in their own image whilst allowing the xenophobic cities of the interior to wither into mere historical monuments. The city centre still carries statues to Lyautey and Foucauld, and churches are still as noticeable as mosques. The fusion of cultures, Moroccan and French, seems so complete and intricate here that one can easily forget that the long battle for independence was chiefly fought on the streets of Casablanca. Morocco's future national and political growth is now insolubly linked with the actions of Casablanca. It is a child of the industrial revolution with many of traditional problems of that transformation, great divisions in wealth and problems in structuring health and adequate housing for a mushrooming city. Alone in Morocco one can talk in terms of class awareness and foresee a time when a larger political role is forcefully demanded by its citizens.

If it is a source of fascination to the politician and speculation for the businessman it has much less to offer the traveller. There are no galleries, museums, ancient monuments or accessible public buildings. The one previous existing distraction—the aquarium is closed for repairs. A tour of the city centre confines itself chiefly to admiring urban parks and 20th-century civic architecture. The streets and shops of the old medina and the quite separate new medina provide the chief amusement. A taxi ride along the coast road passing above the massive port, the enormous new mosque being built and along the lighthouse point to the coastal resort suburb of Ain Diab could complete in a half day a tour of the city.

However if your chief interest is in diving through external distractions to meet some of the people of Morocco, Casablanca could be the place for you. Moroccans are generally pained to see someone alone and are right to compare unfavourably the aloofness of London or Paris to the welcome and hospitality freely given to visitors in Casablanca.

No scene of the film *Casablanca* was shot in Morocco nor does the finished film bear much relation to the city of the past or the present. When the Marx brothers planned their own version of Casablanca they ran up against considerable legal difficulties. A peeved Grouch Marx wrote, 'Up to the time that we contemplated making this picture, I had no idea that the city of Casablanca belonged exclusively to Warner brothers', for so possessive had the producers become of this North African city that they had never seen that they sued anybody who attempted to use 'their' new name.

History

The smart western residential suburb, Anfa, was the site of a Phoenician trading station which was founded in the 6th century BC. It continued in existence under the Arabic conquest of Morocco but was quick to join in the Khajarite revolt against the harsh exploitative rule of the early Arab governors.

Anfa subsequently became the capital of the Berber Khajarite kingdom of Berghoauta. Their faith and political independence was successfully defended against frequent invasions from the orthodox Idrissid and later the Almoravide rulers. Indeed the founder of the Almoravide movement died fighting the Berghouata. The kingdom was finally conquered by Sultan Abdel Moumen in 1149. Few of the defenders were left alive after the final assault on this heretical capital, though the Almohads maintained the use of the port of Anfa for the export of cereals.

By the 15th century Anfa also housed a flotilla of corsairs who raided the Portuguese coast so effectively that Don Ferdinand was forced to send an Armada of 50 ships against this threat in 1468 and again in 1515. In 1575 the Portuguese commander of El Jadida closed the corsair base for ever by building a fort at Anfa which also served to guard the northern approach road to El Jadida. This remained until the Lisbon earthquake of 1755 shattered both the walls of Anfa and the treasury of Portugal.

Sultan Sidi Mohammed reclaimed Anfa and built the present Medina to the east of the ruins in 1770. The walls, fortifications and Grand Mosque of the Medina all date from this period. The Portuguese name for their fort, Casa Branca, white house, alone remained in use though it was neither the Arabic translation, Dar el-Beida, nor the French, Villa Blanche, but the Spanish, Casa Blanca that passed into general usage.

Sultan Moulay Sliman closed the port as part of his policy of isolating Morocco from Europe but it was reopened by his successor in 1830. The tempo of trade increased with exports of wool and corn to Britain whose merchants sold tea, teapots, clothes and paraffin candles in return. An English consul arrived in 1857 when it was a modest town of 8000 inhabitants and he was soon to be followed by the other major powers. In 1898 R. B. Cunningham Graham wrote, 'At Casa Blanca Consuls abound, of course so do Hyenas-that is outside the town-but both are harmless and furnish little sport.' The consuls, foreign merchants and their protected agents were soon to furnish some rare sport. In 1907 the town exploded against their predominant influence and nine French port workers were killed in the streets. This furnished a useful pretext for the French army to land in Morocco the next year. The Resident General from 1912–25, Lyautey, started the process of urban planning and port extension that soon produced its own tempo of commercial dynamism and growth. Morocco's mercantile élite from Fez were quick to move to the coast and join in the development and property boom.

Though the new city was at the forefront of agitation against French colonial rule and still is the centre for contemporary political protest it is linked in the western conscience to three rather spurious events—the landings, the conference and the film. The Casablanca landings of November 1942 have no military significance as the result had already been pre-arranged between the two opponents, the American and the Vichy French generals. Sea sick American troops were landed with great confusion at Safi, Medhiya, Fedala but not Casablanca. The Casablanca conference was held two months later in January 1943. It had no significance for Morocco; Roosevelt and Churchill spent their days planning the invasion of Sicily from a suburban villa in Anfa. The film was released in the winter of 1942 and was lucky to gain the free publicity of landings and conference. It was also fortunate in a last minute change of cast, Ronald Reagan and Ann Sheridan were replaced by Humphrey Bogart and Ingrid Bergman and as an inspired afterthought the director, Michael Curtiz added Dooley Wilson singing, 'As Time Goes By'.

GETTING AROUND

By Air

Taxi to town 150 dh

All international flights and most domestic connections use the Airport Mohammed V which is 30 km out of town on the main P7 route to Marrakesh. Frequent buses leave from the airport to the central CTM station, 20dh a trip. For the odd domestic link you might have to go to Airport de Casablanca, Anfa, accessible by taxi. All the airlines have offices on the central Av. des F.A.R., at no 15 for Air France, at no 4 for Alitalia, at no 17 for Iberia, at no 44 for Royal Air Maroc and Swissair is at no 27.

By Train

Make sure that you are arriving at the port station, 'Gare du Port', rather than the 'Gare des Voyageurs' which leaves you with a 50 minute walk into the centre of town or a 10dh petit taxi ride. There are twenty one daily trains to Rabat for the 1 hour journey, three for Tangier and six for Fez—both routes take about 7 hrs and involve a possible change of trains at Sidi Kacem. The four daily trains south to Marrakesh leave from Gare des Voyageurs. The port station is admirably sited beside the major coastal route for Ain Diab and fronts onto Blvd Mohammed el Hansali which leads straight to the Place Mohammed V, the hub of the city where the major avenues bifurcate off and you find the main gate to the old Medina.

By Bus

The CTM station is on the Rue Vidal which runs behind the Av. des F.A.R. The tall Hotel Safir on the F.A.R. is a useful beacon for the turning to the station. There are 11 buses a day for Rabat, 3 a day for El Jadida, Essaouira and Marrakesh.

By Car

If at all possible try not to drive in Casablanca which has few street signs, competitive

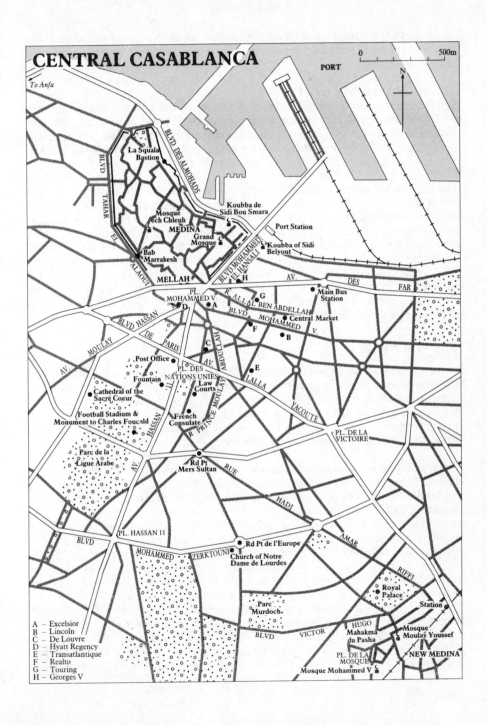

CENTRAL CASABLANCA

To Anfa

PORT

0   500m

N

BLVD DES ALMOHADS

BLVD TAHAR EL ALAOUI

La Squala
Bastion

Mosque
ech Chleuh

MEDINA

Grand
Mosque

Bab
Marrakesh

MELLAH

Koubba de
Sidi Bou Smara

Port Station

BLVD MOHAMMED EL HANSALI

Koubba of Sidi
Belyout

AV.   DES   FAR

H

PL.
MOHAMMED V

D   A

R ALLAL BEN ABDELLAH

G

BLVD   MOHAMMED   V.

Main Bus
Station

Central Market

BLVD HASSAN

MOULAY

AV.

DE   PARIS

F

B

Post Office

C

AV.   ABDULLAH

Fountain

PL. DES
NATIONS UNIES

Law
Courts

E

Cathedral of the
Sacré Coeur

LALLA

Football Stadium &
Monument to Charles Foucald

French
Consulate

R PRINCE MOULAY

YACOUTE

PL. DE LA
VICTOIRE

Parc de la
Ligue Arabe

HASSAN

AV.

Rd Pt
Mers Sultan

RUE

HADJ

PL. HASSAN 11

BLVD

MOHAMMED   ZERKTOUNI

Rd Pt de l'Europe

Church of Notre
Dame de Lourdes

AMAR

RIFFI

Royal
Palace

Station

Parc
Murdoch.

BLVD   VICTOR

HUGO

Mahakma
du Pasha

Mosque
Moulay Youssef

A – Excelsior
B – Lincoln
C – De Louvre
D – Hyatt Regency
E – Transatlantique
F – Realto
G – Touring
H – Georges V

PL. DE LA
MOSQUE

Mosque Mohammed V

NEW MEDINA

traffic, packs of scooter riders and the normal indomitable Moroccan pedestrians who maintain a courageous indifference to cars. The ringroad is however well signposted and an efficient bypass.

GETTING AROUND THE CITY

The old medina and the central parks are in walking distance from each other through the city centre. It is worth catching a taxi for the coastal resort of Ain Diab, the New Medina or the Gare des Voyageurs. Petits taxis can be caught on the Place Mohammed V and the Av. des F.A.R., the fare for Ain Diab 15dh, 10dh for the Gare or the Medina.

TOURIST INFORMATION

The Syndicat d'Initiative, 98 Blvd Mohammed V has a good selection of city maps and lists of cinemas, health clubs, discos and a railway timetable. The Post Office is at the junction of the Blvd de Paris and the Av. Hassan II, open Mon–Fri, 8.30–12.00 where you can make telephone calls. A smaller branch office on 116, Av. Mohammed V. There are plenty of banks, the Banque Populaire on 48 Av. des F.A.R. or the BMCI on 26, Place Mohammed V or 267 Blvd Mohammed V are some of the most convenient.

Emergencies: dial 19 for Police, 15 for ambulance. A 24-hour chemist can be found on Place des Nations Unies, tel 269491. Church services: Notre Dame de Lourdes, Place de l'Europe, mass on Sunday at 10.00 and 19.00; St Jeanne d'Arc, Blvd Moulay Youssef has a service in English at 9.30.

The Old Medina

If you are familiar with any of the Medinas from Morocco's old cities Casablanca will be a disappointment. It was built at the end of the 18th century but has constantly been chopped and changed since. There are few old buildings, few crafts, fewer craftsmen, but the streets are packed and busy enough with the activities of an urban souk. It is not large enough to get lost for long but a walk around the perimeter wall is a good introduction and allows you to visit the few points of interest.

The **Hyatt Regency Hotel** stands conspicuous in the centre of the Place Mohammed V. The road behind, the Blvd Tahar el Alaoui, leads you on a complete 2 km circuit of the old **Medina walls**. The defences look somewhat bedraggled but contrast well with the streams of traffic from this modern city.

Pass the **Bab Marrakesh**, sometimes called the new gate, and continue north past two further entrances. Turn right on to the Blvd Sour Jedid, passing a triangular public garden to turn right on to the busy Blvd des Almohads which passes between the Medina walls and the port. The 18th-century **bastion of La Sqala** can be seen overlooking the site of the old port and 100 m further on a path winds up into the Medina and a quick right turn leads you to the bastion terrace and its view.

Returning to the Blvd des Almohads and continuing on for another 50 m you reach another breach in the ramparts leading directly into the square of Sidi Bou Smara. The first alley on your left, keep left at the next turning leads you to the **Koubba of the Sidi** surrounded by a small cemetery, a charming corner of the Medina shaded by fig trees and removed from the frenetic street life. A wider arcaded alley leads to the **Grand**

Mosque built by Sidi Mohammed in celebration of the recovery of Anfa from the Portuguese. Carrying along on this route will lead you out on to the Place Mohammed V, or you could retrace your steps and continue the circuit along the Blvd des Almohads. Beside the port railway station you will notice the **Koubba of the marabout Sidi Belyout** set in a rough garden. Continue up the Blvd Mohammed el Hansali beneath the walls to return to Place Mohammed V.

The Medina can be crossed from south to north by following the busiest street which is known variously as Rue Chakib Arsalane/Jemaa ech Chleuh/Rue Tnacker, which will lead you from Place Mohammed V to Blvd Sour Jdid. The Medina has a general dilapidated air, well-worn but with few striking buildings. The products for sale are mostly aimed at the cheap local market and it is claimed that you can buy back here what went missing yesterday.

Place des Nations Unies

Heading south from the Place Mohammed V you walk down the Av. Hassan II to pass through the Place des Nations Unies, the administrative heart of Casablanca. Marrast was employed in the 1920s as the architect for most of the official buildings that surround the square. The central fountain operates on Fridays and weekends, to the east of which is the **Palais de Justice**. Next door is the **French consulate** with a statue of Lyautey to the fore. The **Préfecture** is easily recognizable to the south with its slightly incongruous clock tower striking a jarring note with the Classical–Moorish synthesis displayed all around. The concierge can however on a good day let you in for a fine view of town, park and port from the tower. The PTT and the Banque du Maroc sit very solidly on the northern face of the Place. A turning to the right, the Rue Rachidi allows you to admire the **School of Fine Arts** to your right in the old **Church of the Sacred Heart**, which was designed by Pual Tornon in 1930. It is a light, airy white structure designed with sympathy and reference to Islamic forms.

The enormous **football stadium** to the south of the Place is still decorated with a monument to Charles Foucauld, the aristocratic French cavalry officer who disguised himself as an itinerant Russian rabbi in order to explore the interior of Morocco in 1883. He was assassinated in 1916 at his mission post deep in the Sahara in the land of the Tuareg in the Tamanrasset mountains.

This is bordered by the great square **Parc de la Ligue Arabe**. At the far southern end of this wooded park is the inner ring road, the Blvd Mohammed Zerktouni. About 600 metres to the east, left as you leave the park, is the **Church of Notre Dame de Lourdes**, finished in 1956. The interior is hung with some fine tapestries that illustrate the doctrine of the Immaculate Conception and the appearance of the Virgin at Lourdes on the right. The borders have been picked out in blue and red in a deliberate Moroccan scheme, though figurative religious art is of course completely removed from the practice of Morocco.

New Medina

Created as a show piece of colonial paternalism, a new quarter was designed for Muslims to the southeast of the then European city centre. A few of the inhabitants of the bidonville slums were transferred to these elegant thin streets with the wider connecting roads lined with stone built arcades. Here in the new Medina are the largest concentration of bazaars, the stalls and shop fronts of artisans. It is the cleanest, most ordered **souk** in Morocco, lacking vitality but with a fine selection from all the national crafts.

The most elegant arcades are to be found in the area north of the railway line and south of the Blvd Victor Hugo. The high walls of the **Royal Palace**, that enclose a secretive and elegant garden, border the Boulevard to the north. A street surmounted by three picturesque arches leads to the Place Moulay Youssef with its central garden and mosque built by the present king's grandfather in 1938. Two arcaded and arched streets on the left of the Place lead to the larger Place de la Mosque with well kept and shaded central gardens and the **Mosque of Mohammed V** to its south. To the north are the outer walls of the **Mahakma du Pasha**, the combined residence of the Pasha of Casablanca and the tribunal of the Islamic courts finished in 1952 by the French. It is for the moment closed to visitors which is a pity as the interior is a maze of courts decorated in the traditional Moorish styles with carved plaster and wood.

A bridge, the **Sidi Djedid**, leads south across the railway line to the greater extent of the New Medina. The vegetable and spice market of the **quartier Balilida** is off the Rue du Gharb, a delightfully animated court full of the competing colours and odours of the souk. A terrace that runs parallel to the market above, the Rue Taroudant, contains the stalls of herbalists and enchanters. Hedgehogs and turtles are sold live and there are curtains of dried animal and bird skins from which to make charms and love potions. Madame Chrifa Dukkalia, who runs one of the stalls, will tell your fortune from her pack of henna stained cards. The small cones of green, dried leaves from the henna tree are sold as the base for the henna paste that is used for decorating hands and feet and for invigorating and dyeing hair.

A Coastal tour

Catch a taxi in the Place Mohammed V, travel down to the port station beside the Medina and turn left to travel between the Medina and the port.

The Port

The nearest dock to the road is for the fishing fleet, then there is the area dedicated to liners and yachts before the three commercial moles and a great extension that is being finished to the east which is doubling the size of the port, already the fourth busiest in Africa. The export of phosphates dominates the activity of the port with vegetables and fruit despatched to Europe and corn, wood, sugar, oil and manufactured goods imported. Passing level to the protective sea wall, the enclosing port jetty of Moulay Youssef, you quickly understand the need for bathing pools as the beach is revealed. A mass of weathered, disturbingly sharp bedrock extends hundreds of metres out to sea at low tide. The sewage from a city the size of Casa and the Atlantic currents should discourage even an eel from swimming here. Opposite the first large public pool is the **Parc des Expositions** which houses the trade fairs and the **Aquarium**, if it ever reopens, is on the left corner. The Blvd de la Corniche leads on past a crumbling walled **Christian cemetery** to the **lighthouse** on the Pointe d'el Hank.

Ain Diab

Ain Diab is 3 km west, a coastal resort with little attraction for visitors from the west. The bars, the bathing clubs and the mixing of both sexes in a public area with fewer clothes on than normal has a fascination for the less sophisticated Moroccans that it is difficult to share. The shore is lined with a number of clubs who seem to have taken their inspiration from the Club Med. An exclusive members-only policy (though as a foreign visitor you will often be welcomed in), bathing pools, concrete flooring and constant hearty ball games comes close to a vision of purgatory. Upmarket there are a number of new brash modern hotels, the ***** **Riad Salaam** with five restaurants and water exercise pools is the most lavish. There is a new **Saudi Palace** with an associated library and mosque that has been built above it.

Sidi AbderRahmane

Of much greater appeal is the road even further west, the S130, which sheds the smart suburbs of Anfa and Ain Diab to reveal in another 3 km the striking **shrine of Sidi AbderRahmane**. A cluster of whitewashed shrines and sanctuary lodgings entirely occupies a rock headland whose sandy connecting strip is covered by the advancing tide. At dusk you watch the sun being swallowed by the Atlantic and as the whitewashed tombs are flecked with the dying red rays one is certain that man has worshipped here or watched in awe since the dawn of consciousness. Remains of Homo Erectus, the first user of fire, have been found in the nearby sand dunes.

The pleasant windswept stretch of sandy beach with the two small settlements and campsites at **Dar Bouazza** and **Tamaris beach/Hajra Kahla** are 10 km further at a signposted right turn off the S130. This coastal road is a slower but more entertaining route than the inland P8 which goes through **Bir Jdid**, only of interest on Thursday for its **souk**. The roads rejoin at Azzemour, 83 km away.

SHOPPING

There are three commercial art galleries that have exhibitions of Moroccan artists, decorative art from other Islamic countries and works from France and Belgium: The **Galerie Alifba**, Rue Mostafa al Maari, **Galerie d'Art moderne** at 61, Av. Moulay el Hassan-1er, tel 220725 and the **Alif ba** at 46, Rue Omar Slaoui.

LIBRARIES AND CULTURAL CENTRES

Centre Culturel Français, 121, Blvd Zerktouni, tel 259077; the Dante Alighieri Society at 21, Av. Hassan Souktani, tel 200145; Dar America at 10, Place Bel Air, tel 221460; the Portuguese Cultural Centre at 296, Blvd Mohammed V, tel 306128 and the Spanish on 15, Rue Do-Hu, tel 313267.

SPORTS

The chief sports in Casablanca, the businessman's city, are inevitably **golf** and **tennis**. The Royal Golf D'Anfa shares the **race track**, which can be running on Sunday. The club house is usually welcoming to visiting players, the Hippodrome, Anfa, tel 361026, an 18- and a 9-hole course. There is also a golf course at Mohammedia and outside Rabat. Tennis courts are at the major clubs: the Tennis USM at Parc de la Ligue Arabe, tel 275429, the tennis Romandie, Blvd de Libye, tel 361640, Club Olympique de Casa, Cour des sports, RUC Tennis Club, Clos de L'Aviation.

Riding can be arranged at Club Bayard, Anfa, tel 272581 and the Club d'Etrier, quartier des Stades, tel 253771 and **racing** at the Hippodrome in Anfa some Sundays as advertised.

Water sports are constricted by the fierce Atlantic surf and rocky coast. **Swimming** or bathing is generally restricted to large salt water concrete pools along the coast towards Ain Diab. There are both a **sailing and a rowing club** which occasionally function from jetties in the port. RUC Rowing club, Moulay Youssef jetty, Port, tel 225721 and STE Nautique de Casablanca, Delure jetty, Port, tel 225721.

CABARETS AND NIGHT LIFE

The **Theatre Mohammed V** is on the Av. des F.A.R. Morocco, despite its reverence for story-tellers, does not have any tradition of theatre. The hall is used for musical concerts and visiting companies. The shows are well advertised in advance and usually televised.

Casablanca enjoyed a brief notoriety as the sex-change capital of the world but the surgeons of the West have returned home to practise their art in their own, now legal clinics. Casablanca continues to enjoy a heady reputation for sophisticated commercial sexual shows that seems no more than a continuation of the Victorian 'Oriental' obsession. Certainly a night spent in the **discos** at Ain Diab brings swift disillusion to the fantasist. Taxi drivers and hotel porters traditionally have to face the burden of these enthusiastic requests. 'Why else do the French and the Saudis come to Casa, for the aquarium?' scornfully remarked a friend as he sidled up eager-eyed to the reception desk.

A night in Casablanca could begin with a tour of the bar clubs. Start in the city centre at **Don Quichotte** at 44, Place Mohammed V, tel 222051, and move on at will to the **Negresco** on Rue Poincaré, tel 272661, the **Embassy** on 2, Blvd Mohammed V, tel 265707 , the **Puerta del Sol**, 7, Av. Hassan II, tel 222772 and finish at **La Fontaine**, Blvd Mohammed el Hansali. The **Fontaine** has live music for the belly dancers who can be quite direct in their demands for tips whilst the bar flies and bar ladies have expensive and unquenchable thirsts.

The clubs along the Corniche get more reputable and sadly international in their disco tastes as you move away from the port. All can easily be found by taking a taxi along the coast road, the Blvd de la Corniche. The Corniche clubs: the **Bahia** on the Anfa plage, tel 367242, **Le Balcon 33**, at 33, Blvd de la Corniche and also on this road is **La Notte**, tel 367361, **La Reserva**, tel 367110, **Topkapi**, tel 367339, **Le Tube**, tel 367502 and **Wichita** at 13, Blvd de la Corniche. At Ain Diab itself **Le Calypso**, tel 367150, **Le Tangage**, tel 357105 and night clubs in the **Hôtels Tarik, Karam, *** Anfa Plage, **** Suisse** and ******* Riad Salam**.

WHERE TO STAY

There are nine one-star and ten two-star hotels listed in the centre of town and it is very rare to have any problems in finding a room. The hotels, solidly built during the Protectorate, are spacious and largely undamaged by improvements. Arab oil money has poured into the development of a number of ugly hotels at the Ain Diab resort.

The **** **Transatlantique** remains the most elegant hotel in Casablanca at 79, Rue Colbert. Enormous comfortable bedrooms in an old hotel that has escaped redecorations. In the centre of town on a quiet street, calm atmosphere and service, French and Moroccan restaurants, 59 rooms.

238

A pick from the one-star hotels would include: **Du louvre** at 36 Rue Nationale, 32 rooms, tel 273747, **Rialto** at 9, Rue Claude which has 21 rooms and a hammam opposite, tel 275122. The **Touring** at 87, Rue Allal ben Abdallah with 32 rooms, tel 310216 and the **Lincoln**, tel 222408 at 1, Rue Ibn Batouta with 53 rooms and a restaurant.

For your money a two-star hotel provides added grandeur and more efficient plumbing. Choose from either the **Excelsior** at 2, Rue Nolly, 60 rooms, tel 262281 or **Georges V**, 1, Rue Sidi Belyout, 35 rooms, tel 312448.

Camping at the **oasis camp site** in Casablanca on the Av. Mermoz is not recommended. A new site has opened 25 km along the coast road south to Azzemour, the **Tamaris** at Hajra Kahla, which is open all the year, or you could consider camping at Mohammedia.

EATING OUT

Casablanca has the reputation for the best restaurants in Morocco and dinner in any one of the top half dozen Moroccan or French addresses below should show you some very fine cooking. Expect to pay London/New York prices and a totally different quality in food and service.

It is difficult to choose in a city like Casablanca but for Moroccan cooking look first at these three restaurants: **Al Mounia**, 95, Rue du Prince Moualy Abdullah, tel 222669; **El Bahja**, 79 Rue Colbert, tel 260763; **L'Etoile de Marrakesh** at 126, Blvd Mohammed V, tel 271259.

For French cooking and seafood three restaurants beneath the lighthouse on the El Hank rock peninsula: **Le Cabestan**, tel 221060; **Au Petit Rocher**, tel 221195 and **La Mer**, tel 221084 have an international reputation. La Mer was always favoured by Giscard D'Estaing when he visited Morocco as President of France. The other two preeminent restaurants are **Ma Bretagne**, Blvd Sidi Abderrahane, tel 362111, perhaps the most expensive, and the fish specialities at **La Cambuse** at Ain Diab, tel 367105.

For a considerably less extravagant night out try: **L'Etoile Marocaine** at 107, Rue Allal Ben Abdallah, tel 311473, a small unlicensed restaurant decorated in the Moorish taste and serving traditional food at a reasonable price.

Le Petit Poucet at 86, Blvd Mohammed V, tel 275420, was one of the smartest centres of urban life before the Second World War. You can still eat in its dignified cool but faded grandeur or sip anis in a dark corner, and they run a cheaper café restaurant next door.

For a reasonably priced fish restaurant go into the port, past the police customs post to **Le Port de Pêche**, a tranquil place where you can sip sangria whilst you decide what fish to choose and how it is to be cooked.

There are three good Spanish restaurants: **La Corrida** at 59, Rue Gay Lussac, tel 278155 with a garden, **Las delicias**, 168 Blvd Mohammed V or **Tout va Bien**, 64 Blvd du Janvier 11, all serving admirable groaning plate loads of fruits de mer or paella with salads and red wine which can make a splendid meal.

Patisseries and Glacés

The most famous patisserie in Casablanca is **Bennis** at 2, Rue Fkih el Gabbas in the Quartier Habous where you can sample the traditional Moroccan pastries redolent with almonds and honey.

The Blvd du Janvier 11 boasts the two finest glacés, **Glacier Gloria** and **L'Igloo** where the most exotic combinations of fruit, sherbets, ice creams, whipped cream, flavoured milks, juices, teas and coffees can be ordered. A fraise melba costs only 13dh, the Blvd is just below the Place des Nations Unies.

ADDRESSES FOR THE POTENTIAL BUSINESSMAN

Casablanca only really comes alive as a city if you approach it with schemes for importation and exportation of goods. The festivals of the city are almost all commercial, the leather and textile fair is in February, the international fair in April, the building fair in July and the artisan Moussem later that month. Otherwise international summits, Mediterranean or African sporting competitions puncture its calendar and there is a car race in April.

The British Chamber of Commerce for Morocco with 52 years of experience is at 291, Blvd Mohammed V, tel 303760, the American in the Hotel Mansour, Av. des F.A.R., tel 313011. Chambre de Commerce et d'Industrie de Casablanca, 98, Blvd Mohammed V, tel 221431, the Chambre de Commerce Internationale on 4, Rue de Rhone, tel 309716.

The Churchill Club, Rue Pessac at Ain Diab, tel 367280 maintains an English-speaking rule in its premises in the heart of Francophone Africa, a surprisingly popular place for Moroccan businessmen in which to practise their new language skills.

There is a British consul at 60 Blvd d'Anfa, tel 261441 the same address for the British Chamber of Commerce for Morocco, there is an efficient American consular office at 8, Blvd Moulay Youssef, tel 224149.

Pays de Rehamna, the Plateau of Phosphates

Inland from the ports of the Atlantic coast, Casablanca, El Jadida/Jorf and Safi fast roads cross an extensive plateau towards Marrakesh. The coastal region supports a large population of farmers but the great national treasure lies inland in an otherwise great expanse of arid and marginal grazing land. The mines of Khouribga, Youssoufia and Benguerir extract millions of tonnes of phosphates, impressive due to the scale of operation but ugly in detail.

The one feature of interest is the Kasbah of Boulaoune which is well worth a detour from your route across this monotonous plain.

Berrechid

38 km outside Casablanca and 15 km from the International Airport is the crossroads of Berrechid. At the feast of Aid el Kebir a great Moussem is held at the **shrine of the marabout Sidi Ameur ben Lahcene**, close to the railway station and a souk is held every week on Monday.

If you turn left at the crossroads, onto the P13, you pass after 40 km the turning to the village of **Benahmed** which also has a **souk** on Monday. The spoil heaps of Khouribga are visible for miles though you do not pass the mine for another 40 km. **Oued Zem** is 35 km further southeast.

Settat

Continuing due south of Berrechid on the P7 you pass Settat, a town of 150,000 and centre of the province of Chaouia. Moulay Ishmael built a Kasbah here at the end of the 17th century as a staging post on the Marrakesh to Rabat road. There is a train station, a bank on the Place de la Liberté and a hotel on the northern edge of town which overlooks the race course.

This, the **Hôtel M'Zamza**, tel 2366, has a pool, bar and restaurant and would be useful as a base for those planning a late visit to the Kasbah of Boulaoune or the eccentric choice of a 73 km drive to El Borouj on the S104 for the market of the Beni Meskin, and back.

Boulaoune

Buses leave from Settat daily across country to El Jadida and Sidi Bennour, both routes pass through the hamlet of Boulaoune, which still leaves you with an 8 km walk to the Kasbah. There will be more traffic on these roads for the **souks, Had Od Frej**, between Boulaoune and El Jadida, is on Sunday and **Sidi Bennoul** has its souk on Tuesday if you are planning to hitch. Car or grand taxi from Settat would obviously be easier; you take the S105 for El Jadida as you enter Settat and after 11 km pass the scant remains of a Kasbah erected at **Ouald Said** by Sultan AbderRahman in 1870. At Boulaoune, 50 km from Settat, there are vineyards and the **Caves de Bou Laoune**. Turn left on to the S124 for Sidi Bennoul and then shortly afterwards left again on the S128, feeling rather dizzy with these manoeuvres turn left again on to the long drive through pinewoods to the Kasbah.

The Kasbah of Boulaouane

This is one of the least visited but most impressive of the royal Kasbahs of Morocco. Through the flat agricultural plateau the Oued Oum er Rbia has cut out a deep serpentine course. In one of its more violent coils Moulay Ishmael built in 1710 the Kasbah of Boulaoune so that three of its four walls were protected by the natural moat of the river.

The gateway decorated with scallops and its wooden gates still in position is in fine condition. An inscription records its noble founder and the date. Passing through the gatehouse chamber you enter the large enclosed courtyard. To your left is the **Mosque** which you may enter and climb the minaret for a fine view of the encircling walls and the meanders of the river. The tarnished **sanctuary of Sidi Mansana** is in the northeast corner and a hole reveals an underground chamber near the wall. The **Palace courtyard** and tower are opposite, to the right of the gatehouse. Details of the paved mosaic floor can be made out and some plaster work survives on the stone walls. Broken and diminished fragments of white marble bear witness to what was once a delicate pillared courtyard. The **Bath house** is in the southern corner. Beyond the Palace walls an open tunnel descends beneath the fortress's curtain walls to appear in an external bastion. Two thick walls enclose this passage which descends the steep slope down to the remains of an hexagonal tower. The twin walls continue their progress down to the river to provide a secure wharf on the Oum er Rbia. Another low doorway has been cut through the curtain wall that leads out to a natural terrace where there is a tomb to a holy man partly underground.

Returning inside the walls watch out for the air vents of the underground chambers. Four out of the original six vaulted chambers survive and can be entered. The nearest is used by a barn owl that nests in a hole that connects with one of the battlemented towers. Old garrison quarters can be traced in their positions around the remaining areas of the curtain wall. A complete circuit can be made of the **battlements** that provide excellent potentially predatory views of the surrounding countryside and an arch gives out to the village that is stranded on the far reaches of the promontory.

Coming out of the drive turn left on to the S128 to continue alongside the river crossing at the Dar el Mir dam before later rejoining the P7, the main Casablanca to Marrakesh road.

The road south to Marrakesh

On the journey south to Marrakesh there are four villages where you can break the journey. Neither the landscape nor the architecture is of interest but by reading the tribal history of the Rehamna, see page 000, and by day-dreaming after a meal you could extract some entertainment from the journey.

114 km south of Casablanca is **Mechra Benabbou**. There is a restaurant north of the village and to the south, just before the bridge, there are woods that go down to the bank of the Oum er Rbia to make a pleasant picnicking place.

136 km from Casablanca in the midst of the barren plain of the Rehamna is **Skhour des Rehamna** with a **souk** on Wednesday, a few cafés and the **Hôtel restaurant Touristique**.

162 km from Casablanca is **Benguerir**; the spoil heaps of the mines can be seen on the eastern horizon and a military camp with a triumphal gate to the south. The **Hôtel Milano** and almost directly opposite a garden restaurant vie with the grill shops and cafés in the arcades for your attention.

South of Benguerir is the Bahira plain; in the 16th century the Sedd el Mejnoun depression was a lake full of fish and surrounded by woods full of birds.

197 km from Casablanca and 40 km from Marrakesh is the last stop of **Sidi Bou Othman** which has a **souk** on Monday, two Koubbas shaded by jujube trees and the **Auberge la Lorraine** for meals. One and a half kilometres to the northwest a 12th-century Almohad water storage tank has been discovered, on this old crossing point of the bleak Jebilet hills. It was here in 1912 that Colonel Mangin fought against the tribal army of the Blue Sultan, El Hiba, who had come from the Western Sahara to lead the jihad against the hated French. Mangin, having destroyed the fanatical army, marched quickly to occupy Marrakesh and rescue seven French hostages before the end of the day.

Azzemour

The least visited of all Morocco's Atlantic towns, it has few provisions for tourists and a welcome air of unhurried grace and ease. The old Portuguese walled town presents a striking view as you cross one of the three bridges that span the Oued Oum er Rbia, 'the mother of spring', to approach Azzemour. The white walls of the Medina houses rise up directly from the river bank and seem to bleed their colour down into the remains of the riverine fortifications.

On the landward side a long garden square divides the increasingly ruinous and battlemented Medina from the new town which stretches out to the east along the main road, the Av. Mohammed V. The square with its gardens and its backdrop of ancient Iberian walls is the natural centre for the town and has a few cafés and grill kitchens.

HISTORY

The Portuguese walls have long outlasted their creators who ruled Azzemour for less than thirty years.

Before the first Portuguese consul was allowed to land in 1486 this riverside port had enjoyed a long if undramatic history. It was used by Phoenician and Roman merchants when it was known as Azama and continued in existence as a regional centre of the Berber Berghawata Kingdom before the Almohads incorporated it in the 12th century into their Empire.

A Portuguese consul operated for 16 years at Azzemour before he was expelled, but the Portuguese returned in 1510 and three years later had seized control of the town. They immediately started on the construction of the walls and a central Kasbah which were strong enough to resist the siege of En Nasser the following year. The fall of Agadir in 1541 dramatically upset the balance of power and the Portuguese evacuated Azzemour the same year.

After this flurry of activity Azzemour has settled down to another long period of tranquil ease. The Portuguese garrisons which remained at the neighbouring towns of El Jadida and Anfa until the 18th century helped to isolate and hinder the development of Azzemour into a Muslim port.

GETTING AROUND

Azzemour is easily reached from El Jadida, only 16 km away, on the bus which travels every half hour or by grand taxi. There is a bus every half hour leaving from Casablanca to El Jadida for 13dh which passes through Azzemour. The Syndicat Initiative de Tourisme is at 141, Av. Mohammed V, just past the pharmacy and will know if anybody in the Medina is interested in taking lodgers.

The Medina

The aged red **walls** are an impressive site, partly covered in cascades of bougainvillea and punctuated with impressive and very European looking defensive towers. There are three landward gates and two riverine exits that overlook the slow-moving mud red waters of the Oum er Rbia. The northern gate has a stairway to the right which allows you to climb up to the battlements and look down upon the old **Mellah** quarter. Since the great exodus of Jews from Morocco the Mellah is only half occupied by newcomers and many of the houses are falling into ruin. The aerial view of the street plan and internal layout of the houses of a medina with their connecting alleys has a distinct prurient fascination. The Medina is a totally Moroccan creation which was rebuilt after the Portuguese left in 1541.

Dar el Baroud

The battlements lead round to the Dar el Baroud, the crumbling remains of the central Portuguese fortress, with its central dark pillared chamber boasting a decaying gothic stone window frame. It has been described as the powder room but is now used quite frequently for shitting. Whistle or hum as you explore if you wish to avoid potential embarrassment, not that the Moroccans seem particularly ashamed at performing so natural a function in an ancient monument. Near the west gate is a small **synagogue** which is locked, the key is kept at the Syndicat D'Initiative.

The Three Sidis of Azzemour

Rue Moulay Bouachaib, a narrow street, leads from the central Place to the **zaouia of Moulay Bouachaib** which was established at Azzemour in the 12th century. The big town moussem in August does however celebrate a Jewish Sidi, Rabbi Abraham Moul' Niss and there is also a **sanctuary** to an Idrissid marabout, **Moulay Abdullah ben Achmed**.

The Beach

The beach is a 2 km walk to the north, a path leads from below the northwestern tower with its gothic fringe of battlements appearing like an inverted crown and passes through the old raised carved stone tombs of the Jewish cemetery, now completely overgrown, and on through scrubland that borders the estuary to reach the beach. The Atlantic though rough is safer than swimming in the river which has an even more treacherous reputation and a disturbing colour and consistency. The sandy beach fringed by dunes and woodland continues on to El Jadida. Alternatively a tarmac road leaves the Place du Souk for a 2 km drive to the beach and the **Koubba of Sidi Ouadoud** surrounded by a few chalets, and the pool complex of **Haouzia** largely used by railway workers in the summer.

WHERE TO EAT AND SLEEP
The **market** is held behind the Place du Souk on Fridays and Tuesdays. There are three main cafés, the **Café de Atlantique**, a pavilion conspicuously set in the central public garden, the slightly more raffish **Café el Manzah** with its upstairs room giving a fine view of the walls. The **Café le Victoire** is ideal for breakfast as it is next door to the single hotel in town, the first floor **Hôtel la Victoire** at 308, Mohammed V, run in a relaxed amiable manner by Rochdi Larbi, a room costs 25dh a night. The grill cafés and couscous kitchens face the Portuguese walls where the bougainvillea drapes at its thickest in the northwest corner.

El Jadida

El Jadida is both the administrative centre for a rich agricultural province of 800,000 people and a summer resort for the young people of Casablanca and Marrakesh. The general social relaxations and freedoms of a holiday town make it a good place to meet Moroccans as equals. The evening sea breezes and the trouble-free population can be a refreshing contrast to the summer heat and hassle of the cities of the interior. Though out of season El Jadida carries the same slightly injured air of Le Touquet in October.

The 18th-century Portuguese citadel of **Mazagan** is at the heart of the town. Within the sea-moated walls there is a small but complete town that contains El Jadida's most distinctive site, the celebrated **Portuguese cistern**. Around the citadel are the neat avenues of the French-built new town. The hectic pace of post-Independence development proceeds not along the shore line but inland where a large but handsome domed mosque now breaks the skyline.

The 16 km long sandy beach is to the east of the town lined at first by an elegant boulevard that gives way to the wilderness of dunes and a forested nature reserve.

HISTORY
El Jadidi is entirely the creation of the Portuguese though it has been loosely associated with a Phoenician trading station known as Rub Isis. Before the Portuguese arrived the rich grain country of Dukkala province was ruled from either the neighbouring towns of Azzemour or Tit. The Berber tribes of the Dukkala joined their northern neighbour, the independent heretical kingdom of Bergawata in resisting Abdel Moumen, the Almohad Sultan in the 12th century. The Sultan replied to this additional threat by directing tribes of destructive Arab nomads on Dukkala province which was so brutally ravaged that large areas of farm land reverted to pasture.

Some prosperity must have been gradually restored to attract the Portuguese who built the fort of 'el Brija el Jadida' here in 1502. Four years later this was greatly expanded to the present dimensions, and the new town was christened Mazagan.

The Saadian Sultan, Abdullah el Ghalib, gave the defences their greatest test when he besieged Mazagan in 1562 and it successfully resisted all further assaults for the next 250 years until Sultan Sidi Mohammed took the town in 1769.

It remained an empty shell until Sultan AbderRahman resettled the town in 1815 by transplanting some of the Jews from Azzemour to Mazagan which he renamed 'the new one'—El Jadida. Trade revived in the late 19th century but the French protectorate gave the town a new identity as an administrative centre and summer beach resort.

GETTING AROUND
By Bus: The bus station is on the Rue de Mohammmed V, a ten-minute walk from the central Place Mohammed V. Buses leave for Casablanca every half hour and a ticket costs only 13dh. There are at least nine buses a day for Marrakesh, 23dh. Going further south there are four a day for Safi and only one direct for Essaouira, 31dh.

GETTING AROUND THE TOWN
El Jadida is an easy town to understand. The active centre is arranged along the Place el Hansali between the Portuguese city and the Place Mohammed V with the hotels, cafés

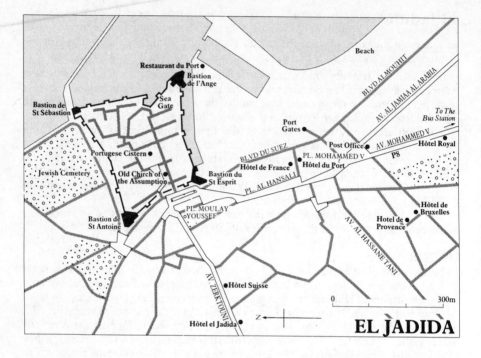

EL JADIDA

and restaurants all within a few minutes walking distance from each other. The **souk** is of limited interest and concentrated along Blvd Zerktouni, though a more lively vegetable and meat **souk** is held every Wednesday below the new lighthouse when the surrounding farmers ride into town to trade.

The Place Mohammed V is ringed with Mauresque public buildings; a Theatre, the Hôtel de Ville, the bank and the Post Office which is open Mon–Fri, 8.00–12.00, 15.00–18.30. The Syndicat d'Initiative for tourism has two charming girls who give out the usual brochures and answer some inquiries, open during normal office hours on the Av. de la Ligue Arabe.

The Hospital is on Rue Sidi Bouzid, on the southern edge of town and there is an after-hours chemist on Av. de la Ligue Arabe.

WHAT TO SEE
The Portuguese Town

The Portuguese garrison escaped the siege of Sidi Mohammed in 1769 by sea. They are recorded to have dynamited the city and trapped the triumphant besiegers in the resulting inferno which is strange, for architecturally the city is an almost perfect survivor of its period and has attracted a number of film directors. Of the five Italian-designed bastions four survive and it was probably this missing gate tower that was blown up by the departing Portuguese. It remained a deserted ghost town until the whole city was transformed into a **Mellah** in 1815 and as trade grew throughout the century a number of European merchants joined the Jewish community within the walls. The Muslim farmers of the Dukkala preferred to settle outside the walls in tents or abode huts. The departure of the Jews in the 1960s has left the Portuguese town with the aura of an historical monument rather than a living community.

Praca do Terreiro

The ramparts are built to the 18th-century requirements of a European siege and the sloping glacis and odd cannon portals can be considered less picturesque than earlier surviving Atlantic fortifications. The city is approached through twin gates facing the Place Mohammed ben Abdallah. The left gate leads to the Praca do Terreiro dominated by religious buildings. The **Grand Mosque** on the left is decorated with an odd pentagonal minaret for it was formed by converting the old lighthouse to sacred purposes. The **Church of the Assumption** on the right, once the centre for the sumptuous ceremonies of the Latin church is now a cultural centre and is subsequently usually shut. The alley to the left, the Rue do Arco, leads to the **bastion of St Antoine**, whilst turning to the right you meet the main axis of the citadel, the Rue Mohammed Al Hachmi Bahbah.

The Portuguese Cistern

This is halfway along the road on the left and is open from 8.00–12.30, 14.00–18.00 for 3dh. It was built in the 16th century as an arsenal and served as a fencing school before being converted into a water cistern. The vast underground chamber is an astonishing site—a flooded Cathedral crypt lit up by a bolt of African sun—and was used by Orson Welles in his film of *Othello*, the noble Moor.

The brickwork of the ceiling is held fast by groins of stone that fan out in a regular confusion of vaults from rows of square dressed pillars that are interspaced with the more delicate form of Tuscan columns. The vaulting is linked to the walls and the floor is a serene level of worn herringbone brick. This is flooded with a few inches of water to create a graceful architectural reflection. For in the centre of the chamber sun light streams, in almost tangible force, through a well head. The sunlight has dressed a few of the pillars in an oozing green lichen that throws in an extra element of colour into the reflection.

The entrance chamber holds a model of the city and an adjacent room contains two broken cannon and a number of Portuguese inscriptions. Ask the custodian to allow you on the roof for a central view of the surrounding walls, towers and roof line of the city.

Porta do Mar

Coming out of the cistern continue along the central street to the sea gate, Porta do Mar, through which the last Portuguese governor departed for the awaiting evacuation fleet. The wide arch still screened by an iron grille is protected by flanking bastions. A communal bakery exists within the walls wafting out gorgeous scents of baking dough.

The Bastions

A gate to the right of this bastion will be unlocked by a guardian to allow you to climb up to the **bastion De L'Ange**. There are two other entrance gates to the battlements at the **bastions of St Esprit** and **St Antoine**; if no one appears ask the guardian at the cistern.

The bastion of St Ange gives a fine view of the harbour and town with the walls lined with bronze European cannon. These are not necessarily captured spoils of war, for obselete but still impressive cannons proved to be popular gifts from 19th-century consuls anxious to win concessions from the Sultan. In the company of a young agile guide you can walk along the battlemented walls around three quarters of the city. The views and the odd scrambling climb are rewarding along all of the wall. The **bastion of St Sebastian** contains the old prison compound and the tribunal of the Inquisition, an impressive austere court house, with a sea view, that was converted into a synagogue as the surviving Star of David testifies. From here you can look outside the walls over an extensive Hebrew cemetery or over the northwestern corner of the town which contains the best examples of surviving Portuguese stone and iron work decoration to the houses. This quarter is the most inhabited and holds a chapel built by the Spanish. For on the death of the young King Sebastian at the battle of Ksar el Kebir the entire Portuguese Empire passed in inheritance to his cousin, King Phillip II of Spain.

The Port

The jetty provides a pleasant view of the sea walls by day and at night the lights of the town flicker in reflection across the slick waves. It was largely rebuilt by German prisoners of war. The **lighthouse of Sidi Bouafi** is to the southeast of the town on a rise of land that affords views down to Cape Blanc. The 57 m high tower was built in 1916 and the guardian will sometimes show you around.

The Beach

To the east of the town stretches a sandy beach which gets rapidly more deserted and delightful the further you travel, while a wrecked ship, torn in two is a useful reminder of the power of the Atlantic surf. The roadside is also decorated with dredged and washed up anchors and buoys whilst opposite is a race course and the stables of the national stud. Take a left turn as the main road heads inland for Azzemour. This takes you beside the dunes, a deserted beach to your left and a wilderness of wildlife and birds on your right.

WHERE TO STAY
Easily accessible from both Marrakesh and Casablanca, rooms can be in short supply during the summer months from June to September. The map marks all the hotels listed below and it could be worth telephoning a booking in advance.

The **** **Le Palais Andalous** is an underused hotel made from a converted palace. A large central mosaic paved courtyard is surrounded by various cool dining or sitting rooms. The bedrooms are arranged off a central balcony above the courtyard and profusely tiled. The beds are high and large enough to require steps that have thoughtfully been fitted. There is a low-key restaurant and a bar. Dinner for 65dh, a double room for 206dh. The hotel is in the new town off the Av. Pasteur, turn right at the Green Cross pharmacy on to Blvd Docteur de Lanouy where the large doors of the hotel will be seen on the right.

The beachfront **Dounia Hôtel** is closed and for sale and so the *** **Doukkala Salam**, Av. de la Ligue Arabe, tel 3737 is now the only hotel that faces on to the sea. If you have come for a beach holiday and don't mind modern hotels you might think of staying here with its pool, bar, disco, tennis court and restaurant.

There are four small clean and functional one-star hotels: the **Royal**, 108, Av. Mohammed V, tel 2839, the **Suisse**, 145, Blvd Zertouni, tel 2816, **De Bruxelles**, 40 Rue Ibn Khaldoun, tel 2072, **De Provence**, 42 Av. Mohammed Er Rafi, tel 2347. The Bruxelles has double rooms with balconies for 47dh, the Provence is efficiently run by an Englishman who with the genius of his race has filled this corner of Morocco with the repressed and slightly camp gentility of Brighton; a double room with a shower for 62dh.

Slightly downmarket but with more character are the cluster of hotels off the Rue de Suez by the port gate. The **Hôtel du Port**, the **Hôtel de France** on the corner and down a side street, the **Rue Lecoul**, opposite the Tonic restaurant you find the **Hôtel du Maghreb** on the first floor up a great airy staircase. On the Place Mohammed V is the **Hôtel Christour**, a double for 45dh. The **Hôtel de la Plage** on the Av. de la Ligue Arabe is above the busiest town bar and close to the beach. It rents a double room for 43dh.

The **Camping International**, on Av. des Nations Unies is a very, perhaps too well, organized site with its own pool, bar and restaurant. It is well positioned on the edge of town, opposite the hotel school and just above the beach.

EATING OUT

The **Restaurant du Port** gives you the best view of the Portuguese citadel walls lapped by the sea and surrounded by bobbing fishing boats. Go through the harbour gates, pass pavilion one and at the far end of the long dock building is this licensed fish restaurant. A long lunch with wine and fresh fish will cost around 100dh a head.

The newly opened **Restaurant El Khaima** is by the camping site on the Av. des Nations Unies. A smartly decorated restaurant serving fish and Italian cooking under a domed roof in an oval dining room with a garden terrace and bar.

Restaurant le Tit, 2, Av. Jamia Al Arabia which runs parallel to the beach. Cheerful service and a good selection of wine; avoid the fish soup which is appalling.

Safari Pub on the Av. Mohammed er Riffi above the place, a busy little licensed restaurant serving grills and crêperie. Three-course menu for 62dh and open until midnight.

On the Place Mohammed V there is **La Marquise** and **Christour**; the Christour has menus for 30 and 42dh, the **Français** for 30 and 35dh.

Cafés

The café **Hammanat** in the middle of the shore-front promenade is an excellent people-watching centre. There are several busy cafés that line the Place Mohammed V and Place Al Hansali and the new Arabic **Café Bahia** has regrettable modern tiles and delicious cakes.

Out from El Jadida

To Marrakesh

The road south from El Jadida passes through the flat prairie farmlands of the Doukkala

Tit, Atlantic Coast

province before giving way to the semi-desert of the Bahira plain to the north of Marrakesh. The road passes beside two Doukkala market towns: **Sidi Smail** which is 52 km from El Jadida and has its **souk** on Monday, and **Sidi Bennour**, another 21 km south which has its **souk** on Tuesday. In November for a week Sidi Bennour becomes a city as thousands of farmers camp to celebrate the saint's Moussem.

Sidi Bouzid

5 km to the southwest of El Jadida, along the S121 coast road, is the unexceptionable beach resort of Sidi Bouzid. The rapid growth of the town may soon claim it as a suburb, but for the moment it is a hatch of bungalows with a summer campsite. Beside the road is its major attraction, two good fish restaurants: **Le Refuge** and **Requin Bleu**.

Moulay Abdullah

Moulay Abdullah is 11 km south of El Jadida on the S121 coast road. It is a small farming and fishing village built within the walls of the ancient city of **Tit**. The ramparts which face the sea have been heavily restored and every August the walls are briefly filled by a tent city which assembles to celebrate the Moussem of Moulay Abdullah.

Ismael Amghar, a companion of the prophet Mohammed, is believed to have travelled to Morocco where he established a Muslim college, the zaouia of Moulay Abdullah at Tit, a trading post of the Phoenicians. Beyond the walls there are dozens of rock-cut **Phoenician tombs** which are being slowly weathered away by the tide.

Both the Almoravide and Almohad Empires garrisoned and adorned this holy town which became a leading base of Islamic orthodoxy against the heretical Berber kingdoms of the coast—the Berghawata and Doukkala, though it was not the Berber tribes but the threat of Viking raids that caused the Almohad Sultan Abdel Moumen to build the city walls, and indeed it was the threat from the sea that caused Tit to be abandoned four

250

centuries later. A Wattasid Sultan, Mohammed el Bertougali moved the entire population to a village near Fez rather than have them paying tribute to the Portuguese. Nearby El Jadida remained in Portuguese hands until the late 18th century, and the mosques and houses of the town crumbled to leave only the minarets and a few doorways surviving. Though the **sanctuary of Moulay Abdullah** as the centre for the annual Moussem remained in continuous use by the surrounding tribes.

Tit remained deserted until the present scattered population of farmers and fishermen moved in to occupy in the 20th century less than a tenth of the area that was last inhabited in the 16th century.

The Almohad minaret

The whitewashed domes and the green-tiled roof of the zaouia of Moulay Abdullah are beside a minaret that was built by Abdel Moumen in the 12th century. This is all that remains of the Almohad sanctuary mosque. The recessed mouldings and window carvings have been compared to the greater and more elaborate towers built by his son and grandson, the El Hassan at Rabat and the Koutoubia at Marrakesh. The walls have recently been cleaned and the missing lantern top is being created out of ugly veneers of new stone. Work is progressing slowly so perhaps the mason is exercising a form of passive resistance.

The Almoravide minaret

Hidden by the rising ground from the road is the sole surviving Almoravide minaret in Morocco. The Almohad Empire destroyed most of the buildings of the preceding Empire which they had fought such a long and bitter struggle to overthrow. Here however the tower has endured though there is no longer any trace of the accompanying mosque. The tower is strongly built from thin courses of stone and the high arched windows have a characteristic simplicity. As you walk closer admire the inset panels, the carved stone relief arches and supporting pillars that delicately frame the alternating double and single windows. The richest form of decoration and arch is reserved for the single window. Some of the nearby farm buildings and barns for the livestock boast fine carved stone doors from the 16th century.

Jorf

6 km on in perfect contrast to ancient Tit is the brand new gleaming chemical complex of Jorf which has just been built beyond the lighthouse of Cape Blanc. Japanese and Spanish capital helped build this, the fabulous world of Moroccan Phosphates III & IV which will take the strain off the present plants at Safi and Casablanca. To add to the intricate confusion of chimneys, gantries and conveyors a petrol refinery, a port and a little fishing harbour have been added. There is a café beside the road which looks over the harbour. A human touch is added by shepherds who quite unconcerned continue to graze their flocks right up to the perimeter fence.

A few km beyond Jorf there are two campsites with their own restaurants, the **Albatross** with its own beach and the **Bar le Brise**, on the landward side of the road which is sealed from the sea by a briney lagoon.

The hotel restaurant **Le Relais** is a delightful sybaritic world of its own. In winter it has two wood fires burning and a well-stocked bar. From May to August the six bedrooms are opened for the use of guests wishing to stay here on full board. The dining room has an invigorating view of sea-smashed rocks and a small sandy beach where you can bask or snorkel whilst preparing yourself for another excellent seafood meal, langouste, homard, huitres, moules, coquillages. Le Relais is 26 km from El Jadida; breakfast, lunch, dinner and room for 150dh per person.

The coastal road to Oualidia for the next 60 km passes along a sandy plain. An almost continuous lagoon shelters behind the natural sea wall. The area is given over to intensive market gardening and salt is extracted in evaporation pans from the brackish lagoon.

Oualidia

80 km from El Jadida and 64 km from Safi on the S121 coast road, Oualidia is one of the least exploited beach resorts of Morocco. It is a quiet village of a place that falls in a scattering of houses and hotels down a hill towards a sandy inland lagoon, filled by the sea which roars in through two breaches in the coastal rock wall. In the summer wind surfers and fishing boats can be hired from the beach and a local **souk** is held beside the road every Saturday. It is appreciated by families from Marrakesh for its gentle charms; safe bathing, good service, a quiet welcome and delicious food have never appealed to the bulk of foreign visitors.

One of the last Saadian Sultans, El Oualid, built a kasbah here in 1634 in order to hold the lagoon port of Oualidia which had become his only secure access to the sea. It was a measure of his desperation that he valued Oualidia as a port and it has now decisively silted up. Only one of the **Kasbah**'s outer walls survives beside the road and it has been decorated with some heavily rusting cannon.

The present king's father, Mohammed V, built his summer villa below the Kasbah which directly faces one of the sea entrances into the lagoon. The walls of the palace villa were made the same colour as the golden sand of the lagoon with details picked out in green. Though still officially royal property no one seems to mind if you cautiously explore its two separate compounds and deteriorating walls.

GETTING AROUND
The CTM bus stop is on the coastal side of the road by the petrol station and opposite the local stalls. A road slips down the terrace a little further on taking you to the lagoon beach and naturally past the hotels and campsite. There are daily buses from both El Jadida and Safi for under 20dh.

WHERE TO STAY AND EAT
The * **Auberge de la Lagune**, tel 105 is beside the main road. There are half a dozen rooms with sea views, powerful hot showers and the busiest local bar. The dining room is large and cool with a terrace overlooking the lagoon where you can have breakfast. Various priced menus starting at 50dh, though the 75dh menu includes the local speciality of oysters.

Down the hill a little is the ** **Hotel Hippocampe**, tel 111, with its own pool and an equal if not greater reputation for food than la Lagune. A room for one is 96dh and there are bungalows available at 84dh for three, menus of 75, 85 and 150dh with supplements for lobster.

The new **Motel a L'Aignee Gourmande** has ten rooms and a 20 m walk for a morning swim. A room for 70dh and fish menu for 45dh.

Opposite is the seasonal camping **Sables D'Or** and at the end of the road is the more ambitious **Chems** complex just below the dunes; this has spaces for tents, caravans and bungalows for rent with its own bar and restaurant. A double room for 110dh, a six sleeping bungalow for 200dh, a seafood meal for 39dh.

Cape Beddouza

Beyond Oualidia on the road south to Safi the intensive pattern of cultivation recedes and the lagoon wall has disappeared. The road takes a more dramatic turn passing along high sea cliffs, through arid grazing and a number of sandy trails lead down to totally deserted sandy beaches. Cape Beddouza, 33 km from Oualidia and 23 km from Safi is one of the most beautiful of these. There is a last great wide expanse of golden beach before the lighthouse at Beddouza. A **maraboutic shrine** has been built on an exposed rocky outcrop in the midst of the sand where the waves break below at the foot of the sanctuary. The lighthouse is protected by charming green and white mock fortifications and a hamlet is spread out below where there is a café-auberge with a fine view of the sea. A turning just beyond the lighthouse, to the right, leads down to the beach.

Cape Beddouza is identified as Cape Soloeis where the Carthaginian admiral Hanno dedicated an altar to the God of the Sea in the 5th century BC on his voyage to discover the gold trade of Guinea. In his day the coast was covered in trees and there were numerous elephants bathing in a lagoon. The altar has disappeared but if you let your spirit wander it is easy to find a suitable spot. Directly below the lighthouse the sea cliffs and caves begin and a puckered sea-battered rock lets in an arm of fuming water. Natural rock arches and overhanging cliffs provide pleasant bowers for Poseidon and his Nereids to sport. An old burial ground is nearby beside a small low almost subterranean **mosque** whose solid stone carved pillars have been cut from the living rock. The **Mihrab** emerges from the mosque like a pillar of salt.

A broken row of street lights stretch a little way along the beach and though there is no established site this is an obviously attractive area in which to camp.

Lalla Fatima

From Cape Beddouza to Safi, 32 km, the coast is composed of a savage cliff face. There are only two accessible beaches, Sidi Bouzid, just above Safi, and Lalla Fatima halfway there. Turn right by the **café Lalla Fatima** to take a 2 km hair pin descent to the beach through a boulder-strewn landslip. In the summer a café is manned beside the small car park but if you plan to pitch a tent or park overnight here watch out for the tides. The beach has a strong atmosphere for it is entirely enclosed by high dramatic sea cliffs whose seams of quartz reflect the setting sun. A Moussem is held here in the last few days before Ramadan.

5 km before Safi the remains of a Portuguese bastion, **Fort Nador**, can just be recognized beside the cliffs.

Sidi Bouzid, by Safi

On the cliff edge a tomb to the marabout Sidi Bouzid has been raised. On either side of this sanctuary you will find the café restaurant **La Corniche** and the restaurant bar **Le Refuge**. Both enjoy fine views over Safi which looks deceptively close but is a 4 km walk away.

A road descends from the cliff restaurants to the rocks, a good area for snorkeling and the nearest clean sea bathing if you are staying at Safi. Sidi Bouzid also has the only campsite, the **camping municipal**, tel 2871 which is open throughout the year, 1 km further towards Safi. It is an attractive site shaded by trees with its own pool, bar and shop, 5dh per person, per tent and per car.

Safi

A successful industrious town, Safi has never appealed to the mass of tourists. The Medina is subsequently an easygoing and attractive place in which to walk and you often have the 16th-century Portuguese remains to yourself: the city walls, chapel, Chateau du Mer and the Kechla fortress. The sardine fish-packing industry and the phosphate plant are to the south of the town which makes that area an uninviting place to swim but by staying here you could give yourself time to visit the excellent beaches that are within 30 km to the north and south of the town.

An element of quixotic romance has been added to this working man's town when Thor Heyerdahl sailed *Ra I* and *Ra II* in 1969 and 1970 from Safi to prove that it was possible that ancient Egypt could have influenced the development of civilization in central America. Ptolemy does at least record that Safi might have been the ancient Punic entrepôt of Mysokaras.

HISTORY

Safi is mentioned by the 11th-century geographer El Bekri as Asfi, a port where the merchants of Marrakesh could sell the products of the trans-Saharan Guinea trade, chiefly gold, slaves and ostrich feathers. In the 14th century a fortified monastery, a ribat, was founded just to the south of the port by the Merenid Sultan Abou Hassan. This was partly to overawe the growing influence of the Mediterranean traders but mainly to discipline the Djebel Hadid to the south.

The European traders proved to be the greater threat and in the early 15th century all contact with the Christians was prohibited and the port was closed. By 1450 the Portuguese had returned and their consul was soon deeply imbedded in local intrigues but they were not the only ones to dabble in politics and, threatened by the Pasha of Safi's increasing reliance on the Spanish, they decided to strike quickly. In 1508 a Portuguese force was dispatched from Essaouira that seized Safi, which was embellished with walls, two fortresses and a cathedral. The fall of Agadir in 1541 caused a dramatic change in policy and the Portuguese abandoned Safi the same year, demolishing what they could.

The following centuries saw the European commercial powers jostling for the right to trade at Safi and the Pasha of the port was a key figure in the Moroccan government. Sidi Mohammed served as Pasha of Safi before succeeding his father as Sultan but during his reign he caused the decline of the port by concentrating all external trade at Essaouira.

Safi now relies on phosphates and fish for its prosperity, as a journey on the coast road south of the town will testify. The smell from the sardine packing factories is unmistakable whilst the pollution from the chemical works creates spectacular sunsets.

GETTING AROUND

By Train
The station is to the south of the town, tel 2408, where the railway travels up to the phosphate mines of Benguerir to connect with the main Casablanca to Marrakesh track.

By Bus
Travelling by bus is cheaper, quicker and easier. The CTM and Chekkouri coaches leave from Rue President Kennedy with frequent runs to Essaouira—17dh, Casablanca—28dh and Marrakesh—20dh. Local buses leave from the Place de Indépendance by the Post Office with hourly services along the coast both north and south. Catch the no 10 for Souria Kedima and the no 15 for Lalla Fatima and Cape Beddouza.

By Car
Arriving by car park between the Medina and the sea by the Blvd du Front de Mer. Cars can be hired from Safi Voyages who represent Europcar on the Place de Indépendance, tel 2935 or from Hertz on 14, Rue de Industrie, tel 3825. The Renault garage is Courdec on Av. Mohammed V and for Fiats go to Du Maghreb on the road to Sidi Ouassel, tel 3391.

TOURIST INFORMATION
The three banks, the BMCE, BMCI, the Banque Populaire and the Post Office are all found on the central Place de Indépendance. The French have a consulate on Rue Chaouki, tel 2797 and there is a Catholic church, of St Vincent de Paul at 16, Rue Chefchaouen with mass on Saturday evening at 19.00 and Sunday at 11.00.

WHAT TO SEE
The New Town

The Place de Indépendance is the central animated square of the town. To the south of the Place is the Rue du Caid Sidi Abder Rahman which is lined with shops and cafés and is the direct route for Souria Kedima. The coastal road, to the right, passes an elegant cliff promenade with a busy central café. If you continued you might notice a small mosque on the right which is all that is left of the **Ribat** founded in the 14th century by the Merenids. Beyond is a **koubba** raised over the grave of **Sid Abou Mohammed Salih**, the patron saint of Safi whose tomb has an associated zaouia lodge.

Chateau de la Mer

The Chateau de la Mer also known as the Dar el Bahar is the stone fortress built by the Portuguese in the 16th century on the shore to guard the old harbour. It was the

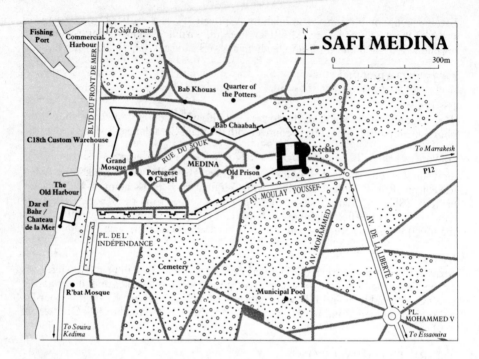

Fishing Port
Commercial Harbour
To Sidi Bouzid
BLVD DU FRONT DE MER
SAFI MEDINA
N
0   300m

Bab Khouas
Quarter of the Potters

Bab Chaabah

C18th Custom Warehouse

RUE DU SOUK
MEDINA
Grand Mosque
Portugese Chapel
Old Prison
Kechla
To Marrakesh
P12

The Old Harbour
Dar el Bahr / Chateau de la Mer

AV. MOULAY YOUSSEF

AV. MOHAMMED V
AV. DE LA LIBERTÉ

PL. DE L' INDÉPENDANCE

Cemetery

R'bat Mosque
Municipal Pool
PL. MOHAMMED V

To Souira Kedima
To Essaouira

governors' residence during their forty years of rule and was used by visiting Sultans until the late 18th century. It was restored in 1963 and is open Mon–Friday, 8.00–12.00, 14.00–16.00, entrance 2dh. A saint's tomb is hidden down a dark passage off the large square paved interior. The old prison can be seen at the foot of the tower where a spiral staircase leads up to the summit to provide a fine view over the Medina. A ramp leads from the central court to a firing platform that commands the sea approaches and is lined with a medley of European cannon. The southwest bastion provides a fine commanding vista of the sea and the surrounding cliffs of the coastline.

Medina

The Medina is the oldest part of Safi, it is roughly triangular in shape tapering inland to a summit crowned by the Kechla, the citadel, fortress. The walls are complete on the landward sides and surrounded by open gardens and weed-strewn cemeteries. Beyond the north wall a stream runs to the sea upon which the potters have for long settled.

To the right at the entrance of the Medina at the central Rue du Socco you can see the 18th-century custom sheds built for the use of the European merchants outside the city walls. The Medina **souk** handles goods for the local market and the stalls of cooked food, fruit and vegetables are likely to be of most interest. There are a number of cafés and the Medina is empty of aggressive hasslers or touting bazaar keepers.

Portuguese Chapel

An alley to the right, Rue Cadi Ayad, enticingly labelled 'Passage touristique et Toilette' leads past the great outer walls of the Grande Mosque. A 100 m on your left is the entrance to the Portuguese Chapel, open 9.00–12.00, 15.00–18.00, which is the choir, all that remains of the cathedral of Safi, that was built in 1519. Cool and dark the roof looms above you decorated with a number of symbolic bosses. The central stone boss of the arms of Portugal is surrounded by a ring of eight. The world as divided between Spain and Portugal by the Borgia pope is easily recognizable, as are the keys of St Peter, an episcopal mitre with two croziers and the arms of the crusading order of St Iago. Continue on through the shadowy stone street hung with buttresses and arches to emerge into the full daylight by penetrating through the outer wall. By walking up the Av. Moulay Youssef you can admire the battlements to your left and the public gardens that succeed a cemetery to your right, the entrance to the Kechla is off the central roundabout.

The Kechla

The two unequal monumental crenellated round towers were built by the Portuguese in the 16th century. The **offices of the Makhzen** were moved up from the Chateau du Mer in the 18th century and a courtyard, garden, towers and new apartments constructed within. At the entrance are two cannon cast in the Hague for the Sultan, in the centre of the internal courtyard is a **Koubba** shaded by an overhanging tree. A broad stone pavement leads up to the large round tower lined with British cannon. To the right a confusion of apartments is arranged around a Moorish courtyard and a sunken garden of cedars and conifers can be reached below. The high white towers, roofed in green tiles, are open and offer excellent surrounding views of the fishing fleet, chateau, potteries and the Medina. The old courtyard jail and mosque can be seen immediately below; the inmates have been moved to the gaol built at El Jadida.

Quarter of the Potters

Leaving the Kechla you can cut across the surrounding open garden space to visit the quarter of the potters. Established above a stream that washes down supplies of clay each year from the hills, the potters of Safi are a well-established guild. A training school and market has been established where the full range of pottery is exhibited and can be freely admired and gently bargained over. The traditional salt glaze blue of Safi on white decorated with entrelacs or geometric patterns is perhaps the most attractive. The more innovative designs are washed with a green glaze or dark burnt yellow and the burnt brown with green and white is also popular. The dusty black with pastel shades and foliate and escriptive decoration looks pretty repellent but appeals to the local market.

The beehive kilns, the underground potter's wheels and masses of chipped and broken ware can be seen on the hill above. The puffing kilns covered with palm leaves provide a vision of centuries of unchanging craft. Beside the Bab Chaabah a new café has been established in the garden. You can pass through this gate to reenter the Medina or continue outside the walls through the Bab Khouas in order to visit the fishing harbour. Home for over 200 boats, Safi is one of the busiest sardine ports in the world, landing over 40,000 tonnes of fish a year. The commercial port further north is being extended and ships out mostly phosphates to the world.

SHOPPING AND SPORTS

The pottery of Safi can also be bought in the Medina. Safi is not a tourist destination and the prices asked for the bold geometrical coloured carpets for sale in or two of the shops in the new town can be encouraging. The **souk** is held on Monday.

Ask at the stud farm on the way out to Essaouira if you are interested in a **ride**. **Tennis** is available on Rue Marceau. **Swimming** at Sidi Bouzid, Lalla Fatima or Cape Beddouza to the north.

WHERE TO STAY AND EAT

The *** **Atlantide**, Rue Chaouki, tel 2160 has 50 rooms, a restaurant, an extensive garden and a bar. The ** **Mimosas** on Rue Ibn Zaidoun, tel 3208 has 43 rooms, a restaurant and bar.

There are a number of cheap hotels in the Medina which are all found off the central Rue de Socco or facing out to sea at the iron railings of the port. The smartest and cleanest of these is the **Hôtel de Paris** which charges 16dh per person; the central cool courtyard has a fading poster of a panther and some worn chairs. The **Hotel Kouar** is the most secretive, off a side passage of the Rue de Socco and opposite the hammam, rooms for 20dh.

The cheaper fish grills and cafés are all clustered around the entrance to Rue du Socco or along the Place Indépendance opposite the Chateau du Mer.

Restaurant Calypso in a courtyard garden off the Place provides a fine three-course lunch of fish, salad and fruit for 40dh.

For a more elaborate meal try one of the two restaurants at Sidi Bouzid, a fine place for dinner where you can watch the most colourful sunset in Morocco. The **Atlantide** and **Mimosa** hotels have licensed restaurants, the latter serves a meal for only 35dh. In an unlikely but surprisingly pleasant position between the canning factories and phosphate works is the **Le Reserve** restaurant.

To Marrakesh

Travelling southeast from Safi to Marrakesh you pass through **Souk et Tleta de Sidi Bougreda** which with its Tuesday market is the last town of interest before entering a barren plain which is broken only by the Jbilet hills north of Marrakesh.

Souira Kedima

The coast road 6537 having passed the last effusions of the phosphate plant leads in 33 km to the dune-girt beach of Souria Kedima. Halfway along a turning towards the sea takes you to the maraboutic **shrine of Jorf el Yhoudi**, the Jews' fort.

Souira Kedima, sometimes spelt Quadima, was mentioned by the geographer El Bekri 'as the old enclosure' which refers to the **Ribat of Agouz**, an Almoravide bastion of which there are no longer any visible remains, although there is a substantial square Portuguese fort which was built in 1521 but abandoned only four years later. It is a sturdy rectangle of 40 m by 25 m with a round tower in the southeast corner. The fishermen use the courtyard as a safe sanctuary for their boats and their shambling shacks are being replaced with a brand new arcaded market with a small attached mosque. There are a few holiday bungalows, a summer camp site and restaurant that serves fresh grilled fish and tagines under a bamboo terrace.

Kasbah Hamidouch

6 km before the beach a rough and awkward track leads off in the direction of the Tensift estuary where a ford allows you to cross the Tensift over to the village of **Dar Caid Hadji**.

From here the track is relatively easy to the 17th-century Kasbah of Hamidouch built by Sultan Moulay Ishmael above the banks of the river which used to flow into the surrounding moat. Girt by towers it contains within the walls the ruins of a mosque, a separate prayer hall and numerous buildings inhabited by the Abid garrison. You can attempt to rejoin the main P8 road which does involve fording the Tensift again; most drivers humbly backtrack.

Safi to Essaouira

Sebt des Gzoula, 27 km southeast of Safi, just off the main P9 road has a **market** on Saturday and in September celebrates the Moussem of Sidi Abderahman Moul Goumri. The roadside village of **Tnine Rhiate**, 9 km further south, livens up once a week for the Monday **souk**.

Talmest is the administrative centre for the region and is at the heart of a fertile pocket of agriculture, 11 km south of the Oued Tensift bridge. At a crossroads, 10 km south of Talmest and 54 km north of Essaouira, there is a turning to the west, the 6611, which takes you on a circuit through the hill country of Djebel Hadid.

Djebel Hadid and The Seven Saints of the Regrada

The Regrada are Chleuh Berbers who spoke the Tachelhait dialect. They have always lived on the Djebel Hadid, the iron hills, a network of broken land between Safi and Essaouira that is covered in a dense maquis and still populated with jackals, wild boar and mountain fox.

The Regraga before the arrival of Islam were monotheistic, perhaps due to the influence of Jewish and Christian missionaries, and they were certainly aware of the Gospels and the Old Testament. They took the reference in John XVI, when it refers to Christ as the herald of an even greater prophet very much to heart. This passage, 'for if I go not away, the comforter will not come unto you; but if I go, I will send him unto you', led to much speculation. The leading men of the Regraga in the 7th century received some mysterious indication that this great comforter had indeed come and was to be found at Mecca which was then, as now, the spiritual centre of Arabia. The prophet Mohammed, who was at that time just one of the many poet theologians of Mecca, identified himself as 'the comforter'. He privately instructed the seven men of the Regraga who took back to Morocco an early version of the Muslim faith. This early version of Islam they diligently preached in their homeland and one by one they were all buried in the hills around the Djebel Hadid.

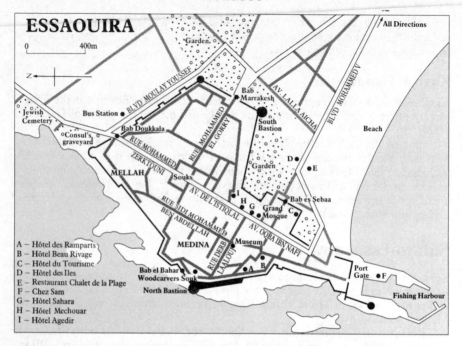

ESSAOUIRA

0   400m

A – Hôtel des Ramparts
B – Hôtel Beau Rivage
C – Hôtel du Tourisme
D – Hôtel des Iles
E – Restaurant Chalet de la Plage
F – Chez Sam
G – Hôtel Sahara
H – Hôtel Mechouar
I – Hôtel Agedir

As some of the earliest Companions of the Prophet their shrines are venerated each year in a 44-day Moussem held in the spring. The pilgrimage starts at the coastal **shrine of Moulay Bouzertoun**, which the women are free to attend and are allowed to discard their usual social restraint, for their honour is under the strong protection of the saint. The biggest event is 12 days later at **Amerkoud** where Sidi Boubekr and his son Sidi Salih are buried. Sidi Abdullah ben Adnas lies alone in his Koubba close to the Oued Tensift whilst Sidi Quasmin, who received the call to Mecca, has the least accessible tomb in the hills to the northeast. Sidi Ali el Khourati and Sidi Aissa bu Khabia are found at the **zaouia Khourati**.

The 6611 takes you on a circuit of the Regrada country that will pass Akermoud and some rough track turnings for Tleta Khourati and Moulay Bouzertoun. **Zaouai Moulay Bouzertoun**, a whitewashed complex of mosque, tomb and sanctuary buildings perched above the beach and surrounded by a few low village buildings, has a particular serene and hospitable air.

Essaouira

This is the most enchanting town on the coast of Morocco. The 18th-century battlements encircle the old town and port which overlook a scattering of barren wave-worn islands. A great sandy bay sweeps out to the south whilst wooded hills dominate the skyline to the east. The quarters of the town, the Medina, the Kasbah and the Mellah fully express the exoticism of Morocco without becoming alarming. The dark alleys are broken with frequent arches and the women of the town are mysteriously concealed under their enveloping haiks. At dusk the call to prayer echoes across the silhouetted skyline unchallenged by the distracting sound of traffic.

Essaouira has a remarkably equable climate, the average temperature is 18° in January and 22° in August. The coastal wind is another constant, and the town will never appeal to the mass tanning market. Bedrooms throughout the year are easy to find and the mixed population of fishermen, farmers, craftsmen, tourists and the multilingual urban youth coexist effortlessly. The town's potential for hassle, after you have found a hotel room, is small, though hashish might be offered in a conspiratorial whisper if you look like a potential consumer. There is one very small racket which involves a tale of woe after which you give a few coins in order to send a letter to America. The only disadvantage is that this con-man only approaches you once whilst he has a large stock of entertaining stories.

HISTORY
Es-saouira, 'the little Ramparts', has been known over the millennia as Amougdoul, Migdol, Mogdoul, Mogdoura and Mogador. The offshore isles are still collectively known as Mogador, a name that probably derives from the Phoenician 'Migdol', a look-out tower.

Phoenician sailors used these islands from at least the 7th century BC, and archaeological evidence has also confirmed that a sizeable settlement specialized in extracting the famous Tyrian purple, red to us, from shellfish during King Juba II's reign. King Juba's son, Ptolemy, was wearing purple when the circus crowds at Lyon cheered this young prince more heartily than their own monarch, the Emperor Caligula. Caligula was infuriated that any prince should be more popular than himself and had Ptolemy, the grandson of Anthony and Cleopatra, murdered, driving Morocco into full rebellion against Rome. A fable records that the dye workers on the island of Mogador destroyed the factory that had indirectly contributed to the death of their last king.

In the 11th century the bay opposite the islands formed the chief port of southern Morocco. King Manuel of Portugal in his quest to dominate the whole trade and coast of Morocco seized Essaouira early in his campaign and built a fort here in 1506. This fell to the Saadians even before Agadir, the main Portuguese base, was recovered in 1541, but the Saadian dynasty who originated from the far south preferred to use the port of Agadir.

The present shape and character of the town is entirely the achievement of Sultan Sidi Mohammed. Agadir had never been loyal to the Alouite dynasty and Essaouria was deliberately created to replace it. In 1760 the Sultan used his captive French architect, Theodore Cornut, to design the walls and street plan of the Medina which has an unaccustomed regularity. The Jews of Agadir were moved north to handle trade with the Christians which was dramatically boosted by Sidi Mohammed's reduction of import duties and free trade policies. By the 19th century the port of Essaouira handled nearly half of Morocco's trade. The commercial connection with Britain was strong and through this port tea was first imported to Morocco, a habit which with the addition of mint and French-imported sugar took the nation by storm. The distinctive Moroccan teapot was first manufactured in Manchester from Andalucian patterns.

The port was also the home of a flourishing and only partly clandestine trade in arms. The Berber caids of the High Atlas, the Arab tribes of the plains and sheikhs from the Sahara all had their commercial agents at Essaouira who purchased arms and munitions and also presided over ransom negotiations.

GETTING AROUND
By Bus: The CTM bus drops passengers at the formal front of the town between the port and the Place Moulay Hassan. Other coaches arrive at the square at the back of the town, by the Bab Doukkala where you find all the ticket kiosks and departing coaches.

The main approach to the town, the coastal Av. Mohammed V, leads directly to the car park between the port and the Place Moulay Hassan. The Place is the social hub of the town lined with cafés, restaurants, a few cheap hotels and the Banque Populaire. At the far end of the Place a right turn takes you down to the central long avenue of the town which leads past the souks to exit from the walls at the Bab Doukkala, the bus, taxi and lorry square. The Post Office is on the Av. Lalla Aicha, the avenue which encircles the town walls.

The Tourist Office, on Place Moulay el Hassan, tel 234, has a beautiful wooden model of the northern ramparts. Friendly girls hand out the usual leaflets and not another scrap of information.

WHAT TO SEE
The Port
The harbour is guarded by two handsome bastions, European in style, but erected by the Sultan Sidi Mohammed in 1769, year 1184 of the Hegira, as an inscription informs you. The seaward bastion, Skala du Port, still holds a line of cannon on a battlemented terrace for the protection of the port which can be visited with the escort of the guardian. Outside this righthand of the two harbour gates a double alley of seafood grills collects everyday to compete relentlessly for business. Gulls cry overhead and a gentle sea breeze wafts away the tempting odours of roasting fish and crabs.

The sardine fishing fleet, the third largest in Morocco, provides a great spectacle of activity in the early morning or after dusk. The quays are otherwise busy with the frames of new fishing boats revealing practically every stage in the elegant production of these sturdy wooden craft.

The Town
Place Moulay Hassan is lined with elegant tall white houses picked out in blue that help give the square a tranquil and intimate atmosphere. The cafés seem to break down the strongest reserve and the travellers who have arrived for a few days but stayed for a few months are quick to offer an exchange of books. The impressive doorway on the right of the square, no 17, once gave entrance to the Tribunal but now to an indoor basketball court.

Skala de la ville
There are three alleys to the left of Place Moulay Hassan. Any of these will lead you through the shade of the high tenements and under connecting arches to the town

battlements, the Skala de la ville, and the round tower of the north bastion. A 200 m terrace is lined with bronze cannon originally cast for Phillip II and Phillip III of Spain. The crenellated walls look out over a rocky shore to the Atlantic and the outlying islets.

Souk of the wood carvers
In the casements and courtyards below the bastion and tower some of the skilled joiners and carvers of Essaouira have their workshops. The root boles of the thuja trees can be seen piled at the doorways and young apprentices at work on the less skilled tasks. The rich resinous smell of the wood is a great attraction and the artisans are usually happy to demonstrate their craft. Wood from the callistrus arteculata has a rich chestnut colour, the root bole, 'racine de thuja', provides a rich confusion of knots whilst the trunk, 'tige de thuja', has a plainer striped grain. Acacia or ebony both have dark woods that are contrasted very successfully with the light pale wood of citronnier. Shells, mother of pearl, strips of silver and copper are also inserted to create astonishingly inlaid tables, chests and cabinets. Essaouira also has the best selection of trays, chess boards, dice cups, thuja boxes and backgammon sets. Similar work seen in other cities is likely to have come from Essaouira and to be more expensive.

You should bargain in the bazaars but the cooperatives in town and the casemate workshops have less time for negotiations and generally offer a reasonable first price. Any hinges and locks should be examined carefully, skill with wood is seldom matched with much love for metalwork.

The Museum
The Museum Sidi Mohammed Ben Abdellah is on the right of the Rue Derb Laalouj which leads from the bastion back to the centre of town. The 19th-century town house of a pasha was transformed into the Town Hall during the French Protectorate with the unfortunate addition of a monolithic central staircase. It is now an unexceptionable folklore museum with a few weapons, kaftans, carpets and jewelry. The notes on Andalucian music and the instruments on display are of greater interest and the designs for decorating the hands, feet and face of women for great festivals have a fascination. Open everyday, except Tuesday, 9.00–12.00, 14.30–18.00.

Medina streets
Past the Museum at the central crossroads, the Rue Sidi Mohammed ben Abdallah can lead you up through the Medina and straight ahead into the dark secretive passages of the Mellah and then out through the Bab Doukkala.

Alternatively continue across down Rue el Attarin to the central axis of the town. A right turning up the Av. Okba ibn Nafi can take you back to the Place Moulay Hassan whilst to your left the Av. de L'Istiqlal leads down a long arcaded boulevard of shops with the market courtyards and fondouqs opening off on either side. The women of the town are well covered in haiks, great drapes of brown or white cotton or wool with which they obscure their figures whilst on the streets, leaving only a pair of dazzling brown eyes glinting through a fold.

The Consuls' graveyard and the Jewish cemetery
Out through the Bab Doukkala on the left, at the seaward corner of the bus square a

gateway gives entrance to the enclosed Christian cemetery. A bustle of assorted European consuls, doctors and priests lie buried here. A much larger Jewish cemetery borders to the south and you can sometimes enter through a small door in the far corner. Schist blocks with their symbolic carvings lie apparently haphazard over the tightly-packed compound incised with attractively carved deep Hebraic script. The Jews of Essaouira were always the chosen intermediaries between the Moors of the interior and the European merchants. The Jewish community subsequently developed enduring relationships with various trading firms and a cosmopolitan scattering of kin. Benjamin Disraeli is one of the most celebrated of these, for his father Isaac, author of curiosities of literature, lived for a few years as a child in the Mellah of Mogador.

Hoare-Belisha who served as both Home Secretary and War Minister to Britain in the 1930s was the third generation descendant of a Mogador–Manchester trader who settled in England. Seeking to impress, a visitor to the town informed the Belishas who still lived in the Mellah of their cousin's great status. To which they glibly replied, glancing briefly up from their holy books, that yes they had heard that young Leslie was for the moment high in the counsels of a Northern city.

Berber souk

The Berber market keeps to the coastal fringe of Essaouira but otherwise has to move slowly north as the town grows. An uninspiring walk past new houses and the large leather factory brings you to the compound where vegetables, charcoal, old and new clothes are sold to a bustling crowd on Thursday and Sunday.

The Beach

The beach to the south of the town, protected from the full force of the Atlantic surf and current, is one of the safer bays in which to swim. The area nearest the town is often occupied by football games and piles of seaweed. As you walk towards the ruined fort the sand gets cleaner and the beach emptier.

Diabat

Along the beach the bulk of a ruined 18th-century fort can be seen, for once not a Portuguese relic but part of Sidi Mohammed's defence system. Built on a rocky promontory the compact walls have split but not disintegrated, and are washed daily by the incoming tide.

Inland is the estuary of the Oued Ksob beside which you can walk to reach the straggling village of Diabat and clamber across the fallen bridge. A right turning off the road south, signposted Tangaro, will also bring you here.

The villagers from Diabat still seem to maintain a noticeably cold air to visitors, for Diabat is still notorious for the multiple beach murder in the late sixties. This brought a climactic end to the hippy settlement that had grown up along the beach in the wake of Jimi Hendrix, the guitarist whose drug consumption, sexual energy and suicide set standards which few have been able to follow. He had attempted to buy Diabat in order to secure the future of the encampment. Yusuf Islam, the Islamized Cat Stevens, spends his summer in Essaouira but his orthodox Muslim lifestyle attracts much less of a cult following.

Beside the road is the ruined compound of an old tanning factory with the engineering equipment from Huxham & Brown, Exeter, quietly rusting away. Towards the shore from the factory and now besieged by dunes and overgrown with shrubbery is the palace built in the 18th century by Sultan Sidi Mohammed, the **Dar ac-Coultone Mahdounia**. A pavilion can be seen in the centre surrounded by the walls of a square keep decorated with low towers on each corner. The eastern tower can be entered through a low bending tunnel which leads to a chamber, which still retains some of its mosaic flooring and a thin strip of plaster carved with Koranic verses remains on the wall. A small balcony of three arches that used to overlook the port now gives out on a prospect of encroaching dunes and a wall of vegetation.

The **Auberge Tangaro** is beside the road to the south, a delightful sanctuary where you can buy fresh squeezed orange juice and sit on the sunbaked terrace listening to the rattle of the wind pump. 7 km further south a dirt track takes you to **Cape Sim** with its windswept dunes, empty sands and fine view of Essaouira.

North from Essaouira

A 20 km walk from the Berber market along a wide strip of empty beach will take you to the maraboutic **shrine of Moulay Bouzertoun**. A double moussem is held every year in August as part of the pilgrimage of the Seven Saints of the Regrada (see above, under Djebel Hadid).

This would be a four-hour walk or a pleasant day trip on hired mules with a picnic. A piste track, left turn off the P10 5 km out of town on the Marrakesh road takes you over increasingly rough going to the sanctuary. The first left turning off the piste leads to the farm house of Inspecteur Wattier who spent much of his life maintaining the surrounding forest and conserving the dunes until his accidental death in 1922. The view from here and the **belvedere du Chict**, the second left turn, is uplifting, miles of empty coast and low woodland stretch between the headlands of Essaouira and Cape Hadid.

The Isles of Mogador

The half-dozen islands are periodically closed to visitors but in the last few years have been accessible to those prepared to charter a fishing boat from the harbour. The largest of the four small islands nearest to the harbour has an 18th-century tower and fort.

Dzint Faranan, the smaller of the outer pair, has some spectacular caves on its northern shore and contains an inland lake. The largest, the **isle de Essaouira** holds all the evidence of human settlement, a villa with baths dating from King Juba's period and various buildings of the dye works. From the shore the prison and mosque built by the Sultan Moulay el Hassan are conspicuous. Raisuni was imprisoned on the island for four years, originally shackled by his neck to a sunbaked wall; he failed twice to escape, killed several guards but with the governor's assistance was granted a pardon on the death of the Sultan Moulay Hassan. The boats only sail to the prison island on Saturdays for those with a nice ear for historical recreation. The islands are one of the few breeding grounds of that most elegant and rare bird of prey, Elenors Falcon, esteemed almost beyond price by the ruling princes of Arabia but with singularly unattractive feeding habits.

WHERE TO STAY

**** Hôtel des Isles, Av. Mohammed V, tel 2329, a well-run hotel with 42 bungalows arranged around a central pool courtyard. It does however obscure the view of the walls and the elegant round tower of the south bastion. Tennis court and pool, opposite the beach and garden, a double for 246dh, menu 75dh.

*** Hôtel Tafouket, Av. Mohammed V, tel 2505, facing the beach with a slightly unpromising exterior, this hotel of 40 rooms is run with a rare blend of efficiency and hospitality. It has its own bar and restaurant but is a fair distance out of town.

Character and convenience

There are four one-star hotels: **Sahara, Du Mechouar, Tafraout** and **Des Remparts**. The Sahara is horribly tidy and organized, almost Swiss, whilst Des Remparts is perhaps the least efficient but still a most enjoyable friendly place in which to stay, run by El Houcienne and his son Mustapha. 30 rooms are arranged around a three-storey interior courtyard. The roof provides a spectacular view perched above the ramparts, and a possible sunbathing spot if you can find a corner out of the wind. It is on the left at 18, Rue Ibn Rochd, a street whose entrance is in the far lefthand corner of the Place Moulay Hassan, where you will also smell a bakery in the morning on the opposite side of the street; tel 2282, bed with bathroom for 45dh.

The cheapest

Hôtel du Beau Rivage, above the **Café de France** in the Place Moulay Hassan. Clean, scrupulously honest with some rooms having a sea view, 18dh a night. The **Hôtel du Tourisme**, Rue Mohammed ben Messaoud, tel 2075, is perched on the Medina walls. Clean simple rooms, cold water and cats, 17dh per person. **Hôtel Agadir**, 33 Rue d'Agadir which is off the Av. de Istiqlal down an alley past the Grande Mosque on the way to the hammam. For 15dh a night you can live in the bosom of a Moroccan family, the secretive entrance is at least half the attraction. The **Municipal campsite** despite its position above the beach, on Av. Mohammed V, is not an attractive option.

The **Tangaro** at Ain Diabat has some gravel where you can park a van and a few rooms with cane furniture and blankets that vary from 45 to 100dh. Run by Giulio Siry with charm and order, the seaview, the sunbaked courtyard, bougainvillea, wind pump and collection of music create a memorable style. Meals for 28 or 40dh.

EATING OUT
The Port

Chez Sam, at the far end of the port, a delightful clapper-built restaurant that first appears to be a stranded boat house. It overlooks the harbour and the fishing fleet. Excellent reputation for fish, they have a menu of 50 or 110dh and serve single drinks. Outside the Port gates the grill cafés serve a plate of sardines with a salad for under 10dh. For crabs and lobster you obviously pay more.

The Beach front

The **Hôtel Tafoukt** serves dinner with menus of 58 or 70dh. Next door the restaurant **Petite Algue** has a patisserie on the ground floor and a formal licensed dining room upstairs with menus for 20 or 30dh which include a plate of local mussels.

Chalet de la Plage, on the seafront opposite the **Hôtel des Isles**, a seafood menu for 60dh and a separate and occasionally musical bar area. Less crowded in the evening after the day trips have gone.

Hôtel des Isles restaurant serves dinner for 75dh each evening in a room overlooking the beach; there is a heavily embroidered tent-bar and a night club.

The Town

There are five unlicensed restaurants that serve cheap Moroccan food around Place Moulay Hassan. The **Essalam** provides the smallest but the cheapest meals at 30dh for three courses. The café restaurant **Bab Lachour** also on the Place provides a meal for 50dh outside or upstairs in a first-floor dining room.

Taking a right turn at the bottom of the Place you pass **Café El Ayounne**, **Toufiks restaurant** and **Café L'Horloge**. Toufiks serves a delicious vegetable tagine and freshly squeezed orange juice for 35dh.

The Riad, 18 Rue Zayone, in the heart of the Medina, but well signposted, serves local dishes in a tranquil traditional atmosphere with imaginative menus. Harara for 8dh, courgette and arguin oil salad 10dh, tagine with potato soufflé 38dh. The Manager, Azriguine el Mostapha, is a charming informative man.

There are a number of good simple cafés in the larger streets of the Medina that serve freshly fried fish, meatballs and kebabs with a selection of well-spiced and seasoned salads; fish tagines can be found for about 14dh.

Cafés and patisserie

Petit Algue on the beach front is good but outshone by **Chez Driss**, an exceptional place founded in 1925 and run by father and son; you can breakfast at one of the tables and try to exercise self-control. Chez Driss is at 10, Rue Al Hajalli.

East to Marrakesh

There is little over which to delay the journey, though the initial scenery climbing up from the coast through forested hills is pleasant enough. The **Koubba of Sidi Amoughal**, the town saint, is just before the main road south to Agadir.

35 km east of Essaouira is the village of **Tleta Henchen**, 1 km off the road, which has a **souk** on Tuesday. 40 km on is the shrine and village of **Sidi Moktar** which has a **souk** each Wednesday.

The **Chichaoua crossroad** just over half the way to Marrakesh, 100 out of the 180 km, is the obvious place to stop for a coffee or a tagine. It has a **souk** on Sunday and a carpet cooperative with shop attached.

Haha, South of Essaouira

The Province of Haha is the most westerly extension of the Atlas mountain range as it reaches the coast between Essaouira and Agadir. It is the most beautiful portion of the Atlantic coast of Morocco. Rough hills scarred with gorges fall down to the coast. A line of forbidding high cliffs, that occasionally part to reveal isolated beaches, seals the land from the sea. The mountain sides are covered in arguin woods, trees that grow nowhere else in the world but cling tenaciously enough to these slopes. Goats climb the trees in order to pluck the fruit, an initially astonishing and improbable sight. This is often enthusiastically pointed out by children wishing to earn tips from photographers whilst their fathers sell bottles of arguin oil. Gentler surprises are revealed with the emergence of a cultivated valley from the wilderness of secretive hamlets and hilltop agadirs emerge on the barren hills.

The main road to Agadir, the P8, follows a delightful twisting changing course that has to be repaired each year after the rains rush off the peaks of the High Atlas and wash away part of the road. A large number of piste tracks of variable condition extend deep into the hill country. An excellent opportunity to explore the rural Berber hinterland for those with a strong car but a limited possibility if you are travelling by bus.

HISTORY

Haha is one of the strongholds of the Berber language, the Tachelait dialect is still widely spoken and off the main road little French or Arabic is even understood. The indigenous tribes long held a reputation for skilful farming and commerce. Leo Africanus who travelled through the region in the 15th century commented on the large number of provincial towns of over 6000 people that were scattered over the land. He was the last to be able to comment on this prosperity, for the autonomy of the province was soon to be broken by the Merenid Sultans in Fez. They despatched a portion of the fierce bedouin Arab tribe of the Ma'quil to settle on the plains to the north and destroy the prosperity of Haha in a series of murderous raids.

A succession of despotic local governors were imposed to rule the devastated land in the succeeding centuries, supported by militias of nomadic cavalry from the plains. A revenge of sorts was however extracted on the Merenid–Wattasid dynasty.

Sheikh Mohammed al Jazuli, from a Berber tribe of the Souss was a great mystic who studied and taught at Fez. His great work, the *Dalail al-Khairat* is still considered a classic Sufi text. He was poisoned and his disciple al-Sayyaf, who came from one of the 12 Haha tribes, accused the Merenids of poisoning his master. Al-Sayyaf left Fez to wage a mobile guerrilla war of vengeance against the dynasty from various bases in the south. For twenty years he carried the remains of his master on an unridden camel until his own death in 1485. Both bodies were buried with great honour in Haha and the tribes, particularly the Shayazima of Afughal, completely identified themselves with the Jazuli vendetta. The movement was strong enough to attract the Saadians who became the leaders of the Jazulis in the 16th century and did indeed eventually destroy the Merenid–Wattasid dynasty.

This episode however did nothing to relieve the despotism of the governors. A British botanical expedition in the 19th century heard tales of the previous governor. He had some hereditary claim to the suzerainity of the region and with great gifts to the Sultan's Treasury kept his power. He tyrannized the province for many years and used the 'leather glove' to enforce his exactions. The victim had quicklime tightly bound into the palm of his hand which was then soaked in water. When a few weeks later, the bindings were removed, only a tattered stump would be revealed.

Eventually a popular rising was planned by all the tribes but the resourceful governor escaped with 22 mules laden with treasure to his friend the Caid of Chichaoua. Arriving in Marrakesh he promptly presented half his wealth to the Sultan and was allowed to retain the rest which enabled him to live in great splendour. His Kasbah in Haha was of course pillaged after his flight and two of his nephews found long dead, entombed in the walls. He had thoughtfully laced his store of honey with arsenic and the rebels' victory feast in his hall finished in mass agony.

The rebellion spread and the tribes descended on Essaouira. In 1847 the Sultan as well as despatching a Harka, an army to burn the land, solemnly cursed the tribes, known as Sokhta. The Haha sued for peace in the customary manner by sacrificing bullocks before the gates of the Sultan's palace, their front legs cut away so that the animals poured out their life blood as if in supplication.

Sidi Kaouki

15 km south of Essaouira on the P8 turn right on the tarmac 6604 and continue 11 km for the **maraboutic shrine of Sidi Kaouki**. Set on the shoreline of a bay, the beach strewn with sea-washed roots and driftwood. The sanctuary is totally encased in a number of bare apartments all with their own eccentric pattern of sea terraces and fragile stairways. Burnt driftwood has soot-stained the interiors in contrast to the external whitewashed walls. A new mosque just been built with a surrounding scattering of dry-stone-walled low cottages. At night the outer Temenos wall is scanned by the rotating light from Cape Sim, the white walls of the sanctuary flash out into the night. A popular pilgrimage is held in mid-August for the saint has a reputation of curing the sterility of women. Throughout the year both men and women make lonely pilgrimages and supplications to the saint.

40 km south is **Smimou**, an unobtrusive town with a pretty arcaded main street. There are some old working salt works just outside the town. For a trip inland turn east 17 km up the route 6606 to reach the **souk of Tnine Imi n Tlit** which is held on Monday, 2 km off the road to the left up a dirt track.

Caid Allal bou Fenzi, 32 km further east on the 6606, has a magnificent view over the hills to the south and west beside the Kasbah. The neighbouring village, **Sebt des Ait Daoud**, has a **souk** on Saturday for the mountain tribe of the Ait Daoud. For the truly determined, four-wheel mountain driver a track of sorts continues across the mountains to rejoin the P40 Agadir to Marrakesh road.

Djebel Amsittene

4 km beyond Smimou a piste track, 6633, to the east climbs up through a landscape of red earth dominated by arguin and thuja trees to an especially fine view from Djebel Amsittene. The track is signposted for Tnine Imi n Tlit, a right at the first turning and a left at the second should get you after 16 km of twisting road to the foot of the summit of 905 m. The complete all round view of the Haha, the High Atlas peaks to the east, the sea to the west is well worth the effort of climbing to this modest height. Beside the tower dwells the guardian beekeeper, one of those courteous tranquil mountaineers that you should remember if you are ever tempted to make wild unflattering generalizations about Moroccans.

8 km beyond Smimou a turning to the west takes you 15 km to the village of **Dar**

Cheikh Taguent and **Cape Tafelney**, the coastal track south, though equally beautiful, has deteriorated quite dramatically.

68 km from Essaouira is **Tamanar**, the local administrative centre. There is a **souk** here on Thursday and some tempting tagines simmering by the roadside. The **Hôtel Etoile du Sud** has rooms for 30dh and makes a convenient stop for coffee, orange juice or a full meal. The Wednesday **souk of Ida ou Trhouma** is off the road to the east, the turning is 10 km south of Tamanar.

Pointe Imessouane

16 km south of Tamanar a right turn can take you on a narrow tarmac road 20 km to Pointe Imessouane, a remote fishing village. The high season for the fisherman is at the end of the summer when the tassergal, a fine fish which can weigh 14 lbs, migrates past this coast.

Just above the village there is the **Berber Auberge** which has a dramatic sea view from its terrace. You can eat and sleep cheaply here in one of the few beds, though most people seem to arrive in a VW van. There is a small strip of sandy beach and rocks you can dive from, a popular base for surfers and wind surfers with its comparatively sheltered cliff lined bay to the east.

Tamri

117 km south of Essaouira the road swings around the river bed at the village of Tamri. Bananas are planted on the estuary floor and sold at the roadside in season whilst euphorbia grows wild on the surrounding hills. The river is partly supplied from the water fall at Immouzer, one of the network of three river valleys that extend east, to form the heartland of the Ida Outanan tribe historically separate from the Haha.

A small beach can be reached from a turning to the right just as you leave the estuary, which has strong Atlantic undertow, for Cape Rhir/Ghir is only some 17 km further south. **Amesnaz** is the first safe swimming beach of the Paradise Plage coast, it is 30 km south of Tamri. The village of **Taghazoute**, 15 km from Agadir, is scruffy enough but the holiday resort nature of Agadir can first be felt at the long beach beyond, where you find the terraced bar restaurant of the **Sables D'Or**.

For Taghazoute beach and an inland trip to the falls of Immouzer, see north of Agadir, page 483–4.

Part VI

MEKNES, FEZ & THE MIDDLE ATLAS

Lakhmis Gate, Meknes

The heart of Morocco is the plain of Sais and upon the plain sit the two Imperial cities of Meknes and Fez. They are the twin pulsating valves that have for centuries fed Moorish culture into the rest of the nation. The Sais plain is low and fertile enough to support an urban population yet it is secured from external enemies by the Riff and Middle Atlas mountains that almost entirely enclose it. The first Muslim kingdom of Morocco was established here, upon the shell of the old Roman capital of Volubilis. This state declined after a century but it left behind a new city—Fez—where Islam, law, literacy, art and skilled crafts had a safe refuge. These civilized resources were at the disposal of any dynasty that could unite the disparate regions of Morocco. One of the greatest Sultans, Moulay Ishmael, turned his back on the preeminence of Fez and in the 17th century attempted to create a new centre for the nation. He built a vast new Imperial city beside the medina of Meknes, whose ruined walls and storehouses remain a powerful testament.

On the southern edge of the plain of Sais there is a continuous thread of towns where the agricultural lowlands first meet the limestone uplands of the Middle Atlas. These towns have acted throughout their long history as both markets and fortified border posts against the nomadic Berber tribes of the highlands. Taza and Sefrou are the oldest and most interesting of these and are both surrounded by a striking and little travelled hinterland.

The Middle Atlas is in total contrast to the sophisticated Moorish culture of the plain. It is an essentially pastoral space, a high partially forested plateau that has always been

271

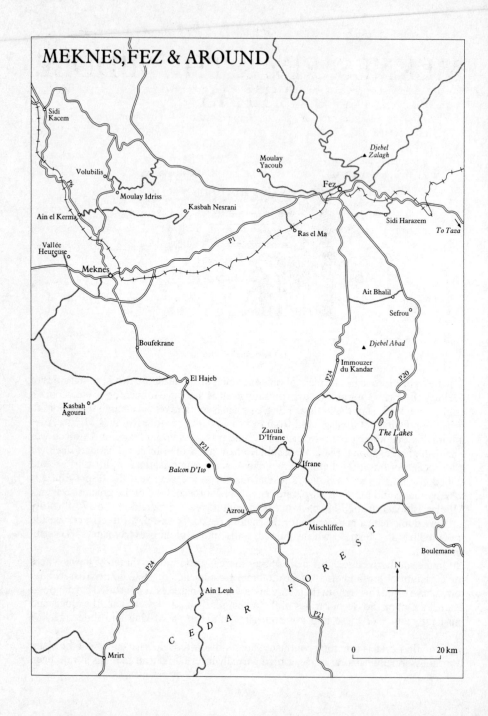

MEKNES, FEZ & AROUND

Sidi
Kacem

Djebel
▲ Zalagh

Moulay
Yacoub

Volubilis

Moulay Idriss

Fez

Kasbah Nesrani

Ain el Kerma

Sidi Harazem

To Taza

Vallée
Heureuse

P1

Ras el Ma

Meknes

Ait Bhalil

Sefrou

Djebel Abad

Boufekrane

Immouzer
du Kandar

El Hajeb

P24

P20

Kasbah
Agourai

The Lakes

Zaouia
D'Ifrane

P21

Balcon D'Ito

Ifrane

Azrou

Mischliffen

C   E   D   A   R   F   O   R   E   S   T

Boulemane

P24

N

Ain Leuh

P21

Mrirt

0   20 km

the realm of Berber nomadic tribes, principally the Beni M'Guid of the cedar forests, the Ziane and the Ait Serri. It boasts no distinguished architecture or ancient areas of settlement. The hill stations immediately south of Fez and Meknes, Immouzer du Kandar, Ifrane and Azrou, provide a change in atmosphere from the frenetic street life of the old cities but apart from a well established tour of cedar forests, ski runs and lakes have little interest in themselves.

The landscape is at its most rewarding in the higher distant regions, like the source of the Oum er Rbia, the Ouzoud gorge and the Ouzoud waterfall. For the moderately adventurous hill walker the Middle Atlas is an unexploited haven of peaks, hidden valleys, kasbahs, lakes and high mountain passes. These can be explored from the principal highland towns, Midelt and El Ksiba or from lesser bases like Azilal, Demnate and Toufinite.

Most visitors continue to see the Middle Atlas plateau as a region to be quickly crossed, an amorphous area, a zone of transition between a Mediterranean and a Saharan flora. Travelling on the road to Marrakesh, across the Tadla plain, an interest in the region's tumultuous warring history brings rewarding insights to the initially un-promising towns of Khenifra, Tadla and Boujdad.

MEKNES

Meknes is at the centre of one of the richest agricultural regions where olives, grain, vegetables and grapes are successfuly grown by thick-set Berber farmers who seem to characterize this region. Despite its splendid Imperial past as the capital city of Sultan Moulay Ishmael, with its present population of half a million, an army base and a university it remains more of a large Berber town than a cosmopolitan urban centre. Meknes is divided into three distinct quarters. The new town with its neat French-built, tree-lined avenues, cafés, bars and hotels is to the east of the Oued Boufekrane valley. On the western hill perches the walled Medina, its skyline a confusion of green, white and golden minarets. To the south of the Medina, through the Bab Mansour stretches the Imperial city, a bewildering, only partially occupied enclosure, surrounded by over 25 km of massive pise walls.

Three days at a hotel in Meknes is enough to visit all the conventional tourist sites. The Medina with its souk, Palais Jamai Museum, Bou Inania Medersa, Mosques, ornamental Gates, tomb of Sidi Ben Aissa and reclusive quarters can easily consume a day. Behind the Bab Mansour within the Imperial city is the Koubbet pavilion, the underground 'slave pens', the tomb-Mosque of Moulay Ishmael, the Heri Es Souani arsenal and the Aguedal tank which requires a 5 km walk to be fully seen and experi-enced. A taxi circuit around the outer forts and walls of the Imperial city could be the prelude to visiting Volubilis and Moulay Idriss on the third day in Meknes.

History

Meknes has had a cyclical past. Vulnerably situated at the heart of Morocco it has inevitably suffered at every succession war but its position, at the centre of a rich

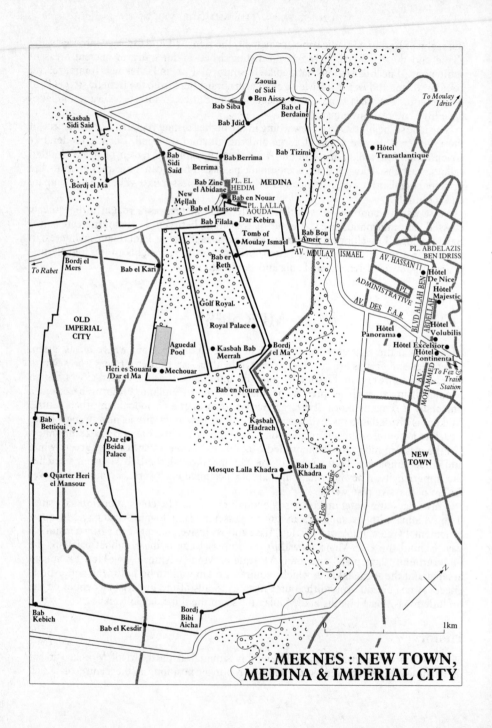

Zaouia
of Sidi
Ben Aissa
Bab Siba
Bab el
Berdaine
Bab Jdid

Kasbah
Sidi Said

Bab Tizimi
Hôtel
Transatlantique

Bab
Sidi
Said
Bab Berrima

Berrima

Bordj el Ma

Bab Zine
el Abidane
PL. EL
HEDIM
MEDINA
New
Mellah
Bab en Nouar
PL. LALLA
Bab el Mansour
AOUDA

Bab Filala
Dar Kebira

Tomb of
Moulay Ismael
Bab Bou
Ameir
PL. ABDELAZIS
BEN IDRISS

AV. MOULAY ISMAEL
AV. HASSAN II

Bordj el
Mers
Bab el Kari
Bab er
Reth
Hôtel
De Nice
Hôtel
Majestic

To Rabet

ADMINISTRATIVE
PL.

Golf Royal.
AV. DES F.A.R.

OLD
IMPERIAL
CITY
Royal Palace
Hôtel
Panorama
Hôtel
Volubilis
Hôtel Excelsior

Aguedal
Pool
Kasbah Bab
Merrah
Bordj
el Ma
Hôtel
Continental
To Fez &
Train
Station

Heri es Souani
/Dar el Ma
Mechouar

Bab en Noura
Bab
Bettioui

Kasbah
Hadrach
NEW
TOWN

Dar el
Beida
Palace

Quarter Heri
el Mansour
Mosque Lalla Khadra
Bab Lalla
Khadra

Bab
Kebich
Bordj
Bibi
Aicha
0
1km

Bab el Kesdir

MEKNES : NEW TOWN,
MEDINA & IMPERIAL CITY

To Moulay
Idriss

To Fez &
Train
Station

Oued Bou Fekrane

agricultural plain allowed the city rapidly to restore its fortune during any period of peace.

Meknes originated as a hill-top kasbah, on the site of the present Medina which was garrisoned by Khajarite Berbers in their revolt against the Arab conquerors in the 8th century. By the 10th century it had grown into the principal market for the powerful Berber Meknassa tribe but was destroyed by an Almoravide army in 1069. A new kasbah was then built around which a settlement reassembled but this in its turn was destroyed by Abdel Moumen, the first Almohad Sultan who, once established in power, designed a new city on a rigid square grid, adding a circuit of walls, mosques and a regular water supply. Meknes Medina still contains recognizable Almohad features, like the Jdid gate, though it has grown and lost its original planned shape. The town flourished under a century of Almohad authority though it was reduced to ruins during the long succession struggle that eventually raised the Merenid Sultans to the throne. Youssef, the same Merenid Sultan who built Fez el Jedid and restored Salé, had to rebuild the Grand Mosque and city walls before he could repopulate the town in 1276. His son gave the town a zaouia and begun work on the Medersa which was finished by Sultan Abou Inan in the 14th century. Close to the political capital of Fez, Meknes was a convenient base to launch rebellions. It was repeatedly embroiled in the confused family politics of both the Merenid and Saadian dynasties but survived this troublesome period intact.

In 1666, Moulay Ishmael was appointed the Pasha of Meknes by his elder brother, Sultan Moulay Rachid. He proved a loyal official and lived like a private person, tilling his own land and gathering money by way of trade. After the death of his brother in 1672, Moulay Ishmael succeeded to the throne. The cities of Fez and Marrakesh led a number of rebellions against the new monarch who determined to create a new capital out of the loyal city of Meknes.

The Imperial city of Moulay Ishmael, 1672–1727

The Medina was left largely undisturbed but a brand new Imperial city was built beyond its southern walls. A slave army of 50,000 Berbers and Europeans were employed to construct its enormous extent. Dozens of palaces were built for his court, for his 500 concubines and four wives, for his few favoured children (from the 800 he sired) and gardens, parks, ponds and pavilions built, improved, knocked down and constantly replaced within the confines of the massive external walls. The Imperial city also served as the headquarters and garrison for a standing force of 25,000 Abids, the disciplined negro slave army by which the Sultan imposed his arbitrary rule. Vast store houses, stables, exercise fields, enclosures for allied nomadic cavalry and armouries held the instruments of war from which the Sultan could quickly dispatch a force to crush the first sign of dissidence.

Moulay Ishmael has been presented to history, mostly through the accounts of missionaries, ex-slaves and the snubbed literate population of Fez, as a megalomaniac tyrant. His rule was certainly arbitrary, bloody and autocratic but his achievements were equal to the suffering he caused; his army and garrisons preserved order, recaptured Tangier, Mehdiya, Larache and Asilah from the Christians, encouraged trade, rebuilt mosques, shrines, whole towns and constructed kasbahs throughout the country. He attempted to reassert orthodoxy in the confused cult-ridden religious life of the country and was the last Sultan to treat the European powers on equal terms. In his correspondence to King James II, he argued in favour of Protestantism and to Louis XIV he made the famous request for the hand of the French King's illegitimate daughter, Marie Anne de Bourbon.

Ishmael's Imperial city did not long outlast its founder; the Abid slave regiments grew reckless and greedy without the stern hand of their master and deposed a succession of his sons. The Lisbon earthquake of 1755 shattered the palace compounds and whilst his son Moulay Abdullah and grandson Sidi Mohammed (1757–90) altered and maintained portions of Meknes, they increasingly returned the business of government back to either Fez or Marrakesh. The focus of the city returned to the Medina and it was the French who caused a revival in fortunes, for like the great Sultan they appreciated Meknes's strategic position and made it their central army base. In a move that Moulay Ishmael could understand they ignored both the Medina and the Imperial city and built a New Town for their regiments.

GETTING AROUND

By Train
The main train station is on Av. de la Basse, just off the Av. des FAR, the Fez road. Turn left and the centre of the New Town is 1 km walk east, or you could get off at the Meknes el Amir Abdelkader station (ex Lafayette) on Rue Alger closer to the centre. There are plenty of trains going off in all directions, 8 a day west to Rabat and Casablanca for 29dh, 8 a day east through Fez and Taza to Oujda and 4 north to Tangier with a change of trains at Sidi Slimane or Sidi Kacem.

By Bus
The CTM coach station is at 47 Blvd Mohammed V on the junction with the Av. des FAR. There are 7 a day to Rabat, Casablanca and Fez and daily buses to Tangier, Ifrane, Azrou, Ouezzane and Er-Rachidia. Other bus companies and local routes leave from Rue Dar Smen by the Bab Mansour or the roadside park just south of the Place el Hedim. A shuttle service of buses, nos 5, 7 and 9, connects the Medina and New Town.

Taxi and Cars
You will find grands and petits taxis below the Place el Hedim beside the road immediately south. Car hire firms all operate from Fez. There is a good Renault garage on the road to Fez and Maroc-France on Av. Hassan II, tel 22858 specialize in Volkswagens.

TOURIST INFORMATION
The Tourist Office is on the Place Administrative, tel 24426; they arrange the hire of guides, 30dh a day. The Syndicat D'Initiative is just south of the Place on the Esplanade de la Foire inside a big yellow gate. The Post Office is also on the Place Administrative and there is a sub-office in the medina on Rue Dar Smen. Banks, the BMCE is on 98, Av. des FAR and the Banque Du Maroc on 33 Av. Mohammed V.

The Hospital Moulay Ishmael is on Av. des FAR, tel 22806. An after-hours chemist can be found on the side of the hotel de ville in the central Place Administrative, tel 23375, though the normal hours are from 8.30–20.30. There are two French Catholic churches, Notre Dame des Oliviers by the Place Poereiam which celebrates mass on

Saturday at 18.00 and Sunday at 10.30 and the Chapelle St Michael, Rue el Merzch, which has mass on Sunday at 19.00.

The Medina

The starting point from which to explore either the Medina or the Imperial city is the Place El Hedim. From the New Town descend across the Rue Boufekrane valley by walking along Av. Moulay Ishmael to enter the walled Medina through the **Bab Bou Ameir**. Then turn right to climb 400 m up the busy Rue Rouamzine and turn left through the **Bab es Smen** to approach the central Place El Hedim, 'the square of destruction'.

Bab Mansour el Aleuj

This monumental gate separates the central square of the Medina, Place El Hedim, from the vast, enclosed Imperial City of Moulay Ishmael. The Bab Mansour has come to symbolize Meknes, reproduced in countless books, articles, postcards and posters.

It is difficult to see it at its best in the day, for the sun shines into your eyes from the east and leaves the Bab Mansour in shadow. The softer evening light picks out the details but even then the gate appears ponderous, over-decorated and the relief too bold. The pillars, torn from the classical ruins of Volubilis, a mixture of Ionic and Corinthian columns, appear empty gestures that distract from the overall harmony. It succeeds as

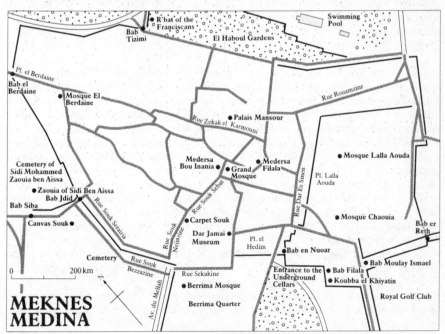

MEKNES
MEDINA

277

architecture in a way that the Sultan might have been content with, powerful, looming, appearing obsessively strong and rigid, its top panel of carved Koranic script a reminder of the strong Muslim orthodoxy of the Alouite dynasty.

The less obtrusive but altogether more agreeable gate to the right, the **Bab Jamaa en Nouar**, was built at the same period; it now gives entrance to a school that has been housed in an old mosque and the gate apartments. Both gates were designed by Moulay Ishmael's court architect, the renegade Mansour el Aleuj, and completed in 1732 during the reign of his son Moulay Abdullah.

Place El Hedim

Looking into this large square from the Bab Mansour the **food market** runs along most of the left hand side of the place, screened by a long row of pottery shops and barbers. It is a wonderful place to gather a picnic: tasting from the glistening cones of flavoured olives, pats of goats cheese, prime fruit and fresh vegetables from the farms that surround Meknes. Here even the dates look polished. At the right hand corner of the Place an alley leads directly to the Grand Mosque and passes on the left a 14th-century town house, the 'Maison Merenide' which has been turned into a tourist bazaar.

At the back of the Place El Hedim is an **enclosed fountain**, seen from across the square the swirl of expanding mosaic tile work flickers through the urban haze. To the left of the fountain you find the Dar Jamai museum entrance.

Dar Jamai Museum

The Dar Jamai is a 19th-century vizier's palace that houses a collection of Moroccan arts and crafts. Like every Moroccan museum it is a disordered presentation of often undated Andalucian-influenced products from Medina artisans and the traditional crafts of the Berber tribes of the Middle Atlas. It is open every day 9.00–12.00, 15.00–18.00 except Tuesday, tel 30863. *Entry 10 dh*

The Dar Jamai has an unobtrusive entrance that is well sited off the busiest sun-drenched square in Meknes. The contrast as you enter through the cool dark twisting entrance passage emphasizes the domestic sanctity of an enclosed Moroccan house. Along this passage are some examples of Andalucian painted wall tiles, their foliate patterns familiar from wood carving but rarely seen in this form in Morocco. Even more surprising is the small collection of miniature paintings that were produced in Meknes.

At the centre of the Museum is a mature **Andalucian garden** well planted with shrubs and often buzzing with birds. It is an attractive calm building; the exhibits are held in chambers whose worn ceramic floors and graceful patina of age greatly contribute to your enjoyment. It belonged to the same brothers who built the Palais Jamai in Fez. They were powerful officials in the court of Sultan Moulay Hassan and descended from one of the Arab tribes that had taken service under the Alouite Sultans, the Oulad Jamai, and become hereditary servants of the government.

In the few chambers off the central garden you can see the silk banner used by Sultan Moulay Hassan for his campaigns, dated 1874–1887 in the Gregorian calendar, and a small display of brilliantly bound compact Korans.

The collection of elaborate keys is entertaining and the other items of wrought ironwork, splendid door bosses and supporting hinges show how much the Gothic borrowed from the Moorish taste.

The vizier's reception room upstairs is fully furnished, a useful antedote to the false sense of Moorish domestic interiors received by visiting the serene interiors of Medersas and empty palaces. For here there is a riot of familiar 19th-century clutter, coloured glass, debased workmanship, painted wood and conflicting plaster work.

The display of 19th-century Fez and Meknes ware is more pleasing; these **ceramics** have a gentler line, warmer, more fluid shapes than seen in today's merely capable rigid geometricism. The contrast with rural domestic pottery is always strong; though geometric in intent the gourd-like shapes of the vessels and the black lines on red show Berber design at its most primitive and retentive.

The collection of Berber **jewelry** makes for an interesting comparison with that offered in today's souks, though the universal style of much native Islamic jewelry holds few surprises. The metal work has a solidity that one can hardly expect now; for these were collections of disposable wealth, while now jewelry concentrates on display. See Jean Besancenot's *Bijoux Arabes et Berberes du Maroc* (Ed de la Cigogne, Casablanca): he reckons that workmanship used to add less than 25% to the metal's value.

There is a fine mixed collection of Moroccan **carpets and killims** from the indigenous Berber tribes of the High and Middle Atlas. The tendency was to produce woven and embroidered killims rather than a true knotted carpet. The carpet collection does also clearly show why few Moroccan carpets have survived beyond the 19th century. The large, thinly spaced knots tied to inadequate backing will not last more than a century unless they have been used as wall hangings. Their admirable warm and simple diamond lozenge design is difficult to find now. The Zayan/Zaian carpet is good example of this, whilst opposite the carpet from Ait Bousba shows the origins of the pictogram, or 'Message carpet', though it is splendidly random and primitive compared with the over busy pattern-book designs found in today's bazaars.

The killims show a natural restraint in embroidery and the designs are all based on harmonious stripes of colour, interspaced with geometrical lozenges, diamonds and triangles. The products from Zemmour and the Beni M'Guid tribal confederation are most attractive and are still being created.

The Bab Berrima and Mellah quarters

Back in the Place El Hedim and looking down the square from Bab Mansour turn left in front of the Museum and walk down Rue Sekkakin. In 200 m you reach Bab Berrima, a busy junction of streets. On the right is the site of the Berrima Kasbah that once defended this section of the Medina although now you can see only a **17th-century gate** and portions of the Medina **perimeter wall**.

On the left the long and comparatively wide Av. du Mellah, lined by cloth merchants and tailors, extends downhill. Moulay Ishmael attracted a large Jewish community to Meknes and built a separate Mellah quarter in 1682, a square enclave projecting from the Medina that was securely enclosed behind its own wall, pierced by three secure gates and governed by Caid Ali, an English renegade. The great Sultan was under the firm influence of his treasurer, the Jewish financier Joseph Maimaran, who was replaced by his son Abraham after his death in 1685. The Jewish community were later moved even further down hill, into the new Mellah outside the walls, and Sultan Sidi Mohammed built the **Bab Berrima Mosque** in the 18th century for this increasingly Muslim quarter of the city. The exterior of the Mosque can be seen by twisting through the gate passage on your right where there are a couple of delicious hole-in-the wall grill cafés.

Bab el Jedid and the zaouia of Sidi Mohammed ben Aissa

From the Bab Berrima walk 300 m along Souk Bekkani on the outside of the Medina wall, a local shopping street which is a mass display of tupper ware, kitchen ware and jeans until you reach the brick-built Bab el Jedid. This translates as the new gate, somewhat contrarily as it is the oldest gate in Meknes, its arched vaults date from the 12th-century Almohad city. In front of the Bab el Jedid there is a good selection of eating cafés and a row of tent makers are busy in their shops cutting canvas and sewing awnings together on their pedal-operated Singers.

Continue beyond the Bab el Jedid keeping a wall on your right behind which is the vast walled cemetery of Sidi Ben Aissa. Just beyond the Bab es Siba, the gate of dissidence, an avenue on the right leads up to the large distinctive green tiled pyramid roof that covers the venerated tomb of Sidi Mohammed Ben Aissa which was built by the Sultan Sidi Mohammed (1757–90). You should not approach too closely nor should you wander through the cemetery decorated with the domed tombs of many revered Islamic saints. A mosque and various courts are attached to the shrine for Sidi Ben Aissa is the founder of the important religious brotherhood of the Aissoua whose influence has spread through-out North Africa. Partly suppressed in the early reforming years of Independence, this ecstatic mystical sect has revived in recent years.

Sidi ben Aissa and his teachings are equally mysterious. He is known to have died in 1523 but there are abundant apocryphal stories about his imprisonment by Moulay Ishmael. He rewarded his followers with branches that he turned into gold and silver and yet during a famine safely recommended a starving man to eat anything so long as it was poisonous, which hopefully illustrates the fundamental Sufi trait of indifference to the values of this world. His followers can harmlessly consume scorpions and cacti and are invulnerable to snake bites during the music and dance induced ecstasy of the brotherhood.

On Fridays you can often overhear Aissoua music and the brotherhood holds a popular Moussem here during Mouloud.

Beyond the shrine, on the left, the city and country meet in a shanty town of corrugated stalls, shafts of spectacular light flicker over the dark piles of vegetables whilst beyond the chicken, pigeon and dove salesmen work amongst cages of live birds.

Medina Souks

Returning back to Bab el Jedid pass through this ancient gate and turn right to follow the Rue des Serairia, the **blacksmith's souk**, interspaced with knife grinders, charcoal salesmen and tool makers. On the left you can enter the Sultan's fondouq, a delightful 18th-century brick courtyard established for the use of armourers.

As the street narrows you enter the centre of the **jewelry trade**—a right turn lets you out by the Bab Berrima, a left turn brings you into the covered **souk Nejjarin**, the central thoroughfare of the Medina lined with the shops of metalworkers, tinkers and carpenters. You soon pass on the right the **Nejjarin**, 'the carpenters' Mosque, which follows the 12th-century Almohad plan even though the visible work is all 18th-century restoration. Beyond the Mosque, again on the right, is the **Dlala Kisaria**, one of a number of interior courts lined with carpet and killim booths that stock the produce of the Middle Atlas tribes. It is one of the easiest and most accessible places in which to bargain for killims with a good range of stock and jovial merchants.

A right turn by the Kisaria can take you down the old dyers street passing the **Sebbarine Mosque** on your left to reemerge at the Place El Hedim by the Dar Jamai museum.

By continuing along the main covered thoroughfare, known as the **souk Sebbat**, you enter the richer and most tourist-oriented area of the souk. Notice the ornately decorated gates of the **Grand Mosque** 100 m further on your right. The Mosque is at the heart of the Medina with five elaborate entrances; it covers the area of the Almoravide Mosque but dates from the 13th-century Merenid rebuilding of the city.

Medersa Bou Inania

Directly opposite is the Medersa Bou Inania; its entrance is below a cupola in the main street and guarded by enormous bronze decorated doors. It was started by Sultan Abou Hassan, the creator of the Salé Medersa but finished and named after Sultan Abou Inan who reigned from 1350–1358. It is open from 9.00–12.00, 14.00–16.00, admission 10dh.

Enter the ribbed dome of the entrance passage and pass through a gate in the cedar screen with the Barakat Mohammed symbol carved above which could be translated as 'The chance for faith'. The tall rectangular court paved with black and white marble squares surrounds the central pool. Around three sides of the court runs a gallery above which are two storeys of students' chambers whilst the fourth face of the court opens into a spacious prayer hall of green and yellow tiles, a carved peacock fan set above the Mihrab.

The decoration of the central court begins with a band of zellig mosaic that is replaced by bands of Koranic script which is carried upwards by all the decorative materials; carved plaster, glazed tile, marble and carved cedar all conspire to carry the word of God. The solid angular pillars of the gallery are saved from stolidity by columns that reach up towards the tiled cornice and restrain the entrelac design of the plaster walls of the chambers.

The delight taken in the beauty of Arabic script, entwined with foliate decoration as seen on highest carved cedar band, can over-emphasize the depth of education that was undertaken in a Medersa. Generations of students phonetically memorized the classical Arabic poetry of the Koran whilst many could never read more than a few lines. The language of the street, Moghrebi Arabic, not to mention the three Berber dialects, are far removed from the language of 7th-century Mecca.

The communal life of the Tolba, the student reciters, is revealed in the ground floor wash room with its long common sink, although the second storey of rooms has an individual and very European looking water closet. Do not miss the view from the roof across the green tiled Grand Mosque and the prominent minarets of the Medina. The double lancet windows of the Touta minaret can be seen almost due west and the minarets of the Ahmed Chebli Mosque and Sidi Kadour el Alaoui to its right.

Leaving the Medersa the rich clothes shops and bazaars of the Kissaria stretch ahead, but a sharp right turn beside the Grand Mosque takes you down Rue Sebab, passing on the left the **Medersa Filala**, built by Moulay Ishmael in the 17th century. It was a smaller and cruder version of the Bou Inania which is not open to the public. Then a right turn down the Rue es Zemmour returns you to the Rue Dar es Smen and the Place El Hedim.

The Northern Medina

The various quarters of the northern Medina remain unseen by most visitors, protected by their confusing labyrinth of streets and this area is easier to approach from the northern gate, the Bab el Berdaine. Walk from the Place El Hedim towards the New Town and having just passed through the Bab Bou Ameir turn right to walk along the Rue des Moulins outside the city walls. Below, in the Oued Boufekrane valley are the extensive El Haboul **public gardens** with formal paths, shaded benches, zoo and an open air theatre. There are also two paying club **swimming pools**, a smaller expensive quieter one surrounded by grass and a larger pool with a diving platform surrounded by orange trees. At the far end of the gardens is the recently restored battlements of the **Bab Tizimi** entrance to the Medina.

Opposite Bab Tizimi is the **R'bat**, the convent of the Franciscan sisters who run a school for Muslim girls. Ring the bell on the small lefthand door and a sister may appear to show you the echoing chapel and a selection of embroidered work for sale. The convent is built over the site of Moulay Ishmael's gunpowder mill, prudently built outside the Medina and far from the Imperial city.

Pass through the Tizimi gate and walk beside the battlemented walls and dip out again to approach the 17th-century **Bab el Berdaine**, 'the saddlers' gate', from the outside. The decorative bands seem to flaunt further the power of its two great flanking towers. It is best admired in a climb from the potters' quarters, down by the Oued Boufekrane, which slowly reveals the extent of the gate as you ascend the hill in a submissive and tired attitude.

Passing through the gate you enter a long inner compound, the Place el Berdaine where there is the clean and admirably unadorned stonework of the **Berdaine Mosque**.

You can then walk down the length of the northern Medina, admiring the undisturbed nature of most of the city with its workshops, separate baths, bakeries and mosques delineating the various quarters.

Half way down, about 600 m from Bab Berdaine, a left turn down Rue Knout brings you to the exterior of the **Koubba of Moulay Ahmed El Ouezzani**, which was the open air sanctuary of this famous ascetic who lived here from 1917 to his death in 1933.

Further down the central thoroughfare which bears a number of different names along its length you pass the **El Mansour Palace**, Rue Karmouni, a richly decorated 19th-century merchant's house whose interior is partly hung with the trappings of a tourist bazaar. In the Medina you may see signs for the restaurant **Zitouna** which though established in a Medina town house has an institutional aroma and caters largely for coach tours.

Imperial City

'I have built these buildings—let those who can destroy them', Sultan Moulay Ishmael.

'We have never seen anything equal to it, neither among the modern buildings nor among the ancient', Ambassador Temim.

The extent and past grandeur of the Imperial city can be appreciated in a 5 km walk broken half way at the café at **Heri es Souani**. Most of the city is in ruins and has been built over by village communities, and the royal palace is not open to the public. The little pavilion of the Koubbet el Khiyatin, the nearby underground store rooms, the tomb of Moulay Ishmael, the Heri es Souani arsenal and the Aguedal tank are the highlights of the Imperial city, though inevitably the abiding image left at the end of the day is a bewildering series of massive walls.

Dar Kebira
Passing through the Bab El Mansour you enter the large interior Place Lalla Aouda, the formal processional square of the enclosed **Dar Kebira**, the old palace quarter of Moulay Ishmael. None of the palaces have survived and it is now just another residential quarter of the city.

The Dar Kebira was finished in 1677 and opened by the Sultan who sacrificed a wolf under the full moon at midnight and set its head above the gateway to the palace. According to the chronicler ez-Zayyani the Dar Kebira contained 24 separate palace compounds, gardens, barracks and two mosques, most of which were destroyed by the Sultan's son Moulay Abdullah. The mosques alone have survived, the **Lalla Aouda** and **Chaouia** can be seen facing the square from where only eunuchs were permitted to make the call to prayer. The Museum of Moroccan Arts in the Oudaia Kasbah at Rabat was originally built as a palace by Moulay Ishmael. It can give some indication of the varied splendours of the Dar Kebira which would have been decorated with columns extracted from Volubilis and decoration looted from the great Saadian palace of El Badi at Marrakesh.

Comparisons with the palace of Moulay Ishmael's great contemporary, Louis XIV, continue to be made. However Versailles with its radial axes of parkland, its draughty uncomfortable interiors and the exterior splendour of its façade can hardly be further removed from the secretive, heavily enclosed pavilion gardens of Moulay Ishmael. The Sultan started work ten years before he received the first reports of Versailles. What Meknes and Versailles share is a roughly equal consumption of material and human lives.

Koubbet el Khiyatin
Passing through the Bab Filala, the pavilion of Koubbet el Khiyatin can be seen in the far right corner of this smaller paddock square. This audience chamber was used for the reception of foreign Embassies and the interminable bargaining over the ransom of slaves. The decorated carving on the walls endlessly repeat in Kufic script 'All jell', glory to God.

Beside the Koubbet is the entrance to the **'prison of the Christians'**, a misleading title for a massive vaulted underground network of storerooms, an impressive and mysterious acreage of damp stone lit by skylights. Intriguing bricked up passages disappear to other decayed sections of the old underground city of cellars.

The Christian slaves were never housed here; at first they lived under the 24 arches of a now vanished bridge, a dozen for the Spanish, the rest shared between French, English and Portuguese. After the fall of Larache, 1700 more Spaniards joined the community and some disused tanneries were converted into a distinct European quarter. The slaves had four holidays a year; at Easter, Christmas, the nativity of St John the Baptist and that of the Virgin Mary, and were ministered to by Franciscan missionaries. These priests were free to travel throughout Morocco (corsairs were forbidden by the Sultan to capture Franciscans), and they collected a tax on brandy sales and gambling from their charges.

The righthand arch of the two ahead enters the exclusive and guarded walled **Royal Golf Club** which has been created out of the central palace garden. Moulay Ishmael kept a delightful menagerie in this garden: four wild asses from Guinea ran wild and two white dromedaries allowed themselves to be washed in soap every morning and wounded storks were cared for. Arab horses that had completed the pilgrimage to Mecca remained unridden and free for the rest of their life, beads and scrolls from the holy city hung from their necks and any criminal was assured of sanctuary if such a horse allowed him to approach. On their death the horses were reverently buried in shrouds and a Koubba raised over their tomb.

The tomb of Moulay Ishmael

Through the lefthand arch the long white Tomb Mosque of Moulay Ishmael extends opposite half a dozen bazaars. The actual prayer hall of the mosque remains closed to non-Muslims but the tomb can be approached providing you are respectfully dressed and tip the guardian, a dirham or two per person. The sanctuary was completely restored by King Mohammed V in 1959. Pass through three preliminary faience courts before arriving at the central fountain court where the pious remove their shoes. The door to the left leads to a lavishly gilded and decorated Moorish hall from where you can look on to the marble tomb of the great Sultan flanked by two clocks, the gift of Louis XIV.

Dar El Makhzen

Beyond the mosque is the **Bab er Rith**, the gate of winds, which reveals a kilometre passage below a stretch of massive double walls. Along this road the Sultan would ride in a chariot drawn by his plump concubines. The Harem had a precarious status for the Sultan cared for few of his children and even less for his concubines (most of his adult sons were exiled to the oasis of Tafilalet). His official wives were however forceful characters. Moulay Ishmael's first wife, Zidana, was a fearsome negro witch who was even allowed out of the Harem when escorted by a suitable chaperone like her ally, the third wife, the English Sultana. She had been captured in 1688, aged 15 en route with her mother to Barbados. Moulay Ishmael returned this surprised mother-in-law to England with presents and a letter for the king.

The wall on the left is the exterior defendable perimeter of the Imperial city, that on the right defines a particular palace enclosure, the enormous Dar el Makhzen, the chief palace of the Sultan which was finished in 1697 and refurbished by Moulay Hassan in the late 19th century. The eastern portion remains to form the present **Royal Palace of Hassan II**. At the end of this long walk turn right below the Water Fort, Bordj el Ma, into the **Mechouar**, a colonnaded space where rulers could receive the ovations of their people. The gate on the right is the main guarded entrance to the palace, whilst a stroll to the left, through an enclosed hamlet clustered around a mosque and out through a gate allow you to admire the extent and width of the outer walls. To the east stretching inside these walls is the **Kasbah Hadrach**, the old barracks of the Bukharis, the crack Guard regiment of the Sultan's negro slave army. This old Kasbah quarter is protected by two gates, the Bab en Nouara and Bab Lalla Khadra by the mosque of that name.

Beyond the Mechouar, an **arboretum** has been established on the left of the road in the pavilioned **park of Ben Halima** whilst on the right a squatter village nestles beside the Royal Palace in the ruins of the **Kasbah Bab Merrah**. Storks nest on decaying pise buttresses and towers, a few cows graze in a paddock that once held a delicate pavilion and a young cripple shelters in a cardboard hut decorated with pseudo erotic pictures cut from the advertisements of the Western press. Broken faience tiles are unearthed as the foundations for a new breeze block are dug in the half shadow of vast soot-blackened brick arch chambers.

Heri Es Souani

The 500 m walk beside pise walls that mask these areas brings you to the Heri Es Souani, also known as the Dar el Ma. This is the most accessible and impressive remnant of the Imperial city, a massive warehouse whose silos held provisions for the court and standing army. A café selling coffee and cold drinks is surrounded by a garden of olive trees which happily grow on beds that rest on the massive roof. From here you can see miles of walls, modern villages and ruins stretching in every direction surrounded by open farmland, itself enclosed by distant mountains beyond. Within the old Aguedal park-gardens to the south a campsite, racecourse, arboretum, military academy and two schools partly fill the enormous enclosed area. To the west stretch the 4 hectares of the **Aguedal tank**, constructed by Moulay Ishmael to assure water for the palace gardens and orchards and now often surrounded by picnicking families. Within the Heri Es Souani you can admire the arched chambers and from the skylights cascades of creeper hang illuminated from the roof. In two of the corners round chambers surround a well where water could be drawn up from 50 m by machinery worked by circulating mules. A roofless area of store rooms, not stables, of 15 rows of 21 broken arches extends southwest, partly overgrown with fennel, that lays further stress on the scale and organization of the Sultan's reign.

Dar el Beida

Southeast of Heri es Souani is the palace and Mosque of Dar el Beida, an elegant arrangement of tiled towers, pavilions and gardens built by Sultan Sidi Mohammed ben Abdallah at the end of the 18th century. King Mohammed V created the military academy here after Independence and though you can admire the exterior, the inner arcaded court and gardens are now, of course, inaccessible.

Heri El Mansour

Below the Academy, still enclosed by the Imperial perimeter wall is the modern settlement of Sidi Ayad and below that the battlemented quarter of Heri El Mansour. This contains the 18th-century **Mosque of Er Rouah**, the Mosque of the stables, built by Sidi Mohammed in 1790 with its own attached Medersa. Turning to the left of the Mosque down the central street you reach the immense walls of the Heri El Mansour, now sadly closed to all visitors. This was considered the chief glory of the Imperial city, a vast beautifully appointed arcaded stable that reputedly held over 12,000 cavalry horses and that was fed by its own aqueduct. The roof has long since fallen and it is now an enclosed wilderness of worn pillars, broken tiles, accacia scrub and arches. Above the stables on the elevated platform created by their roof the Sultan created a formal Andalucian garden, the ornate paths studded with dozens of delicate pavilions that formed the El Mansour palace. Poised above the southern turreted and battlemented outer wall, beneath which the Guich tribes in the government service would assemble; this was the most splendid and fanciful of the Sultan's creations.

As the Dar el Beida and Heri El Mansour are currently inaccessible, most visitors are content to walk beside the Aguedal tank from the Heri es Souani. At the far end of the tank a left turn brings you into the Beni M'Hammed quarter and a right turn along the central avenue takes you out of this modern settlement through the **Bab El Kari**. Below this gate extends one of the most impressive stretches of external wall, the 'wall of riches' whose battlemented and towered defences stretch in an unbroken line a kilometre south to the Borgj el Mers. A road leads from the gate across empty ground west to the Mellah and a right turn climbs up past the taxi rank towards the Medina. A left turn along the Blvd As Salam could allow you to examine the most beautiful gate in Meknes, the towered **Bab Lakhmis**, or you could continue uphill and pass through the **Bab Zine El Abadine** to reenter the Place El Hedim.

FESTIVALS
A Fantasia festival is held in the Imperial city in September, the same month of the Moussem of Moulay Idriss and Sidi Bouzelm. The Aissoua celebrate at Mouloud and a week later the Hamadasha and Dghoughlia sects in Djebel Zerhoun.

SPORTS
There are two club **pools**, **tennis** and **basketball courts** in the Lahboul park below the El Haboul gardens, tel 20415. There is a Hammam at 4, Rue Patrice off Av. Hassan II.

WHERE TO STAY
The ***** **Transatlantique**, Rue el Meriniijine, tel 20002, is one of the deservedly celebrated hotels of Morocco, with excellent food, a pleasant garden and a superb view across the Oued Boufekrane to the skyline of Meknes's medina. The 120 bedrooms are divided into two quarters, the traditional rooms in the old portion of the hotel are the same price but of much greater character. It has two pools, bar, two restaurants and a tennis court. A double room costs 500dh, a single 400dh.

**** **Rif**, Rue d'Accara, tel 22591, is a pleasant hotel in the centre of town with a popular bar, the Bahia nightclub, two restaurants with menus of 86dh and 75dh and a small pool; 221dh for a single, 283dh for a double room. The **** **Zaki**, on the right of the road to El Hajeb, tel 20063, is a glittering new vulgar hotel with bars, disco and pool; a single costs 254dh, a double room for 325dh.

There are four clean and engaging two-star hotels that charge 90dh for a double with a bathroom, a single without costs 57dh. There is the **Majestic** on 19, Av. Mohammed V, 42 rooms, tel 22035, the **De Nice** on Rue d'Accra, 33 bedrooms and a bar, tel 20318, the **Palace** on 11, Rue de Ghana, 32 bedrooms, tel 22388 and the **Panorama** at 9, Av. des FAR, 23 bedrooms and a dining room, tel 22737.

The three one-star hotels are just as comfortable; the **Continental** at 92, Av. des FAR, 42 rooms, tel 20200, is a fine hotel with wide corridors and large bedrooms. A double with a bath costs 70dh, a single without 54dh. The elegant staircase has a fish tank on its bannister. The **Excelsior** at 57 Av. des FAR has 37 recently redecorated rooms, a double room with a bath costs 70dh, tel 21900, and there is the **Volubilis** at 45, Av. des FAR, 33 bedrooms, tel 20102.

There is a good camp site in the middle of the Imperial city, in a pleasant meadow next door to the Heri es Souani arsenal and the Aguedal tank. The **Camping Aguedal/Jnane Ben Hlima** is open all the year, tel 30712, and has a kitchen, restaurant, hot showers and a shop. It costs 17dh for two people with a tent and car, and meals are available from 30dh.

The **Youth Hostel** is close to the Hôtel Transatlantique on Av. Okba Ibn Nafi, tel 24698. 10dh for card holders to spend a night in spartan beds around a concrete yard; this includes a cold shower.

There are a number of hotels in the Medina found along the Rue Dar es Smen and Rue Rouamazin. The **Maroc Hotel** is by far the best and often the cheapest of these, tel 30705, at 103, Rue Benbrahim, just off Rue Rouamazin; 20dh for a single, 30dh for a double with working basins and free showers.

EATING OUT

The licensed restaurants are all in the New Town. There is **L'Hacienda**, off the Fez road, tel 21092, **La Coupoule** on Av. Hassan II, tel 22483, the **Dauphin** on the Av. de Paris, tel 28423, the **Metropolis** on the corner of Av. Hassan II, the **Gambrinus** on Rue Omar Ibn Ass, tel 20258, the **Guillame Tell** on Av. des FAR and the **Poker d'As** on 4, Av. de Paris. The Moroccan restaurant **Al-Ismaili** at the Hôtel Transatlantique has the best food, service, music and view in Meknes. A filling Moroccan salad costs 25dh and a delicious selection of tagines is available from 50dh.

The Medina has some delightful grill cafés by the Bab Berrima and Bab Jedid and a good selection along the Rue Dar es Smen and Rouamazin. The **Café Bab Mansour**, almost opposite its namesake, is particularly good; you can eat couscous and salad here for 12dh and sip tea until midnight.

BARS AND NIGHT LIFE

The bars of Meknes are casual places dominated by locals of both sexes openly drinking. This is comparatively unusual for Morocco and at times you can almost forget that you are a foreigner.

There are four hotels that have bars; the **Transatlantique** (a beer for 12dh) is quiet, the **** **Zahi** is worth a quick drink in order to see the astonishing hall, but the plush red interior of the **Rif Hotel** in the centre of town or the **De Nice** are busier and more relaxing. The Rif has a floor show in its **Bahia club** from 20.00–22.00, admission 50dh.

There are a number of other bars worth checking out; **Roi de la Biere**, **Jour and Nuit** and the **Du Tresor** are all along Av. Mohammed V, the latter at no 33. On the Av. Hassan II at no 3 there is **Bar Vox Brasserie**, at no 11 the **Bar de Centre** and at no 24 the **Bar American**. There is the **Novelty Bar** at 12, Rue de Marseilles and at no 6 the tranquil pastis-sipping atmosphere of **La Caravelle**. The three liveliest places are the **Hacienda**, the **Continental** or the **Club de Nuit**. The Hacienda is out of the centre of town but well signposted off the road to Fez. It has a disco night club, entrance 25dh, and occasional live bands. The Bar Continental is on the corner of Av. des FAR and Av. Hassan II beside the hotel where a series of three dark bars are run by a team of strong

Berber women. Almost opposite is the **Café Français Club de Nuit** at no 73, Av. des
F.A.R., where a beer costs 5dh and the bar closes half an hour after midnight. A door
down from the bar is the cellar **Cabaret Oriental**, a Moroccan night club where live
local bands play each night until 3.00.

Djebel Zerhoun Region

This 100-square-mile network of limestone and metamorphic hills rises abruptly north
of the plain of Sais to divide Fez and Meknes from the fertile Sebou valley. The central
and holm oak forested summit of Djebel Zerhoun is 1118 m high. The lower foothills are
covered in orchards and olive groves that are cultivated by a string of villages; these
mountain villages have a tradition of self-sufficiency and piety intensified by the idiosyn-
cratic spiritual life of the Hamadasha and Dghuglia brotherhoods. The villages on the
northern hills speak the Berber Tarifcht dialect of the Riff whilst the southern villages
speak the dialect of the Sanhajan Saharan Berbers.

GETTING AROUND
Leave Meknes on the P6 to Tangier, turn right after 10 km on to the P28. 8 km later a
right turn takes you on to an unobtrusive tarmac track, the S323, which passes through
the principal Zerhoun villages.

WHAT TO SEE
Many of the villages are still enclosed by stone kasbah walls that shelter the cottages, the
minareted mosque and a zaouia. The views over the plain towards Meknes are superb
and the Homeric dignity of a life spent with olive trees and flocks on the rough hills seems
stamped on the mood of the villages.

Beni Rached

Having first passed beside the hamlet of **Beni Jennad** the village of Beni Rached is
reached 2 km later. Beni Rached holds the tomb of Sidi Ali ben Hamdouch, the founder
of the Hamadasha brotherhood, who died in 1722. Sidi Ali ben Hamdouch was strongly
influenced by the teachings of Bu'Abid Sharqui who founded the maraboutic dynasty at
Boujad. The Hamadasha brotherhood use the intoxication of dance and repetitive
rhythmical music to achieve a state of mystical ecstasy when they become insensitive to
cuts and heavy blows. The Moussem is held here seven days after Mouloud although the
more notorious mutilatory aspects of the cult have been outlawed.

Sidi Ali's tomb is covered by a green cupola in the centre of the long shrine building
just above the therapeutic bath and basin of Ayn Kabir. The dank **grotto of Aisha
Qardisha**, a powerful and sinister female spirit, is 100 m east of the shrine. Aisha
Qardisha is widely feared throughout Morocco. She appears at dusk looking dazzlingly
attractive and seduces men on little frequented streets and then leads them away to their
doom. She can be recognized by her cloven hoofs and like all genies is terrified of iron.
The entrance to the grotto is difficult to spot as it is overhung by a large cult fig tree.

The bare footed saint, **Sidi Hazlyan**, is buried in the southeast corner of Beni Rached under the yellow and white minaret. He was the ascetic but uxorious brother of Sidi Ali from whom about half of the village claim descent. There is a third Koubba in the village, a plain white affair that marks the **grave of Sidi Musa**.

Village traditions credit Caid Bel Shaqur with constructing the **Kasbah** wall. The Caid overreached his authority by demanding the first night with every bride and was subsequently flogged to death by the irate men of Beni Rached.

The pretty stone walled village of **El Marhassyine** is 6 km further where a road leads over the hills below Djebel Zerhoun into the back of Moulay Idriss. The village of **Moussaoua** is 4 km beyond the turning and has a conspicuous green pyramid shrine at the centre of the village which covers the **grave of Sidi Ahmed Dghugli**, a disciple of Sidi Ali who founded the allied Dghuglia brotherhood. The tarmac track stops here and a bad dirt track continues for 10 km to the well-preserved **kasbah of Nesrani** perched on a hill which enjoys a spectacular view to the south. An even worse section of track, for walking only, links Nesrani to the P3, the Sidi Kacem to Fez road.

MOULAY IDRISS

Moulay Idriss is the principal and most famous of the Zerhoun settlements. It is a national pilgrimage site for it holds the tomb of Moulay Idriss, the great-grandson of the prophet, and is governed by its own Pasha and holds the residence of the Caid of the whole Djebel Zerhoun region. It is an astonishingly dramatic site. The two distinct quarters of the town, Tasga and Khiber, are piled up, around and between two massive exposed outcrops of volcanic stone. Surrounded by hills whose rough forests alternate with ordered olive groves, the landscape is in harmony with the spiritual atmosphere, for the Djebel Zerhoun is both a centre of orthodoxy and ecstatic cults.

History

The tomb of Moulay Idriss, 'el Akhbar'—the great—is the venerated heart of the town. He fled to Morocco from Arabia to escape the revenge of the Abbasid Caliphs after the defeat of his family at the battle of Fakh in 786. Grandson of Ali and Fatima, the beloved cousin and daughter of the prophet Mohammed, he was of unimpeachable holy ancestry and although in his practice was a strict defender of Sunni orthodoxy, he is considered by many Shiites to be the rightful 6th Caliph.

Accompanied only by his loyal slave Rashid he arrived at Volubilis in 787 to be welcomed by the Auroba tribe as their Imam. The Berber tribes had in thirty years of war just overthrown the rule of Arab governors. That another Arab, a powerless refugee, should be acclaimed as leader demonstrates just how completely the tribes had accepted Islam. Moulay Idriss is seen as the source of religious and political orthodoxy by which successive Sultans have reigned.

All cities strive to have a traditional association with Moulay Idriss and the claims that he founded this village would appear to be contradictory to the foundation of Fez. His rule was however brief for agents working for the Abbasid Caliph, Harun er Rashid of

Baghdad, poisoned Moulay Idriss in 792. Fortunately a Berber concubine preserved the holy dynasty by giving posthumous birth to a son, and the loyal ex-slave Rashid ruled as regent until he too was poisoned by agents in 807. The precocious child, Idriss II, then started to govern aged 15, and at the end of a long reign was buried in Fez.

In a suspicious coincidence both the tombs of Moulay Idriss and Idriss II were rediscovered in the 15th century after centuries of neglect. It was a period when Morocco was threatened by strong external enemies and the new shrines served to create a focus for a politically expedient orthodox nationalist cult. The present town and sanctuary of Moulay Idriss is mostly 18th-century work, for Moulay Ishmael piously and sympathetically restored the shrine and included some of the pillars that he despoiled from Volubilis. The entire town was closed to Jews and Christians until 1912.

GETTING AROUND
From the Bab Mansour at Meknes grands taxis charge 6dh for a place to Moulay Idriss, or it is only 4dh by bus, with more frequent services on Saturday for the **souk**. Moulay Idriss is 24 km north of Meknes, 10 km along the P6 then right on to the P28 for 14 km. There are two small right turns that approach the town, the second takes you to the car park or on beyond the town into the Zerhoun hills. Volubilis is 5 km away off a loop road to the left of the P28.

WHAT TO SEE
Your first experience of the holy town is likely to be of a busy and dusty bus and car park. Above and ahead a line of stalls leads to the triangular wedge of souks that points towards the sanctuary **Mosque of Moulay Idriss**. To the right of the sanctuary stretches the Tasga quarter of the town and the higher Khiber quarter is to the left. The souk stalls are lined with eyebrows of green tiles that contrast well with the high rising white mass of the double village beyond. Curious reed woven plates, rosaries, golden scarves, grilled food, religious trinkets and embroidered cloth are displayed for the pilgrims and as you near the sanctuary masses of coloured nougat and enormous green candles predominate. An unmistakable wooden bar halts non-Muslims from entering the outermost courtyard, whilst within stretches a whole complex of halls, ablution fountains, prayer halls and the holy tomb of Morocco's first legitimate Islamic ruler. Pilgrims are allowed to stay in the courtyards but in summer the chants and collective enthusiasm seldom allow much sleep. To the right of the sanctuary entrance is the royal guesthouse, to the left the offices of the Habous, the ministry that administers religious endowments. Most of the olive groves in the region are annually leased by the Habous to farmers and the rents are used to maintain the shrine, mosque and schools.

Returning back to the bus park follow the single tarmac road up a steep hill, turn right past the Post Office and climb some stone steps past a famous cylindrical minaret encased in blue and white Koranic script built from stone and faience in 1939. Later the path splits under the shadow of a great vine giving an excellent view down onto the glazed roofs and white courts of the secretive mosque sanctuary of Moulay Idriss. Both paths lead down hill from here towards the sanctuary **souk** although the **Medina of Moulay Idriss** is small enough to allow you to wander freely along its erratic climbing alleys, their secrecy interrupted by surprising views, passing lone cafés and a generally friendly populace.

Roman Baths, Ishmaelite bridge and palace

Follow the tarmac road through the town past the Caid's house, the white-walled cypress enclosure on the hill, a right turn swings around to descend to the stream. Just above the river there is a complete, round open air **Roman bath**, the stones worn by use but still connected to a hot sulphurous spring that oozes up through healing mud, particularly efficacious for rheumatism.

Further on, a **bridge** built by Moulay Ishmael spans the river Khouman and on the other side a path climbs up past a few cottages to deteriorate rapidly into a goat track. By scrambling up this slope of rocky undergrowth you can reach an 18th-century ruined **pavilion palace** that has a fine view over the back of the twin rocks and the terraced houses of the Tasga and Khiber quarters.

FESTIVALS
The massive state festival is held in September. Five visits to the festival used to be considered to equal a pilgrimage to Mecca.

WHERE TO STAY AND EAT
Moulay Idriss has fortunately been kept quite free of hotels, but except during the Moussem it can be possible to find families who rent rooms. Try the cedar-lintelled house of Sidi Fridolla, first right at the prohibiting wooden sanctuary bar, first left and knock at the red door of no 24, 30dh a night. Otherwise there is the **campsite Zerhoun** half way to Volubilis. The dogs of the Zerhoun hills do however keep up an almost continuous nocturnal howl.

The **Baraka de Zerhoun** is on the left of the tarmac hill road at 22, Ain Smen-Khiber, tel 44184. It is a delightful newly opened but traditional restaurant that serves bowls of local Zerhoun olives and freshly made butter. An excellent spiced vegetable salad costs 10dh and a tagine 50dh; it is run by two women in white, Benfares Soad and Tahrzouti Amina.

Courtyard of a Roman House, Volubilis

291

VOLUBILIS

The ruined Roman city of Volubilis sits below the escarpment of Djebel Zerhoun. The triumphal arch, basilica and Capitoline temple are the most impressive free-standing monuments around which the rest of the city lies in ruins. A number of houses have been excavated and though few of the walls are higher than waist height a series of mosaic floors have been revealed. An hour's walk will show you everything of interest. It is an exposed, largely shadeless site and the late afternoon is best when the declining sun gives a warmer and less exhausting glow to the stones. If you want to see the mosaics in their true colours bring a bottle of water to splash on the stones.

Volubilis is open from 8.00–18.30, admission 15dh. There is an open air collection of sculpture and inscriptions by the ticket office and a shaded café bar that serves lunch for 40dh.

GETTING AROUND
Moulay Idriss, connected to Meknes by frequent buses, is a 5 km walk from Volubilis, but there is usually no problem in finding a place in a grand taxi for this short run. If you can find four or five other people you might charter a taxi from Meknes for the day and combine a visit to both Moulay Idriss and Volubilis which will cost between 2–300dh.

History

Volubilis, from the evidence of its visible ruins, appears to be an entirely Roman city. During the period from AD 45 to 285 it reached its peak of prosperity as the capital of the province of Mauretania Tingitania, but it had been in existence for centuries before the first Roman proconsul arrived.

Excavations of the tell mound in the city centre hint at a past that extends back to a Neolithic culture and it came under early Phoenician influence as the Temple of Baal/Saturn attests. The city, which covered 15 hectares in the 3rd century BC, had trebled in size by AD 24 when it was used as the western capital by King Juba II of Mauretania.

Juba II had been educated at the court of Emperor Augustus and took as his wife not some native Berber princess but Cleopatra Silene, the daughter of Mark Anthony and Cleopatra. He employed Roman soldiers and administrators so that Volubilis had in all practical matters passed into the Roman sphere of influence long before Claudius's annexation of Mauretania in AD 45. Volubilis was one of the few cities to side with Rome when later that year Aedemeon led a nationalist revolt against the annexation. The revolt was suppressed in a two-year campaign and Volubilis was rewarded by the Emperor Claudius with a ten-year tax holiday and grants of citizenship. Its loyalty proved it to be the natural choice for the capital and a procurator ruled the province of Mauretania Tingitania from Volubilis for the next 250 years. The city was at the centre of a rich agricultural region (traces of over 50 villas have been found in the immediate area) and grew in wealth by exporting corn, olive oil and wild beasts for the Roman games. It was however on the far southeast edge of the province, defended by a ring of five forts, Sidi Said, Bled El Gaada, Sidi Moussa, Tocolosida and Ain Schkor. There was no road east to Algeria and communication was only possible with the rest of the Empire through ports on the Atlantic coast. Immediately to the east of Volubilis, in the area between Fez and Taza, was the territory of the Baquates tribe. The Baquates were alternately allies or enemies but always remained independent. The city walls, strengthened by forty towers, pierced by eight gates and stretching for 2500 m were built during the reign of the Emperor Marcus Aurelius, 161–180. At this peak the city held a population of 20,000 and the bulk of public buildings, houses and mosaics date from this period and especially from the North African Severi dynasty who ruled the Roman Empire from 193 to 235.

Roman rule of Volubilis ended during the reign of the Emperor Diocletian, AD 284–305, who reorganized the Empire into 101 defendable provinces. In Morocco this entailed a withdrawal of the legions to a much smaller province consisting of a block of northern coastal territory around the cities of Tangier, Ceuta, Larache and Tetouan. Volubilis was sacked in the immediate aftermath but excavations of the cemetery to the west of the town bear witness to a continued if drastically reduced urban life. It survived as a heterogeneous trading community and as a place of refuge for Christians and Jews fleeing persecution in the Roman Empire. During the Arab conquest in the 8th century the city, known as Oualila, was a tolerated enclave and was ruled by a council of Christian chiefs.

The ancient city had one last flicker of fame. A refugee from Arabia, the great-grandson of the prophet Mohammed, arrived at Volubilis in 787. Moulay Idriss was acclaimed Sultan here but though Volubilis was still Morocco's chief city he chose to establish his rule away from its traditions of oligarchy and religious pluralism. Volubilis

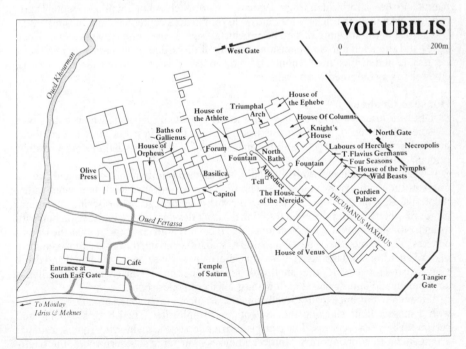

was drained of vitality by the rise of his chosen city of Fez and by the 11th century it had become a magnificent but deserted shell.

The city was only reduced to ruin in the 17th century by Moulay Ishmael's demand for hardcore for the foundations of the Imperial city of Meknes. The Lisbon earthquake of 1755 further shattered Volubilis but not before an English antiquarian, John Windus, had sketched the site in 1722. These drawings were of great use to the team of French archaeologists who started work in 1915, and the digging was greatly assisted by Marshal Lyautey's loan of thousands of German prisoners of war.

The Site

The arch by the ticket office is the old southeast gate of the city. From here a path leads across a largely unexcavated quarter of the city to cross a stream, the Oued Fetassa. Beyond this stream, on the left, squats the first of the many stone **olive presses** and associated storage and separation tanks. The extraction of olive oil was of primary importance to Volubilis as it still is to the villages of Djebel Zerhoun where the techniques have remained unchanged. The olive stones were crushed by a mill stone, then packed in hessian sacks and compressed. The oil was squeezed out then drained into tanks where it was allowed to separate. It was then tapped off from both the heavier oils and watery vegetable refuse, bottled and ready for export. Throughout the city you will find that even the grandest houses have their own olive press. Commerce and manufacture was forbidden to the Roman Senatorial class but anything remotely agricultural, even making bricks, you could do to your heart's content without loosing status. It is refreshing to imagine this grand provincial capital surrounded by piles of crushed olives and the back doors of mansions reeking of discarded black tarry oil. The Oued Fetassa, joined by the Oued Khouman from Moulay Idriss, flowed outside the southern city walls as a combined moat and sewer.

House of Orpheus

A right turn after the oil press takes you to the House of Orpheus, which stands by a conspicuous clump of three cypress trees. This is the largest house of the southern quarter of the city, named like all the mansions of Volubilis after the subject of their principal mosaic.

It is a palatial building firmly divided in the eastern tradition into public and private quarters each with its own entrance. The first, private entrance leads to a room with a dolphin mosaic on the floor. Notice how the diamond lozenges, interlocking circles and airy curls which surround it echo traditional carpet designs. There is also a kitchen with its niche for statuettes and lamps dedicated to the household gods, the genius, the lar and penates. The genius can be best compared to a guardian angel, the lar as a representative of dead ancestors and the penates as twin benevolent spirits who stopped food and drink going off and looked after the sanctity of the family hearth. To the right of the kitchen is an intimate and simply paved bath with its adjacent boiler room.

The second entrance leads directly into the **atrium**, a lavish open air court decorated with a mosaic floor showing the sea goddess Amphitrite pulled by a sea horse and surrounded by sea leopards. The court is surrounded by the main living rooms, a similar arrangement to contemporary Moroccan houses. The large southern room, the **tricli-**

nium (dining room) has a magnificent Orpheus mosaic. The central circular panel shows Orpheus playing his harp, encircled by a ring of trees which like the mammals and birds are seduced by his music—even the sphinx and griffins look tranquil. It is enclosed by a disciplined decorative pattern with two delightful infills that show a pair of mallards feeding from an urn and a pair of Barbary partridges from a bird table. Orpheus amongst other musical triumphs descended to hell in an attempt to rescue his wife Eurydice and, 'so to the music of his strings he sang and all the bloodless spirits wept to hear; . . . And Sisyphus sat rapt upon his stone. Then first by that sad singing overwhelmed, The furies cheeks it's said were wet with tears' (Ovid).

Next door, to the left of the path lie the ruins of the **baths of Gallienus**, an extensive Hammam, notable now for only one section of broken and faded mosaic amongst a series of gaping holes. These public baths were redecorated by order of the Emperor Gallienus, 260–68, which turned them into the most lavish in the whole city. Gallienus is otherwise known for his military reforms. He divided the army between reserve forces and highly trained mounted regiments who could rush to any trouble on the border.

Forum

Passing the ruined Forum baths on the right the path climbs a step to enter into the public square of the city, the forum. To the left of this stood the **Macellum**, a small butcher's souk which archaeologists have discovered was built over a number of ancient temples. To the right of the forum towers the long wall of the **Basilica**, the court house. This would have had two double rows of columns running down its interior length linking two opposing apses. It must have been a ponderous heavy grey building eminently suited for legal proceedings and was completed in the early third century. In front of the basilica are various plinths that commemorate officials, generals and emperors. Perhaps the most interesting inscription is the monument to the North African Severi dynasty, who considered Marcus Valerius Severus an ancestor. He was the chief magistrate of Volubilis when the city sided with Rome against Aedemeon in AD 45 and known to be a native for his father had the Berber name of Bostar.

The Capitol

The raised Capitol with its elegant Corinthian columns stands to the right of the basilica. Now very obvious, it would have been less so when the area was enclosed by a columned arcade. Within this enclosed court an altar can be seen from which thirteen steps advance up to the **Capitoline temple**. This, like the ancient temple on the Quirinal hill at Rome, was dedicated to the trinity of gods, to Jupiter Optimus Maximus, Juno and Minerva. There were two classes of Roman gods, those who protected the state and those who protected the family. The Capitoline triad were the chief divinities of the state. A council would assemble below the Capitol to declare war, generals appeared before setting out to battle and after victory returned to offer crowns of gold and booty. Juno and Minerva, like the Virgin Mary, were appealed to on all manner of occasions but in their Capitoline role watched over the health and population of the whole province.

The temple was dedicated to the Emperor Macrinus in 217, who reigned for a year between Caracalla and his flamboyant nephew the Syrian priest Helagabulus. At sunset the view through these pillars east to Moulay Idriss is triumphantly photogenic. This would have been the usual orientation for a temple, but instead it stares mysteriously at the back of the Basilica.

Returning to cross the forum the path passes to the left of the **House of the Athlete**, labelled 'Maison du Desultor', which contains a crude mosaic of a sportsman who has won a cup for vaulting over a grey horse. Beyond this stand the ruins of some fashionable shops and opposite, on the right, is one of two public fountains that surround the ruins of the city's third and largest public bath which covered an area of 1500 square metres. This, the **north bath**, and the fountains were probably built on the orders of the Emperor Hadrian and fed by an aqueduct that channelled fresh spring water from the Zerhoun hills.

Triumphal Arch

The path now leads across the principal avenue to the magnificent Triumphal Arch, raised in 217 by the governor Marcus Aurelius Sebastenus to the honour of the Emperor Caracalla and his mother Julia Domna, whose defaced medallion bust can be seen on the right. Julia Domna accompanied her husband Severus on his campaign in Britain, 208–11, where she became known as the 'mother of the camp'. She later helped her son Caracalla murder his co-Emperor Geta in 212 but as a North African family who had given Roman citizenship to all provincials this odd couple may have enjoyed genuine popularity in Volubilis. However by the time the Arch was finished they had both been murdered. The Arch remains an impressive monument built from local Zerhoun stone and with little evidence of the reconstruction by French archaeologists in 1933. In 217 it was capped with a bronze six-horse chariot and nymphs that cascaded water into carved marble bowls below. It carried an inscription which thanked the province for this symbol of loyalty and remitted all outstanding debts to the Imperial exchequer though there was a broad hint that the Emperor would be happy to accept a free gift of soldiers and elephants.

From the Arch you look down the broad **Decomanus Maximus avenue** towards the Tangier gate. This central street was faced with a columned arcade which would have been lined by small shops and artisan stalls. Tucked discreetly behind this screen were the large residences of the officials, landlords and merchants.

The **House of the Ephebe**, named after the fine bronze head found here, is immediately north of the Arch. It has an impressive interior courtyard with a central pool around which public rooms ornamented with mosaics are arranged. The most elegant of them, on your right, has Bacchus being drawn in his chariot by leopards and there is also a Nereid riding a sea creature. The private quarters behind the atrium are arranged around their own pool. An old mausoleum had been incorporated into the domestic offices, perhaps for use as a cellar, and even in this opulent mansion you find the ubiquitous olive press.

On the left, walking west, is the **House of Columns** which sports a circular pool in the atrium, beds of geraniums and a famous spiral fluted column which was carved in the early 3rd century.

Next door, the **Knight's House** has a mosaic of a lascivious Bacchus aided by Eros discovering Ariadne, neglected by Theseus asleep on the shore at Naxos. The figures are crude but the god's prurient eyes are alive and the flesh glistens with colour. Ariadne bore Bacchus six children and her bridal chaplet was placed in the stars, the Corona Borealis or Cretan Crown.

House of the Labour of Hercules

Next along, staying on the left of the road, is the House of the Labours of Hercules, named after the crude mosaic found in the dining room. Here in oval frames are strip cartoon images from the life of Hercules; as a child strangling snakes, the capture of Cerberus, the Cretan Bull, cleaning the Augean stable, the Stymphalian birds, wrestling with Antaeus, the Erymanthian boar, the Lernean hydra, Hippolyte's girdle, erecting the twin pillars of Hercules and slaying the Nemean lion. It is thought that the mosaic might have been made during the reign of the Emperor Commodus who had a Hercules obsession, but he was always a popular deity in Morocco, due to his association with the Phoenician Melkarth and the number of his achievements that occurred in Morocco. Another room has Jupiter and his boyfriend Ganymede in the centre and the four seasons in the corners. There are the usual private quarters behind with a back rest bath and frescoed panels painted to imitate marble. It has a number of arches in the front which were rented out to provide space for eight shops, though you enter from a side street that was guarded by a porter's lodge.

Beyond the House of the Labours of Hercules is a row of five smaller houses. The first held an inscription that has identified it as the **house of T. Flavius Germanus**, the second holds a well preserved and amusing mosaic of the four seasons. The third, marked by one crude pillar, is known as the **House of the Bath of Nymphs** after a mosaic which shows three nymphs undressing and dancing beside the Hippocrene spring which is overlooked by Pegasus, an ancient cult tree and a horned wild man—presumably Acteon. Directly behind this house is the north gate which opens out into the extensive western cemetery whilst opposite, across the street, is the **House of the Nereids** whose poolside mosaic is worth a quick look. The fourth house has a disturbing mosaic of four wild beasts; a bull-baiting scene, a lion, a lioness and a leopard eating heads. The fifth house in ruin with no mosaics, brings you to the Gordian Palace.

The Gordian Palace

With its imposing exterior of a dozen Ionic columns, this is believed to have been the governor's residence which was rebuilt during the reign of Gordian III, 238–44. It was made by combining two houses and once, amongst these impassive pooled interior courtyards, bath houses and 74 rooms would have bustled busy secretaries and confidential agents. Inscriptions found in the palace record a series of agreements between the Roman governor and the chief of the Baquates tribe. The frequency of new treaties at the end of the 3rd century suggests a troubled frontier. The last pact made just a few years before Diocletian's withdrawal refers somewhat ironically to a 'Foederata et ducturna pax', a federated and lasting peace. Though strong in atmosphere, the decoration of the palace is restricted to a few columns and some simple geometrical mosaics.

The House of Venus

After the Gordian palace head for a single cypress tree, to the east of the Decumanus Maximus, which was planted in the House of Venus. This house, renowned for its series of mosaics, was also where the superb bronze busts of Juba II and Cato, now in the Rabat museum, were discovered, buried in a protective bed of sand.

Descend into the house past two small halls to arrive in the central courtyard where an 'I' shaped pool is decorated with a damaged mosaic of a series of racing chariots drawn by rival teams of peacocks, geese and duck which include accurate period details of a hippodrome. The large dining room straight ahead used to house the mosaic of the navigation of Venus which is now displayed in the Tangier museum. To the left of this room is a damaged portrait mosaic of Bacchus and the four seasons framed in eight pointed stars. To the right is the celebrated mosaic of the naked Hylos captured by two nymphs, a colourful composition dominated by rippling muscles and erotic curves whilst the two side panels show scenes of guilty Erotes being chastised. Hylos was an Argonaut who joined Jason's crew as the darling squire of Hercules. He went ashore but was seized by two nymphs, Dryope and Pegae, who dragged him away to live with them in an underwater grotto.

The next door mosaic shows chaste Diana with a nymph surprised by Acteon at her bath, her bow hanging from the branches of a cult tree. Acteon is already sprouting horns, for the goddess, in revenge for being surprised, changed him into a stag and he was then chased and devoured by his own hounds.

Returning back to the Forum you get a brief look at pre Roman Volubilis as you pass the tell, an ancient mound composed of fragments of past temples and burial chambers. Across the Oued Fetassa are the foundations of the **Temple of 'Saturn'**, where over 600 stone carved votive offerings have been discovered. It was established centuries before the Roman period as the Phoenician temple of Baal, a semitic horned male deity of the mountains and streams, whose rites and worship continued unchanged under the Roman label of Saturn.

Out from Meknes

North from Meknes

The road and railway follow the same unstimulating route north to Souk el Arba du Gharb. Sidi Kacem, 45 km from Meknes, is approached through a mud gorge cut by the Oued Rdom. In the gorge is the green tiled pyramidal koubba of Sidi Kacem which draws an enormous local moussem each October. The town sprawls beyond, dominated at night by the flickering flames of the refinery tower. From the shanty towns of Sidi Kacem an army of labourers tramps out before dawn to work on the surrounding farming estates, for to the north stretches the wide and fertile Sebou valley. At the crossing of the Oued Sebou is the rural market town of **Mechra bel Ksiri** which has **souks** on Monday and Thursday, and a moussem is held in September by the Koubba of Sidi Kacem Harrocha. 14 km beyond is **Souk el Arba du Gharb** whose hotels and bus connections to Ouezzane and the beach of Moulay Bousselham are listed on page 192.

West of Meknes; the Vallée Heureuse and Dayat er Roumi

The dilapidated Vallée Heureuse gardens are 11 km west of Meknes just off the P1, the main road to Rabat–Salé. They were created by the French prison governor Bagnon as therapy for his inmates. Just before the turning to Sidi Slimane there is an unmistakable stone- and shell-decorated archway through which a dirt track leads to a number of overgrown but ornate car spaces. Ornamental steps lead through a profusion of crumbling decorated basins, pools, flower beds and fountains encrusted with porphyry, marble and red granite. In their working heyday it must have been excessive but now, in partial ruin and covered in cascades of wild roses, brambles, broken palms and wild figs against a background of olives, it has a Fragonard sumptuousness. The natural waterfall flowing over limestone stalagmites contrasts with the wreck of the stone boat island, the Jardin Lyautey, the dead bower and the ruins of a boating pond which you pass as you regain the main road. In the summer a café operates on the terrace from a shack obscured by foliage, whilst the valley is overlooked by the huts of the rural poor.

From the Heureuse gardens there is a pleasant journey through 100 km of farmland, cork and holm oak woods of the **Forest of Mamora**. **Khemisset**, just over halfway, is an uninspiring modern town which has an empty church, an artisanal ensemble where you can buy wood carvings and a **souk** on Tuesday.

15 km south of the town along the S106 is a freshwater lake surrounded by gentle hills. This, the **Dayat er Roumi**, makes a convenient break in the journey and you can fish, swim or picnic by the shore or eat at a restaurant that opens during the summer months. On Friday a **souk** is held by the **Koubba of Sidi Bettache**, 9 km on the road to Maaziz, or you can take a right turn and cut across to the S209 for the Thursday **souk** held at **Khemis de Sidi Yahya**. You would then pass the iron mines of Medinette on the left before rejoining the main road just before Tifflet. **Tifflet** has a **souk** on Wednesday but the village's distinctive pompom hats are held out on poles on all days and hours for the admiration of the passing traffic. From Tifflet it is 26 km to Sidi Allai Bahraui and then 30 km to Salé on the Atlantic coast.

South of Meknes; Kasbah Agourai

The Kasbah of Agourai is 35 km south of Meknes along the obscure but tarmaced route 3065, a pleasant interlude from the city or taken in on the way south to Azrou. This beautiful rectangular kasbah was built by Moulay Ishmael in the early 18th century. It has five towers on each face and the packed pise walls have mellowed into a range of pink and ochre colours. Two small cannons protect the entrance and storks roost on the walls. The kasbah is packed full of low white houses, a conglomeration touched with shades of green and blue within which you find a gently ageing mosque with a faience fountain flowing outside. Water cascades throughout the kasbah from standing pipes and below the outer walls a washing souk has established itself on the lower slope.

A new village has arisen around the kasbah. It has a **souk** on Thursday, a hammam with separate baths for men and women and the **Café El Gazail** on the northern edge of the village on the road to Meknes serves good coffee and light meals. Above the village the graveyard is dominated by the **koubba** that covers the grave of Sidi Said L'Hakusi.

Southeast of Meknes; El Hajeb and the Balcony of Ito

The P21 road runs southeast to Azrou, an attractive journey of 63 km. The roadside village of **Boufekran** is just 17 km out from Meknes but its row of cafés along the dusty central street is a favourite stop for drivers looking for a cheap meal or coffee. Behind the modern village there are the ruins of an 18th-century Kasbah.

El Hajeb, 12 km further south, has more substantial remains. Perched on a terrace of limestone, it is in a typical position for a Berber market on neutral ground between the pastoral land of the nomadic Beni Mtir tribe to the south and the farmed land of the Sais plain. The **souk** is still held every Monday.

The walls of a large kasbah restored by Sultan Moulay Hassan in the 19th century still stand proud beside the road. On the Sultan's death the caid of the Berber Beni M'Tir tribe, Hammou el Hassan, occupied the kasbah. Though chief of under 2000 families he played an active if malicious role in the turbulent political life of Morocco. He encouraged the ill-fated Moulay Cherif El Kittani to claim the throne in 1909 but his candidate was whipped to death on the orders of Sultan Moulay Hafid. Not the least bit discouraged, he fielded two separate candidates in May 1911; these also died horribly but the caid survived to make his submission to the French in 1913.

Cafés cluster around the municipal garden and there is a **campsite** by the road, a pleasant place from which to explore the limestone escarpments to the east and west which conceal a number of caves, rock pools and springs.

The Balcony of Ito is 17 km before Azrou. This is a natural terrace, a cliff escarpment beside the road at 1500 m which has a wonderful panorama over a massive depression full of the eroded stacks of ancient volcanoes through which the Oued Tigrira flows. It is marked on maps as either the **Balcon D'Ito** or the **Belvedere Tigrira**.

Between Meknes and Fez

The 60 km of farmland that stretches between Meknes and Fez can be crossed by any of the frequent buses, trains or grands taxis and takes less than an hour to drive.

El Ghor

It is something of a quest to find this impressive and ancient funerary monument in the middle of the densely farmed plain of Sais. Take the 3110 out of Meknes and turn left on to the 3109. On your right just before a metal hand-railed bridge, a track from the road leads to a circular mound retained by two complete circular bands of well-dressed stone that commemorates some Berber king from the 7th century AD. Its construction suggests use of Roman measurements, and there used to be an altar on the east that was lit up by the first light of the dawn. It is an evocative, mysterious site associated with sun worship where I disturbed two courting farm boys who sped off into the distance on their bicycles.

Ras el Ma

13 km before Fez, on the P1, a right turn on to route 4006 leads 6 km south to Ras el Ma, 'the head of water', one of the springs that feed the Oued Fez. It has always been a venerated site, a koubba and cave can be seen near the spring and Moulay Idriss traditionally received his inspiration to found Fez whilst resting here. A **kasbah** was built here as a base around which tribal cavalry in the service of the Sultan could gather, a convenient distance from the city, which was always something of a temptation to an army held together by the hope of plunder. This kasbah was restored in 1970 and is lived in by a member of the royal family.

Moulay Yacoub

At the Ras el Ma crossroads, or from two other left turns just out of Fez, you can join the route S308 that climbs through 15 km of a gentle down-like landscape to the spa of Moulay Yacoub. This is well served by local buses and grands taxis from Fez.

It is a pleasant holiday resort much loved by Moroccan families who can all indulge in a little quiet hypochondria. Moulay Yacoub is built on terraces above a hot sulphurous spring which fills a series of natural hammams and enclosed pools. In the past it enjoyed a reputation as both a haunt of prostitutes and a cure for venereal disease, although now the waters modestly only cure 'renal and urinary' diseases.

Admission to the warm sulphurous pool costs 2dh or its 7dh for the hammam with separate enclosures for men and women. Swimming trunks are worn in the baths, and souk stalls sell a selection of these as well as soap, beads, towels and candles. You can eat at a number of grill cafés or at the **Restaurant Marhaba** just above the baths. Opposite the village is the rounded hill of **Lalla Chafer** which has a few pine trees growing on its slope. Walking up the hill to the café on the summit is part of the cure. Lower down the valley a new 'scientific' thermal station is being built. Several new sources of hot mineral water have recently been discovered; the last bore sent a bubbling steaming stream cascading down the central steps to everyone's delight and satisfaction.

WHERE TO STAY
There are a number of pensions in the village which has become a favoured sketching ground for Maghrebi artists. Of these the **De la Paix**, the **Grand Hôtel** and next door to it the **Moderne** charge 40dh for a comfortable room. The best is the **Hôtel Lamrani**, tel 122, which overlooks the old working pool and the soon to be opened 'scientific' pool. Large comfortable rooms here cost 50dh.

A summary of rural souks around Meknes
On Monday there is a **souk** at **El Hajeb** or you could travel 64 km the next day to attend **Azrou's souk** on Tuesday though there are smaller ones closer to hand at **M'haya** and **Abouderbala**. On Wednesday **Meknes** holds its souk. On Thursday there is one at **Ain Taoujdate** (30 km east towards Fez and a right turn on to the S310(a) and at **Agourai**. Saturday souks are held at **Moulay Idriss** and **Sebt Jahjouh** (30 km southeast of Meknes on the S223). Sunday souks at **Ain el Jemaa** (35 km northwest along the P4 to Sidi Simane) and at **Sebaa Aioun** (20 km east along the P1 and a right turn on to the S321).

FEZ

'Fez where all is Eden, or a wilderness.'

Fez is the most complete Islamic medieval city in the world. Its history has for a thousand years been the history of Morocco's political, commercial and intellectual life. It is now superseded by the modern cities of Rabat and Casablanca, and to an extent by its own New Town built by the French after 1912.

Much has perished in the long decline from the golden period of Fez under the Merenid Sultans in the 13th and 14th centuries. Chiefly the old mosques, tombs and colleges have survived, respected by each dynasty, every mutinous regiment and pillaging tribe. The medersas are open to non-Muslims but the rest of the vast heritage of religious architecture remains inaccessible. Visitors are left to concentrate on the street pattern, the style of life, the sounds and odours which remain triumphantly unchanged.

The city of half a million is divided into three. Fez el Bali, Fez the old, is the enigmatic and fiercely Muslim medina, a maze of reclusive quarters, fondouqs, medersas and mosques whose narrow streets remain inaccessible to cars. Fez el Jedid, New Fez, is the 13th century Imperial city to the west of the Medina which is still dominated by the royal palace. The French-built New Town is even further to the west, a separate entity with wide avenues and new developments which would be without interest but for its cafés, hotels, restaurants and convenience.

History

Fez was founded in the 9th century as the capital of the Idrissid state, the first Muslim Kingdom of Morocco. A century later the Idrissid dynasty had declined but the city they had established survived. It grew in wealth and remained the acknowledged religious and cultural centre of Morocco, though new administrative capitals were established at Marrakesh and then Rabat. Its golden period of wealth, fame and prosperity was in the 13th and 14th centuries under the Merenid Sultans.

Foundation Legends

As the oldest Imperial city and the centre of religious learning, Fez required a set of foundation myths to set it apart as the destined centre of Morocco.

According to most theories the founder of the Idrissid kingdom was Moulay Idriss, the great-grandson of the prophet Mohammed. He first established his kingdom on two existing cities, Christian Volubilis and Jewish Sefrou. He determined to create a specifically Muslim city and one day whilst travelling between Sefrou and Volubilis he rested half way, at the Ras el Ma spring. He followed it downstream to discover a wide, well watered valley fringed by hills. Encouraged by his first instincts and the prophetic welcome of an aged holy man he established a settlement on the right bank of the river that year, in 799. During the excavation of the foundation walls a golden axe, a 'fas' was unearthed or according to another legend a group of Persian exiles, or Fars, were buried alive. From either the axe or the Persians the new foundation received its name, and a citizen of Fez is known as a Fassi.

Idrissid Fez

Moulay Idriss lived for only another five years before he was poisoned by the Caliph of Baghdad and without his holy presence the settlement dwindled. His son, Idriss II, found it easier to establish a new circuit of walls on the opposite, the left, bank where he built his el Aliya palace and barracks for his 500-strong Arab guard.

It formed a bare nucleus of a city but the turbulent politics of the more prosperous Muslim states in Spain and Tunisia soon provided a flood of refugees to fill Fez. In 818 a civil war drove 8000 Arabs from Andalucia, and they were welcomed by Idriss II and given the right bank of Fez to colonize. A few years later, in 825, another tide of refugees, fleeing from a revolution in the holy city of Kairouan, arrived at Fez and settled around the el Aliya palace. For the next 250 years this settlement pattern remained. Fes el

Andalous and Fes el Karaouyine were two quite distinct cities, enclosed within their own circuit of walls, facing each other across the river bed. The Andalucians had the prettiest women whilst the men were considered strong, brave and good at cultivating the soil. The Kairouan men were considered more elegant, better educated and given to more luxurious living. What they both shared was a strong Arab identity and an urban, Muslim, technical and intellectual culture far in advance of any mere Berber tribe.

The government of Idriss II was firmly based on the Arab and orthodox population of Fez. His administration and army were staffed by Arab refugees, the latter chiefly employed in conquering and converting distant Berber tribes. Idriss II died in 828 after a long and successful reign and his tomb became the focus of the city's pride and identity.

His inheritance was divided amongst a number of warring sons but the ruler of Fez was accepted as the overlord. During his grandson Yahya's reign the two great Mosques of Qaraouyine and Andalous were founded, providing graphic evidence of the prosperity and confidence of the city.

By 917 the Idrissid principalities had become so weak and divided that the Fatimid Empire was able to appoint a governor over Yahya IV, the last Idrissid ruler of Fez. Fatimid suzerainty was replaced in 930 by the Ommayad Caliphate of Cordoba, which dominated the city for a century but after 1031 the two cities of Fez were left without a civilized protecting power. The predominately Arabic population then suffered heavily from the wars of the surrounding Berber tribes. Trade routes were severed and the city, reduced by years of famine, was in danger of disintegrating. Aid was to come from the unlikely source of a recently converted Berber tribe from the Sahara.

Almoravide Fez
For in 1075 the Almoravide leader Youssef ben Tachfine captured Fez. The Fassis could not at first accept the rule of these unsophisticated Berbers from the Sahara, and though the city initially rebelled against its loss of freedom it soon benefited from the firm rule of the Almoravide Empire. It was better suited than Marrakesh to act as the mercantile hub for the extensive Empire which stretched from Spain to West Africa. The Almoravides dismantled the divisive twin walls and erected a single circuit that protected both quarters. The endless neighbouring feuds over water rights ended, for the Almoravides were from the desert and knew all about the efficient collection and distribution of water. Clean mountain springs were tapped and a network of pipes, sewers and mills prepared the ground for the future expansion of the city.

Almohad Fez
After seventy years of Almoravide rule the Fassis presented a united front against the Almohad army that besieged the city from its base at Taza. In 1146 the Almohad commander, Abdel Moumen, at last captured Fez. He built a dam upstream, collected a great head of water which he suddenly released and the resulting flood washed the lower walls clean away. The Almohads then marched into the defenceless city and demolished the remaining outer walls declaring that 'only justice and the sword shall be our ramparts'. They also obscured or demolished any traces of Almoravide rule, on the flimsy basis that the decoration of the previous dynasty had been impious.

Aside from these initial assertions of sovereignty, Fez prospered under Almohad rule and continued its rapid growth and expansion, though Marrakesh, Seville and Rabat were the administrative and military capitals of the Almohad Empire. Later Almohad Sultans ignored the early revolutionary declarations and constructed a massive new perimeter wall. This defined the extent of Fez el Bali and large sections, particularly to the north, are still in place.

Merenid Fez

Abou Yahya, the Emir of the Beni Merin tribe and first Merenid Sultan, captured Fez in 1248. So central had the city now become that this date has been taken by many historians to be the start of his reign and of the Merenid dynasty.

Though Merenid rule was to prove the golden period of Fez, the Fassis never took to the Merenid dynasty, who were mere Berber chiefs of a nomad tribe from the eastern plains. Despite the glittering succession of new buildings commissioned by the Merenids, the city frequently rebelled against its new rulers. No dynasty can win the loyalty of Fez, which seems to be forever attached to the Idrissid line, from whom many of the leading Fassi families claim descent. However the centuries of Merenid rule, from 1248 to 1465, were the peak of the city's power, wealth and renown, against which the present city is but a shadow.

Yusuf, the second Merenid Sultan, reigned from 1258 to 1286 and firmly established Fez as the capital of Morocco. On 21 March 1276 he started work on Fez el Jedid, 'New Fez', enclosed in a double wall 750 m from the turbulent politics of Fez el Bali. Known officially as El Medinat el Baida, the 'white city', a portion of the Oued Fes served as a moat for its outer walls, which were crowned with merlons and reinforced by square towers. The white city held the court and palace of the Sultans, the mint, baths, markets, three mosques—the Great, the Red and the Flower—an aqueduct and separate quarters for the Sultan's Mercenary Guard. Sultan Yusuf was the first Moroccan ruler to build a medersa, a residential college for religious education, which he built in the Medina. It was an archetype which his successors developed and embellished into one of the great glories of Fez.

In 1438 the barracks were enlarged and converted into the first separate Jewish quarter in Morocco. Wealthy Jewish merchants had always been convenient targets in any urban unrest and by placing them within the protection of the royal city, the Merenids bound this community, useful for its taxable wealth and various skills, to their service. One of the more disagreeable services was the preservation of the heads of the executed, in salt, before they were displayed on gates. The word for salt, 'Mellah', soon became synonymous with a Jewish quarter.

The Golden Age of Fez

During Merenid rule it was Fez el Jedid that functioned as the capital city. The Medina, Fez el Bali, was a privileged community with its own forms of administration which provided an ordered continuity, and was removed from the intrigue of the court and arbitrary rule in the provinces. Under these conditions it flowered.

At the beginning of the 14th century Fez el Bali had a population of 125,000. None of the houses were permitted to touch the city walls, which were lined with gardens and cemeteries and pierced by eight gates. Within the Medina there were 785 mosques, 372 flour mills, 135 bakers' ovens, 93 public baths, 467 fondouqs and 80 fountains. Outside the walls potteries, oil mills, sawmills, weavers, tanneries and smiths collected in three industrial zones, the Bab Guisa, Bab Ftouh and along the river banks.

The Medina was divided into 18 quarters which each had a headman agreed upon by the chief residents. The Cadi, a magistrate learned in Koranic law, judged civil cases with a deputy who specialized in marriage and divorce cases. There were 35 secretaries and accountants on the Cadi's staff helping to supervise the financing of pious foundations, hospitals and baths. The Cadi also acted as rector of the university and censor of intellectual life. The various medersas lodged 2000 students in Fez whilst they pursued their studies in the University of Qaraouyine. Lectures were given in the great mosques after the morning prayers, the university library was housed behind the mihrab of the Qaraouyine Mosque and the courts of the various medersa or the houses of professors were used for smaller teaching groups.

There was a hospital for the sick without family and a leprosarium outside the ramparts housed lepers in isolation. The Muhtasib, 'the prefect of manners', kept surveillance over the baths, the honesty of exchanges, weights, measures and organized a weekly inspection of prostitutes by physicians.

There were 150 trade corporations each under the protection of a patron saint, like Sidi Mohammed Ibn Attab for the shoe makers and Sidi Mimum for the potters. The most powerful corporation were the semi-official water and drainage technicians. They and the water jurists alone understood the labyrinthine pipe system that was everywhere acknowledged to be the chief wonder of Fez. It filled fountains, public baths and mosque pools, drove 400 mills and then, 'the river doth disperse itself into manifold channels insinuating itself unto every street and member thereof to pass through countless conduits into sinks and gutters.' Numerically the corporation of weavers was dominant, 500 ateliers employed almost 20,000 workers. But the leather trade won in complexity, three corporations ran four tanneries with separate guilds for each variety of animal hide, for the dehairers, millers of dyes, harness makers, saddle bag makers etc. Muslims served as smiths but superstitiously refused to mix metals, and so damescening, making lanterns and jewelry became a Jewish monopoly. The 300 porters who were licensed to carry goods into the city all came from a tribe in the high valley of the Guir and held their wages in common.

Above the urban hierarchy the Sultan appointed a Pasha as governor of the city. He held enormous power and directly ran the police, criminal trials and ordered executions. The Pasha occupied the Almohad fortress close to Fez el Jedid at the western end of the Medina and supervised the state prison in the towers of the Gate of the Lion.

The Decline of Fez

In 1465, the last Merenid Sultan, Abdul Haqq, was dragged through the streets of Fez el Bali and executed at the start of a revolution. A council of Idrissid Shorfa had planned the insurrection and succeeded in ruling a republic for seven years, but this experiment in democracy was finished by the hereditary viziers of the Merenids, the Wattasids, who marched into Fez at the head of an army. Wattasid authority over the next century was slowly reduced to Fez itself as the Portuguese seized the coast and maraboutic tribal dynasties fought over the rest. An earthquake shattered the town in 1522 and the Saadians occupied Fez 19 years later. The Saadian Sultan Abdel Malik ruled from Fez for two years, from 1576 to 1578 but all other members of the dynasty made no secret of their preference for Marrakesh. Looted by rival armies throughout the succession wars of the 17th century, Fez welcomed the first Alouite Sultan, Moulay Rachid, as a liberator in 1666 and the new Sultan celebrated his authority by building a Medersa.

His brother, Moulay Ishmael, detested the city and appointed a succession of cruel and avaricious governors throughout his long reign, from 1672 to 1727. Though the population declined during this period of victimization, this was a light load compared to the thirty years of anarchy that were to follow. Despite valiant efforts it was not until the reign of Sultan Moulay Hassan, 1873–1894, that decay was checked. He built three administrative palaces that physically and symbolically united Fez el Jedid and Fez el Bali, and it is indicative that most of the substantial Fassi merchant houses date from his reign.

The grip of the European powers strengthened after his death and on 30 March 1912 Sultan Moulay Hafid was forced by the French to sign the Treaty of Fez. The city reacted violently to the surrender of national sovereignty and on 17 April the European population were hounded through the Medina streets, lynched and over 80 mutilated bodies were stacked up before the palace gates. The Sultan's army joined the rebellion and manned the city walls but the following day a French force marched from Meknes and first shelled and then occupied the subdued city.

Sultan Moulay Hafid was removed to Rabat where the government of Morocco has since remained, and Casablanca is now the unrivalled mercantile metropolis. The French built an ordered New Town of regular avenues well to the west of the old city to house the European population in comfort and safety. Fez el Bali is a unique medieval survivor, fallen far from grace but remaining one of the most distinctive cities of the world.

GETTING AROUND

By Air
The Fez–Sais airport is 11 km due south off the P24 road to Immouzer, tel 24712/24799. 2 hr flights to Paris on Air France/RAM and a 12 hr flight to Montreal by RAM. Internal flights to Casablanca, 205dh, Marrakesh, 340dh, Agadir, 500dh, and Oujda, Rabat, Er Rachidia and Tangier. Air France and Royal Air Maroc have a joint office at 54, Av. Hassan II, tel 25516. The airport bus, no 16, leaves from Place Mohammed V or pay 5dh for a place in a grand taxi.

By Train
The main station is on Av. des Almohades in the new town, tel 25001. 8 trains a day to Rabat and Casablanca, 66dh and 47dh and change at Casablanca Gare des Voyageurs for Marrakesh. 4 east a day, via Taza, to Oujda for 60dh and 3 north to Tangier. A taxi ride to the Medina gate, Bab Boujeloud, should be 5dh from the station.

By Bus
The two main bus stations in Fez, from the many, are the CTM depot in the new town on Blvd Mohammed V, tel 22041 and the Bab Boujeloud, tel 33529. There are 7 buses a day to Rabat and Casablanca, 36 and 53dh, 2 for Marrakesh, 54dh, 4 for Meknes, 10dh and daily buses to Tangier, 47dh, Tetouan, 42dh and Ouezzane, 30dh. Travelling east

to Taza and Oujda the Bab Ftouh, to the southeast of the medina, has more frequent services.

By local bus

The no 1 runs between Place des Alouites and Dar Batha, no 3 between Place des Alouites and Place de la Resistance, no 9 from Place de la Resistance to Dar Batha, no 10 Bab Guissa to Place des Alouites, no 18 Place de la Resistance east via Bab Jdid and on to Bab Ftouh, no 19 from the train station to the Place de Alouites.

By Taxis

Fez petits taxis use their meters and therefore appear delightfully cheap. Av. Hassan II, Place Mohammed V, the train station and Rue Normandes, off Blvd Mohammed V (for southern destinations) have grands taxis in the new town. Taxi fares increase by a half after dusk or 21.00 whichever is earliest.

By Car

Car hire offices: Avis is at 23 Rue de la Liberté, tel 20667 and have an airport desk, tel 26746; Goldcar, 2 Blvd Mohammed V, tel 20495; Hertz at the Hotel de Fez, Av. des FAR, tel 22812; Maroccar, 53, Rue Compardon, tel 25376; Transcar, 21 Rue Eduard Escalier, tel 21776; Tourist cars in the Grand Hotel, Blvd Mohammed V; Popular car, 138, Blvd Mohammed V, tel 23898; Zeit, 35 Av. Slaoui, tel 23681.

Garages: there is a Renault garage on Rue D'Espagne, tel 22232, a Fiat, the Auto Maroc on Blvd Mohammed V, tel 23435 or the Mechanique Generale on 22, Av. Cameroun.

GETTING AROUND THE CITY

You will not need to rent a car while you are exploring the city as there are good bus services and plenty of reliable taxis. The broad garden Av. Hassan II bisects the new town and leads at its eastern end to the Place de la Resistance one km from the principal square of Fez el Jedid, the Place de Alouites. At the other, the eastern, side of Fez el Jedid the Place Baghdadi, Boujeloud square and Dar Batha museum border Fez el Bali. The Boujeloud arch is the usual entrance into Fez el Bali but the Bab Jdid (to the south), Bab Ftouh (to the east) and Bab Guissa (to the north) are served by taxis and local buses.

TOURIST INFORMATION

The Tourist Offices are in the New Town, on Place de la Resistance at the end of Av. Hassan II, tel 23460 and the Syndicat d'Initiative is found at Place Mohammed V, tel 24769 for leaflets, maps, hotel information and guides.

Banks are mostly found in the New Town, the BMCE on Place Mohammed V, BMCI on Place de Florence, Banque Populaire and Credit du Maroc on Blvd Mohammed V and SGMB on Av. d'Espagne. In the Medina there is a branch of Credit du Maroc uphill from the Cherratin Medersa.

The Post Office is in the New Town at the corner of Av. Hassan II and Blvd Mohammed V. Open Mon–Friday in summer from 8.00–14.00, winter 8.30–12.00, 14.30–18.00, stamps sold on Saturdays from 8.00–11.00. Branches at Place d'Atlas and Place Batha in Fez el Jedid. The Central Police station is on Av. Mohammed V, tel 19.

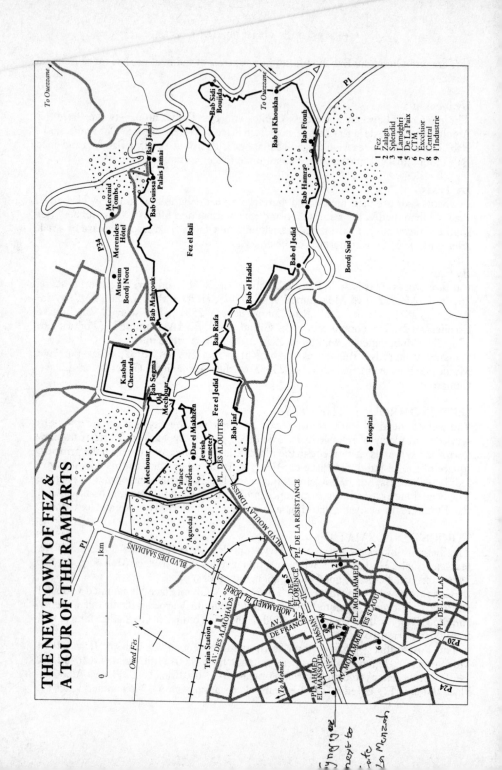

THE NEW TOWN OF FEZ &
A TOUR OF THE RAMPARTS

0   1km

Oued Fès

N

To Ouezzane

P34

P1

To Ouezzane

P1

Merenid Tombs
Merenides Hôtel
Museum Bordj Nord

Bab Jamaï
Palais Jamaï
Bab Guissa

Bab Sidi Boujida

Bab el Khoukha
Bab Ftouh

Bab Hamra
Bab el Jedid

Bordj Sud

Fez el Bali

Bab Mahrouk

Bab el Bali

Kasbah Cherarda
Bab Segma
Old Mechouar

Bab Riafa

Bab el Hadid

Mechouar

Fez el Jedid

Dar el Makhzen
Palace Gardens
Jewish Cemetery
Bab Jiaf

PL. DES ALOUITES

Aguedal

PL. DE LA RÉSISTANCE

Hospital

BLVD MOULAY IDRISS

BLVD DES SAADIANS

Train Station

AV. DES ALMOHADS

To Meknes

PL. AHMED EL MANSOUR

AV. DE FRANCE

AV. MOHAMMED EL DORRI

PL. DE FLORENCE

5

2

9 4 7 8
AV. HASSAN II
AV. MOHAMMED V

PL. MOHAMMED V

PL. DES SLAOUI

3

6

P20

PL. DE L'ATLAS

P24

1 Fez
2 Zalagh
3 Splendid
4 Lamdghri
5 De La Paix
6 CTM.
7 Excelsior
8 Central
9 l'Industrie

There is an all-night chemist in the New Town on Blvd Moulay Youssef by the Place de la Resistance. A French consulate is on Av. Abou Obeida Ibn Jarrah, tel 271418 and a Catholic Church of St Francis on Av. Mohammed Es Slaoui which has mass on Saturday at 18.30 and Sunday at 10.30.

A Tour of the Ramparts

A 15 km circuit of the outer walls by car or taxi is an excellent introduction to Fez. The surrounding hills, particularly at Bordj Sud and the Merenid tombs provide magnificent views over Fez el Bali.

Before leaving Fez try to witness dusk from the hills. Flame coloured light plays on the ochre walls and flickers last over the high minarets. The sky is full of pigeons and swallows enjoying the evening flight, smoke from thousands of kitchens lifts off from the Medina. Then you are hit by the call to prayer.

Fez el Jedid

Leaving from the Place de la Resistance in the New Town take the road for Taza which descends into the Oued ez Zitoun valley. The outer walls of Fez el Jedid rise to your left enclosing the Mellah and the Jewish necropolis which is entered through the Bab Jiaf.

Schools and hospitals cluster around the Bab Riafa which leads to the area that Moulay Hassan developed in the 19th century to unite the Medina and Fez Jedid.

An electrical station on your right marks the site of an old aqueduct and opposite is the **Bab el Hadid**. Just beyond is the **Bab el Jedid**, that provides the only road access into the heart of the Medina, a useful alternative approach.

Bordj Sud

Crossing over the Oued Boufekrane the approach track to Bordj Sud can be seen to your right. This was built by the Portuguese prisoners of the Saadian Sultan Ahmed el Mansur, 1578–1609, as part of a system that was designed as much to overawe the Fassis as to defend them. The fort is in partial ruin with a good field of fire over the Andalous and Karaouyine quarters rising up on either side of the invisible Oued Fes.

Bab Ftouh necropolis

Pass below the vast cemetery of Bab Ftouh studded with the whitewashed koubba of holy men—non Muslims are not usually welcome on this hill. All the great professors of the university of Qaraouyine are buried here and on the summit there is an open air Mosque, a Msalla used for the great feasts of Aid el Kebir and Aid es Seghir. Around the Msalla are the **Koubba of the Sebatou Rijal**, the anonymous seven saints who brought Islam to Morocco.

Sidi Harazem

At the lower eastern corner of the cemetery is a koubba to Sidi Harazem. He came to Morocco from Arabia and in between retiring to a life of poverty and silence taught at the Quaraouyine Mosque. He was so skilful a debater that he silenced the most agnostic and sophistic of genies and has become the patron of Koranic studies and students in general. In the spring the ancient Festival of Sidi Harazem takes place, an equivalent of the European Lord of Misrule is elected and processes up to the great Mosque of Andalous to officiate as the student Sultan for the Friday prayers. Now a humorous affair it was in the past a great occasion for political unrest.

The final resting place of the Sidi's bones is a contentious issue, his bones are not claimed to lie here but in Marrakesh or the nearby spa of Sidi Harazem. Below the cemetery is the gate of **Bab Ftouh** and to the left behind the walls stretches the extensive cemetery of **Bab Hamra**.

The Pottery
The pottery quarter with its distinctive chimney has been moved away from the Medina and is now 1 km east from Bab Ftouh. Here you can watch skilled potters at work, fluent decorators and teams of apprentices cutting faience for the zellig mosaics. The distinctive blue and green glazed tiles are fired here and there is a good selection of work for sale.

Bab Sidi Bou Jida
Otherwise continue east of Bab Ftouh to pass the eastern gate of Bab El Khouka. Bab Sidi Bou Jida is named after the Koubba of that saint which is on your right. He can be compared to St Jude, the patron saint of lost causes, and is greatly favoured by students before exams and women before marriage.

Pass over the Oued Fes and a new tiled auction court built outside the walls. The smell and the sight here is intense, trucks unload raw, bloody skins direct from the butchers and slaughter houses. Forked over by specialists the great wet bundles are bought, packed on to mules and sent down into the medina as the first stage in the long tanning process.

Bab Jamai
Pass the Bab Jamai which gives access to the luxurious **Palais Jamai Hotel**. This incorporates a few rooms and a magnificent Andalucian garden that belonged to a distinguished Fassi family, the Ulad Jamai, that had a tradition of government service. The Jamai brothers, Haj Amaati and Si Mohammed Soreir, served Sultan Moulay Hassan as Grand Vizier and Minister of War. After the death of their master they fell victim to the jealousy of the child-Sultan's Turkish mother and her ally the half-negro Chamberlain, Bou Ahmed. They were imprisoned in Tetouan, their property forfeit and their families persecuted. Haj Amaati died in prison but remained chained to his brother in high summer for eleven days. Si Mohammed survived the ordeal but was only released after fourteen years. On his deathbed he requested that, 'my chains and fetters are to be put back upon my limbs. I desire to appear before God . . . that I might appeal to Him for the justice my Sultan refused me.'

Bab Guissa and the Merenid Tombs
Next door to the Bab Jamai is the 13th-century Almohad-built Bab Guissa above which the road climbs up through the cemetery hill of Bab Guissa. Beside the modern **Merenides Hotel** a track leads towards the Merenid tombs, a crumbling selection of pise ruins and caves. The tombs were established within the extensive walls of an old Merenid kasbah that held this hilltop. Below the kasbah but outside the city walls was the

leper colony. The prominent arched cube was once covered with a pyramidal roof and a marble columned interior court held a simple stone tomb carved with an elegant epitaph and surrounded in a sea of coloured zellig mosaic. In the 14th century this patchwork of enclosed hilltop tombs must have equalled the Chellah in elegance. The view over Fez el Bali from here is unsurpassed. Immediately below stretches the Karaouyine quarter whose two great monuments, the **Qaraouyine Mosque** and **tomb of Idriss II** are immediately recognizable, the latter by its high green tiled pyramidal roof and accompanying tall minaret. Just to the left the great expanse of lower green tiles marks the Qaraouyine Mosque with its whitewashed minaret. This is crowned with a dome, not the usual Moroccan lantern, which faithfully echoes the Great Mosque at Kairouan, in Tunisia, which was founded by Uqba in 683. A dirtier, lower, conventional minaret can be seen to the right, this is the trumpeteer's tower from which the fast of Ramadan is announced. The city below remains defined by its 12th-century walls, the intense urban network is in heady contrast to the hillside olive groves that overlook the medina to the north and south.

Bordj Nord
Beyond the Merenides Hotel is the star-shaped Bordj Nord, the second Portuguese-built Saadian fortress that covered the city with its field of fire. This was converted in 1964 into a **Museum of Arms** and is open every day except Tuesday, 8.30–12.00, 14.30–18.00, admission 3dh for an hour's tour.

There is a small collection of prehistoric Stone and Bronze Age weapons before you enter an impressive selection of European and Moroccan swords, daggers and lances. Some small cannon guard a display of firearms from the 16th to the 20th centuries which leads into a sporting collection and a mass of arms confiscated from the Riff tribes in their brief rising of 1959.

Kasbah Cherarda
Below the fort the extensive square-walled Kasbah of Cherarda can be seen, protected by towers and surrounded on almost all sides by a cemetery. This was built by Moulay Rachid in 1670 to house tribes in the Sultan's service, notably the Oudaia and Cherarda cavalry. It is now divided between a hospital and University buildings and subsequently not open to inspection.

Bab Segma
Passing down its long wall the Bab Segma with its single remaining 14th-century octagonal tower separates the kasbah from Fez el Jedid. A kilometre of wall runs west from Bab Segma to enclose the Royal park, gardens and palace and a left turn before the sports park runs along another monumental 1 km of Royal wall to arrive at the Place de la Resistance.

Fez El Jedid

Though the most famous sites and odours are in Fez el Bali, a walk through the simple street plan of Fez el Jedid and a visit to the Dar el Batha museum is a good preparation for the heady and confusing alleys of the Medina.

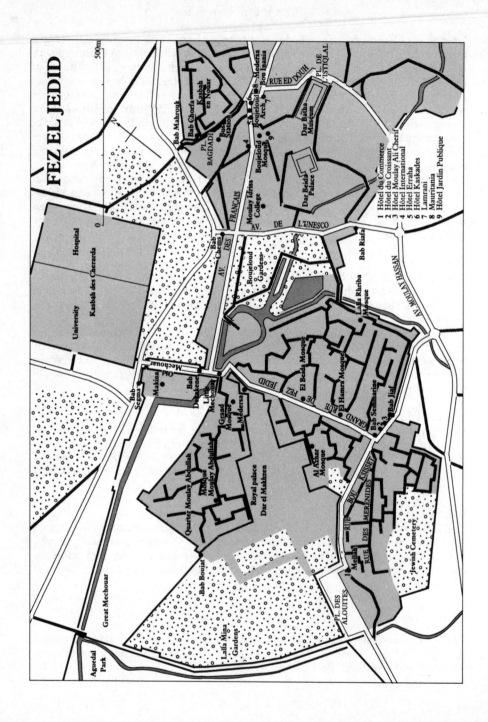

FEZ EL JEDID

500m

1 Hôtel du Commerce
2 Hôtel du Croissant
3 Hôtel Moulay Ali Cherif
4 Hôtel International
5 Hôtel Erraha
6 Hôtel Kaskades
7 Lamrani
8 Mauritania
9 Hôtel Jardin Publique

Bab Mahrouk
Kasbah en Nouar
Bab Chorfa
8 Medersa Bou Inania
RUE ED DOUH
PL. DE L'ISTIQLAL
Bus Station
Boujeloud Arch
PL. BAGDADI
4
Boujeloud Mosque
9
Dar Batha Muséum
Moulay Idriss College
Dar Beida Palace
AV. DES FRANÇAIS
Bab Chems
AV. DE L'UNESCO
Boujeloud Gardens
AV. DES
Boujeloud Gardens
Bab Riafa
Lalla Rhriba Mosque
AV. MOULAY HASSAN

University
Hospital
Kasbah des Cherarda

0

Makina
Bab Mechouar
Old Mechouar
Little Mechouar
Bab Dekakene
El Beida Mosque
RUE DE FEZ JEDID
El Hamra Mosque
Grand Mosque
Medersa
GRAND RUE DE FEZ JEDID
Bab Semmarine
Bab Jiaf
23

Bab Segma

Mosque Moulay Abdullah
Quartier Moulay Abdullah

Royal palace
Dar el Makhzen

Al Azhar Mosque

RUE DES MERENIDES
RUE BOU KSSISET
Jewish Cemetery

Bab Boujat

Lalla Mina Gardens

Mellah
RUE DES ALOUITES
PL. DES ALOUITES

Great Mechouar

Aguedal Park

Place des Alouites

From the Place de la Resistance, in the New Town, the Blvd Moulay Youssef leads in 1 km directly into the Place des Alouites or you can hop on the no 3 bus. This main entrance to the palace was created by King Hassan II between 1969–1971 as the ceremonial guard and great gates proclaim. On occasion this entire square is covered in a patchwork of carpets brought out by Fassis to honour some official guest. The gleaming brass doors were manufactured in the Medina and installed in 1971.

Dar el Makhzen

Christopher Kinninmouth writes that, 'I believe this to be the finest single sight Morocco has to offer; one of the wonders of the world.'

The royal palace, the Dar el Makhzen, occupies half of Fez el Jedid and covers over 80 hectares. Within the walls is an inaccessible city that holds 700 years of pavilions, squares, gardens and palaces. It includes a mosque, the **Koubba of Sidi Mejaed** and a medersa built by the Merenid Sultan Abou Said Othman in 1320. Sidi Mohammed built the **Dar Ayad el Kebira palace** in the 18th century, Moulay Hassan built the present Royal apartments in 1880 and in 1980 another palace was added, the **Dar el Bahia**, for the 12th Arab summit held in the next year.

Mellah

From the Place the Grand Rue des Merenides runs through the whole Mellah quarter. There are few Jews left but a legacy of jewellers' shops, brocade, balconies, small windows with their tracery of iron grille work and an air of business gives the quarter something of its old distinctive atmosphere. Tiny side streets lead off in to a labyrinth of covered passages, underground workshops and timbered houses. By heading south down these you can eventually find your way to the Hebrew cemetery, a great walled enclosure of whitewashed and lettered stones, although you will need a guide to point out two surviving Synagogues, the **Serfati** and the **Fassiyn**, one now a house, the other a bazaar.

The Jewish community had to walk barefooted within the three royal cities and before a mosque. But by the 18th century the Fassi Jews had acquired the right to wear sea rush socks outside the Mellah. As you approach the distinctive crenellated high gate of the Bab Semmarine, restored in 1924, you pass through the glittering displays of the jewellers' **souk**, with innumerable gilded bangles.

Bab Semmarine

The Bab Semmarine used to separate the Mellah from the Muslim quarter and before that marked the southern entrance of the city. Immediately beyond the arch is a covered food market which was established in an old granary built by the Merenid sultans. From the gate the Grand Rue de la Fes el Jedid lined with stalls and cafés runs due north through the city to the outer walls. Along the way, on the right, you pass the **Hamra**, the red, and then the **Beida**, the white, **Mosques** built in the 13th century by the creator of Fez el Jedid, Sultan Youssef. The alleys to the left stop at the perimeter wall of the palace beneath which is the pretty **Mosque of Al Azhar**, built by Sultan Abou Inan in the 14th century, with its fine sculpted gate.

Little Mechouar and Moulay Abdullah

The road opens out to form a small walled square known as the Petit Mechouar which has the gleaming back entrance to the Royal palace and under which the river Fes flows. A small arch to the left is the only entrance into the quarter of Moulay Abdullah. Wandering through this calm residential area you soon pass the entrance of the **Grand Mosque** built by Sultan Abou Yusuf Yaqub in 1276 in just three years. The Sultan Abou Inan was buried here in 1358 and a Koubba raised above his tomb beside the Mosque. The main street leads in 200 m to the other Mosque of the quarter which with its conspicuous slender minaret was built in the 18th century by Sultan Moulay Abdullah. The Mosque has become a principal Alouite tomb, full of the graves of princes and two Sultans including Moulay Youssef, 1912–1927, King Hassan II's grand-father.

The quarter of Moulay Abdullah is almost entirely enclosed by high walls and was chosen by the French as the quartier reservé, the red light quarter, of which there is little remaining evidence.

Returning back to the little Mechouar pass under the **Bab Dekakene** sometimes known as the Bab es Siba. This massive triple arched Merenid gate used to serve as the main entrance into the city and Royal palace until 1971. Ferdinand, prince of Portugal, was imprisoned for six years in this gate. He had surrendered himself as hostage to allow his army to escape after a disastrous attempt to seize Tangier in 1437. His brothers refused to return Ceuta to the Sultan in exchange for his release. On Ferdinand's death his naked body was hung from the gate pierced through the heels like a butchered goat where it swung for four days. His corpse was then gutted, stuffed with straw and put on show for a further 29 years.

Passing through the arches you enter a larger walled space, the Old Mechouar. On the left extends the Makina, the old Royal ordnance factory built and run by an Italian consortium in the late 19th century. Although it now holds nothing more offensive than an export oriented carpet factory you will need permission from the Tourist Office to enter. At the far end of this square on the left is the **Bab Segma**, a Merenid gate built in 1315 which was originally flanked by a pair of distinctive octagonal arches, like the Chellah in Rabat, although only one tower now survives. The smaller gate in use is the **Bab es Smen**, built in the 19th century. Unless you want to walk beside the ramparts outside the city return to the little Mechouar.

From the little Mechouar the Av. des Français leads due east for 600 m to the **Bab Boujeloud**, the main point of entry to Fez el Bali. For 500 years this area was a wasteland, caught between the cities of Fez el Jedid and Fez el Bali. It was developed in the 19th century by Moulay Hassan into the three palace gardens of Dar Batha, Boujeloud and Dar Beida. The Boujeloud symbolically was entered from either Fez el Jedid or Fez el Bali. Only one of these, the Dar Batha, is open as it now houses the **Museum of Arts and Traditions of Fez**. Otherwise the quarter remains dominated by high walls that hide gardens, palaces and pavilions whilst less attractive administrative buildings are more exposed.

To the right of the Av. des Français the entrance to the **Boujeloud gardens** may be open, which can allow you to look into this landscape of trees, sculpted lakes and water gardens. Half way along the avenue is a crossroads. To the left is the keyhole arch of **Bab Chems**, to the right the Av. de l'Unesco divides the closed Boujeloud garden from the inaccessible park, pavilions and palace of **Dar el Beida**.

Place Baghdadi

Along the Av. de Français you pass the Lycee Moulay Idriss and beyond this college a left turn brings you to the Place Baghdadi, a focal point for the local blue buses. Nut, fruit and cake hawkers serve the passengers. At dusk small groups collect around the odd musician or haggle over temporary displays of secondhand goods, particularly in the far left of the square by the solid looking **Bab Mahrouk**, the 'gate of the burned'. This was built in 1214 by an Almohad sultan Mohammed en Nasir. It was first known as the Bab ech Cheria, the gate of justice, as this was the execution square. It received its new name after El Obeidi, a leader of the heretical Riff Ghomara tribe and Ibn el Khatib, a less offensive intellectual of the 14th century, were burnt alive here. It was a savage punishment designed to deny any chance of resurrection.

To the right of the Bab Mahrouk is the **Bab Chorfa**, a strong gate protected by two elegant towers that guards the entrance into the **Kasbah en Nouar**, the Kasbah of flowers, also known as the Kasbah of the Filali. This was the site of the central Almohad fortress which was occupied by the Pasha of Fez during Merenid rule and was renamed the Kasbah of Filali to honour Moulay Rachid in the seventeenth century. The original Mosque can be seen just to the right of the gate. Its façade was restored in the 18th century by Sultan Moulay Sliman at the same time that he repaired the battlements.

Boujeloud

Walk down from the Place Baghdadi into the Boujeloud square, a bustling place of cafés, cheap hotels, taxis, buses, bemused tourists and confident young guides.

The Boujeloud square used to be occupied by another Almohad **Kasbah** which was built over the ruins of an Almoravide fort which had defended this exposed western edge of the city. Foundations of the Kasbah were recently found during building work on ground just to the west of the Boujeloud Mosque.

The famous Boujeloud triple arch was built in 1913 by the French beside an earlier gate just a year after they had occupied Fez. It served as a recognizable border between the native quarter of the Medina and the administrative quarters and Resident General's palace that were established in the Dar Batha and Dar Beida in the first few years of the Protectorate. As you approach you can admire the gold and blue entrelac decoration that represents Fez 'the blue' and the gold-green decoration for Islam on the other face.

Dar Batha Museum

GETTING THERE
Turn right past the Boujeloud arch and right again to continue along the comparatively broad Rue Ed Douh for 100 m to the Place de Istaqlal, another right turn then brings you to the entrance of the Dar Batha museum. Alternatively the no 1 bus runs from the Place des Alouites to the Dar Batha or catch the no 18 from the Place de la Resistance.

The palace of Dar Batha was started by Moulay Hassan and finished by his son Abdul Aziz, 1894–1909. A range of green tiled pyramidal roofs emerge above the red walls to cover the old apartments and galleries that now house the exhibits. A long Andalucian garden stretches down within the walls, its grid of blue and white raised paths pass through mature trees and swathes of shrub and bamboo. It is a delightful place, the tranquillity of the enclosed garden appealing just as strongly as the exhibits. In Sep-

The Court in the Merinid El Atstarin Medersa, Fez

tember concerts of Andalucian music are staged here; it is open every day except Tuesday, 9.00–12.00, 15.00–18.00, admission 10dh for a guided tour.

The cases of exhibits follow no particular scheme, astrolabes, Middle Atlas carpets, stamps, illustrated Korans, pens, Berber jewelry, embroidery, guns, rural pots, coins from either the Idrissids or Alouites are interspaced with blue geometric ware from Fez. The far corner rooms are full of the larger pieces of carved cedar, plaster or stone that have been recovered from restorations and excavations of Fassi tombs, Mosques and Medersa and some of these have been dated to the Merenid and Saadian dynasties. As ever in Morocco the achievements of urban Andalucian culture appear timeless, objects from the tenth to the twentieth centuries have so much in common. The true contrast is with products from the Berber tribes, even ones as close to Fez as Zerhoun or the Riff. Fez's past role as an oasis of technical skill and literate culture for the nation is revealed by this charming jumble of exhibits.

Fez El Bali

The major sites of Fez el Bali, the Bou Inania Medersa, the El Attarin Medersa, the tanneries and the tomb of Idriss II can be seen in a day. The lesser medersas, mosques, reclusive bakeries, bath houses, fondouqs, workshops and hidden alleys of the Medina quarters would take weeks to find—and to fully understand you have to have been born a Fassi.

Guides

Arriving at the Medina, usually at the Bab Boujeloud, accept in advance the need for a guide (and the difficulty of avoiding one) for at least the first day. He can show you intimate parts of the city where an unescorted, intrusive foreigner would not be welcome. Official gold-badge-wearing guides cost 30dh for a morning or 50dh for a day and can be

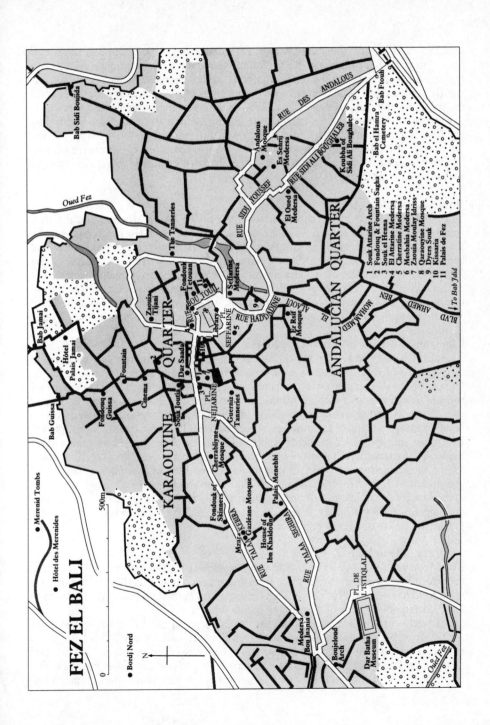

FEZ EL BALI

KARAOUYINE QUARTER

ANDALUCIAN QUARTER

1 Souk Attarine Arch
2 Fondouq & Fountain Sagha
3 Souk el Henna
4 El Attarine Medersa
5 Cherratine Medersa
6 Mesbahia Medersa
7 Zaouia Moulay Idriss
8 Qaraouyine Mosque
9 Dyers Souk
10 Kissaria
11 Palais de Fez

Bab Sidi Boujida

RUE DES ANDALOUS

Andalous Mosque
Es Sehni Medersa

RUE SIDI ALI BOUGHALEB

Bab Hamra
Bab Ftouh
Koubba of Sidi Ali Boughaleb
Cemetery

RUE SIDI YOUSSEF

El Oued Medersa

Oued Fez

The Tanneries

Fondouk Tetouan
Seffarine Medersa

Zaouia Tijani
RUE BOU TOUIL

RUE HADDADINE

EL ALAOUI

Er Reif Mosque

BLVD MOHAMMED BEN AHMED

To Bab Jdid

Bab Jamai
Hôtel
Palais Jamai

Bab Guissa

Fondouq Guissa

Fountain

Cinema

Souk Joutia
Dar Saada

Library
SEFFARINE

PL.

NEJJARINE

Guerniz Tanneries

Cherrabliyene Mosque

Fondouk of Skinners
Mzara Gazleane Mosque
House of Ibn Khaldoun

Palais Menebhi

RUE TALAA KEBRA
RUE TALAA SEGHIRA

500m

Merenid Tombs
Hôtel des Merenides

Bordj Nord

N

Bab Jdid

PL. DE L'ISTIQLAL

Medersa Bou Inania
Boujeloud Arch
Dar Batha Museum

Oued Fez

found at the Tourist Office, the Syndicat D'Initiative and often by the Bab Boujeloud gate. They are a professional body of men and their talk and itineraries through repetition can become uninspiring. Unofficial guides charge less, have a greater incentive to please, although their routes are often given a further erratic twist as they avoid the police for they are officially illegal—but that remains their problem not yours.

Fez exists on trade and to arrive at the Medina with a fixed intention not to buy anything is to miss out on the central life of the city. But see all you wish before making the rounds of the bazaars. Then you can savour the whole ritual of commerce without impatience, delight in the gift of mint tea, the opulent decoration of the large bazaars and loquacious salesmanship.

Boujeloud Gate

The Boujeloud Gate frames the minarets of the **Sidi Lezzaz Mosque** and the **Bou Inania Medersa** in its arch. Beyond the arch is a area lined by a few hotels on the right, food stalls on the left and a small courtyard glittering with embroidered leather and babouches dead ahead. The Medina's two major arteries appear here, the Rue Talaa Kebira to the left and the Rue Talaa Seghira to the right. They run roughly parallel and are both lined with stalls, shops and bazaars. Periodically covered by arches and slats of bamboo they meet just before the central Souk Attarin Arch. This arch and the Place Seffarine are taken as the two central and recognizable points for exploring the Medina.

Clock and Mida of Bou Inania Medersa

Taking the Rue Talaa Kebira, which passes to the left of the two minarets, you approach the Medersa of Bou Inania 100 m on your right before a prominent bridge building. Opposite the medersa gate on the left, high up by a carved lintel of cedar, is a dilapidated row of thirteen windows with a few brass bowls on the sills and the odd surviving water spout. This is known as the water clock, though no description has survived and no satisfactory explanation of its working has been devised. It is subsequently considered to have been the work of a magician Rabbi, and was finished in 1357 in time for the medersa's inauguration. It may not have been a clock but a musical instrument of timed jets of tinkling water on brass, in celebration of the building, beneath which is the ablution court of the Medersa. Men used to be able to enter this Mida, a working portion of the Medersa complex, and admire the court with its central marble basin, stone closets and impressive flow of water. It is now closed, hopefully in order to repair its rich but precarious geometrical plaster and cedar carving.

Medersa of Bou Inania

The Medersa of Bou Inania is the finest and largest in Fez. The **prayer hall** is in active use which saves the spirit of the place from disappearing under the flow of visitors. It is open from 8.00–18.00 every day except Friday morning, though you might be asked to leave during other hours of prayer, admission 3dh.

The main entrance is under a stalactite domed chamber and to the left is a room for the faithful to wash their feet. The central open air court, paved in marble with its central round pool is surrounded by a carved screen of cedar, two lecture halls are off to either side and the large prayer hall seen across a marble moated portion of the Oued Fes. The prayer hall should not be entered by a non-Muslim but the mihrab, the columned hall and the minbar can be examined. From these doors the elegant **minaret** is clearly visible, above the cedar lintelled and green tiled roof, from where the Friday call to prayer is issued. From the first floor the windows of the dark simple cells of the students overlook the sun-baked court. Persevere to the roof for an exciting view over neighbouring roof tops and a barrage of minarets.

The Bou Inania Medersa is a complete expression of the Hispano-Mauresque style, a direct importation of 14th-century Andalucian techniques to Morocco. All the materials, the zellig mosaic, the plaster, marble and cedar carry a range of patterns, in excellent condition, that threaten to overwhelm the architecture. But the geometrical swirls hide a single point, the detail of the floral patterns illustrate a divine symmetry and even the array of stalactites break down into an ordered span of interlocking arches. The cedar screen with its delicate interlocking weave of knots or stars and the plaster entrelacs of the walls insist on a linear two-dimensional frame that invites a further reduction on to the one dimensional single point. All can be seen as witness to the one God, whilst the escriptive Kufic bands which bind the decoration contain lines from the Koran. For a Muslim these are the direct instructions of God dictated by the angel Gabriel to Mohammed:

'"Read in the name of thy Lord thy creator; who created man from a drop of blood. Read, thy Lord is most bountiful, who taught by means of the pen, taught man what he knew not." Accordingly I read these words, and he had finished his task and departed from me. I awoke from my sleep, and I felt as if the words had been graven on my heart.'

A medersa was a residential college for the learning of the Koran but seldom had adequate provision for the maintenance of the students. In practice they often became a finishing school for the children of the privileged. This had an obvious political use, for the Merenid Sultans could counter regional loyalties and divisive spiritual brotherhoods by educating future Caids, Cadis and tribal chiefs within a state-approved orthodoxy. A little of this political dimension has crept into the Bou Inania.

It was built by the Sultan Abou Inan between 1350 and 1357 on an area of wasteland removed from the independent spirit of the Qaraouyine University who feared his intentions. This powerful sovereign (who had deposed his own father) subsequently strove to enhance his new foundation and supercede the traditional university. Its sumptuous proportions and decoration were deliberately designed to eclipse its rival, though the Sultan is remembered for his famous aesthetic response when presented with the costs, 'what is beautiful cannot be expensive at any price; what is enthralling is never too costly.' It is no surprise that several lines praising Abou Inan and his munificent generosity have crept into the decoration of the main court, whilst the dedication stone declares him Caliph, 'the successor' to the prophet.

Rue Talla Kebira
On the left before the covered arch is the entrance to the **Medersa Mida**, just beyond is the **zaouia of Sidi Ahmed Tijani**, one of the two Fassi lodges of this widespread Sufi brotherhood. Continue downhill into the intensity of the contrasting light and shade of the Medina; bazaars, bakeries, grill cafés, zellig decorated fountains and the furnaces of Hammams stoked by a graceful routine of hand thrown wood shavings. The heavily loaded mules of the hereditary Guir valley porters pause for no man. Listen for 'Balak', the muleteers' look-out cry, or run the risk of being knocked off your feet. The rich

odours of olive oil, fresh mint, cedar shavings, leather, fat burnt on charcoal, kif, mule dung and human urine swirl around to mix with the chanting from a Koranic nursery school, the sound of running water, hooves and the overlying babble of business. Buy fresh squeezed orange juice, sweet cakes, fresh bread, fried potato cakes to add another layer of sensual enjoyment. As you begin to climb uphill you pass a row of blacksmiths and beyond this, on the left is an old **Merenid prison** designed like any of the hundreds of fondouqs but with noticeably stronger and heavier arches and colonnades where the prisoners would be chained. It is now the market for the butter and honey wholesalers who can weigh you out a tupperware pot full of the strong tasting Moroccan butter.

The **mosque of Gazleane** can be seen on your right. Just before this, an alley marked by a plaque leads to the house where Ibn Khaldoun (1332–1406), the great historian and sociologist, lived. Just beyond this turning is the **Mzara of Moulay Idriss**, a monument that commemorates the place where the founder rested and envisaged the future city. On the left is the **Mosque of Derb bou Haj** and just beyond that the fondouq of the skinners, where wet hides are scraped clean of fat and tissue in the court. You then pass a distinctive fountain on the right opposite which is the oldest Hammam in Fez.

The cobblers' stalls increasingly dominate the street with their displays of babouches and the second Mosque on the right is called the **Cherrabliyne**, the slipper makers. This was founded by the Merenid Sultan Abou el Hassan, 1331–1351, though only the minaret is original, which is all apart from the gate that a non-Muslim can see. Beyond the Mosque you pass a numer of bazaars to enter the **souk Ain Allou** area dominated by fine leather workers whose distinctive gold-stamped and decorated binding is still known as Morocco work or maroquinerie.

Souk el Attarin

As you near the Qaraouyine Mosque you pass under a modest arch to enter the Souk el Attarin, the souk of the spice sellers and 15 m beyond is the combined carpet warehouse, tearoom and restaurant of Dar Salam. It also heralds the **Kissaria**, the dense network of traditionally expensive shops on an irregular criss-crossing grid of alleys that cluster at the heart of the Medina. Gutted by fire in 1960, the new stalls stock imported goods as well as traditional clothing, jewelry, silver and ornamental metal ware.

Here if not before you may feel the need for a guide. The Attarin arch is taken as the starting point for walks to the Henna souk, the zaouia Moulay Idriss II and the Place Nejjarine, a walk up to Bab Guisa and the approach along the main street to reach the three Medersas that cluster around the great Qaraouyine Mosque.

Henna Souk

Just before the Attarin arch a right turn brings you to the Souk el Henna, a pleasant tree-shaded square where hessian sacks of henna leaves, henna paste, silvery blocks of antimony and kohl are weighed out and sold. There are also stalls of pottery, small drums and containers for sale as well as a more alarming display of the dried skins of lizards, snakes and small predators with hutches of hedgehogs and terrapins for the preparation of magical pastes, aphrodisiacs and love potions. On one side of the square is the **Maristan of Sidi Frej**, a lunatic asylum built by the Merenid Sultan Yacqub, 1286–1307. The sanctuary of Sidi Frej was originally for nursing sick cranes and storks back to health and for the respectful burial of these holy birds when they died. It is now used as a warehouse but the religious ministry hope to turn it into a profitable Andalucian bazaar.

Zaouia of Moulay Idriss II

The first right beyond the Attarin arch, Rue Mjadiyn, leads directly to the zaouia of Moulay Idriss II. Non-Muslims are not allowed into the sanctuary but by following around the wooden perimeter to the right you can get an excellent view of the inside from the edge of the women's gate. Within the darkened sanctuary the tomb can be seen heavily draped in rich embroidered velvet cloth, the ksaoua, and surrounded by baroque brass, flickering coloured candles, glittering lamps, offerings, European clocks and praying women. It is strikingly similar to the saint cults in Spain, Naples, Sicily or Greece and around the corner of the precinct a hole lined by well-worn copper allows the devotees to touch the tomb. As well as being the patron saint of the city he is especially appealed to by boys before circumcision and women before giving birth.

It is not known if the reforming Almoravides or Almohads suppressed the cult but Idriss II's tomb was reidentified during Merenid rule, in 1307 after an uncorrupted body was unearthed here. The present extent of the zaouia was constructed in 1437 but it was the Wattasid dynasty that developed it into a major cult centre. Throughout August the numerous guilds of the city still process to the tomb and offer decorative gifts, animal sacrifices, religious chants and nubas of classical Andalucian music before starting their festivals. In the 18th century Moulay Ishmael restored the shrine which until the 19th century was hung with contracts by which the various towns and tribes tried to establish the exact terms upon which they accepted the rule of each new Sultan. The right of sanctuary, 'horm', is still respected and Sultan Abdul Aziz appalled the Fassis when he arrested the murderer of a European who had taken shelter beside the tomb.

Place Nejjarine

Around the zaouia the lanes are lined with candles, nougat and religious trinket shops. To the east of the zaouia are the packed shopping streets of the Kissaria packed with modern goods whilst just to the west is the calm and pleasant Place Nejjarine, the carpenters' square. A worn but still elegant drinking fountain plays here into a basin of mosaic tiles whilst cedar beams hold a canopy of green tiles. In the morning carpenters can be found at work off any of the surrounding streets, adzing away at a twisted trunk to carve a light but strong plough. The 18th-century Nejjarine fondouq is behind an ornamental gate to the left of the fountain. It is rarely open now, hiding the view of this high and elegant court with its colonnaded floors. This fondouq had, for a Christian, the pleasant combination of lodging theological students and carpenters. It is now awaiting repair.

The covered passage to the right of the fountain can take you back on to the Talaa Seghira towards Bab Boujeloud, passing the restaurant Dar Menehbi about half way. By facing away from the fountain turn right to find the tanneries of the Guerniz quarter which are just before the Mosque of Sidi Moussa. These are the oldest of the three **Fez tanneries** and were traditionally established by Moulay Idriss I. Otherwise any of the alleys to the right of the covered passage should take you back to the souk el Attarin.

Souk el Attarin to Bab Guissa

Off the tourist track a left turn just after the Attarin arch, 15 m before the conspicuous Dar Saada restaurant allows you to enter the **souk Joutia**, the market for salt, eggs and fish. About 40 m beyond the Joutia and 20 m to the right of the main street is an

18th-century fondouq and fountain, the central place of the Es Sagha quarter which used to be the great haunt of jewellers. The elegant carved plaster and cedar colonnades of the fondouq is now one of the centres of the wool trade, raw spun wool is stored here, auctioned off and brought in bright coloured batches back from the dyers to be sold to weavers and carpet makers.

Return back to the main track, the Rue Hormis, and bear left and climb uphill to pass a cinema, a local social centre surrounded with cheap grills and cafés. Off from here is another henna and spice market, the **Place Achabin**. Snaking further uphill you should pass a fountain on your left to enter the quarter of fondouq Guissa or el Yhoudi. In the morning you pass the workshops of farriers, joiners and wood turners with its distinctive aroma of cedar wood and singed hooves. Ask to be shown the original **fondouq el Yhoudi**, high up on the left where the Jewish merchants were based in the 13th century before the Merenids moved them to Fez el Jedid. Replaced several times since then, the fondouq is now used for the sorting, quality gradation and auctioning of tanned and dyed skins. Below the **Bab Guisa gate** is a complex of three buildings, a 14th-century mortuary chamber and a 19th century Mosque and medersa, none of which are open to non-Muslims. To the right of Bab Guisa is the Bab Ferdaous/Bab Jamai where a no 10 bus can whizz you back to the Place des Alouites on the western edge of Fez el Jedid or a taxi on the tour of ramparts.

Medersa el Attarine
100 m from the Attarin arch to the left just as the souk ends are the distinctive bronze doors of the Attarine Medersa, open every day from 8.00–18.00, except Friday morning, admission 3dh.

Built by Sultan Abou Said from 1322–1325 within a confined space it has not the grandeur of the Bou Inania but is a finer more delicate structure. It is at least as rich in the decoration of zellig, plaster and wood but with a lighter architectural touch emphasized by reflecting pairs of arches seemingly supported by thin stone pillars. The plan is familiar, an entrance hall with stairs to the upper floors of 60 student chambers and a central fountain court beyond which is a prayer hall. There are no lecture halls, as in the later Bou Inania, as the Attarine was designed as an addition to the Qaraouyine University, not a possible rival. You may enter the prayer hall, the **Mihrab** is to the right flanked by pillars and lit by coloured glass windows. A bronze chandelier hangs from the cedar ceiling, inscribed with the name of the founder and details of the medersa's construction.

The roof, if the custodian allows you to go up, shares with the Palais Fes restaurant the best view a non-Muslim can get of the Qaraouyine Mosque. The acreage of green tile is most impressive; the tall distant minaret is that of the zaouia of Moulay Idriss II whilst the murky lantern-less minaret is the Trumpeteer minaret from which Ramadan is announced; the nearest is the 10th-century white domed minaret that echoes the Great Mosque at Kairouan, Tunisia. The Mosque's internal court, the Sahn, with its flanking twin pavilions and dazzling blue and white floor is also partly overlooked. The little **Medersa of el Mesbahia**, closed for restoration, can also be partly overlooked. It was built in 1346 by Sultan Abou Hassan and nicknamed 'er Rokham', the Marble, due to his lavish use of Italian marble though the central white marble basin was brought over from a mosque at Algeciras. 200 m to the north of the medersa is the **zaouia of Sidi**

Ahmed Tijani, the main lodge of this influential intellectual Sufi brotherhood that was founded by Sidi Mohammed Tijani in Algeria in the 18th century. Persecuted by the Turks, the founder fled to Fez. The brotherhood was a great ally of Alouite Sultans aiding them in their religious reforms; when Moulay Hafid retired to Tangier in 1912 he wrote a scholarly work in praise of the order.

The Mosque of Qaraouyine

At the heart of Fez and Moroccan culture, it is perhaps appropriate that this Great Mosque should remain such an elusive building. Its outer walls are so encrusted with shops and houses that its shape is lost, whilst the four main gates, of the fourteen doors, offer intriguing but baffling vistas of a succession of pure white colonnades and the simple rush matting with its woven red design. These occasionally frame a turbanned lecturer sitting cross legged against a far wall, a satisfactory romantic image with which to depart.

The Mosque was first built in 859 by Fatima bint Mohammed ben Feheri, a prosperous refugee from Kairouan. This was improved upon by a Fatamid governor in 933 and further enlarged by a governor of the Omayyad Caliph of Cordoba, Abd er Rahman III in 956. The Mosque was then almost entirely remade by the Almoravide Sultan Ali ben Youssef from 1135 to 1143 and finished only a few years before the dynasty fell.

It is a rectangular space sufficient for 20,000 to say their prayers simultaneously. The roof is upheld by spacious round-topped arches supported on sixteen aisles of twenty-one spans. An open air court, the Sahn, of four spans width is at the opposite end from the Mihrab. Within this open court the Almohads placed a marble basin and the Saadian Sultan Abdullah el Ghalib added two flanking pavilions closely modelled on those of the Lion court in the Alhambra palace at Granada. The chief glory of the Mosque remains the central aisle that leads up from the centre of the court directly to the Mihrab. This is embellished with bold and increasingly elaborate carved floral and Kufic script into the plaster as you advance, whilst the domes that span the arches are raised higher and higher as they approach the Mihrab and are ribbed or vaulted with bold stalactite decoration. The carving is in virtually mint condition having been covered by the Almohads two years after they were finished and only revealed in the restorations of 1950. Other hidden treasures are a bronze chandelier from 1203, a Minbar, a pulpit, of precious woods and inlaid ivory from Cordoba and one of the richest libraries of Islam.

Coming out from the Attarin roof, turn left and left again to circle the Great Mosque on Rue Bou Touil. Depending on which gates are open (ten of the fourteen open on Friday), you can see into the Sahn and then into the main body of the Mosque but never on to the central decorated aisle or the domes. On your left you pass the usually locked door of the **Mesbahia Medersa**, then the **fondouq of the Tetouanis**, a fine 14th-century Merenid court, used by Andalucian merchants from Tetouan from the 15th century, which you will be welcome to enter as there is a carpet shop within. There is a less grand fondouq a few doors below and then Palais de Fes, a carpet shop and restaurant in a 19th-century merchant's house with a fine rooftop view.

Place Seffarine

At the southeastern corner of the Mosque, the direction of the Mihrab and prayer, is the Place Seffarine, shaded by fig trees with a pleasant fountain and full of metal workers tapping away at an impressive range and size of pots and kettles. This, like the souk Attarin arch, is a recognizable centre from which to explore this end of the Medina; to the Medersa es Seffarine and the dyers' souk, to the Medersa ech Cherratin or to the Tanneries and the Medersa es Sahrij beside the Great Mosque of the Andalucian quarter.

The Library and University of Qaraouyine

The great library of the University is stored in the white walls between the Place and the Mihrab to which there is no entry. Considering the physical deprivation to the city the library has survived well. It boasts a 9th-century manuscript Koran and an original manuscript of Averrës–Ibn Rachid amongst its 30,000 precious volumes.

The University of Qaraouyine is one of the oldest in the world. Its origins lie in the teaching of the Koran in the Mosque, just as Christian universities much later coalesced out of monastery and cathedral schools. Allied subjects like grammar, theology and Koranic law were taught in informal lectures with an accent on verbal memory rather than debate or written papers. It is claimed that Pope Sylvester III learnt mathematics at Fez a century before Bologna, the first European University, was established. In the 14th century 2000 students, 'tolba', dwelt in the various Medersas to be instructed by the ulemas, the doctors and professors. Ibn Ruchd, Ibn Khaldun, Leo Africanus and Ibn Battuta all participated in the intellectual milieu of Fez. In 1963 the university was 'nationalized', having been the single source of higher education until then. Departments were dispersed to the new town and dependent faculties established at Rabat, Tetouan and Marrakesh.

Medersa es Seffarine

Leaving the Place from the bottom left walk towards the Oued Fes for the inconspicuous door of the Medersa es Seffarine. You may need a guide to find it and to negotiate with the neighbours to open the front and roof doors. It was established by Sultan Abou Yusuf, the founder of Fez el Jedid, in 1280. It was the first medersa in Morocco and it follows the design of a Fassi house, following the practice of professors lecturing in their home when not using the mosque. Formal medersas had long been established in Egypt, Syria and Iraq but with the additional gift of a library the Sultan showed that he was more interested in education than architectural elegance. The arched balcony, extensive vine and ablutions pool have a simple domestic elegance but the prayer hall shows signs of the extravagance that would be unleashed in the Attarin medersa twenty-five years later. You can hardly ever tire of Medina views and the medersa roof has an intriguing prospect over the river mills, houses and bridges.

Dyers' Souk

By continuing left past the Medersa you drop down into the dyers' souk, the souk Sabbighin, which is to the right of the bridge by the river bank. The swatches of bright coloured wool draped over the street to dry are one of the perennially startling and photogenic sites of Morocco. The vats of dye and the grave, grey dressed vat masters are altogether more disturbing. If you are with a guide ask to be shown the riverside mill where seeds and minerals are crushed to extract the raw dyes. The millers wade through the thick pungent waters of the stream raking aside mounds of garbage in order to direct enough water into the workings of the mill. It is a breathtaking vision of mingled squalor, rancid steaming waters and skilled medieval use of water power.

Medersa ech Cherratine
From the Place Seffarine do not continue around the Mosque but follow the Rue Haddadine lined with displays of teapots, kitchenware and jewelry and turn right up the Rue Cherratine. Pass the **Dar Sekka bazaar**, once a mint, to reach the twin bronze doors of the Medersa. This was built by the first Alouite Sultan Moulay Rachid in 1670. It has none of the finesse and exuberance of the Merenid Medersa and perhaps some of the atmosphere of a barracks block, with four solid cedar residential courtyard houses placed in the corners of the extensive court.

Beyond the Medersa you enter a pretty triangular place, the **souk Chemayin** where dried fruit is sold, and passing through you reenter the Kissaria passing several shops that specalize in lambswool hats, tarbouches and embroidered fezzes.

Tanneries
The **Dabbaghin** is the main tannery quarter of the three ancient sites in Fez. It is on a terrace above the River Fes along a well beaten 200 m walk along Rue el Mechattine. The high distinctive smell is enough to guide you. Once there boys will take you to terraces and courts where you can see the operations without being too much in the way.

There is a rush of guilt as you attempt to stifle your initial nausea and notice that you are part of a stream of foreigners who arrive, look repulsed, take photographs, tip and leave. The honeycomb of vats, their assorted colours, processes and levels have an endless fascination. The neighbouring roofs and hills are flecked with drying skins, a tone down in colour from the livid vats of saffron, poppy, indigo, mint and antimony. The scantily dressed tanners are born to their trade and appear like so many human storks, their long elegant legs working through the pools, bobbing down to worry a skin and then striding off to wash at the fresh water standing pipes. The tanneries are worked by a mesh of specialist and cooperative guilds with their own hierarchies of apprentices, craftsmen and master craftsmen. A whole range of processes are undertaken here, 'fresh animal skins' are treated and pounded in alternating solid and liquid vats of urine and pigeon shit. Then scraped, wet died, scraped, perhaps dry died before being trimmed and sorted for the auctions.

The Andalucian Quarter of Fez el Bali
Below the tanneries the conspicuous bridge of **Bein El Moudoun**, the bridge of the two cities, crosses the Oued Fes into the Andalucian quarter. This half of Fez el Bali is a quieter residential quarter; it has the Sahrija Merassa, few shops and hardly any tourists.

Great Mosque of Andalous
From the bridge a narrow lane winds its way towards the Rue des Andalous which almost encircles the Great Mosque of Andalous. There is no view of the Mosque other than that of its decorated gates. It was first built by Meriem, the equally pious sister of Fatima, the founder of the Qaraouyine Mosque, but was largely remade by the Almohad Mohammed en Nasir in the 13th century. The Merenids gave it a fountain and built two nearby medersas for students. They presented an entire library to the Mosque in 1415 but this never developed into a separate university.

Medersa es Sehrij

This Medersa 'of the pool' faces to the southwest of the Mosque. It was built by Abou Hassan between 1321–1323 whilst he was still heir to the throne. When he became Sultan he built another in Fez, the Mesbahia Medersa, and commissioned medersas at Taza, Meknes and Salé. Its rich decoration is currently being repaired and it may not always be open to the public. The simple but harmonious plan, generous central basin and the damaged but early decorative carving of the plaster is well worth examining. From the roof you can catch a glimpse of the neighbouring sister **Medersa of es Sebbayin**, the seven, for here was taught the seven approved styles for the chanting of the Koran. It is currently occupied by students.

Away from the Grand Mosque a first left beyond the Medersa takes you down Rue Sidi Ali Bou Ghaleb. You pass the **Koubba** of this saint on your right just as you enter the quarter of cemeteries. Like the Koubba of Sidi Harazem beyond the walls the saint is not buried here but the shrine remains an important popular cult centre. The ill and the mad surround the Koubba on Tuesday night and wait for the saint to appear in their dreams and suggest a cure. The **cemetery of Bab El Hamra** on the right should not be entered and has a local reputation as the resort of black magicians. At **Bab Ftouh** you can find a taxi for a tour of the ramparts or a no 18 bus back into the new town.

Alternatively turn right beyond the Medersa on to the Rue Sidi Youssef, the 19th-century **Medersa el Oued** is immediately on your left on the corner. The street bends left and in 200 m brings you to the bridge of Sidi el Aouad. The car parking square stretches south, built over the Oued Boufekrane, a tributary of the Oued Fes. This road can lead you out beneath a procession of minarets to the Bab Jdid though the no 18 bus sweeps up here plying the Bab Ftouh to new town route. The tall minaret immediately overlooking the square belongs to the 18th-century **Rsif Mosque** around which a vegetable market collects. From the Sidi el Aouad bridge the Rue Haddadine climbs up into the Place Seffarine.

SHOPPING

Fez el Bali

Any visit to Fez el Bali should naturally expose you to a vast range of crafts. **Sebti Kamal** has a collection of antiques at 3, Place Nejjarine, tel 33505, with illuminated Korans and doors and panels of carved wood, decorated in floral and Koranic verse. One of the most famous bazaars is that of Haj Abbes Mrabeti Merrakchi by Place Seffarine, no 2, Sbaa Louyat Kariouene, tel 34691 who employs some of the most skilled bronze and leather craftsmen.

Fez el Jedid

In Fez el Jedid you will find one of the most distinguished tailors, **Masrour Mohammed ben Lahbib Filali** at 1, Rue Douh, tel 34964, employed by the court to create sumptuous embroidered kaftans at anything between 400–2500dh. Considerably down-market but with a good stock of classical styles of kaftans, gandoras, bernouss and djellabas is the **Palais du Caftan** at 17, Derb el Gueb.

New Town

In the new town begin by looking at the prices of the interesting displays at the **Artisanal**

ensemble on Blvd Allal ben Abdellah, tel 23160. The courtyard is busy with working craftsmen and the carpet looms busy with hundreds of hands twisting, tying and snipping at carpets. Along Blvd Mohammed V at no 40 is **Berrada**, with its impressive collection of incised silver and plate. **La Fibule** at no 5, tel 24947, has a good and firmly priced selection of Moroccan crafts, at no 2 is **Bijouterie 2000** with a fine display of jewelry and fabrics from **Atelier Ghalie Abdelkrim ben Cherif** at no 150, tel 22532. For picnics the central market is found off Blvd Mohammed V, just across the street from the café Zanzibar.

You can buy directly at a 40% discount from the leather factory in the Sidi Brahim Industrial quarter, **Maroquinerie Industrielle de Fes**, Rue 802, tel 41941; the potteries at Ain Khaddous also sell directly, tel 45554 and the carpet workshop in Fez el Jedid, **La Makina**, off the old Mechouar might be of interest, tel 34950 or ask for an appointment through the Tourist Office.

There are three good **bookshops** that stock English titles. The English bookshop, 68 Av. Hassan II, has the largest range but the Libraire du Centre, 60, Blvd Mohammed V and the Hotel de Fes, Av. des F.A.R. are worth a look. Newspapers are sold at all these shops and along the Blvd Mohammed V.

FESTIVALS

The students' moussem of Sidi Harazem is held at the end of April and the two major city festivals of Moulay Idriss II and Sidi Ahmed el Bernoussi are both in September. The French Consulate runs a cultural section which organizes a number of exhibitions and events, 33, Rue d'Afghanistan, tel 23921.

SPORTS

Riding is possible from the Club Equestre Moulay Idriss at the racecourse, tel 23438. **Swimming** in the summer is available at the crowded municipal pool near the Stadium off the Av. des Sportes, admission 5dh, or at the camp site, tel 41537. The Hotel Zalagh, Rue Mohammed Diouri, tel 22531, lets non-guests swim for 20dh.

A **hammam**, entrance 50dh, with attendant masseur, operates in the Palais Jamai Hotel. Or use the hammam Aturki in the Medina for 3dh, turn right through Bab Boujeloud on to Rue Tala Seghira and to the right, first door under the covered arch.

WHERE TO STAY

Of the three five-star hotels: the ugly **Les Merenides**, single 407dh or a double for 514dh has the best view, the **Hotel de Fes** on Av. des F.A.R., rooms from 400dh to 1,800dh, has the most lavish and efficient facilities, but the **Palais Jamai** is alone worth its price.

It was established in 1930 in the enclosed 19th-century palace of a Fassi Vizier. Its position just within the Medina ramparts of Bab Jamai, its extraordinary Andalucian garden, enormous heated pool, tiled hammam, Moroccan restaurant and distinct lack of guests make it an exceptional place to explore the city from. It is featured in many novels, not least Paul Bowles's, *The Spider's House*. A double room costs 520dh, a double room in the old palace wing with genuinely erratic plumbing for 800dh, an extra bed 110dh, a Royal suite for 2000dh and breakfast for 45dh.

New Town Hotels

Removed from the heady medieval sights, odours and sounds of the Medina, the appeal of the new town is in its cleanliness, order and water. The main avenues lined by bars, cafés, bookstalls and restaurants provide a burst of animation in the evening 'passeo'.

Unclassified new town hotels like the **Savoie**, **Regina**, **Renaissance**, **Maghreb** and **Jeanne D'Arc** can be fairly ruthless with their prices during the high demand of the summer. The **Youth Hostel**, tel 24085, is on Rue Moulay Ibn Nouceir. A bed is 10dh a night for card-carrying members, 13dh without, an evening meal available for 22dh.

The nine functional if uninspiring one- or two-star hotels can work out cheaper. The best and most popular of these is the **Central** at 50, Rue Nador off Mohammed V, tel 22333, a single for 37dh, a double with bath 55dh, and there is the **L'Industrie** and the **Excelsior** on Blvd Mohammed V tel 25602, and the **Kairouan** at 84 Rue D'Espagne, tel 23590.

The best three two-star hotels in order of preference are the **CTM**, Av. Mohammed V, tel 22811, the **De la Paix**, 44 Av. Hassan II, tel 25072 and **Lamdaghri**, 10, Rue Kabbour el Mangad, tel 20310.

Double 218dh The newly refurbished **Splendid** at 9, Rue Abdelkrim el Khattabi, tel 22148, with a garden, pool, restaurant and bar is the most appealing three-star hotel and the **** **Hotel Zalagh**, on Rue Mohammed Diouri, the best of its range. It has a hammam, large pool, a popular night club and an excellent view over the Medina, a double for 240dh.

In Fez el Jedid
The ** **Hôtel du Commerce** is by far the most comfortable and attractive hotel, overlooked by the Palace walls and entered from the Place des Alouites. The other three hotels of this quarter are distinctly less appealing, the **Hôtel du Parc** is by the corner of the Grande Rue Fes el Jehdid and the Av. Français; it charges 20dh for a single and 30dh for a double. On the opposite end of the Grand Rue Fes el Jehdid, just before the Bab Semmarin you find the **Hôtel Croissant** at no 285, tel 25637, and opposite the **Moulay al Cherif** with dingy but balconied bedrooms.

Medina Hotels
There are half a dozen basic hotels just in front of the Bab Boujeloud. Noisy, busy and with unreliable water supplies their attraction is in the proximity to the main entrance of Fez el Bali and the evening café life. In summer the heavy demand for rooms can increase the price beyond the usual 25dh for a single and 35dh for a double. In order of preference: the **Hôtel du Jardin Public**, 153, Kasbah Boujeloud, tel 33086, is up a small alley to your right as you approach the gate. **Hotel Kaskade**, tel 33991, is just after the gate and has wide double beds and an old hammam on the second floor. **Hotel Erraha**, tel 33226, to the right of the corner café a block to the fore of the gate. **Hotel Mauritania**, 14, Rue Serrajine, tel 33518, is just inside the gate on the right, and the **Lamrani** one further, tel 34411.

EATING OUT

The top five restaurants
Book a table and examine the menus in advance to check on house specialities which are only prepared on specific order.

M. Larachi, the knowledgeable proprietor of **L'Anbra**, presides over dinner in a colonial villa that displays his antique collection on the road to Immouzer from the new town. For exquisite pastilla, lamb mechouar, fruits, gazelle horns, tea and mineral water allow 110–220dh. 47, Route D'Immouzer, tel 41687/25177.

The **Hôtel de Fes**, Av. des F.A.R., tel 32006, has two restaurants. French cooking is under the direction of Maurice Lupsin; crevettes royales with langouste from Mohammedia and oysters from Oualidia cost 70dh, a supreme of Saint Pierre cloute aux truffles for 65dh. The restaurant **Najjarine** is in a lavish upholstered tent with a traditional band, lavish quantities of porcelain, silver and St Louis crystal whilst a meal of pastilla and tagine costs 90dh.

The Moroccan restaurant **la Koubba du Ciel** on the top floor of the Merenides Hotel, tel 45225, has a spectacular view over the Medina and you can listen to Berber music and dance whilst an enormous Moroccan salad costs only 35dh.

The **Palais Jamai Hôtel**, tel 34331, has two fine restaurants with set menus for 145dh. Philip Dajas presides over **La Djenina** where picatta de lotte aux poivres, 60dh, crevettes royales beurre coraille, 110dh or carré d'agneau aux herbes de provence 140dh can be consumed. The **Al Fassia Moroccan restaurant** is also exceptional. It is above the hotel's Andalucian garden in a hall of the old palace. The service is discreet and the menu comprehensive. A satisfying array of salads costs 35dh, pastilla, 45dh, chicken baked with lemon and olives, 50dh, and cinnamon-couscous pudding, 35dh, 'President Cabernet rouge', 90dh a bottle, which is all accompanied by classical Andalucian music played by a traditional quintet.

Moorish palaces in the Medina

There are several bazaar-restaurants in 19th-century palaces in the Medina. They are closed on Fridays and over any available religious holiday.

The **Palais de Fes**, tel 34707, beside the Mosque of Qaraouyine at 16, Rue Boutouil-Karaouyine, serves a traditional menu; allow between 110–140dh for a full meal and enjoy the rooftop view while you wait. The **Dar Tajine** at 15, Rue Ross Rehi, Palais Haj Ommar Lebbar, tel 34167, prepares traditional lamb and chicken dishes but also serves fish or pigeon pastilla and a fine fish tagine. Allow 75–90dh for a full meal without wine. The **Palais M'Nebhi**, Rue Petit Talaa, Talaa Seghira, tel 33893, occupies a beautiful palace once used by General Lyautey. Haj Sentissi produces the best couscous in the Medina; book a table in advance and be prepared to look at the collection of carpets and pay from 120–160dh for a meal. There is also the **Palais des Merenides**, 99, Zkak Ruaoh, tel 34028 run by Haj Mohammed Lahlou, with menus for 80 or 115dh; and the **Dar Saada**, tel 33343, on the left of the souk Attarin at no 21. The **Restaurant Firdaous** is just in the Medina through Bab Guisa at 10, Rue Jenifour, tel 34343, and serves an enormous meal from 20.00–24.00 of date-harira soup, salads, brochettes, tagines and couscous for 110, 130 or 150dh or you can pay 45dh just to see the evening floor show with a free drink.

French–Moroccan restaurants in the New Town

For a reasonably priced meal that you can prolong over a bottle of beer or wine, walk down the Av. Mohammed V or the Rue Kaid Ahmed.

The **Chamonix** is open until midnight at 5, Rue Kaid Ahmed, tel 26638, where a meal of salad, couscous à la Fassi and fruit costs 35dh. Opposite at no 45 is the **Casse**
Dinner menu 38.50 dh

329

Croute and the even cheaper **Caisse Croute Balkhiat**, tel 26605, at 41, where skewers of kebab, bread and spiced salad cost 14dh. There is the **Mauritania** on 54, Av. Hassan II, tel 24715, or behind the CTM is **Chez Claude**, 4, Rue de Taza.

The **Roi de la Bière**, tel 25324, is a delightful aged but dignified place, a three-course meal for 55dh at 59, Blvd Mohammed V. The **Saada** on 42, Av. Slaoui, tel 23681, serves a menu for 30dh and one of the most famous new town restaurants is **La Tour d'Argent**, a full three-course meal for 60dh, though it has recently lost its licence; it is at 34, Av. Slaoui, tel 22689.

Cheap eating in the Medina

In the Medina there are a number of tiny hole-in-the-wall grill kitchens and café restaurants. The restaurant **Bouayed**, 26 Rue Serrajine or the **Des Jeunes**, 16, Rue Serrajine, tel 34975, both by the Bab Boujeloud stay open late and are clean, quick and honest. Sniff around the Bab Semmarine or the Place des Alouites for a café serving food in Fez el Jedid.

NIGHT CLUBS

The Hotels **Palais Jamai**, the **Volubilis**, Av. Allal Ben Abdellah, tel 23098, the **Grand Hotel**, Blvd Chefchaouni, tel 25511, **Les Merenides**, the **Sofia**, 3, Rue du Pakistan, tel 24266, and the **Zalagh** run night clubs, of which the latter might be worth a try.

Fez to Taza

Travelling directly over the 120 km between Fez and Taza has little to delay your journey.

Sidi Harazem

10 km east of Fez el Bali there is a right turn for the spa of Sidi Harazem which was known until the 17th century as Hammam Khaoulan. It was the favourite spa of Sultan Moulay Rachid who moved the bones of Sidi Harazem here from Marrakesh. The April Moussem of the great Muslim saint is now celebrated here as well at Fez and Marrakesh. The 17th-century **Koubba** and the small **bath house** are pleasant enough but they are dwarfed by the bottling plant, a 4 star health hotel and a very ugly modern concrete spa centre. It is a place of popular piety, full in the summer of trinket sellers, musicians and grill cafés. The snaking stream of 35°C hot manganese-rich water is full of bodies dozingly take the cure and women washing clothes. The squeamish might be put off the shared mineral pool by the liver, urinary and venereal diseases that have driven other swimmers here for a cure.

On the main P1 road 2 km beyond the Sidi Harazem turning there is a bridge over the Oued Sebou and 12 km later the **koubba of Sidi Abd er Rezzak** to the south. The Monday **souk of the Beni Sadden** tribe is held just to the north of the road, opposite the village of **Ras Tabouda**, about 30 km east of Fez. Beyond Ras Tabouda there is a small caravanserai beside the road which gives a first glimpse of Lake Idriss I. If you are looking for a meal along the way stop at the village of **Sidi Abdjelil**. It is on the eastern

330

edge of this dammed lake and has a number of roadside grill cafés. The bridge over the Oued Bou Hellou marks the site of a Roman frontier fort that was established in the tribal territory of the Baquates. 10 km further east is the turning for the Djebel Tazzeka national park.

Travelling directly to Taza, you cross the Touahar pass. The chief town of the Beni Magara tribe, **Mghara**, dominated the summit in the 8th century AD. The power of this tribe was destroyed during the Khajarite wars. This left as dominant the neighbouring Meknassa tribe who founded Taza, though the tribe's name is more directly commemorated by the village of **Meknassa Tahtania** which can be seen 12 km northwest of Taza up route S328.

Djebel Tazzeka

The forested highlands of Tazzeka are one of the two great national parks of Morocco. A 76 km drive through these hills is the best possible approach to Taza but the main site, the **Friouato cavern**, can as easily be reached from the town, in a 24 km taxi ride. To approach Djebel Tazzeka turn left off the P1 at the sign post for Bab Azhar. This tarmac road, the S311, swings under the main road and climbs up through the Oued Zireg gorge.

The cliffs of the gorge reach above, patrolled by circling buzzards, whilst the small river bed can occasionally be glimpsed below. Beyond the Saturday market of **souk Es Sebt** and the neighbouring village of **Bab Azhar** you enter the forested hills. The road twists and climbs through a wilderness of pine, cedar, holm oak and cork to the Bab Taza pass at 1540 m.

Djebel Tazzeka

Just before the summit of the pass a rough track climbs north over 7 km to the summit of Djebel Tazzeka, though the radio aerial on the peak destroys some of the grandeur of this celebrated view over rippling forested slopes from 1980 m.

Daia Chicker

8 km beyond the pass you reach **Bou Idir**, a superbly positioned, decaying French hill station at 1450 m with a liberating view. Below Bou Idir you descend past the damaged entrances of a number of old lead mines to the wonderful serene depression of Daia Chicker. This bowl of pasture has been formed after thousands of years of rain lightly traced with carbon dioxide has dissolved the limestone. Two small lakes seasonally appear, the furthest away drains into the Chicker cave system, a potholers'/spelunkers' heaven of miles of subterranean tunnels. (The Alpine Club, 13 Blvd de la Résistance, Rabat, or the Mountain Federation, 53 Rue Allal ben Abdellah, Casablanca may be able to include you in their next visit.)

Friouato cavern

A signposted turning leads up a twisting tarmac drive to the Friouato/it-Ato cavern, entrance 5dh. A vast number of irregular steps lead down a descending tunnel into an enormous 180 m deep subterranean bowl. This is lit by a 30 m wide cleft in the rocks through which sunlight streams to pick out one moss-covered rock wall. The increasingly erratic staircase descends down the scree slope to the bottom of the bowl. This is quite impressive enough although with a torch you can descend further to view caverns opening up rich in oozing stalagmite and stalactite rock forms. The narrowing tunnel and steps descend to where the water level fluctuates and most amateurs are relieved to halt by the silt deposits which are warm, dank and dark enough for most tastes.

Below the Daia Chicker is the **Pass of Sidi Mejbeur** at 1198 m which provides a memorable view down over Taza Medina and the new town. Taza's strategic position commanding the narrow river valley is triumphantly revealed. To the east of the city there is a small area of cultivable land before the plain of Jel opens up in the widening funnel of desert between Riff and Middle Atlas.

The falls of the river Ras have not flown even in spring for several years now but the dry course is decorated by the twisted trunks of ancient cork trees. At the summit of the falls is a café terrace with a fine view and a full water tank. Then descend through olive groves to the city.

TAZA

This ancient city fortress, poised on a high outcrop of limestone, has a turbulent history. It controls the Taza gap, a narrow valley that separates the Riff from the Middle Atlas and divides the eastern nomadic steppe from the farmed lands of the west. From its high ageing battlements you can survey the surrounding landscape and then explore the dark busy souk that runs straight through the Medina.

On lower ground to the east of the Medina the French built a grid pattern of streets in 1920 from which recent development has extended. The two quarters of the town are still physically apart, divided by an olive grove and a 3 km walk. As the seat of the provincial governor and the region's central market Taza has a certain bustle and the quiet charm of the town has fortunately left it quite stranded from mass tourism.

History

Taza is a frontier, a border town and a national fortress. It has subsequently been involved in a long succession of wars and was used as the central military base by three dynasties during their struggle for power, by the Almohads, Merenids and Alouites. Taza, though vital during the struggle for power, is less useful afterwards and so it has a recurring history, rising in importance during war and declining in peace.

The Meknassa citadel
Though garrisoned and embellished by a succession of dynasties Taza was created by the Berber Meknassa tribe. They fortified the rock in the aftermath of the Khajarite wars but accepted an orthodox Idrissid governor in the 9th century. The Meknassa fortress became a key defensive position against the Fatimid Empire in the early 10th century as it advanced from the east but after a decisive defeat, just east of Taza at Msoun, tribal resistance against the Fatimids collapsed and both Taza and Fez surrendered.

An Almohad capital

The Almohad Sultan Abdel Moumen gained control of Taza early in his long campaign to destroy the Almoravide Empire. He seized the town in 1132 and for two decades Taza acted as the capital of the infant Almohad Empire. The magnificent Grand Mosque in the Medina of Taza dates from this era of importance, a true sister in size and elegance to her contemporaries, the Koutoubia of Marrakesh and the sanctuary of Tinmal in the High Atlas.

Merenid Taza

The Beni Merin in their turn struggled against the Almohad Empire for twenty-five years before their tribal chiefs could reign as the Merenid Sultans. Taza was the first city to fall to these Berber nomads of the eastern plain. The town, close to the tribal homeland, was rewarded by the most distinguished Sultans of the dynasty who each generation added to the stock of elegant buildings with another mosque, a school, bath, medersa, hospital or zaouia which were all encircled within strong outer walls.

The eastern frontier

Plundered and stagnating in the anarchy of the 16th century, it fell as an empty husk to the Saadians, by which time Leo Africanus had found little left to praise in the town beyond its walls. The Saadian El Mansour took good care of these, employing European architects and using his Christian captives to strengthen the defences in case of an advance by the Turks.

The first Alouite Sultan, Moulay Rachid, selected Taza in 1666 as his base. Oujda and the east he already commanded, for his family's influence had advanced north up from the oasis of Tafilalet. From Taza he destroyed the armies of his enemies, the Saadians and Djila, in a series of quick and ferocious campaigns.

His successors continually fortified Taza and the eastern frontier against the Turks and later the French in Algeria. During Abdul Aziz's reign, 1891–1907, the region gradually slipped out of control despite a number of campaigns.

The rogui, 'the pretender' Bou Hamara, proclaimed himself Sultan at Taza in 1902 and though forced out once from the city maintained his rule over the eastern plains and the Riff until he finally fell prisoner in 1912.

The French occupied Taza in 1914 and established a large garrison used in the long conquest of the Middle Atlas and Riff tribes. Active campaigning continued until 1934 but the barracks were converted into the nucleus of the present new town from 1920. The French garrison in Taza witnessed a few more months of fighting when the Riff tribes and the Liberation Army reopened a guerrilla campaign in 1956. After Independence the region has known a long and rare era of peace though a confused revolt in the Middle Atlas in 1959 and an army mutiny in 1974 reasserted its continued strategic importance.

GETTING AROUND

By Train: There are daily trains for Oujda, Fez and Rabat, change at Sidi Kacem or Sidi Slimane for Tangier, at Casablanca for Marrakesh.

By Bus: All buses stop at the train station, though the CTM coaches officially start from the Place de L'Independence. There is a daily bus to Oujda and two for Fez that leave at

14.30 and 18.00 for 17dh. The daily bus to Nador leaves at 16.40. Local buses go directly from the train station to the Medina or a ride in a petit taxi for 10dh.

By Car: Taza is 120 km from Fez and 223 km from Oujda. The new town is full of mechanic shops and there is the central garage on Place de L'Independence.

GETTING AROUND THE TOWN

Taza is a town on three levels. At the bottom by the road is the train station, at the top of the new town, a half hour walk, is the Place de L'Independence and at the entrance to the Medina is the Place Moulay Hassan. The Medina has everything of interest in Taza, the Place de L'Independence has the bars, cafés, hotels, banks and Post Office and the train station, tel 2019, is the transport hub of the town.

TOURIST INFORMATION

The Post Office is by the Place de L'Independence on the corner of Rue Allal ben Abdallah and Mouassa Ibn Noussair, open from Monday to Friday. The Banque Populaire is on Rue Anoual and the BMCE on 24, Av. Mohammed V. The Tourist Office is at 56, Av. Mohammed V, open from Monday to Friday, and Taza tours can be found on Av. Mohammed V, tel 2005. The Moussem of Sidi Zerrouk is held in September.

WHAT TO SEE

Taza's chief attraction should be the magnificent Almohad Grand Mosque but this is off-course, closed to non-Muslims. The **Medina** subsequently has no oustanding attraction but it is a pleasant and unhassling place. A Medina walk has been described that begins at the Mechouar, follows the principal souk avenue to lead past the Grand Mosque and out to the Bab er Rih on the northern ramparts but Taza Medina is small and friendly enough to explore at random.

The Av. Moulay Youssef leads from the New Town to a roundabout at the foot of the Medina where a long staircase climbs up through the Bab Jemaa to the Place Moulay Hassan. Arriving by bus or taxi you sweep beyond this, up beside the outer lower walls and to the left you may catch a glimpse of the **Koubba of Sidi Aissa**, on the road to the campsite, where the Sultan Bou Inania built a lodge and a zaouia for poor students in the 13th century.

Southern ramparts

Entering Taza from the south you pass through the **Bab El Guebor** breach in the ramparts. To the right is the palace of the Pasha, behind which is the 25 m high '**El Bastioun**' a brick-built artillery fortress constructed by the Saadian Sultan El Mansour against the Turkish threat. Inside the 3 m thick bastion walls some 16th-century graffiti of ships can be seen, carved by the Portuguese prisoners captured at the battle of Ksar el Kebir. During the restoration of the bastion in 1916 the entrance to the Kifan el Khomari cave was discovered, revealing Paleolithic finds from the Mousterian culture.

250 m to the left of the Bab el Guebor entrance is the surviving 12th-century **Bab Titi gate** and twice that distance the circular Almohad tower known as **El Sarrasine** guards the western corner of the Medina plateau. The ramparts which wrap Taza in 3 km of wall follow the 12th-century Almohad defences though restorations undertaken by Merenid, Saadian and Alouite Sultans can offer a confusing variety of dates.

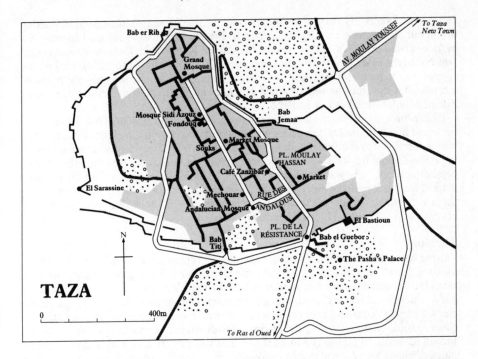

The Rue Bab el Guebor leads directly to the central Place of Moulay Hassan. Cars, buses and taxis park here, the covered food market is to the east and the souks to the west, and the street life is best watched from a table at the café Zanzibar.

Mechouar

On the left you will have passed a mosque and a fountain beside the Rue des Andalous. This twisting alley crossed by arches and buttresses leads to the walled and gated Mechouar Avenue, a formal space established by the old governor's palace and the **Andalucian Mosque**.

The Mosque which retains its 12th-century Almohad minaret is largely hidden from view but a courtyard to the west allows a discreet examination. There is a delightful garden courtyard—public lavatory on the right as you enter the Mechouar, from where you can ask directions for the reclusive and decaying 18th-century governor's palace, tucked in behind the Andalucian Mosque.

Bou Hamara

It was occupied by Bou Hamara, 'the father of the she donkey', who began his spectacular career as the scribe Omar ez Zerhoun. He left Meknes in 1901 accused of forging documents, having last served as the secretary of the Caid of the Beni M'Tir tribe. Travelling as a holy man, on an attractive she donkey, amongst the Riff tribes he developed a considerable following which he enlarged with his considerable rhetorical and magical skills. As support grew he claimed to be Moulay Mohammed, the elder brother of the reigning Sultan, Abdul Aziz. In 1902 his tribal force defeated an army led by one of the Sultan's real brothers, Moulay el Kebir. Bou Hamara subsequently dominated the east for ten years moving between Taza, Selouane and Oujda. He lost the support of the powerful Riff tribe of the Beni Ouriaghel when he sold mineral rights to Christians. Captured, he was confined in a cage on the back of a camel and taken to Sultan Moulay Hafid at Fez in 1912.

There 'he was put into the lions' cage in the presence of the Sultan, while the ladies of the court lined the roof of the palace to witness the execution. The lions, however, too well fed, refused to eat him, but mangled one of his arms. After waiting for some time to see if the King of beasts would change their minds, the Sultan ordered the Pretender to be shot and his body was afterwards burnt . . . terrible as was his end, Bou Hamara himself had been guilty of every kind of atrocity, and had regularly burnt, after sprinkling them with petroleum, any of the Sultan's soldiers that he had been able to capture during his campaigns' (Walter Harris, *Morocco that Was*).

The Souk
Passing beyond the Mechouar you continue along a central street, which, under a variety of names, leads straight through the Medina. On your left you pass the entrance to a small but reportedly charming **medersa** built by the Merenid Sultan Abou Hassan in 1323 which is currently closed, though the neighbouring secondary school has some elegant carved cedar and tilework in its courtyard. The road narrows as you enter the covered souk quarter, passing the **shrine of Sidi Ali er Derrar** before you reach the **Jamaa es souk**, 'the market Mosque' which, if you can get a view of it, has a curious minaret whose tower is wider than its foundation. A number of alleys open to the left of the Mosque to compromise the **kissaria**. The products of the souk are entirely for the local trade and the Medina is delightfully free of salesmen and tourist bazaars, though you can hunt for local basketwork, braided mats and carpets made by the Beni Ouaran hill tribe. Look out for the mint tea café at a fondouq at no 53 and the grain market courtyard. The 12th-century **Mosque and shrine of Sidi Azouz**, the patron of Taza, on the left, marks the transition from the souk to a richer residential quarter of the Medina with its quiet houses guarded by heavy doors and ornate grille windows.

Grand Mosque
The central aisle of the Grand Mosque is aligned with the street but the great clean area of high white wall punctured by a number of green tiled and decorated gates is firmly closed to non-Muslims. Alleys to the right and left allow you to admire the extent of the Mosque and thread your way out to the ramparts. It was founded by Abdel Moumen in 1135 and built to the same plan as the Almohad Mosques of Tinmal, in the High Atlas, and the Koutoubia in Marrakesh. The Merenids adorned the interior; the mihrab, the finely carved stucco panels of the dome, the ivory inlayed minbar and an enormous bronze chandelier can only be seen by a non-Muslim in Charles Terrasse's detailed study, *Le Grande Mosque de Taza, 1943*.

Bab er Rih
The Bab er Rih, the gate of the winds, is a 12th-century bastion with a fine view of the

surrounding mountains. Low squat huts hug the edge of the fortress and the clearly defined garden plots extend east to the olive groves. To the west Moulay Rachid built a palace, the **Dar el Makhzen**, of which there is little trace, only the view and the cool winds remain unchanged. From the Bab er Rih turn right and walk beside the ramparts back to the Place Moulay Hassan.

WHERE TO STAY

The Salam chain run the **** **Friouato Hotel** which is found off the new town to Medina avenue set in its own garden. It has a pool, tennis court, bar, restaurant and 58 rooms, tel 2593; a double room costs 250dh.

The ** **Grand Hotel du Dauphine** is the best place to stay, an old and comfortable hotel with balconied bedrooms that overlook the Place de L'Independence, a sweeping staircase, an ancient switchboard and an enclosed pinewood bar. There is also a restaurant, tel 3567; a single room for 45dh or a double with a bathroom for 110dh.

If full there is a reasonable and cheaper alternative opposite, the **Hotel Brasserie**, tel 2347, a single for 25dh, a double for 40dh but try to avoid the noisy **Hotel de La Gare** by the train station.

EATING OUT

The streets of Taza New Town have more bars than restaurants and the town has more of a reputation for beer than food. There are a few grill cafés in the Medina that concentrate around the Place Moulay Hassan, and in the New Town the cheaper cafés are found along or just off Av. Mohammed V. A more formal meal is available for 40dh at the **Dauphine** or a 28dh menu from the **Majestic** at 26, Av. Mohammed V or for 80dh from the **Hotel Friouato**.

Taza to Oujda

From Taza a desert plain extends across to the eastern city of Oujda. This bleak expanse is broken by a scattering of eucalyptus groves and a few dusty towns. A defenceless area that stretches between the two citadel cities, it has been a natural battleground and most travellers still hurry across, which leaves the few places of interest—Msoun, Gouttitir, Debdou, the Za canyon and Za waterfall—largely undisturbed. Msoun is only 28 km east of Taza but all the other sights can be explored from Taourirt which has a couple of basic hotels.

HISTORY

To the north of the plains is the territory of the sedentary Riff hill tribes. South from these hills has been dominated by nomadic pastoral tribes. The most famous of these were the Beni Merin, a Berber but Arabic-speaking tribe who controlled the Moulouya valley in the 12th century. Periodically employed by Almohad Sultans in wars of conquest, they developed an increasing taste for the power and wealth that could only be won in warfare.

In 1248 an Almohad army retired from the Algerian frontier after their Sultan, Es Said, had been killed. This demoralized force, shadowed by Beni Merin scouts as it limped across the desert, was massacred as it struggled across the river Moulouya. From this ruthless act the Beni Merin chiefs grew greatly in reputation. Taza and the entire eastern plain fell instantly into their power, to be followed by the great city of Fez.

Msoun

The Kasbah of Msoun commands the ground to the north of the road and the approach to the Oued Msoun ford. This secure compound was built by Sultan Moulay Ishmael in the 18th century. Each face is protected by four turrets that stud a battlemented wall and even the wooden gates are still in place. Within the walls are some olive trees and the dusty hamlet of the Haoura tribe, a semi-nomadic group of shepherds who are absent from their kasbah home for most of the year. It is a strange but attractive place that houses a complete community and has a shop, Post Office, school, mosque and tea room with a view due south to the peak of Djebel Ouarirth.

A great battle was fought here in AD 933 when the Berber Meknassa tribe, who held Meknes and Taza, were destroyed by the Fatimid Empire, who in that century ruled all of North Africa.

36 km east of Msoun is **Guercif**, a village at the centre of an oasis of agricultural lands irrigated by the Oued Melloulou and Moulouya. The surrounding orchards and gardens provide welcome shade for a picnic, but the village has small appeal and the listed campsite even less. From Guercif a road follows the Moulouya valley southwest to Midelt; this the least visited oasis valley of Morocco is best approached from Midelt, see page 346.

Gouttitir

Between Guercif and Taourirt look out for a left turn to Gouttitir. It is a hamlet only a kilometre from the road which is established beside a natural hot water mineral spring. Men have use of this natural Hammam, hidden from immediate view by the steep cut bed of the stream, until dusk when it becomes the women's property. The café **Sidi Chaffi** with its enormous spacious hall and cool arcades echoes to almost continuous reggae. Haffid can rent you a hut for 30dh and fix a light meal.

Taourirt

Taourirt kasbah is crowned by radio aerials for it is still in active use by the Moroccan army who still value its commanding view of the Za river crossing. It has been in continuous occupation but its most active period was from 1295 when it became a Merenid base against the Ziyanids of Tlemcen. By the central crossroads there are four grill cafés to the south and half a dozen cafés that serve breakfast. There are two hotels, the very basic **Riad** on Blvd Mohammed V, 25dh for a room, or the slightly smarter **El Gaada**, tel 3, to the left on the road to Debdou. A busy local **souk** is held by the crossroads on Sunday morning.

Out from Taourirt

A road marked Beni Koulal follows the river south of town almost to the entrance of the dramatic Za river canyon. Do not accelerate past the bollards as the road ends in a lethal cliff drop. A dirt track by the Koubba and cult tree of Sidi Mazark allows you to walk to the gorge.

A 53km drive south of Taourirt through the land of the Haoura nomads, the desert plain of the Sedjaa of Tafrate takes you to the hillside village of **Debdou** surrounded by orchards and woods. The nomadic but Arabic-speaking Beni Merin tribe controlled the kasbah before they fought their way to the throne. Elevated to higher concerns the kasbah was given to some cousins, the Beni Ouatta in the 15th century, who were destined to eventually succeed the Merenids to the throne. The kasbah was then occupied by the Berber-speaking Haoura who have not yet developed similar political aspirations. South of Debdou a tarmac road climbs through forested hills towards the **El Ateuf kasbah** and a mosque built by Caid Goarich.

6 km west of Taourirt leave the main road and travel north, downstream towards the dammed Lake of Mohammed V. The falls are 9 km along this tarmac road. Pass the buildings of the colonial farm, the distinctive white koubba and about 1 km further a dirt track to the right leads to the Za falls. A delightful cascade of water falls over the hard pebble pudding rock into a large and swimmable bowl below complete with gravel beds, caves and drying rocks. The river valley makes a pleasant unconventional camping ground.

Taourirt to Oujda

The border city of Oujda and the mountains of Beni Snassen are described at the end of Part IV 'Tangier, the Riff and the Mediterranean coast'. You can find details of Nador and the beach of Qariat Arkmane there which can be reached on a road that turns north for the sea 27 km east of Taourirt.

21 km further east is the Tuesday **souk of El Aioun** from where a bumpy tarmac road approaches the camel cave in the Beni Snassen mountains. El Aioun was founded by Moulay Ishmael who built a kasbah here in 1679. He recruited the Berber Beni Snassen tribe to his army but found it convenient to guarantee their obedience by having a garrison within striking distance of their homeland. Sultan Moulay Hassan restored El Aioun kasbah in 1876, at the same time that he strengthened Selouane and Saidia against the growing threat of French expansion from Algeria. A zouaia of Sheikh Bou Amama (1840–1908) was welcomed to El Aioun, as this Sufi brotherhood increasingly devoted itself to resistance against the French. Just to the south of the town is a cemetery where many of the martyrs of this resistance are buried and koubba raised over the more celebrated mujahadeen.

50 km east of El Aioun, just south of the road, a Moroccan army was destroyed by the French at the battle of Isly. The leader of Algerian resistance, Abd el Kader, had retreated into Morocco in 1843 and had been joined outside Oujda by the army of Sultan Moulay Abder Rahman. The French general Bugeaud, ignoring both the border and the declared pacific intentions of the Sultan, boldly advanced into Morocco. On 13 August 1844 he attacked the combined Moroccan–Algerian army on the banks of the Isly which though it was dry in this midsummer month flowed blood that day for 6 km downstream into Oujda.

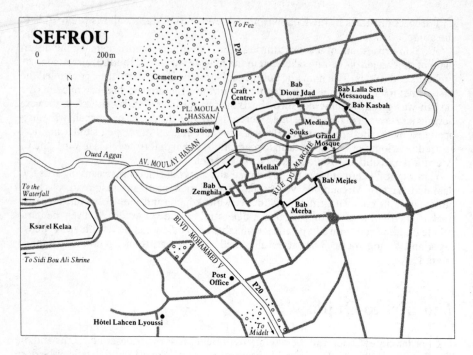

Sefrou

Sefrou is on the border between the fertile Sais plain and the limestone plateau of the Middle Atlas. It is the market of the indigenous Berber Ahel Sefrou tribe, its prime position allows the pastoral tribes to the south and the sedentary agriculturists to the north to meet and trade in mutual security. Numerous petty springs flow from the base of the plateau to water the surrounding gardens and cherry orchards of the region. The walled Medina remains at the heart of this prosperous town of 45,000, the twisting Medina alleys span either side of the steep banked Oued Aggai which is occasionally spanned by an elegant bridge.

HISTORY

It is an ancient town whose Berber population was converted to Judaism by missionaries perhaps even before the fall of Jerusalem in AD 71.

Moulay Idriss I is recorded to have lived for three years outside Sefrou at a Ksar called Habarnoa (between 787–792), whilst he converted the town and its surrounding tribes to Islam and planned the foundation of Fez. Firmly established astride the 'trik es soltan', the Tafilalet to Fez caravan trail, the town prospered from the Saharan trade in the 12th century. The Bedouin Arab invasions of the 13th century endangered numerous Jewish communities to the east and on the borders of the Sahara, and refugees from Tafilalet and Algeria settled in Sefrou to establish an influential Israelite community who have all emigrated in the last three decades.

The town has returned to its old ways as a regional market that supports a flourishing artisan community. The **souk** is held on Thursday and the cherry harvest is celebrated in June with several memorable days of music, dance and feasting. The patron saint of the town, Sidi Lahcen Lyoussi, is venerated with a Moussem in August.

GETTING AROUND
There are frequent buses that travel the 28 km between Fez and Sefrou but services south are less reliable. Buses leave Fez from Bab Boujeloud and arrive at Sefrou's main entrance to the medina, Bab Lamkam.

TOURIST INFORMATION
The Tourist Office is found on Blvd Hassan II beside the Aggai bridge, tel 60380. The Post Office, BMCE and Banque Populaire are all found on Blvd Mohammed V.

The Medina
The crenellated ochre pise walls of the city have been continuously restored although there are a few sections that survive from the 18th century. Nine gates pierce the ramparts, five enter the Medina quarter and four the old Mellah quarter on the south bank of the Oued Aggai which is spanned by four connecting bridges. Opposite the bus station on Place Moulay Hassan there is a busy garden café, a fountain and two gates, the **Bab Taksebt** and the **Bab Mkam**. The Bab Mkam on the left leads past the **Echebbah Mosque** above the river bank and you pass a wall plaque which indicates the height of flood water in 1950 which drowned 30 in the Medina. Remaining on the north bank you pass the zaouia and **tomb of Sidi Lahcen ben Ahmed**, an 18th-century saint, to enter the **souks**, a network of streets lined with green booths where the skilled tailors, embroiderers, cobblers and carpenters practise their trade before your eyes. One of the city's three fondouqs can be found behind the souk, its central courtyard packed with farmers' donkeys on market day. The **Grand Mosque of El Kebir** was restored by Sultan Moulay Hassan in the 19th century, its white arcades and minaret are perched on a terrace above the river bank but are closed to non-Muslims.

The Mellah
The bridge in front of the Mosque looks out over pine and fig trees growing out from the high river banks and down over trails of decorative rubbish and hanging fragments of cloth. The mixture of water and effluent flows down over worn rocks to fertilize the lower gardens. Over the bridge enter the Mellah, the distinctive Jewish quarter with its more regular streets, angular buildings and brown balconies. The white café immediately to the left of the bridge is the regular gathering spot for the war veterans. From here the Rue du Marché continues through the Mellah, passes a covered market on your left to the Bab Merhba, outside of which the Thursday souk used traditionally to be held. A less conspicuous entrance west of Bab Merhba passes the largest Hammam, the **Essalam baths** and by twisting through narrow dark alleys you cross a bridge and return to the Place Moulay Hassan through the Bab Taksebt.

The Artisanal Centre
Below the crenellated walls in a small garden just to the north of the Place Moulay

Hassan are the Artisan display rooms, full of leatherwork, pottery, ironwork and the distinctive embroidered textiles of Sefrou. Admission free, open Mon–Sat, 8.00–12.00, 14.00–19.00.

Jardin Public
A pleasant shaded public park with a swimming pool can be entered from the Place Moulay Hassan immediately to the west of the city through which flows the river which is crossed by another bridge.

Oued Aggai waterfall
Walking west from the park you pass the twin gates that guard the entrance to the separate walled **ksar of El Kelaa**. To the right a road follows the river upstream for 1 km passing numerous caves, some of which were venerated as tombs of holy men by both Jews and Muslims. The caves are known as **Kef el Mou'men** or **Kef el Yhoudi** according to your religious loyalty. The enduring myth of the grotto of the seven sleepers has a Sefrou version and there is an ancient tradition that the prophet Daniel is buried here. The falls are dramatic in winter but have been diminished since 1977 due to a new pumping station. It is however possible to climb down into the rock pool and enjoy an alfresco shower and then absorb a beer from a hotel bar that overlooks the fall.

Sidi Bou Ali Srhine
Taking a left turn in front of Ksar El Kelaa it is possible to walk up 2 km of steep road to the shrine of Sidi Bou Ali Srhine, placed spectacularly on the edge of the limestone plateau that overlooks Sefrou. The green pyramid roof of the Koubba, its white outbuildings, café and trinket stalls is a much frequented shrine whilst below is the **holy spring of Lalla Rekia**. Each year to propitiate the spirits of the spring and ensure a continuous flow, a black cock, a white hen and a black billy goat are sacrificed, their necks cut and the blood mixed with the flowing water.

The nearby fort, known to the French as Prioux but now called Sidi Ali Ben Ziane, is still in use as a training ground but a track skirts below it to provide an improvement on the already excellent view over the new town, Medina, gardens and distant mountains.

WHERE TO STAY AND EAT
The ** **Hôtel Sidi Lahcen Lyoussi**, tel 60497, has a garden with cherry trees, a pool, restaurant, bar and only 22 rooms. It is a friendly but still tranquil place; a four-course dinner costs 75dh, a double with bathroom 175dh. The **Café Lafarine**, a secluded house surrounded by a garden just past the Medina on the road to Fez, rents rooms from 25–40dh.

Above the town beside the Sidi Bou Ali Srhine shrine there is a hotel café which charges 40dh a room. The camping ground is beside the road to the shrine. It has a fabulous view, is well shaded by trees and equipped with a cool underground cellar.

The **Cascades Hôtel** by the Oued Aggai falls charges 50dh for a room that overlooks the river, there are 5 rooms in the hotel and beer for sale at the bar. You can also drink at the bar café **La Poste** next door to the Post Office on Blvd Mohammed V.

Ait Bahlil

It is possible to walk north from Sefrou over the limestone plateau to the neighbouring village of Ait Bahlil or travel 7 km north on the Fez road and turn left on the CT 4006.

Bahlil has a picturesque upper town where rows of blue and white houses climb up a narrow valley to the now dry source of a spring. Several small and elegant bridges crisscross the elaborate stone encased dry stream bed, though the spring reappears at the foot of the town to fuel the washing souk. Two old mosques decorate the skyline of this photogenic village which is full of venerable but cheerful old men in turbans. There is a charming friendly dottiness in the air and the town has an enduring genealogical fancy that they are descended from the 1st-century Roman garrison, in particular from the Christian portion of the Second Legion. The houses often hide old underground dwellings, cool cellars cut into the limestone hill which served a double purpose of security whilst the excavated rubble can be profitably burnt and sold as lime.

At the western edge of the upper town is the café **Derb el Kebir** where men play interminable card games and the grill window provides an entrancing view north to Fez and the plain du Sais.

The Sebou Gorge

Travelling east from Sefrou on the route 4610 you first see the gorge 23 km from town as you cross a bridge over the Oued Sebou. The ruins of an earlier bridge are framed below whilst the walls of the gorge open to the south. You can walk up the valley below its massive stone face studded with caves.

The village of the Beni Yazgha tribe, **El Menzel**, is 8 km east. It is the centre of a pocket of tightly cultivated land, an oasis of olive groves that shade terraced gardens. Just past the mosque you find the central café, shaded by high mature trees where a number of shops and grill cafés have collected. From El Menzel you can take a piste track south for 12 km to the settlement of **Ain Timedrine** and the nearby **spring of Ain Sebou**, the lush, almost tropical, vegetation contrasting strongly with the burnt hills.

Trik es Soltan—South from Sefrou to Midelt

The 'trik es Soltan' is the old route by which caravans brought goods from Timbuctoo across the Sahara to Tafilalet and then up to Fez. It is the least travelled of the routes south across the Middle Atlas plateau but with your own vehicle you can as easily tour the lakes and a cedar forest from this road as from Ifrane and Azrou.

Leaving south from Sefrou is the **koubba of Sidi Youssef** on a summit that guards a nearby spring. Along the road are circular towers where crushed limestone is burnt to be sold throughout Morocco for lime. The village of **Annoceur**, on the left 24 km from Sefrou at 1345 m, marks the final limits of the irrigated lands; south of here only a few areas of orchard cultivation break an immense arid pastoral plain. 3 km east of Annoceur a classical inscription was discovered in 1960, this created a flurry of excitement as historians reassessed the extent of Roman rule but it is now thought to have been dropped by a passing caravan that was carrying antiquities from Volubilis to decorate a palace in the Tafilalet.

3 km beyond the Annoceur turning is a right turn for Dayat (lake) Aoua whilst 2 km south is the piste track for Dayat Afourgah and Iffer suggested in the lake tour, see page 349. Once you have crossed the Tiz-n-Abeknas pass at 1769 m, the right turn to join the tour of the cedar forest, on route S309 is only 9 km further south, see page 351.

Boulemane

A scattering of red-roofed houses of the old French post of Boulemane is 76 km south of Sefrou. It is in a dramatic position 1700 m up the Recifa gorge, at the foot of Djebel Tichchoukt and surrounded on almost all sides by cliff bluffs and scree slopes. There are two garages in Boulemane and the café restaurant **Essada** with its central stove pipe, as it can be as cold here in the winter as it becomes hot in the summer.

South of Boulemane you can take an obscure foray along the dead end road to **Immouzer Marmoucha** which is 55 km east at the foot of Djebel Bou Iblane. Getting there you would pass the **Ifkern ksar** on the Oued Sebou, the **Ait Makhlouf ksar** of the Marmoucha tribe poised below Djebel Issouka before reaching Immouzer des Marmoucha at 1639 m, the central village of the Marmoucha hill tribe of shepherds. A track from Immouzer climbs for 30 km to **Talzemt**, an old French army post where a ski lift is reportedly still operating.

70 km south of Boulemane you rejoin the Meknes–Midelt road, the P21, near Boulojoul, crossing a high desert plain that at the pass of Souiguer nearly exceeds 2000 m.

Midelt

Midelt is at 1500 m, a sprawling roadside market town with a population of 16,000 set in the centre of the Middle Atlas plateau.

Midelt was the central ksar and souk of the Ait Idzeg which guards the crossing of a fertile valley floor. The Ait Idzeg, before the French pacification, were a sedentary Berber tribe of 1000 extended families that occupied the high slopes of Djebel Ayachi. In a time-honoured pattern they were threatened by tribes from the south of the Atlas, in particular by the Ait Atta who each summer drove their herds from the Sahara up into the Atlas mountains. Each year they moved further north and stayed longer until portions of the tribe became firmly established in the Middle Atlas. The Ait Idzeg, who were on the front line of this creeping threat, joined the Ait Yafalman confederation of tribes that on every occasion and every issue opposed the Ait Atta.

The French when they advanced into the Middle Atlas established a garrison beside the Ait Idzeg ksar. The ksar has now disappeared to leave an initially commonplace atmosphere of a garrison town dominated by French-built telegraph lines and red tiled chalets.

It is however well placed to break a journey and explore the Middle Atlas hinterland. Midelt is 192 km from Meknes and 154 km from Er-Rachidia and has hotels, cafés, garages, a Banque Populaire and a souk. The town has a reputation as a friendly and useful base for walking to the surrounding ksar or driving into the mountains. The horizon to the south is dominated by the peaks of Djebel Ayachi, 'the mother of the waters'.

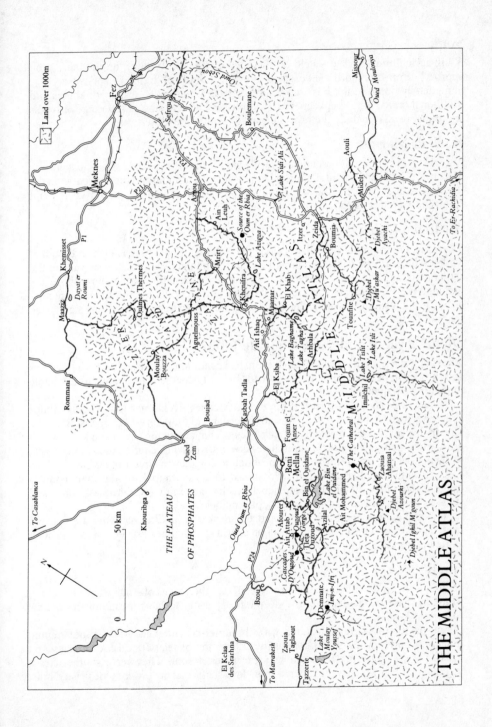

THE MIDDLE ATLAS

Souk

A big agricultural market is held on the edge of town on Sunday, on the left as you approach from the north. The small courtyard **Souk el Jedid** is open every day immediately opposite the bus stop where there is a reasonable display of killims and traditional crafts. The shopkeepers are hospitable and also stock a full range of fossils and minerals that include the brown crystal known as the 'desert rose'.

Kasbah Meriem

A weaving and embroidery school for local girls is run by Franciscan sisters just outside Midelt. Take the 3418 road signposted for Jaffar and Tattiouin and the convent is on the left. You can see the girls at work and samples of work, carpets, woven killims and embroidery are for sale.

Ait Idzeg ksar

There are a number of ksar-villages along the valley floor both to the north and south of Midelt which can be walked to in half an hour. The tightly confined pise walls of the settlements and the neatly terraced beds and petty orchards hardly show above the denuded plain and create spectacular shifting views. The **ksar Pilo**, the most picturesque, is 9 km south of Midelt along the valley which can be reached off the signposted road to Tattioune.

Djebel Ayachi and the Cirque de Jaffar

The rough tracks to the west of Midelt are in bad condition even from May to September and the circuit of mountain and forest roads below Djebel Ayachi is now more suitable for landrovers than cars.

The track 3426 which turns off the P21 to Meknes, 15 km north of Midelt, climbs above the inhabited plateau de L'Arid to the cedar and thuja forested heights. After the forestry hut of Mitkane turn left on track 3424 to climb up to the Cirque de Jaffar which has a celebrated view of the forests and peaks to the west. The continuation of this track, washed away in parts, returns down to Midelt to complete a circuit of 80 km.

An adventurous alternative is to drive or taxi 15 km south to Tattiouine where mules can be hired for the 20 km climb to Djebel Ayachi—an exciting wilderness of forest and stone in delightful contrast to the bleak plateau below.

Any mountain further west, like Djebel Mu'asker at 3277 m, is better approached from Tounifit which can be reached along a tarmac road that starts 48 km from Midelt along the P33 to Khenifra.

Aouli

25 km northeast of Midelt on the tarmac S317 are the gorges of Aouli where the Oued Moulouya has carved out a long and steep walled passage through the mountains to flow east.

You pass across a region dotted with the deserted entrances to work-out mining tunnels of different ages and complexity. Leave the plateau after 12 km to descend beside the river gorge that travels down to the mines of Aouli. They were a source of lead, copper and silver which was extracted from deep shafts that burrow into the twisted hills.

Massive disentangled rusting mining machinery stands idle in the deep gorge that is occasionally filled by a torrential mountain river. Great metal flood doors remain to protect the empty apartments and villas and the river is crisscrossed with a number of metal cat walks and bridges whilst dark mine shafts beckon from the hill side. Until 1979 3000 men were employed here; only a very few remain, who now herd goats and fish the stream.

Moulouya Valley

South of Midelt a left turn on to the tarmac S329 could take you along the least travelled oasis valley of Morocco. It follows a line of bleak settlements along the Oued Moulouya and crosses the desert plateau of the Rekkam to reach, in 263 km, **Guercif** on the Fez to Oujda road. There are no hotels, a few basic cafés and petrol is available only at the two chief villages of **Missour**, 96 km from Midelt and at **Oulat Ouled el-Haj**, 146 km.

From Midelt a trip to Tamdaflet and back, 126 km, allows you to visit some of the most interesting Ksour on this otherwise long and hot bleak journey. 16 km east of Midelt turn right off the P21 after the Ksar of Zebzate and reach the **Ksar of Amersid** in 18 km. **Ksar Seghern** is 10 km later where a left turn leads in 3 km to the banks of the Oued Moulouya where there is a group of over a dozen Ksour, containing over 2000 people who are collectively known as Ksabi ech Cheurfa. The Arab population moved here from the Tafilalet to settle on one of the alternative trade routes to Fez which was protected by a kasbah built by Moulay Ishmael. 8 km from Seghern you pass **Saidia Ksar** and in 11 km reach **Tamdaflet**, a modern settlement on the Oued Moulouya.

WHERE TO STAY AND EAT

*** **Hôtel Ayachi**, on the southern edge of town, is enclosed by its own garden and surrounded by tiled chalets, tel 2161. It has 28 rooms, a double for 168dh, a restaurant where dinner costs 65dh, whilst a bar is at the back.

Hôtel Mimlal has 7 rooms and charges 50dh for a double; it sells beer and wine at the bar and a menu for 30dh is available. It is on the left as you enter town from the north, with a raffish boozey atmosphere. The **Hôtel Roi de la Biere** in the centre of town has ten cool rooms, a double for 60dh and a single for 35dh and no beer. If this is full the **Occidental** and the **Terminus** are two basic hotels in the centre.

Apart from eating at the **Ayachi** or **Mimlal** there is a cheap and discreet place to recommend at 15, Rue des Essayaghine, opposite the CTM where Fatima Tazi produces a fine tagine or couscous.

South to Er Rachidia

Only 30 km south from Midelt you cross the watershed of the Atlas at the pass of the camel, the Tiz n Talghemt, which reaches 1907 m. There is a distinctive transition from the northern forested face of the mountain range to the desiccated south facing slopes. The climate, vegetation and culture south of the pass is Saharan. Settlement is restricted to fortified villages along the valleys whose dry river beds cover a network of khennegs that feed the small gardens with water. The ksour of this mountain region are occupied by the Ait Idzeg tribe whilst the dry slopes and plateau are grazed by the Ait Haddidou, a fierce nomadic tribe who were a vital part of the Ait Yafalman confederation. The Ait Haddidou, who were distinguished by their cohesion, their costume and their particularism, were notorious raiders and descended from their secure mountain valleys to pillage caravans from the lower slopes of the Middle Atlas to Tuat, deep in the Saraha.

The road which follows the 'trik es soltan' route from Tafilalet to Fez is pockmarked with kasbahs, ksar, caravanserai and French Foreign legion forts to protect farmers, merchants and isolated garrisons from these raiders whose chiefs only surrendered to France a few years before the Second World War.

Descending 12 km you pass **N'Zala,** where there is an eight-towered Foreign Legion fort to add to the succession of half empty disintegrating ksar and caravanserai. 6 km further south is the substantial **ksar Ait Kherrou** of the Ait Idzeg that guards the entrance of the gorge of the Oued N'Zala, whilst beyond there is a waterhole known as the **fountain of Ain Chroub ou Hrob,** which translates as 'Drink and run'.

Rich

75 km south of Midelt a turn to the west leads 3 km to the settlement of Rich beside the banks of the Oued Ziz at the centre of a dry high mountain plain. It is a village that has grown from a ksar to become the commercial and administrative centre for the southern-most ksour of the Ait Idzeg that hide in the plain of Oudlalas fed by the water of the upper Oued Ziz. To the south is the dramatic High Atlas face of Djebel Bou Hamid, whose slopes appear golden in the evening light.

A central garden of pine trees exists at the entrance of the village where a collection of battlemented stalls sell kebabs and boiled eggs. The **souk** is usually held on Sunday and there are two basic and friendly hotels on the road to the souk compound; the **El Massira** on the corner above a café has grilled windows on its rooms that overlook the souk gates.

Ziz

7 km south of Rich the ksour of Ait Krojmane tribe marks a crossing of the Ziz. The east turn to Gourrama allows access to the string of ksar that follow the valley, their yellow walls punctured by the region's style of high arcaded arches and windows. The Ziz snakes gently through the mountain plain but has carved a dramatic gorge in its descent south. After the Legionnaires' tunnel the passage is through vast bleak gold and red cliffs that hem in two beautiful oasis kasbahs of **Amzouf** and **Ifni.** At the foot of the gorges the river is caught in the Ait Atmanes dam and forms the Hassan Addakhil lake. The dam was finished in 1971 and payed for by a special tax on sugar. Below the lake a few drab red modern military kasbahs stretch beside the road along the 16 km to Er-Rachidia, see page 457.

Immouzer du Kandar

On the first substantial rise in the land above the agricultural plain from Fez is the hilltop settlement of Immouzer on the edge of the limestone plateau that marks the beginning of the Middle Atlas. In the summer this open town with its park and twin lakes shaded by deciduous trees is a refreshing change from the exhausting heat, odour and vitality of Fez. Although the town is built beside the ruined walls of an old kasbah, the dominant architectural features are the square red-tiled European houses and hotels. This popular summer hill station has a relaxed bar and café life and a three day Apple fête is held in July to celebrate the harvest.

GETTING AROUND

At least four buses a day leave for Fez and Ifrane, 5dh, or travel by grand taxi to move east to Sefrou.

A **souk** is held every Monday in the interior of the decayed **Kasbah of Ait Segh-rouchen**. The walls of the kasbah are barely discernible and the entrance is through a double arch to the left of the town's mosque with its conspicuous high roof and dormer windows. Within this muddled compound are the characteristic underground dwellings of the region. They are well used and often lived in like the two at the bottom of a shortpassage; turn right as you enter the gate. The kasbah also contains a number of carpenters' workshops whose aromatic wood shavings are burnt in the nearby Hammam to heat the baths.

Out from Immouzer

A dirt track leads 10 km east of Immouzer to climb near to the top of **Djebel Abad**, where a tower at 1706 m affords a splendid introduction to the topography of the area: Fez in the plain of Sais, Meknes fringed by the Djebel Zerhoun, the Riffs in the far distance and the Middle Atlas ranged to the south.

8 km below Immouzer du Kandar on the road to Fez a sharp left turn down the narrow route 4633 brings you to the river Cheggag and the **Ain Chiffa spring**, a verdant oasis in high summer, and the fresh water has been trapped to fill a pool.

WHERE TO STAY AND EAT

The best place to stay and eat in Immouzer du Kandar is the ** **Des Truites**, tel (06) 63002, a family run hotel, bar and restaurant with 17 simple rooms. A single room for 63dh, a double for 87dh, and allow 130dh for breakfast and a hearty dinner with wine.

If this is full try the **Royal**, tel 63080, a functional two-star hotel with a bar and restaurant by the lake. They charge 140dh for a single room, 175dh for a double and 75dh for dinner. There are cheaper rooms available from the **Hôtel du Centre**, a double room for 30dh, and there is a large well-organized campsite which runs from April to September on the edge of town towards Ifrane.

The Lake Circuit

This circuit can be as easily attempted from Immouzer, Ifrane or Sefrou. 9 km south of Immouzer and 16 km north of Ifrane on the P24, a left turn leads to **Dayat (Lake) Aaoua**.

It is a long attractive sheet of water, a natural depression formed from dissolving limestone, its banks fringed by mixed woodland and surrounded by rounded low hills. A blissful tranquil scene for anyone enduring the summer in a Moroccan city but the ducks, red pedaloes and lakeside reflections have less appeal for a European eagerly seeking the desert and 'Islamic sensations'. The **Hôtel Chalet du Lac** overlooks the lake and rents boats, and a thin Gallic patroness provides over the bar and kitchen, rigorously maintaining standards and obedience from her dogs. There are 26 rooms, a single with breakfast costs 120dh, a four course meal 95dh.

Dayat Afourgah and Iffer

Continue on the tarmac road beyond the hotel to reach in 16 km the Fez–Sefrou–Midelt road, turn right and about 2 km later a sign will indicate a track on the right. This allows you to pass the tinted Dayat Afourgah which drains through a cavern in the limestone to the quite separate Dayat Iffer, the water appearing filtered and cool in this crater lake.

Dayat Ifrah

Then turn left on to tarmac which in 5 km reaches the Dayat Ifrah, a great circular bowl of water in a natural depression. Around the lake's edge horses pasture and nomads gather in their black tents to water their herds, whilst two rival hamlets exist on the opposite shore each with its own mosque.

Valley of the Rocks

5 km further on the dirt track you arrive at Dayat Hachlaff, now no longer a lake and hardly even a reliable spring. The Dayat Hachlaff is at the foot of the valley of the rocks. The hill to the west, the double peak of Lalla Mimouna, is named after a holy woman hermit who died having been raped by the genies of the woods. The right track, in bad condition, passes through the weather sculpted rock forms, thought to be the genies petrified by avenging angels until the day of judgement, after which you could eventually rejoin the road at Dayat Aaoua. To the left, route 3325 passes a large circle of carved stones before reaching the road for Ifrane.

Ifrane

Ifrane was established in 1929 as a summer hill station for the French officials and has remained despite Independence a favourite gathering ground for the rich and influential. The town is a collection of well-built stone houses with high pitched red tiled roofs set in their own gardens, often named after French flowers, that look prim and self satisfied behind their green shutters. Ifrane is a graphic demonstration of how strongly the present ruling class have absorbed the manners and tastes of the French colonial administration.

The skyline is dominated on one side by the massive square bulk of the Hotel Mischlieffen and on the other by the king's new palace, a Gothic chateau of yellow stone walls and a green roof. Ifrane's 'season' is from June to September and a brief flurry of activity during the winter when the king comes to ski or walk and his court comes too, occupying every bed in town.

GETTING AROUND

Buses leave from the Post Office, there are at least seven buses a day north to Fez, 11dh, through Immouzer, and four south to Azrou. There are cafés and a Post Office in Ifrane but no bank though Travellers Cheques can be cashed at the Mischlieffen hotel.

CASCADES DES VIERGES

Below the king's palace a network of paths follow the regulated and extravagant meanders of the river Tizguit which flows down to the west of Ifrane as the 'Cascades des Vierges'. At night this area is flooded by street lights and illuminated globes.

The Cascades flows down from Ifrane towards Meknes to dissipate in the agricultural plain. A minor tarmac road, the S309 to El Hajeb, follows close to the serpentine river banks, braided and overhung by walnut trees for 7 km to the **zaouia of Ifrane**. This is an unpretentious settlement, a scattering of huts that have spread around the mosque, college building and koubba, though many of the occupants are of distinguished Shorfa ancestry. The limestone caves all along the river length were a favourite resort for ascetics who lived in holy poverty, removed from the wicked temporal cities in the plain. A number of their tombs can be found by following the rough track below the zaouia whilst upstream the shaded bank is a popular picnic spot.

SPORTS
There are short runs and ski lifts at Mischlieffen and Djebel Hebri which is equidistant from Ifrane and Azrou. Ski equipment can be hired in Ifrane from the café restaurant **Chamonix** and the club at **Mischlieffen** serves food and hot drinks. **Skiing** is possible anytime between December and March but never predictable. In practice there are only a few random weeks a year when there is enough snow.

WHERE TO STAY AND EAT
Stay in Azrou or Immouzer rather than Ifrane. The ***** **Mischlieffen** is brash and expensive, a double for 350dh, dinner for 100dh, tel 41972. The *** **Grand Hotel**, Blvd de la Poste, tel 6407, is a monument to the mock-Alpine taste, the interior heavy with a mass of brown painted and varnished wood, a single for 159dh, a double for 193dh. The joyless ** **Perce Neige**, Rue des Aphodelles, tel 6210, has a bar, restaurant and a double room costs 137dh, a single 108dh and dinner 75dh.

The campsite however is a large and well shaded paddock of grass on the eastern edge of Ifrane beside the Meknes road. They charge 4dh per person, 3dh for a tent and 3dh for a car. The municipal pool is in a wire compound on the northern edge of Ifrane, open throughout the summer for 3dh a day.

There are a few cafés in Ifrane along Av. Jramchek, the **De la Rose** can provide a three-course meal for 30dh.

Cedar Forest

The Atlas Cedar, closely related to the Cedar of Lebanon but quite distinctively tall and conical compared to its famous brother, grows best between 1500 m and 2000 m. A good specimen can grow in 200 years to a height of 60 m and a circumference of 2 m although exceptional individual trees have survived for 500 years. Large acreages of this indigenous natural forest were felled to make sleepers during the creation of the national railway system, whilst the forest around the Col du Zad south of Azrou on the P21 road to Midelt looks dangerously diseased with alarming stretches of dying trees. There are still magnificent stretches and a 52 km circuit around Ifrane provides an easy and stimulating introduction.

Leaving Ifrane on the S309 you pass through an area of inferior pine wood and the treeless Middle Atlas plateau before turning left on to the S3206. As you climb the Tiz-n-Tretten pass you enter the right altitude for these magnificent trees. The cedar groves isolated on rises in the land further emphasize their height in contrast to the surrounding pastures. At the summit of the pass, at 1934 m, there is a fine view south to the distant peaks of the Middle Atlas. Then you pass close to the local 'hills' of Djebel Mischlieffen at 2036 m and Djebel Hebri at 2104 m, old volcanoes that have risen above this forested mountain plateau where a few ski lifts have been planted on their slopes.

Turn right after Djebel Hebri to join the P21 to Azrou, a few km later a track on the right, the 3387 marked Cedar Gourand, winds for 5 km through a spectacular belt of the forest. Sunlight pierces through the branches, the track shifts to thread through the massive trunks whilst the resinous red bark emits a delicious odour.

Colonel Gourand, Lyautey's second-in-command from 1912–14, was named Resident General in 1917 and the finest cedar in this forest was given his name in recognition of his calm, solid leadership. The extent of the tree is quite remarkable, the trunk is over 10 m in circumference, and any doubts about recognition are dissolved by the surrounding trellises of mineral and fossil salesmen. Continue on the track to descend on to the P24 Azrou to Ifrane road where there are fine views of the plateau and rounded volcanic outcrops to the north.

The route from Azrou to Khenifra via the source of Oum er Rbia passes through less visited tracks of the cedar forest. For another foray into Morocco's ecological climax, see below.

Azrou

This Berber town of 45,000 people is caught in the banks of steep wooded hills that face a distinctive puckered volcanic outcrop of rock. From this, for 'Azrou' translates as 'rock' in the Berber dialect, the town derives its name. Moulay Ishmael built a kasbah here in 1684 to guard this junction of the Fez–Marrakesh and Meknes–Tafilalet routes. There is little trace of this government kasbah but the rock remains unaltered but for the frequent changes of clothes laid out to dry on its flanks and the gold crown on the summit. Azrou by the 19th century had fallen out of the government's control and into the expanding territory of the Beni M'Guid, a nomadic Berber tribal confederation who originated from the Sahara.

The French, after they had subdued the Middle Atlas, recruited Berber Highlanders for the lower posts in the army and administration of the Protectorate, first educating them at the College Berbere at Azrou. The college authorities unsuccessfully attempted to wean the Berbers from Islam and carefully stressed the history of Berber–Arab conflict. This clumsy attempt to divide and rule had little effect but the influence of 'Azrou graduates' is still strong particularly in the FAR, the Force Armée Royale.

GETTING AROUND
There are four buses a day to Meknes, 67 km south, and seven for Fez, 77 km away, for 15dh. The Fez bus stops at Ifrane and Immouzer. Four buses to Marrakesh pass through a day but these often start from Fez or Meknes fully booked, though there are often seats spare on the daily Er-Rachidia bus, 38dh a ticket.

The buses depart from the large triangular space that opens out above the rock, the Place Hassan II, and immediately above this you find the Place Mohammed V, a pleasant small space fronted by cafés whose green glazed tiles flash in the sunlight. Here you find the Banque Populaire and BMCI, cafés, shops and the cheaper hotels.

MARKETS
Azrou as an old market town of the Beni M'Guid has a tradition of weaving and craftsmanship. Killims and natural wool blankets can often be found for sale at the Tuesday **souk**. The Azrou **Ensemble Artisanal** is an unusually stimulating centre; it

maintains traditional patterns, creates new designs and is experimenting with figurative tapestries. There is also a stone- and wood-carving school, the quality is good but the prices are firm, a new killim cushion cover costs 68dh here. The Ensemble is below the rock on the left, open 8.30–12.00, 14.30–18.00, Mon–Sat.

WHERE TO STAY
** **Panorama**, tel 2010, 36 rooms, bar and restaurant is tucked away from the town centre without the benefit of a good view.

The two one-star hotels are much more attractive but with few rooms are worth booking in advance. The **Azrou** on the road to Khenifra, tel 2116, has 10 rooms, a busy bar and restaurant whilst the **Cedres** on Place Mohammed V, tel 2326, has 9 rooms, a café and a licensed restaurant; a single for 48dh, double for 62dh and 5dh for a boiling hot bath.

Behind Place Mohammed V, in the Place Moulay Hachem ben Salah, cheap basic rooms can be found in the **Hôtel Salaam**, **Beausejour** and **Ziz**. The Ziz charges 25dh for a double, the Beausejour with its balcony views 36dh for a double. There is a **youth hostel** 1 km out on the Midelt road, tel 8382, and a summer **campsite** by the town pool, admission 3dh, behind the rock.

EATING OUT
Le Relais Forestiere on the Place Mohammed V is an immaculately clean little restaurant, where you can eat a 35dh lunch freshly prepared by Madame Idijer and listen to her Minerva Radio.

South from Azrou to Midelt

The cedar forests extend south of Azrou for about 15 km trailing off after you pass the conspicuous volcanic cone of Djebel Hebri to the left. A further 16 km south through pine woods and decayed cedars you reach the hamlet of **Timahdit** at 1342 m and then pass through a confused terrain of old volcanic activity whose craters fill to form small lakes.

The hamlet of **Bekrit**, 48 km from Azrou, marks the far edge of the forest and the entry into a pastoral landscape dotted with nomad tents in the summer. A left turn 4 km later leads to the **lake of Sidi Ali**, a beautiful long stretch of water, full of fish and one of the favoured summer watering points for the Beni M'Guid nomads.

10 km on you cross the Col du Zad which at 2178 m divides the catchments of the three great rivers of Morocco. If you were a rain drop falling to the north you would flow down the Oued Sebou into the Atlantic below Mehdiya Kasbah, falling to the south or east you would drift down the Oued Moulouya to flow out into the Mediterranean at Saidia beach and landing to the west you would join the Oum er Rbia and pass out into the ocean at Azzemour.

After the hamlet of **Ait Oufella** there is right turn 4 km to the south which leads to **Itzer**, a worthwhile diversion on Monday and Thursday in order to coincide with this important local **souk** which in the lawless past used to be held under the ksar and patronage of the saintly family of Sidi Boumoussa. From Itzer you pass through **Boulojoul** after the Sefrou junction and through **Zeida**, a manganese mine on the Khenifra junction, before reaching Midelt which is 125 km south from Azrou.

Azrou to Khenifra

The 112 km from Azrou to Khenifra along the P24 is across an uninspiring stretch of Middle Atlas plateau. 11 km from Azrou the village of **Assaka-n-Tatsa** has a **souk** on Sunday. **Mrirt**, half way between Khenifra and Azrou, is the biggest settlement of the region for a lead mine operates in the hills just west of the town. Mrirt has a **souk** on Thursday where you may find distinctive killims all but concealed under a mass of sequin embroidery. To the east of Mrirt a road in 11 km leads to **El Hammam**, the central village of the Ait Segougou tribe who enjoy a reputation for weaving fine carpets. Finding the nomadic weavers is more difficult; rough tracks fan out from El Hammam to a number of small settlements that hold periodic markets that fluctuate with the movement of the herds.

Source of the Oum Er Rbia

A slower but greatly preferable alternative is to travel from Azrou to Khenifra through the territory of the Beni M'Guid tribe, a land of cedar forests, Alpine meadows and mountain streams. It is a spectacularly beautiful journey which could allow you to explore or camp at the source of the Oum er Rbia river and the lake of Aziga. There are no cafés, buses, hotels or petrol pumps between Ain Leuh and Khenifra and the road can often be blocked by snow in the winter.

Ain Leuh

19 km west of Azrou on the P24, turn left on to the S303 and travel 13 km to Ain Leuh. Or you could leave Azrou from the south, travelling for 3 km on the P21 before a right turn on the 3398, a track that passes through 24 km of cedar forest punctuated by magnificent views to the north before arriving at Ain Leuh. It is an old souk of the Beni M'Guid tribe that was adopted as an administrative centre by Sultan Moulay Ishmael in the 18th and the French in the 20th centuries. The steep roofed Alpine houses of the 1920s spill down from the heights to the brown houses and terraced gardens that surround the market. The **souk** for the Beni M'Guid is officially held on Mondays and Thursdays but trade can continue all week.

Climbing beyond the village, hill-top promontories crowned with rich dark stands of towering cedar give way to clear natural meadows of grazing land. Mountain huts, their walls of wooden boards pierced by stove pipes, interchange with the broad sweep of the brown black 'Khaima' tents, contrasting styles that perfectly reflect the need of each season.

The Source

43 km from Azrou you cross two bridges, a track on the left just past the second leads directly to a large pool. It is full of entangling weeds and on its far side the cavorting force of the river threatens to drag any swimmer away to his doom. The trickling stream on the right, fed by a tranquil round pool is one of the three salt springs you pass before reaching

the main torrential cascade of the river whose banks are overhung with trees. Springs just above the river level gush out great volumes of water which noisily rush out enraged and foaming from hidden limestone caverns and miles of natural tunnel. A few minutes' walk upstream brings you to the main waterfall which drops into a smooth round red bowl carved from the great cliff face that looms up above, the Djebel Sang. The bluff on your right gives a good prospect back over both falls and cascades. There are over 40 springs in the immediate area and you can continue upstream to discover a series of smaller secretive falls and pools that stretch back 15 km into the mountains.

Aguelmane Azigza

12 km south of the source a tarmaced and signposted turn leads to Aguelmane Azigza. This lake, introduced by a great Alpine meadow is partly enclosed by limestone hills dressed in a mature cedar forest. A recent rock fall on the opposite cliff face has cleared a path through the forested slope and left a deep ravening cleft. Back on the road, the 3845, a slow descent gradually sheds the cedars and then pines to enter the farmed red soils of Khenifra which is 30 km west of the Aguelmane Azigza.

Khenifra

This extensive market town stretches along both banks of the Oued Oum er Rbia, surrounded by the folding hills of the Middle Atlas. The houses of Khenifra are painted a deep red with doors and windows picked out in green which reflects the region's fierce red soil and spring vegetation.

It is the centre of a great mountainous pastoral region, horses and mules remain in constant daily use and the cavalcades that ride in from the hills to attend the souks provide a memorable spectacle. It is also well placed for an exploration of the Ziane mountains to the west or the source of the Oum er Rbia to the east.

Khenifra was until the 17th century a fortified enclosure where one of the dominant and turbulent Ziane hill tribes wintered their herds. Sultan Moulay Ishmael recognized its strategic location and spanned the Oued Oum er Rbia with a bridge that was guarded by a government kasbah whilst a walled enclosure served as a caravanserai for passing merchants to provide the nucleus around which the town grew.

In the late 19th century Sultan Moulay Hassan recognized a tribal chief of the Ziane tribes, Moha ou Hammou ez Zaiani as the Caid of Khenifra. Moha ou Hammou ruled vigorously, he established markets, baths, a mosque and fondouqs in Khenifra. He gained in authority and ambition during the weak rule of Moulay Hassan's son Abdul Aziz and asserted himself as a tribal warlord, his cavalry squadrons preying on caravans and raiding up to the walls of Meknes in the years that preceded direct conflict with the French. However by November 1914 Hammou had been forced back on his mountain capital by an advancing French column. Khenifra was stormed with the loss of 600 lives but the undaunted Hammou continued a guerrilla campaign against the French garrison which for years could only be supplied by convoys protected by armoured cars. The resistance diminished after Hammou died in battle, attempting to raise a general rebellion against France in 1921.

The modern extent of the town dwarfs the scant relics from the 18th and 19th centuries. Moulay Ishmael's bridge remains astride the river and the view from it across to the central riverside Medina quarter is rewarding. This quarter at the entrance to the town contains an old mosque, a zaouia, the kasbah and a souk. On the other bank of the Oued Oum er Rbia across the old bridge are the walls of the kasbah built by Moha ou Hammou. There are a number of pleasant gardens and public spaces in the town, a pretty terraced garden leads down from two hotel restaurants to the river bank and a race track can be found beside the road south of town.

The weekly **animal souk** is held below the bus station on the Tadla road out of town. There are separate corrals for the auction of cows, sheep, goats, mules and horses with fondouqs to hold the mounts of the travelling farmers. The busiest **souk** is held on Sunday and a smaller one on Wednesday.

GETTING AROUND
160 km from Fez, 82 km from Azrou, 129 km north of Beni Mellal and 300 km from Marrakesh, Khenifra is well served by buses plying the Fez–Marrakesh route. The BMCE bank have a branch at 13, Blvd Mohammed V.

WHERE TO STAY AND EAT
By the river a road leads up to the garrison gates of the FAR depot, whose sentries wear a ceremonial uniform of a rather fetching green turban, red cloth belts and baggy lightly striped trousers. Here you find the liveliest corner of Khenifra at the two restaurant hotels, the **Voyageurs** and the **France**. A clean double room at the Hôtel de France costs 80dh, a single 60dh. There is also the **Café Bar de la Poste**, a petrol pump, a bazaar and an Alimentation Generale.

If you are looking for a bath and a swim there is a four-star hotel, the **Mouha ou Hammou Azzayani**, tel 6020, up on the hillside new town. A double room here costs 240dh, a single 190dh, dinner 79dh.

Ziane Highlands

This rugged area of mountains, none of whose peaks exceeds 1600 m, is a westerly extension of the Middle Atlas. It is a land sharply cut by a number of steep valleys whose small streams collect to drain into the Atlantic through the Oued Bou Regreg which flows out between Salé and Rabat. The region has always been dominated by the Ziane Berber confederation and in particular by the mounted nomadic clans whose herds of cattle, sheep and goat are moved up from the lowland pastures into the central highlands for the summer. In the southern region this is reflected in separate souks for the summer and winter.

Passing through this landscape with its fleeting glimpses of moving herds and distant tents powerfully reinforces the interest of the local souks. The people still rely on horses, mules and asses for transport and turn every highland souk into a pageant of riders. At the head of the hierarchy of elegance are those who own a horse, cavaliers who sit astride on a tooled leather high pommelled saddle with bucket stirrups, elaborate trappings and reins. A step below is the more common sight of a strong docile mule ridden on ancient well-worn killim saddle bags and controlled by simple rein of rope. At the bottom of the scale of dignity are the owners of donkeys, sitting side saddle on straw panniers or well back to avoid strain on the ass's spine. The cavalcades that depart into the hills, the hooded cloaks trailing along the spine of their mounts after the trading, eating and gossip of the souk is over provides an intense romantic image.

Local buses travel for the souks but otherwise this region can only satisfactorily be explored by car, mule or motorbike. 34 km west of Khenifra along the 2516 is the crossroad **souk of Aguelmouss** set in the centre of a wide plain. The souk is held on Saturday morning, a delightful transitory affair, and there are four bedrooms available from the café where you can begin negotiations for the rent of a horse. A right turn at the Aguelmouss crossroads now travels to **Mrirt** on the P24 whose **Thursday souk** is well attended. A left turn takes you 42 km to the town of **Moulay Bouazza**, the spiritual heart of the Ziane. Moulay Bouazza is one of Morocco's great mystical instructors who developed Sufi doctrines here before his death in 1176. His tomb and accompanying mosque were restored by Moulay Ishmael in the 17th century. There are a couple of cafés near the mosque. You can get the best view of this tightly packed red settlement that clusters around a tomb in the fold of the hills by travelling up the one-way road to the administrative 'Cercle'. The road from Moulay Bouazza to Oued Zem, 60 km on the S131, passes through the most beautiful scenery of the region, volcanic plugs rise up from the forested valleys and hills to create an entrancing broken wilderness scenery.

Continuing north from Aguelmouss along the 2516 in 8 km you cross a ford of the Oued Marrout in the middle of a plain dominated by granite tors. Massed blocks are piled securely on each outcrop, the natural vents used as chimneys for the rude shelters of passing shepherds. Fine clay is washed from these hills into kaolin pipes which have always been eagerly sought and dug up to sell to the potters of Fez and Meknes.

Oulmes

The small settlement of Oulmes is reached in 18 km, and 4 km beyond this hamlet there is a left turn for **Oulmes a Thermes/Tarmilate** which is a bottling plant, a hotel and a few houses at the centre of a pleasant wooded plateau of limestone. Oulmes mineral water and Sidi Ali sparkling water are extracted and bottled here to be sold throughout Morocco. Rich in carbonate, calcium, magnesium, bicarbonate of soda and according to the label 'radioactive' they assist intestinal, hepatitis, anaemia and arthritis sufferers. A very thin twisting road, now closed to traffic, descends in 2 km to the hot water source of Lalla Haya at the foot of the valley where the hot mineral water emerges at 43°C. The bottling plant jeeps can take you down on a tour for 70dh and the surrounding hills of the plateau are dotted with caves, wooded groves and streams which can be explored in walks from the hotel.

The **Oulmes Hôtel** is an interestingly remote and unusual holiday base; it is closed from July to August but reopens for the September shooting season. There are some well preserved wild boar heads in the hall and a small store of local wood carvings. It has a restaurant and a lift, a single for 107dh, a double for 130dh.

El Harcha 17 km west of Oulmes is at the heart of a scrubland and forest reserve populated by wild boar and panthers. The road skirts the foot of Djebel Mouchachen which at 1086 m gives an extensive view over the Ziane mountains and the lowland region to the west. **Tiddas,** the administrative centre for the Zemmour tribe is 20 km on; it has a **souk** on Monday and around the shrine of Sidi Abd el Hadj a moussem is held in September, a great gathering point for Berber horsemen. **Maaziz** at the conjunction of the Oued Tanoubert and Bou Regreg is on the border of the highlands and the plains and has a **souk** on Sunday. It is also a road junction, a right turn on route S106 for Khemisset 30 km or a left turn to Rommani 29 km.

Khenifra to Midelt

This route has a dramatic mountain climb for the first third of the distance before it ascends the bleak Middle Atlas plateau. It can be blocked by snow anytime from December to February.

Leaving south from Khenifra on the P24 to Tadla a small road to your left, 17 km out of town, leads in 16 km to the village of **El Kbab** whose **souk** on Monday is well attended by skilled local craftsmen of the Ichkern tribe. It was here that Father Albert, who had spent several months with the ascetic Charles de Foucauld in the central Sahara, established himself as a doctor from 1928 to 1959. He wrote his *Dictionnaire de physchologie linguistique*, in a hermitage which still survives above the village.

Returning 8 km back towards Khenifra a left turn takes you straight on to the P33 Midelt road to pass the village of **Azrou n Ait Lahcen** and the lake of **Aguel Baghane.** Another lake, the **Aguel Tagha,** is hidden high up to the south; its tranquil surface provides the suitably secretive source of the Oued Moulouya, that flows northeast to the Algerian frontier. After the lake the road climbs to the Tanout ou Filal pass, which at 2070 m marks a distinctive change in landscape. The rolling Alpine meadows of the foothills are now replaced by the windswept mountainous plateau of the Middle Atlas, broken by outcrops of granite boulders and high peaks looming to the south.

The journey could be broken at a café in one of the few villages besides the road. **Aghabalou n'Serdane** is 18 km from the pass, **Sidi Tiar/Tamaroute** 9 km beyond that and **Boumia** the largest of these settlements is a further 18 km east, 3 km off the road. Boumia has a **souk** on Thursday and a tarmac track extends 34 km south to Toufinite.

Toufinite

This small administrative post for the Ait Yaha tribe, built below the Djebel Mu'Askar peak and besides three ksar boasts a basic café. It is an unusual but excellent entrance to the mountainous hinterland. A rough track travels due west below the peaks of Djebel Oujjit at 2781 m and Djebel Toujjit at 2690 m to reconnect with the Es Ksiba tarmac road 40 km later. Another track leads east of Toufinite to swing around the slopes of Djebel Mu'askar and then south up a mountain valley full of inhabited pise ksar of the Ait Yaha, the most noticeable of which, **Ksar Agoudim** is 18 km from Toufinite. Beyond Agoudim the road naturally deteriorates as you cross the Atlantic–Mediterranean watershed and enter cedar forested mountain slopes. A third alternative from Toufinite is to travel back along the road to Boumia for 13 km and take a track to the east which leads in 12 km to a fine group of ksour which guard the downstream entrance to the Oued Ansegmir gorges.

Returning to the main road there is only the **Zeida Manganese mine**, 18 km east of Boumia on the junction with the P21 Meknes road, and Midelt is another 30 km south.

Khenifra to Tadla

The red soil of Khenifra fades into yellow as you enter an area of intensive olive cultivation. The road runs below a limestone escarpment, crossing small streams fed by mountain springs and a succession of small village presses sell their own olive oil. These communities have a long tradition of sanctity and are often grouped around active zaouia. The great maraboutic dynasties of Djila and Boujdad that once ruled this region originated from such humble foundations.

23 km south of Khenifra you pass through village of **Es Sebt** whilst the neighbouring settlement of **Maamar**, inland to the south, guards the ruins of the capital of the maraboutic dynasty of Djila. The Djila dynasty were poised in the 17th century to succeed the Saadians. Their authority extended over Rabat, Fez and Meknes but their power was shattered in a few years by Moulay Rashid and by 1668 their zaouia lay in ruins. The **tomb of Sidi Bu Beker** can be traced surrounded by the ruins of the Mosque.

After a brick factory you reach the Midelt turning and the roadside *** **Hôtel TransAtlas**, tel Khenifra 30. It has a circular red courtyard, bedrooms that face inwards towards the swimming pool with a detached roadside air, bar and constant television that gives a mid-West motel-like atmosphere. A single with a bath and a lavatory 138dh, a double 168dh.

The village of **Zaouia des Ait Isehak** is 6 km beyond, set a few km to the west of the road. The villagers claim to be descended from an isolated garrison of Moulay Ishmael's negro slave regiment. The zaouia was under the influence of Djila and Sultan Moulay Rashid studied here as a young man. Here he learnt theology and absorbed the tactics, geography and political weakness of his future enemy.

Passing through the settlements of **Ouaomenia** and **Dechra el Oued** in 26 km is the larger village of **Zaouia esh Sheikh**. There are a few basic hotels beside the road south of the village, the best of which is the **Hôtel café Rif**, whilst at the central bus stop area there are a number of cafés under the shade of white arcades where good tagines are served for lunch. **Souks** are held here on Wednesday and Saturday.

El Ksiba

22 km before Tadla a turning south off the main road leads in 7 km to El Ksiba, most charming of this string of villages, 1050 m high at the entrance to a forested mountain valley and surrounded by orchards and groves of apricots, olives and oranges. El Ksiba before the 19th century was just the central souk of the Ait Serri tribe. Sultan Moulay Hassan, in order to restrain the influence of his capable but ambitious Caid of Khenifra, made a local chief, Moha ou Said, the Caid of El Ksiba to be an equal power in the region. Caid Moha ruled over 5000 families and with subsidies from the Sultan built the Kasbah of Saarif at El Ksiba. This has not survived but the **Sunday souk** is still a central

rendezvous for the hinterland settlements and a pretty Mosque flanked by two zaouia is found at the top of the village above a neat garden of rosemary hedge and roses. Beside this is a café and beneath it arcaded stalls sell fruit and grilled snacks. Peugeot taxis group around the petrol station and you can browse through the book and nut shop, through collections of wicker baskets, sandals, gumboots and the radio repairs.

On the way out there is a cascade of spring water and to the left a semi-circle of official buildings, the Gendarmerie, the Post Office and **Hotel Henry IV** which has a bar, restaurant, courtyard parking and a pleasantly aged but clean interior. A single costs 59dh, breakfast 12dh and a filling dinner 51dh. South from the village the route 1901 enters a narrow valley full of toy-like wooden bungalows under mature glades of poplar and silver birch with a stream-fed swimming pool and a basic campsite.

Atlas Crossing and Imilchil

Though El Ksiba is pretty enough its chief attraction is as an access point for the Imilchil September marriage fair and the adventurous crossing of the Atlas mountains to Tinerhir. The crossing is possible from November to April when the snow has melted, though there is no hotel, bank or petrol along the 220 km of rough mountain tracks between El Ksiba and Tinerhir. It is an exhilarating journey, although scenically this treeless belt of high plateau cannot compare with the accessible foothills at either end. In summer with patience and a tent it is possible partly to walk and to buy lifts in the infrequent trucks that ply this route.

The first 40 km to Imilchil are tarmaced. 3 km from El Ksiba the road climbs the Tiz-n Ait Ouirra pass to reach the Oued Drent valley, continuing through twisting hills and forested slopes for 30 km until the Tiz-n-Ifar pass. 7 km after this pass a turn south, at the village of **Tiz-n-Isly** puts you on the mountain road, 1903, for Imilchil. Lake Tislit and the Ksar of Tassert at Imilchil are 61 km south after the crossing of the Oued Ouirine.

Every year at Imilchil the Atlas tribes congregate for a grand Moussem in the second or third week of September. (The date is arranged on a lunar calendar and changes each year.) This is the famous marriage fête of the Ait Haddidou tribe where young men and women from different clans can briefly meet before deciding on their mates. This serves a useful function in restricting consanguinous marriages and some of the hazards of an impulsive choice are checked by the ease and frequency of divorce and a trial period of three weeks. The fête is well attended, not least by camera-happy tourists who stay in 'caidal tents' arranged each year by the Salaam Hotel chain. Otherwise you can join the nomadic encampments along the dung-infested shores of the saline lake Tislit and Isli and enjoy the unrivalled opportunity of admiring the clothes, jewelry, dance, music and artefacts of the Berber hill tribes who form a transient city of tens of thousands.

From Imilchil the worst 100 km section of the Atlas crossing awaits; the most common route is to take one of the tracks that pass through **Takkat**, **Timariyne** and **Agoudal**. Then on to Ait Hani along route 3445 which crosses the Tiz n Tirherhouzine pass at 2706m. From Ait Hani 'route' 3444 goes down to Tamttatouche and follows the Oued Todgha through the Todra Gorge to Tinerhir.

Kasbah Tadla

The province of Tadla, a plateau irrigated by the Oum er Rbia, has always been a much fought over and prized possession. Djila, a local maraboutic dynasty, led the Tadla tribes in the 17th century and seemed capable of succeeding to the Saadian throne. These halcyon days were destroyed by the Alouite Moulay Rachid who destroyed the Djilan army and sacked the capital on 24 June 1668. Frustrated from winning political power the Tadla tribes maintained a long feud against the Alouite Sultans.

Moulay Rachid's brother, Moulay Ishmael, was equal to the challenge. He established a line of strongpoints to hold the Tadla plain and keep the road to Marrakesh open. An Abid regiment was placed in the new Kasbah of Tadla on the banks of the Oued Oum er Rbia and rival regiments of cavalry garrisoned at Kasbah Adeksane and Ait Ishak. In 1700 he unified the command and appointed a son, Ahmed er Debhi, Pasha of Tadla Province. Ahmed was also trusted with the command of another 3000 Abids and enlarged Kasbah Tadla to create a provincial capital.

This pacification did not long outlast the reign of Moulay Ishmael and in the 19th century two government armies were defeated in battle by coalitions of Middle Atlas tribes. Moulay Sliman's army in 1818 was trapped in the Serrou gorge and destroyed in a night attack. The Sultan was captured and feasted for three days before being firmly but respectfully escorted back to Fez. Moulay Hassan secured order in the plain but even this capable sovereign could not secure the mountain valleys and a vizier lost an entire army which was trapped in the Boutferda gorge in 1885. The French occupied Kasbah Tadla in 1913 but suffered a rare defeat at El Herri in 1914 before they subdued the Tadla tribes in a campaign from 1915 to 1917. The training camp to the west of Tadla maintains the military history of the town. It is now a pleasant place of trees and gardens that surround the severe and noble beauty of Kasbah Tadla.

An enceinte of steep crenellated walls drops down from the kasbah almost to meet the river. Within these 18th-century walls a village community exists among the old store-houses and barracks whilst a shop has colonized the kasbah gate. One of the two mosques is in a high state of ruin and the **Governor's palace, the Dar el Makhzen,** is filled with squatters. On the town side of the kasbah wall a park has been created whilst a road below the walls leads down to the river beside more terraced gardens, market arcades and the battlemented minaret of the mosque. Moulay Ishmael's bridge of ten arches still carries traffic across the Oum er Rbia, whose height is now controlled by a small dam. A small square fort holds the slight ground on the other bank.

GETTING AROUND
There are four buses a day that do the hour trip to Beni Mellal and three for the 20-minute ride to El Ksiba, although both towns are 30 km away. The **souk** is held on Monday.

WHERE TO STAY
There are three cheap characterful hotels in Tadla all within listening distance of the bus stop. The basic **Hôtel Restaurant Des Allies**, Av. Mohammmed V, tel 172, is the most comfortable and if this is full the **Hôtel de Atlas** and the **Café Oued Umbra** also rent a few rooms.

Northwest of Tadla

The region west of the fertile Tadla plain has been long dominated by the Seguibat and the Beni Meskin nomadic tribes. On the edge of this semi-desert plain, only 25 km west of Tadla is the holy town of Boujad awash with mosques, koubba and zaouia. **Oued Zem** is 22 km beyond, where the road divides for Casablanca or Rabat.

Boujad

Boujad was in the 19th century the most important town in the whole central region of Morocco between Meknes and Marrakesh, a holy town equal to Ouezzane or Moulay Idriss, although now it is merely one of a string of provincial markets that functions after the growing seasons of March and September, and is home to a population of 15,000.

In the 16th century, Sidi Mohammed Bu'Abid ech Chergui, known as the patron of Tadla and the master of horsemen, established a zaouia here. He was a celebrated Sufi mystic who died in 1600 and his descendants were respected by the surrounding tribes for possessing the power of giving the 'baraka' blessing. The agglomeration of sanctuaries, colleges and storehouses became the accepted capital for the surrounding nomadic tribes after the authority of Tadla Kasbah decayed. The saintly dynasty of Boujad arbitrated disputes and acted as an intermediary for the tribes in their relations with the Sultan's government. Sultan Sidi Mohammed destroyed the power of the zaouia and razed the town in 1785; most of Boujdad dates from subsequent rebuilding.

GETTING AROUND

The town is just off the P13 road, a 24 km taxi ride north of Tadla and 22 km south of Oued Zem.

The centre of the town, the Place du Marché, is a vast paved open space surrounded by trees and the outer arcades of the white houses of the Medina. The zaouia was rebuilt in the mid-19th century after the death of Sidi Mohammed. It is found to the southwest of the town, surrounded by houses that are still occupied by his descendants. The **souk** is no longer held in the centre of town but beside the main road on Wednesday and Thursdays.

The old town that surrounds the Place du Marché is encrusted with tombs of the saintly dynasty. The largest **shrine** is that of **Sidi Othman** where a number of courts give on to the koubba raised above the tomb. This you can enter for a fee and in the company of a guide, and manifesting great interest and many tips it is often possible to enter a few others.

In the quarter of the Beni Meskin ask to be shown the **sanctuaries of Sidi Abd el Kader Ziz** and **El Hibi**. In the quarter of el Kedrin is the **Mosque of Sidi Slimane** which you reach from the corner of the Place du Marché by the Hôtel Essalyn; turn left and left again by the bridge and you naturally pass beneath the great square minaret and lantern of the mosque.

The various shrines and a single palm tree are found along the yellow stone path that snakes its way through the el Kedrin quarter. The **mosque and tomb of Sheikh**

Mohammed Bu'abid ech Cherki with its tall lantern minaret is entered through a pyramidical arch. The shrine of Sidi Mohammed ech Cherki has a hammam beside it and holds an inner courtyard lodge for men and women pilgrims, two of whom have been honoured by burial in the inner court. By day the outer court is full of pilgrims resting against the walls, the air full of the music of song birds. The **koubba of Sidi el Maati** is found within its own courtyard that holds an old fig tree also full of birds. The **shrine of Sidi Larbi** is covered by two green domes. Opposite a little mosque on the Rue Sidi Salah is the **tomb of Sidi Salah** whose courtyard is full of practical aids. Two palm trees provide shade and there is a room set aside for women to henna their hair and a well spring for washing.

Just out of Boujdad on the road north to Oued Zem you pass on a hill a spectacular array of five white koubbas, that include the **tomb of Sidi Abdesalam** and **Lalla Hania**.

Just before Oued Zem a tarmac road, the route S131, leads through the distinctive scenery of the Ziane highlands to arrive at **Moulay Bouazza** from where you could continue round through Aguelmouss to Khenifra, see above.

WHERE TO STAY
You will find the basic **Café-Hôtel Essalyn** in a corner of the Place du Marché.

Oued Zem

This is an efficient ordered modern town of 20,000 that has grown in the wake of the phosphate mines. The skyline is dominated by the vast spoil heaps from the Sidi Daoudi mine to the north, one of the busiest of the Khourigba phosphate mining complex from where a railway line, built in 1918, travels to Casablanca. The town is in a natural slight depression that used to trap a seasonal stream. To the north a few traces of the original **Kasbah** by a roadside cemetery can be seen, whilst to the left as you enter, a tree-shaded lake has been created.

In the centre of town there are a number of good roadside cafés offering a good lunch of spiced salads, chips and kebabs for 17dh. It is often an error to imagine that modern Moroccan towns have lost their ability to surprise, for just as I was starting lunch the town fool stripped naked and rolled in the dust at my feet.

From Oued Zem you can take the P13 to Casablanca, 150 km or the P22 north to Rabat, 169 km. The road to Casablanca is across a flat plain punctured by the mining spoils.

The Rabat road shares the mine spoil view for a while but the Khaloua pass tips you on to the hills of Zaer and Ziane. **Ez Zhiliga**, 10 km north of the pass, is deep in this territory and is where the Neghamcha tribe gather for the **Thursday market**. **Rommani** is 32 km further where the Ouled Khalifa assemble for the **Wednesday souk**. At Rommani a turn to the west takes you on a tour of the Ziadia country, see page 226; a turn to the east for Maaziz into the Ziane Highlands, see page 358, or carry on due north for Rabat.

Tadla to Beni Mellal

The direct road, the P24, for the 30 km between Tadla and Beni Mellal has no distractions. **Kasbah Zidania**, 16 km to the west, is marked on some maps. It was built by Moulay Ishmael but makes a disappointing foray across a flat agricultural plain as the kasbah ruins are enclosed within the prohibited fence of an electrical generating station.

A more rewarding journey passes a number of villages which sit at the spring line of a limestone escarpment, surrounded by olive orchards.

Just south of Tadla turn left off the P24 on route 1662 for 18 km to the village of **Tarhzirt/Taghzirt**. Protected by a disintegrating kasbah the ancient settlement of Tarhzirt is split in two by a gorge, its low houses hugging the ascending slopes whilst the stream runs clear between.

Zaouia Fichtala is 5 km south from Tarhzirt on route 1674 to Beni Mellal. This quiet hamlet was once known as Tefza, which the Saadians made the capital of Tadla province to commemorate the destruction of a Wattasid army and the capture of the Sultan here in 1536.

Ait Said/Foum el Anser is framed by limestone cliffs and split in two by a slight gorge fed by half a dozen springs. The village, only 10 km from Beni Mellal, is surrounded by caves decorated with fantastic rocks, believed to be miners petrified by a genie who guards the secret mineral wealth of the hills.

Beni Mellal

The Tadla Plain is littered with the previous capitals of this valuable but turbulent province. Beni Mellal is the current seat of power, a rapidly expanding largely modern city of quarter of a million prospering from the electricity and irrigation water that the Bin el Ouidane dam provides. Orchards of olives and oranges extend around the city to form an oasis in comparison with the sun-scorched plain. The houses of Beni Mellal rise up the limestone slope to the Aisserdoun spring, above which the conspicuous Ras el Ain Kasbah crowns a prominent bluff.

GETTING AROUND
The bus station is now at a smart new terminal on the edge of town on the bypass road from Khenifra to Marrakesh, tel 2035. The most efficient garage in town is the Belkhoya on Blvd Mohammed V.

TOURIST INFORMATION
There are three banks in Beni Mellal, the BMCE on Av. Mohammed V, the BMCI at 87 Rue de Marrakesh and the Banque Populaire on Blvd Mohammed V.

WHAT TO SEE
The oldest central portion of the town was erected within the walls of a **kasbah** built during the reign of Moulay Ishmael. Scattered fragments of walls and gates can be found amongst the houses, alleys and shops that surround the central rectangular Medina square, the arcaded Place de la Liberté where the clothing bazaars and cheap hotels are found. But the French new town, the Medina and post-Independence housing have no great distinction.

A signposted tourist route encircles the town to climb above the town to the **Ain**

Asserdoun spring. This is a welcome sight; cool fresh water flows through a series of contrived cascades and meanders and out through an ornamental public park into the olive groves. From Ain Asserdoun a tarmac road climbs 1 km to the **Ras el Ain Kasbah**. The best view is from a distance, for this stone fortress has been heavily restored and surrounded by a tarmac carpark. The view from the terrace over Beni Mellal is fine but climbing the restored staircase of the Kasbah corner towers can be nauseous as they are usually covered in shit.

WHERE TO STAY
Beside the road to Marrakesh are two neighbouring and indistinguishable four-star hotels used by coach tours and those dying to have a swim or a bath. The **Chems**, tel 3460 and the **Ouzoud**, tel 3752 both have a pool, restaurant, bar, fine view and a tennis court. They charge 185dh for a single and dinner costs 79dh.

Otherwise stay at the *Auberge du Vieux Moulin, on the Tadla end of Av. Mohammed V. It has a bar, a decent restaurant, ten rooms and a worn comfortable interior. A single room for 61dh, a double for 70dh. Or try the *Gharnata, a modern comfortable hotel at the heart of the new town on Blvd Mohammed V, tel 3482, with 14 rooms. There is also a third one star hotel in the new Medina, the **De Paris**, tel 2245, which has also got a bar.

The cheap hotels in the barely discernible Medina quarter are not very appealing. The arcaded **Hôtel El Fath**, tel 7142016, no 15, Place de la Liberté is the best with a courtyard surrounded by two floors of rooms, 17dh per person, whilst directly opposite is the **Hôtel Marhaba**. In the new town on Blvd Mohammed V is the still cheap but clean **Café Hôtel des Voyageurs**.

EATING OUT
The licensed restaurant **Al Bassatine**, tel 2247, is 100 m on the left travelling out on the Fkih ben Salah road. The waiters wear green plush and gold embroidery and though the interior hall can at a moment's notice be filled by coachloads you can eat a pleasant meal on the terrace overlooking an orange grove, a full menu for 70dh. Otherwise the hotels **Gharnata** and **Auberge du Vieux Moulin** serve good filling meals.

South to Marrakesh

The direct route south from Beni Mellal to Marrakesh, the P24, runs across an arid plain, passing irrigated orchard estates but is largely a colourless journey. For the first 70 km the Atlas foothills stay within view. A number of roads turn east into the mountains most attractive of which are those to Oulad Mbarek, the Bzou Cascade and especially the Ouzoud gorge.

Oulad Mbarek and Timoulit

The villages of Oulad Mbarek and Timoulit are worth visiting for the **souks** on Monday and Thursday. About 11 km west of Beni Mellal on the P24 turn south at the hamlet of Oulad Moussa and travel a couple of kilometres to Oulad Mbarek. Timoulit is 6 km beyond on a passable but deteriorating road. It has its **souk** on Monday and was the chief village of the N'Oumalou tribe, one of the component clans of the great Berber Ait Atta confederation. The N'Oumalou were the northernmost vanguard of the Ait Atta whose homeland is south of the High Atlas. In their progress they were closely following the route of the Beni M'Guid, another Berber Saharan tribe who fought their way north to richer grazing lands.

Beyond Timoulit there is a road which climbs over the Tiz-n-Ghenim pass at 1802 m to **Ouaouizaght**, a market town and pilgrimage centre. From Ouaouizaght a tarmac road takes you for 15 km beside the lake to the Bin el Ouidane dam where you can lunch, return to the Marrakesh road or continue along the Mid Atlas plateau.

Back on the Marrakesh road, 23 km from Beni Mellal, a right turn could bring you in 16 km to the busy Saturday souk held at **Souk es Sebt des Ouled Nemaa**. The distinctive sugar factory at **Oueled Ayad**, 46 km from Beni Mellal, marks the left turn for the Gorge Ouzoud el Abid.

Ait Attab and the Ouzoud Gorge

A thin twisting tarmac road winds up to cross the Atlas foothills at 1000 m and provides tremendous views back over the plain. Passing through an area of scrub wilderness you descend into a Berber mountain valley that appears completely content in its isolation, the surrounding hilltops and their cleared area of land crowned by inhabited square towered kasbah. The road leads directly to Ait Attab, the small central village of the valley with three cafés, pretty yellow arcades and a **souk** on Wednesday. From Ait Attab a dirt track leads to the green tiled **tomb of Moulay Aissa ben Idriss** where a Moussem is held on 24 March. Aissa, one of the sons of Idriss II, died fighting the Ait Attab tribe of this valley, who were finally converted to Islam only after Aissa's death, for each spring a whirlwind emerged from his grave and then destroyed the crops of the valley. Reduced to starvation, the Ait Attab took the advice of a holy man, converted to Islam and built a tomb over Aissa's grave which they honoured each spring with a Moussem.

A new tarmac road leads 7 km from Ait Attab to just short of the gorge entrance. This is a remarkable dark high narrow wall of stone through which the river flows down towards the Ouzoud falls. It is a wonderfully impressive and isolated canyon, the only sound that interrupts the gurgling water and singing birds is likely to be the echoing call of a goatherd gathering together his flock. High up above the entrance to the gorge is a deserted **Kasbah**, an excellent place in which to camp, though Berber farmers of this valley are often hospitable to the few travellers. A dirt track continues and crosses the river by a metal bridge and then twists uphill in 20 km to the falls of Ouzoud. This makes an enterprising walk. There are frequent buses from Beni Mellal to Ait Attab and food and beds are available at the **Ouzoud Falls** which has enough visitors for you to arrange a lift from there.

Back on the Marrakesh road the bridge over the Oued Imsaoune is reached 72 km from Beni Mellal. It is a traditional junction point where the police often man a checkpoint. At the dusty square of the **Oued Abid** hamlet there are seven cafés that prepare simmering tagines, grilled kebabs and oranges for the passing traffic. A turn to the south just beyond the bridge on route 1810 leads in 11 km to the cascades and village of Bzou. Turn left up into the village opposite a roadside café and follow the road to a dirt square. Then bear right drawn by the sound of trickling water to find a clear pool fed by a spring trickling down an extent of stalagmite rock. Two channels drain the pool in a series of natural cascades of the Oued Tamla to disappear into a scrub wilderness.

Back to the Oued Imsaoune bridge and on to Marrakesh you pass through **El Kelaa des Sraghna**, a large modern town of 40,000 overlooked by the sterile black volcanic hills of the Jbilet that stretch west to shield Marrakesh from the baked wind of the Bahira plain. El Kelaa was enclosed only a few decades ago within kasbah walls and traditional **souks** are held here on Fridays and Sundays. 30 km south you pass through the large village of **Tamelelt** which has a **souk** on Tuesday, and in a further 50 km you approach the outlying irrigated gardens and palmery of Marrakesh.

Central High Atlas

This journey is considerably more awkward than catching the fast bus from Beni Mellal and Marrakesh. Without your own vehicle it requires patience and a number of taxi rides or infrequent and slow local buses. The Cascade D'Ouzoud/Ouzoud Waterfall and the kasbahs at Tazzerte are however two of the more memorable, mysterious and un-exploited sites of Morocco. The Cascade D'Ouzoud is familiar from hundreds of Tourist Board posters and though only 20 km walk from the Ouzoud Gorge is approached on an entirely different route.

Afourer

20 km out of Beni Mellal a right turn, the S508, leads in 6 km to Afourer which is dominated by the hydro-electricity plant that runs from the waters of dammed lake of Bin el Ouidane perched high in the hills above you. To the left before the village is the roadside **Hôtel Tazarhoute** which has a pool, bar and restaurant. The rooms are expensive, a single for 123dh, but you might want to eat here; a complete meal costs 50dh.

Behind the village you climb the hill in a series of dramatic hairpin bends. The view back is dangerously distracting but a belvedere has been built at one of the best viewing points 12 km from Afourer. The extent of the Tadla plain is spread out below, the lush irrigated estates of orange and olive groves appear as oases in the denuded expanse.

Bin el Ouidane

A canyon has been cut through these arid mountains by the Oued Ouzoud, whose water is collected by two streams that extend 200 km east, draining the scarred plateau caught between the peaks of the Middle and High Atlas. Ruined stone-built agadirs dot the canyon summits as you approach the concave vault of the Bin el Ouidane dam. A slip road leads down to the **Auberge du Lac** hotel and a **campsite**. They have a superb position beside the slow wide river and look up at the dam and across to cave entrances in the limestone canyon wall of the opposite bank. The campsite is open in the summer but the Hôtel du Lac runs throughout the year. It has a few bedrooms that open on to two separate terraces, a cavernous bar and a restaurant. The hotel is full of local hunting and fishing scenes and half a dozen pointers lounge around; tel 5. A double for 67dh, a three-course meal for 50dh.

The lakeside area is now administered as a military region, for the road passes along the top of the dam, its 300 m wide and 130 m high walls hold back 1 billion square metres of water which irrigate the Tadla plain and produce most of Morocco's electricity, a tempting target for any terrorist.

Beyond the Bin el Ouidane lake you travel across 26 km of Atlas plateau, a bleak but farmed expanse punctuated by pise kasbahs to **Azilal**, an uninspiring official post at 1360 m that straggles, wind-blown and dusty, along the road. There is a **souk** held here on Thursday and a basic **Hôtel Restaurant Tahanouton** the edge of the town which is a useful base for an approach to Bou Gemez.

Expedition to Bou Gemez and Zaouia Ahansal

It is possible to visit the reclusive valley of Bou Gemez in the summer by foot, mule or landrover. This is not a casual tour but of appeal for those who might wish to camp and walk in one of the most beautiful and unspoilt Berber valleys of Morocco.

The road 1807 to Ait Mohammed, 20 km south of Azilal is tarmaced but beyond is a 30 km mountain track, usually inaccessible from November to February, which leads up to the lower slopes of Djebel Azourki at 3690 m. This track divides below the peak, to the right it descends west over 30 km into the beautiful isolated valley of Bou Gemez, the barren stone fields giving way to terraced gardens overlooked by the occupied Kasbahs of the Ait Isha tribe. The chief village of the valley, **El Had**, has a **souk** on Sunday and the track ends at the **Kasbah of Agouti**. Above the valley the sacred snow-covered peak of **M'Goun**, 4071 m, one of the great summits of the High Atlas, can be seen looming to the south.

At the head of the valley, to the east, is the **lake of Izourar**, around whose shore the nomadic Ait Haddidou tribe assemble each summer to find water and grazing for their herds.

Zaouia Ahansal

Leaving the valley continue east at the junction, along track 1807 for 28 km to the **zaouia Ahansal**, crossing the Tiz-n-Ilissi pass which has some fossilized tree trunks at 2650 m.

The **zaouia Ahansal** is around the koubba at the head of a valley dotted with small villages and beautifully decorated kasbahs of the saintly Ihansalen clan who mustered 200 families in the first French census in 1930. At the focal point of the four largest and aggressive tribes of the central High Atlas, the zaouia presided over the many local disputes, the focus of a republic where 'Anarchy was mitigated by holiness'. The zaouia also handled negotiations with the Sultan; they sent a delegation to Moulay Hassan when he attempted to resolve the disputes of the tribes from his court established at Tafilalet. The Ihansalen consider themselves descendants of the 16th-century saint, the ally of Dada Atta who established the Ait Atta confederacy. The community is celebrated in Ernest Gellner's classical anthropological study, *Saints of the Atlas*. North of Zaouia Ahansal an arduous 30 km mountain walk leads to a famous rock formation known as the Cathedral on the opposite bank from the Ksar of Tiliouguite.

Cascade D'Ouzoud (The Ouzoud Waterfall)

20 km from Azilal along the Demnate road, route S508, is **Ait Taguella**, a scattered collection of hill-top agadirs surrounded by almond trees and patches of cultivation. Just beyond a right turn leads for 16 km through similar scenery to the hamlet of **Et Tleta Ouzoud** that consists of three houses poised above the Ouzoud waterfalls. It remains a friendly, undeveloped place, expanding naturally in the summer as visitors are seduced into camping here for a week, though there are rooms and meals available throughout the year. Barbary apes come down from the hills, there is no electric light but candles and an immense quantity of cool refreshing falling water.

Several streams plummet 100 m into a pool, the water thundering past a rich mixture of vegetation and oozing stalagmite rock whilst the spray caught by sunlight forms a shifting rainbow. The immediate plunge pool has dangerous currents but you can swim in any of the ones strung out below. This rich natural site set deep in the Atlas and fringed by massive glowering low hills at night has a universal pantheistic appeal, a perpetual celebration of the unadorned earth.

From here you could contemplate a 16 km walk upstream to the Gorges, or paddle through the river pools downstream for a while or take the 20 km old track, now impassable to vehicles, that leads across country to Azilal, passing the **Akka-n-Tisekht**, an impressive devil's punchbowl enclosed by tortured cliffs.

WHERE TO STAY

To the right of the car park through an arch you can camp under a vine terrace by the river bank above the falls. Or you can rent the elegant verandah café room that sleeps four from Thami Abassi who cooks omelettes, prepares salads and tagines to order. Or stay at **Mohammed's**, to the left of the large central house, where half a dozen rooms surround a little orange tree in a courtyard. In the summer, beside the path on the way to the falls, you can camp at the bamboo **Café Ouzade** or one of its seasonal rivals. All are cheap and equally delightful.

Demnate

Back on the road it is 22 km to **Tannant**, an administrative post established by the French on a hill with a fine prospect of three massive peaks 50 km to the south. From the west there is Djebel Ghat at 3825 m, then Djebel M'Goun at 4071 m and Djebel Azourki at 3690 m and just south of Tannant on the river are the Oued Tainit falls.

Demnate, 26 km south from Tannant, is a town still largely contained within its crenellated pise walls positioned on the high edge of an intensively cultivated fertile valley that appears conspicuously green from the massed olive groves. Above Demnate begins the bleak or partially forested slopes of the Atlas highland plateau.

The town's **kasbah** was held by a succession of caids from the Glaoui clan. Abdelmalek was the most celebrated of these; he was a boy of great beauty and bravery, the favourite son of Madani, the ruthless and able founder of Glaoui power. His early death aged 17 in a tribal skirmish is credited with breaking his father's heart. The kasbah was on a nearby hill around which the French erected the administrative offices of the 'Cercle'. The Sunday **souk** is an animated picturesque affair held by the town's old storage tanks and there is an attractive old mosque and zaouia within the walls.

WHERE TO STAY

There are a couple of basic hotels if you have to stay a night at Demnate; the **Iminfri**, the **Fetouka** and the **Zakovia** are on the main street just inside the triple-arched gates of the town.

Imi-n-Ifri

A tarmac road twists east of Demnate 6 km to Imi-n-Ifri, an astonishing natural bridge over which the road passes and a stream flows underneath. The river bed is full of washed boulders and its steep bank and the bridge are liberally decorated with stalagmites. The bleak isolated mountain slopes, crests of distant snow, pine forests and freak wafts of mist and cloud give the bridge a strange malignant atmosphere. Half an hour's walk up stream is a grotto where animals are sacrificed on the 14th day after Aid el Kebir to the spirit of the spring. The spirit destroyed an evil genie who was fond of attacking the women of Demnate. The body of the genie materialized on his death but instantly rotted and was consumed by hideous caterpillars who metamorphosized into crows. These birds attempt to disrupt the annual sacrifice and their defiant shrieks can be heard throughout the year echoing over the valley and hills.

Various good gravel roads are being extended beyond the bridge and there is even plan to push these to the isolated valley of Bou Gemez. The signposted road to Tifni, first right, second left, crosses some spectacular gorges before climbing the Tiz-n-Outfi at 2150 m.

The Demnate olive groves stretch 15 km west of the town to include the pleasant village of **El Arba des Hamadna** which has its **souk** on Wednesday and an imposing kasbah away on the high land to the south.

A turn south leads in 12 km to the **Ait Azdel lake/Moulay Youssef dam** at a crossroads 16 km from Demnate. The lake teems with black bass and in the summer there are boats hired out to fishermen. Turning north at these crossroads leads to the **zaouia Taglaout**, a regional branch of the great Naciri college of Tamegroute on the Draa. This zaouia restored an earlier water system in the early 18th century which was improved upon in 1840 and further embellished in 1971 to create the Ait Azdel lake.

Tazzerte

10 km west of the dam crossroads is the village of Tazzerte which is dominated by four massive decaying kasbahs of the Glouai clan. The village is divided by an olive-shaded irrigation ditch. There is a mosque in each half whilst all four kasbahs are in the eastern section overlooked by the brown hilltop **Koubba of Sidi Mohammed Mustafa**. This koubba contains a sacred black stone in a niche, kissed by pilgrims and replaced with an offering of money or barley. This grain impregnated with the saint's holiness is made into couscous which is eaten over the grave during the saint's anniversary. The women of the village tie clothing and hair on to the bushes in promise of an offering should the fragment blow free and enable their prayer to be granted.

Arriving at the village you will be taken to see the guardian of the kasbahs, a venerable slightly crippled gentleman who used to be one of the Glaoui's shepherds and who delegates a tour to one of his sons. The strong outer walls of the **Caid's Kasbah**, the smallest detached four square building at the far west was built by Madani el Glaoui,

1866–1918, who reached his pinnacle of power as Grand Vizier and Minister of War to Sultan Moulay Hafid in 1909. The vast extent of the neighbouring **palace Kasbah** is the work of his younger brother Thami el Glaoui, 1879–1956, who led the clan after his brother's death and established an empire within an Empire, ruling and subduing the troublesome south for the French as the feared Pasha of Marrakesh. Stout towers and walls enclose a large garden adjacent to the courtyard shell of the kasbah whose white plastered walls enclose a half acre of rubble. The controlled decoration of windows and cornices and the traceable proportions of the elevated chambers hint at its past elegance.

East of Thami's palace is the high double-arcaded court of **Si Hammou's Kasbah**; the graceful controlled horseshoe arches directly support columns whose lotus capitals are linked by a decayed cedar balcony. The towered staircase is quite unsafe and the view from the top amongst the merlons, stork and hawks' nests precarious but memorable. Si Hammou ben Mohammed was the xenophobic nephew of Thami and a ferocious tribal warlord who maintained his embarrassing hatred for the French but remained caid of the High Atlas kasbah of Telouet until his death. Hammou married Madani's daughter, Lalla Hamina, and the high standard of internal decoration is likely to have been commissioned by their son Abdallah, a favourite of Thami who adopted him on his father's death. This kasbah was occupied as late as 1966 whilst the others fell empty soon after the Pasha's death in 1956, after which King Mohammed V banished the most guilty members of the clan from Morocco.

The least impressive of the four is **Si Omar's Kasbah**, built by a son of Madani's whose other responsibilities at Demnate and especially at Talioune must have borne heavily on his time at Tazzerte.

A **souk** is held at Tazzerte on Monday though this takes second place to that of **Sidi Rahal**, 7 km west of Tazzerte on the 6112, which has the busiest local souk on Friday, as well as a zaouia, a café and a garage. The **tomb of Sidi Rahal**, credited with great magical powers—flying on carpets is just one from the long catalogue of his skills—is respected by Jews and Muslims alike. The Sidi has a moussem in August by his tomb which is 2 km to the west near the bridge over the Oued Rdat. Along this route, the 6112, there are two turnings for **Ait Ourir** which has a big **souk** on Tuesday before you reach the main P24 road 17 km outside of Marrakesh.

Part VII

MARRAKESH AND THE HIGH ATLAS

The Koutoubia Mosque, Marrakesh

Marrakesh

Marrakesh the 'Red' is the heart that beats an African identity into the complex soul of Morocco. The city walls, overlooked by the Koutoubia minaret, are framed against the towering blue wall of the High Atlas mountains. It promises so much but at first may seem to contain nothing more than a vast transitory souk. The Jemaa el Fna, the celebrated square at the centre of the Medina, is full of visiting farmers and Marrakesh can appear less of a city and more like a walled market fair. It is strikingly African compared with the Atlantic character of Casablanca and the intense Arab attitude of Fez; yet it is not some desert border town but a city with a long and proud record as an Imperial capital.

The Phoenicians, the Romans, Arabs and even a great-grandson of the Prophet ruled over a mere portion of Morocco, a patchwork of coastal hills and the northern Atlantic coast. The Empire of Morocco was first created by a Berber tribe from the depths of the Western Sahara and not by any of these distinguished, alien powers. They were the first to forge a Moroccan identity by linking a vast continental hinterland to the civilized lands of the northwest. Marrakesh was the Berber capital, a city founded where they embraced Islam and an urban culture on their own terms. Here they brought together, like heraldic symbols of the future state, palm trees from the desert and craftsmen from Andalucia.

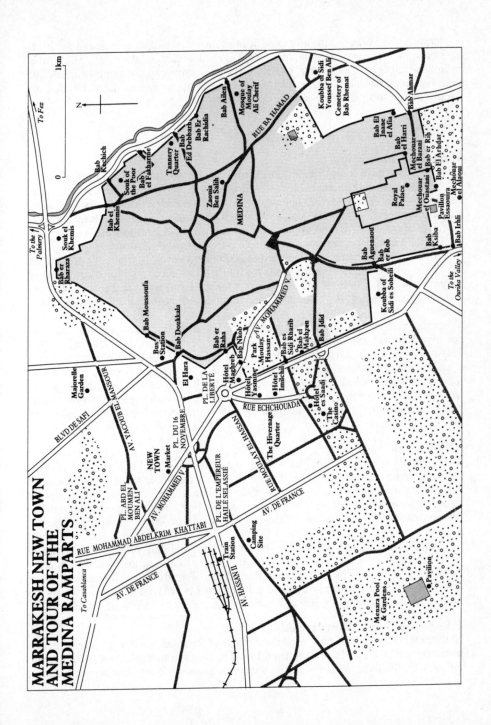

Marrakesh has retained its aura of African exoticism, whilst its guaranteed dry heat, the heady atmosphere of its souk, its celebrated monuments and the nearby High Atlas mountain valleys have a universal appeal. It is a fascinating city, the central objective of most visitors to Morocco, but be aware that you will not be alone, Marrakesh is, after Agadir, Morocco's chief tourist destination.

History

Almoravide foundation

Archaeologists have found the site of Marrakesh almost continually occupied since Neolithic times, but the modern city has its origins as an Almoravide garrison in the 11th century. In 1062 Abu Bekr, the commander of the Almoravides, threw up a wall of thorn bushes to protect his camp, and amidst his tented army built a fortress, the Ksar el Hajar, the tower of stone. In 1071 he appointed a cousin from his Lemtuna tribe, Youssef ben Tachfine, to command the new garrison. Youssef began the construction of a mosque beside the ksar, and barracks for a guard of 2000 negro slaves. Marrakesh's position on the border of three agricultural regions meant that it soon eclipsed the older towns of Aghmat and Nfis to become the main market for the farmers of the Tensift valley, the nomadic pastoralists of the plains and the Masmuda Atlas tribes. It still has that feel to this day.

Youssef ben Tachfine became increasingly involved in Imperial conquest, annexing northern Morocco and then Spain to the Almoravide Empire, and it was his son Ali ben Youssef, born of a Christian concubine, who embellished Marrakesh into a major Islamic centre. He built the great circuit of walls, two large mosques, palaces and fountains, which were all superbly decorated by Andalucian carvers. Almoravide desert technology also improved the city's seasonal water supply, building long *khettera* (pipes) which carried water underground from the High Atlas mountains to the houses and gardens of Marrakesh.

Almohad rule, 1147–1247

After decades of war, the Almohads finally took Marrakesh in 1147 when a Christian mercenary regiment betrayed the Bab Aghmat gate. After three days of licensed plunder to purify the city of its obstinacy, Sultan Abdel Mouman began the process of removing all memories of Almoravide rule. It was he who built the Koutoubia, over the ruins of the Almoravide kasbah and mosque, and moved the Imperial quarter to the south, where it is today.

Abdel Moumen was succeeded by two more great building sultans, Abu Yaacoub Yussef and by Yaacoub el Mansour, whose palaces and sophisticated Andalucian court had little in common with the puritan Berber origins of the dynasty. After only a century of rule, Almohad authority had decayed so far that in 1247 Marrakesh itself, the national capital, was sacked. Twenty years of increasing anarchy left the city an empty husk.

A Provincial City of the Merenids

By 1269 the Merenids had imposed their rule over the south, restoring Marrakesh as a provincial city, but ruled Morocco from Fez. Their most noticeable contribution to the city was the building of a number of medersas although none have survived intact.

Marrakesh was occasionally used by Merenid princes as a springboard for their dynastic ambitions, and indeed for twelve years, from 1374, a separate Merenid principality was established on the city. This frontier was indicated by an early European cartographer, and western maps for centuries afterwards mistakenly divided Morocco between the Kings of Marrakesh and Fez.

Saadian Renewal

The Atlantic coast to the west of Marrakesh had fallen to the Portuguese in the 16th century. The city fell effortlessly into the control of the Saadians who in 1524, after the death of the last Wattasid Pasha, sent a garrison to occupy the deserted kasbah. The real struggle was fought out at the siege of Portuguese Agadir and against Wattasid armies for the possession of the Tadla plain. Marrakesh was the secure capital of Mohammed ech Cheikh, unaffected by Wattasid revivals, Fassi revolts, tribal dissidence, Portuguese or Turkish intrigue that interrupted his conquest of Morocco elsewhere. Mohammed ech Cheikh was assassinated in the High Atlas by a Turkish assassination squad, and six of his sons were killed by the Caid of Marrakesh to make way for the most capable heir, Abdullah el Ghalib.

Marrakesh enjoyed a golden age during the rule of Abdullah el Ghalib and that of his half-brother Ahmed, known either as el Mansour, 'the victorious', or el Dehbi, 'the golden'. During this period, Abdullah founded the Mellah, rebuilt the Kasbah and the Ben Youssef Mosque with its medersa, built a hospital and the new Mouassin Mosque. Ahmed built the incomparable El Badi Palace and the Saadian tombs, and sprinkled the city with fountains, fondouqs, libraries and hammams. During the 16th and 17th centuries, sugar, saltpetre, cottons and silk were produced in Marrakesh which combined with items from the Saharan trade: slaves, gold, ivory, gum arabic and ostrich feathers were exported through the Atlantic ports.

Alouite rule

After 1610 Marrakesh, though it housed a number of Saadian princes in magnificent palaces, was controlled by a series of local marabouts, until the first Alouite sultan, Moulay Rachid, seized the city in 1668. The reign of his brother Moulay Ishmael though it was good for most of Morocco, was disastrous for Marrakesh. The city was repeatedly sacked in a twenty-year war fought between the Sultan and his rebellious nephew who was based on Taroudant. Though Moulay Ishmael carefully reformed and restored the religious shrines of the city he stole away its secular life. He moved all government to Meknes and despoiled the great El Badi Palace less than a century after its completion. The twenty-year anarchy and vicious wars that followed Moulay Ishmael's death in 1727 almost destroyed the city completely.

Later Alouite sultans checked the city's continual decline, by alternating government between Fez and Marrakesh. The Medina, the mechouar, the gates, gardens and pavilions of Marrakesh are now substantially as these sultans left them. The comparative order and prosperity of Moulay Hassan's reign (1873–1894) is revealed in the large number of opulent merchants' houses and the palaces of Bahia and Dar Si Said built by viziers during the minority of his son, Abdul Aziz. They are however pale copies of a magnificent past and it is symptomatic that the various efforts to reestablish industry in this period, principally sugar and gunpowder factories, failed. Even a steam-driven olive oil refinery fell victim to local superstition and jealousies. On the eve of the 20th century there were no wind or steam mills in the city, and trade depended on pack animals being safely escorted past the Rehamna tribe to Mogador.

Growing European influence was bitterly resented, and culminated in the lynching of Dr Mauchamp after he attached an aerial to his roof in 1907. Personal resentment against Dr Mauchamp was intense, from both resentful native healers and city traders who were infuriated that with his aerial the doctor could discover prices in Essaouira days before they could. The city mob for their part were convinced the aerial was a sorcerer's device, for it was well known on the streets, and with some truth, that Mauchamp had great knowledge of the occult. It proved to be one of several incidents which provided the excuse for the French landings in Casablanca in the same year. The French were opposed by a Sheikh from the Western Sahara, El Hiba, who declared himself sultan at Tiznit in 1912 and raised all the southern tribes to his standard. The blue-veiled Sheikh held court from an encampment city outside Marrakesh for a few heady weeks before leading the tribes north to liberate Fez. This army was slaughtered at Sidi Bou Othman, and Marrakesh was occupied the same day without bloodshed. French troops held the city but for the war south of the mountains they employed the caids of the High Atlas, the Glaoui, Gondaffi and M'touggi.

Marrakesh became an important centre of French influence in the south. They built the new town, 'Gueliz', to the west of the city around their enormous army barracks, and adorned the region with roads, hotels, pylons, railroads, schools, irrigation works and hospitals. Apart from the use of roads these technical advances were to the benefit of colonial farmers and the caidal allies of French. The chief ally was Thami el Glaoui, the fabulously wealthy Pasha of Marrakesh who ruled a Medina in which an estimated 16,000–27,000 registered prostitutes lived. Independence in 1956 brought a swift and bloody end to his corrupt regime.

Marrakesh today houses a rapidly expanding population of half a million. It is the most important administrative and industrial centre of the south and earns valuable foreign currency as a tourist destination. It is still a natural market place with a cultural life that retains both the splendour of its periods as an Imperial capital and the traditions from the rural Berber hinterland.

GETTING TO AND AROUND MARRAKESH

By Air
The Marrakesh–Menara international airport is 5 km southwest of town and also has regular internal flights to Agadir, Casablanca, Ouazazarte, Er Rachidia, Fez and Tangier. Tickets can be bought from Air France and Royal Air Maroc who share an office at 197, Av. Mohammed V, tel 31938.

By Train
The station is off Av. Hassan II, a five-minute walk west from the Place du 16 Novembre on Av. Mohammed V, tel 31107. Seven trains a day travel north to Casablanca where you can connect with trains to Rabat, Fez, Meknes, Oujda. There is a direct overnight train to Tangier that leaves at 20.15.

By Bus

CTM and other bus companies all depart from the depot just outside the Bab Doukkala on Place Mouarabiten. There are at least half a dozen daily buses to the beaches at El Jadida and Essaouira for 25dh, but even for these well-covered routes try and buy tickets in advance. Buses to Agadir cost 35dh, to Fez 60dh, Ouazazarte 40dh and Casablanca 38dh. The ten-hour trip on the morning bus to Zagora costs 70dh and there are currently 5.00 and 16.30 departures for the eight-hour trip to Taroudant costing 45dh, or a 3.00 departure which uses the more dramatic Tiz-n-Test pass. Buses to Ourika valley leave from the Bab er Rob.

Local buses leave from the Jemaa el Fna and cost 1dh. No 1 goes right along Av. Mohammed V to below the Gueliz hill, no 3 along Av. Mohammed V and Av. Hassan II to the station, no 4 along Av. Mohammed V and then on to the El Jadida road, no 5 on to the Beni Mellal road (useful for Souk el Khemis), no 6 to the Quartier Industriel (and the youth hostel), no 7 to Av. Hassan II and further northwest, no 8 along Av. Mohammed V and Av. Hassan II, no 10 to Bab Doukkala and the Safi road and the elusive no 11 to the airport via the Menara gardens.

By Taxis

Bargaining for taxis is part of Marrakesh life, but you will never be able to compete with Marrakeshi women and their forceful cries of 'Wahd dirham' (one dirham) as they leap aboard. Prices fluctuate in tune with your desperation, destination and charm. Grands taxis are found in the Jemaa el Fna and by the Bab er Rob, and a place to the Ourika valley can cost only 10dh. As a group you might want to hire a taxi for a day in Ourika or up the Tiz-n-Test, for which you will have to pay between 200dh and 300dh. Petits taxis are found at Jemaa el Fna and along Av. Mohammed V. They should cost 5dh per person—15dh for three to the train station, though the run to the airport is usually about 40dh. For a horse-drawn taxi that seats five, 20dh an hour is a price to aspire to, but it may be easier to settle a general price for a tour of the ramparts and gardens.

By Car

There are plenty of car-hire firms in Marrakesh. Avis is at 137, Av. Mohammed V, tel 33727, and Europcar at 59, Rue Mansour Eddahbi, tel 48484. You'll find Hertz at 154, Av. Mohammed V, tel 34680 and they also run a desk at the Hôtel Palais el Badia, tel 31680. Others include Locoto, at 48, Rue de la Liberté, Interrent at 63, Blvd Zerktouni, tel 31228, Budget at 213, Av. Mohammed V, tel 33224, Afric Cars at Station Aguedal on Blvd Zerktouni, tel 31239 and Tourist Cars at 64, Blvd Zerktouni, tel 31530

Car parts are available from Union Pièces Autos, 18, Blvd Mansour Eddahbi, tel 31790 or the Centre Européen de l'Automobile, 18, Blvd Moulay Rachid, tel 34527
Garages: Ourika, the main Fiat agent, is at 66, Av. Mohammed V, tel 30155 and Tazi for Renaults on Rue Bab Agnaou, tel 22339.
Parking: You can park anywhere off the Av. Mohammed V in the new town, in any big hotel or at the Jemaa el Fna in front of the Foucauld Hotel. There is also a car park in an old covered bus depot immediately beside the CTM Hotel.

Bicycles can be rented from Foucauld Hotel on the Jemaa el Fna at 35dh a halfday, 60dh a full day or from big four-star hotels in the new town like the PLM Toubkal or El Andalous.

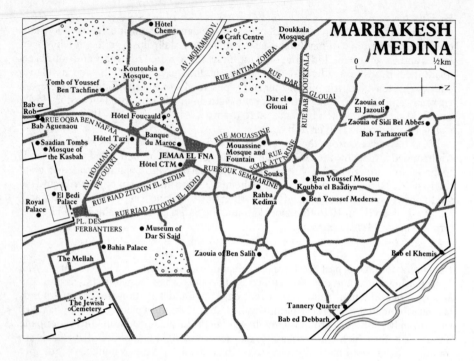

TOURIST INFORMATION

The Tourist Office is at Place Abdelmoumen ben Ali on Av. Mohammed V, open 8.00–14.30 in July and August, 8.00–12.00, 14.00–18.00 the rest of the year, tel 30258. They give away familiar free leaflets with maps, lists of hotels and arrange the hire of guides.

The main Post Office is on Av. Mohammed V at Place du 16 Novembre. There is a good sub office—a Moorish public building on the southern side of the Jemaa el Fna. This is open Mon-Fri, 8.00–14.00 and has telephones for international calls.

Banks: BMCE is at 144, Av. Mohammed V, BMCI on Rue Moulay Ishmael, Banque Populaire at 69, Av. Mohammed V, and Credit du Maroc and SGMB on Rue Bab Agnaou just off the Jemaa el Fna.

WHAT TO SEE

Marrakesh is an easy city to orientate yourself in. The straight central street of the new town, Av. Mohammed V, runs with the Koutoubia minaret, which is just west of the Jemaa el Fna, as its focus. The areas around Av. Mohammed V and the Jemaa el Fna support most of the offices, hotels, cafés and banks. The minaret of the Koutoubia Mosque and the Jemaa el Fna are the dominant images in the Medina of Marrakesh. Even if you avoid all other conventional tourist sites, and explore only the most reclusive quarters of the Medina, these two will remain at the centre of your experience of Marrakesh.

The souk of Marrakesh opens to the north of the Jemaa el Fna and this, the most immediately accessible area of the Medina, is described first. The next section covers the monuments in the northern Medina. The principal attractions, the Ben Youssef Medersa and the Koubba el Baroudiyn, are fortunately the easiest to find but for those looking to escape the coach tours a walk through the undisturbed northern area is included. The area to the south of the Jemaa el Fna, which contains the monuments of Imperial Marrakesh, the Palace of El Badi, the Saadian tombs, the Bahia Palace and the Museum of Dar Si Said, is covered in a third section. This is followed by a tour of the Medina ramparts and a description of the gardens of Marrakesh.

The Koutoubia

The **minaret** of the Koutoubia Mosque appears at its most elegant from a great distance. Approaching Marrakesh from the High Atlas, the tower rises magnificently above the barely perceptible city and only then can you begin to understand the veneration in which it is locally held. So compelling a tower draws you close in to the wasteland and half-garden that surrounds it, though you gain little by examining it at close range. Its stature dwindles and the interior of the mosque is of course closed to non-Muslims.

The wasteland around the Koutoubia Mosque was, ironically, the centre of the original city. The Almoravide Sultan Ali ben Youssef rebuilt his father's Kasbah Mosque and added a new palace to the south, on the site of the present Koutoubia, but these were razed to the ground when Abdel Moumen captured the city in 1147. This Almohad Sultan immediately started on a new mosque but the work was pushed forward too quickly. It was found wanting, incorrectly aligned to Mecca amongst other faults, and was dismantled soon after its completion. The sole trace was a stumpy little minaret that survived into the 19th century. But archaeologists have uncovered its foundations, which can be seen in the dusty area between the Koutoubia and Av. Mohammed V, and for the specialist there are also traces of the Almoravide palace to be seen.

Abdel Moumen, undeterred by this first failure and the scale of his existing projects, two enormous mosques at Tinmal and Taza, ordered a fresh start. This, the Koutoubia Mosque, followed the same plan though it was slightly wider and, obviously, on a different orientation. The interior is dominated by a forest of horseshoe arches which rest on solid square pillars that are decorated by flanking pairs of carved columns. It is a severe but dignified white space that reflects the puritan Almohad creed. Five domes, decorated with stalactites, which rise along the 'nave' aisle as it approaches the tall mihrab prayer niche naturally focus the attention of the worshippers. At the opposite end to the mihrab is the open air Sahn court which, before the construction of medersas in the 13th century was the customary place for lectures on the Koran and Islamic law.

The minaret, due to the vagaries of the site, was positioned in the northeast corner of the mosque and was not finished until the reign of Abdel Moumen's grandson, Sultan Yaacoub el Mansour, 1184–1199. From its 12 m by 12 m base it rises to almost 70 m. It was built from an internal ramp that climbs between its double walls. This connects six chambers that increase in delicate ornamentation as they ascend. Each face of the minaret has a different decorative scheme and the boldly carved lancet windows are a study in Almohad design. The decoration culminates in the rich interlinked arches of the upper storey, above which is a last surviving band of faience decoration. The rough stonework of the tower decreases in size as it rises. This work would have originally been obscured by plaster and decoration as the recently restored minaret of the Almohad Kasbah Mosque shows. Fortunately no such similar work is planned on the Koutoubia.

Above the tattered faience band a battlement of merlons frames the domed minaret which is built on a strict 1 to 5 proportion to the tower, the golden rule for all Maghrebi minarets. On the summit a wooden gallows flies a blue or green prayer flag on Friday beside three golden balls surmounted by a tear. These are thought to be the gift of Sultan Yaacoub el Mansour's wife, who melted down all her jewelry for the globes in penance for having eaten three grapes during Ramadan.

The new mosque was enclosed by streets where hundreds of copyists, scribes, binders and booksellers kept stalls. It is from this surrounding souk of books, the 'kutubiyyin', that it takes its name. For its inauguration in 1158 Abdel Moumen had a spectacular trophy to display, for he had just acquired from the conquered city of Cordoba one of the four original copies of the third Caliph Othman's official compilation of the Koran. From these all later texts descend.

300 m east of the Koutoubia lies the great central square of the Medina of Marrakesh, the Jemaa el Fna.

The Jemaa el Fna

Jemaa el Fna is popularly translated as 'the place of the dead', a suitably chilling phrase which adds a mysterious whiff of exoticism and savage justice to an otherwise undeniably lively place. A less entertaining but probably correct translation is 'the mosque that came to nothing'—a sly reference to the Saadian sultan Ahmed el Mansour's abortive attempt to build a mosque here.

It has always been at the centre of Medina life and started as the formal Mechouar in front of the Kasbah of the Almoravides. When the Almohads moved the Kasbah quarter to the south of the city, official processions were increasingly staged there. The Bab er Rob and the Bab Aguenaou at the entrance to the Kasbah quarter were used for executions and the exhibition of the salted heads. But in essence the Jemaa el Fna has always been as it is now, a popular forum for entertainment, celebration, riots, gossip and business.

At dawn it is an empty wedge of tarmac, surrounded by parked cars, shuttered cafés and bazaars, an area of no architectural interest. As the morning progresses a perimeter is formed by lines of barrows selling nuts and fresh squeezed orange juice, and the edges of the square erupt in a sea of shops. The centre is filled by a random and changing assortment of snake charmers, story-tellers, acrobats, dentists, water sellers, scribes, monkeys, clowns and dancing boys—who during the day direct most of their skills to camera-carrying tourists.

But at dusk the Jemaa el Fna comes into its own, and returns to its true audience of visiting Berber farmers from the plains, desert and mountains. Lines of kitchens set up their groaning tables, braziers and benches beneath hissing gas lamps. Here you can dine on a great assortment of salads, vats of brewing goat-head soup, fresh grilled or fried vegetables, chickens, fish and mutton. You can move from table to table trying different platefuls and break off to wander among the musicians and the storytellers. Sharp young street kids hiss 'hashish', veiled women offer trinkets, or sit beckoning by their stock of woven baskets and woolly hats. Blind beggars cry 'Allah' as they extend a bowl or fix you with one accusatory rheumy eye. Innocent looking children with beguiling almond eyes solicit, or try rather clumsily to pick your pockets. From worn tarot cards, the waddle of sacred doves, ink dots, cast bones or your palm, incidents from a possible future will be divined by hunched figures perched on low stools, surrounded by the instruments of their trade. As the evening progresses the crowds thin, the kitchens close and leave small knots of musicians surrounded by a crouching audience furtively smoking from their pipes.

This is the time to seek out powerful music influenced by the spiritual brotherhoods: the Aissoua, Derkawa, Hamadasha and Gnaoua, freed from the irrelevancies of a tourist audience. The repetitive rhythmical music produced on drums, flutes, crude violins and ginbris, a long, few-stringed guitar, is far removed from light entertainment. Shuffling dancers are animated by a spirit that plays upon piety and continence at one moment and sends lewd, erotic displays in the next breath.

The Jemaa el Fna is a rich but undeniably exhausting carnival. It encapsulates much of the fascination of Morocco: the difference, colour and energy of its alien culture, compounded by a rarely diminished sensation of being a stranger on the edge of any understanding. If you haven't found a nearby hotel bedroom, there are a number of cafés that surround the place, where you can rest and watch in comparative serenity and stock up on loose change.

The Medina Souk

South of the Jemaa el Fna stretches the great souk of Marrakesh. It is a triumphant, labyrinthine market place, a glittering display of all the traditional arts and regional crafts of Morocco, grouped together by trade in separate but interlinking streets and court-yards. Compared with the wood-carving areas at Essaouira or the various craftsmen in Fez it has relatively few workshops, though there are turners, carpenters, weavers and tailors to be found.

The souk is not best appreciated at the tail-end of a bemusing and exhausting tour. It should be dipped into, chosen areas gently explored and discovered at different hours of the day. The traditional trading period is in the morning, but the hours before dusk are the busiest for traffic, both human and motorized, and the souk becomes so packed that the crowds of people seem to sway and move in unison.

For your first visit employ a guide to show you the main streets and features. Then, armed with a little knowledge of the street pattern you can afford to explore, the earlier in the morning the better.

Rue Souk Semarine
Along the northern edge of the Jemaa el Fna a range of bazaars and the Ouessabine Mosque hide the main arched entrance to the principal street, the Rue Souk Semarine. Here, before entering the souk proper, you can find a pottery and a spice market. The whole area is often obscured by shifting displays of clothing laid out on canvas. These pavement vendors are constantly on the look out for police, operating against an echoing soundtrack of bird whistles and hustling calls.

Rue Souk Semarine is, however, easy enough to identify. It is broad, well paved and shaded from the sun by a high trellis cover. Commercially, it is dominated by the cloth merchants, whose shelves groan under the weight of hundreds of bolts of bright silks and embroidered cloth for kaftans. Interspaced amongst the cloth merchants are tailors, and they have been joined by a number of upmarket bazaars, whose hidden halls are stacked full of carpets, and who accept all manner of credit cards.

Rahba Kedima

About 150 m along Rue Souk Semarine the first and second right turns lead into the Rahba Kedima, the old corn market. Until the 19th century, it was forbidden to export grain, as it was considered immoral to profit on feeding Christians to the discomfort of poor Muslims. This open courtyard usually has a few vegetable stalls at its far end, but it is dominated by spice and jewelry stalls. The latter are hung with necklaces of amber which are often synthetic. The strange hanging curtains of dried eagles, mountain foxes, hedgehogs, snakes, porcupines, lizards and unnamed grim relics in pots are real enough however. These ingredients are used in the concoction of love potions, stimulants and aphrodisiacs—a balancing form of female magic which helps to correct the many male-dominated features of Moroccan life. The trinity of Maghreb cosmetics are prominently displayed: silvery blocks of antimony which are ground into kohl—a powder which both outlines the eyelids and stimulates an attractive watery sheen that protects eyes from soot and dust, henna in all its variety—green leaves, powder or ready made pastes for dying hair and for the intricate decorative tattooing of hands, face and feet which you may have noticed, and the pottery saucers of cochineal which is used as a rouge. Also look out for sacks of dried Dades roses, a deliciously fragrant and cheap pot pourri.

On the right as you enter the Rahba Kedima is the **Souk Larzal** where wool is auctioned in the morning to spinners and dyers. Next on the right is the pungent **Souk Btana** where raw sheep and goat skins are sorted, dried on the roof tops and sold to the tannery guilds.

'Criee Berbere'

Halfway along the opposite side of Rahba Kedima square an entrance leads to the narrow 'Criee Berbere', a tight enclosed space lined with displays of killims, killim cushions, killim waistcoats, carpets and woollen burnous. Most of the trading is done from the shops but auctions of goods are often held in the morning and evening. Moroccan auctions are distinctive affairs: the sellers walk around with odd composite bundles of stock, shouting the current price in the hope of attracting a larger one. Nothing seems to get sold very quickly.

This auction square was used before 1912 for the sale of slaves, at dusk on Wednesdays, Thursdays and Fridays. These auctions were only for the disposal of stock at the lower end of the domestic market however, as influential clients would expect private and advance viewing. Galla women were considered the most attractive but girls of the Hausa country fetched the best prices as they were considered more cheerful and neater. In the 1840s about 4000 slaves were sold in Morocco every year but by 1870 there was such a glut that prices dropped below £2. Even before the glut the common exchange rate was 2 slaves for a camel and 10 for a horse.

A left turn from here leads you past a selection of turtleshell bellows to the main street or you can retrace your steps to Rue Souk Semarine.

The Kissaria
Just past the Rahba Kedima turning Rue Souk Semarine splits into the **Souk el Kebir** and the **Souk Attarin** on your left. Souk el Kebir passes a jeweller's alley on the right, before the alleys of the Kissaria open up on your left. The Kissaria is traditionally the heart of the souk and in Marrakesh specializes in clothes with a great variety of stalls selling modern western clothes, traditional cotton gandoras, woven blankets and arrays of western-influenced open-necked female kaftans. Continue along Souk el Kebir, passing the aromatic stalls and small courtyards of the carpenters and wood turners who make wooden screens and book holders. On the righthand side, after an arch labelled Souk des Sacochiers, a skilled craftsman makes elaborate embroidered saddles and all the trappings of an Arab cavalier. Almost opposite at 127, Souk Chkaria, craftsmen will Morocco-bind a favourite book for you although covers for video cassettes are currently more in demand.

At the far end of the souk bear left through **Souk Cherratin**, a collection of alleys where you find a few leather, wood and metal artisan stalls. This will lead you into the long souk of 'babouches', a delightful street of tightly packed stalls selling yellow, grey and white slippers and the more exotic gilded velvet. The Kissaria alleys are now on your left. At the end of the slipper souk, a right turn takes you west towards the famous **Souk des Teinturiers**, the alley used by the dyers. Here, cascades of brightly dyed wool dry from the terrace above, and it is a memorable and striking sight. To the right of this alley is the coppersmiths' souk, more carpenters, a courtyard used for selling olive oil and beyond that is the **Souk Haddadine**, the blacksmith's souk, which is surrounded by charcoal sellers.

Returning back to the Souk des Teinturiers you pass a shop selling unpressed felt hats and genuine Fezs before reaching the Mouassine fountain on your left. A left turn past the Mouassine Mosque takes you down the wider and uncomplicated Rue Mouassine which, lined with cloth, carpet and tourist bazaars, brings you back to the Jemaa el Fna.

Medina Monuments
There are two monuments open to non-Muslims in the Medina of Marrakesh, the Saadian Ben Youssef Medersa and the Almoravide Koubba el Baroudiyn. They are the finest buildings in Marrakesh, some would say in all Morocco, and no visit, however short, should exclude these architectural treasures. They are relatively easy to find as they are both associated with the Mosque of Ben Youssef which is just to the north of the souk.

You can, at best, only look at the rest of the Medina monuments from the outside. They are described in a long walk through the northern Medina which passes a number of fondouqs, fountains, the zaouia of Sidi bel Abbes, the zaouia of el Jazouli, the Dar el Glaoui and the Mouassin Mosque before taking you back to the Jemaa el Fna. If you are short on time or energy leave this for your next visit.

The Mosque of Ben Youssef
From the Jemaa el Fna head down the main souk artery, the Rue Souk Semarine/Souk

Almoravid Koubba el Baroudiyn, Marrakesh

el Kbir for 450 m, turn left at the far 'Y' junction and then right under an arch and left again to reach an open square. This is usually occupied by at least one football game and the Mosque walls are draped with long spinning strands of tailors' silk. Ahead stretches the green tiled roof and minaret of the Mosque of Ben Youssef. A mosque was first built here by the Almoravide Sultan Ali in the 12th century as the central mosque of the Medina. It was then twice as large as the present building. The Saadian Sultan Abdullah el Ghalib attempted to make Ben Youssef the most popular and esteemed mosque in Marrakesh. By this time it was in ruins, and he had to rebuild it entirely, along with the neighbouring medersa, and to cap his work he presented it with a large library. Nor, however, did this survive the well-intentioned improvements of his successors. What you now see dates entirely from the early 19th century, when an ancient and beautifully carved Almoravide fountain was also destroyed.

The Mosque and its rectangular cluster of buildings are encircled by a path. To the right is the Medersa and to the left, behind a wall, is the Koubba of Baroudiyn, its white dome barely noticeable from the dusty square.

The Koubba el Baroudiyn

Rediscovered in its sunken position in 1948, Gaston Deverdun exclaimed that 'the art of Islam has never exceeded the splendour of this extraordinary dome'. The Koubba is all that remains to hint at the glory of 12th-century Almoravide Marrakesh. It appears as a small kiosk covering a shallow ritual washing pool in the outer ablution courtyard of the mosque, and is still surrounded by brick cisterns and latrines. However it introduces many of the shapes that become so familiar in later Islamic architecture.

The plan itself is simple enough, a rectangular two-storey domed structure pierced by arches. At ground level a pair of scalloped arches face each other with twin horseshoe arches on the longer faces. These silhouettes are repeated in the rows of three or five inset window arches of the upper storey, where scallop and horseshoe have been joined by an impaled turban motif. A battlement of merlons frames the dome which is decorated with a band of interlocking arches and surmounted by a series of diminishing seven-pointed stars.

Standing inside you look up into a dome of astonishingly bold, confident, solid yet supremely elegant and disciplined carving. The remains of a Kufic frieze announcing its creator, Ali ben Youssef, can just be made out. Above this rests an octagonal arched dome, its interlaced scallop arches infilled with rich foliate carving upon which hang shell-shaped palmettes. The corner squinches are framed by muqarnas, elegant spanning arches, that in later centuries degenerated to appear like dripping stalagmites. The muqarnas ring a seven-pointed star that frames an eight-podded dome which in turn echoes the triumphant deep carving of the central cupola.

Both the exterior and interior carvings play with the strong African light to make pools of dark shadow and contrasting patches of light. It shows much of the confident architectural origins of the Hispano-Moorish style. The gradual debasement of this style into a mere veneer of decoration can be seen progressively at the Medersa, the Saadian tombs, the Bahia Palace and finally in the modern hotels of Marrakesh.

Medersa of Ben Youssef
The medersa is open every day except Friday morning, 8.00–12.00, 14.30–18.00.

It was founded by the philanthropic Merenid Sultan Abou Hassan in the 14th century as part of an educational programme that established Koranic colleges in Fez, Taza, Salé, Meknes and Marrakesh. In 1564 it was replaced by the Saadian Sultan Abdullah el Ghalib who ordered the building of the largest medersa in Morocco, a feat which was completed in under a year. It was part of his ambition to make the Ben Youssef Mosque a rival intellectual centre to Fez. Dedicatory inscriptions to the Sultan can be seen on the lintel of the entrance gate and along the prayer hall.

You may have to knock at the inconspicuous door to the right of the covered arch to enter. A long twisting passage then leads to the entrance hall, a secretive Marrakeshi feature not found in any Merenid medersa, which have proud portals and direct entrances. The rectangular marble basin just off the hall was carved for a vizier of the Omayyad Caliph of Cordoba in the 10th century. Its figurative carving of heraldic eagles and griffins in swirls of vegetation is a rare survivor in puritanical Morocco. It was brought as Almoravide booty to decorate their new mosque, survived the Almohads and was at length moved by the Saadians across the road to their new medersa. From the hall, stairs lead up to over a hundred plain wooden chambers where students lived, each sharing small courtyard skylights. This is another distinctive feature, for earlier medersas used windows overlooking the central courtyard to provide a central decorative theme.

The open **courtyard**, a great interior space of peace and silence, centres on a marble basin and is flanked by two galleries of solid pillars. Directly opposite is the entrance to the prayer hall. The richness of decorative detail never disturbs the graceful simplicity of the plan. An initial height of zellig mosaic is broken by two bands of tile and plaster, carved with Koranic inscriptions, which lead up into the ornate plaster and cedar carving. The courtyard has a distinctive unhurried harmony, a grandeur touched with an element of severity not found in the more intimate Merenid medersas.

The **prayer hall** is divided into three by four marble columns, and a further four enhance the arched mihrab which carries the two traditional inscriptions of the Muslim declaration of faith.

The *tolba*, the reciters, or students were allowed to lodge here for six years whilst they memorized the Koran and studied the commentaries and laws. In the summer they wandered through the country, begging, listening to marabouts and reciting their verses throughout the night at rural festivals.

The northern Medina

North of the medersa stretches the great bulk of the Medina, without souks, bazaars, guides or many tourists. Modern houses have for the most part replaced the pise buildings, but the streets retain their labyrinthine design and you can freely wander through this living maze, catching glimpses of old fondouqs, mosques, hammams and bakeries. The following route takes you past the notable sights of the area and will give you a feel for this less explored section of the Medina.

Turn right from the medersa and left down a covered passage. As you reemerge into daylight you face a crossroads where the Rue Baroudienne joins the Rue Amesfah. Both these two streets are lined with a number of elegant 16th- and 17th-century **fondouqs**, which are still used as artisan and tradesmen's courtyards. They are well worth having a discreet peep in.

Turn right up Rue Amesfah, passing several more fondouqs, the most elegant of which is beside the monumental decorated fountain on the left, the **Chrob ou Chouf** which translates as 'drink and admire'. A left turn by the fountain, up Rue Diar Sabboun, takes you into Rue Bab Taghzout, which is often half filled by a souk of secondhand clothes.

The **Bab Taghzout** used to mark the northern edge of the city, but in the 18th century Sultan Sidi Mohammed ben Abder Rahman extended the walls to include the zaouia suburb of Sidi bel Abbes, one of the seven saints of Marrakesh, within the city.

Es-Sebti, the seven saints of Marrakesh

Combinations of seven saints or seven sleepers reach back beyond Islam and Christianity to an older universal myth, and in Morocco Ceuta, Djebel Hadid, Fez and Marrakesh all share in this common tradition. In the 18th century, Sultan Moulay Ishmael removed various unorthodox Berber aspects of the annual celebration of Marrakesh's 'es Sebti', and at the same time he rebuilt the sanctuaries of the historical, orthodox saints. A new week-long Moussem of the Es-Sebti was established, which began at the shrine of Sidi Iyad, moved on to Sidi Youssef bin Ali, Sidi Abd el Aziz, Sidi el-Ghawzani, Sidi es Suhayi and Sidi ben Sliman before culminating here at the major shrine of the city, that of Sidi bel Abbes.

Shrine of Sidi bel Abbes

The direct approach to this zaouia is through an arch lined with an expensive and elaborate arcade of jewellers. The zaouia, mosque and tombs are forbidden to non-Muslims, but by going to the left or the right of the main entrance you get impressive views into the extensive complex and of the great pyramidal shrine.

Sidi bel Abbes, 1130–1205, was born in Ceuta but moved south to establish a hermitage outside Marrakesh. His learning, moral sermons, miracles and ascetic life-style gained him a popular following. Sultan Yaacoub el Mansour invited him into the city and presented him with buildings and funds for his good works. Centred on his shrine, these continue today with city merchants supporting the zaouia in running a number of schools, hostels and in feeding the blind each evening. A number of potent legends still circulate in the city, that Christians venerate Sidi bel Abbes as St Augustine, and that he haunts the minaret of the Koutoubia each night until he is certain that all the blind have been fed.

The zaouia rose beside his grave in the cemetery of Sidi Marwan which was then just to the north of the city walls. The existing buildings are the work of the 18th-century Alouite Sultan Sidi Mohammed ben Abder Rahman, who apart from extending the city walls and rebuilding the entire shrine complex added a further gift of a medersa courtyard with two flights of horseshoe arches.

The Zaouia of Sidi ben Sliman el Jazouli

Turning back through Bab Taghzout, a right turn takes you past the covered Souk el Mjadlia and out below the zaouia of Sidi ben Sliman el Jazouli, another of the seven patron saints of Marrakesh. Its distinctive green pyramid roof and neighbouring mosque can be seen from alleys to the north and south of the zaouia, but the street beside it is closed to non-Muslims.

Sidi ben Sliman el Jazouli was one of the great Sufi mystics of Morocco, whose followers went on to found important religious institutions throughout the country. El Jazouli's *Book on the Manifest Proofs of Piety* remains a seminal mystical text. As well as his spiritual teaching, he was a leading figure in the struggle against Portugal and his embalmed body became a powerful totem in the jihad. Buried at Afugal in Haha province for a few decades, his body was brought to Marrakesh by the Saadians in 1523. Six Saadian princes were murdered soon afterwards in a palace coup. They were buried together under a single koubba beside El Jazouli's shrine, giving a further bizarre resonance to the legend of the seven.

Below the zaouia walk down to a dusty crossroad square. Ahead and to your right you will see the minaret of the Sidi Bou Ameur Mosque. Turn left beneath this to walk down Rue Dar el Glaoui.

Dar el Glaoui

On the junction between Rue Dar el Glaoui and Rue Bab Doukkala is the massive bulk of the Dar el Glaoui, the palace of Thami el Glaoui, Pasha of Marrakesh, which was built in the early years of this century. Its magnificent interior remains firmly closed though there is supposedly a plan to make it more accessible.

Dar el Glaoui was a place of legendary hospitality which from the 1920s to 1950s entertained an international social élite including Roosevelt, Churchill and Patton in its heyday. Beautiful Berber girls or boys, opium or marijuana, Lafitte or Latour were offered to guests with the freedom and nonchalance with which other Moroccan houses offer a glass of mint tea. Compliant European females could rely on a parting gift of emeralds and society figures fought for the chance to have been the Pasha's friend for a night. But behind the pampering of sophisticated guests lay French 'loans', illicit taxes, bribery, blackmail and protection rackets, and it was common knowledge that the thousands of Marrakesh prostitutes had the Pasha as their ultimate pimp.

Only hours after the Pasha's death in 1956 a crowd broke into the Dar el Glaoui. Such was their hatred for the Pasha, who had allied himself so closely to the French colonists, that they preferred to destroy rather than loot the palace and even the cars were smashed and set on fire. The mob then had their vengeance on the traitorous henchmen and officials of the Pasha, who were hunted through the streets of the Medina. They were treated like the cars, beaten, stripped and then burnt alive on the rubbish dump outside the Bab Doukkala. It is said that Sultan Mohammed V would not eat for seven days when he heard of this brutality, even though the men killed had been his bitterest enemies.

From the Dar el Glaoui you can walk due west along Rue Bab Doukkala, that runs to the gate of that name to look at the **Mosque of Bab Doukkala** on your left. This was built in 1558 by Lalla Messaouda, daughter of a Caid of Ouazazarte, wife of a Sultan and a redoubtable mother. Whilst in exile in Istanbul she educated two sons, the great Saadian Sultans, Abdel Malik and Ahmed el Mansour. All that can be seen is the slender elegant minaret to the northeast of the mosque and the elegant **fountain of Sidi el Hassan**, named after one of the founding professors of the medersa which used to be attached to the mosque.

Returning back to the Dar el Glaoui walk east for 300 m until you reach the prominent crossroads with Rue Mouassin. Just up the street to the left is the **mosque and shrine of Sidi Abdel Aziz**, another Sufi disciple of El Jazouli who died at Marrakesh in 1508 and has entered the pantheon of the seven saints. Whilst on this crossroads look out for the gates to half a dozen fondouqs, some of which may be open. Try 192 or 149 Rue Mouassin, which will reveal courtyards surrounded by galleries which are supported by high simple pillars and graceful cedar beams.

The Mouassin Mosque

Right at the crossroads and 150 m down Rue Mouassin is the Mouassin Mosque, a monumental building established by the Saadian Sultan Abdullah el Ghalib in 1560 complete with baths, medersa and exterior fountain. The Mosque has an equivocal local reputation. It is named after a prestigious local Shorfa family, but during the building of the foundations a 14th-century Jewish plague cemetery was unearthed. This is considered to have reduced the sanctity of the site and rumours of a curse released in disturbing the grave of a Cabbalist rabbi began to circulate. The Mosque is largely hidden from non-Muslims by the surrounding buildings, and unfortunately the gates and stumpy minaret give little indication of the reported magnificence inside.

The impressive triple-bayed **Mouassin fountain** with its ornate portico is in a small square to the left of the Mosque. In the far corner of the square, beside a large vine growing up the wall, is the door to the secretive café Maur Abouid. The café, built over a bridge, has a wonderful view from its sunbaked roof. Glimpses of tranquil courtyards and hidden koubbas show how much of the city remains hidden, even here in the heart of the Medina. The café is draped with vines and cats, and dotted with an assortment of aged benches and photographs.

Walking beneath this bridge you enter the Kissaria at the heart of the souk, but by continuing down the bazaar-lined Rue Mouassin you resurface at the western corner of the Jemaa el Fna.

Imperial Marrakesh

The Marrakesh of the Sultans has grown up since the 12th century in what now forms the southern area of the Medina. Here, the Almohads first established their kasbah, palaces, barracks and a royal Mosque. Successor dynasties continued to develop the southern quarter into an Imperial city, but in a typically Moroccan way paid scant regard to the achievements of their predecessors. The Royal Palace of King Hassan II therefore, which is not open to the public, stands on ground that has seen a dazzling succession of pavilions, courts and gardens.

The glories of Imperial Marrakesh include the massive and very impressive ruins of the 16th-century Saadian El Badi Palace, which contrast perfectly in their state of decay with the Saadian tombs, which have survived completely intact from the same period. Apart from two 19th-century viziers' palaces, the Bahia palace and the Museum of Dar Si Said, you can also lose yourself in the dark alleys of Marrakesh's ancient Jewish quarter, the Mellah.

To get to Imperial Marrakesh from the Jemaa el Fna, walk south down the café-lined Rue Bab Aguenaou to a crossroads dominated by the Tazi Hotel. To your right is the Place Youssef ben Tachfine. The original tomb was destroyed by the Almohads but Youssef's cult revived and this traditional Berber holy place was consecrated to his memory by the Merenids in the 14th century. The symbolic tomb in the **koubba** is left open to the sky, the only dome that the spirit of this desert warrior will accept.

Returning to the Tazi Hotel, a walk down Rue Oqba ben Nafaa takes you 600 m south. The intermittent wall on your left is not an old city wall but marks out the inner city, the Kasbah quarter of Sultans, the Imperial city.

Bab Aguenaou

The official entrance into the Kasbah lay through the Bab Aguenaou. You will find this distinctive carved gate on the left just before the outer Bab er Rob, where a potters' souk, taxis and local buses collect. Aguenaou is a Berber word that translates as 'the mute ram without horns'. A less prosaic but more logical translation names it the Guinea Gate— the southern gate leading to black Africa, the homeland of the Sultan's negro guards. It was built on Sultan Yaacoub el Mansour's orders in 1185, and has added prestige as one of the few stone structures in this city of pink pisé. It is carved from local 'blue' Gueliz stone which is still being quarried to the north of Marrakesh. The semi-circular frieze has been delicately cut but is surprisingly assertive and strong.

Kasbah Mosque

Passing through this gate you approach the Kasbah Mosque. It was finished in 1190 by the Almohad Sultan, Yaacoub el Mansour, renowned for his great building works. The long white exterior wall is capped with merlons and for once left free of encrusted buildings to give an indication of its impressive extent. Neither the wall nor the recently restored but well proportioned minaret, on the northwest corner, however, give much indication of its age.

To the Almohad mosque the Merenids added a famous medersa which was destroyed in a gunpowder explosion in 1569. The Saadian Abdullah el Ghalib restored the damaged mosque, which has since been touched up every two hundred years, first by Sidi Mohammed in the 18th century and recently by Hassan II. For a Muslim the principal approach is through the great domed north gate which looks across the extensive open sahn court to the domed mihrab flanked by four Omayyad columns of jasper. Beside the mihrab a door gives entrance to the enclosed garden courtyard of the 16th-century royal necropolis—the Saadian tombs.

Saadian Tombs

A tight thin passage to the south of the Mosque was cut through the protective Saadian walls in 1917 for the use of non-Muslims (just to the left of the stork's nest on the ruined wall). This is open every day from 8.00–12.00, 14.00–18.00, admission 3dh, in the company of a portly guide, tips accepted. The tombs are one of the most visited sites in Morocco and in order to recapture some sense of serenity and isolation go as early in the morning as possible.

Coming from the passage you enter an ancient rectangular enclosed garden, planted with trees, cascading shrubs and rosemary hedges. This is the ancient cemetery of the Shorfa, the descendants of the prophet, which had been in use for centuries before any Saadians arrived in Marrakesh. The identity of most of the open-air mosaic graves is lost but a Merenid Sultan, Abou Hassan, was buried here in 1351 to be followed by the first Saadian sultan, Mohammed ech Cheikh in 1557, whose tomb was covered by a simple koubba.

The existing koubbas were all built by Mohammed ech Cheikh's third ruling son, Ahmed el Mansour. He built a pavilion around his father's simple tomb, where he also buried his mother Lalla Messaouda in 1591. He then built the hall of twelve columns to be his own mausoleum and attached to it a prayer hall. The extraordinary interiors of both koubbas can be examined from their thresholds.

The Prayer Hall

The first hall, on your left as you enter, is the prayer hall which extends south of Ahmed el Mansour's tomb. Four clean pillars support elegant high horseshoe arches which, with the skylight, divide the roof space into eight rectangles. The decorated mihrab niche can be seen to your left. Although it has the most pleasing dark, simple sepulchral quality of them all, this was never intended as a tomb. It contains, however, a plethora of them, most the resting places of Alouite princes from the 18th century. There is a sad little nest just to the left of the mihrab where half a dozen plague victims, the children of Sultan Sidi Mohammed, were buried between 1756–1777. The large tomb to the right, surrounded by a wooden balustrade, is one of the many attributed tombs of the Black Sultan, the Merenid Abou Hassan. He is also thought to be buried in the hall of three niches, at the back of the Saadian Tombs, and at the Chellah, Rabat.

The Hall of Twelve Columns

The central mausoleum of Ahmed el Mansour has three central tombs surrounded by a colonnade of twelve decorated marble pillars. The upper plasterwork is so intensely carved as to appear like gilded lace. The dome is even more fantastically rich, and prolonged inspection induces an almost physical sense of nausea. Decoration has overwhelmed form to produce a heady mystery, a pointillist scattering of reflected gilded light and depth that verges on a spiritual unworldliness. But it is with relief that you concentrate on the layer of white script interwoven with black flowers, the lower area of zellig mosaic and the clean sober tombs at ground level. The central tomb is of course that of Ahmed el Mansour, who died in 1603. To his right is his son and successor Zaidan, who died in 1628 and to his left that of his grandson Mohammed ech Cheikh II who died in 1655. There are 33 other tombs of Saadian princelings although only 15 are identifiable by their inscriptions. Immediately behind the tomb of Ahmed el Mansour is an inscription commemorating his father.

The Hall of Three Niches
Through this magnificence a small darkened room can be glimpsed to the right, known as the Hall of Three Niches. An inscription in the middle niche commemorates Ahmed el Mansour's elder half-brother, the great building Sultan of Marrakesh, Abdullah al Ghalib. The large tomb at the back is the aforementioned alternative tomb of the Black Sultan, Abou Hassan who died an exile in the High Atlas in 1351.

Crossing over unidentified Shorfa tombs, the passage that leads into the Kasbah Mosque is on the left. This used to be covered by another dome but now the three sheikhs' tombs are left open to the elements.

Second Koubba
Ahmed el Mansour enclosed an original koubba with an outer decorative shell and in the process created an extra hall which is overlooked by two ornate loggias. The loggias' slim white marble pillars bear a lintel of carved cedar that supports the green tiled roof. The inner koubba is decorated with stalactites and contains four tombs. Ahmed el Mansour's mother, Lalla Messaouda, is buried in a niche next to the wall on the right, beneath a commemorative inscription. The tomb to her left is that of the Sultan Abdallah el Ghalib, to his left that of Sultan Mohammed ech Cheikh, who died in 1577. The final tomb is that of the mad Alouite Sultan Moulay Yazid, who reigned for three years before he died in 1792. The main hall, where a number of Saadian and a few 18th-century Alouite princes are buried, is refreshingly clear of decoration other than the tranquil patterns of zellig mosaic.

To find the El Badi Palace, return to Bab Aguenaou, turn right, walk for 150 m and turn right again on to Av. Houmman el Ftouaki. After about 600 m you will arrive in the dusty place known as the **Souk du Mellah**, where oranges, fruits and olives are often sold. From the Souk du Mellah pass through one of two gates to the right into the Place des Ferblantiers, a large rectangular fondouq where metal workers can be seen at work. Amongst other unusual processes strips of unused Safi canning metal are cut to make intricate brass lanterns. Passing through the southern gate, the Bab Berrima, you enter into a double walled space familiar to anyone that has tramped the Imperial city of Meknes. The outer wall delineates the Imperial Kasbah quarter from the civil Medina, the massive wall further south, decorated by stork nests, encloses the El Badi Palace.

El Badi, 'The Incomparable'

A right turn at the Bab Berrima takes you to the palace entrance, open every day from 8.30–18.00, admission 3dh. Throughout June a magnificent **national folklore festival** is held in the palace, a fascinating opportunity to hear the distinctive varieties of Berber tribal music and the chants and dances of the Sufi fraternities. Every evening from 21.00–24.00 sound and light shows are staged, admission to which costs 40dh. Also in June the small pavilions to the north and southwest of the palace are opened, and you can see a collection of excavated ceramics and an old minbar from the Koutoubia.

The El Badi Palace was started in 1578, five months after the Battle of the Three Kings put enormous wealth from Portuguese ransoms and captured booty into the hands of Ahmed el Mansour, the 'victorious'. The efficient management of the Souss sugar trade and the capture of Timbuctoo, in 1598, added to this wealth, and el Mansour also became known by the honorific el Dehbi 'the golden'. The Sultan employed the finest craftsmen in the world, and Montaigne, on his travels through Italy, noticed sculptors carving marble pillars of extreme height and delicacy for the palace.

Entering the palace, now in ruins, through a series of crumbling walls, you find yourself in a massive empty rectangular courtyard. It is crossed by a rigid grid of paths which lead to a central pool 90 m long with an island, and which flank four sunken gardens. The paths were in fact raised to allow room for a great vaulted underground water system. The four sunken gardens would have been planted with sweet-smelling flowers: roses, violets, jasmin, acacia farnesiana, hollyhocks and orange with high cypress, palm and olive for shade. A Moorish garden drew its chief glory from arrangements of trees and running water, and flowers were almost entirely prized for their scent.

In the centre of each of the four massive walls, pavilions were built, flanked by smaller pools and fountains. The largest of these was known as **Koubba el Hamsiniya**, the pavilion of fifty pillars. Opposite it stood the crystal pavilion, to the north was the green hall and to the south 'the Hayzouran' named after the Sultan's favourite negro wife.

On the southeastern corner of the courtyard, a gate now gives entrance to a smaller series of yards and cellars. In the shadow of the present royal palace, it is an intriguing area where you can see the slave pens, old potteries and baking ovens.

These ruins only constitute the ceremonial court of the palace however; el Mansour's private apartments for himself, four wives, dozens of concubines, children and ministers extended to the south and west. In his book *Black Sultan*, Wilfrid Blunt describes 'walls and ceilings incrusted with gold from Timbuctoo . . . gaily decorated boats to entertain the King and his guests in the cooler hours of the evening . . . . Its vast halls were filled with fountains, and in looking glass ceilings far overhead the fish appeared to swim, reflected from the cool waters of marble basins. There was a domed hall where golden stars set on a blue ground gave the appearance of the heavens themselves. Long fish ponds between the alleys ended in grottoes and arbours.'

El Badi, an almost impious borrowing of one of the 99 names of God, was finished in 1603 only a few months before the death of its creator. Descriptions of the celebratory feasts and inaugural gifts are of almost unsurpassable splendour. During a lull in one of the festivals, the aging Sultan asked his fool for a compliment on the palace, to which was returned the famous reply 'that it would make a fine ruin'. Before the century was out, in 1696, Moulay Ishmael fulfilled this prophecy by stripping the palace bare in order to embellish Meknes, a process that took twelve years.

The Mellah

From the Bab Berrima, Rue Berrima runs east of the El Badi outer walls down through the Mellah and Berrima quarters past intriguing dark entrances into the heart of the

Mellah. You eventually emerge, after 600 m, in a Mechouar outside the present royal palace, whose walls and guards are distinctly off-putting.

Some hundred years after it occurred in most of the other cities of Morocco, the Jews of Marrakesh were moved into the Mellah and Berrima quarter in 1558 on the orders of the Saadian Abdullah el Ghalib. Here, the Sultan created a secure quarter for them beside the royal palace, protected by walls and entered through only two gates. They were a talented community of traders, metalsmiths, bankers and linguists, a useful and valuable asset for Sultans who have seldom shared the anti-Semitism of their populace. The community was governed by an 'ulemaa', a council of rabbis, ruled by a separate caid, and maintained its own cemetery, gardens, souks and fountains.

For some time the Jews had prospered as middlemen between Moroccan Muslims and Christian merchants but were recurrently accused by the populace of spying on the outbreak of war. This anti-Semitism grew with the strength of Portugal in the 15th and 16th centuries. Where learned rabbis had once been invited to lecture in mosques, it became accepted practice that if a Jew strayed into a mosque he was given the choice of immediate conversion or being burnt alive. They had to remove their hats and shoes when walking past a mosque and in a royal city were forbidden to wear any shoes at all outside their own quarter.

But within the Mellah walls the community grew into one of the most populous and overcrowded in Morocco. Before 1936 there were 16,000 Jews living here, but with the foundation of Israel in 1948 and the Suez crisis in 1956 the community disintegrated, moving either to more tolerant Casablanca or emigrating.

Only a handful of Jews are left but the distinctive tall, cramped houses cut by low but regular narrow streets remain. Within the quarter, mostly to the north, the traditional Jewish specialist trades of jewelry, textiles and tailoring remain. At the centre of the quarter is the small **Souweka Square**, with its fountain. If you are interested in visiting the **old synagogues** which have now been converted into houses and shops, you should find a young guide here or ask advice from the Jewish-American hostel in the Mellah. On the eastern edge of the Mellah is an extensive Jewish cemetery separated from the Muslim cemetery by the city's outer wall. Until recently it was a wilderness of shrubs and mating dogs, but now it is kept secure and the tombs frequently whitewashed.

The Bahia Palace

To find the Bahia Palace, return to the Place des Ferblantiers near the El Badi Palace, and follow Rue Zitoun el Said opposite the Bab Berrima. After the road bends round to the right, you will see the long garden entrance to the palace ahead. It is officially open from 8.30–12.00, 14.30–18.00, but in practice the guardians who show visitors round are often at prayers or otherwise detained, and the door locked.

If you do manage to gain access, you will find a perfect contrast to the vast sunbaked simplicity of El Badi. The Bahia, 'the brilliant', contains a series of paved courtyards, dark interior reception halls and Andalucian gardens, built by two generations of 19th-century grand viziers.

Si Mousa was vizier to Sultan Sidi Mohammed ben Abder Rahman, and his son, Ba Ahmed, served Sultan Moulay Hassan and became the powerful regent of the child Sultan Abdul Aziz. Their choice of architecture was highly traditional, and as father and son gradually amassed over 8 hectares of the city they created a maze of passages, connecting doors, courtyards, gardens and pavilions. However, fortunes created by the Sultan's officials always return to their master eventually. Ba Ahmed was exceptional in having been able to enjoy his father's inheritance and his own wealth until the hour of his death. A provincial caid or pasha in Morocco could expect to be squeezed of his ill-gotten gains any time after only a decade in office. Not until Ba Ahmed lay dying did the Sultan's guards quietly replace the viziers at the doors of the Bahia palace. Before the corpse had grown cold, they stripped it of all portable possessions, and a few days later nothing remained but the great empty building—as it is seen today.

The great marble-paved courtyard is surrounded by a gallery of living rooms, and the cool green and white paved Andalucian gardens are seductively attractive. But the interior reception halls, with their formless and technically debased plaster work and decoration painted on boards are uninspiring. However, the gothic complexity of plan and the ghosts of French and Moroccan courtiers (it was lived in by the Resident-Generals after 1912) give it an undeniable charm. The guided tour shows you a mere third of the palace whose garden, the arset Ba Ahmed, used to stretch 600 m east to Bab Rhemat.

Dar Si Said—Museum of Moroccan Art
Continue past the gates of the Bahia Palace on Rue Riad ez Zitoun el Jedid and turn right past the mosque to find this reclusive Museum. It is open from 9.00–11.45, 14.30–17.45, but closed on Tuesdays.

Si Said was the idiot brother of Ba Ahmed, though they shared the same slave mother and powerful vizier father. He held a number of court posts as extra sinecures for his brother whose palace communicated with Dar Si Said by an underground tunnel. Dar Si Said is more modest and attractive in plan than the Bahia Palace, and greater attention has been paid to the detailed decorative work.

The Museum is the usual extraordinary Moroccan mixture of unlabelled, common-place items from the souk and one or two exceptional pieces. The **collection of carpets** by the Arab tribes from the plain, the Rehamna and the Oulad Bou Sbaa, and those from the Berber tribes in the High Atlas, Glaoua and Ait Ouaouzighte, are worth attention. Harmonious red and orange shades and crudely wrought geometrical shapes indicate the oldest. Even here, figurative shapes betray the influence of pattern books, and preface the often hideous picture rugs found in the souk.

The **Berber jewelry** display is not exceptional, but has some interesting, character-istic heavy brooches, decorated with enamel, crudely shaped stones and filigree work. The emblems and symbols which recur, such as the Hand of Fatima, are familiar throughout the Islamic world.

Also of interest are the ornate and sometimes beautiful pieces of **carved cedar**—heavy dark doors, frames, screens and jambs, which includes work recovered from El Badi Palace. Swords, muskets, pouches, decorated powder horns, embroidery and domestic metal work can also be seen.

The Ramparts

A 16 km walk around the city walls of Marrakesh would be arduous at any time of the year. Travelling in the morning by horse-drawn cab, bicycle or taxi is a much more pleasurable alternative. The trip can be broken at Bab Khemis for the souk, and Bab ed Debbagh, for a look at the tanneries, but the rest of the gates are likely to be only of passing interest. A circuit of the walls would ideally end with a leisurely afternoon picnic in the Menara or Aguedal garden.

The Walls
Alarmed by the growing Almohad threat from Tinmal, the Almoravide Sultan Ali ben Youssef decided to protect Marrakesh with walls in 1126. He asked his generals for tactical advice and consulted his astrologers for an auspicious date to start work on them. Within a year a 10 km circuit of 9 m high walls, defended by 200 towers and pierced by twenty gates had been built. This has been constantly repaired and occasionally expanded but still substantially follows the 12th-century plan.

The pise walls respond with a dazzling range of colours to different degrees of light. They glow with a changing hue of pink, ochre, gold and brown against the startling backdrop of the High Atlas peaks and clear blue sky. The walls wind through places defined by a wilderness of dusty graves, elsewhere they are overhung by rustling palms or interrupted by frantic streams of traffic. Elsewhere they are found decorated with drying skins, sheltering a souk, a passing flock or enclosing the processional court of the palace of a king. The walls are a shifting pattern of colour and life, at once both monotonously extensive and the city's richest aesthetic treat.

A Rampart Tour
Leave from the Jemaa el Fna, where horse cabs, taxis and bicycles are easy to find, and move along the Av. Mohammed V passing the town hall on your right and the orange-tree shaded park of Moulay Hassan opposite. Crossing through the line of the city walls at the Bab Nkob breach follow the walls to the right, passing the double crenellated towers of Bab er Raha in the corner to approach Bab Doukkala.

Bab Doukkala
The massive but unequal towers of this Almoravide gate are now isolated to the left of the modern entrance to the Medina. If the doors are open go in to examine its dark, twisting defensive passage. The gates guarded the road to Doukkala, the fertile coastal region between El Jadida and Safi which is occupied by Arabic-speaking Berber tribes who were considered to be among the more loyal and dependable subjects of the Sultan. Just within the gate, to the right, is the impressive extent of the modern, green tiled law courts.

The area outside the gates, despite being used by a busy and modern bus station and passing fairs, retains a melancholy air. To the south of the bus station is the cemetery and **koubba of Sidi Bennour**, which belonged to the El Hara, the old leper colony.

Pass two small gates, Bab Boutouil and Bab Moussoufa, to reach the **palmery of Sidi bel Abbes**. Behind the walls is the zaouia of Sidi bel Abbes, a complex of schools, charitable hostels and shrines. Though he was the patron saint of Marrakesh, the zaouia was a suburb outside the city until the walls were extended in the 18th century.

Souk and Bab el Khemis
The northern end of the Medina has spilled beyond the walls around the Souk el

Khemis, the 'Thursday market'. Fruit and vegetables are sold throughout the week here, though livestock trading is still concentrated on Thursdays.

From the souk enclosure a road passes between the cemetery of Sidi Ahmed Ez Zaouia and a lunar landscape of baked mud and refuse to approach the old Almoravide Fez gate which when rebuilt became known as Bab El Khemis. Just before the gate, on the left, is the **Koubba of Sidi el Barbouchi**, the saint of the slippers, and straight through the gate is the **zaouia of the Sufi Derkawa brotherhood**. The road to the left leads to a series of yards where scrap, broken machinery and bruised food are traded by the most impoverished on the ground of the old Christian cemetery. It is a powerful, disturbing place, threatening only through its misery. It was at the centre of the insurrection of January 1904. A revolutionary mob led by the cobblers' guild marched under black flags to the cemetery and there exhumed the graves of Christian missionaries. The skulls were impaled to serve as standards that led the mob in its assault on the money lenders in the Mellah, the merchants in the souk and the kasbah of the Pasha.

Returning outside the city follow the road south, beside a magnificent stretch of wall and an extensive cemetery through which snakes the dry bank of the Oued Issil. The cemetery is often flecked with the bright colours of drying skins as you approach Bab Ed Debbagh, the tanners' gate.

Bab Ed Debbagh

The entrance to the tanners' quarter is beneath the ancient Almoravide towers of Bab Ed Debbagh and through a twisting three chambered entrance passage. By one of the gate towers there is a door to the precarious roof which, if open, provides the best view over the courtyards of the tanners.

If the gate is closed there will be no difficulty in finding a young guide to take you on a quick tour of the tannery vats. They are at their busiest and least pungent in the morning.

Move south, past Bab Er-Rachidia, to reach **Bab Ailen**, a strong portal named after a Berber tribe that inhabited land to the east. In 1130 an Almohad army descended from the High Atlas to besiege the city. They concentrated their assault on this gate but were driven off by Almoravide cavalry who sallied out from the neighbouring gates. Just within the gate is the minaret and shrine of the **Cadi Ayad Mosque**. This was built by Sultan Moulay Rachid to hold the tomb of Moulay Ali ech Cherif, the holy ancestor of the Alouite dynasty. Two later Sultans, Moulay Sliman (1792–1822) and Sidi Mohammed ben Abder Rahman (1859–1873), chose to be buried here beside him.

The angle in the southeast corner of the walls is filled by the enormous **cemetery of Bab Rhemat**. To the east stretches a modern suburb and a green tiled koubba peaks over the houses to your right. This shrine covers the grave of a 12th-century saint, Sidi Youssef ben Ali who is remembered for his great piety—he continued to praise and thank God even for the gift of leprosy that killed him. The twin towers of the **Bab Aghmat/Rhemat** were betrayed by a Christian regiment in the service of the Almoravide Sultans, who opened the gate and the city to the Almohads in 1147. You could pass under the gate and continue for a kilometre, along Rue Ba Ahmed, to see the exterior of the **zaouia of Sidi ben Salih**, its carved minaret inset with green tiles rising above a jumble of roofs, arches, passages and gates. This complex was built in the 14th century by the Merenid Sultan Abou Said Uthman.

Continuing outside the city walls pass beside the cemetery wall to reach **Bab Ahmar** which was rebuilt by Sultan Sidi Mohammed in the 18th century. The gate was reserved for the use of the Sultan on the feast of Mouloud. The quarter within the gates used to house the barracks of the negro Bouakher regiment who had a religious cult based around a jujube tree that grew from the gate. To the south stretches 3 km of walls that enclose the Aguedal, the private gardens of the Sultan.

Pass through Bab Ahmar to enter a number of processional squares or **mechouars**, arranged to the south of the Dar el Makhzen, the royal palace. From Mechouar Barastani pass through the gate of wind, the Bab er Rih, to enter the smaller Mechouar El Ouastani. In the southwest corner a double wall allows private communication between the palace and the Aguedal and just before this a left turn through Bab El Arhdar may be left open for the use of the public. Beyond is the great Mechouar of the Alouites. The **pavilion of Essaouira** in the middle of the southern wall and an artillery magazine in the corner were both built by Sidi Mohammed in the 18th century. The pavilion was used for diplomatic receptions, parades and for reviewing Fantasia displays. Pass out through the city walls at Bab Ighli.

Travelling south from Bab Ighli you would pass the **Koubba of Sidi Amara** on the right before reaching the **Sqallet el Mrabit** in 800 m. This elegant ramped fortress was built by Sidi Mohammed to house a mobile squadron from the 600 cavalry he kept permanently posted against the Rehamna tribe. Beyond it you can see the white Mihrab of the **Msalla**, an open air mosque used during religious festivals.

Just north of Bab Ighli pass **Bab Ksiba**, the entrance to the Derb Chtouka quarter, once the site of an Almohad fortress. In the 19th century this was still a government kasbah, occupied by the Mokhazines who guarded the Sultan's prison.

Bab er Rob and Bab Aguenaou

After extending the city to the south in the 12th century the Almohads were left with a

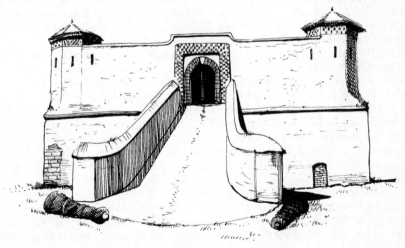

Eighteenth-century fort of Squallet el Mrabit

potentially vulnerable angle in the southwestern wall which they protected by building the Bab er Rob. Grands taxis and local buses stop here, and a **souk** of cheap pottery and fruit extends around the gate which is named after raisin juice, perhaps a memory of an old souk of dried fruits or a morbid reference to the executed heads that were displayed from the battlements. Just through Bab er Rob is the most elegant gate in Marrakesh, the Bab Aguenaou. This carved stone arch gave entrance from the city to the Imperial City.

To the west of the Bab er Rob the walls are hidden by the **cemetery of Sidi es Soheili**, another of the seven saints of Marrakesh whose koubba is beside the Medina cemetery gate, Bab ech Charia. Swinging outside the cemetery you reach the long wall that contains the garden of the Mamounia Hotel, whose entrance is just through the Bab Jdid. North of Bab Jdid is the **Bab Makhzen** which used to directly enter the Almoravide Kasbah and is still reserved for the use of the king. This is no inconvenience as **Bab Sidi Rharib**, just 200 m north, leads directly back on to Av. Mohammed V and the Jemaa el Fna.

Gardens

There is no better way of sheltering from the afternoon heat and hassle of Marrakesh than by picnicking in the Aguedal or Menara garden. The market in the New Town on Av. Mohammed V sells everything you need: wicker baskets, wine, cheese, fresh bread, pâté and a bewildering selection of olives, nuts and fresh fruit.

The Aguedal

These gardens were established in the 12th century by the Almohad Sultan Abdel Moumen. Two enormous tanks were built and filled by khettaras that tapped the Ourika stream, but by the 18th century the walls had decayed, the water had been diverted and tribesmen grazed the orchards. The present garden is the creation of Sultan Abder Rahman (1822–1859) who reclaimed the water rights and rebuilt the walls, but his successors had to keep a constant guard against tribesmen, especially the nomadic Rehamna who enjoyed nothing more than raiding the Sultan's garden.

In the 19th century a succession of pavilions were built in the gardens, most notably the **Dar el Beida** for the harem of Moulay Hassan. However its primary purpose was always to be an efficient and very profitable private agricultural estate. Two visitors from Kew who saw it in 1840 estimated that its 40 acres produced at least £20,000 a year.

When the Royal family is not resident in Marrakesh visitors are allowed to go down through the orchards to the 200 m square main tank, the 'Sahraj el Hana', the pool of health. The pavilion of **Dar el Hana** was raised beside the tank. You can still enjoy its tranquil rooftop view south to the Atlas peaks and then join the knots of Moroccan families by picnicking under the shade of the surrounding trees. On the far side are the ruins of a gunpowder factory.

From the roof of the Dar el Hana you might in 1873 have witnessed the death of the Sultan Sidi Mohammed ben Abder Rahman who drowned whilst boating with his son in the tank. The forlorn almost wistful acceptance of fate is beautifully expressed in the official epitaph: 'he departed this life, in a water tank, in the expectation of something better to come.'

He was not the only sultan to die in the Aguedal gardens. On 9 April 1672 Sultan

Moulay Rachid, after the feast of Aid el Kebir, took a spirited horse to gallop away his ennui through the orange groves of the Aguedal. In the morning the court poets sang, 'the tree's branch did not break the skull of our Imam out of cruelty; nor from ingratitude, unmindful of the duties of friendship. It was out of jealousy of his slender figure, for envy is to be found even among trees.'

Menara Garden
The Menara is 2 km due west of Bab Jdid. If you are in no hurry, leave from Bab es Sidi Rharib and wind your way through the **Hivernage**, a tranquil garden suburb of villas and hotels with the casino at its centre. Some recent buildings that toy with a new North African style display an extravagant fusion of Egyptian and Moorish architecture which may be of interest.

The Menara is an agricultural estate of irrigated olive orchards and gardens that have been planted around a massive water tank. Like the Aguedal, the tank was built by the Almohads in the 12th century, but what you now see was established in the 19th century by the Alouites. Sidi Mohammed ben Abder Rahman replaced the outer walls, refurbished the tank and built the green tiled pavilion in 1869 to replace a ruined Saadian minzah. It has a tranquil view over the great expanse of water from its open balconied first floor, if you can arrive independently of the constant stream of coaches. Away from the pavilion and the click of cameras you can enjoy a quiet picnic by the basin or in the orchard.

Majorelle Garden
The Majorelle is a small privately-owned botanical garden. It is open from 8.00–12.00, admission 5dh, and found in the New Town just north of Av. Yaacoub el Mansour between the Blvd de Safi and the Av. El Jadida. It was created by a French artist Louis Majorelle (1859–1926), and is now owned by the French couturier, Yves Saint Laurent. It is an immaculately manicured walled garden full of pavilions and paths that snake through an admirably lush botanical collection, especially strong in cacti.

Mamounia Garden
This mature, formal garden was established in the 18th century by an Alouite prince who was also responsible for building the garden's central pavilion. It was lent to visiting diplomats before French rule when it was turned into a luxury hotel. The 300 m long sweeping wall of bougainvillea, the quiet undisturbed half-dozen regular plots of olive and palm trees is supposedly reserved for residents. Ignore this restriction or if need be, buy a cup of coffee on the terrace.

The Palmery
Follow the Fez road for a kilometre past the Souk el Khemis then take a signposted left turn for an 8 km drive through the palmery to the north of the city. The Almoravides are credited with planting the palmery but palms in Marrakesh are useful only for wood, shade and desert imagery, for they are too far north ever to bear fruit. Olives or oranges would be a more useful crop and the palmery has a deserved aura of neglect. The pise walls, fragments of irrigation systems and barren palms might be entertaining if you are not travelling further south, but it has increasingly become colonized by villas and time-share holiday homes.

FESTIVALS

The annual national folklore festival is held from the end of May to early June in the El Badi palace, see for details. The fantasia festival is held outside the city walls at the end of July, the Moussem of Sidi Abdel Kader ben Yassin is in September and the fair of contemporary arts is held in November. South from Marrakesh the Moussem of Setti Fatma at the head of the Ourika valley is held in August, the Moussem of Sidi Boutamane in September and the zaouia of Moulay Brahim holds its Moussem after Mouloud.

FANTASIAS

Fantasia evenings are staged several times a week and are bookable through the larger hotels for around 240dh a head, directly from Chaouia, opposite the airport, tel 23653 or El Bordj on the road to Casablanca. Though arranged for the benefit of tourists they are undeniably well managed and are impressive stage events seen at their best in the added romance of the night. Torch-lit entrances lead to caidal tents where traditional food is cooked before your eyes whilst skilled musicians and dancers entertain, leading to the finale of a spectacular fantasia charge of Arab cavaliers.

SHOPPING

Before going into the souk, check out the prices and quality from the **Artisanal Centre**, which is along Av. Mohammed V within the Medina walls. There are two moderately interesting art galleries, the Lamp of Aladin at 99 and 70 Rue Semmarine and Al Yed at 66, Rue El Mouassine.

The best range of **books, guides and newspapers** is from the elaborate but not overpriced kiosk in front of the Mamounia Hotel.

HAMMAM

There are hammams throughout the Medina. There are a couple on the Rue Zitoun el Kedim that are used to accepting Europeans but the most magnificent interior is undoubtedly at Hammam Dar el Bacha on Rue Fatime Zohra, with both male and female sections.

SPORTS

There is an 18-hole **golf course** 4 km out of town on the road to Ouazazarte. There is a **tennis** club off Rue Ouaddi el Makhazine and courts and intructors at most four star hotels. The popular municipal **pool** is in the Moulay Abdessalam garden, entered from Rue Abou El Abbes Sebti, opposite the artisanal ensemble on Av. Mohammed V, entrance 3dh. **Skiing** at Oukaimeden is possible from November to March. **Hill walking and climbing** in the Toubkal National Park throughout the year. For skiing and climbing details, see the Djebel Toubkal and Oukaimeden sections in the High Atlas, below.

WHERE TO STAY

The attraction of Marrakesh is centred firmly around the Jemaa el Fna, and cheap hotels like the **CTM** that overlook this central square of the Medina are booked up early in the day. In the summer you may find that a hotel with a pool is more important than a view of the Jemaa el Fna. In that case there are three hotels, the **Imilchil, Koutoubia** and **Yasmine** just beyond the ramparts which are small enough to have some character, have a pool and are not dominated by tour groups. Going further up-market the **Chems** has got the best position of a four-star hotel, and the **Es Saadi** is the least pretentious luxury hotel.

The ***** **Es Saadi Hôtel** on Av. El Qadissa, tel 48811, is beside the casino at the heart of the Hivernage quarter of the new town. It also has a splendid garden, and delicious food with attentive but unpretentious service. A double room cost 590dh, and dinner 200dh.

It is impossible to talk about Marrakesh hotels without mentioning Winston Churchill's favourite haunt, the **Mamounia**. It has however recently undergone redecoration which has introduced a tacky casino, conference centre and banqueting hall. The porters wear more gold braid than an admiral but the garden, view and cooking remain superb. It has 179 rooms, 49 suites, 3 villas, 6 bars, 6 restaurants, 8 boutiques, etc., and is found on Av. Bab Djedid, tel 48981. The international set that used to go to the Mamounia are increasingly using the new ***** **Tichka Hôtel**, whose interior designed by the American Marrakesh socialite Bill Willis has already given it a certain cachet. It is however surrounded by other hotels and is situated in the uninteresting far northern edge of the New Town off the road to Casablanca. A single costs 280dh and a double 380dh, tel 48710.

Just west of the Koutoubia off Av. Hoummane el Fetouaki and almost opposite the Mamounia Hôtel is the well positioned but inconspicuous **** **Chems Hôtel**, tel 44813. It is a functional motel-like place with its own car park, pool, bar and small garden. A single costs 190dh, a double 240dh.

In the New Town just west of the ramparts and south of Av. Mohammed V are a couple of three-star hotels with small swimming pools and tranquil gardens. The **Imilchil**, Av. Echouhada, tel 31453, charges 159dh for a single room, 193dh for a double; breakfast costs 21dh and dinner 86dh. The **Koutoubia** is at 51, Av. El Mansour Eddahabi, tel 30921, and has 60 rooms; a single for 110dh, a double with bath 140dh. The **Yasmine**, on the confluence of Rue Boualaka and Av. des Remparts, tel 46142, is a quiet place with a pleasant worn interior. It has no bar or restaurant but a downstairs café.

Classified one- and two-star hotels in the Medina

The * **CTM** is the first place to head for. It has a balconied roof terrace which overlooks the Jemaa el Fna and a cool courtyard around which large comfortable bedrooms are arranged. It is worth trying to book a room in advance, tel 42325. Singles without a bath cost 45dh, a double with a bath 81dh. Breakfast is now served on the terrace and the maids Brika or Fatima take in washing.

The ** **Foucauld Hôtel** with its Moorish interior, hip baths and licensed restaurant is found below the wooded park to the south of the Jemaa el Fna on Av. El Mouahadine, tel 25499. It has a pleasant warm character like its manageress, the English-speaking Maria, who charges 100dh for a double room with bath, 70dh for dinner, 6dh a beer and rents bicycles.

The ** **Grand Hôtel Tazi**, on the corner of Rue Bab Aguenaou and Av. Hoummam el Ftouki has 60 comfortable and well decorated rooms, a restaurant and roof terrace bar, tel 42155. A single costs 90dh, a double with bath 110dh. If full try the clean but less characterful **Hôtel Minaret** which has just opened behind the Tazi at 10, Rue Dispensaire.

The ***Hôtel Ali**, Rue Moulay Ismail, tel 44979, has a central courtyard café-restaurant on the ground floor of the hotel. It is not a first choice but it is central and rooms are scrupulously clean, at 80dh for a single.

The ***Hôtel Gallia** is on Rue de la Recette, second left off Rue Bab Aguenaou. A discreet small hotel with 20 rooms, tel 45913/25913; it costs 80dh a single, or a double with bath at 101dh.

Unclassified Medina hotels

The unclassified hotels should charge between 20–25dh for a single and 30–45dh for a double room. They are small and can fill up quickly though you should find a room within a minute's walk of the Jemaa el Fna by working your way through this list. Do not get angry if the prices rise in periods of peak demand, for unlike the classified hotels they are bound by no legal requirements.

The **Hôtel du Café de France** and **Oukmaiden** overlook the Jemaa el Fna and are the first to be filled.

Off the Rue Zitoun el Jedid signs indicate the **Hôtel Essouria** and **Smara**, which have pleasant internal courtyards, and the **France** and **Sahara** hotels.

Off the Rue Zitoun el Kedim (facing the CTM Hotel this narrow arched alley is to your left) are found the **Amis**, tel 42515, and at no 197 the popular and friendly **Hôtel de France**, tel 43076. Beyond that is the **Chellah**, tel 41977, which has a cool central court.

Off the Rue Bab Aguenaou there is a good selection to check out. Along Rue Sidi Boulakate, the first left turn, is **La Jeunesse**, tel 43631, the **Afrique**, **Nouzah** and **Eddakla** and along the second left turn the **El Allal, Hillal, El Farah** and the deservedly popular **Hôtel Souria**.

Youth Hostel and Camping

The new Youth Hostel, tel 32831, is on Rue el Jahid in the Quartier Industriel, a five-minute walk from the train station. It costs 15dh a night and is open to cardholders only.

Camping Municipal is on Av. de France. It is an unappealing site partly shaded by eucalyptus but patrolled by all the more desperate hustlers.

EATING OUT

Marrakesh has a large number and range of restaurants to choose from, and though its culinary reputation doesn't match that of Taroudant, you will eat well here.

The top five restaurants

La Maison Arabe, opposite the Bab Doukalla mosque at 5, Derb Ferrane, tel 22604, is the oldest and most celebrated restaurant in the city, but has a variable attitude to guests, who must book in advance. **Le Restaurant Marrakechi** at 52, Rue Banques, tel 43377, is the busiest of this group, and has a roof terrace which overlooks the northern end of the Jemaa el Fna. **Restaurant Relais Al Baraka**, tel 42341, is at the opposite end of the Jemaa el Fna in the far lefthand corner beside the Commisariat de Police. Here you can eat in the tranquil fountain court or in two flanking dining rooms. **Le Restaurant**

Marocain and the **Marrakesh L'Imperiale**, under the direction of Alain Senderens, are at the **Mamounia Hôtel** and stand comparison with the leading kitchens of the world. Allow £50 a head for dinner with good wine in the Mamounia. For the other three, prices start at around 250dh and it is advisable to book and consult the menu in the morning. Many traditional dishes need longer preparation times.

'Moorish palaces'

Marrakesh contains a number of palatial 19th-century merchants' houses that have been converted into restaurants. The interiors are rich with mosaic tile work, fine brass, carpets and successions of courtyards, but they tend to specialize in over-jovial block-booked tours and belly-dancing spectacles. The interiors are well worth looking over for the price of a cup of coffee or tea, and menus are around 90dh a head without drink.

The **Dar es Salam** and **Riad el Bahia** are on Riad Zitoun el Kedim. The **Bahia**, tel 41350, and the **El Gharnata** are off Rue Zitoun el Jedid near the Bahia Palace. The **Ksar el Hamra** is at 28, Rue Goundaffi and the **Riad** on Av. Hoummane el Fetouaki, tel 25430. **Dar el Baroud** is easily found at 275, Av. Mohammed V, opposite the **Koutoubia**, tel 45077, where lunch costs 140dh, and dinner 250dh or 220dh.

New Town/Gueliz

For a quiet lunch or dinner, prolonged over a bottle of wine, there are a number of restaurants on or just off the Av. Mohammed V. Four of these serve Italian menus. **Villa Rossa**, Av. Hassan II, tel 30832, specializes in fish and there is **La Trattoria** on 179, Rue Mohammed Beqal, tel 32641, **Catanzaro**—a pizza house on Rue Tariq-in-Zyad and **Restaurant Jackline** on Mohammed V, tel 47547. Of the licensed restaurants with French and Moroccan cooking, **La Taverne** at 23, Blvd Zerktouni (opposite Hôtel Tachfine) has a separate bar and fountain courtyard and serves a four-course menu for 50dh. The following are all pleasant, relaxing places as well: **Le Regent**, Av. Mohammed V, tel 30657; **Le Petit Poucet**, Av. Mohammed V, tel 31188; **Jacaranda**, 32, Blvd Zerktouni, tel 30069; **Bagatelle**, 107, Rue de Yugoslavia, tel 30274, and **Les Ambassadeurs**, 6, Av. Mohammed V, tel 31451.

In the Medina

You will find that the food tastes much better from the central grill cafés in the Jemaa el Fna than from any of the more restful balcony cafés. An honourable exception can be found in the northeastern corner of the Jemaa el Fna where **Cher Chegrouni** at no 4–6 offers a nourishing meal of soup, salad, brochettes and sweetened yoghurts for 12dh, and remains in the shade during lunch. The service is friendly and honest if a little erratic.

Otherwise try any of the cafés along Rue Bab Aguenaou, particularly the **Café Restaurant Oriental** at no 33 or the **Restaurant Etoile de Marrakesh** which serves dinner for 25dh up to midnight. The licensed restaurant at the **Foucauld Hotel** has a filling five-course 100dh menu, and you eat in a high Moorish dining room with a fan and tranquil service. The **Grand Hôtel Tazi** has not got such good cooking but the bar tends to stay open longer. A salade niçoise costs only 15dh. For a state of the art Moroccan patisserie, the **Café El Badi** on Blvd Fatima Zohra, tel 44369, offers a lift, terrace view and an impressive menu of delicious fattening drinks and cakes.

Bars

Outside of a restaurant the only place to drink in the Medina is in the Tazi or Foucauld

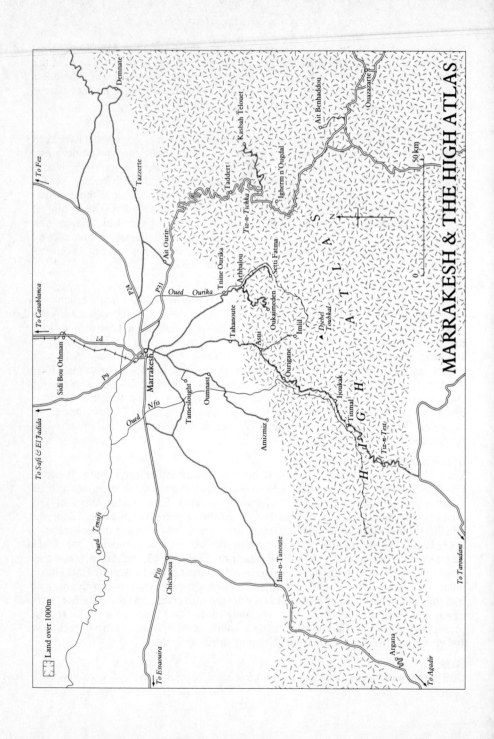

MARRAKESH & THE HIGH ATLAS

Land over 1000m

To Fez
To Casablanca
Sidi Bou Othman
To Safi & El Jadida
To Essaouira
Chichaoua
Imi-n-Tanoute
To Agadir
Argana
To Taroudant
Tiz-n-Test
Tinmal
Ijoukak
Amizmiz
Ouirgane
Oummass
Tameslought
Marrakesh
Oued Nfis
Oued Tensift
Oued Ourika
Tahanoute
Asni
Imlil
Oukaïmeden
Djebel Toubkal
Setti Fatma
Arbhalou
Tnine Ourika
Aït Ourir
Tazzerte
Demnate
Taddert
Kasbah Telouet
Tiz-n-Tichka
Ighcrm n'Ougdal
Aït Benhaddou
Ouarzazate

HIGH ATLAS

50 km
0
N

Demnate

Ld
P9
P24
P31
P10

Hotels, where beers cost 6dh, whisky 20dh. In the New Town there are a large number of bars to visit without having to stray into any of the tourist-dominated hotels. These are a male preserve, and can be unsettling for Western women. They chiefly serve half-litre bottles of beer in quick succession. The prophet Mohammed said that wine is both a great sin and a great advantage to man, but that the sin is greater than the advantage. Hangovers also seem particularly intense in the African sun.

The **Ambassadeurs** is at 6, the **Negociants** at 108 and the **Regent** at 34, Av. Mohammed V. The **Bagatelle** is at 101 and the **Fiaree** at 33, Rue Yugoslavia. The **Haouz** is on Av. Hassan II, the **Iceberg** on Av. el Mouahadine, **L'Escale** on Rue Mauritania, the **Marché** at 44, Rue de la Liberté, the **Poste** on Rue el Imam Malik, the **Renaissance** at Place Abdelmoumen, the **Taverne** on Blvd Zerktouni and **Tony Bar** on Rue Abou Bekr Esseddiq.

Night Clubs

Le Temple de la Musique is the busiest of the big hotel night clubs and is found in the **PLM Hôtel N'Fis** on Av. de France, tel 48772. There is also the **Charleston disco** at Place Abdelmoumen, tel 31136, below the **Grand Café Atlas**, and another in **Le Marrakesh Hôtel** in Place de la Liberté. The **Negociant** at 108, Av. Mohammed V, tel 31094, and the **Sahara Inn**, Av. Abdelkarim El Khattabi, tel 34388, could be looked in on and the **Mamounia Hôtel**, tel 48981, now has a night club and its own casino. The main casino is in La Hivernage quarter, and apart from the tables of roulette, baccarat and pontoon, it also stages concerts and entertainments as well as running a night club, tel 47267.

As an eccentric alternative you could investigate hiring your own folklore troupe from El Haj Allal at 96, Rue Mouassine or from Eddibyn Mohammed at 160, Rue Mouassine or Haj Mohammed Baba at 36, Derb Dabachi.

North, West and East from Marrakesh

There is little entertainment in the arid plains out from Marrakesh. On the route north to Casablanca, the **kasbah of Boulaoune**, which is described on pages 241–2, provides the sole reason to break your journey. If you are travelling east to Beni Mellal, the **Ouzoud gorge** would make a rewarding diversion and the **Cascade d'Ouzoud** in the Central High Atas is well worth an expedition from Marrakesh in its own right, see page 369. Travelling west to the coastal towns of Essaouira, Safi, Oualidia and El Jadida there are only a few cafés and rural souks at which to break the journey. For details look in Part V, The Atlantic Coast from Tangier to Agadir. Though the landscape is unstimulating there is always the poetry of Arab tribal names and a recent vivid history with which to entertain yourself. **Skour des Rehamna**, a dusty roadside hamlet 100 km north of Marrakesh, recalls the dominance of the Rehamna, the greatest and fiercest of the Arab tribes of the Plain.

The Arab Tribes of the Plain

Before the 12th century a tiny minority of Arabs lived amongst the Moroccan Berbers, concentrated in the city of Fez. Large-scale Arab migration into North Africa began in

1050 when two impoverished Bedouin confederacies, the Hillal and Sulaim, entered Egypt from the Arabian desert. They advanced west with their herds and families, destroying the ancient cities and farmland of the North African shore. Ibn Khaldoun was referring to these tribes when he wrote that 'the Arabs are incapable of good government and bring the desert with them'.

Though never a unified force the Arab tribes could field an army of 50,000 warriors and their success drew other impoverished tribes from Arabia to follow in their wake. The Arabs were first defeated by the Almohads at the battle of Sitif in 1152 but instead of pushing the Arabs back east the Sultan began to recruit individual tribes into his service. Unlike his Berber forces, the Arabs had no political ambitions or regional loyalties. As nomads, they could be dispatched with ease to any province. Their ruthlessness and ferocity could be relied upon, and the Sultans would set Arab tribes against a particular dissident Berber region and award them what grazing land or plunder they could seize.

The Merenids employed the Maql Arab confederacy during their border wars but then adroitly directed these alarming and powerful allies south into the desert. In the Sahara the Maql (also known as the 'sons of Hassan'—the Dawi Hassan) separated into their component tribal factions and established a predatory authority over the indigenous Berber tribes of the south. In the lawless desert their ferocious martial spirit was kept intact. It was common for an Arab tribe to refuse to brand their herds as 'all animals are potentially ours.' These Arab tribes remained valuable military allies for any ruler who dared use them.

The Rehamna

In the 16th century the Saadian Sheikhs recruited one of these Maql Arab tribes, the Rehamna, from their grazing grounds in northern Senegal. They placed them on the coastal plains in order to contain squadrons of Portuguese cavalry who had, in 1515, nearly captured Marrakesh. The Rehamna disposed of this threat but increasingly converted the plain between Marrakesh and the coast into their own domain. By the 17th century they had refused any obedience or further service to the Sultan. They were a proud nomadic tribe and scornfully rejected cultivation, for 'with the plough enters dishonour'. They concerned themselves with increasing their herds, escorting or plundering merchant convoys and raiding their neighbours.

On the first sign of government weakness the Rehamna would revolt. In 1859 for instance, the defeat at Tetouan and the accession of a new Sultan led to a Rehamna siege of Marrakesh. All communication was cut, outlying rural souks were raided and the deserted crops efficiently harvested. The new Sultan Abder Rahman was quick to take up the challenge. By 1862 the Rehamna were dispersed and only spared the full extent of the Sultan's revenge by the intercession of a revered holy man. The tribe's best land, along the Rivers Tensift and Nifs, were confiscated and given to a coalition of rival Arab tribes.

The next Sultan, Sidi Mohammed Abder Rahman, had to deal with a resurgence of Rehamna aggression. He established a standing force of 600 cavalry at Marrakesh to police the plains and invited Uld Billah, the caid of the Rehamna, to a magnificent banquet. The caid was detained at the end of the dinner and remained a hostage until the Sultan's death in 1873.

The Rehamna had no loyalty other than that to the tribe and in 1912, Al-Ayyadi, the Caid of the Rehamna, allied himself firmly with France. Rehamna cavalry fought alongside the French against the Blue Sultan, but the Rehamna landholdings were too central, extensive, and rich in phosphates for France to permit Caid Al-Ayyadi the feudal authority they allowed the Berber High Atlas caids. Instead they encouraged a rivalry between Al-Ayyadi and Thami el Glaoui that was fought in the magnificence of their palaces and the prodigality of their entertainments. To fuel this duel of taste Al-Ayyadi recklessly sold tribal lands until his death in 1964. Pride had achieved what no Sultan could—the destruction of the Rehamna.

The Oulad Bou Sbaa

Halfway between Marrakesh and Essaouira you pass the town of **Chichaoua** which was the chief souk of the Oulad Bou Sbaa, 'the sons of he of the lions'. They first established themselves in the Tafilalet and Draa valley in the 13th century. Half of the tribe were recruited by a Merenid prince, Abou el Abbas, in his struggle for the throne and were later posted on land between Marrakesh and Essaouira in order to control the Berber tribes of Haha. Their carpets were much sought after in the 19th century, and in 1936 a cooperative was established at Chichaoua to maintain their quality.

The other half of the tribe stayed in the Draa until the Berber Ait Atta confederacy pushed them further south into the Western Sahara. There the Oulad Bou Sbaa carved out a new territory for themselves, but in 1910 they were destroyed in one of the last great tribal battles when they literally resisted the Reguibat to the last man.

West of Marrakesh there are couple of dusty **souks** off the main road by the bridge over the Oued Nifs and the banks of the Oued Tensift. The names, **Tnine des Oudaia, Sebt des Ait Imour** and **Sidi Chicker** recall the Arab tribes, the Oudaia, the Ait Imour and the Oulad Sidi Chicker who were settled on the Rehamna's best land by Sultan Abder Rahman in 1862. The Oudaia were one of the most loyal components of the Alouite army and were placed in a number of key fortresses like Fez el Jedid, the Oudaia kasbah of Rabat and that of Temara.

The High Atlas

The highest and most dramatic range of mountains in North Africa, the High Atlas, rise immediately south of Marrakesh. This jagged horizon of ethereal blue peaks is a lodestone that draws visitors out from the city of Marrakesh. The High Atlas can be crossed by only three mountain passes of which only one, the Tiz-n-Babaou that links Marrakesh to Agadir, is open all the year. The Tiz-n-Test that connects Marrakesh to Taroudant and the Tiz-n-Tichka to Ouazazarte are cut off by falls of snow and rocks for several weeks every year. As well as these crossings three other tarmac roads intrude into the mountainous region, allowing easy access to the Ourika valley, Djebel Oukaimeden and the village of Amizmiz.

The Berber Tribes of the High Atlas

Long before Marrakesh was founded the Berber tribes of the region practiced a seasonal migration. In the winter they brought their flocks down to the plains, planted crops during the brief spring and then through the summer slowly worked their way back up to the cooler Alpine grazing of the highland peaks. The foundation of a strong central authority at Marrakesh in the 11th century disturbed this pattern. The Almoravides with their desert technology improved the irrigation of the plain and established efficient gardens and a sedentary population on the most fertile tracts. Arab tribes in the service of the sultans were rewarded with tracts of Berber tribal land below the foothills of the Atlas. By the 19th century most of the Berber tribes had been expelled from the plains by the fierce cavalry of these nomadic Arab tribes. The Berbers either stayed to work as sharecroppers on the plain for an alien landlord or moved up into the mountains in order to remain free sedentary farmers.

Souks

There is a string of traditional Berber **souks** where the plain meets the High Atlas foothills. The closest to Marrakesh is **Tnine de Ourika** but this Monday souk has become a favourite destination for coach tours. **Ait Ourir** and **Tazzerte** have much less visited souks the same day, **Tameslought** and **Tahanaout** have a souk on Tuesday, **Amizmiz** on Thursday and **Sidi Rahal** on Friday.

Tiz-n-Babaoun, the road to Agadir

This is the fastest and least dramatic of the crossings of the High Atlas. Agadir, which is 275 km southwest of Marrakesh, can be reached in five hours' driving. Few visitors seem prepared to break their journey and despite the volume of passing traffic this highland region remains surprisingly unspoilt.

A fast busy road, the P10, leads due west of Marrakesh for 74 km across to Chichaoua. There is an older, slower tarmac track (routes 6453 and 6403) that winds across country from Marrakesh to Imi-n-Tatoute, passing close to the Wednesday **souk of Guemassa** and a **kasbah at Had des Mjatt**.

Chichaoua

At the central crossroads traffic stops to take advantage of the half-dozen cafés that serve brochettes and delicious long simmered tagines. A **souk** is held every Sunday and an artisan centre attempts to maintain the high traditions of carpet-making set by the Arab tribes of the plains, see above. To the south of this dusty town there are beautiful calm garden estates ringed by cypress tress which stand tall and elegant, their dark green silhouettes piercing the horizon of low bleak pink hills. 3 km to the east of Chichaoua, by the dry river bed, traces of a Saadian aqueduct and a sugar refinery have been discovered. It is a sobering thought that despite the advances of the last 70 years this region is still far removed from the prosperity it enjoyed in the 16th century.

Imi-n-Tatoute

The village of Imi-n-Tanoute, 47 km south of Chichaoua, is perched at the entrance to the High Atlas pass. It is built on the hard dry land that rises above the cultivated valley and hosts a busy **souk** on Monday. There is a choice of cafés in the central Place where it is possible to rent a a basic room. By the river bed, surrounded in olive groves, is a 19th century **kasbah** which with the **kasbah of Boubaoute**, 34 km to the east, straddled the territory of the M'tougga tribe, who were accustomed to the rule of a dynasty of caids. In the 1850s a M'touggi caid had briefly extended his rule west over the neighbouring coastal province of Haha. His nephew who succeeded him, Abdel Malik M'touggi, maintained a slave guard of 500 men who were all mounted on grey horses and distinguished by a silver ring in their ear. Caid Abdel Malik M'touggi's greatest hour was in 1911 when he was appointed Pasha of Marrakesh by Sultan Moulay Hafid, and his men held all the kasbahs north of the High Atlas. The next year the new Pasha was caught between the French army advancing from the north and the forces of the Blue Sultan from the south. His political manoeuvres were so quick and convoluted that in the words of Gavin Maxwell, 'the M'touggi could scarcely be said even to have kept a foot in both camps.' His footwork was adroit and he survived with his feudal domain intact to become a lesser ally of the French.

The most dramatic M'touggi kasbah on this route is found above the **hamlet of Mintalous**. Perched on a hill of grey, slate-like stone, the ruined kasbah has a fine view over the terraced gardens and almond orchards of the valley below and its deserted interior can be visited in half an hour's walk. It is a small traditional structure built from double layers of the surrounding grey stone, two water tanks still work and the heavy wooden gates remain in place, stamped with characteristic circular designs. The M'touggi, men of the plains, had continuously to master the highland tribes of the Bemsire and Ida ou Ziki in order to maintain their control of the whole of this strategic pass.

30 km south of Imi-n-Tatoute is the roadside **Café Populaire** and just beyond it a seasonal waterfall. Another 20 km and on your right you should see a striking cliff face of dried stalagmites left by a seasonal waterfall beneath which a Berber village squats.

The turning to **Argana** is to the left, about 60 km south of Imi-n-Tatoute. It is a village astride both banks of the Oued Ait Moussa. On the west bank are the ruins of a hill top **agadir**, on the other a neat square little **fort** built by the French below which a **souk** is held on Tuesday—the souk El Jemaa. A dirt track runs from here, along the valley of Ait Mousa, passing an impressive gorge before reaching the secluded villages of **Timesgadioune** and **Aglagal**. From Argana a number of other tracks extend into the mountains. The most attractive of these climbs towards the summit of Djebel Aoulime which at 3555 m is 25 km due east of Argana as the crow flies. The mountain is well in the territory of the Berber Seksawa tribe who had always remained quite independent of the authority of the M'touggi caids.

Returning to the main road pass turnings to the villages of **Bigoudine** and **Tassadent** before reaching the shores of the new dammed **Lake of Tamzaourt** before reaching the cafés of **Ameskroud** which are less than 50 km from Agadir.

Tameslought and Amizmiz

The turning to the peaceful village of Tameslought zaouia, surrounded by miles of olive and orange groves, is 15 km south of Marrakesh along the S507, the tarmac road to Amizmiz.

Turn right by a five towered garden enclosure with its imposing white arch bayonet entrance tower inhabited by a family and their donkey. An olive press has recently been established and the ruins of a pavilion and a koubba are just visible in the olive groves south of the town.

Arriving at crossroads, take a left fork into the central **souk** area. Arcades line the fronts of three great pyramidal roofed shrines that hold the tombs of this saintly dynasty and the **zaouia mosque** can be seen on your left. Beyond is the entrance to the rambling mass of the Tameslought **kasbah** where you be can shown over some of the apartments by their present occupants for a few dirhams.

The Tameslought zaouai was founded in the 16th century by Abdallah bin Hossein el Hassani, a holy man famed for his miraculous powers and so knowledgeable that the superstitious referred to him as the man of 366 sciences. By the 19th century the spiritual reputation of the zaouia had diminished though its wealth remained. The sheikh of the zaouia invested in the first machine-powered olive oil press in Morocco which he established here but it was so efficient that the rival neighbouring mill owners organized a 'Luddite' riot against this foreign machine. The sheikh, increasingly isolated and alarmed for his wealth, soon arranged to be placed under British protection and received the British MP Cunninghame Graham in 1897. He left an account of the kasbah, 'its crenellated walls, flanking towers, and dome shaped roofs. It had innumerable courts, a mosque, a women's wing, a granary, baths . . . a garden where water trickled in a thousand little rills; canes fluttered, rustling like feathers in the air . . . and over all the air of decadence, mixed with content.'

Amizmiz

The village of **Oumnast**, watched over by two kasbahs, is 10 km south of Tameslought and 8 km further is the **Oued Nifs dam** behind which a long lake stretches. This was the first dam built by the French, finished in 1935, and was named after the romantic ruins of the nearby **Kasbah of Lalla Takerkoust**. 20 km past the dam you approach Amizmiz, passing the licensed **Hôtel de France** where you can take a room for 30dh. It has half a dozen ground floor bedrooms that open on to a pretty wall garden partly covered by an extensive vine. Below the garden is the shell of a French settlers chapel.

On the other side of the river, known as the Oued Anougal or Oued Amizmiz, is the bulk of the village beside a ruined **kasbah** of deep red pise. There are some older ruins above the river gorge which have been empty since the the turn of the century. For it is told 'that the caid oppressed the people of the town and district beyond the powers of even Arabs and Berbers to endure; so they rebelled, and to the number of 12,000 besieged the place, took it by storm and tore it all to pieces to search for money in the rose pink walls.'

Amizmiz also holds a **zaouia** founded by Sidi el Hossein ben Messoud and an old **Mellah** quarter. There were Jewish communities in most of the lowland Atlas markets, who spoke ironically of the caids as their dear friends, in that they all owed money. One of the busiest and least tourist visited **souks** is held in Amizmiz every Tuesday where you are certain to find local Berber pottery for sale.

South of the town a dirt track road leads through some attractive rough woodland about 20 km to the hamlet of **Midinet**, where a path approaches the summit of Djebel Erdouz at 3575 m.

The Ourika Valley

The Ourika is a narrow valley that cuts deep into the High Atlas. As you intrude south down the valley, the mountains rise ever more precipitous and the area of cultivation further diminishes. At the head of the valley constricted terraced gardens, their walls constructed from rounded river boulders, their bright crops shaded by the slender trunked almond trees, appear like some vision of the promised land. The gardens are productive throughout most of the year as the Ourika stream which drains the face of Djebel Toubkal seldom runs dry.

In the summer when Marrakesh can feel like a dehabilitating furnace, the Ourika valley has a gentle trickle of cool clear water, a breeze in the trees, trout in the river and the oleanders will have just burst into flower. Small flour mills operate above the river bed, fed by irrigation ditches that double as a source of power. For this constancy of supply the valley pays an occasional but high price in the winter. Sudden fierce rainfall brings a flood from the hills which can rip out the sides of hills, burying houses in mud and boulders or sweep all away in a great torrent of water.

In the past the people of the Ourika valley were in a powerful position since they controlled the water supply to the city and gardens of Marrakesh, for old Moroccan law did not acknowledge the rights of any user down stream. In practice this meant that no ruler of Marrakesh could afford to have a hostile power in control of the valley and it has always been closely associated with the affairs of Marrakesh. This is still true today, and the lower reaches of the valley are lined with the villas of the richer Marrakeshis. It is a traditional place to relax, with a good selection of licensed restaurants and small hotels beside the road. You can camp at the head of the valley or just use it as a midday escape from the city.

From the Bab er Robb, in Marrakesh, a fairly continuous stream of buses and grands taxis ply the road to Ourika. A place in a grand taxi should cost 12dh, though you might have difficulty in finding a taxi to Oukaimeden in the summer months.

South from Marrakesh

28 km from Marrakesh a dirt track to the right leads to the hamlet of **Aghmat**. This was, until the arrival of the Almoravides, the principal town of the region. There is little now to show of a city that until the 14th century boasted medersas and royal tombs. But because of its association with El Mutamid, the poet-prince of Seville who died here, exiled by Youssef ben Tachfine, it might make a romantic picnic spot.

At the entrance to the Ourika valley, 33 km from Marrakesh, you pass through the Monday **souk of Tnine Ourika** which has for that one day become a destination for coach tours, and for that reason alone is usually well worth missing. On the opposite side of the valley, across a bridge, is the settlement of **Dar Caid Ouriki**, the house of the Caid of Ourika. The ruins of the kasbah and its garden are approached through the encroaching hamlet of farms. Dramatically placed below a geological fault, the ruins retain a certain aura. Abdallah, caid of the Ourika in the 19th century, was an early ally of the Glaoui, an alliance confirmed by his marriage to one of Madani's six daughters. This relationship did not however stop Madani's brother Thami el Glaoui from removing Abdallah and appointing his own brother Mohammed El Arbi to the influential caidship.

Oukaimeden

Getting to Oukaimeden, 'the meeting place of the four winds', provides at least half the excitement. 10 km south of Tnine Ourika at the village of Arhbalou, a right turn and a road of 30 km takes you up to the foot of Djebel Oukaimeden. The road mostly climbs within sight of a mountain stream, the Asif Ait Legay, which has cut a series of steep canyons and waterfalls in the side of the mountain. You pass a number of stone and pise built Berber hamlets that perch amongst carefully tended terraced gardens, bramble hedges, orchards and above suicidal cliffs. Climbing to Oukaimeden, at 2600 m a number of altitude belts gradually dispose of olive trees, almond, henna and walnut leaving a barren area of windswept rock. Providing there is no cloud cover there is a continual and magnificent changing view over the valleys of the High Atlas or out north to Marrakesh.

The settlement of **Oukaimeden** is an ugly assortment of skiing chalets and huts sheltered by a rising platform of barren rock. The face of the mountain is scarred by the pylons required for the half-dozen ski lifts. You pass a small dammed lake, stocked with fish, and a barrier at which you must pay 5dh to enter the resort. In winter it provides the best skiing in the country, and in summer it makes a good base for walking. What is more, it has the most accessible collection of stone carvings in Morocco. There is no view from Oukaimeden but a superb view from the Tizerag TV relay station, at 2740 m, which is 2 km drive beyond the resort.

Stone Carvings

There is a map in the French Alpine Club, CAF, in Oukaimeden, marking the stone carvings, but the Club is often locked up and inaccessible. Ask to be guided by any of the locals to the half-dozen carvings. The French had, in their efficient way, built protective shelters which have all now rusted down to a few inches. You can, if you don't like being guided, look for these tell-tale signs just to the right of the road above the dammed pond as you enter the town. You will find a number of shafted stone knives, Aztec-like ritual knives, some circular or stellar-solar shapes with rings, snake-lightening bolts, a male hunter beside a small deer and an elephant with mouse-like ears and a penis but no tusks.

WALKING
The most immediate objective for walkers is the sharp peak of **Djebel Oukaimeden** whose summit is at 3273 m, but to the south east rises the higher and more distant peak of **Djebel Angour** at 3616 m. From Oukaimeden you can walk southwest to Imlil and the Tiz-n-Test via the CAF refuge at Tacheddirt. Climb to the end of the chair lift and then follow the track until a path leads off to the right. The Tacheddirt pass, 2314 m, is about two hours' walk away and from there you descend to the CAF hut.

SKIING
The National Ski Centre of Oukaimeden is open from November to March. The snow is variable and the best conditions are usually from February to March and often coincide with an impassable road. The skiing is Scottish, icy in the morning, wet in the afternoon and with some potentially surprising patches of rock. There are half a dozen button lifts and a 1660 m chair lift. It's 60dh for a day pass and 60dh a day for ski hire from the local shop.

WHERE TO STAY
The *** **Hôtel Imlil**, tel 03, is a comfortable wood-lined Alpine chalet where dinner costs 85dh, a single room 137dh and a double 169dh. The ** **Hôtel Juju**, tel 05, is similarly wood-lined but a bit busier and cheaper. It has a bar, menus at 42 and 67dh, a single room for 73dh or a double for 89dh.

Setti Fatima

Back on the Ourika valley road you reach the village of **Ighref** 5 km after the Oukaimeden turning at Arhbalou. This used to be an entirely Jewish community but only a few remain and the Jewish charity school is now full of young Muslims.

About 24 km from Arhbalou lies **Setti Fatima**, the hamlet which at 1500 m is the virtual edge of human habitation in the Ourika valley. The last kilometre of road to Setti Fatima takes the form of a small walking path and even this is continually being washed away. Across the stream from the hamlet, a path crosses below a café with rooms, beneath which you can camp, and continues up to a system of seven water falls. Each of the falls has a cool pool hidden in a secretive combe, shaded by walnut trees whose fruit is raided by Barbary apes.

Following a path from the café above the main river you reach the green tiled **Koubba** of Setti Fatima, a popular burial ground as the tell-tale head and foot stones indicate. The grille windows of the shrine are covered in a web of cloth knots left by supplicants. This is the centre of a four-day moussem held in August which attracts Berber farmers and shepherds from all over the High Atlas.

For the adventurous there is a 10 km walk up the valley to the hamlet of **Timichi**, from where it is another 10 km to the CAF refuge hut at Tacheddirt. From Tacheddirt it is a relatively simple walk to either Imlil or Oukaimeden.

WHERE TO STAY AND EAT IN OURIKA
The hotels get gradually seedier and the accommodation cheaper as you proceed up the valley. All give Arhbalou as their address but despite this are easy to find, strung along beside the road.

First you pass the **** **Ourika Hôtel**, tel 04, which has a good view, a bar, a pool but a slightly soulless air. A double room costs 230dh, dinner 80dh and breakfast 24dh.

The **Auberge Marquis** has a few rooms to rent. The bar can be lively and the tranquil licensed restaurant serves some of the best food in Ourika. A salad costs 10dh and a delicious chicken cooked with lemon and olives 70dh.

Le Lion de l'Ourika, tel 453–21, has an over-elaborate dining room and uniformed waiters, 10dh for mint tea or 130dh for a large meal.

The **Kasbah Restaurant** further on to the left, has been established in an old Glaoui pavilion. It can be overrun with coach tours but retains a certain chaotic style. A full meal costs 80dh. Almost directly opposite is the **Hôtel Amnougar**, which is a popular week-end base for Marrakeshis. They charge 160dh for a double room and have a bar, pool and dining room, tel 28.

Lastly there is the ** **Auberge Ramuntchko**, tel 118, which has 12 bedrooms, a bar and cooking which varies enormously, depending on how much they like each guest.

Where the tarmac road gives out, at the hamlet of Asgaour are two cafés, the **Atlas** and the **Toubkal** which are good for light meals and might let you sleep on the roof. If you want a room you could try the dirty **Hôtel Chaumiere**, 30dh a night, which does however have an attractive garden terrace that overlooks the river. In Setti Fatima itself the **Café les Cascades** rents out its four bedrooms for 10dh and prepares meals to order, or you can camp beside the café on shaded grass listening to the music of the river.

To the Tiz-n-Test

The Tiz-n-Test pass crosses the High Atlas to link Marrakesh and Taroudant in 200 km of mountain road. It can be closed by snow or made more dangerous by ice any time between December and March. Each year some portion is destroyed by falling rocks or a swollen mountain stream. It is worth intruding. You have the opportunity to climb the highest mountain in North Africa, to visit the only mosque open in Morocco and admire a succession of ruined kasbahs. Or you might simply come for the clear air, to walk in the high valleys and stay in memorable hotels.

GETTING AROUND

At least half a dozen buses a day leave the main Marrakesh bus station, the Bab Doukkala, for Asni, calling at the Bab er Robb stop on their way south. Tickets are 12dh for the two-hour trip. Alternatively a place in a grand taxi will get you to Asni in three quarters of an hour for 12dh.

There are four buses a day that climb south of Asni. The 5.00 and 6.00 departures from Marrakesh cross the Tiz-n-Test to reach Taroudant about 8 hours later. The 14.00 bus only travels to Ijoukak, which it should reach by 16.00. The 18.00 bus crosses the pass by night and then goes east to Taliouine which you reach at about 2.00 in the morning. Or you could bargain with a grand taxi and hire him for between 200 and 300dh for a whole day trip up to Idni.

Tahanoute and Moulay Brahim

31 km from Marrakesh on the Taroudant road, the S501, you pass the strikingly picturesque village of Azrou Tahanoute on the other side of the river bed. A cascade of pise houses surrounds a great rock which shelters the shrine of Sidi Mohammed El Kebir, whose festival is celebrated at Mouloud. It was the subject of Winston Churchill's last painting in 1958. Tahanout proper is a kilometre further, an ancient market place on the border of the mountains and plains where a **souk** is held each Tuesday.

Beyond Tahanoute the road climbs up through the gorge of Moulay Brahim shortly after which a turning to the right leads up to the hillside **zaouia of Moulay Brahim**. A maze of streets extends in a confusion of levels, courts and paved passages around the central shrine. This has a distinctive green pyramidal roof and a wooden bar has been placed below the minaret as a barrier to non-Muslims. The rest of the village with its cafés, pilgrim trinket stalls and hill views, is open and the population pleasantly welcoming. You could stay in the centre of Moulay Brahim in the basic **Hôtel Afoulaki** which lets out rooms for 40dh. To the west a dirt road passes through numerous reclusive hillside villages before reaching Amizmiz 65 km away.

Asni

15 km south of Tahanaout is Asni, a pleasant roadside village which is the local administrative centre and has a **souk** on Saturday. You could stay at the Youth Hostel which boasts a well and charges only 10dh for a bed, or the **Grand Hôtel du Toubkal**, tel no 3, which has an ornate Moorish dining room, a pool, garden, a bar, caged Barbary apes and only 19 bedrooms. A double room costs 193dh, a single 159dh and dinner 75dh.

Toubkal National Park

From Asni a partly tarmaced road leads up to the hamlet of Imlil which is the centre for hill walking in the Toubkal National Park. The road follows the right bank of the Oued Moulay Brahim, climbing from Asni at 1150 m to Imlil at 1740 m in 17 km. On Saturday, for the souk, there is a regular truck shuttle between Asni and Imlil. Other days of the week you will have to wait until the grand taxi is ready to do the trip. A seat in either costs 12dh. Café meals are available in Imlil and some of the mountain villages but prices can be high and rise steeply with the altitude. As there are kitchens in the hostels many walkers bring provisions from Marrakesh and stock up on fresh vegetables, eggs and fruit at the Saturday morning Asni souk.

Imlil

The approach road passes low stone houses of the Berber Gheghaia tribe, farmers and herdsmen who have tenaciously created fertile garden terraces from a wilderness of stone. The dress of the High Atlas women compensates for a life of continual hard labour with a fantastic panoply of colour. Village life around the climbing centre of Imlil remains surprisingly undisturbed. It provides an insight into the reality of a highland culture and a lifestyle that has been consistently over-romanticized. The level of dirt is always surprising but the back-breaking daily labour, clearing stones from the fields, hunting for firewood, grazing and water is awesome.

The hamlet of Imlil is an initially disappointing cluster of cafés and shops centred on an hostel run by the French Alpine Club, for the ascent of Djebel Toubkal, at 4167 m the highest mountain in North Africa, is the primary objective of those who come to Imlil. It has a correspondingly hearty air, full of an international community of sportsmen with their well-meaning advice, backpacks and bright kagouls.

A night in any of the Alpine Club hostels, including use of the kitchen and a tip to the guardian, will be between 20 and 30dh. Escaping a little from the outward bound atmosphere of the hostel an omelette and salad at the **Café Resta** in Imlil costs 8dh, and hiring one of the three bedrooms of the **Café Soleil,** run by Azaym Brahim, will cost 40dh a night.

Djebel Toubkal

Preparation

Climbing Djebel Toubkal between April and November requires no skills other than determination to scramble up innumerable scree slopes, whilst between December and March the snow and ice make the mountain face dangerous even for skilled climbers. Strong shoes or boots, a hat and dark glasses during the day and a sweater and sleeping bag will be needed even on a midsummer's night. Detailed local maps, experienced mountain guides and donkeys can all be found at Imlil. Maps should cost 40dh, mountain guides from 60 to 90dh a day and donkeys about the same. Take added tiredness from the altitude and midday heat into your plans and try to drink only bottled or well water. Most people find themselves resting for a night at the Louis Neltner hut before climbing to the summit in the morning.

The climb

The hillside village of **Aremd/Around** is a good hour's walk from Imlil but you can easily find it by following the river path up hill. It is the largest settlement of the valley and the Berber farmers are well used to creating a little income by renting out rooms, space for tents and selling meals. Staying in a mountain village is in many ways preferable to Imlil and there is even a small but expensive grocery stall here.

From Aremd the trail zizags up the valley. The path crosses over the stream about two hours later, just before the hamlet of **Sidi Chamharouch** where soft sticky drinks, cooled by stream water, are sold. Just beyond the hamlet a concrete bridge crosses a gorge to the **koubba of Sidi Chamharouch,** a popular and venerated Berber shrine. As with many of the mountain cults, a Muslim saint has been created out of traditional beliefs in the spirit of the mountain and the guardian of the spring. It is offensive to local custom for a western tourist to even cross the bridge to approach the koubba. In 1840 a botanist ignored local advice and insisted on climbing Toubkal and was nearly lost in a fierce gale which suddenly arose. 'The Atlas tribesmen discouraged the expedition from ascending the mountain top, the sanctuary of the djinns. One of the Chleuh carried with him a live cock under his arm. In a state of utmost excitement he now proceeded to cut the animal's throat, in order thus to appease the wrath of our supernatural foes. But the storm, now almost a hurricane, raged with increasing violence' (Hooker & Ball).

From Sidi Chamharouch it is a three-hour climb up the zigzagging path to the Louis Neltner hut at 3207 m. This is sited on the tree line beyond which stretch the completely barren boulder and scree faces of Djebel Toubkal. The hut is run by the French Alpine club and charges about 20dh a night.

From Neltner the summit is another three-hour climb up a reasonably clear approach along the south corrie. It is crowned by a tripod, and the view south to Djebel Siroua and north to Marrakesh is at its most magnificent in the clear hazeless light of the morning.

Lake Ifni

Returning back to the Neltner hut you could consider a four-hour walk to Lake Ifni. This involves an hour's climb up to the Tiz-n-Ouanouns pass and a three-hour descent through scree slopes and stone fields to this deep secretive mountain lake encased by broken shattered hills. In the summer the lakeside is an important watering point for sub-Saharan herds and a seasonal hamlet of shepherd huts will often be found occupied. The lake can be fished for trout and dried animal dung from the shores burnt to keep the flies and mosquitoes away.

The track continues south and a three-hour walk brings you to **Amsouzerte** where you can eat and sleep at **Omar's**. From Amsouzerte you could be guided to **Assareg** which is connected to **Aulouz**, on the Taroudant to Ouazazarte road by taxi.

East and West from Imlil

Having achieved the ascent of Djebel Toubkal you may want to tackle some of the less frequented tracks. East of Imlil is the village of **Tacheddirt** which has another Alpine Club hut and is a mere four-hour walk away. From Tacheddirt you can ascend **Djebel Angour**, 3616 m, or walk to one of the hotels at Oukaimeden or Setti Fatima at the head of the Ourika valley. West from Imlil there are trails to the hotels at Ourigane on the Tiz-n-Test pass.

These are all ambitious two- or three-day expeditions. They will require a guide, a mule to carry the luggage and much earnest planning, map consulting and bargaining. But you may have already found that in Imlil it is difficult to bring conversation round to any other topic.

Ourigane

Returning from Imlil to the Tiz-n-Test road the hamlet of Ourigane lies 16 km south of Asni. It consists principally of two hotels whose gardens face each other across a stream, which drains the western face of Djebel Toubkal to merge with the Oued Nfis just below Ourigane. 4 km south of Ourigane watch out for the hilltop **agadir of Tagadirt n Bourd**, to the right of the road.

WHERE TO STAY, EAT AND RIDE
The ****** Residence La Roseraie**, tel 4, has 30 bedroom suites scattered amongst a calm and mature garden which contains a magnificent swimming pool. The central building has a drawing room, bar and restaurant where a portrait of Caid Gondaffi by E. Varley hangs. Below the hotel are **riding stables**. A day riding in the hills on one of the quieter of these elegant Arab horses costs 500dh and includes dinner at the end of the day. Between April and June there are week-long riding expeditions organized into the

mountains costing 3500dh, and including 2 nights spent at the hotel. The cheapest rooms start at 325dh for a single, a double for 630dh and dinner for 120dh.

The ** **Le Sanglier Qui Fume**, tel 9, maintains an even more distinctive atmosphere which Paul Bowles described in 1959: 'Lunch outside in the sun at Le Sanglier Qui Fume. Our table midway between a chained eagle and a chained monkey, both of which watched us distrustfully while we ate . . . Madame is Hungarian and lives in the hope that people coming through Ourigane will speak her language or at least know Budapest . . . obviously disappointed in us.' There are 16 bedrooms in the garden of this riverside hotel which has a pool and a few pet boars and storks. The food remains excellent, the dining room is dominated by large dogs and a collection of kasbah oil paintings by Holbing, an ex-German professor in Marrakesh. The garden can be full on Tuesday, as a coach tour stops here, but otherwise the atmosphere in Madame Thevenin-Frey's garden reigns unchecked. Two old dwarf twins can often be seen selling minerals by her gates. A single room for 84dh, a double for 102dh, dinner for 70dh.

The High Valley of the Nifs

From Ourigane the road climbs through steep wooded hills beside the river to emerge 30 km later into the high valley of the Nifs. It is one of the most hauntingly beautiful places in Morocco, an archetypal vision of a secret valley surrounded by a jagged horizon of snow-capped mountains. Flowing through this upper valley is the river Nifs: found in gentle aspect, a stream of slow moving cool clear water full of darting trout, whilst orchards, terraced gardens and hillside hamlets line its banks.

Walks around Ijoukak

The roadside settlement of Ijoukak, 200 m after you cross the Agoundis stream is at the entrance to the valley. This hamlet is lined with 4 grill cafés in a row, the last one, run by Brahim Ait Ougadir, serves delicious lentil and onion soup and tagines to order. You can ask for rooms to rent and may find yourself in a splendid spartan bedroom equipped with candles, blankets and bottles of water for washing.

Just by the bridge a dirt road leads up the pretty Agoudis valley passing through the villages of **Taghbart** and **El Maghzen**. The road ends just past El Maghzen, about a three hours walk from Ijoukak. A trail then continues climbing up the increasingly narrow and steep valley which is punctuated by hamlets for another 8 km until you reach the final edge of cultivable land at **Ait Youb**.

Another good day's walk from Ijoukak is to take the right turn at Taghbart, cross the river and then climb up the side of Djebel Oucheddon, 2840 m.

The Gondaffi kasbah of Talaat n Yacoub

Just out of Ijoukak you pass a left turn that leads up to Souk Larba Talaat n Yacoub. It is a quiet dusty administrative settlement but its two market courtyards, the arch below the **Mosque** and the **Café Tinmal** can look pretty enough when filled for the Wednesday **souk**. From the souk you can look over the road down on to the **kasbah of Taalat n Yacoub**.

To the right of the road a small sculpted stone pavilion stands beside a water tank. An audible trickle of water descends to irrigate an orchard that stretches down to the Nifs river bank and the sprawling ruins of the Gondaffi kasbah of Talaat n Yacoub.

The kasbah is built of pise and timber on stone foundations and is at least the third to have stood on this site. The existing structure largely dates from after 1906 but it is already in a precarious state. Most of the stairways and upper storeys have fallen in but if you are prepared to nose around amongst the ruins the columned prayer hall, reception room, great dark granaries and the slim interior court overhung with balconies can still be made out.

Perched right beside the river and overlooked from the opposite bank by the Tisi Nemiri, the hill of stones, it is quite clearly unsuited to defence. It never served as a fortress but as the palace and administrative court for two generations of Gondaffi caids who ruled the Tiz-n-Test pass and the Nifs valley. It held an assorted population of 1200 servants and slaves and a harem of 300 women. A small **Mellah** beside the kasbah held a Jewish community who provided vital personal skills such as pastry cooks, silversmiths and financial agents.

R. Cunninghame Graham has left a description of Caid Si Taieb Gondaffi holding court in 1901: 'forty years of age, thick set and dark complexioned . . . not noble in appearance but still looking as one accustomed to command; hands strong and muscular, voice rather harsh but low, and trained in the best school of Arab manners, so as to be hardly audible . . . His clothes white and of the finest wool . . . his secretaries never stopped opening and writing letters, now and then handing one to the caid . . . slave boys, in clothes perhaps worth eighteen pence, served coffee.'

Si Taieb, a Caid of the High Atlas

Si Taieb succeeded his father as caid of the Gondaffi tribe at the age of twenty. His father after a lifetime of rebellion had sued for peace with the government and sent a legendary gift to the palace at Marrakesh: a hundred male slaves each led a horse and a camel, which was followed the next day by a gift of a hundred slave girls each leading a cow and a young calf. He also sent his son to join the army of Sultan Moulay Hassan; in 1883 he was confirmed as Caid of the Gondaffi and sent home. The young caid once in power launched an aggressive expansion. He had at his disposal a tribal force of 5000 men and his own negro slave guard of 500. By 1900 he had trebled the size of his domain, a fact which increasingly drove the rival High Atlas caids, the Glaoui and M'touggi, into an alliance against him. In the words of the latter, 'he is a hill man who has discovered the plains. It will not be easy to get him out.' In 1906 they siezed their chance for Si Taieb had been called to Fez. Their combined forces descended to plunder the Nifs valley and burn the kasbah of Taalat n Yacoub.

Si Taieb returned to find his homeland in desolation and for six years he never left the valley. Lyautey, the French Resident General, was the only man who could entice the warrior caid from his mountain realm. In 1912 the lowland kasbahs of Amizmiz and Aguergour were returned to Si Taieb, at a stroke returning the caid to his pre-1906 position. He was supplied with arms and money for the conquest of the Souss valley. After the capture of Taroudant in 1913 he was honoured by being created Naib, the representative of the sultan in the south. In 1917 he was appointed Pasha of Tiznit and for seven years he remained in command of this frontier of the desert war. In 1924 he retired to his mountain kasbahs where he died four years later, aged 65.

After his death his feudal authority was dismantled and replaced by the even rule of French officials, whilst his lands were divided between his son Lhassen and two nephews. A pleasant white house of spacious courtyards can be seen attached to the end of the kasbah of Talaat n Yacoub. This is the house of the caid's grandson, an electrical engineer from Casablanca.

Agadir N'Gouf

Above the road on the left, about 2 km south of Talaat n Yacoub, the hill top Agadir N'Gouf can be seen. This square castle commands excellent views over the valley and looks as ancient and as strong as the hills. It was built in 1907 as a strong point, the year after the Glaoui and M'touggi had ravaged the valley. Fearing their return the caid kept what he treasured most—his horses—safe in the agadir, stabled around the enormous central court, which was built around a fissure on the hill. Large reception rooms were added later and traces of their elaborate carved plaster work can still be seen. The agadir is now completely uninhabited. It is easier to approach from the north where a path winds down the valley.

Tinmal

Another 3 km south and the Almohad **Mosque of Tinmal** emerges high up on the opposite bank of the river, a fortress of the faith with its high walls and strong towers. It is usually empty of tourists yet must be considered one of the most memorable sites of Morocco, the sole survivor of the 12th-century city of Tinmal and the only mosque in Morocco that a non-Muslim may enter. Its striking position, deep in the High Atlas mountains, is only equalled by its extraordinary history.

A track leads down from the road to a broken bridge which can be scrambled across without too much difficulty. Small boys lie in wait for visitors and will enthusiastically lead you up to the custodian of the mosque, Mohammed Filali, who may be found in the company of one of his three hazel-eyed daughters. On Fridays the village of Tinmal use the mosque and it is consequently not open.

The Mosque

You enter through a small but sturdy door in the corner of the main tower which used to be reserved for the Imam, the leader of the prayers and the Khatib, the pronouncer of the Friday sermon. The mosque is now roofless but this increases rather than distracts from the splendour of the interior. Deep shadows cast by the surviving brick columns and horseshoe arches contrast with an expanse of sunbaked wall which reflect the sunlight to give the whole interior an enchanted roseate glow.

The central tower has been placed immediately above the mihrab, the arched niche which indicates the direction of Mecca. The dome above the mihrab and the arches that link with the domes underneath the two corner towers have been richly decorated to draw the worshipper's attention naturally in this direction. The central aisle would also have boasted more elaborate details. All the other aisles would have been supported by horseshoe arches, embellished by bas relief columns of which a few survive. At the opposite end to the mihrab is the sahn, the open air court of ablutions which has its own entrance arch and would have contained a central fountain. Either side of the sahn are two prayer halls which, screened and provided with their own entrances, could be used by women. The original gates of the mosque are supposedly still in position. Those piled up are from the Koutoubia at Marrakesh, secondhand gifts from the sister mosque built by the Almohads.

In its prime the whole mosque would have been kept spotlessly white. The three towers, built of brick, are an unusual feature in that they are built above the actual prayer hall of the mosque. Most minarets are quite free-standing, structurally independent and rarely aligned with the mihrab. The corner minaret towers were crowned by lanterns but the central one did not reach much higher than it does today. You can climb up its crumbling staircase and look south down the Nfis valley to the Gondaffi kasbah of Agadir N' Gouf which crowns the central hill.

Ibn Tumert and Tinmal

Ibn Tumert was a religious reformer who desired to enforce his puritanical doctrine over the Muslim community. A Chleuh Berber, he was born in one of the small villages on the northern slopes of the Anti Atlas mountains and travelled east to Mecca to study at all the intellectual centres of the Islamic world. He was a well known and controversial figure before his return to Morocco, and by 1124 he had selected Tinmal to be the citadel of his theocratic state.

It became a place of total obedience where he trained the mountain tribes for war against all who would not accept his authority. Dancing, music and singing were banned, art placed under his severe direction and codes of dress established which denied any ornamentation. Ibn Tumert lectured the Berber tribes in their own dialect but taught them the Arabic Koran in a characteristically authoritarian manner. Long lines of warriors would each be given a word of the Koran as their name and by obediently calling out their new names in turn could learn whole suras of the Koran. As a capstone to his authority Ibn Tumert gradually led his community to recognize that he was the 'Mahdi', the prophesied successor of Mohammed.

After two years at Tinmal he led a series of expeditions that enforced his authority in the valleys of the High Atlas, which was consolidated in 1128 by a bloody forty-day purge of the tribes. In 1129 three Almoravide armies attempted a joint assault on Tinmal and though these were beaten off, Ibn Tumert's own siege of Marrakesh that same year ended in a costly defeat. The death of Ibn Tumert in 1130 was kept a secret from his followers for three years whilst his chosen successor Abdel Moumen consolidated his authority. In 1148 he captured Marrakesh which became the administrative capital, while Tinmal degenerated into the Almohad cult centre, secure treasury and favoured burial ground.

In 1154 Abdel Moumen subtly shifted the Almohads from a movement of religious reform to a dynasty invested in his own family. The great mosque of Tinmal was finished as a triumphant cult centre in the same year that Ibn Tumert's own children, grand-children and cousins were quietly disposed off.

Tinmal village

Leaving the mosque, walk through the hamlet of Tinmal which has a ruined kasbah at its centre, a mosque, Koranic school and an old water tank which produces a regular crop of edible frogs. Past the village the old city walls of Tinmal lead up from the river bank to the heights above. Tinmal was both the first and the last bastion of the Almohads. It was finally stormed in 1276 by the Merenids who though they respected the great mosque left no house standing, no tomb undefiled or citizen of Tinmal alive. However, the historian Ibn Khaldoun who visited Tinmal a generation later found Koranic reciters had returned to the mosque. When they entered the valley in 1924 French administrators found the area around the mosque covered in old shrines of which there is now no trace.

Walking back towards the broken bridge over the river you pass an olive press on your right. This was built from the savings of 16 years' emigrant labour in France. The owner is usually happy to show you the mill, explain the process and finish by selling a litre or two of Tinmal olive oil.

Mzouzit

A few km south of Tinmal you pass the village and ruined kasbah of **Mzouzit**, beside a school, on the opposite bank of the river. A track passes through the village and leads after about a 7-hour walk to the hamlet of **Arg**. This makes a convenient camping base for those wishing to climb the two mountains to the north and south, Djebel Erdouz, 3575 m and Djebel Igdet, 3615 m.

Tagoundaft kasbah

5 km from Mzouzit, the kasbah of Tagoundaft is perched high up on a pinnacle of rock at 1600 m, overshadowed by a curtain wall of mountain. Tagoundaft has resisted all sieges and invaders but now its stone walls are being slowly dismantled and carted away for building rubble by the villagers. The remains of the great tower, aqueduct and overgrown water tank can be examined after a half-hour walk up a mule path. The real reward for the climb is the view and the sense of impregnable security you feel from the kasbah's position.

A daughter of the caid was placed in Tagoundaft kasbah whilst there was fighting in the valley. The commander of the kasbah grew over-familiar with his charge. Rather than compromise her honour and that of her father she calmly walked out of the highest window of the tower.

Idni

The hamlet of Idni is 4 km south of Tagoundaft at the foot of the long climb up the Tiz-n-Test pass. It is a traditional stopping place, a chance for one last calm cup of tea before tackling the Tiz-n-Test pass. The **Hôtel Alpina** is now closed after the death of its eccentric proprietor, Madame Gipolou in 1985. The **Café Igdet** and the village store directly opposite have inherited the passing trade, providing snack meals and tagines to order. The café has a small open-air courtyard with three or four spartan rooms for 10dh a night. If you stay here you will meet Bassin Mohammed who trades in minerals and Berber jewelry.

Tiz-n-Test

From Idni the road climbs the 18 km to the summit of the Tiz-n-Test pass, at 2100 m. It was opened by the French on 10 November 1928 by a convoy of 30 motor cars. Some of their initial sense of achievement can still be imagined crossing the pass today. The road is narrow and often alarming, traversing long mountain slopes to twist suddenly in a tight hairpin bend and expose an unfenced vertical cliff face. The odd scarred relic of a fallen vehicle encourages all but the flashy local drivers to select a lower speed and gear. Crossing in the night, stabs of light can be seen on some improbably high and distant slope that warn you of the convoluted route to follow.

A kilometre before the summit of the pass watch out for a turning to a TV relay station. This leads to a viewing platform which has easily the best view; both south over the Souss to the Anti Atlas and north to Djebel Toubkal. Beyond the actual summit there are a couple of cafés and the familiar mineral displays.

The descent south is possibly even more dramatic. The road drops 1600 m from the Tiz-n-Test summit to the Souss valley in under 30 km. As you descend the mountain road you pass hamlets that cling to barren steep walled valleys whilst the Souss valley shimmers verdant in the distance—an exotic and mysterious land that beckons to the traveller.

At the P32 road junction Taroudant is 51 km west, Taliouine 67 km east.

Tiz-n-Tichka

The Tiz-n-Tichka pass crosses the High Atlas from Marrakesh to Ouazazarte and can be blocked any time between December and March. It is an exciting memorable journey, though on a perfectly safe road, that climbs twisting up through forests to the treeless summits of the pass. Just beyond the summit is the turning for the **Kasbah of Telouet**, the chief attraction of the journey, and further south a sub-Saharan landscape of bleak twisted rock presents itself where permanent habitation is restricted to the oasis valleys that drain the Atlas slopes.

It is 200 km along the P31 from Marrakesh to Ouazazarte. There is a two-star hotel at **Ait Ourir** and basic accommodation at **Taddert** and **Igherm**. If you are travelling by bus get off at Igherm as you have a better chance of finding a taxi for the drive to Telouet than at Taddert.

To Telouet

Ait Ourir, 38 km southeast of Marrakesh and off to the left of the main road is one of the string of market towns that nestle at the foot of the High Atlas. Good farm land stretches below and the Tuesday **souk** is usually busy and empty of tourists. A well-built Glouai residence can be seen to the south of the town but is inaccessible as it now houses an orphanage.

Ait Ourir makes a tranquil and unusual base for exploring the region. You could stay at the ** **Hermitage Hotel**, tel 2, which has a bar, restaurant, pool and garden. A double room costs 90dh and dinner 40 or 80dh. There is also a good licensed restaurant nearby, the **Tamaris**, which is right beside the bridge over the river Zat, that collapsed in December 1987.

The ruins of the 12th century Almoravide **fortress of Tasghimout** are 10 km along the secondary road that links Ait Ourir to Ourika, route 6702, a dirt track leads uphill just after the village of Amanouz. Tasghimout was built by Sultan Ali ben Youssef in 1125 when it was known as the fortress of El Halal, and somewhat confusingly Ibn Khaldoun mentions Tasghimout as one of the towns founded by the Almohad Sultan Abdel Moumen. The walls that follow the natural line of the escarpment can be traced and one gate, the Bab el Mohaddin, survives.

Beyond Ait Ourir the road climbs quickly up into the foothills passing below the prominent **Koubba of Sidi Lahoussine**. Just before the koubba a dirt track leads almost due south to the village of **Tidili des Mesfioua**. This was the centre of the Mesfioua who alone of the Berber tribes succeeded in resisting the Arab tribes of the plains and held on to their area of the fertile plain of Haouz. They also preserved their traditions of tribal democracy and up to the 20th century suffered no autocratic caid to rule over them.

12 km south of Ait Ourir a tarmac road turns right up the Zat valley passing through a series of Mesfioua villages where the timeless, tireless pace of subsistence farming continues undisturbed by tourism. The road ends at **Arba Talatast** overlooked to the west by the twin peaks of **Djebel Yagour**, 2723 m and **Djebel Meltsene**, 3588 m. The slopes of Yagour have some of the best preserved prehistoric carved stone whilst the summit of Meltsene is still rumoured to be used for the old Berber sacrifices celebrated on the equinox and solstices.

Back on the main road, the P31, you climb through dramatic mountain scenery, the slopes covered in mixed woods of oak, pine and juniper. Perhaps the best view of these Mesfioua mountains is from the pass of Tiz-n-Ait Imguer, at 1470 m, with a particularly good view southeast to Djebel Tistouit whose summit looms up to 3224 m.

Having passed the hamlet of **Ait Barka** and the **Auberge Toufliat** watch out for a left turn in about 5 km. This if you have time and a good car is a worthwhile detour off the beaten track along a passable mountain track that leads in about 2 km to the Glouai kasbah of **Had Zerekten** and then 5 km on to the village and agadir of **Arhbalou**.

Taddert is a roadside village poised below the last 15 km of twisting road that climbs to the Tiz-n-Tichka summit. Though unpromising at first sight with it cramped cafés it has an auberge and a small camping site, whilst a number of paths lead away from the fumes of truck exhaust to pise farm houses placed idyllically beside the terraced banks of mountain streams.

The summit of Tiz-n-Tichka, 'the gate to the pastures' is 2260 m high. From this central point in the High Atlas a windblown desolate expanse extends in all directions though the immediate environment is ringed by the now customary mineral stalls. 4 km further on there is a left turn for the kasbah of Telouet.

Telouet

The **kasbah** is 21 km east from the main road on a tarmac drive that leads across stunted pine and mineral-stained soil which has given the ground a sanguinous hue in keeping with its reputation. Eventually you glimpse a minaret that rises from the low village of El Khemis Telouet which is separated from the sprawling extent of the kasbah by the Oued Mellah. A café in the village serves good basic meals but there are no rooms available for the night.

Three generations of caids of the Glouai tribe built extravagant structures out of wood and pise to form the kasbah. Most of Telouet is subsequently an area of unrecognizable leached and shapeless mud banks. Broken spars and wattle frames protrude like the bones of some decaying Leviathan. This area of ruin is screened from immediate view by the most recent stone-built, **White kasbah** built by Caid Brahim between 1934 and 1955 with its layers of towers, buttresses, crenellation and curtain wall.

The road skirts the village to approach the kasbah from behind. Melted forms of old walls grow stronger where a few families squat with their chicken, dogs and children in the more weather-resistant corners. A gateway directs your approach through narrow walls that open into a large paved courtyard. Even the minaret of the kasbah mosque has been infected with the universal crumbling.

Government custodians conduct tours of the main reception rooms of Caid Brahim's White kasbah for 20dh. The haphazard evolution of the palace becomes apparent in the eccentric route to these rooms which affords tantalizing glimpses of dark corridors, subterranean staircases and obscure sun-baked terraces. The dusty long echoing corridor to the reception rooms provides an astonishing contrast to the massive assertive confidence of these halls. The vulgarity of display mixes with detailed Moorish craftsmanship of the highest order to silence the visitor. A ornate grille window frames a significant view of the old kasbah of Telouet on the edge of the village with barely two of its walls left standing. The old kasbah is the size of a traditional fortress of a mountain caid and would have boasted little decoration beyond crenellated towers and motifs embossed into the pise of the exterior walls. Inside the rooms would most likely have been small, dark and infested. The halls of the white kasbah of Telouet are of another order and though now empty of furniture the absence of rich cloth, carpets, worked metal and wood seems merely to enhance the grandeur of the interior. The roofs above are still secure and you are allowed up to enjoy the excellent view. They were once decorated with great expanses of green glazed tiles but these now lie in shattered heaps at the foot of the outer walls.

On the way out the custodian may point out a large windowless room, the **cinema**. Edward G. Robinson was Caid Brahim's brother-in-law. The screening of the latest fantasies from California seems bizarrely appropriate in this last outlandish product of feudal grandeur.

The rest of Telouet is not officially accessible and for the pragmatically minded is securely locked up. Every year the buildings become more dangerous but the custodians can sometimes be tactfully encouraged to take you around.

The route to the kitchens, Hammou's kasbah and the harem is through another delightful maze of passages. The kitchens are vast and recognizable chiefly by their blackened walls. The mixture of soot, melting pise and exposed beams is impressive only in its size and the imminent danger of final collapse. Telouet was entirely staffed by slaves except for one salaried French chef. Over a thousand slaves fled overnight when the news of the death of Thami el Gloaui reached the kasbah.

At the heart of Telouet, physically and emotionally, was **Hammou's kasbah**, a stark square keep formed from massive walls and dark and featureless inside. Hammou was the cousin and brother-in-law of Madani and Thami and remained violently opposed to the French who he would not permit to enter his feudal domain. He was the Caid of Telouet and ruler of the traditional mountain territory throughout the phenomenal growth in Glouai power until his death in 1934. Stories of his occult powers blended with the grim truth of his violent, xenophobic and sadistic nature. Sloghis, hounds that could singly kill a wild boar, trailed behind each guest who entered the kasbah like some canine thought police, while the final bloody resolution of a tribal feud too often ended at the hands of Hammou in his labyrinthine cellars. These have long since collapsed to bury this grim underworld.

The **harem courtyard** is beyond Hammou's kasbah and is approached through a number of chambers. The central courtyard was equipped with large pools of water which have now cracked and drained. Cool chambers open from this internal space which due to some trick of design are not overlooked by any battlemented tower. Two ornamental fruit trees survive and in spring still fill this breezeless space with the scent of cherry and apricot blossom. After the initial pleasure of discovery, the languid introspection and sterility of the harem creep back to repossess the spirit of the place.

Beyond these identifiable features you can wander freely amongst the curtain walls and acres of complete ruin. Banks of pise now and then astonish you with their range in height that hints at some past extravagant form. Fragments of carved cedar, carved foliate arabesques and shattered tiles can be glimpsed deeply buried in what first appears to be just leached soil.

It may seem extraordinary that such a place as Telouet should not be better preserved, but for a Morrocan Telouet is a monument to treason on a vast scale. The Glouai were totally identified with the most extreme French colonial ambitions right up to 1956. Thami el Gloaui was deeply involved in the deposition of Mohammed V and his officials had extorted and stolen for years. Allied with the French they had hunted down those who worked for independence and fought against the Liberation Army.

The Glouai had risen to fortune by aiding Sultan Moulay Hassan in completing a late crossing of the High Atlas in 1893. The sultan rewarded them with a position at court and left behind at Telouet a royal gift of arms. They prospered; Madani el Glouai served as minister of war for Abdul Aziz, grand vizier for Moulay Hafid, and his brother Thami ruled as pasha of Marrakesh, whilst from the arsenal held at the kasbah of Telouet they were able to enlarge their tribal domain in the High Atlas. By 1907 the Glouai had become key national figures but their greatest hour came in 1912 as the allies of the French. They undertook the expansion of French rule south of the High Atlas and created an empire within an Empire for themselves in the process. Thami succeeded his brother Madani in 1918, inherited Telouet on Hammou's death in 1934 and only the collapse of French power in 1956 could topple this aged but still avaricious warrior. Within a year of independence the Glouai were either dead, in prison, or exile, their lands confiscated and their tribesmen disarmed. Each year the kasbah moves closer to its sentence of gradual decay.

From Telouet a track continues for 15 km to another Glouai kasbah, that of **Anemiter** which, while as not as large as Telouet, is considered its superior in position and beauty. Anemiter kasbah is at the head of the Oued Ounila from where a rough track follows beside the river bank for 30 km, passing a number of kasbahs before reaching the road at Tamdaght and Ait Benhaddou. This was the route of the old Marrakesh to Ouazazarte crossing, but with Hammou ruling in Telouet the French decided to bypass the kasbah completely and cut a new route for their road in 1928. Telouet's ancient relevance astride the Atlas crossing was severed for ever, it decays in a cul-de-sac of its own making. It is as if history and geography are in tacit agreement over its destiny.

South from Telouet

Returning to the main road the summit of the Tiz-n-Lebsis pass at 2125 m is reached 4 km south of the Telouet turning. 2 km below is the village of **Aguelmous**, close to the head of the Assif Imini stream which the road closely follows down to Ouazazarte.

Igherm n Ougdal is another 6 km south. It has a classic rural four square basic kasbah and a basic hotel with a bar if you need to stay the night. If you have come by the Tiz-n-Tichka by bus there is a much greater chance of finding a grand taxi, for the trip to Telouet, in Igherm than at Taddert.

Descend past the village of **Agouim** in 8 km. The Franciscans established a craft cooperative here to keep alive the old skills of carpet-making, blanket-weaving and embroidery. It is still functioning and selling its wares. Just before you enter the village a dirt track on the right, the 6849, leads in 30 km to the much praised **agadir of Sour**. For the more adventurous this provides a back route to Djebel Siroua and Djebel Toubkal.

25 km south of Agouim, a tarmac turning crosses the Asif Imini stream for the manganese mines of **Imini**. This can be taken as a convenient border between the region of the High Atlas and the sub-Saharan world of the southern oasis valleys. **Tiseldei kasbah** which perches above its village in an attitude of feudal power is 6 km north of the Imini mines, whilst 2 km south you reach Iflit, the first ksar in the valley, occupied by the Ait Zineb tribe. A scattering of ksour increasingly line the river bed before you reach the road junction of **Amerzgane** where a **souk** is held on Sunday. For the journey from Taroudant west to Amerzgane, see Part IX. 2 km beyond Amerzgane is the **ksar of El Mdint** and then that of **Tadoula**, two beautiful towered agglomerations surrounded by their palmeries that get a fraction of the tourists that flock to **Ait Benhaddou**. The right turn to Ait Benhaddou is 10 km further east though again you pass close to the almost equally splendid, and neglected, **Ksour of Tikirt and Tazenntout** only a short distance beyond. This area, its distinctive history and the town of Ouazazarte, only 15 km further east, is described in the beginning of Part VIII.

Part VIII

THE SOUTHERN OASIS VALLEYS

Taboula Kasbah

Human settlement south of the High Atlas could not exist without the handful of oasis valleys that drain the southern slopes of these mountains. The valleys of the Draa, the Dades, the Todra, the Rheris and the Ziz stretch south into the Sahara and allow cultivation to intrude for a hundred miles into an otherwise unforgiving environment. The average annual rainfall in the region is a mere 68 mm and but for the oasis valleys this sub-Saharan region would only support a few drifting nomadic herds.

As it is, due to irrigation techniques which have developed over thousands of years, these valleys produce a considerable agricultural harvest. Above all, they are dependent on the palm tree. The date palm is the farmers' one commercial crop and provides vital shade beneath which all other plants are grown. Its roots hold the soil from erosion by the desert wind. A beam cut from a palm trunk is the basis for most pise desert houses, palm leaves are the wattle for floors and walls. They also provide kindling for fires and plaited create mats and bowls. The hollowed trunk forms a bucket.

There are four and a half million date palms in the southern oasis valleys which produce 95,000 tons of dates a year, of which at least a quarter is exported. Each region produces dates with different qualities, some are prized for their size, some for their sweetness, others can stay fresh for years whilst others are only good enough to be fed to the goats. The best eating dates are found in Zagora.

The date palm has attracted an almost mystical respect. In the 4th century AD, the Roman author Amminaus Marcellinus wrote, 'It is said that the female trees produce fruit when impregnated by the seeds of the male trees, and even that they feel delight in

428

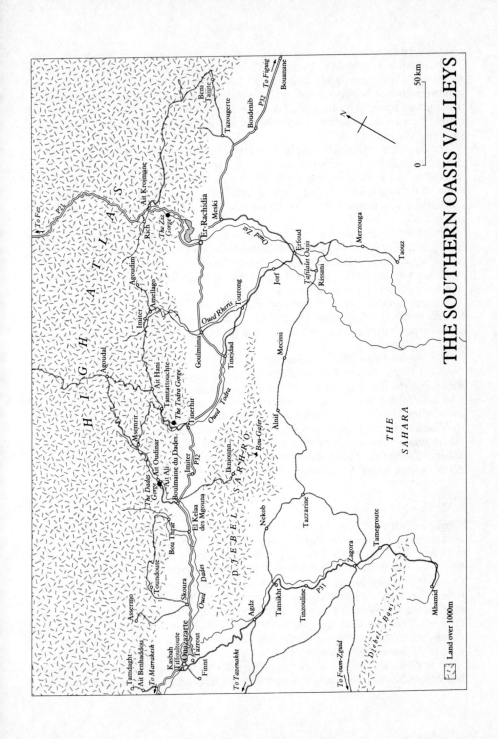

THE SOUTHERN OASIS VALLEYS

their mutual love, and that this is clearly shown by the fact that they lean towards one another, and cannot be bent back by even the strongest winds. And if by any unusual accident a female tree is not impregnated by the male seed it produces nothing but imperfect fruit, and if they cannot find out what tree any female is in love with, they smear the trunk of some tree with the oil that proceeds from her, and then some other tree naturally conceives a fondness for the odour; and these proofs create some belief in the story of their copulation.'

The date is in fact a single-sex plant but to sympathize with the south you must glory in the palm. Imagine the scene of the harvest, eager barefooted boys shinning up the tattered trunks to slice off the tendrils of fruit with a blow of a machette, young children catching the dates as they fall through the branches, women chanting as they shred the fallen fronds and men with a more serious demeanour, sorting, weighing and packing the dates.

The other remarkable feature of the desert south is the numbing beauty of the sky. The light at dawn and dusk is an explosion of fast-fading colours and shadows which more than compensates for the baking oppression of the day. A desert night awakes a child-like wonder at the stars. Palm trunks rear up like pillars of a pantheistic temple to frame the endless configurations of the night.

For a visitor there is an embarrassment of riches. The oasis valleys are lined with literally hundreds of distinguished and still inhabited kasbah and ksour. The valleys all share in the elegance of the desert night and the contrasting beauty of bleak desert and intense cultivation.

The outstanding sights of the region are the village of Ait Benhaddou, the journey down the Draa valley to Zagora, the Dades gorge, the Todra gorge, the sand desert at Merzouga, the Ksour of the Tafilalet and Figuig oasis. No one who has the time should miss any of these but it is equally important to drop off from an ambitious itinerary and spend a few days in one community. There is enormous charm in walking beside the trickling irrigation streams that thread through the palmery gardens and an even greater satisfaction in allowing yourself to become lazy in the heat. Absorb some of the gentle pattern of agricultural life and daydream amongst the exotic poetry of the past, full of the deeds of conquering Arab tribes and French Legions.

History

As well as their relative agricultural riches, the southern oasis valleys have been important for their position on the trade route from Fez to Timbuctoo. Domination has always been fiercely contested, and the valleys have existed in a state of uneasy truce with the nomadic tribes from the surrounding desert plains. From within their fortified villages, the ksour (singular—ksar), the inhabitants negotiated annual treaties with a local nomad tribe who would protect the crops and escort their trading caravans. The balance of this relationship was often distorted if a militant nomadic tribe became strong enough to establish their own kasbah in the valley. But in their turn they would often become dependent on another, fiercer desert tribe. The ksour of the oasis valleys were also in a state of constant feud with each other.

From earliest times the cultivation of the valleys was undertaken by a serf caste, the black Haratine, who are thought to be the remnants of an ancient race which populated the area before the Berbers spread south. They were never incorporated into the Berber or Arab tribes but intermarried with negro slaves from West Africa. They tended the palms and crops in return for a share of the harvest.

The only thing that would bring a brief period of peace and authority to the south before it degenerated into its habitual feuding, was the emergence of some startling new force like the 11th-century Almoravide and 12th-century Almohad Empires. Then, in the 13th century, the Merenid Sultans directed their dangerous allies, the Maql Arab tribes, away from central Morocco to the south. This ruthless Bedouin Arab confederation defeated the Berber pastoral tribes and established a harsh predatory authority over the region until the 16th century.

In the 16th century a turning point was reached when a Saadian Sheikh from the Draa valley emerged as the leader of the Jihad which united all the southern tribes against the Portuguese coastal forts, and carried his heirs to the throne of the Sultans as the newly formed Saadian dynasty. At the same time a new and powerful force was emerging in the south. A Berber chief from Djebel Saghro, Dada Atta, forged a supertribe, the Ait Atta, who overthrew the rule of the Maql Arabs. The Ait Atta quickly managed the transition from liberators into overlords and in their turn dominated the south for three centuries. They did not, despite their fearsome military reputation, remain unopposed. The Ait Yafalman, a defensive confederation of tribes north of the Dades river, managed to defend their grazing grounds effectively from Ait Atta domination.

The two dominant khums (subdivisions) from the five which made up the Ait Atta supertribe were the Ait Alouane and the Ait Khabbache. The Ait Alouane became semi-nomadic and garrisoned kasbahs on the Draa and Dades in return for a proportion of the crops and grazing rights around the valleys. The Ait Khabbache remained entirely nomadic and ranged the desert steppes; merciless camelborne raiders that left many a smouldering ksar in their wake.

The present ruling Alouite dynasty earned its original prestige when Moulay Ali Cherif organized resistance in the Tafilalet oasis to these desert raiders in 1631. The military genius of his son, Moulay Rachid, 1666–1672, allied to the Arab tribes of the eastern desert, elevated the Alouites from southern regional politics to the Sultan's throne.

But the Ait Atta, surviving the elevation of their rivals, remained dominant in the south. They defeated the royal army led by Sultan Moulay Ishmael against their stronghold of Djebel Saghro in 1679. None of the armies led south by successive sultans, notably Moulay Sliman 1792–1822 and Moulay Hassan 1873–1894, against the Ait Atta fared much better. From 1903 to 1908 the French army began to advance west from their posts in the Algerian Sahara. But their invasion of central Morocco in 1907, the First World War and then the Riff rising delayed the final conflict between France and the Ait Atta until 1934. Following the Ait Atta's capitulation after the heroic defence of Bou Gafer, the last bastion of southern resistance was crushed and the Pasha of Marrakesh, Thami el Glouai, lorded over the southern valleys supported by garrisons of the French Foreign Legion.

Independence for Morocco in 1956 came not a year too soon, for the south was rapidly degenerating into its familiar anarchy as armed bands of the Liberation Army fought the Glouai caids. Independence brought stability and pride back but it also closed the disputed Saharan border with Algeria. The oasis valleys, once the conduits of the rich

Saharan trade, were now placed on the outer fringe of a national society. A consistent pattern of drought and disease has hit farmers in the last few decades and though the population has increased since 1940, over half the men now travel north of the Atlas to make a living.

Like all of Morocco the south is administered by a strict hierarchy of officials but in the absence of much commercial activity officialdom appears more sharply defined than elsewhere. The Moqqadan, the village headman, reports to the Caid of a rural commune. The Amal of a Cercle has authority over several Caids but answers to the Governor of a province. This powerful official is chosen by the King but left under the supervision of the Minister of the Interior.

Ouazazarte

Ouazazarte does not live up to the exotic elegance of its name. It first appears as a one-street town set on the edge of a dusty windblown plain. Hidden behind this main drag however, built from stone that camouflages with the arid surroundings, lies the administrative centre for much of the south, governing a population of half a million. Ouazazarte is centrally positioned just off the crossroads that connects Agadir, Marrakesh, Zagora and Er-Rachidia.

In recent years a burst of energetic development has invigorated the town, based on those most ephemeral of industries, film and tourism. Both have been attracted by the consistent dry hot climate of Ouazazarte and while the town itself contains little of interest, it is a useful base for visiting the surrounding kasbahs. It is also a convenient transport centre and you will inevitably pass through the town or stay here whilst you are travelling in the south.

The construction of the El Mansour ed Dahbi dam to control the irrigation of the Draa river has formed a lake to the east of Ouazazarte. But even in this water-obsessed region it is a surprisingly unimpressive site. The water is brown and ebbs and expands within a large bowl of washed gravel.

The new lake partly obscures the fact that Ouazazarté lies on the confluence of three important river systems, the river Ouazazarte, the Dades and the Draa, making it an important strategic stronghold. In order to control the southern oasis valleys rulers have consistently garrisoned the low hills above this river junction and the Almohad sultans built a kasbah, the Irherm N'Ougelid, the fortress of the kings, here which was occupied by the succeeding dynasties.

More recently, after Sultan Moulay Hassan's death in 1894, a three-year tribal war broke out throughout the entire south. This allowed the Glouai brothers, Thami and Madani, to gain control of the kasbah at Ouazazarte, almost immediately due south of their High Atlas home, the kasbah of Telouet.

The Glouai kasbah at Ouazazarte, known as the Taourirt Kasbah, became the centre for the expansion of their authority throughout the oasis valleys. In 1928 the French Foreign Legion, by this time allies of the Glouai, established the now unimpressive fort under which the present modern town has grown.

GETTING AROUND
Practically everything in Ouazazarte can be found along or just off the Blvd Mohammed V, the main P32 Agadir to Er-Rachidia highway as it passes through the town.

By Air

The airport is 1 km northeast of the town with flights to Paris, Casablanca, Marrakesh, Er-Rachidia and Agadir. Tickets and flight information from the Pan Africa and Sir Tourist booking agencies at 55 and 19, Blvd Mohammed V, tel 2203 and 2199 respectively, or directly from the airport, tel 146.

By Bus

The CTM station is on Place Mohammed V. Departures for Marrakesh currently leave at 7.30, 12.00, 12.45 and 16.00. The journey takes six hours and costs 33dh. Travelling east to Tinerhir the buses leave at 6.00 and 12.00, and the four-hour journey costs 29dh. Buses to Zagora are better served by local lines which leave from a separate station 100 m away in the Place Mouhadine, though a CTM bus leaves for Zagora at 12.00 costing 45dh.

By Taxi or Car

Grands taxis leave from Place Mouhadine and cars can be rented from a Hertz office on Blvd Mohammed V. Budget car hire have recently established a sub-office at Residence El Warda, Blvd Mohammed V, and a desk at the airport, tel 2043.

TOURIST INFORMATION

The Tourist Office on Blvd Mohammed V, tel 2485, can help with advice on hotels, local souks and festivals. There are two tourist-oriented festivals a year, an artisan display in May and a Moussem in September. The BMCE and Banque Populaire are on Blvd Mohammed V, and the Post Office is on Place Mohammed V near the CTM bus station. Pharmacie de Nuit is also on Blvd Mohammed V. Ask at Chez Dimitri for Doctor Apostolakis in an emergency.

WHAT TO SEE

The old Glouai **kasbah of Taourirt** is on the eastern edge of the town. Encroached upon by artisan stores and official offices this extensive towered and battlemented building retains little of its original grandeur. As a 19th-century pise building it has survived well, but has inevitably been reduced by decay and the growth of the town. Its central core is under long and continuous restoration.

A small portion of the kasbah is open for a fee of 8dh from 8.00–18.00. You enter a paved courtyard which holds a Krupp cannon, a gift to the Glouai from Sultan Moulay Hassan in 1891. The cannon was instrumental in the rapid growth of Glouai authority over the south. It could, with a few shells, reduce the strongest tribal kasbah to ruin. In numerous tribal battles the heads of massacred defenders were heaped high up around the Krupp armament to almost obscure the barrel.

The kasbah is still partly occupied but you can walk upstairs and along cool white passages to visit two small rooms decorated with carved and painted plaster and cedar. The rooms are known as the dining room and the salon of the favourite. They are meagre in comparison with the rooms of the opulent confident palaces that the Glouai built after 1927 throughout the south. A centre of power in the period of Madani el Glouai's authority, it inevitably declined after it was inherited by his eldest and idiot son, Muhammed al Arbi. In 1949 it still housed 1500 servants, slaves, employees and craftsmen.

You may want to plunge down the valley to the left of the official entrance and wind your way through the lively inhabited village that still clusters at the foot of its walls. The streets and houses metamorphose from the indeterminate pise circumference of the Kasbah Taourirt, which looks at its best viewed from the gravel bed of the Oued Ouazazarte.

In the ground floor of the kasbah there are some booths full of local crafts whilst directly opposite over the road is an artisan centre and a café.

WHERE TO STAY

There has been a rapid growth in luxurious new hotels built in a row along the rising land behind Ouazazarte. Completely self-contained and insulated from everything but the sun, they are closely tied to the upmarket package tourist trade of Agadir. Beyond a drink and a quick exploration of their gardens and pool designs they have little appeal. These include the inaccessible **Club Med**, members only, tel 2283, the ***** **Riad Salam**, tel 2206, the **** **PLM Azghor**, tel 2612: 325dh for a double, menu 100 dh, the **** **PLM Karam Palace**, tel 74826: 460dh per person, dinner 110dh and the **** **Tichka Salam**, tel 2206: 500dh for a double.

If you want a comfortable hotel with a pool whilst you pass through Ouazazarte, the **** **PLM Zat** has only 60 rooms, tel 72070, and a double costs 325 dhs. It is much simpler and quieter, on the eastern edge of town, and has a fine view over the lake towards the Kazbah of Tazrout.

The ** **La Gazelle**, tel 2151, has rooms at 81dh for a double and is on Blvd Mohammed V, on the left as you come into Ouazazarte from Taroudant and set back reclusively from the road. There is a small plunge pool above the car park which is filled in the summer and there are 30 bedrooms arranged around a neatly labelled botanical garden courtyard. It has a restaurant, bar, a tranquil atmosphere and its only disadvantage is a long walk from the centre of town.

In the centre of town along the Blvd Mohammed V are three cheap clean hotels. The **Essalam** has a three storey cat-walk interior and rooms at 26dh a single. Directly opposite at no 24 is the **Royal**, where rooms are 21dh a single, 42dh a double, and here the rooms are arranged around a courtyard. Behind the Royal is the small **Hôtel Atlas** on 13 Rue du Marché, where a single costs 20dh. The other side of the low bridge that crosses the river bed from Ouazazarte, immediately on the left, is the **Hôtel/Restaurant La Vallee**, a friendly open place that serves good tagines. A double room in this new hotel costs 70dh.

Camping

On the eastern edge of town, the campsite is next to the municipal pool, which has just been awarded a triumphal arch. It is a welcoming place that has a good view south and is run by Haj Aouis Boujamaa. A tent in the campsite serves breakfast, lunch and dinner. The charges are 16dh a night for two with a tent and car, whilst dinner costs 30dh.

EATING OUT AND DRINKING

The interiors of the new big hotels are worth inspecting over a drink, otherwise the town bar is at the restaurant **Chez Dimitri**, on the Blvd Mohammed V opposite the Essalam Hotel. It is still run by Dimitri, an ex-soldier of the French Foreign Legion who has become something of an institution. Ouazazarte closes early in the evening, but if you politely tap on the door at Dimitri's they are often ready to let you in or sell you a bottle of wine. The supermarket next to the Essalam is the last opportunity to buy wine before heading south or east of Ouazazarte.

Outside of the hotels there are few independent restaurants. **La Gazelle** which has a licence and a Moroccan and European menu for 45dh is worth considering, but you can get a reasonable meal from three café restaurants in the centre of town: from the **Restaurant el Salam** on Av. Prince Heretier Sidi Mohammed, behind the Hotel Atlas, which serves a good couscous for 25dh or the **Restaurant el Helah** at 6, Rue du Marché, which serves a meal of lentil soup, tagine and fruit for under 25dh, or the **Restaurant du Sud**, by the CTM bus station on Blvd Mohammed V, which stays open until after midnight and serves a 16dh tagine.

The old **Glouai Kasbah of Tiffoultoute** is one of the most distinctive places to eat in the Moroccan south. It is 5 km west of Ouazazarte, at the turning to Zagora. Wander through the massive gates, an empty courtyard and you will find yourself in an echoing hall surrounded by dining rooms. If there is a coach party eating you can avoid their cheerful noise by eating on the roof beside a crumbling stork nest and peer over the battlements at the bulk of the kasbah to the south. There are copious set menus for 45 or 65dh, which serve sugared melon or grapefruit, tagine and cinnamon couscous pudding and the licensed restaurant is open for lunch and dinner; service is performed by a seductive uniformed imp, Bass Ilahcen.

West of Ouazazarte

Ait Benhaddou

This celebrated village of kasbahs is 22 km west of Ouazazarte. A north turn off the main P31 road leads in 10 km to Ait Benhaddou which is seldom found without tourists. It is however one of the most memorable sites of the arid south. It is a village entirely composed of tightly packed kasbahs, their red pise battlemented towers creating a rich and confusing array. Above this fortified cluster perches a hilltop **agadir**, its communal keep protected by an outer curtain wall. A recent addition to the splendour of Ait Benhaddou has been made by some passing film company who have erected a few more towers and a magnificent entrance gate.

The decorated towers of the kasbahs provided vantage points from which to pursue murderous local feuds but were vulnerable against a determined assault. Even before the use of cannons the walls of a kasbah could be easily sapped by diverting a stream alongside the mud foundations, which then dissolved taking the walls with them. The hilltop agadir was used for the safe storage of goods and the harvest. When an external threat proved large and imminent enough the local feuds were disbanded and the village moved uphill to within its cramped but secure walls.

There is a licensed restaurant at the car park. To get to the village, descend past a few shops to the river bank where you can hire a mule to take you across the gravel bed of the salt river, the Oued Mellah. Elegant small girls appear the other side and forcefully adopt you and show you around their village, taking you into the interiors of the few inhabited kasbahs where you will be offered mint tea and can watch courtyard life thick with chickens, rabbits, sheep and the odd cow. It is rare for a month to go by without Ait Benhaddou being used as a dramatic backdrop for a fashion article or film. The village has notched up credits in *Lawrence of Arabia* and *Jesus of Nazareth*.

The Kasbah of Tamdaght

If you crave seclusion after Ait Benhaddou, continue a few km further along the road to where a bridge has collapsed. The Kasbah of Tamdaght is a 20-minute walk from the bridge and has subsequently been cut off from the steady stream of coaches that visit Ait Benhaddou. The kasbah is perched above the meeting point of the Oued Mellah and Oued Ounila, commanding the old approach to the Tiz-n-Tichka crossing of the High Atlas. An orchard surrounds its walls and the custodian will happily show you the view from the surviving roof. An audience chamber with a ceiling of stained satin blue cedar beams has a terrace that overlooks the high walled and stone paved courtyard where slow circles of dancing women would have entertained the Glouai caids and their guests. Tea is offered and small tips scornfully returned by the women of the house.

As you return to the main P31 road look out for a series of kasbahs due south of the junction and particularly for **Mdint**. They are seldom visited but almost equally as beautiful as Ait Benhaddou, sitting astride the Oued Ouazazarte.

South of Ouazazarte

The **Kasbah of Tazrout**, the stork kasbah, whose towers can be seen across the lake from Ouazazarte, can be reached by walking east along the gravel bed of the lake. Each year crystals and semi-precious stones are washed down from the mountains and left stranded in the gravel, so you should keep your eyes open. The kasbah can also be approached along a track, a left turn off the road to Zagora. Beyond Tazrout, somewhere along the south bank of the lake, there are some hidden caves of refuge and you can ask at the Hotel de la Vallee for a guide if you are interested.

If you feel like a rural expedition while in Ouazazarte, the isolated oasis village of **Finnt** is usually hospitable. It lies a few kms along a piste track off to the left of the road to Zagora, 7 kms south of Kasbah Tiffoultoute (see above under eating out). On your arrival you will be taken by small boys to have mint tea with the village headman.

The Draa Valley

A dozen rivers drain the hidden valleys of the High Atlas and pour their water into the lake at Ouazazarte. The Draa has carried its contribution through the bleak eastern end of the Anti Atlas and flows due south to Zagora to dwindle and dissipate beyond in the Sahara. In exceptional years the river will briefly flow the whole 1000 km of its course to empty in the Atlantic. Polybius, the classical historian, records that the Draa was once infested with crocodiles, a fact which is corroborated by a French hunter who is recorded as shooting the last crocodile living in a Saharan oasis in 1929. In most years it is lucky if the Draa provides enough water for the 200 km oasis valley that clings to its banks in an otherwise harsh desert landscape.

The contrast of the bare sun-baked rock and the lush verdant fertility of the riverine palmeries, sharply defined beneath the achingly clear desert sky, is an astonishingly beautiful and powerful sight. Far be it from man to attempt to transgress the limits of nature around him.

The Ksour and Kasbahs of the Draa

It is only later that you can focus on the extraordinary architecture of the valley. There are no scattered huts amongst the terraces. All habitation has been concentrated in fortified villages, ksour. No plot of fertile irrigated land is wasted. The ksar and kasbahs are drawn up at the edge of the palmery and built on the desert wasteland, built on the desert and with the desert; for every wall has been formed from wet local earth pounded into compact shape between boards and then allowed to bake in the Saharan sun. Walls rise up from the ground the same colour and texture as their surroundings, and when their period of use is over, melt back effortlessly into the landscape. None of the walls of the ksour in the Draa are over a hundred years old, though the sites have probably been in continuous use for centuries.

The walls and towers are astonishingly rich and varied in design. Arches, arcades, balustrades, battlements, crenellations and covered terraces are all used in a profusive and bewildering organic originality. The silhouettes seem to make reference to Gothic fortresses, to Edwardian border castles and to Nineveh, to Tyre, to Babylon and to Egyptian Thebes.

Maps, sign posts and guides find a bewildering variety of names for each village. Forget your western desire to be sure of them, and simply concentrate on the rewarding architecture.

HISTORY
The Draa is a Berber-dominated valley which, like its neighbours, has always been under the influence of the surrounding nomadic tribes. The sedentary population of the valley, currently 80,000, is a mix of Berber and Arab, although some villages proudly claim exclusive descent from only one of these groups. There was a limited population of Jewish artisans who have now gone, and a much larger and still resident population of Haratine. The ksour provide adequate defence against feuding neighbours but little protection from a determined outside attack.

The nomadic Sanhaja and Zenata Berber tribes disputed possession of the Draa for centuries, the former from the southern desert, the latter from their principality at Sigilmassa. Here too, the fierce Maql Arabs descended in the 13th century, and remained the dominant power for three centuries.

But it was the 16th and 17th centuries that witnessed an extraordinary burst of activity in the region. The sheiks from the Draa Zaouia of Tamegroute led a nationwide jihad and rose to become the ruling Saadian dynasty, whilst a general Arab–Berber nomad war engulfed the Western Sahara. In 1546 two thousand Tuareg warriors sent by the negro

King of Songhai raided the Draa and 45 years later a Saadian army crossed the Sahara in the opposite direction and conquered his capital of Timbuctoo.

During the Saadian decline the Tazeroualt dynasty then the Alouites held the Draa in fief but by the 18th century the Ait Atta ruled supreme. The French finally destroyed Ait Atta power in 1934 which consolidated the empire within an empire that Thami el Glouai had been establishing in the southern valleys.

Since Independence in 1956 the Draa has been at peace and feuding has been limited to a sartorial rivalry between the village women. The competing styles of dress are dominated by a choice between a black or dark blue haik but this is picked out by highly individual assemblies of sequins, coins and poster bright embroidery. Note also the use made of contrasting red and purple stockings.

Tiz-n-Tinift

Leaving Ouazazarte on the Zagora road, after 13 km you pass the guarded entrance to the **El Mansour dam**, which controls the lake at Ouazazarte and the flow of the Oued Draa.

The road then climbs the denuded deserted slopes of the eastern Anti Atlas. The harsh contours, the heat and the barren wilderness serve only to emphasize the beautiful valley ahead. With every kilometre you travel south you shed the comparative modernity of Ouazazarte. Below the Djebel Tifernine pass lie the oasis hamlets of **Ait Saoun** and **Ouika**, 41 km south of Ouazazarte. The road climbs up out of this valley on to the slopes of Djebel Anouart.

The Tiz-n-Tinift pass, 3 km further, crosses over the Djebel Anouart at a height of 1680 m, providing a magnificent view: the Anti Atlas to the west, the confusing mass of Djebel Saghro to the east and the peaks of the High and Middle Atlas to the north. Meanwhile, the surrounding slopes reveal violently twisted striations, compounded in weird patterns. The road descends beside a steep valley where one or two palms precariously exist in the beautiful but permanently dry bed of the Oued Tansift. The first view of the Draa valley is only a few kms short of Agdz, 68 km south of Ouazazarte, where the sharply defined mass of palms follow the Draa river bed.

Agdz

Agdz is the administrative centre of the Northern Draa. The old military kasbah and the outlying keep-like office of the Caid overlook the town square from a slight hill to the east. At the Caidat, groups of immaculately robed and turbaned farmers assemble in winter to renew their leases, their braided cross belts holding ceremonial daggers and emboidered leather purses.

The square is festooned with carpets which hang by day in a barrage of colour from the windows of the surrounding houses. There are several cafés and bazaars clustered around. The **Café Communal** and **Resto Nadhah**, directly opposite each other, both provide tea, cheap salad and brochettes. The **souk** is held just south of the town in an enclosure beside the road on Thursdays with a smaller affair on Sundays.

To the north of the town the palmery extends up towards the ksour of **Rbat** and **Issafen**. Buses always stop at Agdz and Tinzouline further south, and both are convenient points at which to break a bus journey and explore a portion of the valley.

Tamenougalt and Timiderte

Beyond Agdz on the left bank of the Draa is the conspicuous Ksar of Tamenougalt, the old citadel of the Berber Mezguita tribe, who dominated this area of the valley. There is a slight chance of picking up bilharzia in the south and you might not care to wade across to visit the interior.

The Glouai kasbah of Timiderte is the next to appear further south, looking square and strong on the opposite bank. This was built in 1938 by Caid Brahim, the eldest son and heir of Thami, Pasha of Marrakesh. The interior is light and palatial, contrasting sharply with the traditional interior design of the neighbouring ksar, dominated by small, dark, hot and insect-infested chambers.

The ksar was designed as a fortress to hold the stock of animals, women and children and a very few possessions in security. Male social life was led outside its restricting walls, under palm trees, in the mosque or whilst grazing herds on the barren slopes.

Tansikht and Tinzouline

At Tansikht, 93 km from Ouazazarte, there is a basic mint tea café near the bridge over the Draa. A left turn here continues on tarmac for 20 km, travelling through a dry tributary of the Draa. The valley framed by hills gradually opens out into an arid plain which is periodically grazed by nomadic herds and dotted with distinctive black tents. The road continues across a desert plain to lead to the oasis palmeries of Nkob and Tazzarine.

Back on the road to Zagora, the ksar of Tansikht marks the end of the old territory of the Mezguita. The village of **Oulad Atman** is 14 km south, just on the right of the road, and is dominated by the **kasbah of Dar Caid Arabi**. The use of a few lines of decorative green glazed tiles on this kasbah echoes the colour and shape of palm fronds which is the origin of this decorative style. On the opposite bank you can see the **village and kasbah of Takhite**. A little further at **Idgaoun** you will get your first view of the high truncated pyramid form of the kasbah towers, prevalent in the southern Draa.

Tinzouline is the largest village between Agdz and Zagora. It has a couple of roadside cafés and a colourful **souk** on Mondays. The whole village is ringed with kasbahs in various forms of growth and decay. Inquisitive drivers could follow the sign post to some two-thousand-year-old Libyo–Phoenician rock inscriptions, 7 km down a track to the west of the village.

Azlag

The pass of Azlag lies 25 km north of Zagora. This miniature gorge marks the entry into the palmery of Ternata, the territory of the Arabic-speaking Oulad Yahia and Roha tribes.

Zagora

Zagora was founded on the western bank of the Draa by a tribe of pure Arabs in the 13th century, though on the eastern side of the river there is evidence of a much earlier foundation. An extensive ruined 11th-century Almoravide fortress clings to an extraordinary black volcanic core, Djebel Zagora, a burnt sugarloaf of a mountain that rises up from a green bed of palms.

The modern settlement of Zagora is an uninspiring dusty length of street. It is however the ideal base from which to explore the surrounding palmeries and ksour which are of such interest and charm that you become almost fond of the town itself.

GETTING AROUND
Buses leave for Ouazazarte at 7.00 and 17.00, tickets cost 29dh, whilst a place in a grand taxi should cost only 35dh with the advantage that you can leave at any time of the day. All the town cafés, the Post Office, Banque Populaire, cheap hotels and restaurants are on the main street, the Av. Mohammed V which culminates in the Cercle, the administrative offices of the Supercaid of Zagora. In front of the entrance to the Cercle is the well-photographed sign, 'Timbuctoo 52 days by camel' which, due to an impassable frontier, has not been possible in the last 25 years. It was the route of the Saadian expedition, 'the army of the day' that conquered Timbuctoo in 1591.

The older low pise houses of Zagora are found by the thin strip of palmery that borders the Draa river bank. The road south crosses the river bed of the Draa on a bridge just south of the Cercle.

Djebel Zagora

Having won control of the desert tribes, the founder of the Almoravide movement, Ibn Yacin, first advanced north to strike against the Emir of Sigilmassa, by Rissani in the Tafilalet. By 1050 he controlled the Draa and the Tafilalet oasis but after an early rebellion against his puritan rule he established two fortresses, one in the Tafilalet and one on the slopes of Djebel Zagora.

The 11th-century **Almoravide stone fortress** still hugs the face of Djebel Zagora, a rare surviving monument from this dynasty, for the Almohads systematically destroyed any evidence of their predecessors. The quadrangular outer stone wall and interior cisterns can be visited by crossing the Draa bridge and turning sharply left on the way to the Camping Montagne.

A military post on top of Djebel Zagora stops you climbing to the summit of this dominant black outcrop. You can however climb high enough to enjoy an excellent view of the green palmery which snakes north and south, encrusted with ksour and hemmed in by hills. To the north you should be able to look over Djebel Rhart to see the peaks of Djebel Saghro, whilst to the south the escarpment of Djebel Bani rises out of an adjacent plain. Dawn or dusk allows you the clearest view before the sun drains both you and the colour of the sky.

Amazrou

South of the bridge is the palmery and ksar of Amazrou which offers a delightful shaded place in which to walk. Paths from the **Camping D'Amazrou** and the **Hôtel La Fibule Du Draa** fan out at random through the pise walled plots of barley and vegetables overhung with fronds of strong palm. In the village your hand will be charmingly but

440

firmly seized and a child will lead you to the Jews' kasbah and the sand dunes before escorting you home for mint tea. Jewelry or carpets may be offered for sale but with such graceful artistry that salesmanship approaches a court ritual. You may at the very least find yourself walking away with the profiles of gazelle, camel and hares made by children out of twisted and matted palm leaves.

The souk

The Zagora market occurs on Wednesdays and Sundays to the north of the town where there is also a modern date trading cooperative. The dates of Zagora and the Draa are excellent and the date sellers will allow you to taste from the many different qualities and varieties. Ask for 'boufeggous', which is renowned for both its sweetness and long storage life. The salt miners of Taghaza, in the central Sahara, used to live off an exclusive diet of Draa dates and corn though they all starved when no caravan could reach the outpost for several years.

Opposite the Tinsouline Hotel there are a few jewelry stalls which sell the distinctive indigo dyed cotton cloth of the blue men and the bright embroidered black shawls of the women. The Moussem of Moulay Abdelkader Jilali is celebrated at Zagora at the same time as the feast of Mouloud, the prophet's birthday.

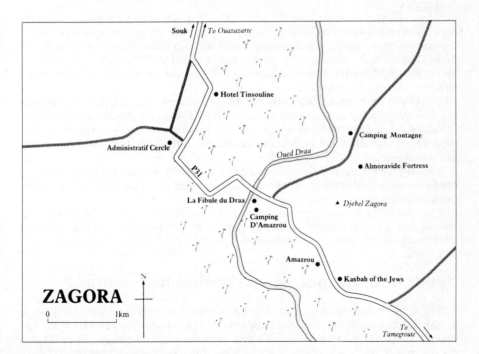

WHERE TO STAY AND EAT

The *** **Tinsouline Hôtel** has a pleasantly faded pink kasbah design and a pool, garden courtyards and rooms overlooking some palmery gardens below. The entrance is well signposted and just off Av. Mohammed V. The hotel water tower provides an excellent view of Zagora, and the hotel is relatively peaceful as the new four-star hotel is drawing off the bulk of the coach parties. There are 90 rooms, at 200dh a double, tel 22.

La Fibule du Draa is just out of Zagora, on the right having crossed the bridge south of town. It is a restaurant with a few beautifully appointed rooms that share a communal shower. The garden is set on the edge of the Amazrou palmery and has a tent and pavilion. 20 more rooms are being built to a restrained and harmonious design. It is well worth booking one of the 45dh rooms in advance, tel 118.

On Av. Mohammed V you will find a number of simple hotels. The best of this bunch is either the * **Vallee du Draa**, which has 14 rooms and a bar, tel 10, or the **Hôtel Palmerie**, which has a reliable water supply and rents a three-bed room for 92dh, or lets you sleep on the roof terrace for only 5dh.

The new **** **PLM Hôtel Club Reda** has just been finished, its plush fittings enclosing a central courtyard with four pools. The interior, particularly the domed hall, is not a success and though there is no reason to stay here, a 35dh breakfast in the courtyard allows you to watch a fluttering of pink and white maids.

Camping

In a depression on the edge of the Amazrou palmery, just beyond La Fibule du Draa, is the **Camping d'Amazrou**, 5dh per person, 3dh per tent. Slightly less popular, but with considerably more space, less shade and better facilities is the **Camping de la Montagne de Zagora**. It costs the same amount and you will find it 1 km beyond the bridge, first right. Camels for the desert tours are stabled here, and the Almoravide fortress is in view.

The **Hôtel Restaurant des Amis**, the **Hôtel Palmerie** and the **Hôtel Vallee du Draa** all serve good cheap meals for around 25dh with beer, on street tables in the centre of Zagora. There are a few basic grill cafés deeper in the town towards the river bank, but the **Hôtel Tinsouline** and **La Fibule du Draa** do provide the best environment for eating in Zagora.

The licensed dining room in the Tinsouline is hung with the work of Fatima Hassani, one of the most celebrated contemporary naive artists in Morocco, and the four course menu costs 80dh.

The service in the unlicensed La Fibule du Draa is relaxed, but the delicious spiced tagines, salads and fruit juices eaten in the garden are well worth the wait. Dinner costs 49dh and breakfast 10dh.

South from Zagora: Tamegroute and M'hamid

22 km south of Zagora on pot-holed tarmac is the unpretentious looking village and zaouia of Tamegroute. It was a celebrated centre of Islamic learning as early as the 11th century, part of the reforming impulse which, further south in the Sahara, exploded into the Almoravide movement. By the late 15th century the Saadian sheiks were the masters

of the Sufi lodge at Tamegroute, whence they travelled north to Taroudant to organize the jihad against Portugal.

A koranic school was reestablished here in the 17th century by Abou Abdallah Mohammed Bou Naceur, who assembled a great library for his students. The school still functions as part of a national system of theological colleges and Tamegroute is an acknowledged centre for the widespread Naciri Sufi brotherhood.

Modern classrooms, a 20th-century concrete **medersa**, the desiccated walled garden of the college and the ancient **library** are easily found in the centre of this small settlement. The library contains a wonderful collection of Koranic commentaries, law books, astronomical guides, histories of Fez, dictionaries and tomes on mathematics. Some of the volumes are over 700 years old whilst a few are written on gazelle vellum with rich ornate decorative gilding and generations of marginal notes and references in coloured inks. The Arabic script runs from the back of the books to the front, and from right to left across the pages. This, and the wallet-like protective leather bindings are the distinctive Islamic features of this collection.

It is rare to be given access to religious buildings in Morocco. At Tamegroute you are allowed to visit the library and the courtyard that surrounds the freshly restored tomb of the founder where they are also busy restoring the mosque. The medieval mixture of scholarship and faith here is reinforced by charity. The ill and mad collect around the founder's tomb both for a cure and for their subsistence. The large house above the koubba is still lived in by the descendants of the founder, and from its ornate grill windows the reclusive saintly women of the house watch the celebrations of the annual Naciri moussem.

There is also a **pottery** in Tamegroute. The products are primitive and solid in design, but finished with an attractive irregular green glaze that suggests both palm trees and the banners of Islam. A market is held on Saturdays and you can eat well at either the roadside **Restaurant de l'Oasis**, or the **Restaurant du Draa**.

Tinfou

Tinfou and its sand dunes lie 7 km south of Tamegroute. Here you will find the **Auberge Repos-Sable Tinfou**, owned by two of Morocco's leading artists, Fatima Hassani of Tetouan and her husband, Hassan el Farrouj of Salé, and run by their son. It has a plunge pool and some traditional rooms off the main courtyard to rent for 30dh; the walls are covered in paintings and tagines are available at all hours of the day. The sand dunes, reached down the neighbouring dirt track, are best climbed at dawn or dusk, in bare feet, but are not comparable in extent with the Erg Chebbi, east of Erfoud.

M'hamid

To cross Djebel Bani from Tinfou and visit M'hamid, the end of the Draa and an historically important post on the Saharan trade route, you require an official guide and the permission of the Supercaid at Zagora. The guides cost 50dh a visit and permission is given by a Ministry of the Interior official in an office that holds files with intriguing titles like 'political parties'. The town taxis charge 300dh for a return trip to M'hamid.

M'hamid is the very last gasp of fertility from the Draa. It used to be an important market for the nomadic tribes, and an oasis staging post for trans-Saharan trade. The creation of closed national borders and the continuing tension between Morocco and Algeria has turned it into a dead end. Even in 1965 it boasted some magnificent and ancient kasbahs, but it is difficult to square these descriptions with the modern desolate and wistful outpost and one has to assume that border skirmishes destroyed these monuments. Windblown sand seems to be rapidly burying the palmery and piles up against the low mean houses. The three old courtyards for the **Monday market** still exist below the dozen official buildings and a greater extent of sprawling pise huts to the south. Of the three restaurants the **Sahara** is the only one open, stocked with tins and lethargy, and it is forbidden to stay here for the night.

The Saadian Sultan Ahmed el Mansour (1578–1602) kept a garrison of Christian renegades here at the Ksar Ksebt el Allouj as a link with his garrison at Timbuctu on the Niger river. Lektawa, a settlement further south of M'hamid where the gold dust of Wangara, brought across the Sahara during Ahmed el Mansour's reign, was minted into dirhams, no longer exists.

King Mohammed V made clear Morocco's claim to the Sahara in a speech at M'hamid in 1958 at a time when the French still occupied Algeria. It was once symbolically attacked by rockets from the Polisario in 1980, and here one gets a sense of the ageless quality of desert life: great heat, little water, a sense of exterior menace, life restricted to the confines of an oasis controlled then as now by armed men. Of the golden trade of the Moors, of caravans protected by hired nomads, there is no trace.

To get there, follow the road out of Tinfou, as it surprisingly ignores the breach in the mountain made by the Draa and climbs over the Djebel Bani to the west before descending into the plain. The Ksour of **Nesrate** and **Beni Hayoun** are tucked in the great expanse of palms to the east of the road.

Tagounite is a dusty modern settlement set in a hard baked plateau. It has an impressive market area on the right as you pass the town gates and a **souk** on Monday and Thursday, when you can buy a meal in one of the town cafés.

Out of Tagounite you climb another spur of the Bani mountain chain at the Tizi Beni-Selmand. A piste track, currently forbidden, at the northern face leads on your left to the ancient Berber **necropolis of Foum Mja**, whose mortuary houses date back to 800 BC. The pass is commanded by a ruined tower and a black stone agadir is visible on your left. Descending you enter the Mhamid el Ghouzlane, the plain of the gazelles, and reach the palmery and ksar of **Oulad Driss** whose pise walls are in immaculate condition. 15 kms further south lies M'hamid.

Expeditions from Zagora

Camel trips
The hotels in Zagora all arrange a number of short-range camel trips. There are two basic varieties: a day trip to the sand dunes outside Amazrou or an evening ride over nearby hills to a bonfire-lit tent where dinner is prepared and musical entertainment provided. Prices should be bargained for. La Fibule du Draa offers a whole day's ride for 150dh, or 250dh for an evening ride and dinner, not unreasonable prices providing you realize you are paying for entertainment that is not too adventurous.

Desert Crossings

It is advisable to check with the police at Zagora who will tell you if you need the caid's permission to travel. At the moment anyone can travel east, but restrictions may apply in moving west. The only route that it is possible to hitch a lift from passing trucks on is east from Tansikht on the Draa to Rissani in the Tafilalet, passing through Tazzarine and Alnif. In all of these there are cafés in which to sip tea while waiting. To make this journey you can also book a 120dh place in a landrover at your hotel. It leaves from the vegetable souk on Wednesday afternoon, arrives at **Rissani** by midnight so that you are there for the Thursday **souk**.

Travelling by car it is wise to have two spare tyres, all official papers, something to dig with, sleeping bags, your own picnic supplies and plenty of water. A compass and map may sound a little melodramatic when you are merely following a dirt road but sand storms can quickly obscure the tracks and leave you completely disorientated. Every year about half a dozen tourists die in the Moroccan and Tunisian Sahara. Curiously enough drowning in desert flash floods exceeds death by dehydration.

West to Tazenakht

If you want to avoid returning through the Draa to Ouazazarte on your way to Taroudant or Agadir, you can try the partly tarmaced journey from Zagora to **Tazenakht** on the Taroudant/Ouazazarte road. It is normally possible, even in a hired Renault 4, though as far as the village of Bleida the road can be soft. Once you pass Bleida the going is comparatively good with tarmac after the village of Arhbar taking you up to Tazenakht.

To Tata (254 km)

The routes from Zagora and especially Tagounite have, due to the desert war, been closed to normal traffic for many years now, which makes this newly accessible route all the more attractive to attempt. The long range of the Djebel Bani is the dominant feature of the journey, broken by the old tributaries of the Draa to provide a few inhabitable oases.

Foum-Zguid is the first breach in the mountain wall, 124 km west of Zagora. You can catch a lorry here on Sunday or Wednesday from Zagora for 40dh. It is the southernmost administrative village of a group of ksour that occupy a palmery. It has a **souk** on Thursdays, a café with rooms and a police passport check. Buses leave here on Tuesdays, Thursdays and Saturdays for Tazenakht and on to Ouazazarte. The nearby **Ksar of Smira** has a **souk** on Mondays.

After Foum-Zguid the piste track follows the 800 m deep breach in Djebel Bani cut by the Oued Zguid to travel on the southern face of the mountains. 52 km further along the Zguid river bed is the oasis of **Mrimina**, and its **shrine of Sidi Ahmed ou Mohand**. The piste then follows the Oued Tissint to the **Tissint** breach where five ksour guard their famously delicious date palms. Passing through the rock canyons of the Tissint breach, the track takes you 20 km on before you reach the **Kasbah of Joua**. 15 km on from Joua is the little oasis community of **Akka Iguiren**, which has two rival villages in their separate ksars. If you want a detour you could try the very rough track that leads north for 40 km past the Koubba of Sidi Bou Tazert to the much larger palmery of **Akka**

Irhen. Here there is a well preserved agadir, a koubba in the cemetery and a Glouai-built kasbah, where the caids posted their representative to rule and tax the far-flung oases after they had rebelled in the late 1920s.

Back to Akka Iguiren it is only 30 km to Tata, which lies on the tarmac road that runs between Taroudant and Bou-Izakarn (see Tata for details).

East of Zagora

This provides a number of interesting alternatives which are all currently open.

A rough track suitable for landrovers starts just south of Djebel Zagora and continues up the less visited eastern bank of the Draa to rejoin the tarmac road at the Tansikht bridge. Portions of this or the whole 100 km can be arranged through the hotels. La Fibule du Draa does a day tour for 150dh.

Tazzarine Oasis

A circuitous loop through Tazzarine Oasis from Zagora to Tansikht is an excellent introduction to desert travel. 87 km of rough track east of Zagora leads to Tazzarine, including an awkward climb up the Tizi-n-Tafilalet, just passable in a Renault 4. As an added incentive, by the village of Ait Ouazik there is a dry valley reportedly containing over 200 rock carvings, but if you want to be sure of finding these you would be wise to hire a guide. Tazzarine is charming. It has a petrol station and you can stay in the **Café Hôtel Bougafer Tazzarine** for 40dh a night.

The enchanting oasis palmeries of **Mellal** and **Nekob** lie on the road west to Tansikht, below the massive Djebel Saghro. Back from Nekob the road to Tansikht is good, the last 20 km tarmaced.

Alternatively, continue east of Tazzarine on the flat rather featureless plain to **Rissani**, stopping at the **Alnif oasis** where there is a café and a military checkpoint. From Alnif you continue under the foothills of Djebel Ougnat passing through Achbarou and Mecissi. This is certainly an exciting way of approaching the Tafilalet, although the old caravan routes ran slightly further south, on a line Zagora–Tissemoumine–Fezzou–Mecissi.

The Dades Valley

Pay no attention to petulant tourists who claim that once you've seen one kasbah you've seen them all. Each oasis valley has a distinctive character but you cannot expect to appreciate this by merely staring through the windows of a passing car or bus. Be prepared to break your journey, taking it easy during the middle of the day but walking along the river bed during the perfect conditions of early morning and dusk.

The Dades is known, by promotional brochures if no one else, as the valley of a thousand kasbahs. For settlement takes the pattern of family based kasbahs scattered along the fertile bed of the river, rather than fortified village ksour sited at regular intervals above the palmeries. A wider belt of cultivable land also robs it of the exotic constriction of the Ziz, Draa or the Tafilalet. The Dades, apart from this greater feeling of space, is also a busier and more commercially successful valley. It harbours a greater diversity of crops, employment and a steady population level of 80,000. More than this the valley alone retains a geographical relevance as an east–west transport route which has been denied the other valleys since the closing of the Saharan border.

A large proportion of the Dades kasbahs are in a high state of ruin but these can be compared with the few that have been kept in perfect condition and remain in active use. Increasingly, the population has moved from the valley floor and lives in modern villages beside the road. The new houses are just saved from box-like blandness by pleasant little decorative embellishments, odd cornices and battlements which have been inherited from kasbah architecture.

Of all the southern oasis valleys, the Dades has the most undisturbed pattern of Berber settlement. The women have a brightly coloured diversity of dress and ornament but some of this may be hidden by the heavy dark blue cotton haiks of the region. The High Atlas slopes to the north of the Dades were the grazing ground of warlike Berber nomads that were never subdued. So whilst Arab tribes ruled the population of the Dades, from the 13th to the 16th centuries, they never felt secure enough to settle here permanently themselves. The same pattern was repeated when the Ait Atta confederacy emerged dominant in the 16th century. The Ait Alouane, a sub-tribe of the Ait Atta, garrisoned key kasbahs in the Dades valley but could never relax their guard or expand to the north for the land was defended by their fierce rivals, the Ait Yafalman confederacy. Both Berber tribal confederacies buried their rivalry in order to resist the French throughout the 1920s and 1930s.

The Dades valley starts as a mountain stream running south from the peaks of the High Atlas, cutting the Dades gorge before it is forced to flow west to Ouazazarte by the rising mass of Djebel Saghro. It has cut a deep but broad river bed through this high land mass where a continuous oasis culture exists. The road, although it travels beside the valley, largely passes along on the flat and dull surface of a sub-Saharan plain.

Setting out east from Ouazazarte the main road, the P32, nears the Dades at the town of **Skoura**, then misses the valley until it approaches the town of **El Kelaa des Mgouna**. From here it runs above but in view of the valley until Boumalne du Dades where the road forks, north up the Dades gorge or continues east to Tinerhir. Stopping at Skoura, El Kelaa des Mgouna and the Dades gorge would provide a good basic itinerary. Even if you hate kasbahs have a look at the Dades Gorge.

East from Ouazazarte

The 42 km journey from Ouazazarte to Skoura on the P32 skirts across an uninspiring sub-Saharan plain. The only break is a right turn, 19 km out of town that leads up to the **Restaurant du Lac** which is open from May to September. It has a commanding view over the lake and of a kasbah occasionally marooned by the rising water on the end of a peninsula. As you approach Skoura the road passes close to the Dades valley—a good opportunity to stop for a five-minute walk up through the palmery to visit a magnificent pile—the **kasbah of Amerhidil**—on the left bank of the river, an example of the distinctive local style of thin tapering towers.

Around Skoura

Few people break their journey at Skoura, just off the road to the left, despite the chance to wander along the maze of paths that thread through pise walls and shaded palmeries to a number of kasbahs. It is a new town built on an ancient site between two tributaries of the Dades just before they converge on the main Dades river bed. Though geographically close it is completely removed from the half glamour and slick tourist hotels of Ouazazarte. Skoura has just one unclassified hotel, the **Nakhil** which charges 25dh for a single room and provides cheap but not elaborate meals. A **souk** is held here in a cluster of bamboo stalls on Monday and Thursday.

Aiso, 'the ape man of Skoura' used to be the prime attraction. He was a small, imbecilic and impotent creature with a large nose, heavy brow ridge and a winning smile. He would not suffer any clothes and remained perfectly happy running through the palmery with the village dogs. A succession of well-intentioned tourists presented Aiso with clothes, blankets, money and food which, although he had no regard for them, made him many friends in the village. Sacheverell Sitwell in 1938 immediately recognized Aiso as, 'something of a familiar type, known as pin head' amongst old wealthy families. He was not a missing evolutionary link but a degenerate of siphilitic forebears.

Sipping a cup of mint tea on the tables outside the Hotel Nakhil you will be able to recruit a local guide. Ask to be taken on a tour of the immediate surrounding kasbahs: **Aichal, Ait Sidi el Mati, El Kebbaba** and the maraboutic **fortress of Sidi Mbarek ou Ali** with a distinctive koubba. There are also the two kasbahs the Glaoui built here, the **Dar Toundut** and **Dar Lahsoune**.

To the south of Skoura a dirt track, the 6843, climbs for 40 km through the bleak twisted hills of the Djebel Saghro massif to the mine of Bou Skour. This is an arduous one-way journey that will take you deep into the original core territory of the Ait Atta tribe. The track also provides an hour walk to **Sidi Flah**, the central hamlet astride the Dades river bed.

To the north of Skoura there are two even more adventurous possibilities. A dirt track, the 6829, follows one of the old and most difficult of the caravan crossings of the High Atlas—the Tiz-n-Fedbral—between Skoura and Demnate. **Ait Souss** is just outside Skoura but 40 km later even a landrover will have difficulty in climbing the entrance to the pass, north of the mountain village of **Assermo**.

For an even more rewarding trip below the valleys and foothills of Djebel Ighil M'Goun (4071 m), follow a 100 km circuit of route 6831 which would bring you back on to the Dades valley at **El Kelaa des Mgouna**. For this you would need a landrover but some indication of the country can be had by travelling the first and easiest 25 km to look at the hilltop agadirs and kasbahs of the Ait Yafalman around the villages of **Toundoute** and **Tabia Ait Zaghar**. The track leads off to the right just after Skoura on the main road to El Kelaa des Mgouna.

East of Skoura the P32 draws away from the Dades to cross the Tiz-n-Taddert pass, 1370 m. After this there is a fine cluster of kasbahs to be seen around **Imassine**, which is 20 km from Skoura. A further 22 km of dull road follows before reaching the **kasbah of Ait Ridi** which marks the entrance into the wide and fertile river beds of the Dades and its tributary the Oued M'Goun. The ksar **Ait Ba Ahmed** guards the bridge over the Oued M'Goun whose banks are lined by terraced fields of vegetables, plots of barley shaded by almond trees and divided by low rambling hedges of rose bushes. Almonds have supplanted palm now for the valley, not much below 1500 m here, is too high and cold in the winter for palms to be successfully grown. 10 km beyond the bridge you travel into the midst of the valley to approach the town of El Kelaa des Mgouna.

El Kelaa des Mgouna

The town sits at the foot of a bluff of rock that separates the two verdant valley floors of Dades and M'Goun. It is the base for some dramatic opportunities to explore the hinterland of mountains and kasbahs but is itself an uninspiring and inoffensive roadside settlement. A **souk** is held on Wednesday but you can buy the local rosewater at any time of the day or week from shops whose shelves are filled with little else.

Roses are grown as hedgerows that divide up the gardens of the valley and their flowers are harvested in May, when a celebratory harvest fête is held. Over 700 tons of petals are picked every year and then processed in the modern rosewater factory camouflaged as a kasbah, a disguise that is only spoiled by two chimneys that emerge to be seen to the right as you travel east from El Kelaa. Rosewater is exported as the basic stock for many scents and prized as a formal handwash throughout the Islamic world.

Tours from El Kelaa des Mgouna

The **Roses du Dades Hotel** organizes an hour tour of the finest local kasbahs for 100dh. A whole-day tour, taking from 9.00–15.30 with a minimum of 6 people costs 350dh each, and a two-day ride, visiting numerous villages, kasbahs and including dinner, entertainments and a bed in the kasbah Taourirte costs 550dh.

Directly opposite the Café Rendezvous des Amis on the main road is the **Bureau des Guides et Accompagnateurs**. The office is bedecked with maps, piles of equipment and is run by a group of young Moroccans as a cooperative. They organize three basic expeditions. The M'Goun Gorge tour, due north from El Kelaa, spends eight days in the mountains and walks an average of about 20 km a day. The Djebel Saghro, due south, is a seven-day expedition that is only attractive in the cooler season, any time between October and April. The southern High Atlas is the reverse for it is only open in the summer, after the snow has melted, between March and September. Costs are 175dh a day for the guide, 80dh for a mule and muleteer and 145dh a day for food and lodging. These three trips are obviously best organized well in advance but shorter cheaper walks can be arranged at short notice. Address: Bureau des Guides, Djebel Saghro, El Kelaa des Mgouna Centre, Ouazazarte.

If you are short of time and money and want a quick feel of the surrounding countryside, walk a little way north of the town to the **Glaoui kasbah**, which is perched on a dramatic outcrop of rock and commands the entrance to Bou Tharar and the M'Goun gorge. Or ask to rent a mule—by far the best way to explore the upstream of the Dades valley.

WHERE TO STAY
Les Roses du Dades, tel 18, is the only, rather expensive, hotel in El Kelaa des Mgouna. Its modern silhouette crowns the rocky bluff above the town, defiantly out of

harmony with the rest of valley. Nor has it aged particularly well, but once inside the hotel the magnificent views, its corral of elegant horses, sheltered swimming pool and bar rapidly win you over. A beer costs 12dh, a double room 230dh.

Travelling east from El Kelaa, new roadside villages predominate, though there are some wonderful old relics scattered along the valley floor. Notable are the **Kasbah El Goumt** and the collection of kasbahs that overlook **Souk Khemis du Dades**, although neither are accessible from the road without a scramble.

Boumalne du Dades

The main attraction of the small administrative town of Boumalne du Dades is its transport facilities for the Dades Gorge. It lies just beyond the turning to the Gorge, over a bridge which crosses the Dades.

A pleasant yellow and white arcade shades a row of shops and cafés which overlook the fertile valley. In 1937 Boumalne consisted of just a fort, a café and a brothel. For some the attractions of the town might just have diminished since then but the **Café Atlas**, by the covered Wednesday **souk**, is still the place to stop for tea. On the hill above the town a range of administrative offices face out, in some vision from Kafka, on to an empty dreary desert plain beyond.

The local cemetery holds the tomb of the ascetic Sidi Daoud, who lived in Ouazazarte from 1822 to 1859 but returned to Boumalne to die. On the first anniversary of his death pilgrims left palm branches over his grave but these were turned into angry hissing snakes. The frightened pilgrims correctly divined the cause of the saint's anger and promptly raised a koubba over his grave. Every year at the time of his festival flour is left at the head of the grave for three days. It is then baked and fed by the saint's female devotees to their husbands to assure fertility.

WHERE TO STAY
It is cheaper and considerably more entertaining to stay in the Dades gorge. The best hotel in Boumalne is the *** **Hôtel Al Madayeq**, tel 31, which has a pool, bar and restaurant. A double room costs 265dh. The hotel terrace has a view over the sturdy simple kasbahs on the valley floor but its interior is chiefly remarkable for a small glass viewing window in the side of the pool. Dwarfed by the hotel is a neighbouring restaurant, the diminutive but well signposted **Soleil Bleu**.

The **Shell garage** on the way out of town to the east lets out a few basic rooms as does the **Café Bou Gafer**. Both charge 45dh for a double room.

The Dades Gorge

To get to the Dades gorge retrace you steps west from Boumalne along the P32. Take the turn to the north signposted 'Mserhir' beside the bridge over the Dades, about 500 m from town. Bus rides cost 16dh for the two-hour journey and usually leave at 14.00 from Boumalne to Msemrir. Alternatively you can take a taxi or negotiate a lift in a truck.

This part of the valley has a relaxed air with none of the daily hassle that you may have become used to. The few cheap hotels all serve good dishes from fresh local produce and are locked in amicable competition with each other. If you have time this is a place to stay rather than just visit.

The gorge itself lies 25 km up from the turning, but the valley which leads to it is certainly as interesting. It has been described as a sabre cut in the High Atlas—a long verdant river bed surrounded by scarlet scarred slopes. The brilliant range of red and cardamine soils contrast with a golden backdrop of denuded treeless hills. It is too high for palm trees but almond and walnut provide shade for the intensely worked gardens.

Six km from the entrance of the valley you pass a ruined kasbah used by the Glaoui caid of the valley. The **Café Meguirne**, 14 km along the road, run by Hassani Haddou and his young brother, marks the approach to the **Kasbah of the Rocks**. This approach to the series of Ait Atta kasbahs is dominated by dark red eroded volcanic rocks which change their shape, form and character at different angles and distances. At first they are a great barrage of aggressive points angled menacingly at the sky in some cartoonist's image of massed arsenals of ballistic missiles. They alter as you dip down into the green valley floor becoming increasingly phallic, a monstrous exhibition of lingham totems. This too melts before your eyes, dwindling to sprouting mushrooms before taking on the contours of a brain that finally suggests a placenta bed. It is with some relief that eroded golden limestone cliffs further up the valley are content to assume the form of sacred hawks and mother goddesses astride gaping caves.

The **kasbahs of the Ait Atta** stand below the volcanic rocks and look fragile and impudent beneath such a powerful and massive natural formation. Their walls imitate perfectly the colours of the surrounding soil, topped with delicate towers lanced by double window frames, their summits crowned with corner battlements. It is a place of obsessive beauty and form, a place to plan picnics amongst the hanging rocks, to sketch and to dream.

The maraboutic **ksar Ait Ali** lies 3 km before the bridge over the Dades at **Ait Oudinar** which marks the end of the tarmac, 23 km up the valley. A little further up the road the river emerges from the gorge and a tributary joins the Dades. The gorge's floor is taken up by the river bed and makes a delightful cool walk, wading upstream with the narrow walls of rock looming above and cutting out the fierce sun.

A good gravel road continues above the gorge to **Msemrir**. The gorge is hidden for about 5 km and the climb up a number of hairpin bends to **Imiadzen** is rewarding for the views back over the valley rather than for the chance to stare down into the gorge. Imiadzen has a café and is 7 km beyond the gorge entrance.

WHERE TO STAY

By the Rock of the Kasbahs is the **Tamlatte Hôtel** which has the best view in the area and hires basic rooms for 17dh, a double for 28dh. The **Hôtel Kasbah de la Vielle Tradition** is just 100 yards before the Tamlatte. It has a spacious hall, above which hangs a balcony and a few clean simple rooms with cane ceilings. A double room costs 25dh.

At Ait Oudinar, just by the bridge, is the **Auberge des Gorges du Dades** run by Haj Zahir Youssef. The food is excellent, a tagine costs 20dh and ask for goat's cheese from the patron's herd. A double room costs 30dh and camping space is available on earth beside the river.

451

Right beside the gorge entrance is the **Camping Tesorin** which also rents a few rooms for 25dh. Opposite is the **Hôtel La Kasbah**, run by Saabi Hammou, a friendly place which leans against the rock wall. A double room and dinner both cost 30dh.

The Battle of Bou Gafer and the Ait Atta

The road east from Boumalne to Tinerhir, 53 km, crosses a featureless desert plain.

For the adventurous, just out of the town of Boumalne on the right is a rough track (route 6907) which leads off into the Saghro mountains. The town of **Iknioun** is the administrative and market centre for the whole desolate mountain region, and from it another dirt track, route 6909 takes you down to Tinerhir. However, heading east out of Iknioun on the 6908 you should reach the village and copper mines of **Moudou**, from which, if you ask for a guide and a mule, you can make the one-day journey to the battlefield of Bou Gafer, although you should be prepared to camp.

The Ait Atta, lords of the oasis valleys for three centuries, were the last of all the tribes of Morocco to surrender to the French invaders. 25 years after the original Casablanca landings, the French army opposed the two brothers, Hammou and Hassou Ba Selam, who led the Ait Atta tribe at their ancestral mountain stronghold of Bou Gafer. For a whole month, 1000 Ait Atta warriors resisted the assaults, the bombardments and the aerial bombings of the French before falling to the final assault of the Foreign Legion on 25 March 1934. The ground is still covered with the debris of the month-long battle, which is remembered with pride every year by an official celebration in Ouazazarte.

Back on the Boumalne–Tinerhir road the plain is broken by two oases. **Imiter** is the most appealing, 20 km to the east with its oasis dominated by a ksar of over a thousand inhabitants and a separate group of associated outlying kasbahs. An Ait Atta oasis, **Timatrouine**, lies 10 km further on, 23 km before Tinerhir.

Tinerhir and the Todra Gorge

Tinerhir may at first seem just one of a string of dusty administrative centres and indeed a consistent feature of the town is wind coming off the mountains and whipping up small whirlwinds of sand. It is, however, an old and well established town, with a mixed population of farmers and craftsmen, on a high bank of the Oued Todra where the river leaves the protective folds of the High Atlas and flows out across the mountain plateau. At 1350 m, Tinerhir looks over a magnificent dense palmery. This band of vegetation hugs the river bed and leads 12 km north of Tinerhir to the celebrated canyon of the Todra Gorge. The gorge, a dramatic geological rift in the mountains, is the destination for most travellers, but the town and the palmery have their own, more delicate charms.

GETTING AROUND
Tinerhir is 169 km from Ouazazarte and 141 km from Er-Rachidia. Buses and taxis all arrive and depart from the central arcaded garden square, Place Principale. There are two CTM buses to Ouazazarte a day, currently leaving at 9.00 and 16.00 on a journey which takes five hours and costs 32dh. There is one bus a day to Er-Rachidia leaving at 14.00, which costs 18dh for the three-hour ride.

Travel to the neighbouring towns of Boumalne or Tinejdad by a place in a grand taxi. A taxi ride up the valley to Todra Gorge should be 7dh per person. Mules can be rented, ask at the hotels, and think in terms of 10dh an hour.

Tourist Information: The Banque Populaire is on Blvd Mohammed V, the name the P32 assumes in town, and Tinerhir's **souk** is held on Tuesdays.

WHAT TO SEE

The Kasbah

The ruined Glaoui kasbah still dominates the town from its hill to the west. Two great keeps are surrounded by outer yards and the whole wrapped up in a curtain wall. It was a deliberately palatial structure, built to overawe and impress the hostile natives. Their behaviour to some extent mirrored the kasbah, and the Ait Atta tribe, when they finally succumbed to the French in 1934, asked only that they be not governed by the hated Glaoui. Increasingly ruined, covered in debris and slogans, it is a powerful image of the mighty French allies fallen. The severe lines of the whitewashed courtyard pillars now dribble with soluble mud stains. The confident grandeur is now mocked by scrawling graffiti.

The kasbah is bricked up once a year, but local boys make a new entrance in order to use the sheltered courtyard for football and you may have to grub around a little to find their new hole. The view of the palmery from the kasbah, or from the neighbouring Saghro Hotel looks out on to one of the largest and richest oasis of the Moroccan south.

The town

Behind the Todgha Hotel on the Place Principal in Tinerhir, an animated network of streets leads down to the river bed. You pass the hiring corner where journeymen sit behind their trade tools, and descend downhill past booths of native jewelry. Tinerhir's most characteristic product is the small delicate wrought iron grilles that decorate and protect local windows. Every stage of manufacture has a cluster of workshops with forges twisting, shaping and fixing before passing their work on to the framers and carpenters. As you descend, the town sheds its regularity to blend effortlessly into the confused patchwork of the palmery gardens and orchards.

The palmery

Entering the palmery from the heat, dust and light of a desert day you pass into a different environment. It is easy and pleasant to loose yourself amongst the palmery paths, absorbing the different quality of colour, odour and the flickering density of light. At dusk, the range of colour in the mud pise walls of the kasbahs and the renewed energy of the inhabitants creates a brief but glorious pageant.

The palmery is populated by the clans of the Ait Atta. With few strong exterior threats, the domestic architecture celebrates the petty feuds of the area symbolized by family-sized fortified kasbahs rather than ksour. Many of them are in good condition and you can hire mules and guides in the town in order to explore them. The **Kasbah of**

Amitane, 6 km north of Tinerhir, has some particularly good Berber brick and tile exterior decoration.

There are some ruined agadirs on the rough hills that overlook the palmery which you will notice from the road, the 6902, to the gorge. 12 km north of Tinerhir the palmery ends at a village built around the **zaouia**, the religious college, **of Sidi Abdelali**. 500 m beyond the zaouia, the water from a spring on the left reputedly cures female infertility.

The Todra Gorge

Shortly beyond this you enter the Todra Gorge, just past the Hôtel El Mansour where the tarmac ends and a gravel track fords the Oued Todra. Following the gravel river bed the massive walls of the gorge rise steeply to cut off the sunlight.

There are two hotels tucked beneath the canyon at its peak height, where two facing cliffs soar and bulge 300 m above them. The grandeur of the cliffs declines quite quickly beyond the hotels, but if you are lucky you can sometimes spot mountain goats and eagles by walking just a short way beyond. As late as 1950 the French Foreign Legion picketed the heights to discourage snipers from picking off tourists. In an attempt to maintain the threat of rural menace and a slight state of suspense amongst walkers, panthers are enthusiastically rumoured to roam the hills.

A spring in front of the hotels flows all the year and harbours some very small shrimps. Try walking up the gorge at night; the contrast of pitch black looming mountain and the sliver of sparkling sky is peculiarly powerful.

Walking to the Dades

Very fit, serious walkers might want to try the mountainous track that connects the Todra and Dades gorges. It is also possible to drive the route in a landrover, though the worst section, from Todra to Tamtattouche, has been worn away in flash floods and is currently pretty bad.

Beyond the Todra Gorge, it is a 16 km walk to an isolated village called **Tam-tattouche**, where a Hotel-Camping-Restaurant receives few visitors, though the patron speaks some French. From here, by turning left you face the most arduous stage of the journey, a 40 km walk to **Msemrir** on the Dades, and have to climb through a 2800 m pass to do so. Msemrir has a café where you can sleep.

From Msemrir, the gravel road to the Dades is in good condition and there is a daily bus to Boumalne or a good chance of a lift. Otherwise it is a mere 18 km to the first hotel at **Ait Toukhsine**.

If you think this is too tame, you could follow the 6902 track 15 km from Tamtattouche to **Ait Hani**, an old ksar of the Ait Haddidou tribe. This dominates an ancient Atlas crossing. With a landrover you could drive the 150 km of mountain tracks across the Tiz-n-Ouano pass at 2706 m, past Imilchil Kasbah and the lakes of Tislit and Isli, before descending to the Hôtel Henri IV at El Ksiba (see page 360). On foot in the summer you may be able to hitch on Berber trucks, but you may find yourself waiting for a couple of days in remote villages.

WHERE TO STAY

The *** **Saghro-KTH** is the most efficient and comfortable hotel in Tinerhir, positioned conspicuously beside the ruins of the hilltop kasbah. Its strong yellow outer walls marry pleasantly with the surrounding ruins. A separate enclosure led to by a covered passage brings you to the windproof open air pool and some surrounding rooms. The hotel, tel 1, has a restaurant, a bar and 65 rooms. A double costs 180dh.

The three cheaper hotels are all found around the square. The ** **Hôtel Togdha**, tel 9, charges 81dh for a double and 68dh for a single. There are 38 rooms, a restaurant, café and a bar. It contains large cool interior public rooms and is decorated with a remarkable false woodland first-floor balcony which overlooks the garden square. The plaster statuary scattered throughout the hotel was made by Bucher, an Austrian who fell in love with a local girl and now lives in Ouazazarte.

The **Hôtel Restaurant Salam** has double rooms for 27dh including working showers, and there is also the **Café Hôtel Oasis**, which has four basic rooms, rented from 25–40dh a night.

The palmery, north of Tinerhir towards the gorge, must be one of the most pleasant places to camp in the south. Gentle cool breezes come off the Atlas to rustle the palm leaves, olives and oleanders. The **Camping Atlas** is the smallest and tidiest of the sites, with raked gravel, two showers and three lavatories. The **Camping du Lac (Garden of Eden)** split off from **The Source of the Sacred Fish Camping** about ten years ago, and has the best café-restaurant. The Source of the Sacred Fish is delightfully unorganized and contains reclusive patches of beaten earth amongst the palms. The site borders the cool clear water of the Oued Todra that issues from the gorge. It received its curious name in an attempt to protect the round tank of pet carp from possible poachers by giving them semi-divine attributes.

If you want to sleep in the palmery but not camp, the **Café-Restaurant Azlag**, just after the bridge, has excellent bedroom views from its few rooms.

You can also stay in one of the three hotels in the gorge. **Hôtel El Mansour**, at the entrance to the gorge, has two palm trees growing through the centre. It is the smallest and most basic place but avoids the sometimes overcheerful tour groups that collect at the other two hotels. A double room costs 35dh.

The **Hôtel des Roches** and the **Hôtel Yasmina** have been in their dramatic position since 1932. The towering rock walls that loom directly above and the spring of fresh water at their foot make them an enticing place to stay. The cleft of sky visible at night, hemmed in by the mountainous walls, appears as a crescent charged with a full field of stars. The generators and tour groups do tend to keep going until 2am however. The des Roches has 10 rooms and charges 20dh for a single and 25dh for a double. The Yasmina charges 30dh a single, 45dh a double or 10dh for sleeping on the roof. Both hotels have showers and basins outside.

For 350dh you can take a day's horse tour inland from the Todra Gorge and every year expensive landrover trips are organized by these hotels to the High Atlas Moussem and Marriage Fair at Imilchil, held in September.

EATING OUT

The **Hôtel Saghro** and **Todgha** have the only licensed restaurants in Tinerhir. **La Gazelle d'Or**, in the central public garden, serves a good couscous or tagine for 20dh. Behind the Togdha Hôtel going down towards the river, the market area contains a number of cheap and good grill cafés. All the campsites have grills going, but the best is the **Camping du Lac**. The **Yasmina** and **Des Roches** hotels in the gorge are both

Sacred Fish Spring, Tinerhir

licensed and serve a three-course Moroccan dinner in their tents or dining rooms for 45dh, whilst the **El Mansour** charges 25dh.

Tinejdad

Tinejdad is 40 km east of Tinerhir. It is the chief village in a scattering of ksour that occupy an area watered by the Oued Todra and known as the palmery of Ferkla. It has always remained free of Arab settlement and is entirely occupied by Berbers and Haratine. The **Ksar Asrir** on the western edge of the palmery is considered one of the finest. Very few people stay here, but if you want to explore a lesser known palmery the **Hôtel Restaurant Tizgui**, run by Brahim and Said, is a clean friendly base and has working showers.

East to Erfoud

From Tinejdad you can go directly to Erfoud, in the Tafilalet oasis, on route 3451, although no bus service covers this road. The **Ksar of Mellab**, 17 km east of Tinejdad, marks the end of the Ferkla palmery, and the landscape turns considerably less interesting.

Tourong, an isolated settlement 20 km later, sits in the midst of a beautiful palmery which has grown on the junction of the water courses of the Oued Todra and the Oued Rheris. The bleak surrounding hills are studded with the ruins of two hill forts and a tower, all that remains of the endless border disputes between the rulers of the Dades and Tafilalet and beside the road a koubba stands guard over a long graveyard of savage black rock head and·foot stones.

After Tourong, small sand dunes drift across the road and whirls of desert dust prepare you for Erfoud. Long lines of feggaguir/foggara, subterranean tunnels collecting the moisture from the soil, seem like giant grey mole hills across the arid plain.

456

19 km before Erfoud you pass through the **palmery of Jorf**, which has a **souk** on Wednesdays. A black stone fort outside the village overlooks the ruins of a grey pise palace with a picturesque chain of three Moorish arches.

Just 11 km from Erfoud lie three beautiful ksour, beside the Oued Rheris. The **oasis of El Bouiya** on your right has a recently discovered Berber necropolis with a stone-built cairn.

East to Er-Rachidia

Alternatively, you continue the 83 km to Er-Rachidia along the P32. The first 24 km to Goulmima is the bleakest passage, but east of there the line of the High Atlas and particularly the summit of Djebel Timetrout marches with you to provide a changing view. Apart from exploring around Goulmima, the isolated oasis **hamlet of Tarda**, a right turn 23 km before Er-Rachidia, would make an interesting picnic spot.

Goulmima

Like Tinejdad, this is a modern village that functions as the local centre for over twenty ksour which occupy the oasis palmery known as **Gheris of Charis**. It is of much less interest than the surrounding hinterland but it does contain a pleasant campsite shaded by eucalyptus trees.

The palmery is watered by the Oued Rheris, for long the fiercely held territory of the Ait Morghad tribe. The ksar towers of this region are noticeably high and strong, a local architectural style that reflects the long struggle against raids by the Ait Atta. The **ksar of Tilioune**, 15 km downstream from Goulmima, is traditionally held by pure Arabs, an odd outpost left behind by the Maql Emirate in this otherwise Berber sea.

To the north in the steep valley cut in the High Atlas by the Rheris are the beautiful but distant **kasbahs of Imiter and Agoudin**. The road north is passable for the first 20 km, to **Tadirhoust**, but gets increasingly rough after this. Imiter lies just down a left turn 35 km later, and Agoudin is a further 23 km on the right. This is, therefore, a mountain track foray only for the well-equipped and kasbah-obsessed.

Er-Rachidia

Like the majority of towns along the P32 in this area, Er-Rachidia is a fairly boring military and administrative centre. Its attraction to tourists is the transport it offers to the Ziz valley and gorge and the Tafilalet oasis and sand dunes to the south. Situated in the middle of the valley of the Ziz, the town first came to prominence as the forward base of the French Foreign Legion in their turn of the century advance from Algeria. Their fortress was known as the Ksar es Souk, after its neighbouring market. To this day, Er-Rachidia retains a military presence, and the one-street town does not even compare favourably with Ouazazarte.

However, there is something to be said for spending a night in Er-Rachidia. An early start gets you to the Ziz Gorge or valley in the cool morning air and its gentle light. The

restful uncompetitive atmosphere of the town may also be welcome before the fren-
eticism of the Tafilalet, and before or after the long journeys to Fez and Figuig.

GETTING AROUND
The bus station, taxi rank and cafés are all easily found on Av. Moulay Ali Cherif. The
bus to Fez, a 12-hr journey, costs 60dh. The bus south to Rissani takes two hours and
costs 12dh. East to Figuig a daily bus currently leaves at 6.00 for 53dh, an 8-hr journey.

WHAT TO SEE
You can take a good walk north from the town towards the Atlas mountains, through
olive groves beside the Oued Ziz, passing the deserted Ksar of Targa, the Ksar of
Azzemour and the Ziz damn finished in 1971. At **Targa**, abandoned like most of the
ksour after the disastrous floods in the 1960s, a red-walled empty mosque looks out high
over the steep bank of the river terrace. Throughout the interior you find the decaying
structure of empty houses, broken pillars and olive presses. The site looks strangely
similar to a classical ruin and feels suitably haunted, though many of its previous
inhabitants now live in pise or concrete houses built to the north of Er-Rachidia.

Ask at the Rissani or Oasis Hotel to hire donkeys which allow you to explore the valley
to the north or south, riding in the summer along the dry river bed of the Ziz.

The Er-Rachidia **souk** is held on Sundays in a big enclosure on the western edge of
town. There is a smaller affair on Thursdays. Since the town is not a tourist destination,
the market is a pleasantly unspoilt rural affair, at its most animated in spring and autumn
when the farmers have got something to sell.

WHERE TO STAY
Unless you need a swimming pool the **Hôtel Renaissance** is the best value, at 19, Rue
Moulay Youssef, tel 2633. A single room costs 47dh, the showers work well and it is used
by all the passing Moroccan businessmen. The Café-Restaurant downstairs serves the
best couscous and tagine in town.

The *** **Oasis** at 4, Rue Abou Abdallah, tel 2526, has 46 rooms and though you might
not stay here (a double costs 113dh), the hotel has a bar and a licensed restaurant. You'll
find it just behind the cinema.

The ** **Meski**, tel 2065, is on the right as you enter Er-Rachidia on the Tinerhir road.
It has a slightly shabby air, but does boast a small swimming pool which is sometimes full.
A double room costs 89dh and the dinner menu is 48dh.

The **** **Rissani** is the swimming pool choice. It is beside the bridge over the Oued
Ziz as you travel east from the town centre. It has 60 rooms, a bar, disco, tennis court and
pool, but is used by passing coach tours.

EATING OUT
The **Restaurant Terminus**, Av. Moulay Ali Cherif, offers a filling three-course menu
in its garden for 25dh. The central **Imilchil**, on Av. Moulay Ali Cherif (where else), has a
shaded terrace beside the Tourist Information booth, where you can lunch for 20dh. For
watching morning and evening café society, when the street of Er-Rachidia comes alive,
the Imilchil, the **Patisserie Al Hamra** and the **Lipton** are best.

The Valley of the Ziz

North to Rich

The source of the Ziz rises just south of Midelt, at the foot of Djebel Ayachi in the High Atlas, which reaches 3500 m. If you are not planning on travelling north towards Fez over the Tis-n-Talrhmet, 'the pass of the she camel', a trip from Er-Rachidia through the Ziz gorge to Rich and back is well worth the effort.

Beyond the dammed lake, the Ziz has cut a majestic trench through the Atlas mountains. The cliff walls of the gorge rise serenely to enclose two beautiful oasis villages, **Amzrouf** and **Ifni**, and their kasbahs.

Just to the north of these through a tunnel built by the French Foreign Legion is a wider mountain plateau landscape, through which the Ziz flows in gentler aspect.

The **ksar of Ait Krojmane** marks the second place where the road crosses the Ziz and a left turn here towards Gourrama gives access to a string of ksour. They include lovely melting yellow buildings with unusual triple-arcaded window terraces. The town of Rich, 98 km from Er-Rachidia, lies 7 km north of this crossing (for continuation see page 348).

South to Rissani

The Ziz valley south of Er-Rachidia is spectacular in a grand natural manner, thick green vegetation on the valley floor contrasts with the surrounding golden red hills. Here the Ait Khabbache, the only camel breeding Khum of the Ait Atta, were the tributary overlords. The Ait Khabbache disputed their domination of the Sahara as far south as the Tuat oasis with their great rivals the nomadic Dounia Menia.

The flood of 1965 swept all of the old buildings of the Ziz valley clean out from the river floor. The diverse pattern of settlement, the rambling ksour, and the patchwork of irregular orchards and gardens were destroyed, 12,000 palms were uprooted and 25,000 people left homeless. As a result, the valley is now a pattern of regular terraced gardens with none of the complexities of generations of inheritance and subdivision. New villages are arranged in regular lines way above the edge of cultivable land.

Source Bleu Meski

This campsite, 22 km south of Er-Rachidia, is the traditional stopping point on the Ziz and a good base from which to explore the valley floor. It is named after a spring of clear blue spring water which issues from a natural cave and from there flows into a large weathered concrete tank. It was built by the Foreign Legion, anxious to find a place in which to swim free from bilharzia and snipers. Carp of various sizes swim about with you in the tank, and can be hand fed. There is a restaurant that serves slightly disappointing food, but the loo, permanently flushed by spring water, is a treat. The sunken open air showers are fun, but the spring is a very popular stop and the tents are cheek by jowl. **Camping Bleu Meski**, tel 249, charge 20dh for a car, a tent and two people, and serve indifferent tagines for 20dh, couscous for 22dh and 20dh for a steak.

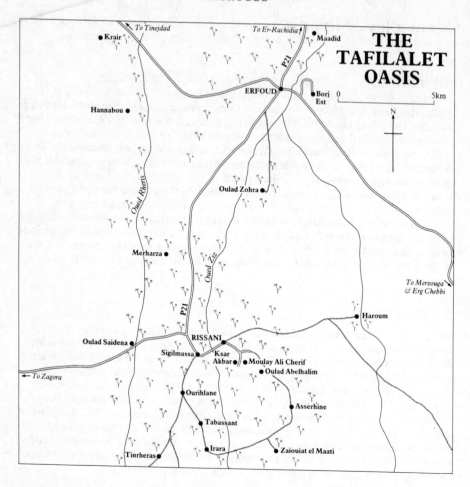

THE
TAFILALET
OASIS

On the opposite bank stand the ruins of the **Meski Ksar**, reportedly destroyed in 1890. You can struggle across the braided streams through the oleanders to its walls made from rounded riverine stones. The entrance spirals beneath higher walls, past a wreckage of olive and grain mills.

11 km south of Meski there is a spectacular panoramic view of the valley, where fossils are displayed for sale beside the parking place. The village of **Aufous,** variably spelt Aulouz and Aufouss, has three surviving ksour which you see as you enter, a zaouia and a **souk** on Thursdays. Further south and slightly off the road nearer the river are the less accessible **Ksour of Zrigat, Zaouia Jedid** and **Douia.** Douia marks the end of the Berber-occupied Ziz.

The Ziz continues south running parallel to the Oued Rheris, and together they form the oasis of Tafilalet. **Maadid,** 73 km from Er-Rachidia on the left of the road, is the first of the Tafilalet ksour. These tend to be much larger, are occupied entirely by Arabs and have a secretive intensity in contrast to the openness of the Berber communities.

The Tafilalet: Erfoud, Rissani and Merzouga

The region of the Tafilalet has a brooding haunting atmosphere quite distinctive from all other oases and desert valleys in Morocco. It is a natural depression in the desert fed by the Ziz and the Rheris, but they never meet other than in a capillary network of irrigation ditches. The ksour are memorable, mysterious places and are not particularly welcoming. The combined population of the Tafilalet is 80,000, and **El Jorf**, the largest ksar in the west of the region, houses 6000 people. More so than anywhere else in the south, the cultivation of the 700,000 palm trees is the principal if not single occupation of most of the inhabitants.

Outlying palmeries thrive, but the central and southern belt is the last to receive water, and this has proved disastrous in the current long drought. On top of this the area has been harassed by Bayoud Palm sickness. This used to be treated by magic, which proved to be at least as efficacious as the twenty-year inconclusive scientific study of this mysterious disease.

At times like this, the vital position of the date palm in desert husbandry becomes clear. Felling palms has always been regulated by religious traditions and it used to be unlawful to sell a living tree. During difficult periods, the only way for a date palm owner to raise money was through loans secured against the date crop. The trees remained inviolable. Gathering the harvest before the traditional date was also a punishable offence. The mystique of these vital trees is recognized by Islam, and saints' tombs are often placed in the densest groves. The Koran has a vigorous description of Christ's birth amongst the protecting palms; sura XIX describes Mary's labour: 'and the throes came upon her by the trunk of a palm. She cried: "Oh would that I died ere this, and been a thing forgotten quite!" And one cried to her from behind the palm tree: "Grieve thou not, thy Lord has provided a streamlet at thy feet and shake the trunk of the palm tree toward thee it will drop fresh dates upon thee"'. Christ is considered by Muslims to have been one of the succession of prophets leading up to Mohammed, though they do not believe he was the son of God.

HISTORY

The Tafilalet oasis, homeland of the current ruling dynasty, has a rich and remarkably important history for it was the key to the great wealth of the Saharan trade for a thousand years. The capital of the Tafilalet was over this long period the near legendary city of Sigilmassa, whose ruins lie to the west of Rissani. According to an ancient but dubious tradition the city was established on the site of a Roman marching camp known as Sigillum Massae. Its historical foundation was in AD 707 when the Arab conqueror of Morocco, Musa ben Nasser, established a garrison here. Sigilmassa soon became the entrepôt for Saharan trade and attracted large communities of Arab and Jewish merchants.

Shortly afterwards the Tafilalet showed the first of many signs of independent spirit. In 740 Berber tribes revolted throughout Morocco against the harsh rule of the Arab governors. Sigilmassa became a stronghold of the Khajarite heresy, which was as much a movement against the rapacious Arab governors of Tangier as a theological schism and it was only purged of heresy in 960 after the Fatimid ruler of Tunisia sent an army across the desert.

The period of the Almoravide and Almohad Empires was one of liberation from the rule of a succession of petty tyrants but the decay of a strong central authority changed the prosperous oasis into a war zone as the successor states of Merenid Morocco and Zayanid Algeria fought continuously for its possession. Both the Merenids and Zayanids employed Arab tribes in their border wars and the decay of both dynasties in the 15th century allowed these Arab tribes to emerge dominant in Sigilmassa.

In the 17th century, the Alouites, one of the most respected of the Arab families of the Tafilalet, arose to organize resistance to a triple threat posed by desert raiders and the armies of the Berber dynasties of Djila and Tazeroualt. Moulay Ali Cherif was the first to be recognized as Sultan but it was his sons who established Alouite rule over all Morocco. The Alouite sultans, ruling from Fez and Marrakesh, used the Tafilalet as a depository for their many unwanted children and potentially troublesome wives or relations. As a result, many distant relatives of the Royal Family, who are also known as Filali, still occupy the palmeries and ksour of the region.

The Ait Khabbache of the Ait Atta who dominated the Ziz valley held an equivocal relationship with the oasis, but one which did not hinder them from completely destroying the fabled city of Sigilmassa in 1818. They did however in the next century come to the aid of the oasis in its resistance to the French. A battalion of the Foreign Legion and Senegalese infantry first occupied the Tafilalet in 1916 but both battalions were wiped out in a surprise attack on 9 August. Another French outpost upstream fell in September when the Ziz was diverted to sap its walls. After two years of fighting the French had controlled the spread of the rebellion but had only reestablished their front line at Erfoud.

The French garrison at Erfoud had to wait until 1931 before they were given permission to attack the rest of the oasis to their south. When they did they were led by de Bournazel, a charismatic officer known to the tribes as 'the Red Man'. De Bournazel always wore a distinctive scarlet uniform but seldom bothered to carry a weapon. He led a charmed existence untouched by any wound throughout his long and celebrated military career in Morocco. After the conquest of the Tafilalet he ruled as an enlightened military governor from 1932–1933. But he died the following year from a stomach wound, the first and last bullet to hit him leading the final campaign in the conquest of Morocco, the assault on the Ait Atta stronghold of Djebel Saghro.

The Tafilalet has often been at variance with the rest of Morocco. Its mood seems to encourage a wilful separatism and fierce patronage of lost causes. As late as 1957, the Caid of Tafilalet, Addi Ou Bihi, led a brief and confused revolt. He died many years later of dysentery in a prison in Rabat.

Erfoud

Erfoud is a small town of dusty red buildings, built by the French in 1930s beside the Ziz and below their fort as the administrative centre for the Tafilalet. Planted with eucalyptus and tamarisk, and surrounded to the north and west by palmeries, it is a dull town but a useful base for exploring and the obvious staging post for going on to the major attraction of the region, the sand dunes of Merzouga, and the kasbahs of Rissani.

The town preserves its military origins in its large quadrilateral plan; two avenues run parallel towards the river bed where they lead into opposite sides of the main square. The entrance to Erfoud's courtyard souk is on the northern edge of this square, and in the market you can find barrows of different varieties of dates, fossils and carved desert stones for sale. After the date harvest is over in late September, Erfoud celebrates in October with a fête of dates. Telephone the big hotels a week or two in advance for a precise date.

From the square a bridge, known as the Bab el Oued, crosses the river and a track climbs up a hill to **Bordj Est**, East Fort, the old French strongpoint, which enjoys magnificent views over the surrounding palmery.

GETTING AROUND
The two-hour bus ride from Er-Rachidia to Erfoud costs 12dh. CTM buses leave from Av. Mohammed V, tel 18, in Erfoud for the continuing 22 km south to Rissani, or you can catch a grand taxi for this and any other trips that do not involve desert crossings.

TOURIST INFORMATION
There is a Post Office and international telephone office in Erfoud, and a Banque Populaire on Mohammed V and in Rissani.

WHERE TO STAY AND EAT
By far the smartest hotel in the Tafilalet is the old **** **Salaam**, which has a swimming pool but where a single room costs 221dh and a double 283dh. The dinner menu is 86dh, and is served by waiters in dinner jackets, initially a little surprising after struggling your way down to the desert outpost. Erfoud is not a pretty town and this hotel on the edge of the settlement on a slight hill with a view of the palmery is therefore quite alluring. If you are not a guest you can use the pool for 10dh. There is also the newer **** **Sijilmassa Hôtel** on the southern edge of the town on the right of the road, an open-plan affair with none of the fading dignity of the Salaam but the same prices, tel 80.

The ** **Tafilalet**, tel 30, off Av. Moulay Ismail, has double rooms at 131dh. The bar is decorated with enormous posters of cool lakeside woodland scenes, but elsewhere plush embroidery is dominant. Jeep parties to Merzouga take off from here. The menu for dinner is 58dh.

The unclassified hotels are not very appealing and have varying supplies of water. The most reliable are **Les Palmiers** at 36, Av. Mohammed V, 30dh a bed, or **La Gazelle** at the other end of the avenue over the crossroads. La Gazelle, tel 116, has a coolish downstairs cellar where you can eat for 35dh.

The **campsite** is on hard stone ground on the easterly edge of Erfoud, and it also rents clean but empty rooms at 6dh a night. Pitching your tent costs 3dh. The municipal pool is directly opposite the campsite, and is open from June to September.

As far as eating is concerned, apart from the hotels there are some roadside cafés which serve light snacks only.

West from Erfoud

For more details of the route 3451 to Tinejdad, see Tinejdad itself. There are some interesting communities close to Erfoud on this route, and it is always worth bearing in mind that the most obscure ksour and palmeries can often be the most rewarding to visit. Receiving few strangers, they gently welcome you, take you on a tour of the gardens and irrigation systems and offer you mint tea. Such experiences are a far cry those who travel quickly to Erfoud, visit the dunes and then rush off to the next sight.

East from Erfoud

Erg Chebbi, the Sand Dunes of Merzouga

Fed on images of the desert that involve great crescents of sand, few visitors can resist the temptation of refuelling their fantasies by visiting the one large patch of sand desert in the Moroccan south, the Erg Chebbi.

The attractions of Merzouga have remained undiminished by the steady flow of romantics. Note however that in high summer the few rooms and even the roof space at the four small cafés at the foot of the dunes are often booked by 16.00.

The great massed piles of golden sand rising up from a bleak black desert plain is an impressive site even in the crushing heat of midday. To climb to one of the sand peaks just before dawn is the ideal after a night spent in one of the dune-side cafés. The shifting colours, rippling shadows from the crests of the dune and the rapid change in temperature make the effort worthwhile. In spring snow on the peaks of the Middle Atlas can be quite clearly seen. A dinner of tagine mopped up with fresh bread and eaten by gas or candle light and the expectations of the morning create an entertaining atmosphere. Half a night spent sleeping rough on the roof is a restless experience for the clarity of the desert sky and the lack of any distracting urban light creates a quite dazzling display of stars, accompanied by the excited chatter of shooting-star spotting.

GETTING THERE
The Hôtel Tafilalet in Erfoud runs landrover tours to Merzouga, 400dh for a nine seater landrover, and in high season does an evening trip for 50dh. There will be no shortage of people offering themselves as desert guides, in fact not surprisingly there is usually quite a glut.

If you have your own vehicle there is no need for a guide as the route is quite straightforward from Erfoud. Do not, however, attempt this in a sand storm or after rain. Allow two hours, remembering that dawn is around 6.00. Cross the bridge east of Erfoud's central square and pass below the hill conspicuously crowned by Bordj Est. Continue along this surfaced road and join the dirt track when the tarmac ends. By following the line of telegraph poles you cannot fail to reach Merzouga and the dunes, passing a small settlement with a café and fossil stalls on the way. Be prepared to dig or push yourself out, particularly as you approach the dunes and cafés.

Coming from Rissani, take the road south of town and the first tarmac left turn should be signposted to Merzouga. After 1 km take the first good dirt track road on your right, continue through palmeries and then cross the dry river bed where there is a café and a tent to eat in on the far bank. Then head for the line of Erfoud to Merzouga telegraph poles, and on a clear day the dunes should already be in view.

If you do not have transport, lifts can normally be arranged with fellow tourists. Otherwise there should be a few trucks coming in and out of town at Rissani on market days, and a lift will cost you around 10dh.

WHERE TO STAY

The desert track runs south beside the sand dunes and there are various tricky drives leading to the four disparate cafés. The **Yasmina**, the **Etoile de Sable**, the **du Sud** and the **Auberge Erg Chebbi** are all friendly places, renting out a few rooms and roof space, preparing meals for the evening and selling soft drinks. The Yasmina is perhaps the best, where 45dh pays for both dinner and a bed.

The track leads on to the hamlet of **Merzouga**, where a **souk** takes place on Saturdays. There is a soldier posted at the town's gate and you will need to have your passport and sign the visitors' book in order to pass through.

The **Café des Amis** is in Merzouga, and on the other side of the river is the **Hôtel des Palmiers**, below a water tower. The highest sand peak of the dunes, about 150 m, is immediately above the hotel, and is favoured by sand skiers. The Hôtel des Palmiers charges 100dh for a room that sleeps 4–5, or 50dh for a double.

Trips from Merzouga

The **Ksar of Taouz** is 24 km south of Merzouga, on the left bank of the Oued Ziz, and is as far as you are allowed to go. Beyond is the Algerian border where the strategic road to Tindouf runs across an immense Saharan plateau, the Hammada du Guir, south of which stretches a vast sand desert, the great Eastern Erg. Fossils are a major trading item in the area, and if you are determined to find your own you should visit the **valley of the black rock** below a slight hill between Merzouga and Taouz though you will need a guide to find the familiar spiral shaped goniatites which are reputed to proliferate here. On the way back from Taouz you could take a slightly different route and go by the **lead mines of Mfis**.

From November to March a lake which forms just west of Merzouga is visited by over 72 different sorts of migrating birds, including pink flamingos.

South from Erfoud

Rissani, Sigilmassa and the Ksour of the Tafilalet

Rissani has 2000 inhabitants, many of whom prefer to stay in their 18th-century ksour, but a small selection of contemporary buildings line the single road where you will find the bank, hotel, bus stop and entrance to the souk. Though useful, these unattractive modern structures are the only blot in a great scattered bowl of ancient ksour and palmeries.

However, the wind that gathered the Erg Chebbi to the east is usually in evidence, and combined with the drought, which has been most intense and prolonged here, it gives the whole area a feeling of lingering fatalism, where dust-saturated air suffocates weakened, struggling palms.

The **souk** of Rissani is much larger and busier than that of Erfoud. Its long random lines of precarious looking stalls sell all manner of food and farmers' requirements on Sundays, Tuesdays and Thursdays.

Ksar of Rissani

The central Ksar of Rissani is a maze of dark, almost troglodyte passages and layers of small dwellings. Great towers, decorated at their summit by ornate brickwork, guard each corner and face of the long ksar wall. The impressive gates are picked out in green and white paint or plaster and green glazed tiles. Within, all is confusion for a stranger. Great lengths of dark passages lead into further blackness, and sudden hopeful pools of light offer three alternative dead ends.

The population adds greatly to the mystique. Imagine generations of impoverished Filali princes existing with pride on their inheritance of a few palm trees, exiled to the heat and stagnant society of the Tafilalet. Strains of Arab, Berber, Haratine and negro and Christian renegade soldiery have been bred into the population. The women of the ksar are entirely covered in unadorned black, and hardly a crack shows in the reclusive envelope of material through which to catch even a glimpse of almond eyes.

Sigilmassa

The ruins of Sigilmassa lie just five minutes walk to the west of Rissani on the road from Erfoud. The site is little more than an extensive mound of melted pise with odd fragments of ceramics and wood, flashing out from the enveloping earth. There are a few stretches of wall which a guide might try to enthusiastically describe as the Great Mosque or Palace. Here lie the ruins of the first Arab and Islamic city of Morocco, which for thousands of years was embellished with gardens and running water, and was fabulously rich from the products of trans-Saharan trade: ebony, gold, ivory, ostrich feathers and negro slaves.

The Shrine of Moulay Ali Cherif

The unmemorable tomb of the founder of the Alouite dynasty is 2 km out of Rissani to the southeast. The shrine was rebuilt after a flood in 1955 carried the older structure away. It is unmistakably a modern building, an unsuccessful exterior through which it is forbidden for non-Muslims to enter. Walter Harris, who accompanied the Sultan Moulay Hassan on his tour of the south in the late 19th century, suspected that the ailing Sultan had in fact come more to pray at the tomb of his ancestor than to exercise his authority and collect taxes. He describes the final approach to the shrine: 'Mounting on his great white horse, saddled and trapped in green and gold, with the canopy of crimson velvet held over his head, rode the Sultan, while huge black slaves on either hand waved long scarfs to keep the flies from the sacred person'.

Ksar Akbar

Behind the shrine, and also approachable from the road, is the Alouite Ksar Akbar. Built in about 1800, it held its full quota of redundant concubines and threatening royal children, but now it is an empty, melancholic place, its gates alone in a good state of repair. You can visit an interior courtyard within the enclosure which used to hold some of the royal treasury, that derived from tariffs on the cargoes and caravans of the slaves from the Sudan. Two houses in the Akbar are still occupied, and the children will amuse you by throwing blocks of mud down a deep well in the lefthand corner whilst trying to sell woven reed plates.

The Kasbah of Oulad Abdelhalim
A further 2 km southeast on the circular road from Rissani, this Kasbah is a magnificent structure and well worth visiting. It was built in 1900 by Moulay Hassan's elder brother, Moulay Rachid, who had been appointed governor of the Tafilalet. You enter through the side of one of the decorated corner towers and arrive in a large enclosed square to face the more impressive and ornate internal gateway. Two towers, still rich in plaster-work and capped with tiles, flank the gate, and on the left as you proceed through it is a small mosque. The third and final court is entered through an increasingly decayed and twisting passage, its large doors now stuck forever open. It has a cloister of horseshoe arches and four cool chambers leading off it in the traditional pattern. Delicate fragments of mosaic and plasterwork are picked over by the most obvious occupants, some busy chickens and an assertive cockerel.

Southern Ksour of the Tafilalet
From Oulad Abdelhalim the road continues to take you on a tour of some of the larger ksour: **Asserhine** with its pool, **Zaouiat el Maati**, **Irara**, **Tabassant**, **Ourihlane** and back to the ruins of Sigilmassa and Rissani. The tarmac has deteriorated in places but if you can find the road to Ksar Tinrheras, route 3462, you can enjoy a superb view of the surrounding palmery, the distant Atlas and the sand desert to the east.

The upper third of the towers in all the ksour are decorated with a beehive complexity of chevrons, crosses, lines and bands of holes, set into pise walls with a profusion and artistry distinctive to this area. Theories on the origins of kasbah design abound, and some mileage has been made out of that idea that the Tafilalet, the first Arab city of Morocco, was the most similar to Mesopotamia, where artisans recreated the architecture of the Tigris and Euphrates on the banks of the Ziz and Rheris.

The progression of visitors over the years has bred quite a hard attitude into the local children, who seem the most vociferous in Morocco. However, the ksour are worth the effort, and there has to be some price to pay for such quick access to medieval interiors of magical darkness and light.

WHERE TO STAY
The only hotel in Rissani is the **El Filalia** in the centre of town by the bus stop. They usually charge 20dh per person, but prices can increase with the enormous demand in high summer. You can eat couscous or tagine in their upstairs dining room, among pinball machines. The doors will either be battened down against the dust or you will have a view out over the main street. The hotel water can smell quite strongly of paraffin, but there is a basic hammam 20 m to the left as you leave the hotel.

Er-Rachidia to Figuig

For those seeking isolation or Algeria, the day-long journey to Figuig, 405 km east, runs between a continuous escarpment to the north and land draining away into a desert plain to the south. The route is scattered with bleak mining and military posts but of more interest are the small oasis settlements along the course of the Oued Guir and its tributary the Oued Ait Aissa, both of which, predictably, drain the southern slopes of the High Atlas. The bus breaks its journey whenever you imagine the landscape to be at its most desolate, where a tenacious Berber farmer and his wife cheerfully disembark with supplies of sugar, Omo and seed corn for their invisible home.

Herds of camels and goats around scatterings of tents betray the stronger nomadic influence on this desert borderland. Over this land too, the nomadic tribes of the Dounia Menia, the Oulad Djernir and the Ait Atta fought for centuries. In 1908 a charismatic holy man, the Sherif Moulay Lahsin, secretly supported by Sultan Moulay Hafid, briefly united the tribes in resistance to the French who were advancing west from their posts in Algeria, and the road passes through a number of battle grounds where the conquest was resisted.

Tazougerte

For 70 km east of Er-Rachidia, the P32 follows below the bulk of Djebel Aguelmouss, whose summit is at 2113 m. A rough track on the left follows the Oued Guir's breach through the mountains. The Kasbah of Tazougerte lies 10 km north up this striking valley. Beyond the kasbah is a reliable water supply, the Tasoumit spring, which you can also visit. A track extends northeast from here past the **Koubba of Sidi Abdallah de Belkassem** for 43 km across the plateau of Snab to the mines of **Beni Tajjite**. From Beni Tajjite a series of rough mountain paths lead to **Douiret-Sbaa**, hidden in the folds of Djebel Taforalt. This secretive zaouia was the Sherif Moulay Lahsin's mountain base but it was burnt and ploughed over by the French.

Boudenib

From Tazougerte the road hugs the course of the Oued Guir. A broken palmery follows the river bed for 30 km, scattered with largely ruinous ksour, though 26,000 date palms are still cultivated. Boudenib, 18 km from the Tazougerte turning, is a dusty military town with pleasant pink and white arcaded shops around its central garden square.

During the construction of the new fort a French cavalry regiment charged the Boudenib palmery in an attempt to clear the area of snipers. In the confusion of the palm groves and walled gardens the enthusiasm of the charge was checked and the troopers were overwhelmed by warriors who dropped from the trees. Boudenib was however eventually forced to surrender and you can still find Borj Sud, south fort, to the south of the palmery.

On 1 September 1908 the Moroccan tribal force assembled by the Sherif attacked the new fort. Brave to the point of madness, thousands of warriors launched wave after wave of attacks on the well protected fort throughout the day. Many more thousands of tribesmen died on 7 September attacking French relief troops on the plain of Djorf, but not before their veiled leader had delivered an unanswered and strangely prophetic challenge to the French army: 'Know that since your arrival in the Sahara, you have badly treated weak Muslims. You have made our country suffer intense harm, which tastes as galling to us as a bitter apple. Come out from behind your walls, you will judge which is nobler, the owl or the hawk'.

The next 150 km or so are scattered with a few sights, if you feel like breaking your journey. The **Ksour of Sahli**, east of Boudenib is entirely populated by a clan of Shorfa, the descendants of the prophet Mohammed. **Bounane**, 57 km east of Boudenib, an oasis town on the Oued Ait Assa palmery, gives access to **Takounit Kasbah**, 5 km north, and the isolated **Ksar of El Hajoui** 10 km south. **Ain Ech-Chair**, another 67 km further on, is a small pise village at the foot of the crumbling walls of an almost empty ksar.

El Menabba, 18 km beyond Ain Ech-Chair, is a small military post just before the turning to the now closed P19a border road. On 17 April 1908, the French force advancing to build Borj Sud camped here. As Douglas Porch describes in *The Conquest of Morocco*: 'A wave of several thousand Moroccan warriors, stripped naked and well oiled, had crept close to the French camp from the east. In the confusion of the light and without the tell-tale pair of trousers or jellaba it became difficult to distinguish friend from foe. It was like a riot in a nudist colony, though 19 soldiers were to die and another 101 would be wounded before breakfast'.

Bouarfa

Bouarfa perched below the pass of Djebel Bouarfa is 50 km from Menabba and 287 from Er-Rachidia, and is unassociated with any palmery or oasis cultivation. It is not an oasis but the modern centre for the desert southeastern province which is still officially considered a military region.

The best of the town's two basic hotels is the **Tamlatte**, on the left of the Oujda road beside the mosque. It occasionally wafts with the delicious odour of myrrh which permeates from next door where, less exotically, they wash the dead. Food is best from the café restaurants below the hotel next to where the buses park.

Bouarfa has a cottage industry of weaving durable carpet rugs from cloth scraps. The silvery kaleidoscope of colours and knotted texture is seen in many more Moroccan homes than the average tourist bazaar rugs. There are looms throughout the town and the one at 45, Blvd Mohammed V sometimes has a small stock for sale.

Bouarfa to Figuig

There is nothing to impede your view of the 118 km of desert between these two outposts. All to be seen are some impressive mountains and a scattered suburb of nomadic encampments around Figuig, largely composed of Arab herdsmen who have left Algeria.

The peak behind Bouarfa is Djebel Bouarfa, a mountain rich in copper and manganese and 1819 m high, and to the north of the road you can see Djebel Klakh which is also mined. Half way to Figuig the shape of Djebel Melah, again on the left, becomes dominant (1721 m) and as you reach within 30 km of Figuig you pass between Djebel Maiz (1950 m) to the north and Djebel Grouz (1839 m) straddling the border to the south. If you are driven to climb any of these, do inform the authorities to avoid any later misunderstandings.

Figuig

In the far southeastern corner of Morocco is the oasis of Figuig, an elliptical basin of palmeries surrounded by dark volcanic hills. Seven unequal and feuding Berber villages

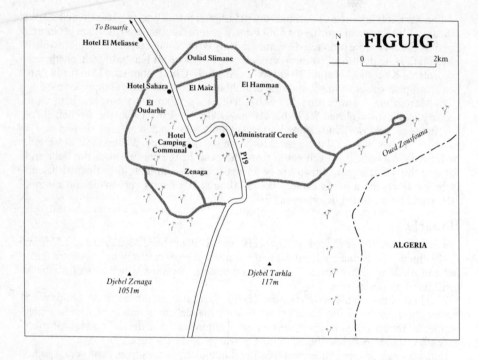

guarded the twenty springs and gardens from each other by a series of walls and towers. If there was a severe enough external threat they created a united front as Figuig city, 'the Berber island in an Arab sea'.

Figuig is a noticeably religious settlement with a gentle practising piety. The chants from the various zaouia and mosques sound especially entrancing in a desert dusk when the sun falling behind the surrounding wall of black mountains lights up the white wall of a koubba with the last few minutes of its gentle diffused and coloured light.

HISTORY

Figuig has always been a strategic site, a secure base for the control of the desert routes, not so much trans-Saharan caravan routes as the overland passage to Mecca. Considering its position it is surprising that Figuig's loyalty has always been to the Sultan of Morocco, though for much of the past he was a conveniently distant figure.

The dominant theme of Figuig's history has always been the fierce rivalry between the ksour, disputing over land and water rights. Unlike some other desert outposts, the ksour of Figuig were seldom dominated by any nomadic tribe. The individual ksar contracted alliances with one of the various rival nomadic tribes, who fought each other over grazing rights. The permutations and politics of this shifting pattern of rival ksour and tribes were endless.

Figuig prospered in the 19th century, as an inviolate base for desert raids into French-controlled Algeria. The French Armee d'Afrique garrisoned Beni Ounif, just 8 km

470

south of Figuig in 1900, in an attempt to control the town. This division is mirrored today, as Beni Ounif is the Algerian border control post.

After Independence, the old pattern of feuding emerged once more with a modern political slant, and in 1959 the militants of Ben Barka's socialist party, the UNFP, fought the old guard under the Caid of Figuig. Fighting since has twice returned to Figuig, in 1963 and over the winter of 1975 when Moroccan and Algerian border units fought in the streets.

With its road and rail connections, Figuig remains an immensely valuable strategic site for Morocco—a Moroccan thumb on an Algerian artery.

GETTING AROUND

The buses arrive on the Blvd Hassan II which has all the cafés and hotels along it, a Banque Populaire and the pretty courtyard of the craft shop. Foreign currency, drink and picnic food should all be procured before arriving in Figuig. Despite being one of the two official border crossings between Morocco and Algeria, the town remains enticingly remote and little visited. It is 350 km south of Oujda and 405 km east of Er-Rachidia, with little in the way of comfort along either route. Travelling by bus gives you a certain level of intimacy with the local population and plenty of time for sleep. Cars allow you to pursue the odd detour, picnic under some palms or travel through the cool and brilliance of the night. Road conditions are fine from both directions.

From Figuig, there are four buses to Bouarfa a day. The 6.00 meets the Er-Rachidia connection, the 8.00 allows a long lunch in Bouarfa until the 14.00 bus. There are four buses between Bouarfa and Oujda a day, another eight-hour journey, though you may be able to catch the weekly night freight train.

THE ALGERIAN BORDER CROSSING

Relations with Algeria are currently improving and the crossing is not too troublesome. At the moment, you have to buy 1000 Algerian dinars (about £140) at the border with French francs, although travellers' cheques, sterling and US dollars have recently been accepted.

No visa is required for British citizens, but they are required for US and Canadian passport holders. Your passport may need to be stamped in Figuig as the Moroccan border post is sometimes not manned. If you are driving, check that you have your green card, registration documents and driving licence.

The border is 8 km south of Figuig and there is only one taxi in town.

WHAT TO SEE

First impressions of Figuig are of a line of square modern buildings ending at an administrative cercle and the army headquarters. Inevitably, behind the road the traditional pattern of pise ksour reveals itself. The ksour are almost urban in style, and distinctively feature long outer perimeter walls embracing cultivated areas of the palmery. These, where they still stand, are punctuated by conical perimeter towers, built with a stone base and a very narrow crawl entrance which allows access to an upper platform lined with a row of sniping holes. The oasis is a Berber Zenata stronghold, the same group that inhabits the Riff, and although none survives in the north they also maintained bitter feuds up there from a similar system of towers. Of the seven rival ksour, it is now only easy to distinguish four separate communities: El Oudarhir, El Maiz–Ouled Slimane, El Hammam and Zenaga.

El Oudarhir, on the right as you enter the town, is in increasingly ruinous condition but if you like them it has some excellent dark subterranean passages to explore. Scattered throughout this ksar are over a dozen koubbas, one of which is next door to the oldest surviving mosque of the oasis, whose minaret you may climb with the permission of the Caid. There are two sources of water in the ksar, one a hot spring, the other salty.

The **Ksar of El Maiz** is on the left of the road, opposite, and is not easy to distinguish from the **Ksar of Ouled Slimane**. This is another satisfying warren of alleys and individual buildings. Perhaps the most amusing of the original ksour is **El Hammam**, with its celebrated hot water spring, where one can still bath in the natural hammams. The women's hammam can be found by wandering through the palmery of El Hammam to the south. There is a maze of irrigation ditches and isolated shaded water tanks. Follow any water course upstream, along the network of levels and channels and you should arrive at the effluent of the hammam. The male hammam is further uphill and less easy to track down. A dark rock-cut staircase leads steeply down in a twisting subterranean passage to an echoing stone-vaulted pool in whose warm waters you can immerse yourself. There are reportedly over a hundred steps underground—I lost count when I crashed heavily into the wall, and a torch or a candle would be advisable. Above the hammam is the Zaouia of Sidi Bou Amama, for long a centre of desert resistance to the French.

The most successful of the ksour is **Zenaga**, to the right of the road to the Algerian frontier. At the bottom of the oasis depression, the recent lowering of the water table has not affected its gardens and palmeries. It is the richest, most intact and confident of the communities of Figuig. You can attempt to walk to Zenaga, wandering through the baffling paths of the high walled gardens with their astonishing variety. You will catch small glimpses of the underground water channels where tunnels and pipes crisscross at different levels and flow in opposite directions. In the enthusiasm of Independence the government tried to regulate water rights in Figuig, but the inspectors gave up trying to understand the baffling complexity of the system after four years.

Zousfouna

1 km before Zenaga, a turning to the left takes you to the valley of the Oued Zousfouna. A string-like palmery extends along the river bed, a pleasant place to walk or picnic throughout the hot afternoon and there are various viewing points looking south. The hills that surround Figuig give the area an inward intensity, an almost urban feel of containment quite different from the sense of isolation and distance you might expect. In order to find a lingering view of the great expanses of the desert you would have to climb one of the surrounding hills, and it is well to clear any such climb with the police in this sensitive frontier town.

WHERE TO STAY, EAT AND BATHE
You can stay in Zenaga at the **Auberge de la Palmerie**, tel 62. A single costs 28dh and the cooking is good.

The **Hôtel El Meliasse** is by the garage on the right as you enter Figuig. It has cool cavernous rooms, two small balconies and showers, at 30dh a single, 50dh a double.

The **Hôtel Sahara** is in the centre of town, where very basic rooms are rented for 15dh. The official hammam, 2dh entrance, is just outside the Sahara, and chants percolate upstairs from a nearby zaouia on Friday evenings. The **Hôtel Camping Communal**, Blvd Hassan II, has an excellent view of the Zenaga palmery from its terrace café and rents 5 rooms at 30dh or camping in the grounds. You can use the pool for 10dh.

The Meliasse Hôtel has a café. Otherwise there is the **Café Fatah**, or the busy central **Café Oasis**, opposite the garden square, which is full of soldiers in the evening. Figuig menus seldom stretch much beyond salads, omelettes, cakes and the odd brochette, however.

Part IX

AGADIR, THE SOUSS VALLEY AND THE ANTI ATLAS

Falcon

The Souss and the Anti Atlas is the most distinctive and self-contained region of Morocco. It is an area of striking physical beauty and the landscape is deeply imbued with history and an older and abiding sense of spiritual mystery. The people are noticeably less aggressive to travellers, the climate is attractive throughout the year and the availability of cheap flights to Agadir makes it the ideal introduction to Morocco.

The semi-tropical Souss valley is sealed to the north by the great peaks of the High Atlas and to the south by the Anti Atlas mountains. To the east these two mountain ranges meet to form the holy mountain of Djebel Siroua. Geographical isolation from the rest of Morocco has bred a strong regional identity. The people of the Souss and the Anti Atlas have a tradition of dissidence and independence from central government that is continued today in strong support for the socialist opposition party, the UNFP. Though the accessible and fertile areas, like Agadir and Taroudant, have a mixed population, the region is still dominated by the Chleuh group of tribes who speak the Tachelhait Berber dialect. Through accident or proud design the Chleuh have maintained a racial purity which has preserved characteristic features. A Chleuh is typically slight with a lithe almost delicate frame, great flexibility, grace and powers of endurance. Pronounced cheek bones give a broad look to the head and a slight impression of Central Asian or Inca ancestry.

The Chleuh are famous for their industry which was originally directed to war and creating orchard gardens from the bleakest of landscapes. They evolved skilled specializations: the metalwork and weaponry of the Ida ou Kensous has been prized since the

474

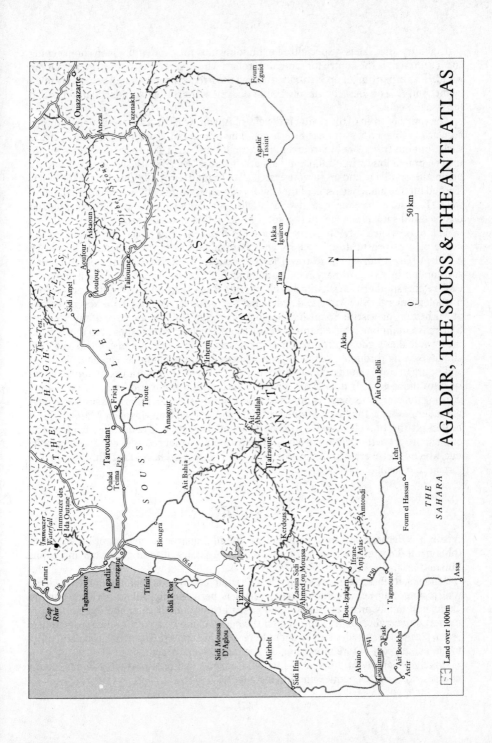

AGADIR, THE SOUSS & THE ANTI ATLAS

11th century, the Akhassa specialized in'building mosques, the Ammeln in shopkeeping and Tazeroualt is the centre for Chleuh acrobats who dominate circuses throughout the world. The expansion of opportunities during the French protectorate was quickly filled by the Anti Atlas tribes: the Ida ou Gnidif became waiters, the Issendal chauffeurs and the Issagen cooks.

The transport hub of the region is the city of Agadir which has an international airport, regular coach services and car hire firms. The attraction of this modern resort city is slight, but out from Agadir stretches an unspoilt hinterland and coast. To the north are the celebrated long white sands of Taghazoute, alias 'Paradise Beach', and inland, the mountain top village and mysterious waterfall of Immouzer des Ita Outane. To the east is Taroudant, the ancient capital of the region, contained within an ancient circuit of ochre walls. Taroudant has surprisingly few 'sights' but with its old hotels, fine cooking and busy relaxed souk it is a city to stay for a while, rather than just visit.

The pink-walled city of Tiznit has a quite different aura mixed from a recent but heady past of prostitutes, jewellers and blue sultans from the Sahara. It is also an excellent base from which to travel further south. To the oasis village of Tafraoute, surrounded by extraordinary rock formations high in the Anti Atlas mountains or to explore the southern coast: the beach of Sidi R'bat with all its wildlife and curious mythology, nearby Sidi Moussa d'Aglou and its troglodyte fishermen, the seven beaches of Mirhelt or the wistful Spanish art deco town of Sidi Ifni. On the edge of the Western Sahara is Goulimine whose Saturday camel souk has been over-exposed to tourism but the town makes a good introduction to the desert. If this appeals you can take the Tata circuit, passing through a string of oasis villages before reaching Taroudant.

The argan tree is an unofficial totem that symbolizes the mysterious and independent spirit of the region. It does not grow anywhere else in the world. A tenacious, slow-growing thorn tree, its wood is indestructible by insects. Argan leaves are similar to olive but fuller in shape, the flowers appear in June and a green fruit ripens by March. This is beaten off the branches and fed to herds, though goats will climb the slenderest of branches to graze the fruit themselves. A heavy orange-coloured oil is extracted from the nut, which is recovered from the animal dung. This is used in cooking, for lamp fuel or turned into soap.

AGADIR

Agadir is a Berber word for a communal fortified granary—an inappropriate rural and tribal name for a city whose history is full of the affairs of foreign powers and ruling Sultans.

As a result of an earthquake in 1960, Agadir is now a completely modern city, a well-planned, all-season resort town, which is permanently full of package tourists. Compared to any other city in Morocco, Agadir is strangely calm and open, empty of mystery and verging on the bland. But if the hassle in the rest of the country is getting to you, a pleasant restful day can be spent here, walking up to the ruined kasbah and down to the fishing port before swimming on the magnificent beach.

It is the chief city of the south, a useful transport centre for catching flights, buses, hiring cars, cashing cheques and buying alcohol.

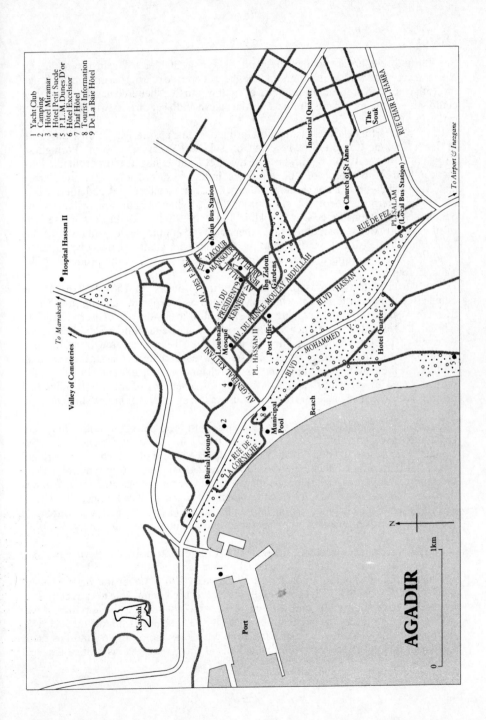

1 Yacht Club
2 Camping
3 Hôtel Miramar
4 P.L.M. Dunes D'or
5 Hôtel Excelsior
6 Diaf Hôtel
7 Tourist Information
8 De La Baie Hôtel

AGADIR

Kasbah

Port

Valley of Cemeteries

To Marrakesh

Hospital Hassan II

Main Bus Station

Industrial Quarter

Church of St Anne

The Souk

RUE CHAIR EL HAMRA

To Airport & Inezgane

RUE DE FEZ

P.L. SALAM
(Local Bus Station)

BLVD HASSAN II

Hotel Quarter

BLVD MOHAMMED V.

BLVD HASSAN II

Post Office

Ibn Zidoun Gardens

AV. DU PRINCE MOULAY ABDULLAH

PL. HASSAN II

AV. GENERAL KETTANI

AV. DU PRESIDENT KENNEDY

Loubnane Mosque

AV. DES FAR

R. EL MANSOUR

R. YACOUB

Beach

Municipal Pool

RUE DE LA CORNICHE

Burial Mound

N

0   1km

History

Sun-burnt foreigners are not new to Agadir, they are its lifeblood. The history of the city has repeatedly shown that it withers and dies when deprived of external influences. Since the 15th century European traders have been drawn to this sheltered bay. For here they could cut out the merchants of Fez and Marrakesh and deal directly with the Saharan caravans.

In 1505, a Portuguese merchant built a fortified trading post at Agadir. This, the castle of Santa Cruz de Cap du Gue, he profitably sold seven years later to the Portuguese king. The castle at Agadir rapidly became the largest and easily the most profitable Portuguese fortress in Morocco. The governors' influence spread inland but the Berber and Arab tribes united under the Saadians, began to retaliate and had the enclave under an intermittent sort of siege from 1515. When Agadir finally fell to the Saadian Sultan Mohammed ech Cheikh in 1541, the whole chain of Portuguese forts to the north were abandoned as untenable and unprofitable without Agadir. During the 120 years of Saadian rule Agadir enjoyed a golden period of prosperity, exporting locally produced sugar, cotton and saltpetre as well as the products of the Saharan trade.

The wheel of fortune was reversed under the Alouites. In 1687 Sultan Moulay Ishmael conquered the region which had existed as a separate state for fifty years. Though weakened by Moulay Ishmael the fatal blow to Agadir was delivered in 1760. The city had joined in yet another regional revolt and in revenge Sultan Sidi Mohammed determined to destroy the port. First he moved the all-important Jewish middlemen north to his new trading development at Essaouira to where he increasingly diverted all trade. Only then did he formally forbid any merchant to visit Agadir and close down the port. Assisted by the fact that the slave-worked plantations of the West Indies had destroyed the demand for sugar from the Souss valley, by 1819 Agadir had shrivelled to a mere village.

It remained a rural backwater until one of those petty incidents in the diplomatic poker game, the Agadir crisis of July 1911, propelled it back into fame. By the end of the 19th century, France had divided North Africa into agreed areas of influence with Britain, Spain and Italy, but had deliberately excluded Germany. Under the pretence of helping the Moroccan sultan assert his independence a light German gun-boat, *The Panther*, was dispatched to anchor off Agadir, which was then still unoccupied by France. The wheels of cynical colonial diplomacy spun into action and German support for Morocco's independence was dropped in exchange for several million square miles of French West Africa.

During the French Protectorate Agadir slowly regrew into a sizeable town, a pleasant unhurried place with a mixed international population of 35,000 by 1959.

Thirteen minutes before midnight on 29 February 1960, Agadir was destroyed and half its inhabitants buried alive in an earthquake. It proved impossible to extract most of the bodies from the rubble, and with cholera spreading amongst the survivors it was decided to bury the city and citizens in one mass grave. The burial mound, the Tell, is to the north of the modern city, inland from the port. Now there can be almost as many holidaymakers in the town's 15,000 hotel beds as there were victims of that leap year night disaster.

GETTING TO AND AROUND

By Air
Agadir–Inezgane airport is 8 km southeast of town, on the left of the P30 road to Tiznit, tel 31106, and has a good range of domestic flights. The airline offices are all on Av. General Kettani. The telephone number for Royal Air Maroc is 22793, for Air France 23145 and for Sabena 23793.

By Bus
There is an ambitious national plan to link Agadir and Laayoune on to the railway system and put a tunnel under the straits of Gibraltar. Until these projects mature buses will remain the easiest way of travelling to and from Agadir. All bus lines leave from Av. Yacoub el Mansour. As ever, you should buy tickets as early as possible. There is an early morning bus to Casablanca, currently leaving at 7.30, the 5-hr journey costs 90dh. There are four buses a day to Taroudant, 2 hrs for 12dh, six to Essaouira, 3 hrs for 45dh, four to Tiznit, 2 hrs for 18dh and two a day covering the 4-hr drive to Goulimine. Local buses to Inezgane, Taghazoute (no 12) and Tamri (no 14) leave from Place Salam. Bear in mind that Inezgane generally has a better range of departures for all points east and south with at least four daily buses to Marrakesh, Taroudant, Goulimine and Ouazazarte.

By Taxi
Taxis are found by the bus station and along the Av. des FAR. It is a quarter-hour journey to Inezgane bus station where you can find places in grands taxis plying the regular runs to Tiznit and Taroudant.

By Car
Agadir has a good range of car hire firms, and the bigger agencies allow you to return a car to any of their other depots. Afric Cars, Hertz and Interrent are all found on Blvd Mohammed V, Europcar on the Av. des FAR and Avis on Av. Hassan II. Rent-a-car/Location de voitures, tel 23750, has the cheapest with a Renault 4 for just over 1000dh a week. Mopeds can be hired at the beach or along Blvd du 20 Août.

Agadir has a number of specialist garages: Renaults can be mended at Castano on Av. El Moukouama, and Fiats and Fords at Auto-Hall, Rue de la Foire.

TOURIST INFORMATION
It is easy to find your way around the modern town with its wide avenues running parallel to the beach. The most striking feature is that there are no hasslers. The Tourist Office is on the southwestern corner of the central shopping mall, on Place Hassan II. They hand out a colourful city map and can give suggestions on coach excursions, festivals and 'Fantasias'. Actual tickets are brought from hotels or travel agents. Banking hours are Monday to Friday, 8.15–11.30 and 14.30–16.30. The Algemene Bank Morokko which cashes Eurocheques and stays open on Saturday morning is opposite the distinctive Post Office on Av. du Prince Moulay Abdullah. You can make international phone calls from a small office at the side of the Post Office and the big hotels will usually change travellers' cheques.

The telephone number of Hospital Hassan II, Route de Marrakesh, is 22477. Alternatively, you could dial 22685 for a French-speaking doctor. A 24-hour chemist can be found in the central shopping mall next to the Municipal Hall. The police are in Rue 18 Novembre, tel 19, and the Catholic Church of St Anne, on Rue de Marrakesh, has Mass on Saturdays at 18.30 and on Sundays at 10.00 and 19.00. The Hotel Salaam, tel 22120, is also helpful in an emergency.

The Kasbah Ruins

The only real 'sight' of Agadir, the ruins of the old government kasbah, provides an excellent vantage point from which to view the whole town and the port. It is a long and steep but rewarding climb, or you can drive or take a taxi up.

The kasbah was built by the Saadian Sultan Mohammed ech Cheikh as part of his prolonged jihad to remove the Portuguese from Morocco. Having fortified the site in 1540, he was able to expel the Portuguese from their precious harbour of Agadir the following year.

Above the entrance gate is an inscription in Arabic and Danish, inveighing you to fear God and honour the King. For in 1746 Danish merchants had achieved a monopoly position in the Souss sugar trade and helped rebuild the kasbah. Justifiably suspicious of both the tribes and the Europeans, in 1752 Sultan Abdullah kept a mixed garrison of Christian renegades and Turkish mercenaries in the kasbah.

In the anarchic years before the French Protectorate, the kasbah was no longer an official garrison and was lived in by the villagers of Agadir. Before the earthquake it held a warren of over three hundred houses. You can easily discover the traces, twisted sheets of corrugated roofing, old electric cables and shattered reinforced concrete beams within the ramparts. There are also several old water cisterns which are well-worth avoiding.

The Tell

Below the kasbah, inland from Blvd Mohammed V is the site of Portuguese Agadir and possibly that of Phoenician Rusadir. The 1960 burial mound of city and population now hides any traces. Trees have been planted on the mound but the monument to the dead remains uncompleted. It is visited by surviving relatives and is inappropriately the favourite practising ground for car driving instructors. A small track from here crosses the main bypass to take you to a valley of cemeteries. Here, Christians, Jews and Muslims are buried in separate fields and cacti proliferate on the bleak slopes above.

The Town

The town itself is not a place of architectural elegance, its low regular buildings, wide tree-planted avenues and central pedestrian shopping zone faithfully echo the auto-mobile-fixated garden suburb of the West. Apart from the beach-front hotels the only buildings with individuality are the Hôtel de Ville, the Grand Mosque, Le Tribunal and the concrete bunker-like central Post Office—designed by the architect Zevaco.

The Beach

The beach, on the other hand, is magnificent, and one of the safest places to swim on the whole Atlantic coast. The foothills of the Atlas at which you can gaze while floating leisurely in the sea, rise steeply north of the town. At the northern end of the beach by the port there is a car park and showers are available at a number of the café-bars on the terrace. Further south the beach is increasingly dominated by large hotels. Rows of sunbeds, camel rides, deck chairs, wind surfers and water skiing instructors await their customers.

The Port

If you want to wander without shopping, the port is the most lively and intriguing quarter of Agadir. The fishing fleet, combined with that of Safi to the north, is the largest gatherer of sardines in the world, landing more than 160,000 tonnes a year. Outside the port gates is a small square full of tables where fresh fish is served. Inside the gates is a massive fish market and a series of cafés for the fishermen. The Yacht Club is a restaurant and bar open to all with a good view of some of the harbour's activity. In order to leave the central docks for the fishing fleet, a new harbour is being built for general trade in bulk agricultural goods and a small yacht marina constructed by the beach.

SHOPPING

A kasbah of pink concrete has been built off the Rue Chair el Hamra to house market stalls. It is surprisingly attractive and has been adorned with some impressive wooden gates. Some tourist bazaars have been fitted on the north face, but the delightful animated confusion of a Moroccan marketplace has already taken control. As far as shopping is concerned you should avoid the colourless street-front shops in Agadir. Taroudant and Tiznit a few hours away have intriguing souks and maintain their traditions of craftsmanship. The **Crown English Bookshop** in the central shopping mall has been run since 1986 by Dan Bacon. Here you can find piles of holiday fiction, R. Collomb's *Atlas Mountain Guide*, English–Moroccan Arabic dictionaries and the Penguin *Koran*.

The **Uniprix** on Place Hassan II has all basic foods, mineral water, spirits and wine at under 30dh. Stock up here whatever direction you are going, as the only other off-licence in the south is at Ouazazarte, and only Marrakesh and Casablanca compete in range.

WHERE TO STAY

All the hotels in Agadir have been built since the earthquake and share the town's air of efficient uninspiring domestic convenience. However, you may need to stay a night in Agadir to fit in with bus or plane connections, or to sample the nightlife.

Of the dozen large four- or five-star beach hotels, the **PLM Les Dunes d'Or**, tel 20150, gives you the most intense experience of the insulated well-equipped luxury world of Agadir tourism. A double room with bath comes at around 250dh. Bear in mind that just under half of all Moroccan tourist revenue comes from this one town.

The ** **Miramar** (tel 22673) on Blvd Mohammed V at the northern edge of town is above the harbour and has a bar, restaurant and only 12 rooms. A double here costs 150dh. Another small comfortable hotel is the * **Petite Suede** with 16 rooms with a double for 86dh. It is inconspicuously tucked in behind a bank off Blvd Hassan II and only 200 m walk from the beach.

Facing the square where the buses leave from is the * **Excelsior**, on Av. Yacoub el Mansour, right in the middle of all the lively cheap grill cafés which surround the transport hub. The **Hôtel Diaf** on Av. Allal ben Abdellah is clean with powerful showers and seems to attract a good proportion of passing oddballs. If it's full, there is the **Hôtel de la Baie**, almost opposite, tel 22724, on Av. du President Kennedy, where a double costs 78dh. There is a campsite on Av. Mohammed V, tel 29540, an efficient but tightly packed site throughout the year.

Inezgane, once a separate town, is now just a suburb to the south of Agadir. It has three hotels of character that are removed from the mass tourist blandness of Agadir and better placed for the airport and the southerly bus and car routes. The **Provençal**, tel 31208, has rooms arranged around an abundant courtyard garden with a pool. There is an adjoining busy local bar, a restaurant, and the hotel is littered with various hunting trophies. A double costs 175dh, and the *menu du jour* is 75dh. **The Pergolas**, tel 30841, has no pool but instead the best French cooking in the south of Morocco under the direction of Mme Mirabel; a double costs 125dh.

The **Pyramides**, tel 30705, is easily found on the Route de la Perpiniere de l'Oued Souss, a quiet broad avenue that leads to King Hassan's newly expanded Agadir palace. The hotel is tranquil, has a pool and bar, and you can rent horses here to ride in the surrounding estuary which teems with wildlife.

EATING OUT

The cheapest, and to some extent the most amusing place to eat in Agadir, is at one of the grill cafés in the bus stop area. If you want to dawdle over your food a little the Rue des Oranges off Blvd Hassan II has a number of good cheap restaurants. At no 19 is **L'Amirauté**, a good reputation for fish with a large choice of Moroccan specialities and efficient friendly service. Three courses will set you back less than 50dh. There is also the **Tanalt** opposite, with a Moroccan menu at 40dh, and the **Daffy** at no 2 where they serve hot prawn pil-pil for 20dh.

The middle ground of Agadir restaurants, well advertised by neon signs with photograph menus in all the languages of Europe are all filled by jolly tourists. The best place to escape from an Agadir evening is **La Pergola** in Inezgane, see above. It has a number of menus which start from 90dh and following the culinary tradition of Touraine serves the best French food in the south of Morocco. It is popular with local businessmen and the more discerning and knowledgeable French tourists.

NIGHTLIFE

All the large beachfront hotels operate their own cabarets and discothèques. These are designed to entertain block-booked holiday groups and can be dreadful. Perhaps the worst is the **Salaam Hôtel**, where they organize Arabic fancy dress and belly dancing competitions. The **Hôtel Atlas** and the **Sahara Hôtel** go to some lengths to employ good resident bands who generally play from 8–11 when the disco takes over. The **Byblos Disco**, part of the **Dunes d'Or Hôtel**, is considered the most lively. The **Rendezvous**, a nightclub in the centre of the town, has the least institutional atmosphere.

Of quite a different order is the **Corniche Restaurant Bar** run by Ziki Brahim on the beachfront. From ten in the evening to three in the morning you can hear relevant, contemporary Moroccan bands play here. It is an absorbing, busy place, the music constantly changing and improvising in the style of jazz, though it and the audience are entirely Moroccan. The waiters provide an entertaining background of frenetic activity. Nearby is the **Jour et Nuit**, an elegant grill café and bar that stays open throughout the night, gradually collecting all the sleepless souls. If you don't feel like spending a night in a hotel, these two places, facing the moonlit deserted beach, are the perfect preparation for a dawn bus departure.

Taghazoute Beach

A mere 16 km north of Agadir lies Taghazoute Beach, a broad sweep of clear pale sand in a sheltered bay which is a justly celebrated alternative to hotel-dominated Agadir. At the centre of the bay, hardly visible from the road, is a campsite, the only accommodation, divided so that families are on the right and bachelors in a separate compound to the left. Beyond these camping grounds on the beach front are a couple of café-restaurants and a grocery stall.

The rock terrace on the north face of the bay is covered with the palm leaf umbrellas of the extensive **Sables d'Or Restaurant**, where beer in hand you can watch the sun descend.

Beyond is the village of Taghazoute, a small unpretentious roadside affair whose life is based around three cafés: the **Florida**, the **de la Paix** and the **Café Gibraltar**, which is opposite the other two in one of the arches of the vegetable souk.

The village has entered into hippy mythology as a centre for cheap winter living. The rocky coves of the coast provide camping sites and driftwood, whilst the surf provides exhilarating sport. Taghazoute village is the social centre for this community where meat, kif and vegetables are easily bought. The colony's busiest days have gone, though an obstinate rearguard of the acid revolution remains, mixing uneasily with the current generation of earnest European students who turn up. One or two genuine bums can normally be discovered in the melange. The police have forbidden the rent of rooms in the village and once in a while clear the coast, driving herds of muttering free spirits into the restrictions of an official campsite. Their traditional camping grounds are north of the village, where the atmosphere of mild degeneracy ends at a rock bluff just north of the old anchor warehouse, the Almadraba Bou-Inden.

Another group of Europeans has drawn its camper vans up on the shore of Taghazoute. The retired divide themselves into strict language and nationality compounds like some echo of the Crusades. They pickle themselves on spirits, sun and romantic fiction, adding a frisson to their adventure with the whispered tale of Germans hanged in Inezgane, a rumour that circulated as far back as the 1930s. Throughout the months of June, July and August, both these groups are swamped by Moroccan families escaping from the cities. They settle in one vast encampment by the seaside throughout the long summer holiday.

Cape Ghir

Amesnaz Beach, 11 km north of Taghazoute, is the last stretch of open sand and reasonably safe swimming before you reach Cape Ghir which is also spelt Rhir. This dramatic wave-dashed headland is where the High Atlas meets the Atlantic and is marked by a lighthouse. 40 km north from Agadir Cape Ghir marks an ancient Berber tribal boundary. To the north are the lands of the Haha Confederation (see page 267), whilst to the east and south stretches the highland territory of the Ida Outane.

Immouzer des Ida Outane

To visit the hilltop village of Immouzer and its mesmerizing waterfall, take a right turn at Tamraht, 12 km out of Agadir on the P8 coast road. A single track tarmac mountain road, the S7002, twists through dramatic scenery 50 km to Immouzer.

The turning at **Tamraht village** is lined with banana stalls and some quiet cafés. The road passes through banana groves, giving the area its nickname—Banana Valley—but the most beautiful stretch is reached when the plantations have been replaced by palm woods, and the road runs beside the smooth river-polished rocks, limestone gorge walls and bathing pools of the Oued Asif n Tarhalt. At the roadside, piles of hollowed out palm trunks are sold as curious but largely inadequate buckets and flower pots. Half way through this area of palms is the **Café de la Palerie**, a delightfully relaxed hut surrounded by a clearing where a rabbit tagine lunch costs 29dh.

The **Café Restaurant Tifrite**, a few km further on, is a more substantial place. The dining terrace overlooks a stream and the lush river floor. It has an effusive patron, a shop and serves tagine at 30dh. It marks the end of the palm gorge and the beginning of the long climb to the hard worked mountain plateau and the village of Immouzer.

Immouzer des Ida Outane is a white mountain top administrative village which contrasts with the red stone and pise hamlets that are scattered throughout the territory of the Ida Outane. A Berber tribal confederation, they have always occupied the western reaches of the High Atlas and have a reputation for industry, cultivating the most remote mountain valleys and grazing the highest slopes. Despite the fact that the Ida Outane were almost fully occupied by their own struggle against the environment, they still managed to throw some surplus energies into an intimate patchwork of local feuds. In all this they represent a typical, balanced Berber commonwealth and enjoyed practical independence from governments and national history until the arrival of the French in the region in 1927.

The **souk** is held here on Thursdays, an absorbing, busy place in early summer for Immouzer is celebrated for its honey. The hives feed from an exotic range of mountain herbs. Honey made purely from marjoram or marijuana is greatly prized for its medicinal qualities, though afficionados relish the mixed aroma of a highland blend. A festival of honey is held each year in July.

WHERE TO STAY

Immouzer has one hotel, the ***** Auberge des Cascades**, tel 16, a delightful place perched on a natural mountain terrace which enjoys a magnificent view and is surrounded by a mature garden with a pool, bar and restaurant. The hotel has fourteen well-decorated rooms and a double costs 175dh. Look out for the series of black and white prints produced by a local artist.

The Waterfall

A left turn at the central Caidat, the dramatically sited office of the Caid which is built on a cliff-edge stalagmite, takes you down a twisting narrow road 4 km to the roomy **Café Restaurant le Miel**, surrounded by benched displays of cheap minerals and fossils. From here, it is only a short walk through olive groves to the foot of the falls.

The Immouzer or Oued Tinkert falls are not dramatic for the volume of water, which never exceeds three healthy streams, but because of the rock formation, pools and heady air of mystery. The rich mineral content of the river has caused, over millennia, great blanket sheets of rock to be draped down over the mountains where the water has passed. Even living bushes and mosses can be seen encased in a stiffening layer of tufa deposit and the viscous water appears to slide in reluctant waves rather than plummet. The blanket of deposited rock has been rent in places to reveal secretive dripping caves glistening with wet moss and fern. Strange, powerful intriguing shapes are formed within the shadows.

The central fall of the three collects in a plunge pool before rushing down a natural rock-cut sluice to enter a perfect grotto. Here golden polished rocks with soft intricate curves loom up from their secretive depths through a deep sonorous pool of deathless blue water. This beautiful natural swimming pool is set in an enveloping bowl of stalagmite rocks which are greened by small growths of moss and hedged with dangling fig branches. At various ages steps have been cut in some of the rocks, now used as diving platforms. It is an enchanting place, serene and mysterious when empty, but not without a certain pagan charm even when full of desporting swimmers and bathers basking on the rocks.

East of Agadir to Taroudant

Taroudant is 80 km from Agadir along the P32 road, the route used by all the bus companies. On Thursday you could break the journey halfway at **Oulad Teima** in order to visit the **souk**. Travelling by car you could take a longer but more interesting journey along the Marrakesh road, the P40, which climbs below the argan foothills of Djebel Lgouz. 37 km out of Agadir, a right turn on to the 7016 puts you on the back road to Taroudant. Near the village of **Sidi Moussa** and visible from the road are the ruins of the **Caid's garden**, an overgrown walled enclosure that makes an ideal picnic spot with its ruined towers, paths, tanks and wildlife.

Taroudant

Taroudant is enclosed by an enormous rectangle of golden ochre battlemented walls, threaded with fortified towers. These walls are some of the best preserved in Morocco and the chief architectural glory of the town. Olive and orange groves spread out in all directions from the very foot of the defences. High Atlas peaks rise to the north while the Anti Atlas to the south are often obscured by a vapour that rises from the verdant intensity of the Souss valley.

Taroudant has always played two unchanging roles, that of chief market town of the

Souss and that of a strategic citadel commanding the major trade routes. It has, even more than Marrakesh, an African rather than Mediterranean identity. Its ancient walls contain not a venerable city of monuments but a market in a constant state of flux. The modern houses inside the spectacular walls are anti-climactic, but the central souk is one of the most enchanting and relaxing in Morocco. Taroudant has the best cooking in the south and a number of excellent hotels. It has never appealed to the bulk of the tourist trade, and consequently there are comparatively few foreigners about. All the better.

HISTORY

Taroudant has always been at the centre of the politics of the Souss valley. Its only period of national importance was during the 16th century as the original capital of the Saadian dynasty.

The Almoravides took the city in 1056, early in their rise to power, but it regained its independence under the Almohads, fellow Chleuh Berbers whose power base, Tinmal, is less than 100 km away. The Merenids had no such understanding with the city. They settled Arab tribes around the city, built a kasbah and enclosed Taroudant with great walls, ever a sign that a ruler has little confidence in a people's loyalty.

The great period of the city's history began in 1510 when the first Saadian, Mohammed al Quaim, a sheikh from the Draa valley was invested as Emir of the Souss by a fellow Sufi master at Taroudant. He and his sons led the jihad, holy war, against the Portuguese on the coast from their headquarters at Taroudant. They captured Marrakesh fourteen years later but continued to embellish Taroudant. This was not foolish loyalty but a continued interest in the region's very profitable trade in sugar, cotton, saltpetre and gold.

The seeds of Taroudant's destruction were sown in her resolute support of Sultan Moulay Ishmael's chief rival, his nephew Ahmed ibn Mahrez. When Taroudant eventually fell by siege to the Sultan in 1687 it was entirely destroyed: its population slaughtered or enslaved, its treasures and buildings looted and burned. It was repopulated by soldiers from the Riff, and its decline compounded in the 18th century when the port of Agadir was closed and the products of the Souss became less competitive. The region and its principal city fell into a state of acute and continual tribal dissidence.

In 1912 El Hiba, the Blue Sultan, having lost Marrakesh to the French after the battle of Bou Othman, retreated to Taroudant. The French armed the retinues of the great High Atlas caids and sent them south to attack El Hiba. Taroudant fell and its brutal sacking caused a brief fluttering of moral misgiving from the French High Command though this was soon forgotten due to the Blue Sultan's continued resistance from the Anti Atlas mountains.

GETTING TO AND AROUND

Bus: The most dramatic bus connection is the 5.00 SATAS departure for Marrakesh, going over the magnificent Tiz-n-Test, at a cost of 45dh for the 8 hours. There are four buses a day to Agadir, 80 km west, and tickets are only 12dh. These are often full, so buy your ticket well in advance, or go by grand taxi. Remember that Inezgane 12 km south of Agadir has a better range of bus connections to the south than Agadir, if you are planning on a quick connection.

From Taroudant, there are currently two buses a day to Tata and five to Ouazazarte. Ouazazarte is three hours away, and Taliouine, a useful stop, half way along the route.

On foot: Taroudant has hardly spilled beyond the extent of its ancient walls and is not a difficult city to walk in. Roads into the town inevitably lead to one of the two central squares, the Place Tamoklate or the Place Assarag. CTM buses and blue petits taxis for local trips gather in Place Tamoklate, and the local souks open off it in a labyrinth of rough fondouqs and manufacturing stalls.

The main street of the town is lined with shops and café-restaurants appealing largely to local custom and leads from the righthand corner of Place Tamoklate to Place Assarag. This is the hub of traveller's Taroudant. Its larger open space is partly covered with café tables and it is lined by cheaper hotels. The Banque Populaire, the bar of the Hotel Taroudant, the entrance to the tourist souk, grands taxis and the SATAS bus depot are all to be found here.

The Ramparts

Taroudant has few buildings of age or interest. It has seen too many pillaging armies for even many historical descriptions to survive. However, this is more than compensated for by the city walls. Their colour looks best at dusk, when the hue of gold, pink and orange contrasts perfectly with the olive green of the surrounding groves. The walls have been repaired whenever required and substantially follow the original Almoravide pattern. Small parts date from the Merenid rebuilding, but they consist mainly of 18th-century work. The early Saadian kasbah walls enclosed the area of the Makhzen, the government quarter of the city, now partly occupied by the Palais Salaam Hotel.

The indented battlemented entrance to Taroudant beside the hotel is flanked by orange trees which from March to April bathe the area with the rich perfume of orange blossom. Horse drawn carriages which will take you on a tour of the ramparts can be found at the Palais Salaam, which also hires out bicycles. If you go by foot, it is just possible to scramble along the battlement walkway, the stretch by the Bab el Khemis being one of the easiest. Even here the pise walls have decayed to make it quite

Taroudant, Street Scene in the Medina

487

adventurous at times. Rain has melted the fabric of the thick walls to create twisting holes, some just large enough to act as intimate spiral staircases down which you might like to squeeze.

The Souk

The entrance to the tourist **souk** is by the Banque Marocaine on Place Assarag. The Taroudant souk is small compared to those of Fez and Marrakesh, but is perhaps the most enjoyable to shop in. You can afford to wander aimlessly for the size and temper of the town discourages hard hassle. Down the first turning on the left you can buy incense, spices and dried roses.

Taroudant is the chief city of the Chleuh, with their long tradition of excellent craftsmanship. It is, along with Tiznit, one of the best places to buy or commission native Berber jewelry. The worked silver has a solidity and confidence of style which is not easy to find elsewhere. Strap sandles, looking a little like those worn by Roman legionnaries, are also made at souk stalls.

You will also see the usual incised grey marble 'African' animal carvings. But of much greater interest is the work of Taroudant sculptors who prefer the warm colours of locally mined limestone. The linear and decorative obsession of Moorish art has been rejected in favour of firm rotund and figurative work. The studio workshops are well worth looking out for and the prices are not extravagant. If you're keen on the local cloaks, the heavy ochre brown of a shepherd's burnous or the finer and lighter black wool ones complete with cavalier hoods and tassles, can be bargained for. Also difficult to find elsewhere are the cured skins of wild Atlas mountain foxes, those of smaller predators and the usual goat and sheep skins.

The Tanneries

The skins for sale at Taroudant are cured just outside the city walls—turn left out of Bab Khemis and right after 100 m to reach the tanneries. Though not as impressive in scale and complexity as the tannery quarters of Fez or Marrakesh the distinctive vats, procedures and odours have a continual fascination and are undeniably photogenic. It is possible to buy a fox fur hat throughout the day but the morning is the best time to see the tanneries in action.

WHERE TO STAY

The entrance to the **** **Palais Salaam Hôtel**, tel 2312, is well signposted and found through a gate in the city walls just off the road to Ouazazarte. The 19th-century palace of the Pasha of Taroudant, it is both the most interesting, accessible interior in Taroudant and an outstanding hotel. Silhouetted battlements enclose the whole complex and overlook its main pool which is surrounded by a luxuriant garden of high palms. The rooms all open on to small verdant Moorish courtyards, and have an unusual split level design with their sleeping areas upstairs. The public rooms retain the original decoration of the palace which is intimate rather than grandiose, and the dignified service and environment attracts guests for weeks rather than just a passing night. The hotel boasts three dining rooms, two pools, a cocktail bar and an efficient helpful reception desk. Prices are 283dh for a double, 221dh a single, and the menu for dinner is 86dh.

The ** **Hôtel Saadiens** on Bordj Ennassim, tel 2589, has 57 rooms and a terraced restaurant, a small pool and is pleasant and clean but is obviously no comparison with a four-star Hotel.

The * **Hôtel Taroudant**, on Place Assarag, has 31 rooms that open on to a garden courtyard covered in masses of bougainvillea. In the town centre, it has a street bar, a good licensed restaurant and a worn, relaxed, distinctive character, like its proprietor. A single costs 47dh, a double 61dh. The excellent full Moroccan menu is 55dh and beer 6.5dh.

At the **Hôtel de la Place**, Place Assarag, bedrooms 9, 10, 11 and 12 open out on to a roof terrace, where you can take breakfast overlooking the square. They cost 35dh whereas the less appealing rooms on the first floor go for 25dh.

Place Tamoklate contains the **Hôtel Restaurant El Warda** with balconies overlooking the square. You can eat a 45dh three course menu in the animated first floor café or on the terrace. There is a smart patisserie on the ground floor for breakfast. The prices of the rooms are flexible, and you should make certain that they are firmly established. A double can be 45dh.

La Gazelle d'Or is the most exclusive five-star hotel in Morocco. It was converted from a house built by a French baron just before World War II. It is 2 km out of Taroudant, first left at the petrol station on the road to Amezgou. A semi-circle of ten cottages flank the central dining room. The whole hotel is isolated in ten hectares of garden whose lawns are still cut by hand. Buffet lunch is served by the pool, surrounded by an orange grove with a fine view of the High Atlas. There is a small stable of Arab horses for the guests. Prices are very high. A double room costs 1340dh, and a fairly skimpy buffet lunch is 250dh a head excluding the cost of a glass of water. The dinner is excellent, served by waiters dressed like acolytes for a sacred feast. Three quarters of the guests are British, which gives this small hotel the atmosphere of a rather unfriendly house party—the perfect setting for an Agatha Christie. The hotel is closed in July and August, and telephone bookings are often refused, but try 2039/48.

EATING OUT

Taroudant is renowned for its cooking, and you will eat well at any stall café in the city. The **Restaurant de la Place** on Place Assarag has tagines for 12.5dh and brochettes at 2dh each.

The licensed **Hôtel Taroudant** will give you a delicious four-course meal for 50dh, from either the Moroccan or French menu, and the **Restaurant Tout Va Bien** on Place Tamoklate serves a particularly good couscous and you can bring your own wine. The **Café Nada** on Rue Ferk Lahbab stays open at all hours serving harira and tagine. The **Hôtel Saadiens** is licensed, and serves its Moroccan menu on a balcony overlooking the street.

Eating at the **Palais Salaam Hôtel** is a treat, but you will have to book a table at the hotel reception in the morning and choose your dishes in advance if you want to eat in the Moroccan restaurant. Try a Berber 'Caprice' cocktail beforehand at the pool, or a cheaper 8dh beer.

Excursions from Taroudant: Freija, Tioute and Amagour

Freija

To get to the oasis and kasbah of Freija, drive 8 km east of Taroudant to Ait Yazza and turn right for the Souss river bed. The bridge has been down for years but you should have no difficulty crossing the gravel bed. The kasbah has a spectacular position on the south bank overlooking the crossing. It is now an inhabited farm building, but you can wander up a snaking path and descend through prickly pear hedges past a koubba. Below, on the other side of the road, are the ruins of an extensive palace which is also inhabited and which shelters within its walls the village school.

Tioute

The Tioute turning is 12 km from the Freija crossing of the Souss, right off the Tata road. About 5 km of gravel track takes you to the village of Tioute enclosed by a verdant palmery garden that is hemmed in by the surrounding hills. In this beautiful hidden valley are the ruins of the extensive **Caid's kasbah**, on a promontory of high land just beyond the village. The kasbah was part of the extensive feudal holdings of the Glouai Empire and though damaged by the 1960 Agadir earthquake there are a few surviving chambers that retain their painted plaster decoration. The ruins of the **Mellah**, the old Jewish quarter, are found a little further on, beside a spring that is trapped to fill a tank. A venerated rabbi from this community is buried below the walls of a ruined agadir that crowns the nearby hill. The villagers identify this agadir as an old Portuguese fort and though there are no records that support this it is odd to find bricks being used in this region.

Amagour

For the adventurous, or those with four-wheel drive, you can continue 40 km beyond Tioute via the village of Tinouainane to the picturesque villages of Amagour and **Adrar ou Aman**. They stand above a great breach cut out of the Anti Atlas. An ancient volcanic crater much used as a sanctuary by migrating birds is 15 km walk out of Amagour. Ask for a guide in the village.

Taroudant to Ouazazarte

Oued Aissa, 26 km east of Taroudant is a pleasant verdant village with a kasbah on the right of the road. The turning for the **Tiz-n-Test** is 53 km from Taroudant, and the start of one of the most spectacular roads in Morocco, leading you across the High Atlas to Marrakesh.

Sidi Amel

The village and shrine of Sidi Amel is 6 km before Aoulouz, along a short track leading up to the right. The white minaret of the mosque can be seen from the road. The guardian and school teacher are humorous, welcoming men always ready to entertain the odd visitor with a cup of tea, and Sidi Amel is high enough to offer clear views over the tropical-looking Souss valley.

The guardian will happily show you into the mosque's worn ablution courtyard with its well of fresh cool water. The shrine of Sidi Amel is separate from the mosque, identifiable by an elegant koubba. The moussem is held here in the last four days of the year, a survival from old Berber and Western European rites when the new year was calculated on our solar calendar rather than as it is now in Morocco, on the Islamic lunar cycle.

Djebel Siroua

To get right off the beaten track, just before the elegant spanning bridge over the Oued Souss at Aoulouz is a piste turning. After 8 km a left turn leads to a waterfall 10 km away—the only place outside the Soviet Union where the bald-headed Ibis may be seen.

Many will feel that this is enough, but it is a mere prelude for the drive straight on and over the Djebel Siroua to Anezat 100 km east on the Tazenacht–Ouazazarte road. The dirt track which at times climbs to 2500 m, has been covered by a Renault 4 though a four-wheel drive would be securer and more comfortable.

Djebel Siroua rises on the right, its empty volcanic crater touched all year round with snow. It was a sacred mountain to the Masmuda Berbers and is the junction of the two great ranges, the High Atlas and the Anti Atlas. Bulls were sacrificed every year at its summit and pools of animal blood have still recently been seen near the crater. The mountain is the territory of the Ait Ououzguite, a transhumant tribe who move in the summer to the higher slopes for new crops and pasture. The villages are austere dry stone creations crowned by agadirs which are still used to store wool, cereals and carpets when the village seasonally migrates. At this time, a saint from the Tamgrout zaouia is invoked to protect the agadirs, and two guardians are left behind with a complete code of bylaws for their administration.

Well water and freshly baked bread are available from the villages. Some have a school master who will speak French, though he will be on holiday from June through August. Otherwise navigation and communication in Berber can be difficult, and there are more tracks and villages with similar names than appear on any map. Even if you don't get across it is an extremely exciting foray into undisturbed tribal land. The route should take you from Aoulouz to Innouzia–Ouennin, Aoufour, Askaou, Askaoun, over two passes and down to Tachokchte, Tammellakout and Anezat on the main P32 highway.

Aoulouz

Aoulouz, on the south side of the Souss river, is a small but busy market town. The **souk** is on Sundays and Wednesdays, and the market area down from the main road on your right. Just beside the bridge on the left is an inhabited four-towered **kasbah**, which has delicate exterior stalactite plasterwork on the upper towers. It has a delightful situation with the Souss river bed breaking through the mountain wall behind. There are beds available in Aoulouz at the café with no name at 6 Blvd Hassan II at the far end of the avenue on your right just before the main souk. They protest that they are not a hotel, but rent out rooms. The café is a good base for wheedling information about the more obscure taxi and truck routes into the Djebel Siroua, which includes a local service to Assarag which will be of interest to mountain climbers.

Taliouine

You will notice before you arrive at Taliouine that there are no longer any argan trees. This Soussi tree has its easternmost frontier at the Kasbah of Innouzia–Ounnenine.

Taliouine, halfway between Taroudant and Ouazazarte, is often ignored by travellers rushing to the dubious attractions of Ouazazarte. It is a beautiful steep-walled oasis valley full of almond trees, agadirs, high villages and kasbahs perched on bleak hills and echoing architectural details across to each other. The clean, cool mountain air makes it an exciting place to walk and there is a five-day expedition organized from Taliouine to climb Djebel Siroua (see below).

The **Glaoui kasbah** sits conspicuously on the valley floor, just east of the village, a massive palace surrounded by carefully cultivated terraces shaded by thin almond trees. Four square towers feature shell motifs cut in plaster above the windows. The caretaker, a strange title for one who inhabits a disintegrating domain, lives in the tower with his television aerial protruding. The surrounding courtyards and additional outbuildings are occupied by 25 families of the ex-servants of the Glaoui, who are normally happy to talk and show you around the exterior. The small detached pavilion on the hill was used as an estate office where rent was gathered in coin and kind.

WHERE TO STAY AND EAT

There are two contrasting hotels in Taliouine, the **Hôtel Ibn Tumert** and the **Auberge Souktana**. Ibn Tumert, tel 30, low, open and modern, is above the kasbah, a red stucco building with a featureless interior. The view of the kasbah and the surrounding mountains is superb, and it has a large pool, a bar and a good restaurant. It has 106 rooms, a single costs 80dh and a double 100dh. The four-course dinner menu is 90dh.

The Auberge Souktana, on the left of the main road below the kasbah, is a delightful and cheap alternative. Get there early to make sure you get one of the four bedrooms, though you can camp in the garden if not. The Auberge is run by Ahmed and his French wife Michelle, and has a relaxed and friendly atmosphere. Basic amenities come in the form of candles and barrels of water, and dinner is served communally and leisurely for 35dh. Ahmed organizes a five-day expedition to Djebel Siroua. These are usually planned well in advance for specific groups in the spring or autumn months and costs start from 120dh per person per day. The usual route is to stay a night at the villages of Akhtamana, Tmgoute and Atougga for the climb to the summit and then a two-day return to the road on one of a number of local routes.

East to the Oasis Valleys

Out of Taliouine the road climbs through the progressively bleak hills of the Anti Atlas, a cluster of mosques and koubbas at **Irhaki-Tinfat** being the sole distraction. The Tizi-n-Tarhatine pass at 1886m divides the watersheds of the Souss and the Draa, though it seems to make no difference at all to this forbidding and waterless landscape.

Tazenakht

This village has little to recommend it except as a refuge from the heat and savage landscape. It specializes in the carpets of the Ouzguita women, a fact you won't be able to miss. If you like these harsh geometric designs, the artisan cooperative has lower prices and a better selection than you will find in the souks of Fez, Marrakesh or Taroudant. The vivid lozenges and diamonds are a hallmark of highland carpets, reflecting the dominating pattern of the mountains, their harsh silhouettes and bold forms.

Tazenakht is also the last stop before a couple of desert crossings east. You may want to stay at the **Hôtel Zenaga**, tel 32, to get an early start on either of these. It charges 40dh a double, and the restaurant in the back room runs up a good chicken tagine for 24dh. Both the crossings are currently open, and there should be no reason for this to change, but it is always safest to check with the police at Tazenakht on conditions and any permission that may be required.

The S510, a tarmaced road for 44 km, leads from Tazenakht to the copper mine at Bleida. Beyond the mine it continues beyond as a dirt road that follows the Oued Tamsift valley to make an alternative approach to the village of Agdz on the Draa valley.

22 km out of Tazenakht along the S510 a turning leads due south for 70 km along a new road to the oasis of **Foum Zguid**. This has recently become accessible by buses which now pass through Tazenakht on their way south three times a week (see page 445).

If you do take either of these routes you will miss little of interest on the way to Ouazazarte. 28 km north of Tazenakht a dirt track road from the village of **Anezal** provides wonderful escapades into the villages and agadirs of the Ouzguita tribe on the slopes of Djebel Siroua. The river beds of the Tamgra and the Tamassint, just before the hamlet of Anezal, have small patches of palm and oleander to shade a picnic.

53 km beyond Tazenakht, the bridge over the Oued Tidili was swept away by its river in full flood in March 1988, taking a lorry with it. The previous November the Finnish Ambassador and his wife were drowned east of Zagora in a similar flash flood. Water when it comes to the desert is as dangerous as when there is none. The bridge has been repaired and here the P32 road east splits. For the Tiz-n-Tichka pass north to Marrakesh, see pages 423–4.

South of Agadir to Tiznit

Beyond the Oued Souss, Inezgane and Ait Melloul, you leave the populated estuary and take the open road for Tiznit.

The **forest of Ademine**, a belt of scrub wilderness which you pass through quickly on the edge of the Souss valley, is the snake charmers' favoured area for hunting for new twisting, rearing performers. The undulating coastal plain of the Souss is farmed by the Chtouka tribe of the Chleuh Berbers. Once a dry grassland prairie, the water from the Youssef ben Tachfine dam which traps the Oued Massa now allows many more crops to be raised during the spring and autumn.

Tifnit

33 km out of Agadir, a turning to the west takes you 10 km down a tarmac track, the 7048, to the beach of Tifnit. It is a curious and alternative village, a community that attracts a drifting population of camper vans, hippies, local soldiers and fishermen. The village, an anarchy of low grey stone huts, has been built on a sand spit that extends out to sea and

looks like a fledgling Phoenician colony. Low doors, wells, drifting sand dunes and the inherent complication of the pathways reassert the Moorish style after Agadir's international boulevards. A basic café exists amongst it all, whose sand terrace and floor is threatened by each and every high tide. You can live off fresh water from the well, fresh fish and bread—a simple ascetic diet in imitation of Christ.

Sidi R'bat

Back on the road to Tiznit, look out for a right turn, 6 km beyond the village of Tiferghal, signposted for **Tassila**. A deteriorating track at Tassila leads on for 8 km to the small village of **Massa**, and the divine isolation of Sidi R'bat. Massa which is now just a line of farmers' plots leading down to the estuary, was in the 17th century, a thriving port much visited by Genoese and Portuguese traders.

The Oued Massa flows down out of the Anti Atlas mountains to this wide brackish estuary, which is sealed from the sea by a tidal sand bar and surrounded on both sides by dunes. It holds an astonishing wealth of wildlife and is a sanctuary for migrating birds. At dusk, flight after flight comes to the water, and geese congregate silhouetted on the skyline of the southern dunes. The frogs cannot be ignored, as their chorus becomes almost deafeningly vociferous.

The **Complexe et Balnéaire Sidi R'bat** is one of the most glorious places to camp in the whole of Morocco. It is fortunately further on along the beach, out of ear shot of the frogs, and a coastal breeze keeps the midges at bay. Rooms are available around the wide open courtyard, which houses a café, bar and restaurant. Camping is 5dh per person, whilst a double room costs 45dh. Even after a week of walking along empty beach and through the protected dunes full of wildlife it is a difficult place to leave. There is an alarming plan to develop this reserve into a nature park, with elephants and gazelles, and the sympathetic manager of the Complexe, Marcel Hamelle, has already been told to go.

Sidi R'bat has earned itself a mythical place in the history books on several accounts. It is the beach where the Arab conqueror Uqba ben Nafi rode his horse into the sea to show Allah that there was no land further west for him to conquer for the true faith. The siting of a **ribat** here, a fortified monastery for the propagation of the faith, shows that conversion was not immediate, and in fact was not widespread in this area until after the 11th century. The beach is believed to be where the prophet Jonah was disgorged by the whale. There is a more sinister tradition that states that the man of destiny, the Antichrist, will first be recognized at Sidi R'bat, rising naked and sublimely beautiful from the sea. Staying here, you begin to understand something of the nature of myth-making.

Returning back on to the Agadir to Tiznit road, you will cross the Oued Massa where an assortment of kasbahs and forts of every age guard the strategic crossing. Armed soldiers on the bridge give a sense of historical continuity.

Tiznit

On the arid edge of the plain of Souss, facing the foothills of the Anti Atlas, stands the city of Tiznit. The approach road passes modern silos and pylons but the heart of the city is still the Medina which is encased by a complete circuit of over five kms of massive pink-ochre walls.

Though it is strongly identified with the Blue Sultans, the desert warrior Ma el Ainin, and his son El Hiba, Tiznit was actually founded by Sultan Moulay Hassan (1873–94) in the hope of creating a centre of stability in the dissident south. The Sultan encased over a dozen existing kasbahs in the present outer wall and established the city's reputation for jewelry by settling Jewish artisans within the walls.

Ma el Ainin was a courageous Muslim nationalist, an Idrissid Sheikh from the Sahara who with the support of Sultan Moulay Hassan and the desert tribes fiercely opposed the French who were advancing north from the Senegal and west from Algeria. The failure of either Sultan Abdul Aziz or Moulay Hafid to resist the French landings in central Morocco encouraged Ma el Ainin to declare himself Sultan in 1910, and take command of all the tribes of Morocco in jihad (holy war) against the French. His army was defeated at Tadla, and he retired to die that October at Tiznit.

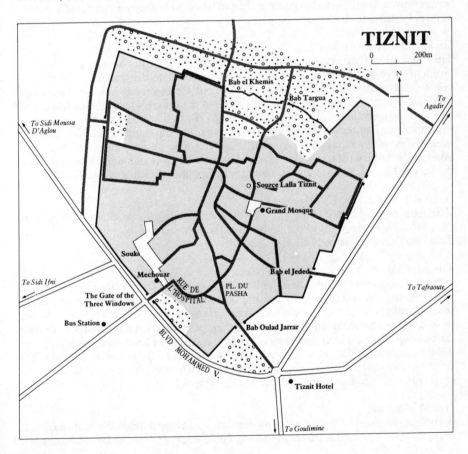

But his son El Hiba, who had inherited his father's striking looks, intelligence and authority, continued the resistance. He declared himself Sultan at Tiznit in May 1912 after hearing that Sultan Moulay Hafid had in the Treaty of Fez surrendered the whole of Morocco to the French. Known as the Blue Sultan by virtue of the fact that he never discarded his litham, the indigo desert veil, the whole of the south rose under his leadership. Marrakesh threw open her gates to his holy army, which streamed north from the city to liberate Fez. They were massacred by the French army that lay waiting with their machine guns and howitzers at Sidi Bou Othman. In May 1913 El Hiba's former allies, the chiefs of the High Atlas, now in the pay of the French, ousted him from Taroudant but he continued his resistance in the Anti Atlas until he died, at Kerdous, in 1919. Control of Tiznit then passed to the High Atlas Lord, Si Taieb Gondaffi, who was made Pasha by the French. El Hiba's younger brother, the poet Merebbi Rebbu, continued a guerrilla war of resistance until his final capitulation in 1926. Tiznit is now the provincial capital, a town of 45,000. Despite only 5% of the surrounding province being cultivated, chiefly with argan and almond trees, there are over quarter of a million farmers in the hinterland.

GETTING AROUND
The Place Mechouar is at the heart of the Medina through an entrance guarded by a distinctive pair of tall towers pierced by three windows. The Banque Populaire and the best café-restaurants are all in the Mechouar, but the larger cafés lie on the avenue outside the three windowed towers. This leads to the square whence buses leave, and where you will also find the Post Office and CTM Hotel. There are two buses a day that cover the 7-hr journey east to Tata and two for the 2-hr trip south to Sidi Ifni. There at least half a dozen buses a day to Goulimine and four to Tafraoute. For the more established routes a place in a grand taxi is almost as cheap as and more convenient than the buses. The journey to Sidi Ifni costs 15dh, Goulimine 15dh and Agadir 20dh.

WHAT TO SEE
Within the circumference of the walls, Tiznit is a delightful town to explore. At dawn or dusk the pink brown walls of the houses and the light blue of the windows and doors flicker and glow in harmony with the heavens.

The Mechouar
Tiznit has a deserved reputation for craftsmanship, and particularly for metal work and silver jewelry. Between the Mechouar and the outer wall is the **jewellers' souk** where you will find a profusion of bracelets, necklaces, rings and brooches in traditional Berber style. The Soussi merchants entice you into their bejewelled lairs, plying you with mint tea and clichéd sales patter. The hand of Fatima, a symbol of good luck which wards off the evil eye, is a constant motif. It is an ancient symbol that was part of the regalia of the Assyrian kings and has been included into the Muslim heritage by being named after the chief lady of Islam, Fatima the daughter of the prophet.

Grand Mosque
A road to the right of the Mechouar, the Rue de l'Hôpital leads down through the triangular Place du Pasha, past high walls that hide a cemetery, to the Grand Mosque. It

was here that El Hiba was acclaimed Sultan by the blue-robed Saharan tribes: the Tekna, Reguibat, Tidrarin and Delim. The minaret of the mosque is studded with curious little perches. An odd tradition says that the souls of the dead rest here in order to gain virtue by their proximity to the prayers of the faithful. This is not at all in line with orthodox teaching which dictates that souls wait for the Day of Judgement with no more sense of the passing centuries than a good night's sleep. However if you can discreetly linger during the evening and listen to the plain chants of the women, it becomes understandable that the souls should wish to congregate here.

Though the architecture is unusual in Morocco, 'perched mosques' are common south of the Sahara. There is a good example in Timbuktu.

The Spring/Source of Lalla Tiznit
Further into the town you reach the spring of Lalla Tiznit where clear blue water fills a basin. Lalla Tiznit was a Mary Magdalene type, a reformed prostitute who became strong in faith. She was martyred, but Allah recognized her holiness and marked her death by creating a cool refreshing spring that is now kept topped up by a pumping station.

Bab Targua and Bab El Khemis
Continuing north you should reach the outer walls and the towers that protect the Bab Targua and Bab El Khemis gates. The inside staircases are still just about safe and the roof provides a precarious view over part of the town and the decaying private walls that once divided up the valuable and now dwindling olive groves outside.

Tiznit is largely empty of student guides and you can happily wander around getting lost in the old streets. Portions of the original pre-city kasbahs jostle amongst the street pattern in pleasant contrast to recently built breeze-block houses.

SOUKS, SPORTS AND FESTIVALS
The Thursday **souk** is held just out of town on the Tafraoute road and is well worth attending in the growing season.

Tennis can be played at a court on the road to Mirhelt and you can pay to use the Tiznit Hotel **pool**, though the sea is close enough.

The Moussem of Sidi Abderrahman is held in August in Tiznit. The Moussem of Sidi Ahmad ou Moussa, on 3 August for six days, is the great festival for acrobats, and is held 35 km east of Tiznit off the Tafraoute road.

WHERE TO STAY AND EAT
The *** **Tiznit Hôtel**, tel 2411, is just off the main crossroads on the road to Tafraoute, the Rue Bir Enzarn. The rooms face into an interior courtyard, thick with maze-like rosemary hedges which surround a low pool where there is a bar. A professional band of musicians and dancers perform by the pool every evening from 18.00–20.00. A large Moorish dining room, where you can eat dinner for 65dh, looks west towards the walled town. A double bedroom is 174dh, a beer 8dh. The night club downstairs opens after 20.00 with some native dancing at about 22.00.

The * **Hôtel Mauritania**, tel 2072, is on the left of the Goulimine road, close to the Tiznit Hotel. It has a raffish atmosphere, 16 bedrooms, a double for 67dh and the town's busiest bar.

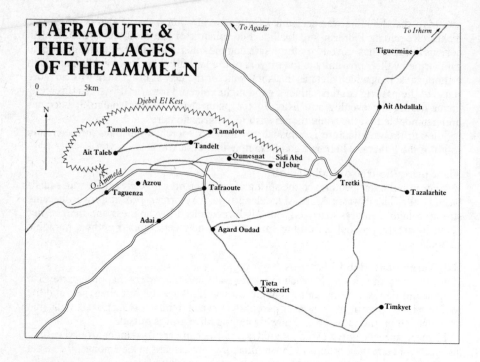

**TAFRAOUTE &
THE VILLAGES
OF THE AMMELN**

The **CTM Hôtel**, tel 2211, is outside the town walls, facing the Post Office on the large dusty bus square. It is clean and a room without a shower costs 20dh a night. There is a good cheerful little restaurant on the first floor.

Inside the walls a number of small pleasant hotels line the Place du Mechouar. There is little to choose between them, though the **Hôtel Atlas** is the most popular and vies with the **Hôtel Bon Acceuil** for the best and most varied tagines in their pleasant ground floor cafés. Most of the Mechouar hotels have their own roof terraces for a pleasant smoke at dusk.

Sidi Moussa D'Aglou, Tiznit Beach

17 km from Tiznit is the sea and village of Sidi Moussa, which you can reach by hitching a lift on the lorries that go to pick up building sand, though taxis are probably more convenient. At first, Sidi Moussa appears to be dominated by electric cables, one of which is rather mysteriously connected to a koubba, a distinctive, whitewashed saint's tomb. The **Motel Aglou** faces directly towards the sea and has fifteen romantic rooms all with their own terraces, a tranquil cushion strewn café and a courtyard for cars and tents. A double room costs 45dh. The **Café Restaurant Ouazize** serves a quite delicious fish tagine, has decorated water basins, outdoor showers and has a general store.

Facing the sea, the best beach is on your left, where the acrobats of Tiznit practise on the wet sand. To your right is a lagoon coming out of curiously weathered rocks. Beyond a path leads to the wave-dashed shelves on which local fishermen perch. Houses, with elaborate portals and doors, have been tunnelled into the sand cliffs to make a troglodyte village.

On from Tiznit

From Tiznit there are three interesting choices. The road inland leads through the Anti Atlas mountains to Tafraoute and back to Agadir; the inland road to Goulimine passes through the village of Bou Izakarn and the road to Tata which takes you in a broad sweep through oasis settlements to bring you to Taroudant or the southern coastal route through Sidi Ifni that takes you on to Goulimine and the entrance to the Western Sahara.

Tafraoute and the Anti Atlas Mountains

The round trip to Tafraoute is one of the most classically beautiful journeys that you can make in Morocco. The astonishing grandeur of the Anti Atlas mountains, the contrast between oasis greenery and bleak mountain slopes and the extraordinary lunar landscape around Tafraoute are the major physical attractions. On the human side, the independence of the mountain Berbers, their dress and architecture and the welcoming tempo of their life wooes you into a distinctive relaxing pace.

It is an excellent opportunity to get in some out of the way piste travelling if you have a car, but if not, the walking around Tafraoute is a treat in itself.

GETTING AROUND
Tafraoute is situated on a loop of road, route 7074, which runs from Tiznit to Agadir. It is 144 km from Tiznit. There are four buses from Agadir to Tafraoute a day and even more on Wednesday, when the **souk** is held. This direct journey takes about 5 hrs.

The approach from Tiznit is the more impressive of the two routes. Four buses leave Agadir for Tiznit a day, a 2-hr journey, and four buses leave Tiznit a day for Tafraoute, a 3–4-hr journey. Landrover taxis occasionally make a run from Tiznit to Tafraoute and on to Irherm, which would make an exhilarating journey. Leaving Tafraoute you have a choice of four daily buses to Agadir and three to Tiznit. There are a few hotels outside Tafraoute, but it is the best base for any exploration of the Anti Atlas.

Tazeroualt

20 km east of Tiznit, where the coastal plain gives way to the foothills of the Anti Atlas, is the village of **Assaka**. The road crosses the Tazeroualt river, which drains north into the Youssef ben Tachfine dam. Five kasbahs hug the fertile river bed and over the river a rough piste track leads 7 km south to the **Souk Sebt d'Ouijjane**.

Beyond Assaka the road penetrates into a steep gorge decorated with the strange twisting trunks of arguin trees. A righthand turning 40 km from Tiznit takes you 11 km on a tarmac road to the **Zaouia of Sidi Ahmed ou Moussa**, a fascinating side trip.

Sidi Mohammed ou Moussa was an Idrissid marabout who founded the zaouia before his death in 1563. His son, Sidi Ali Bou Dmia, established the state of Tazeroualt which in its heyday during the mid-17th century ruled over almost the entire south: the Souss, the Dades and the Draa. Sultan Moulay Hassan finally destroyed the principality in his campaign of 1882, founding Tiznit as the new bastion of central authority in the area. Illigh, the capital of Tazeroualt, was left in ruins but the zaouia itself survives as a functioning religious centre.

The village of **Zaouia Sidi Ahmed ou Moussa** has a small **market** on Tuesdays, but is totally transformed for the moussem which starts on the third Thursday in August and lasts for six days. Acrobats in circuses all over the world come from this region, and Sidi Mohammed ou Moussa is their patron saint and protector. The moussem is their annual celebration. At other times of the year you can see them practising on nearby beaches, particularly at **Sidi Moussa D'Aglou**. The village runs beside the dry bed of the stream, which is punctuated by deep stone wells from which women draw endless pitchers of water. The zaouia itself is the complex of whitewashed buildings that clusters around the mosque and its old tower. Sanctuary walls enclose the burial hill above the village, and a gatehouse guards the approach to the green tiled pyramidal roof of Sidi Ahmed's tomb. A horseshoe arched arcade inside provides shade for the pilgrims, and a snaking sacred way leads up the hill past smaller stone tombs to the summit.

The large souk courtyard lies between this hill and the river bed. Beside the river sits a pink café, just before two stone arched bridges, one an attractive ruin, which lead 4 km to **Anou-Illigh**. Now largely abandoned, the site of the old capital of Tazeroualt is littered with the barely recognizable extent of ruined palaces and the tombs of the various Idrissid marabout princes.

Kerdous

Tirhmi, back on the main road, boasts the **Café Moderne**, a useful stop before advancing up the hairpin bends that take you to the Col du Kerdous. This valley used to be the sanctuary of El Hiba, the Blue Sultan, who led the tribes of the south in resistance to the French until his death in 1918. Merebbi Rebbu, his younger brother renowned for his poetry, fought on until 1926. At the summit of 1100 m, a hotel, an incomplete jumble of styles, has been in the process of construction for many years. It has an astonishing position, perched with an eagle's eye view down over the valley but an unhappy incident from the past has brooded to create a doom-laden atmosphere.

A tarmac track turns right just past the 'hotel', and leads 3 km to a kasbah of astonishing tranquillity. The wall above the heavy wooden studded door has been inset with green slate, a perfect example of the traditional Berber geometric and eyebrow decorative patterns. A small koubba and mosque lie to the right and a rough track crosses over the stream bed and continues the 10 km to **Souk Tleta des Ida Gougmar**. This used to be one of the old trading routes that led south from Taroudant through the mountains to Ifrane Anti Atlas and the start of the Saharan caravan crossings.

The Territory of the Ammeln

As the mountain plateau after the Kerdous pass gives way to high mountain valleys, groves of palm are joined by the slender trunks of almond trees, and you enter the territory of the Ammeln tribe. Their reputation for commercial acumen is mirrored by the plethora of local souks. You will find a basic **Hôtel–Café–Restaurant, La Victoire**, at **Tizourhan**, 67 km from Tiznit. A piste turning just before the village leads to **Souk Khemis des Ait Oufka**, and beyond it on an evil 110 km track to **Foum el Hassan**. **Souk el Tnine**, 13 km from Tafraoute, has a Monday market, and **Arba n Tafraoute**, 4 km further, has its **souk** on Wednesdays. **Souk el Had de Tahala**, 7 km before Tafraoute, buys and sells on Sundays.

The entire valley leading to Tafraoute is inhabited by Ammeln Berbers, a division of the Chleuh. Due to the limited resources of land and water in the area, they developed into outstanding grocers and now run corner stores in practically every town and city in the country. They are said to have the same proverbial financial caution elsewhere attributed to Scots and Jews and they are also tenaciously loyal to their homeland. As a result, as you approach Tafraoute you will notice that the villages have a scattering of modern houses amongst the traditional pise and stone architecture. These are often built by absent Tafraoutis, though they are little used until retirement. Weddings and other family occasions are an excuse for week-long extravagant hospitality, and cosmopolitan reunions of Belgian mine workers, Tangier estate agents and wholesalers from Casablanca.

Tafraoute

In Tafraoute the pise houses have, due to expatriate prosperity, been entirely replaced by large modern square red ones. The village of 1700 people is not, architecturally, very exciting. However, for several km around Tafraoute you will have been aware of the bizarre and massive rock formations for which the area is so famous. Set off against the rich green of the oasis, from all over the village you see glimpses of these weird shapes in red and mauve granite, which seem like daily meteorite showers on Mars. Soaring peaks and silhouetted rock fields, created by slow cooling extrusions of igneous red lava, create illusions of gravity defying rocks balanced precariously and improbably on thin summits. The ideal time to see this landscape is in mid-February, when the contrasting lush growth of barley and delicate almond blossom is at its peak.

Almond trees are between 4 and 10 metres high, with thin black sinuous branches, tight pink and white blossom followed by bright green lance-shaped leaves. The fruit is green, drying to a leathery pouch with the familiar nut inside. It has two varieties: Dulcis, the cultivated, edible variety, and Amara, its wild sister, which grows tenaciously on high mountain slopes and produces a bitter narcotic oil, spiced with poisonous prussic acid. The wood is reddish in colour and used for veneers. In mid-February you may be lucky to catch the almond blossom festival, the dates of which vary from year to year, but this can also be a period of low cloud and rain.

Tafraoute has three hotels, a campsite, cafés, a patisserie, garages and petrol stations. The Post Office (open 8.30–12.00 and 15.00–18.30) and the Banque Populaire (open 9.00–11.30) are both on the small Place Hassan II.

WHAT TO DO
You can effortlessly spend several days in Tafraoute, walking and exploring the surrounding markets and oasis villages. The most celebrated area to walk in is the **Vallée**

des Ammeln, the Valley of Almonds, on the road to Agadir. A string of villages surrounded by spring-fed gardens nestles at the foot of the vast, towering thousand-metre wall of Djebel el Kest. There are two dozen kasbahs, intricate braided irrigation ditches and walled terraced gardens with small orchards of fig, olive, almond and palm to explore. Though it does not matter enormously, perhaps the best place to start is at the village of **Oumesnat**, 7 km out of Tafraoute. From here you can wander by a network of paths through over 27 villages. The road follows the valley east, so it is more tempting to walk west to the **ksour of Tamalout, Tandelt, Tamaloukt** or even **Ait Taleb**, 14 km from Oumesnat.

Other nearby villages which you might wish to visit include the **oasis of Adai**, 3 km from Tafraoute on the Tiznit road. You will recognize it by its abrasive pink minaret. It is set in a remarkable landscape, gripped and overawed by the chaos of threatening red granite rocks.

Alternatively, 4 km south on route 7075 is the village of **Agard-Oudad** and the well-known rock formation called 'Le Chapeau de Napoleon'. Considering that the French pacification of the Anti Atlas in the 1930s was only achieved with a fair amount of indiscriminate aerial bombing, it seems strange that the French are so admired, although I have decided that this particular name must be a joke. If you walk 500 m south of the rock, it looks just like a Barbary ape sucking its thumb. If you continue another 1 km, you will be surprised by the rock paintings of the Belgian artist, Jean Veran, in a perfect setting for his grandiloquent style. The track continues south 17 km to **Tasserit** and beyond to the isolated mountain palmery of **Timkyet**, a possible destination for the adventurous in four-wheel drive vehicles.

There are some fine prehistoric rock carvings of animals which are best found by asking for a guide at the **Hôtel des Amandiers**.

WHERE TO STAY

There are two small cheap hotels in the centre of town—the **Tangier** and the **Redouane**. Sometimes the Tangier will let you have a room for 12dh, or a double for 20dh, but the prices can dramatically increase for the Wednesday **souk**. The Redouane is cooler, slightly more spacious and you can book a room (tel 66) for 18dh or a double for 23dh. The showers usually work and cost 5dh.

The *** **Hôtel des Amandiers** is a not entirely successful modern mock-kasbah design above the town, which makes up for its slightly gloomy interior with an undisturbed view of the fantastic surrounding rocks and a varied garden. The rooms are spacious but simple and there is a bar and a restaurant. The pool seldom seems to be full, but would be wonderful in its attractive secluded rock garden if it were. The Amandiers has 60 rooms and accepts telephone bookings on tel 8. A double room costs 265dh and a three course dinner 80dh.

WHERE TO EAT

Tafraoute has a deserved reputation for careful and skilful cooking, and you will eat well throughout the town. A civilized three-course Moroccan menu with good service, wine and an unhurried atmosphere can be had at the **Hôtel des Amandiers**.

The **Restaurant l'Etoile du Sud** has a certain intense style. It serves meals, after rosewater hand baths, in a caidal tent in a garden littered with three broken gramophones amongst other bits and pieces. A complete menu with a drink is only 38dh.

The **Café Atlas** at 2, Place de la Marché is a less pretentious affair though a band often drifts between the tables. The house *hors d'oeuvre* is a delightful collection of indigenous flavours—three low bowls filled with local apricots, pure argan oil and Amallou, a paste of argan oil and finely crushed almonds, which you eat on bread. Otherwise they serve harira for 12dh, vegetable tagine for 25dh and chicken tagine for 30dh.

The **Tangier** and **Redouane** hotels have cafés, the Tangier being less dominated by Europeans and serving a large tagine for 36dh and couscous for 12dh.

There are two possible routes out of the Anti Atlas beyond Tafraoute, one to Irherm, the other to Agadir. Both begin by continuing 7 km beyond Oumesnat to Sidi Abd el Jebar and its koubba, where the road begins to climb out of the oasis.

Route to Irherm

20 km out of Tafraoute there is a turning to the right which leads you over the Tizi-n-Tarakatine at 1500 m. The road is new and sweeps you through the hills to the small village of **Ait Abdallah** where there is a compound for the **market** on Wednesdays. The café is open all week but only prepares food on souk days. An old military kasbah, fringed by wire defences still in place, sits above the village, but the skyline is dominated by the dramatic peaks of the surrounding grey mountains.

The tarmac ends at the village, but a rough piste track, suitable for four-wheel drive, crosses the rounded red hills of the mountain plateau of the Iberkakene to **Irherm**, on the Tata–Taroudant road. The mountain crests are crowned with dry stone-walled agadirs of crude structure, similar to the debased iron age hill forts of Britain. A lefthand turning after Tiguermine leads you 3 km to the fine **Agadir Tasguent**, on the left before the village of **Et Tleta des Idouska**. Rejoining the main piste you come upon an astonishing mountain panorama before **Azoura**, a village clinging to the side of a mountain and the centre for the Idaou Zekri, a sedentary tribe who occupy over 75 ksour in the region. If you arrive at Irherm on a Friday, you will find the **souk** in progress.

Route to Agadir

The turning to Tizi-n-Tarakatine marks the end of the Tafraoute oasis though the mountain scenery beyond remains dramatic. Argan trees cover the hills and small eminences of land are crowned with fortified farmhouses. These have an almost Apennine feel, whereas the stronger and more aloof agadirs have been compared to Greek mountain-top monasteries.

36 km from Tafraoute a piste road on the left will take a normal car to the Thursday market at **Souk el Khemis des Ida ou Gnidif**, whence a different track loops you back to the main road.

The village of **Tioulit**, 46 km from Tafraoute, is a spectacular example of the homeland of the Illalen, a confederation of 18 tribes who occupy the mountain plateau between Tafraoute and Ait Baha. The **Fortress of Tioulit** dominates the village from its magnificent position on an outcrop of rock.

The agadirs of the Illalen are known to have contained as many as 300 compartments, in several storeys either side of a central aisle. Here families could safely store their valuables and grain. A custodian maintained propriety in the agadir, which was often used by the heads of families for council meetings and elections.

Ait Baha

Ait Baha, 82 km from Tafraoute, is the old border between the plain of the Souss and the rougher independent tribal lands of the Anti Atlas. When Wyndham Lewis visited the French colony of Morocco in 1931, 'a few kilometres further on was the ultimate frontier of Dissidence—that is to say the territory of the mountain cantons that have not made their submission to the French.'

Ait Baha also has its **market** on Wednesdays, and is served by two daily buses from Inezgane at 11.00 and 16.00. If you wish to stay here, the **Hôtel Café Tafraoute** has a pleasant, tranquil and cool interior, and a room will cost you 20dh.

Beyond is the territory of the Ikounda, one of the fifty fractions of the Achtouken who occupied the grazing of the argan hills surrounding the Souss valley. **Imi Mgoun**, 'the great entrance', a key tariff gathering spot on the old trading route to the Sahara, was in their possession. The Ikounda were pacified early by the French, allowing the scholar Montagne to translate their rare written code for the management of communal agadirs. Every contingency was covered: 'he who fornicates with a she ass inside the agadir, in view of the porter, or in view of any other witness, will pay a fine of 2 Dirkem to the Oumanas, and 3 saas of corn to the she ass'. Few contemporary legal codes pay such respect to the outraged feelings of donkeys.

Biougra, 33 km from Agadir, is the centre of this steppe land, and comes alive for the moussem of Sidi Said Cherif in May.

Inland to Goulimine

15 km out of Tiznit you reach the beautiful town of **El Had Reggada**, a collection of associated but rival ksour girt by strong exterior walls. A koubba is perfectly placed above the southern gateway, and a **souk** is held here on Saturdays.

Another fortified settlement, the village of **Talaint**, which has a **Wednesday market**, lies to the left of the road 7 km beyond El Had. After Talaint you begin a steep climb to the pass of Tizi Meghert at 1067 m where the twisted shapes of ancient argan trees dominate the rough slopes. Beyond the pass a turning leads in 2 km to the Tuesday market of **Souk et Tleta des Akhsas**.

Bou Izakarn

Bou Izakarn marks the foot of the southern slopes of the Anti Atlas. By now the palm has taken over from argan trees.

The fortified exterior walls of this oasis palmery have only recently been breached by the growth of the village. It is strange to think that until as late as 1935 these walls served a vital purpose in protecting this agricultural village from the depradations of nomadic raiders.

The palmery gardens are to the east of the village, an enchanting land where plots of wheat, vegetables and cropped grass grow beneath the protective shade of palms. A few cafés are clustered around the Tata turning, where a regular bus now operates to Ifrane Anti Atlas, 40 km east. You can also catch taxis here.

The **Café de la Poste** used to have beds but now directs you to the ** **Hôtel Anti Atlas**. This has a cool interior with pool and card games in near continual progress and looks out on to the sunbaked roadside terrace through three well-proportioned arches. There are a few rooms off a small but mature courtyard garden beyond. The bedrooms have thick cool walls and their own bathrooms. A double costs 81dh.

The Friday **market** is easy to find, as loudspeakers now add to its bustle, on the southern end of town beneath the town walls. Goulimine is 40 km south through a dry valley, where soil consolidation schemes fight a double and unequal battle against the climate and goats.

The Tata Circuit

The Tata circuit, the 450 km journey from Bou Izakarn to Taroudant, has only been possible by car or regular bus since the opening of the Tata to Irherm stretch of road in November 1988. It is a spectacular journey passing between the austere, scarred landscape of the Djebel Bani mountain chain and the edge of the Saharan plain but broken by a number of intriguing oasis settlements. This is a desert region, but it is a much more palatable introduction than heading south into the Western Sahara. The roads are good, though they do not always follow exactly the routes shown on maps—of which no two are in total agreement—but on the main route there is no question of getting lost. The region has a freshness and charm as yet untouched by overfamiliarity with the ways of tourists, and a reputation for hospitality and interest in passing travellers. Though it is possible to stay at hotels or cafés in Bou Izakarn, Ifrane Anti Atlas, Akka, Tata and Irherm, you may well find yourself invited to stay along the route by local people.

Tata is the principal oasis on the route, with a bank, a post office and some well-stocked shops. It also has the most comfortable hotel, the **Hôtel Renaissance**, to use as a base for exploring the area, and the best food.

All the oasis settlements survive by tapping the underground drainage of the southern slopes of the Anti Atlas mountains. The oases occur at khenegs, breaches in the long wall of the Djebel Bani escarpment towards which the water flows. The escarpment runs from Tantan to Zagora, dotted with settlements which used to form an important West–East trade route.

GETTING AROUND

There is a daily bus service that connects Tiznit to Tata via Bou Izakarn. The bus currently leaves Tiznit at 4.30. The Agadir to Tata bus also passes through Tiznit, at 11.00, and it may be possible to join that. Onwards to Taroudant, there are buses from Tata on Tuesdays, Thursdays and Sundays leaving at 8.00. In the other direction, there are buses from Taroudant to Tata on Mondays, Wednesdays and Saturdays. Taxis can be found to ferry you between Bou Izakarn and Ifrane Anti Atlas, particularly on souk days, but otherwise they are thin on the ground. If you are hoping to hitch a lift or take a place in a grand taxi, it is useful to remember that traffic will be going to Goulimine souk on Saturdays, to Bou Izakarn and Irherm on Fridays and Ifrane Anti Atlas on Sundays. But more so than with many routes, the flexibility of a car (you could hire a Renault 4 in Agadir) greatly increases your options.

Ifrane Anti Atlas

Not marked on some maps, but just beneath Tabahnift, the village of Ifrane Anti Atlas is itself unexceptional. A long triple row of pink painted concrete and stone houses, it is a small, expanding administrative centre, whose Caid governs a rural commune of 11,000. However, its setting is magnificent. Ifrane lies 10 km north of the P30 road, 14 km out from Bou Izakarn, across a large bowl dotted with over 20 ksour which appear to be carved from the barren mountains.

Above Ifrane, the exposed, twisting strata of the red and gold hills is matched by the colours of the strident exterior walls of the dozen ksour that exist in various states of decay just to the north of the new town. Verdant terraced plots, shaded by palms and olives, are ranged beside the white polished boulders of the river bed.

Ifrane Anti Atlas is an ideal base to stay and do some leisurely exploration of desert life. To the east and west of the town lie village ksour and a delightful, mature walled garden can be found to the east of the town, below the conspicuous red stones of a low volcanic hill. Knock repeatedly and the gardener should appear to show you around.

North of Ifrane, on the track to Tabahnift village you pass an old and increasingly ruined area of pise built ksour, surrounded in biblical juxtaposition by cemeteries and threshing grounds. Further along this road is a Jewish necropolis, which is visited once a year by the descendants of this ancient Jewish community, now scattered in Tel Aviv, Casablanca, New York and Caracas. This track, the old caravan route, climbs for another 35 km to the Kerdous pass, on the main road between Tiznit and Tafraoute, see page 500.

Ifrane's **souk** is on Sundays between 6.00 and 12.00, divided, as is usual in Morocco, into areas of livestock, vegetables and dry goods. The chief attraction is not so much the wares on display but the immaculately dressed Berber farmers riding in from the surrounding country for this weekly social occasion. Hard-working farmers stroll hand in hand through the souk, their blue or white gandouras crossed by the shoulder strap of an embroidered satchel and a fresh laundered turban tightly bound around their heads. An air of ancient cultural dignity, of grace, hospitality and tolerance hangs lightly over the population. A pair of exquisite men, their hats rakishly tilted and their eyes aggressively hennaed wander through the agricultural market, nodding and greeting without a flicker of ridicule.

WHERE TO STAY

There are three basic hotels in Ifrane. The **Hôtel Anti Atlas** is at the foot of the town, just above the walled caid's house. Bedrooms equipped with rush mats and mattresses surround a small garden of orange trees and basil. A room costs 30dh, and filling tagine can be ordered from the hotel café which is also used for local music festivals.

The **Café Restaurant de la Poste** is by the mosque at the top of the town and overlooks the river. A room here with a straw mat for a bed costs 20dh, or you can rent roof space for 10dh. The town's premier café is the **Café du Paix**, where a number of rooms have recently been added above the first floor tearoom, costing between 15 and 30dh a night.

Timoulay, Taghmout and Taghjicht

Back on the main road by the Ifrane turning, you pass **Timoulay Ifla** (upstairs) and **Timoulay Izder** (downstairs). The former is a minotaur's warren of ruined walls on the edge of an inhabited village, the latter a more fertile oasis palmery guarded by a kasbah.

26 km east of the Ifrane turning is the oasis of Taghmout. The balcony of the **Café Bani**, beside the main road, provides the best opportunity this side of Tata for a lunch of omelette and salad. A right turn off the road leads through the palmery, a tightly packed ribbon of settlement sandwiched between twisted dark hills behind and wind-blown desiccation in front. You will find a few shops before the track continues to an outlying hamlet which hosts a Sunday afternoon football match.

On the opposite side of the road is the long palmery oasis of Taghjicht, its thin belt of palms and dozen associated ksour largely hidden from view by great mounds of baked clay and natural walls of mud.

Amtoudi, the Agadir of the Iznaguen

3 km out of Taghmout a left turn leads in 10 km through the **Tainzert palmery** to the Monday market of the Adai tribe, **Souk Tnine d'Adai**. The 12th-century Agadir of **Iznaguen**, the fortified granary of the Ait Assa, is a further 11 km to the northeast along a good dirt track which enters into a palm-lined gorge. The agadir is on a prime strategic site and its stone walls and strong gateway are in impressive condition, considering that this is probably one of the oldest surviving tribal forts in Morocco. The view of the surrounding Anti Atlas landscape is well worth the steep climb, though you can rent mules at the café below, where if you order a tagine it will wait simmering for your return.

Further up the river bed there are some natural pools of polished rock, supposedly safe for swimming, though some of the rivers from the Anti Atlas carry a risk of bilharzia. Returning back to Souk Tnine d'Adai, a right turn drops you further east on the main road.

If you are in the mood for more agadirs, some 55 km further east a right turn travels for a few km along the bank of the Oued Tamanart to the agadirs of the **Ait Herbil** and the **Aguerd**, framed by dark hills.

Foum el Hassan

Icht is a small settlement, 77 km east of Taghmout, where the police often operate a checkpoint. Foum el Hassan, the larger neighbouring settlement lies 6 km to the south.

It first appears as a small dusty military post, the market square shuttered and lifeless, but by crossing the wide gravel bed of the Oued Tamanart you enter an extensive and prosperous palmery. The Ait ou Mribet tribe dominated this oasis from their Ksar of Imi Ouagadir, and they claim to be descended from Christian Berbers established here in the 13th century.

There are few architectural traces of the ksar left, and the farmers now live in low pise houses above the palmery. Wandering through the maze of paths that enclose walled oasis gardens, you will see palms shading crops from the savage sun and irrigation water which runs through the plots throughout the year. Each spring the irrigation canal that runs deep below the gravel bed of the Tamanart is dug out and cleaned, for without constant attention these oasis settlements would wither away.

By following the irrigation stream you pass through a gorge, the Foum, that has been eroded through the high peaks of the Djebel Bani. At the junction of the Oued Tamanart and the Oued Tasseft there is a well and a grove of trees in which to rest. Along the lower banks of these rivers just before their junction, there are two prehistoric carvings etched into red stone, if you are prepared for an industrious half-hour search. The reward for finding them lies in their age and the hunt rather in the aesthetics of the carving.

Ait Oua Belli

From Icht, 40 km of desert stretch between you and the twin villages of **Tisgui el Haratine** and Ait Oua Belli which bestride a breach in the wall of Djebel Bani.

The **agadir** of the Ait Oua Belli is perfectly positioned at the summit of the hill which guards the gorge. The exterior wall is in good condition and individual family storage chambers and the communal water basin can be seen. A half-hour climb to the summit is amply rewarded by the view: to the north, three dry river beds dotted with palm trees stretch into the distance; to the south extend the irrigation works that feed the green pockets of this oasis, whilst beyond stretches the glimmering extent of the Sahara.

Akka

Following the main road another 40 km you arrive at Akka, the chief village and military garrison for a group of several ksour which cultivate an extensive and rich oasis. Official dusty red buildings lining the road, armed guards, abandoned defensive sand walls and stone emplacements are at first inhibiting, but the village is worth exploring.

Behind the veneer of new buildings you will find old Akka, which still contains graceful pise arches, elaborate metal grilles and well-jointed stone walled corrals. The old souk quarter straddles three arcaded courtyards of gradually diminishing grandeur, of which the last has an old central watering well. The products of Akka's oasis orchards were celebrated, its rich sweet dates and all manner of dried and fresh fruit were prized additions to the monotonous diet of a desert crossing.

The great merchants of Fez and Marrakesh all kept agents at Akka, for it was an acknowledged marshalling point for trans-Saharan caravans. Two tracks leave Akka for Tindouf, now in Algeria, and from there the caravans would cross the Sahara to Timbuktu. The journey of goods from Fez to Timbuktu took 130 days, the camels often travelling seven hours a day for seven days without water. The trade was chiefly in salt, exchanged for slaves and gold. The slave survivors of the return desert crossing would be rested at Akka and sold to waiting agents. Those who were too unfit to find a buyer were left to join the local Haratine community who cultivated oasis orchards and gardens. The last slave caravan was seen skirting the Western Sahara in 1956, and Mauretania only officially abolished slavery in 1981.

Akka is one of the richest areas in Morocco for discovering **prehistoric stone carvings** and you will need to hire a guide to find them even if you only intend to travel a few km east to **Oum el Alek**. If you are hunting the stone carvings you could stay at the **Café Hôtel Tamdoult**, at 20dh for a basic room.

One of the most enduring images of Akka is the stuffed camel which acts as a sentry to one of the barrack compounds on the main street. Since it is a serving member of the garrison you are forbidden to photograph it.

70 km out of Akka towards Tata you pass a few outlying settlements, the most notable of which is **Touzzonine**, an unchanged and accessible oasis village. Here you can study the traditional building techniques—stone-based foundations, palm trunk beams, cross-thatched with palm leaves and plastered with mud pise create proportions consistent with the surrounding habitat, and within this there is an astounding diversity of individual features. The community fight a continuous battle with the environment and the ruins of a settlement to the north stand as a menacing warning of decay. The road on to Tata follows an escarpment, a natural wall of black rock grazed by goat and camel herds.

Tata

Tata is an attractive pink new town built beside a river bed and sheltered from the desert winds and dust by a ring of hills. It is at the centre of a network of three river beds that drain the southern slopes of the Anti Atlas mountains. The beds are mined with irrigation canals, which feed the scattering of palmeries and gardens cultivated by the 20 or more surrounding ksour.

The population of Tata is a roughly equal mix of Chleuh Berber and Haratine. The Haratine serfs have, since Independence, risen from their depressed status and now cultivate over half the available land for themselves. Both groups speak the Berber Tamazight dialect in preference to Arabic, and hold a **souk** on Tuesdays and Sundays.

The ksour of Tata have a quite distinctive look and identity that make them appear like a scattering of Mycenean acropolis. An indeterminate mix of walls and houses cluster tightly around a rise of barren rock. Dark wide window portals, uncluttered by frames or grilles, stare out to impassively survey the surrounding patch of fertile cultivation. **Tiggane, Agarzagane, Taguent** are just a few of these striking sites that you should walk out and explore.

Tata has a shaded central garden square, three hotels, a bank, a post office and plenty of cafés that serve a delicious selection of salads, soups, grilled meats and tagines. Stay at the * **Hôtel de la Renaissance**, 96 Av. des FAR, tel 42, where a double room costs 67dh. The hotel, run by young Kahim Brahim, is perched on the river terrace and looks over the dry bed towards a koubba. The bedrooms are comfortable, the water works and the house cooking and fresh squeezed orange juice are delicious.

Opposite the hotel are some stone steps that climb a hill dominated by a pink administrative block. From here you get a good view of the extent of the town and you can see the tarmac road that travels east. It stops dead at the edge of town and the dust track to Zagora takes over. You should check with the Tata police before starting on this adventurous desert route, which is briefly described on page 445–6.

From Tata a magnificent new road has been carved through the rock desert. The road took six years to build and two weeks after it was opened, in November 1987, torrential rains tore out over a dozen bridges. It is an exhilarating route—the geological strata are clearly visible in all their extraordinary convolutions, and you pass only one small settlement before reaching the narrow cultivated Issafen mountain valley, 52 km from Tata, heralded by a string of three decaying hilltop agadirs.

Issafen

Issafen is too high for palm trees; olive, almond, walnut and henna trees dominate the valley. Here, stone walled houses have replaced the desert pise, and the all enveloping embroidered black cloak, the haik of the oasis women, gives way to the blue and purple smocks of Berber mountain women. The purple is contrasted by red edging or scarlet socks, and hair is swept back in a scarf fixed with a narrow striped fillet of material.

The men of Issafen used to be notorious raiders until the Sheikh of the Ait Haroun placed the whole valley under a curse. Famine decimated the families of the valley before the leaders agreed to solemnly swear to the Sheikh that they had renounced their careers of pillage.

In the midst of the valley is the **Kasbah of Tamghirt**, a stone-built keep in immaculate condition, a reminder of warlike days. Beyond is a gaunt, completely ruined and melting village, a Gomorrah-like vision of total destruction. A **souk** is held each Thursday at **Khemis Issafen** at the head of the valley. Irherm is 38 km north over a bleak and twisting mountain road that crosses the Tiz-n-Touzlimt pass at 1692 m.

Irherm

This small whitewashed village is set in the centre of a mountainous plateau 1700 m above sea level. Low fruit trees grow in embattled windswept orchards, but it exists chiefly as a market for the highland hinterland. Mountain tracks fan out from Irherm and it is possible to travel to Taliouine, Tafraoute and Amagour on these roads. Irherm hosts a busy vegetable **market** on Wednesdays and Fridays, and has a petrol station, four cafés and a number of mechanics who repair the damage done by mountain tracks. These mechanics follow a long tradition, for Irherm is the chief village of the Ida Oukensous, craftsmen renowned in the past for their metal work, producing swords, muskets and inlaid powder horns. Now they concentrate on clutches and suspensions.

The **Café de la Jeunesse** has a few rooms to rent, which might be useful for anyone planning to hitch a lift with a truck or climb Djebel Akhlim, the 2531 m summit 15 km east of Irherm.

The road to Taroudant runs through broken hill country that does not compete with the earlier splendour of the route. Argan trees reappear as you approach their natural habitat, the Souss valley.

9 km out of Irherm the Saturday market for the Indouzal, **Souk es Sebt des Indouzal**, can be reached by a left turn off the road. A further 31 km and there is a splendid view across the Souss valley to the High Atlas mountains, and a café has conveniently planted itself nearby. The road then makes a long twisting descent through rough foothills and their wild arguin groves.

A few km before joining the main Taroudant to Ouazazarte road, a turning to the **Tioute Kasbah** leads off to the left, whilst the **Kasbah of Freija** can be seen above the Oued Souss crossing. These Souss valley kasbahs are well worth visiting and are covered in the section on the city of Taroudant, which lies 8 km to the west; see page 490.

Southern Coastal Route to Sidi Ifni

24 km beyond Tiznit you pass through the village of **Souk Arba du Sahel** before you reach the coast at Gouzirim. The road is violently twisting, so that the view of the Atlantic from here to Sidi Ifni is constantly shifting in and out of view.

Mighleft/Mirhelt is 15 km further on and initially appears a rather unattractive jumble of block-like houses. It is in fact a friendly, hospitable village served by a dazzling array of beaches. A single yellow arcaded highway contains a string of cheap hotels and a small covered vegetable market. The **Tafkout** is possibly the best hotel, but if full try the **du Sud** or **Farah** before going to the **Atlas**. The Tafkout charges 15dh a night and has a roof terrace full of tanning flesh. The downstairs café provides some cool nooks and day beds as well as a good basic menu. Every evening local boys play a vast range of music from Syrian love songs to Madonna impersonations here.

Above the village, crowning the hill, is a French fort in an attractive-looking state of ruin. The view is worth the climb but the interior consists only of a fairly recently deserted barracks and stables. Some interesting pornographic graffiti and mermaids can be seen in the far corner.

Staying in the relaxed atmosphere of Mirhelt you have a choice of six **beaches**, known locally as Fish Beach, Camping Beach, Coquillage Beach, Hotel Aftas Beach (only open in high summer), Plage Sauvage and Marabout's Beach. The last, 3 km from the hotels, is the most dramatic, if a little overawing to sunbathe and swim in. The **koubba complex of Sidi Mohammed ou Abdallah** sits in front of a massive upsurge of igneous rock, rising up through the middle of the sandy beach with outlying tendrils of natural rock that form arches and caves. It's a very potent place in which to watch the sun sink.

Mirhelt's appeal is very strong, and many people come out from Sidi Ifni to spend weeks just living here. A typical day takes in the late morning social at a café, a little shopping for fruit and vegetables, a hot walk down to a beach followed by supper on Hotel Aftas Beach and music back in 'town' in the evening.

Sidi Ifni

Sidi Ifni is a lugubrious town, a tranquil vacuum, perched on sea cliffs in which to while away the time. It is a Spanish-built town surrounded by old military barracks and high hills and existed as a Spanish enclave, a bastion of Imperial pretension, from 1934 to 1969. The political isolation from this period is still palpable in this geographically isolated town, where, in a time warp, Hispano-Berber architecture gently decays swathed in recurrent sea mists.

The Spanish relationship with Sidi Ifni is based on two small periods of rule separated by four hundred years of absence. This is a pattern repeated along many of the anchorages along the Saharan coast of Morocco.

The Spanish crown took over the fort of Santa Cruz de Mar Pequena which had been built as a commercial venture by merchants from the Canary Islands in 1476. For a generation this isolated tower above the beach was used as a secure base for slave raiding expeditions into the interior. It was swept away by the Saadian-led jihad in 1524.

Three hundred and fifty years later the Spanish were granted the right in the 1860 Treaty of Tetouan to build a fishing station on the coast of Morocco opposite the Canaries. However they did not take advantage of this until the region had been pacified by the French, and only arrived to build the town of Sidi Ifni in 1934. They refused to surrender Sidi Ifni to the newly Independent Morocco in 1957 which led to a little known but violent desert war. The Moroccan Liberation Army supported by local tribes stormed the outlying Spanish forts but the town itself was successfully defended by the Tercios, the Spanish Foreign Legion. The Moroccan government cut all land communication with the enclave which was eventually ceded back to Morocco in 1969.

Sidi Ifni is also haunted by the memory of an ill-fated Scotsman, George Glas, who in 1764 chose the ruins of the Spanish fort as the foundation for a trading post. The venture failed, the ship that took him away mutinied, the crew stole his goods and cast his murdered body into the sea.

GETTING AROUND
Whatever your map shows, there is a good tarmac road to Sidi Ifni from Tiznit or Goulimine. A place in a grand taxi from Goulimine costs 10dh, from Tiznit 13dh, and there are occasional and slower local buses that stop at Mirhelt before travelling 33 km on to Sidi Ifni.

WHAT TO SEE
There are no remaining traces of the Spanish slaving tower or George Glas's trading post to be found. The 20th-century Spanish town, weathered art deco, is however full enough of quirky architectural surprises. Place Hassan II, the old Plaza Espana, has a mature Andalucian garden and is ringed by the major buildings of interest. A camouflaged, closed Catholic church and the large locked-up Spanish consulate, set the tone of limbo for the whole town. They lead the way to a broad baroque sea-cliff stairway to the beach in a prime state of wistful decay. The lanterns on either side have been truncated at varying and random heights and one or two of the fat balustrades have exploded. The concrete prow of a building in the shape of a boat looms high above the shore to threaten the Hôtel Ait Bamrane. The empty pool beside the hotel and a seaside sign warning against bathing complete this bizarre pattern of neglect.

Isolated by a Moroccan land blockade from 1957, an all weather dock was vitally important to Spanish Sidi Ifni. To this end the most quixotic of all the remaining structures of Sidi Ifni was built, a concrete island constructed some 700 m out into the sea. A cable car rusting beneath the connecting pylons still links this extraordinary grey fort with the shore, though it is no longer in use. Ships docked at the fort to unload their supplies, but since recovering Sidi Ifni in 1963 the Moroccan government has totally ignored this device and has just finished building a brand new harbour.

The airport must have been a more practical solution to the blockade, though pilots would have had to deal with both banks of sea mist and clouds which lower themselves off the surrounding hills. This airfield is now overgrown and grazed by herds of goats. The surrounding plethora of official military buildings are guarded by bored but armed soldiers.

A vegetable market operates everyday in the small central **souk** in the town. On Sundays, the market for the Ait Bamrane tribe assembles above the airport, and includes a collection of clowns and magicians. The women of Sidi Ifni seem particularly beautiful, and wear wind-torn tie-dyed indigo saris, navy blue and black. The local Moussem is held in the last few days of June.

Oued Noun

For an expedition out of town, follow the dirt track that leads south towards the new harbour. Running parallel to the coast, it passes the **shrine of Sidi Ouarsik** and reaches the estuary of the Oued Noun. This was the location of a rare example of Moroccan–Portuguese cooperation. In 1481 John II of Portugal accepted the Sultan's invitation to build a fort here in order to evict the Spanish from the coast. There is no trace of Fort Guader now left. **Plage Blanche**, 50 miles of empty white beach, see page 517, stretches between the estuaries of the Oued Noun and the Oued Draa. Its emptiness is broken only by the remote fishing hamlet of **Aoreora**.

The track continues along the north bank of the Oued Noun passing near river-cut limestone gorges before reaching the village of Tilioune.

WHERE TO STAY AND EAT
The **Hôtel Belle Vue**, tel 5072, on Place Hassan II, has comfortable bedrooms with views over the sea, a bright orange stucco interior and decidedly eccentric plumbing—for whilst neither shower nor basin produced any water, the lavatory bowl had the rare luxury of being flushed with hot water. There are two bars and beer also available on the terrace overlooking the central garden. Rooms are 69dh for a single, 81dh for a double with shower, and a restaurant which serves fish in the summer when available.

The **Hôtel Beau Rivage** which peers above the skyline with its imposing blue balconies as you enter Sidi Ifni has the busiest and most welcoming bar in town. The interior is less imposing but it has a full and reliable menu where you can eat a meal of three courses for 24dh.

The **Hôtel Ait Bamrane** is on the small area of beach, Av. de la Plage, a tranquil almost deserted place which also has a bar. A room costs 77dh for a double, and the phone number, though you are unlikely to need to book a room, is 5173.

The **Café Hôtel Suetra Loca** used to be the evening haunt of the Spanish legion as the battered football game and heroic oil painting demonstrate. It has a few rooms at 35dh for a single, and sells coffee and cakes downstairs.

South of Sidi Ifni

The road to Goulimine has been repaired and now constitutes a beautiful and easy climb over the surrounding hills. There is a market on Wednesdays at **Souk el Arba de Mesti**, which is about 25 km before Goulimine.

Goulimine

There are two Goulimines. On Saturday morning it is a much-hyped tourist destination, streams of day trip coaches leave Agadir for Goulimine, 'the gateway to the Sahara and the camel souk of the blue men'. Otherwise normal Moroccans dress up as 'Blue Men' in order to act as desert guides or jewelry salesmen.

The rest of the week Goulimine is a quiet administrative and market town of 150,000 people on the border between the sedentary farming of the Anti Atlas and the pastoral nomadism of the Western Sahara. A gentle, relaxed town, where visiting farmers and teachers are happy to talk to you about the realities of desert life—of waking up in the middle of a dark night with their new wife screaming with mysterious pain and not a doctor, a telephone or even a light anywhere in the wilderness for many miles.

Its position has always been valued, since it commands the northern bank of the Oued Noun, a string of oasis settlements to the east and was an important base for the Saharan caravan trade. Black hills overlook the town from the north where white stone emblems proclaim the three faiths: to God, King and country.

The discovery of a trade route across the Sahara to the 'Bilad as-Sudan', the land of blacks, as it was known, was first achieved by the Berbers of the Draa and Noun rivers in the 8th century. Goulimine was the first centre of this profitable trade which swapped salt mined in the Sahara for West African gold and it was a key link in the communications chain of the Almoravide Empire, which stretched in the 11th century from Spain to Ghana.

Its position inevitably declined from these days of gold and glory. New Saharan trading routes were discovered and the desert aristocracy of the Almoravide Empire was destroyed in 1147. But in the 19th century caravans were still being dispatched from Goulimine to Timbuktu. The abolition of the slave trade by the French in the 1930s destroyed the last remaining commodity of the Saharan trade. When the caravan trade had been active the Tekna and the Reguibat, the Berber Saharan tribes known as the 'Blue Men', had made a living by selling their 'protection' and their livestock to merchants at the great camel market of Goulimine. There was a continual demand for desert-reared camels for even the most efficiently run caravan consumed a heavy toll of animals in a desert crossing.

GETTING AROUND
Whichever direction you arrive from, north or south, you will find yourself in the central Place Bir Nazarine, a roundabout affair surrounded by the main cafés, the bank and the Post Office. Buses for Tiznit and Tantan usually leave from here as well. Av. Mohammed V leads off downhill to the town market, otherwise originally known as Place Hassan II.

WHEN TO GO
Think about timing your arrival, if possible, to coincide with one of the moussems; of Sidi Mohammed Ben Amar at Assrir at the end of May, and at Ksabi in mid-June, or with that of Sid Laghazi at Goulimine at the end of June.

Camels and the Goulimine Souk

No tourist brochure fails to mention the camel market. Where once the market of Goulimine must have been as full of deals as a secondhand car auction, camels as transportation died suddenly in the 1930s with the joint end of the slave trade and arrival of trucks to the region. Now they are raised purely for meat and status, and those that are paraded in front of tourists are not for a hard-working life in the desert but for the butcher. The herds have in the last 15 years been greatly depleted by long drought and by the war in the Western Sahara.

The much-visited Saturday market takes place between 7.00 and 12.00 just out of Goulimine on the road to Tantan. During the growing season, from October to April, it is a bustling lively affair. The upper compound is devoted to dry goods, the lower to livestock. Randy hobbled bulls rampage through corrals of sheep, goats and donkeys to get at beautiful cows. The farmers dress for the occasion and spend most of the morning disparaging their neighbours' flocks. In high summer there is obviously little happening in a Saharan agricultural market, but the camels are still paraded. Their eyelashes are a source of endless admiration and they earn a good income in photographic fees.

Camels came to the Sahara as weapons of war. The Persian Empire brought them from Asia in the 6th century BC, and Alexander the Great rode a camel across the Egyptian desert to visit the oracle of Zeus-Ammon at the oasis of Siwa. The first picture of a camel in Africa is that issued by Pompey's lieutenant, Lollius, in 64 BC. Camel breeding was only perfected in North Africa in the 5th century AD and to this must go much of the credit for Islam's initial lightening advance. Arabian camels are not successful in a cold climate, which partly explains why the Berber tribes in the mountains effectively resisted Arab conquest whilst those tribes on the plains quickly succumbed.

When camels appear fatigued on long journeys, they are sung to. There is a whole repertoire of such songs for a trio of voices, and 'it is worthy of observation how they renovate the camels, and the symphony and the time they keep surpasses what anyone would imagine'.

The Town

The town market off Place Hassan II is overlooked by cafés with first-floor terraces. The entrance to both the **Café Khalima** and the **Café Ali Baba** are off the passage to the souk. The shopping is remarkably low key for such a celebrated market town. The meat market with its joints of camel and hooves sold for stock is worth a look.

From the market, a climb up the slight rise to the old kasbah, an attractive pink pise ruin, provides you with a good view of the town and its surroundings. However like many of Morocco's monuments it suffers from being used as an outside lavatory.

Guedra Dancing

Guedra, the ancient dance of the women of the desert, is put on all over Goulimine for the benefit of tourists. The **Hôtel Salaam** arranges dances on Saturday evening, and puts on daily lunch-time displays for coaches from Agadir in tents at the oasis of **Ait Boukha**. On Saturdays at 12.00 and 21.00 there are performances at the **Hôtels Mauritania** and **L'Ere Nouvelle** for 20dh. Though less reliable it is well worth checking the smaller and generally more intimate performances at the **Rendezvous des Hommes Bleu Café** on Friday night, and in high summer the hotel at Abaino organizes the odd display on Saturday. Guedra is performed on the knees, due to the low height of nomadic tents. It is a dance of the torso and arms and contains a traditional and extensive range of erotic references. The women of the desert were traditionally much freer than many of their Islamic sisters elsewhere. Touareg women even had their own tents, where young warriors competed for their attention by reciting complimentary verse, performing heroic deeds and bestowing gifts of fresh meat. As a result Guedra was continually suppressed by Islamic reformers.

Accompanied by a deeply repetitive musical rhythm, in its natural habitat it has its own tantalizing pace which requires all of the night and much of the following morning. The tourist performances are a mere introduction, and can seem a slightly depressing travesty when rows of slab-faced Europeans begin to look restless after half an hour, partly because the dancers are professional rather than inspired.

Excursions from Goulimine

There are several memorable trips to be made from Goulimine, to oasis palmeries, a hot spring, a beautiful deserted beach and distant oases.

Assrir and Ait Boukha

A road leads 11 km southeast of the town to the oasis village of Assrir, where the Moussem of Sidi Mohammed takes place at the end of May. Assrir has always been an important desert centre, and a vestige of its old great July **camel market** is still held here every year, and attracts a great number of tourists. Traces of the ksar mud pise walls are considered to be an 11th-century Almoravide foundation for the core tribe of this dynasty were the Lemtuna, who then inhabited this region. Nearby is a watery pit where clay bricks are still shaped and left to bake out in the sun.

The road continues for 6 km to Ait Boukha, a much larger oasis palmery. Here you will probably be led by some charming child to have mint tea at home and a look at some jewelry for sale. A baked track leads beyond the oasis upstream to a dam holding back an enchanting little lake. In the rock walls of the river terrace camp fires are made. The village boys come in the morning to smoke the butts left behind by the camper van tourists.

Abaino

The hot springs of Abaino are 15 km out of Goulimine up a right turn off the Sidi Ifni road. The spring by the koubba is now almost permanently dry, but the faithful still hang out fragments of sweat-stained cloth by the bush overhanging its dry cave.

The naturally heated baths however are well organized and have two separate enclosures for men and women. 5dh entrance lets you soak in a hot mineral pool while the sun bakes down on the corners of this open air enclosure. Swimming trunks should be worn by men, and costumes or knickers by women. Black buckets are used for more personal washing. For a more direct experience of the holy water, you can lie naked in the steamy underground tunnel that issues from the baths.

The **Hôtel Abaino** is pleasantly chaotic. It has two great thick-walled courtyards with bedrooms off them, various areas to sit, a licensed restaurant and a bar. A double room costs 40dh or you can camp in a small compound.

Plage Blanche

Plage Blanche is a long and very beautiful deserted beach south of the Oued Noun estuary, 64 km from Goulimine. Take the road to Sidi Ifni and turn left on the S7101, a good tarmac road which leads 16 km to Ksabi and then gives way to a rough track for the rest of the journey. If you want to stay here you will need to bring all your provisions and what you need to sleep in. In high summer you should be able to find a place out to the beach in a grand or landrover taxi.

Assa

If you want to leave all traces of tourism and comfort behind, a tarmac road, the 7093, leads southeast to the total isolation of Assa, an ancient fortified Tekna camel and goat market 108 km from Goulimine. You pass through **Fask**, a simple oasis community fringed by hills, where there is a café and petrol. You can also stop at **Targoumait** before Assa, which is, in the words of an official posted there for two years, 'hot'. Bear in mind that there is no hotel anywhere along this route.

Part X

THE WESTERN SAHARA

Tantan

Goulimine, once a great Saharan market town, marks the geographical frontier between the sedentary villages of the Anti Atlas and the nomadic pastoralists of the Sahara. Although quite a number of tourists visit its somewhat dubious Saturday souk, very few venture further south into the heat, dust and bleak conditions of the Western Sahara. And there is certainly little of beauty to justify the great distances and discomfort involved. However, the disadvantages are a vital part of the attraction of this inhospitable terrain. It is a land of adventurous travel rather than tourism.

The desert of the Western Sahara is primarily hammada, a vast flat stony plain, an arid wasteland without prominent features. The Atlantic Ocean is largely inaccessible from the land, as it pounds against the foot of savage cliffs, and most of the soil is poisoned by residual deposits of salt.

For many travellers, the unimprovable nature of the land is a threatening and powerful contrast to what they know—the settled almost domestic state of nature in the West. For those who have been educated to believe in man's ability to improve his environment, the desert can appear as a shocking and emphatic negative. For here the landscape is fixed in an immutable harsh form; you exist by following the pattern for survival, a pattern which offers little scope for alternatives.

Similarly, travelling in the Western Sahara involves very few choices. Due to the forbidding nature of the land and the recent war, in which the Algerian-backed Polisario were fighting Morocco for possession of the Western Sahara, it is important to keep to the main routes. There are many checkpoints, areas of interest may well be occupied by the military, monuments damaged and the population suspicious of your motives.

The last couple of years have, however, opened up areas which you could never have

518

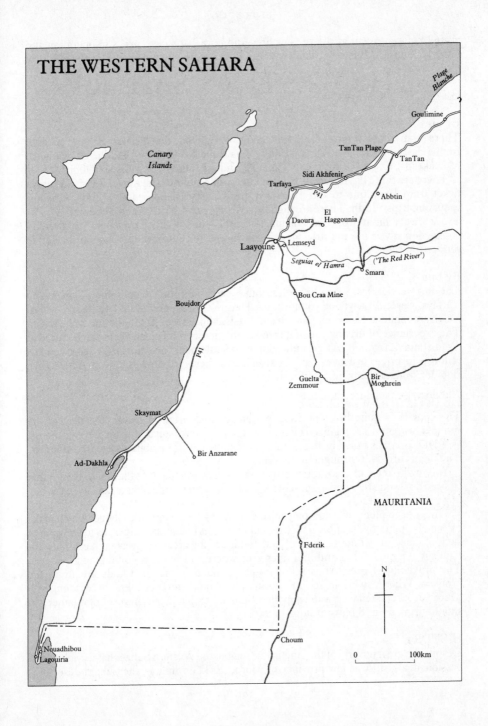

THE WESTERN SAHARA

Canary
Islands

Plage
Blanche

Goulimine

TanTan Plage
TanTan

Sidi Akhfenir
Tarfaya
P41
Abbtin

Daoura
El
Haggounia

Laayoune
Lemseyd

Seguiat el Hamra
('The Red River')

Smara

Bou Craa Mine

Boujdor

P41

Guelta
Zemmour
Bir
Moghrein

Skaymat

Bir Anzarane

Ad-Dakhla

MAURITANIA

Fderik

N

Choum

Nouadhibou
Lagouiria

0   100km

visited before, except at risk of your life. And now that a ceasefire is in operation and King Hassan II is finally speaking with the Polisario, the area may shortly become even more accessible.

GETTING AROUND

By air

There is an efficient grid of air connections throughout the Western Sahara. A flight from Laayoune to Rabat costs 1190dh, Laayoune to Tangier 1410dh, Laayoune to Marrakesh 1300dh, Laayoune to Tantan 225dh, Tantan to Marrakesh 590dh.

There are three flights a week between Laayoune and Ad-Dakhla for 370dh. A return ticket from Laayoune to Las Palmas in the Canary Islands costs 1120dh, or short excursion trips 810dh. There are flights on Wednesdays, Fridays and Sundays. There is also a direct flight from Ad-Dakhla to Agadir for 760dh. This could be a useful connection if you are not driving, as it allows you to return quickly without having to retrace the route north.

By bus

The bus service from Agadir to Laayoune passes through Goulimine, Tantan and Tarfaya. Beyond Laayoune you must use landrover taxis, grands and petits taxis, all of which are found at Laayoune, Smara and Ad-Dakhla, as well as Goulimine and Tantan. The experience of driving yourself through the desert is ideal, and cars can be hired at Agadir and Laayoune. As an inducement to settlement, petrol in the area is greatly reduced in price, just over half the usual, and there are now pumps at Ad-Dakhla, Boujdor, Smara, Laayoune and Tantan.

HEALTH AND WEATHER

The climate is quite bearable from November to March. However, the heat of the summer brings on a recognized medical symptom of unreasonable anger. Villa Cisneros, as Ad-Dakhla was called by the Spanish, was known by its inhabitants as Villa Neurosis. The nights are cold throughout the year.

You might keep an eye out for snakes, rats and scorpions. Not that there is a lot that you can do if you are bitten as most of the snakes you find in the Sahara, and even the bite of a palm rat, is deadly.

Always keep plenty of water on you, and if driving take extra cans of beer which make extremely popular gifts at the police checkpoints. It is of course dangerous to stray out of sight of the roads without a guide. Sandstorms are the greatest threat, and can blow for ten days at a time. The sand infiltrates everywhere and reduces visibility to a few feet. The proximity of precipitous sea cliffs along much of the road adds greatly to the problem. When driving in serious storms you should stop, and test the wisdom with which you calculated your water supplies. Remember that ideally in very hot weather you should drink up to 8 pints of liquid a day.

HISTORY

Despite the great poverty of the land in this region, the Western Sahara has as violent and passionate a history as any province of Morocco. The whole of the Sahara desert was occupied by the great Berber tribal confederation of the Sanhaja when Rome ruled the North African coast from the 1st to 5th centuries AD.

From the 7th century, the Sanhaja pioneered the use of the camel, an animal imported from Asia, in crossing the Sahara to reach the gold mines on the Niger. Islamic missionaries who came in the wake of the Arab invasion used this route to spread the faith amongst the desert tribes.

It was the enthusiasm and passion of these missionaries, converting in such barren territory, that shaped Morocco's early national history. Early in the 11th century, Ibn Yasin, a missionary from the Souss valley, established a fortified monastery on an island off the Saharan coast. Though the identity of the island is not known for certain, it was possibly Tidra off the Mauretanian coast. The men of this monastery were of the Lemtuna tribe, a branch of the Sanhaja. Known as Al-Murabitim, the Almoravides, they emerged in 1043 to conquer and establish an empire that stretched from Spain to Ghana. It was a dramatic but brief period of desert supremacy and unity. However even before the Empire had been properly subdued the Almoravide rulers had moved to Marrakesh, preferring to rule from this central and more temperate position. It was however a magnificent achievement that a tribe from the Western Sahara was the first to establish an indigenous Islamic authority over the whole of Morocco.

The 13th century saw a dramatic reversal as the Western Sahara fell under new, fierce overlords. The Merenid sultans, having got what they wanted from their dangerous and barely controllable Bedouin Arab allies, directed them away from the rich heartland of Morocco towards the south. These Arab tribes, known as the Maql, or 'sons of Hassan', established feudal emirates over the Berber tribes of the Sahara, usurping the best land and demanding a percentage of the harvest and herds. When the Berber Lemtuna tribe did eventually reopen the struggle against the Maql Arabs they were completely defeated over a 30-year period of war. After this time, whatever the truth of your lineage it became fashionable and expedient for Berber tribes to claim Arab origins.

Also in the 13th century the Spanish and Portuguese built a number of towers along the Saharan Atlantic coast from which to raid the Maghrebi interior, although not a stone of these structures now survives. Their ploy was to catch Berbers or Arabs, and to hold them to ransom for a greater number of negro slaves. It was not until the Saadian-led jihad (holy war) of 1524 that these slave raiding enclaves were decisively banished.

The end of 19th-century saw the Spanish returning to the Western Saharan coast after an absence of 600 years. The last remnants of the Spanish Empire, Cuba and the Philippines, had just been lost to the USA and to make up for the indignity of having no colonial Empire, the Spanish claimed control of a vast area of the Western Sahara. It became known as Rio de Oro or the Spanish Sahara, though in reality the Spanish only controlled two fortified and intermittently besieged posts, now known as Lagouiria and Ad-Dakhla.

From 1895 the actual ruler of the Western Sahara was Sheik Ma el Ainin, who presided over the nomadic tribes from his capital of Smara. From here, with the support of the Sultan, he organized resistance to the French, who where encroaching on Morocco from both the east and south. He, his sons, notably El Hiba, and other relations remained at the forefront of resistance right up until final French victory in 1934. Only after this were the Spanish able to impose their rule on the area inland from their two coastal forts, the last area in Africa to succumb to colonialism.

A period of armed colonial peace lasted 22 years. In 1957, after achieving independence from France, the Moroccan Liberation Army, supported by Tekna and Reguibat
Berber tribes, launched a coordinated attack on the extant Spanish Saharan positions.
But with the help of the French, the Spanish were able to repel these the following
year.

The development of a Saharan national consciousness, separate from Morocco, was
fostered by the Spanish in the following years through broadcasts and elected, though
powerless, tribal assemblies. Added to this, the development of phosphate mines at Bou
Craa gave the Saharans, for the first time, an economic base for a separate nation whilst
the 1963 Morocco–Algerian border war created a future sponsor for the Saharans in the
neighbouring Algerian republic.

However, before they could become independent, the Saharan nationalists, the
Polisario, had to overthrow Spanish rule. In the 1970s they launched a guerrilla
campaign against their overlords, and the Spanish, who in one week's fighting used up
the equivalent of five years' phosphate profits, now faced the facts and prepared to quit
the region.

Meanwhile, in 1974 King Hassan II of Morocco had agreed with Mauretania to the
south to divide the Western Sahara. In November 1975 he orchestrated 'The Green
March', when 350,000 Moroccan citizens crossed the border into the Spanish Sahara to
reclaim the lost province. The Spanish government, in the midst of Franco's terminal
illness, was caught unprepared. They surrendered sovereignty of the territory quickly,
without even calling a referendum.

The Moroccan armed forces who had been protecting the green marchers (green,
incidentally stood for Islam, not ecology) ended up fighting the Polisario movement by
the end of the year. The figures are greatly disputed, but between 10–30,000 Saharans
subsequently left the area, objecting to Moroccan rule. They walked in a less publicized
march to the Polisario-run refugee camps in Tindouf, Algeria, which were established
and funded by the Algerian government. From these camps the enlarged Polisario waged
a fast-moving, mobile campaign of hit and run raids. Mauretania, crippled by this
guerrilla war, left its half of the Western Sahara in 1979. Morocco promptly occupied the
entire territory.

The construction by the Moroccans of immense sand wall defences throughout
the 1980s, now longer than the Great Wall of China, reversed the war's trend in
Morocco's favour. The Polisario were reduced to fighting a desultory perimeter war,
unable to penetrate the wall into the centre of the province. In January 1989, the
Polisario and King Hassan II met face to face for the first time in peace talks held at
Marrakesh, and a truce was declared in the desert. Both sides were pleasantly
surprised by their adversaries, and the omens for more detailed negotiation seem
good, inshallah.

The Moroccan government has invested millions in the Sahara, building roads,
airports, fishing ports and the city of Laayoune, not to mention their spending on the war
itself. To a stranger, removed from the politics of rival nations, it seems extraordinary
that anybody should ever have fought to possess so desolate a piece of land. That such a
war has been so recently fought gives travel in the Sahara its piquant interest—the
traveller as eyewitness to the strange passions of mankind.

From Goulimine to Tantan

The road from Goulimine takes you through arid rolling hills for 80 kms, and it is surprising to see how much of this low land is productive during the brief spring. In the last 40 km of the journey to Tantan, the gradual transition to desert begins as great scree slopes of sand appear on the hills to the west. At the crossing of the Oued Draa, there is a small ruined tower and the first of many police checkpoints. The river is an ancient boundary which also, until 1934, marked the limits of French military power. The French frontier was held to the west by Fort Foum on the Draa and to the east by Fort Aioun in this, the Draa valley.

In exceptional years, the Draa river runs for a few days along its entire length from Ouazazarte. In the past it was a more substantial feature, which the classical historian Polybius records as being infested with crocodiles and which also gets a mention in Pliny and Ptolemy.

Tantan

For those travellers who find the Saturday tourist explosion in Goulimine disappointing, Tantan provides a perfect and powerful antidote. The view as you descend on the town from the north is enticing, its great cluster of sand-yellow houses dominated by a military kasbah and overlooked by the bright green dome of the mosque of Sidi Mohammed Laghdal. Despite forming the major base for the 1975 Green March, Tantan itself is, however, a completely unexploited, dry, dusty administrative town. Water and electricity supplies fluctuate, and the busiest aspect of Tantan life is the sight of tractors pulling water tanks. They make up for their lack of brakes with free use of the horn.

GETTING AROUND
The town is ranged off the long Av. Mohammed V, which turns off the main road south to run parallel to the bed of the Oued Ben Khlil, a tributary of the Draa. The military kasbahs that surround the town are in use, and in this sensitive area they are closed to visitors. Walking along Av. Mohammed V and up the hill to look at the exterior of the domed Mosque is about the extent of the cultural tour of Tantan.

On the main avenue buses depart for Goulimine, and Laayoune and there is a vast number and variety of taxis.

Typical for this town, the annual moussem is particularly elusive, and tourists may be quoted dates in October, May, June and July. A parade of camels is promised.

WHERE TO STAY
The major hotel in Tantan is the **Royal**. It has the only bar and pool in town but is currently forbidden to visitors as it is reserved for Moroccan army officers. You should check this, as with the ceasefire things may rapidly change down here. Whatever the situation at the Royal, there is no problem finding a bed in Tantan. Along Av. Mohammed V there are small squares devoted to landrover taxis, grands taxis, petits taxis and finally much the largest space for coaches. At each square there are clusters of small

hotels and two one-star hotels, **L'étoile du Sahara** and the **Amgala**. The well advertised **Hôtel Dakhla** at the coach square has clean rooms, brightly painted balconies and is, for Tantan, comparatively busy.

WHERE TO EAT
The shrub-shaded **Le Jardin** café-restaurant, on Av. Mohammed V is the centre of Tantan's social life. You can sip tea and eat cakes here overlooked by a large concrete jaguar. For eating there are lots of small grill cafés cooking brochettes along the avenue, but do not expect much activity before dusk. Next door to the Hôtel Dakhla there is a smart little **patisserie**. You can get into some fierce bargaining with a powerful and well-hennaed lady at no 360 over vast stripey blankets and tie-dyed shawls. The **cinema** is open on Mondays, Wednesdays, Thursdays and Sundays, showing a diet of violent American and kung-fu, and hopelessly romantic Indian films.

Tantan Beach

On the coast west of Tantan, this is an uninspiring collection of bourgeois villas built on a grid pattern above a sandy and tranquil beach. Construction is still continuing, and a new mosque has been built. The overall impression is of a rather bizarre attempt to suburbanize the desert, with one or two hopeful wind-battered 'For Sale' signs erected by those who have already tried and failed.

A piste track is used by camper trailers and vans which park above the beach. The **Café d'Etoile de l'Océan** and immediately below it the combined **Café, Patisserie and Librairie de Fez** provide a light lunch of salad, omelettes and very occasionally fresh fish from their terraces, both of which have views over the sea.

Just south of Tantan beach a brand new fishing port has been constructed as part of the great development plan to open up the Saharan seaboard to settlement. At the moment, only the infrastructure is in place, and maybe it will take off, but currently there are only a few visiting ships, no resident local fishermen and the **Café Restaurant du Port** seemed genuinely surprised to be asked for fresh fish. The canned products of the Safi-Agadir fishing fleet are proudly pointed out by the café's owner. The restaurant is beside the hanger-like and deserted fish market. Watch out for the bored police and customs guards at the port gates, who are a little over-thorough in their search and can be light fingered, particularly over cassettes.

South to Tarfaya

South of Tantan the road crosses a section of the earth quite terrifying in its aridity and lifelessness. The desert is flat baked stone, and to the horizon lies a complete, ugly and brutal wasteland rising some 50 km inland in a series of cliff terraces. The ground is poisoned with salt, and rain if it occurs runs off to collect in stagnant depressions, quickly turning so saline that it is poisonous to everything but a very few, low inedible shrubs. First impressions suggest that you have entered into the etchings of Doré's illustrations of Dante's Hell.

From Tantan Beach onwards you are largely denied access to the sea by flaking sea cliffs. But there are three points at which it is accessible, where at the Oued Chebarka,

Oued Fatima and Oued el Aouina the road dips down to cross barren salt estuaries and their sheets of lifeless water. The presence of this water round which no vegetation grows on the bare rock emphasizes the harshness of the environment. They were used by the Tekna Berbers as salt pans, producing the valuable trading commodity with which they bought gold and slaves from the negro kingdoms to the south. In turn these chattels were sold on to Spaniards from the Canary Isles who fortified these estuaries.

At these three points you can escape the desert and enter the refreshing but turbulent currents of the Atlantic. Driftwood can easily be gathered from the shoreline and camps made in total isolation.

Sidi Akhfenir is a hamlet which appears to consist of 16 identical café restaurants. In the few kilometres either side of this truck stop you will notice little shacks on the cliff edge belonging to line fishermen. They eke out an existence providing fish for the passing trade.

About 20 km beyond Sidi Akhfenir the remains of the clifftop **Koubba of Sidi Lemsid** can been seen. The traditional ancestor of the tribe of the Ouled Tidrahin, the saint's shrine has been badly damaged by the war. The Tidrahin are an indigenous Berber tribe of Sanhaja stock who lost their grazing grounds and hence their prestige to the Arab Delim. By the 18th century they had become a tributary to the Delim, but unlike other Berber groups their spiritual ancestry and powers earned their overlord's respect, and they remained desert herdsmen rather than take up the despised life of fishermen, the last resort of the fallen in the Western Sahara. Below the cliffs and scattered stones of the koubba, the sea enters into a vast tidal estuary where great wet boulders dotted in the immensity seem like beached whales.

As you continue towards Cape Juby and the town of Tarfaya, whisps of sand increasingly build up to form dunes whose sculpted shapes gradually dominate the harsh monotony of the flat stony hammada. Some of these small sand dunes drift across the road.

Rejoining the shore before Tarfaya, you come across the melancholy and outstanding feature of this section of the coast, known as 'the graveyard of sailors'. Wrecked hulks rising above the sea, continuous sand-flecked wind, and the knowledge of the endless pattern of violent sea death deprive this elegant stretch of long serene beach of some of its intrinsic appeal. It has a lingering impassive fascination. The Canary current has an onshore pull of 6 knots, and beneath it the shallow ocean floor is littered with violent reefs. Fog, offshore sand storms extending to the Canaries, a shapeless, deceptive coast, abnormal refractions and magnetic anomalies are a few of the problems for ships off this coast. The group of three shipwrecks just outside the safety of Tarfaya harbour are charged with the full mocking malignity of fate. The Spanish grain ship *Monte Altube* was wrecked here bringing food as recently as 1972. There is a lone café for melancholic reflection 25 km before you reach Tarfaya. The fate of the crew of *The Medusa* lingers in the salt and sandy air: shipwrecked, some of the men drifted on a raft off these shores for days and indulged in one of the worst cases of cannibalism ever recorded.

Tarfaya

260 km south of Tantan and 115 km north of Laayoune, it is somewhat disappointing to find that there is no hotel in Tarfaya—just a few bungalow cafés and stalls, partly

obscured by banks of wind-blown sand. In all contexts, Tarfaya has been bypassed. The road runs straight past the town on to the south.

HISTORY

Tarfaya has a curious history. It was built in 1878 by a British adventurer, Donald Mackenzie, who from 1867 had been an itinerant trader in the Sahara, the only European who was respected by the fierce xenophobic tribes. He named it, of course, Port Victoria. In 1888 Mackenzie's manager at the trading post was murdered in a tribal raid. The Sultan paid him compensation of £5000. Though the French were increasingly dominating the Saharan market from their bases on the Senegal river, Mackenzie continued trading, but the British government put increasing pressure on him to sell his post. This he eventually did in 1895, selling to the Sultan for £50,000.

After that, Port Victoria was used by the Sultan to supply the desert ruler Ma el Ainin with materials for building Smara and with a flow of arms for fighting the French in Mauretania. It had incidentally been ceded to Spain in the European carve-up of North Africa at the Conference of Berlin in 1885, but they did not colonize and rename it Villa Bens until 1916, when the Spanish captured a German submarine unloading Turkish Korans and Krupp arms for El Hiba, Ma el Ainin's son.

The great source of wealth in the Sahara in the last 50 years has been the salaries and budgets of alien administrations. And for some time, Tarfaya, as Villa Bens, took its share. From 1920 to independence in 1956 it was the Spanish headquarters for the Southern Protectorate of Morocco. After 1958 the Spanish administered the colony that they had retained, the Spanish Sahara, from Laayoune, and the Moroccan government administered their southern frontiers from Tantan. The newly-named Tarfaya returned to obscurity.

This fate seems little threatened by the updated fishing facilities now on offer. The rich fishing banks off these coasts have traditionally been exploited by fishermen from the Canary Isles. In the early years of the desert war the Polisario ran small craft along the coast and machine-gunned any vessels they found close to it. This, combined with current delicate fishing negotiations with Spain, now represented by the EEC, has left the harbour largely empty.

The ruins of Port Victoria, a conspicuous grey ruin on an old islet, and the rest of the Spanish-built barrack structures, are still heavily guarded. Villa Bens was built to withstand constant sniping raids from the local tribes who were amongst the last in Africa to be pacified by the Europeans.

The route to Laayoune, Tah and Daoura

South of Tarfaya you pass through the central belt of sand desert, the Erg Lakhbayta, broken by two great salt basins, the **Sebkha Tah** and the **Sebkha Deboua**. The Tah in particular was intensively mined for its salt deposits, the great currency of the desert. From 1958–75 it was the border post between Morocco and the Spanish Sahara, and in November 1975 it was the starting point for the Green March.

Further south beside the road is the oasis of Daoura which was the stronghold of the Izarguin tribe. Daoura was famous for its productivity and the crops were protected in the 19th century by two clay-walled and corner-towered forts. These were distinctive structures in a land that otherwise held only tents. The architectural primacy of Daoura was further confirmed with the construction of the region's first walled mosque. Now a scattering of sand-blown huts, a café and a few palms give little indication of how past generations valued Daoura.

Laayoune

An extraordinary creation, Laayoune is a city of 100,000 people not yet 30 years old, set in the middle of the desert. It was built by the Spanish after Tarfaya returned to Morocco in 1956, and is now maintained almost purely by national will. Since 1976, Morocco has poured £600m into the Saharan province and Laayoune appears to be largely composed of the offices and the machinery of government. The population is a mix of a minority of Saharan nomads and a larger proportion of Moroccans from the north, attracted by government-sponsored building projects, double wages, generous loans and tax-free imports.

Long-term economic survival for a settlement this size is however more difficult to envisage. The surrounding desert is beyond man's power to improve. The **Bou Craa mine**, due east of town, holds only 2% of Moroccan phosphate reserves and has been producing less than half what is needed to make it profitable. It is a fully automated process, and like the new fishing port at **Laayoune Beach**, 30 km west of the town on the sea, it is not reliant on the town for survival. The only ancient and productive thing in Laayoune is the lagoon on the river bed to the west of town. Here, in defiance of nature, mullet somehow manage to cross drifting sand dunes to breed each year in the brackish water.

Laayoune's most important function seems to be as a bulwark of Moroccan nationalism. Its population would easily dominate a territory-wide referendum on the future of the Sahara, to Morocco's advantage. The city exists as a powerful symbol of the forces of nationalism in Africa. Here the vocabulary of European imperialism is reworked, and it is Morocco's historical destiny to bring culture and civilization to the south. There is no apparent awareness of how ironical this sounds coming from a nation that recovered its own independence only 30 years ago.

GETTING AROUND

It is easy and more intriguing to walk around Laayoune. The original Spanish town runs along the western lagoon terrace. The new city monuments are uphill to the east and beyond these stretch the neat straight avenues of the Moroccan new town.

The airport, to the east of town, has flights to Agadir, Casablanca, Dakhla, Smara, the Canaries and Tantan, tel 223346. Royal Air Maroc's offices are on Place Bir Anzarane, tel 224077.

Car hire is organized from the unusually helpful Tourist Office. They have a café, and an uninspiring display of crafts for sale in their new offices on Blvd Moulay Abd el Aziz, tel 223375. A landrover with a driver costs 500dh a day and a Renault 4 from 140dh a day with a mileage charge. They can also put you in touch with Saharan Tours, tel 223133, who at the moment concentrate on day trips for excursionists from Agadir and trips to the Canaries, but are planning more enterprising forays.

The Banque Populaire is on the Calle de Sol, and the BMCE is on Place Hassan II.

WHAT TO SEE

The Spanish settlement was built overlooking the riverbed of the Seguiat el Hamra. The terrace above the bed has become the depository for much of the town's rubbish and is constantly worked over by a few goats and rats. Above it stands the closed Spanish cathedral and some curiously shaped houses with white domed roofs which echo traditional designs in their attempt to create cool interior space. Walking uphill you will pass the kasbah-like exterior of the Spanish-built **Parador Hôtel**, which contains by far the most pleasant environment in the town, amongst its small pool and gardens.

Above the hotel spreads the recent Moroccan development of the city, including a massive concrete football stadium, the airport to the south and the new central mosque, finished in 1983. From the mosque, the **lagoon** is seen enclosed by golden sand dunes, providing perhaps the single good view in Laayoune, much reproduced on posters. However entrancing, do not swim in it.

Near the mosque is an astonishing area, Mechouar Square. On one side of the square is a glittering modern glass pavilion, 'The Hall of the Green March', which contains a photographic exhibition of the great event. The rest of the space is designed for the tribes to congregate in to show their allegiance to the king when he comes on a tour of inspection. The slightly alarming portrait of him in dark glasses and black boots with a riding crop which you see on walls all over the country was taken here. The space is unashamedly theatrical and overawing. When necessary the tall Islamic space-age towers floodlight the central area which is ringed by great sweeps of white canvas stretched back in taut cable-held suspension. A midnight descent of helicopter loads of Gulf sheiks seems forever imminent.

WHERE TO STAY

The **Club Med** runs two extremely comfortable hotels which are either booked full for some important national event or near empty. Of the two, the Spanish-built **Parador** has the more tranquil atmosphere. The **Al Massira Khadra** is directed towards tour groups from the Canaries, Agadir and passing cruise liners. Both have cool tiled courtyards, well watered gardens, small but delightfully welcome pools and several restaurants, bars and public rooms. The Parador with its 31 rooms is on Rue Okbaa Iben Nafeh, tel 224500, and charges 400dh for a double, and 9dh if you just want a beer. The Al Massira Khadra on Rue de la Mecque, tel 224225, charges 390dh for a double and 700dh for a suite.

The new **** **Hôtel Nagjir**, with its red and black leather interior design, charges 184dh for a double. There are two two-star hotels. The **El Alia**, which has a restaurant, is the base for Saharan Tours, and is consequently decorated with some interesting camel saddlery in the hall. The dull **Hôtel Lakoura**, on Av. Hassan II, charges 147dh for a double.

If you have arduously driven or bussed down to Laayoune, retreating to a moneyed enclosure may seem self-defeating. The **Hôtel Marhaba**, directly opposite the Aghrab Cinema on Av. Hassan II, is the busiest and most efficient of the cheap hotels, which all charge 30dh for a room. Going towards the river bed there are also the **Sidi Ifni**, the **Farah** and the **Sakia Elhamra**. The **Hôtel Rif** has an excellent position on the terrace edge below the cathedral, but is currently closed, though it may reopen one day.

WHERE TO EAT, DRINK AND DANCE

There are three good cheap Moroccan cafés below the **Aghrab Cinema**, which is incidentally open every day at 7dh a show. Otherwise, go to the **Parador** with its Moroccan restaurant, grills by the pool and its international dining room. The **Al Massira Khadra** has its own restaurants, a night club and glitzy interior bars. The **Nejjib** has just finished building a large downstairs disco and bar, and they have not carried the international bordello taste of the front hall down there.

Routes from Laayoune

Laayoune sits on the main road south. From here, you can continue due south to Boujdor and Ad-Dakhla, the furthest south that tourists are currently allowed to travel. Alternatively, if you have had enough of the unremitting landscape and weather you could take the road to Smara and from there return to Tantan.

South of Laayoune to Boujdor and Ad-Dakhla

Laayoune Beach

The 20 km road between the town and the beach is lined with devices erected to stop the sand dunes drifting on to the road. They are doomed to failure but are constantly assisted by busy mechanical diggers.

Laayoune beach is just to the north of the port complex with its separate phosphate jetty and terminal. There is a single café among the few houses outside the port which can run up any mixture of eggs and tinned food. It seems slightly ridiculous to swim off Laayoune beach which is beside the one area of industrial and domestic effluent in a region otherwise largely devoid of human life. Safe sandy beaches are however rare enough in the Western Sahara.

Boujdor lies 200 km south, on a tarmac road with some surprisingly bumpy patches. Access to the sea is effectively prohibited by a continuous line of savage, crumbling cliffs on which cormorants nest unmolested. Only the sight of an occasional disintegrating shipwreck breaks the disturbing monotony of crossing the desert. Do not get excited by Lemsid, the main attraction marked on the map. It was once graced by the koubba of Sidi Mohammed Bou Gambour but both the settlement and the shrine have been destroyed in recent fighting.

Boujdor

The most memorable feature of Boujdor is the police checks: one outside the town, one in the headquarters and one just as you leave. Do not attempt to speed up the process, even if you have to stop and wake up the friendly guards who manage to doze in huts amid a staggering density of flies. Your mother's maiden name and your whole holiday route may be requested, tea offered and the rival attractions of different Moroccan cities debated. Small gifts of cigarettes and canned drinks are cheerfully accepted in exchange for the tea, and make a welcome distraction from form filling.

Boujdor's most prominent building is its lighthouse, around which cluster a nest of official white buildings and a large military compound of red-coloured buildings. Built by the Portuguese, the lighthouse was dedicated to Henry the Navigator, whose zeal saw the Portuguese past this alarming cape, with its consistently strong northerly winds, by 1434. It was rebuilt in 1965 after the 1957 Liberation Army kidnapped the keepers and damaged the tower.

The civil quarter of Boujdor starts through the arch. It consists of a single street, the Av. Hassan II which leads down to the fishing port. There are almost enough buildings along it to form a respectable village. Of these the café notable for its film posters on the left as you walk down Hassan II is the most sociable place from which to watch village life. Opposite on a street corner is Rashida's café, where a line of cooking pots proffer delicious fish tagine, spiced onions with raisins and hot aromatic vegetable sauces.

The port area marks another brave attempt to harness the natural resources of the Sahara to economic advantage. A fish market, freezing plant and desalination unit are all being built. The local fishermen are still using lines from small offshore boats and dare not venture too far from this one harbour, isolated as it is in an otherwise immense and vicious coast. The area has always been inhabited by successive waves of defeated tribes who have been forced off the inland grazing on to the coast to scrape a despised living from fishing and gathering shellfish. Great prehistoric midden heaps of shells over 3 km long have been found along the coast, strewn with stone tools and fragments of decorated ostrich's eggs.

The beach looks promising but the sand in fact gives away at the shore edge to a rather sharp area of wave-cut rock platform—an ideal place for the amateur rock pool naturalist but not for swimming. Along the shore European camper vans collect in the winter and form ghettos. There are no beds for hire in Boujdor, but if you spend time in the town it would be rare for you not to be offered some form of hospitality.

The road from Boujdor to Ad-Dakhla was completed in February 1988 and is now open for unescorted traffic. The opening of a petrol station at Boujdor was vital in making the road to Ad-Dakhla possible for all normal cars. The route runs through the same grindingly barren, flat Hammada desert. About 147 km out of Boujdor, you leave the coast to follow the valley of the Oued Assag and climb out through some comparatively entertaining low canyons. The monotony of the journey acts powerfully on your imagination. Flaking caps of shell deposits on these low hills can appear as great cascades of molars falling from the crumbling skulls of innumerable decapitated giants. Natural caves have been weathered and cut out by the wind, providing possible refuge from the sun, with their delicate and crumbling pillars. Menhirs have been erected from great slabs of rock by the road construction crews.

Skaymat, marked on all maps and by a profusion of road signs, is eagerly awaited but an enormous disappointment, being no more than a dirt track turning to **Bir Anzarane** and the now disbanded road builders' encampment. The road returns to the coast after Skaymat and there are various adventurous opportunities to clamber down to the sea.

If you want a swim, the obvious place to stop is some 70 km before Ad-Dakhla, where the Moroccan–Mauretanian frontier was for the three years from 1976 to 1979, before Mauretania gave up all interest in the Western Sahara. The frontier lies along a canyon which is easy to walk down. The cliffs of the canyon are white, with pink and yellow striations, and the compressed shell deposit gives the eroded stacks an entrancing uniformity of height. Here, whale bones from past millennia extrude from the tufa, crossed by the delicate contemporary tracks of the desert fox. The canyon descends to the sea, the cliffs growing above you until you arrive at a perfect beach sealed by white cliffs, astonishingly beautiful by day and if you can stay to see the sun sink into the Atlantic, you will not regret any of the distance travelled.

10 km further south, you reach the turning for **Hassi Labyad**. Latest information suggests that at the moment you are only allowed to follow this, the southern, road some 20 km before being politely turned back by soldiers. I was informed that there were still large numbers of Libyan mines in the area. It is not yet possible even to fly to **Lagouiria** on the present Mauretanian frontier, where the monk seal has one of its last secure breeding grounds. From there it would theoretically be possible to cross into Mauretania at Nouadhibou, 'desired of the fox', where an iron ore train heads to Choum and Federik, deep in the Sahara. Mauretanian currency regulations and prices are a discouragement however. Visas cost £50 and even the simplest bedroom £15.

Ad-Dakhla

This town, then known as Villa Cisneros, was founded by the Spanish in 1884, on the end of a long spit of land which runs parallel to the mainland and almost encloses a bay called the Rio de Oro. Now, the military flavour of Ad-Dakhla first assails you at the first checkpoint as you arrive at the neck of the land spit. Armed soldiers guard a system of pillboxes and shelters carved into yellowish white tufa rock. You are led into a crumbling yellow pise hut set into a tufa hill where trenches lead up to a command post. The shelter is decorated with recovered pieces of shrapnel and sturdy benches made from great sea-washed timber baulks. The soldiers preserve the immediacy of the slightly intimidating atmosphere by strictly forbidding photographs, whilst talking of the beauty of Ad-Dakhla as they hand you a glass of mint tea. Your own familiar details are taken, and by now you will have learned not to wince at the harsh description, 'celebateur' if you are unmarried.

At this stage the peninsula is quite wide, and all the way down to the town itself the road follows the inland bay. Beyond the first checkpoint on your left the first of the four inland bays is dramatically revealed to you, a vast expanse of clear tide-washed glistening sand, whilst just to the north of the road moulder a string of largely abandoned tufa barracks and hill forts. As well as the three further bays, the inland sea holds the intriguing 10 km long basalt **island of Herne**, which used to be a flamingo colony. It is thought to be the 'Cerne Island' which Hanno, the Carthaginian admiral, used as a stopping point. As you progress further down the peninsula, the long line of forbidding white cliffs which border the African Saharan shore can be seen across the lagoon-like bay. With its long, flat, empty beaches this bay would make one of the best imaginable areas for sand yachting. Someone ought to establish a workshop fitting wheels on sailboards here.

Shortly before you enter the town you pass **Fisherman's Cove**, an area where you can camp and park. There are no mussels to be gathered here, but plenty of winckles which are best lightly steamed and eaten with pepper. Sole and rouge are caught and local fisherman are free with advice. You can always buy what you fail to catch. Two smaller secluded bays follow, lined with empty pink beach chalets built by the Spanish forces. These include an old naval tapas bar which, according to its fading sign, was known as **F21 at 10'36"**. If the situation does stabilize in the Sahara, these chalets may well be renovated.

The peninsula ends at **Point Durnford**, named after a midshipman on a British marine survey ship which landed here in 1821. Sometimes you can see the masts of a World War I German merchant raider sunk off the point. The town of Ad-Dakhla itself is completely dominated by the military. At the height of the war the airport was constantly buzzing with helicopters, ferrying troops out to isolated posts. The harbour and jetty, where elegant patrol craft are moored, is under the control of the navy. The road into town, bedecked with an arch, passes two large military compounds which are being decorated with stone turrets. The **souks**, to the left and then to the right of the main road are stocked with goods for 'garrison man': awesome quantities of aftershave, thermoses, pen-knives, trinkets, suitcases and tight fitting underpants. The **Spanish Cathedral**, and its garden square where the benches are designed to cast shade, is the only non-military structure of any size upon which it is safe to gaze at and photograph.

GETTING AROUND
In 1988, Ad-Dakhla is as far as the casual visitor can go. No buses operate further south than Laayoune, though there is a steady stream of lorries and grands taxis which cover the route during the night. A place in one of these costs 200dh for the 540 km.

WHERE TO STAY
Facing the airfield there are three hotels, **Pension Atlas**, **Hôtel Oued Eddahab** and **Hôtel 14 Août**. The **Hôtel Bahia**, just behind Bar Juan on the coast road, has 4 or 5 beds to a room. The newest and cleanest place to stay is the **Imlil**, to the right of the main road by the second souk area. All the hotels charge 26dh a bed, and the cost of a room varies with the number of empty beds you are prepared to pay for in exchange for a little privacy. The hotels are all full of soldiers on leave and have a barrack-like atmosphere, sustained by the heavy tread of boots and corridors full of lovat green.

BATHING, EATING AND DRINKING
Water is in short supply in the hotels, and the only practical places in which to wash are the hammams. **Le Bain de la Marché Verte** is in a reddish building, just behind the long white igloo hut off the souk streets, and the **Bath Sahara** beyond that. Both cost 5dh and admit women from 10 to 5, and men from 6 to 10 in the evening.

There are pleasant cafés sprinkled throughout the town. Desert draughts are played in most, usually with stones against bottle tops. A local variation has a dice stick indicating how many squares you can cross in one go. Once you have arrived here, there is not a great deal to do, so sorting out which café to eat in can be prolonged into the major activity of the day. Heavily spiced fresh fish tagine, if you like it, is the very best Ad-Dakhla has to offer.

The **Café Terminus** on the road back out of town has a quieter civilian atmosphere than the town centre. The tables here are full of incessant card games. There is, however, no need to avoid the company of the soldiers who are generally charming and courteous. It is interesting to observe that the formal military salute serves as a mere token introduction to a more effusive system of fraternal greetings which seems to ignore rank completely.

The **Bar Juan**, the only bar in Ad-Dakhla, has a notice forbidding the consumption of beer by Muslims. This only seems to apply to the premises, as there is a constant stream of camouflaged carry-outs. Antonio, the monosyllabic proprietor, is like some titular deity of fortune, having served the legions of Spain, Mauretania, Sahara and Morocco with his blend of fag ash and indifference. Beers are 10dh. Opposite the bar, inside the barrack gates, is an enormous model of a Moroccan teapot.

SHOPPING
The continual odour of cloves is the most distinctive feature of Ad-Dakhla's shops. Here, lengths of blue or black Chinese cotton to shield you from the sun and a few twigs with which to clean your teeth seem more useful than affected. Otherwise you could think about bargaining gently in the evening for tie-dyed cloth or long striped blankets. The shops are run by the Spanish-speaking indigenous population, of which the Delim tribe used to be the most dominant force. A notoriously cynical group, they were much employed by the Spanish. An old Saharan joker would point to a vulture and remark that the Delim must be about to arrive.

East from Laayoune to Smara

Lemsid

Lemsid's spring is one of the most reliable sources of water in the entire province and used to enjoy the holy status of a sanctuary, where feuds were forbidden, where travellers could rest in safety and where alliances could be negotiated. It lies about 19 km east of Laayoune, along a turning signposted Lemsid/Lemseyed, which is overlooked by a stone monument.

Below is the small oasis of Lemsid, surrounded by a few vegetable plots and date palms. Seldom is shade more welcome. Touring visitors are taken here and treated to mint tea and brochettes on the palm matting. Three brown tents have been pitched nearby to form a small theatre for musical entertainments in the evening.

The area scraped clear for the car park is rich in worked flint tools. All over the Western Sahara, the desert wells are situated on vast knapping floors, which have never been adequately studied. The distribution of these Homo Erectus tools, dated 400,000 to 50,000 BC, tells us that the wet period of the Sahara, which produced the rock carvings of elephants, cattle and hunters was an exception. Homo Erectus was as dependent as we are today on the same few sources of water.

Dcheira

Across the river bed, in grim contrast, is the old camp and fortress of Dcheira, a Spanish compound largely deserted but still forbidden to visitors. Here, in January 1958, the Moroccan Liberation Army and the Reguibat and Tekna tribesmen united in an attack which nearly liberated Spanish-held Laayoune. However the Spanish, reinforced by French units from Mauretania, counter-attacked in February and advanced up the Seguiat al Hamra to retake Smara, which they had lost.

Bou Craa

If you want an entirely non-touristic diversion to the frail economic pulse of the Western Sahara, try the phosphate mines of Bou Craa. Along the continuing Smara road, small tin huts can be seen guarding the depressions where barley is cultivated if there has been any rain. Seldom more than 50 metres in diameter, the cultivation and guarding of these precious fertile beds was the task of the Haratine serf caste, who are a mix of negro and the original pre-Berber black inhabitants of the Sahara. They surrendered a large proportion of the crop to their nomadic overlords. Pylons and the phosphate conveyor will also have been marching parallel to the road. The conveyor runs over 100 km to the port, with the belts stretching 8 km between 12 relay stations. 50 km before Bou Craa there is a single café.

The final stretch of road to Bou Craa, after passing the old sand wall defences at the Smara turning, is like one vast expanse of raked gravel. It is as if a megalomaniac Japanese Emperor had turned a whole province into a Japanese garden. You pass four small river beds whose fantastically wind-bent acacia trees serve to prolong the illusion with evidence of bonsai.

Bou Craa is literally a pit, or rather four pits. It is initially slightly disappointing to find that there are not hordes of swarthy miners glistening in the heat as they labour with picks. In fact, miners are rather hard to find. Everybody is a technician operating or trying to mend enormous trucks and diggers built in America.

The miners' compound is very hospitable, and houses two pools, a café, a kitchen and one of Morocco's greatest surprises. Casablanca doesn't even have a zoo but here in the Sahara you find one. Mostly with empty cages, admittedly, but there is an undeniable ape and a reclusive duck. The surrounding trees are fed with water pumped up from subterranean levels and attract a large number of migratory birds. Outside the compound there is a small tradesmen's shanty town, selling to the garrisons of soldiers in the area, passing convoys and miners. It presents a fairly grim scene—old hardboard and corrugated iron stalls and cafés around a yard where a central mass of flies partly obscure an assortment of sheep horns and unsaleable refuse in the middle.

Beyond Bou Craa is a military zone. It is 140 km to **Guelta Zemmour**, an old watering-point of the Reguibat, where there is a Spanish fort and what was the front line with the Polisario. Guelta Zemmour is on the edge of the Tiris desert, one of the driest areas in the whole of the Sahara and also one of the most hotly contested areas in the recent war. In 1981 it witnessed three distinct battles. In March it was besieged by 1500 Polisario. The attack was relaunched in October when the 2000-man Moroccan garrison was overwhelmed. In November a combined Moroccan ground and air assault stormed the post, only to evacuate it a few weeks later as the strategy of the sand wall was enforced.

In good years the Guelta Zemmour water might be available for six months of the year. There are only 24 other waterholes of lesser reliability in the whole vast area to the south. The traditional importance of these is reflected in a precise local vocabulary. *Bir* means well, *sania* a well more than 20 m deep, *hassyn* denotes a permanent supply, *metfia* a natural rock cistern, *ajdir* a rare natural well, *ain* a spring and *daya* a lagoon.

Smara

Smara

Back on the Laayoune–Smara route you return to an area which supports nomadic herds. Surprisingly, the grazing along the banks of the Seguiat al Hamra, which runs between Smara and Laayoune, is the richest in the whole of the Western Sahara. It was continually fought over, but by 1907 the Reguibat tribe had won control. They still possess the land, moving their herds in family groups of two or three tents. The tents are now bright white, to the great advantage of the inhabitants and of aerial surveillance. As you cross the Oued el Kachbyine, a tributary of the Hamra, you enter into an expanse of pinkish yellow rolling hills. 25 km before Smara you pass a range of brown hills, where a saint's koubba nestles in the mountain folds. 5 km before Smara the desert turns black, as the disturbing dead colour of the basalt stones dominates the sand. Passing through the control point you pass the ruins of **Ma el Ainin's palace** to the far left and military barracks to your right. The town is chiefly composed of a broad main street of yellow-painted houses that climbs up a hill whose summit is dominated by tall radar masts.

HISTORY
Smara has always been an area of hidden prestige, and it is ringed by the largest concentration of prehistoric rock carvings in the Western Sahara which have been cut into the dark Devonian stone. It is insolubly linked with its founder, the Blue Sultan and the hero of the resistance against France, Ma el Ainin, literally 'water of the eyes'. Ma el Ainin's father was an Idrissid—a descendant of Morocco's first Islamic ruler, the chief of the Berber Galagnia tribe and the sheikh of a Sufi brotherhood in the desert. By the age of seven Ma el Ainin already knew the whole of the Koran. As an adult he was widely respected for his miraculous powers as well as his 300 scholarly works. Based at first on the Bir Nazarin water hole, he realized that a single focal point was needed to unite the tribes in resistance to the French and Spanish. In 1884 work began at Smara, 'the

rushes', where he moved in 1895 whilst organizing resistance to the French advance from the south. The help Ma el Ainin received from the Sultan included skilled workmen from Fez, Tangier and Tetouan to help in the construction of his kasbah.

The settlement, now all but disappeared, was partially fortified on the terrace of the Oued Seluan. Constructed with dry stone walls, the domes and some interiors were plastered and washed in white or ochre. The dominant building contained the domed central rooms of Ma el Ainin, where he bathed and the council room where he dispensed justice as the Khalifa of the Sultan. These were surrounded by the houses of his four official wives, and ranged beyond were storerooms, cisterns and enclosures for camels and tents. Only the great mosque partially survives. A triple line of bleak black stone arches represent the original interior area of 81 arcades which was in fact never completed. Ma el Ainin also established a Koranic school for boys and a celebrated 450-volume library. Those few documents that survived were apparently removed by the departing Spanish in 1975.

Ma el Ainin died in 1911 in Tiznit where he is buried, his army having been defeated the previous year by the French at Tadla. The jihad was continued by his son El Hiba, but he too suffered defeat at Sidi Bou Othman outside Marrakesh the next year whilst a French force penetrated the Sahara to sack Smara in 1913. The Spanish Legion arrived here in 1934, building their barracks to the east of the ruins. Since then Smara has remained a military focus, and in 1958 and 1979 was at the centre of two fiercely fought battles.

WHAT TO SEE

The town, surrounded by the desert of black stone, shows few traces of the 50 wells dug and the 200 Draa palms planted at Smara by Ma el Ainin. The skyline is dominated by a great red and white communications tower. Smara is almost entirely military and any walk on the edge of the settlement is usually forbidden.

The central yellow arcaded street is pleasant enough and enlivened by camouflaged jeeps, stacked with fuel cans and decorated with whip-cord wirelesses, and veiled passengers nestling carbines in the back. I asked the police if the road east was closed for tourists. They answered, smiling, 'to all the world'.

The ruins are not easily accessible, as a military communications post has been established immediately behind and a collection of damaged tanks and personnel carriers have been piled to one side. The army posts resolutely refused entry on the same day that the *Matin du Sahara* published a special two-page appreciation of the national importance of the site.

Below the ruins on the dry river bed are the remains of a double cupola complex which gave access to the subterranean water flow. Both this and the **koubba** that presides over another well, with its photogenic weathered ancient thorn tree, are in the usual shocking shit-covered state. Their condition was rather unreasonably blamed on the Libyans.

WHERE TO STAY, EAT AND BATHE

The hotels **Erraha** and **Chabab Sakia el Houra** face each other at the intersection on the main street. They both have clean beds and passable water. This is stored in an old oil drum which is topped up daily by a donkey cart which does a morning delivery from the modern pumping and desalination plant. The Erraha has a first-floor sitting room with a view of the street through an ornate grille. Both hotels charge about 20dh a person.

The two best cafés for eating are on the left of the central crossroads. The hammam, with male and female sections, is to the right of the football pitch, left at the crossroads. The arch on the right of the crossroads leads you to the market and eventually to the Place de l'Unité, where the fortress tower for the mosque contradicts the army camps which are decorated with false koubbas and minarets. A garden at the centre of the square is bordered by the **Patisserie de l'Arc en Ciel**, where pilots meet in the evening and enjoy three sorts of fruit juice and waitress service.

TEA WITH THE REGUIBAT

Smara is the chief town of the province, and has schools and two shops which provide everything for the nomad's tent. Whatever the effects of Morocco's investments in the Sahara, the bulk of the indigenous population of this region lead an unchanged existence shepherding their herds of goats between the scant areas of pasture. To witness, even for the space of three cups of tea, the ritual of nomadic life is to be rewarded for the tedium of desert travel. Pick a group of tents from the road to Tantan or back to Laayoune at random, park and walk. The light can make the distance deceptive, but a long walk gives you time to recall the savage actions with which Paul Bowles accredits Reguibat bands.

The tradition of hospitality can usually be invoked by enthusiastic admiration of the herd, but it would be brash and indiscreet to approach too closely without first waiting for the almost inevitable invitation. The tents are called *khaima* and usually measure 4 metres by 12. Their floor is generally of woven reed, but canvas is slowly replacing the patchwork of heavy brown cloth which constituted the fabric for the tents. The walls are often decorated with striped blankets and a few carpets and ornate gilded leatherwork may be kept aside for special occasions. Tents are divided into two equal sections by a cotton screen, often made of hanging clothes, restricting the view between the sexes but not the conversation. In spring, with the surplus of milk, butter fat, congealed inside the skin of a young calf, gently sways on a stick frame. Bowls of milk bobbing with clots of cream and steeped in sugar are offered as well as the ubiquitous tea. Couscous, rice and millet is eaten with meat, but this latter is consumed surprisingly rarely.

To communicate with the Reguibat is to touch the history of the desert. They and the Touareg are the only Berbers who still use the Tifinagh, an ancient alphabet derived from the Phoenicians and incorporating styles from Libyan script, though this is now only used for place names. Questioned about the city of Laayoune, a tribesman replied, 'Yes, Laayoune used to be the grazing ground of the Erkhal family of the Reguibat.' A tree, its branches illustrating the various tribes, clans and families of the Reguibat, may be drawn in the sand for your education. The silence, the smoothing out of the sand, the different ways of measuring achievement.

The road from Smara to Tantan

Petrol must be bought as you leave Smara. The only permanent settlement on the 220 km drive to Tantan is **Abbtih**, 140 km out of Smara, and there is no petrol there. Abbtih consists of four official bungalows, a decaying army fort on the red hills and a mosque with its graveyard. There is no longer a market there, but there are two cafés selling tagines.

LANGUAGE

The official language of Morocco is Arabic, though 40% of the population speak one of the three Berber dialects as their first language. However, Moroccans seem to have a natural linguistic ability, and in the cities they will typically speak Arabic, possibly know one of the three Berber dialects, learn French or Spanish at school and may also know a little English, Dutch or German.

Throughout Morocco you will be understood in all but the most rural areas by speaking French, and may do so with the added confidence that you are both using a second language. Even in the depth of the countryside it is not unusual to find a well-educated school teacher or migrant worker who has returned to his village, and who will be produced to ease communication. Despite the official Arabicization policy, French remains the language of higher education, technology, government and big business.

Spanish is understood and spoken in Spain's old colonial possessions in the far north and south of Morocco, the Riff and the Western Sahara. Hotel porters, guides and hustlers can usually be relied upon to know some English. It is in short easy to travel and communicate in Morocco without learning Arabic. However, if you can learn even a few phrases or greetings you will not only give great pleasure, undoubtedly you will also earn goodwill which may be useful in any transaction or relationship.

Arabic

Classical Arabic and modern Arabic as spoken in Cairo or Mecca are very different from the official language of Morocco—Moghrebi Arabic. That is not to say that those with knowledge of these forms will not be at a great advantage.

Pronunciation

Moghrebi Arabic is a very guttural language, but this does not mean that it should be hard sounding. As a general rule, hard consonants should be pronounced as far back in the throat as possible, thereby softening them slightly. In particular:

'q'	should be pronounced more like a 'k', softened by being vocalized from further back in the throat
'gh'	should sound like a purring 'gr', again from the back of the throat, a hardened French 'r'
'kh'	like a Gaelic 'ch', pronounced from the back of the throat, as in the Scottish 'loch'
'j'	again a softer sound, like the French pronunciation of the letter, as in 'Frère Jacques'
'ai'	should sound like the letter 'i' as you would pronounce it when reciting the alphabet
'ay'	should sound like the letter 'a' as in the recited alphabet

ENGLISH	FRENCH	ARABIC
Basic		
Yes	Oui	Eeyeh/Waha
No	Non	La
Please	S'il vous plaît	Minfadlik
Thank you	Merci	Shokran/Barakalayfik
Good	Bon	Mizeyen
Bad	Mauvais	Meshee mizeyen
Meetings and greetings		
Sir	Monsieur	Si/Sidi
Madam	Madame	Lalla
Hello (informal)	Bonjour	Labes
Hello (formal)	Bonjour	Salam Alaykoom
How are you?	Comment allez vous?	Ooach khbar'ek?
Fine	Ça va bien	Labes
Good morning	Bonjour	Sbah l'khir
Good afternoon	Bon après-midi	Msa l'khir
Goodbye	Au revoir	B'slemah
Good night	Bonne nuit	Leela saieeda
Very basic conversation		
My name is . . .	Je m'appelle . . .	Ismee . . .
What is yours?	Et vous?	Smeetik?
How do you say . . . in Arabic?	Comment dit-on . . . en Arabe?	Keef tkoobal . . . Arbia?
I don't understand	Je ne comprends pas	Ma fhemshi
I don't know	Je ne sais pas	Ma arafshi
Look out!	Attention!	Andak/Roud balek!
Help!	Au Secours!	Ateqq!
Excuse me	Excusez-moi	Smeh lee
Sorry	Pardonnez moi	Asif
Never mind/such is life	C'est la vie	Maalesh
No problem	Pas de problem	Mush mushkillah
I've lost . . .	J'ai perdu . . .	Msha leeya . . .
Travelling and directions		
Train	train	tren
Bus	autobus	l'kar/tobis
Airplane	avion	tayara
Car	voiture	
When is the first/ last/next . . . ?	Quand est-ce que le premier/dernier/prochain . . . part?	Waqtash . . . loowel/l'akher/ lee minbad?
Where is . . . ?	Ou se trouve . . . ?	Fayn kayn . . . ?

. . . a hotel	. . . un hotel	. . . otel/fondouk
. . . a campsite	. . . un camping	. . . mookhaiyem
. . . a restaurant	. . . un restaurant	. . . restaurant
. . . a lavatory	. . . un W.C.	. . . vaysay
. . . the bus station	. . . la gare d'autobus	. . . mahata d'lkeeran
. . . the train station	. . . la gare	. . . mahata d'ltren
. . . a bank	. . . une banque	. . . bank
. . . a chemist	. . . une pharmacie	
. . . a post office	. . . une poste	. . . bousta/barid
ticket	billet	bitaka/beeyay
express	express	mostaajal
fast	rapide	saree
straight	tout droit	neesham
left	à gauche	al leeser
right	à droite	al leemin

At a hotel

I want a room	Je voudrais une chambre	B'gheet beet
Do you have a room?	Est-ce que vous avez une chambre?	Wesh andik wahid beet?
Can I look at it?	Est-ce qu'on peut la voir?	Wesh yimkin nshoof?
Is there . . . ?	Est-ce qu'il y a . . . ?	Wesh kayn . . . ?
Where is . . . ?	Ou se trouve . . . ?	Fayn kayn . . . ?

At a restaurant

The majority of restaurants in Morocco which have menus will have the dishes in French. The following list of foods takes this into account.

What do you have to eat?	Qu'est ce que vous avez à manger?	Ashnoo kane f'l-makla?
. . . to drink?	. . . à boire?	. . . f'l musharoubat?
What is this?	Qu'est ce que c'est?	Shnoo hada?
big	grand	kbir
small	petit	sghrir
plate	assiette	t'b-sil
knife	couteau	moos
fork	fourchette	forsheta
spoon	cuiller	malka
glass	verre	kess
bread	pain	l'hobs
eggs	ouefs	beda
oil	huile	zit
salt	sel	l'melha
pepper	poivre	lebzar
sugar	sucre	azoukar
The bill please	L'addition s'il vous plaît	L'h'seb minfadlik

540

VEGETABLES/SALADS	LEGUMES/SALADES	LKHOUDRA/CHALADA
olive	olive	zitoun
rice	riz	rouz
potatoes (chips)	pommes de terre (frites)	btata (btata mklya)
tomatoes	tomates	matesha
onions	oignons	l'basla
spiced bean soup	harira	harira
mixed salad	salade Marocaine	chalada

MEAT/POULTRY/FISH	VIANDE/VOLAILLE/POISSON	L'HEM/ /L'HOUT
beef	boeuf	l'habra
mutton	mouton	l'houli/kabch
chicken	poulet	djaj
pigeon	pigeon	lehmama
fish	poisson	l'hout
sardines	sardines	sardile

FRUIT	FRUITS	FAKIHA
oranges	oranges	leetcheen
grapes	raisins	l'a'arib
bananas	bananes	banane
almonds	amandes	louze
dates	dattes	tmer
figs	figues	kermus
peaches	pêches	l'khoukh
apricots	abricots	mishmash

DRINKS	BOISSONS	
(mineral) water	eau (minerale)	l'ma (mazdini)
mint tea	thé à la menthe	dial neznaz
(white) coffee	café (au lait)	qahwa (bi lahlib)
beer	bière	birra
wine	vin	sh'rab
orange juice	jus d'orange	leetcheen

Common Moroccan dishes

The Moroccan menu is delicious but not very varied. You will find most of the following on an average tourist menu:

spicy meat stew	Tagine de viande	Tagine l'hem
spicy fish stew	Tagine de poisson	Tagine l'hout
chicken stew with olives and lemon	Tagine de poulet aux olives et citron	Tagine djaj
couscous	couscous	couscous

kebabs	brochettes	katbane/brochette
meatballs	boulettes de viande	kefta
pigeon pie	Pastilla	B'stilla
roast lamb	agneau roti	mechoui

Buying and Bargaining

NUMBERS   NOMBRES

1	١	un	wahed =
2	٢	deux	(class. tnin) jooj =
3	٣	trois	tlata =
4	٤	quatre	arba =
5	٥	cinq	khamsa =
6	٦	six	setta =
7	٧	sept	seba =
8	٨	huit	tmenia =
9	٩	neuf	tse'ud =
10	١٠	dix	achra =
11	١١	onze	hadach =
12	١٢	douze	etnach =
13	١٣	treize	tlatach =
14	١٤	quatorze	arbatach =
15	١٥	quinze	khamstach =
16	١٦	seize	settach =
17	١٧	dix-sept	sebatach =
18	١٨	dix-huit	tmentach =
19	١٩	dix-neuf	tsatach =
20	٢٠	vingt	achrin =
21	٢١	vingt et un	wahed u achrin =
22	٢٢	vingt-deux	tnin u achrin =
30	٣٠	trente	tlatin =
40	٤٠	quarante	arbain =
50	٥٠	cinquante	khamsin =
60	٦٠	soixante	settin =
70	٧٠	soixante-dix	seba'in =
80	٨٠	quatre-vingts	tmanin =
90	٩٠	quatre-vingts-dix	tsa'in =
100	١٠٠	cent	mia =
200	٢٠٠	deux cents	mitin =
300	٣٠٠	trois cents	tlata mia =
400	٤٠٠	quatre cents	arba mia =
1000	١٠٠٠	mille	alef =

How much?	Combien?	Bsh hal?
Too expensive	trop cher	Ghalee bzef
Do you have . . . ?	Est ce que vous vendez . . . ?	Wesh andik . . . ?
I am looking for . . .	Je cherche . . .	Bgheet . . .

something	quelque chose	shihaja
This is no good	Ça ne va pas	Hadee meshee mizeyen
I don't want any	Je n'en veux pas	Mabgheet shee
I've seen it already	Je l'ai déjà vu	Shift ha badas
Okay!	Okay!	Wakha!

BOOK AND RECORD LIST

A interesting selection of available paperback reading on Morocco would include:
Morocco That Was, Walter Harris (Eland Books), £4.95
Lords of the Atlas, Gavin Maxwell (Century), £4.95
Journey into Barbary, Wyndham Lewis (Penguin), £3.95
The Voices of Marrakesh, Elias Canetti (M Boyars), £3.50
Moghreb el Acksa, R. B. Cunnighame Graham (Century), £5.95
Love with a Few Hairs, Mohammed Mrabet (Arena), £2.95
The Spider's House, Paul Bowles (Arena), £4.95

Photographic introductions
Haut Atlas, l'Exil de Pierre, Jelloun and Lafond (Paris 1982)
Morocco, Shirley Kay (Quartet), £7.50
The Moors, Michael Brett (Orbis), £10.00

Biography
Lords of the Atlas, the house of Glouai 1893–1956, Gavin Maxwell (Century)
Black Sunrise, Wifrid Blunt (Methuen)—a biography of Sultan Moulay Ishmael
El Raisuni, Rosita Forbes (Thornton Butterworth).

History
History of North Africa, C. E. Julien, edited by C. C. Stewart, translated by J. Petrie (London 1970)
History of the Maghreb, Abun Nasr (CUP), £8.95
The North African Stones Speak, P. MacKendrick (Croom Helm), £25.00
The Almohad Movement in North Africa, R. Le Tourneau (Princeton, 1969)
Fez in the Age of the Merenids, R. Le Tourneau
Medieval Muslim Government in Barbary, J. F. P. Hopkins (London, 1958)
An Introduction to History, Ibn Khaldoun, edited translation (RKP), £6.95
The Jews of Islam, Bernard Lewis (RKP), £18.95
The Berbers, R. Montagne, (London, 1973)
Arabs and Berbers, edited by E. N. Gellner (London, 1973)
A Survey of North West Africa (OUP, 1959)
An Account of the Empire of Morocco, J. G. Jackson (London, 1968)
Letters from Barbary 1576–1774, J. F. P. Hopkins (OUP, 1982)
Marrakesh, Gaston Deverdun (editions Nord Africaines, 1959)
The Golden trade of the Moors, E. V. Bovill (OUP) £2.95
The Moorish Empire, The Land of the Moors, The Moors—all 3 by Budgett Meakin (London 1899, 1901, 1902)
Morocco, Nevill Barbour (London, 1965)
British policy towards Morocco in the Age of Palmerston, F. R. Fleurnoy (London, 1935)
The Conquest of Morocco, Douglas Porch (Cape), £15.00
The Conquest of the Sahara, Douglas Porch (Cape), £15.00
Rebels in the Rif, David Woolman (OUP)
The Ait Ouraghel of the Moroccan Rif, D. M. Hart

The Ait Atta of Southern Morocco, D. M. Hart (1984)
Resistance in the desert, 1881–1912, Ross E. Dunn (Croom Helm, 1977)
Quaids, Captains and Colons in the Maghrib, K. J. Perkins (New York, 1981)
Man, State and Society in the Contemporary Maghrib, W. Zartman, editor (Pall Mall, 1973)
Politics in North Africa, C. H. Moore (Boston, 1970)
The Commander of the Faithful, J. Waterbury (CUP, New York, 1970)
The Spanish Enclaves in Morocco, Robert Rezitte (1976)
The Western Saharans, background to conflict, V. Thompson and R. Adloff (Croom Helm, 1980).
Western Sahara, roots of a Desert War, Tony Hodges (Croom Helm), £16.95
Spanish Sahara, John Mercer (Allen & Unwin, 1976).

Travel
Their Heads Are Green, Paul Bowles (Peter Owen)
Seventy One Days Camping in Morocco, Lady Grove (Longmans, 1902)
Tafilalet, Walter Harris (Blackwood, 1895)
Adventures in Morocco, Gerhard Rohlfs (Sampson Low, 1895)
Morocco, Edith Wharton (Century), £4.95
Kasbahs of Southern Morocco, Rom Landau (Faber & Faber, 1969)
Travels in Africa and Asia, 1324–54, Ibn Battuta (RKP), £5.95
A Description of Africa, 1600, Leo Africanus (Hakluyt Society edition of 3 volumes published in 1896.
Reconnaissances au Maroc, Charles du Foucauld (Paris, 1884).
El Idrisi, Description of Africa and Spain, (Leyden, 1866).
A Visit to Wazan, R. S. Watson (London, 1880)
Travels across the desert to Morocco 1824–28, R. Caillie (London, 1968)
Morocco that Was, Walter Harris (Eland Books), £4.95
Journey into Barbary, Wyndham Lewis (Penguin), £3.95
The Voices of Marrakesh, Elias Canetti (M. Boyars), £3.50
Moghreb el Acksa, R. B. Cunnighame Graham (Century), £5.95

Anthropology
Ritual and Belief in Morocco, Edward Westermarck (London, 1926)
Women of Marrakesh, 1930–79, Leonara Peets (Hurst), £12.95
Saints of the Atlas, Ernest Gellner (Weidenfeld & Nicolson, 1969)—an academic study of a holy dynasty in the High Atlas
Moroccan Dialogues, Kevin Dwyer (Johns Hopkins, 1982). Recorded conversations from the Souss valley.
Moroccan Islam, Tradition and Society in a pilgrimage centre (Texas, 1976)
A Street in Marrakesh, Middle Eastern Women Speak Out (Texas, 1977)
Saints and Sorcerers, Nina Epton
Doing Daily Battle, interviews with Moroccan women (Women's Press), £5.95
Beyond the Veil, the sexual ideology of Islam, Fatima Mernissi (Al Saqi), £4.95
The House of Si Abd Allah, Henry Munson

Art

The Splendours of Islamic Calligraphy, Abdelkebir Khatabi and Mohammed Sigilmassa (Thames and Hudson, 1976)

Islamic Ornamental design, Claude Hurbert (Faber and Faber, 1980).

La Peinture Marocaine, Mohammed Sigilmassa (Paris, 1972).

Les Arts Traditionnels au Maroc, Mohammed Sigilmassa

Pattern in Islamic Art, D. Wade (London, 1976)

Costumes et Types du Maroc (Paris, 1942)

Bijou Arabes et Berberes du Maroc, Jean Besancenot (Casablanca, 1954)

Le Maroc de Delacroix, Maurice Armand

Islamic Monuments in Morocco, R. B. Parker (Baraka Press, USA)

Terrasse has published detailed studies on the grande Mosque at Taza and the Mosque of Qaraowyn at Fez.

Art of Islam, Language and Meaning, Titus Burkhardt

Moorish Culture in Spain, Titus Burkhardt

Islam

The Koran (Penguin), £6.95 or *The Koran* (OUP), £1.95

Islam, Alfred Guillaume (Penguin).

An Introduction to Sufi doctrine, Titus Burkhardt

Ideas and Realities of Islam (Allen and Unwin), £2.25

Anthology of Islamic Literature, edited by James Kritzeck (Penguin).

The Tijaniyya, Abun Nasr (London, 1966)

Flowers and Birds

Ornithology of the Straits of Gibraltar, Irby (1879)

The Birds of Britain & Europe with North Africa and the Middle East, Heinzel, Fitter & Parslow (Collins), £5.95

Flowers of the Mediterranean, Oleg Polunin and Anthony Huxley (Chatto and Windus), £3.50

Les Oiseaux de la Tingitane, Pineau and Giraud Audine (1979).

Cooking

Fez, Traditional Moroccan Cooking, Z. Guinaudeau, translated by J. E. Harris (J. E. Laurent, Rabat, 1957).

Secrets of Moroccan cooking, Fetouma Benkirane (Sochepress)

Moroccan cooking—the best recipes, Fetouma Benkirane, translated by Shirley Kay (Sochepress).

Moroccan cooking, Robert Carrier.

Recordings of Moroccan music

Brian Jones presents the Pan Pipers of Jajouka (Rolling Stone, London)

Berberes du Maroc (from the far south) (Le Chant du Monde, Paris)

Festival de Marrakesh, Folklore National du Maroc in 2 vols

Music of Morocco (Ethnic Folkways Library, New York)

Ballads and songs of the Sephardic Jews of Tetouan and Tangier (Ethnic Folkways Library, New York)

Rais Lhaj Aomar Ouahrouch—Musique Tachelait (Ocora, Paris)

Lyrichord, 141 Perry Street, New York, NY 10014, publish a good selection including the Rwals from the High Atlas and a collection of Moroccan Sufi Music.

Moroccan fiction in translation
The Sand Child, Tahar ben Jalloun (H. Hamilton)
Heirs To The Past, Mother comes of Age, The Butts—3 novels by Driss Chraibi (Heinemann), £1.50
Messaouda, Abselhake Serhane (Carcanet), £6.95
A Life Full Of Holes, Yesterday and Today, the Jealous Lover, by Larbi Layachi
For Bread Alone, an autobiography, Mohammed Choukri (Arena), £2.95
Love With A Few Hairs, The Lemon, M'Hasish, The Beach Café and The Voice, The Chest, Marriage With Papers, The Big Mirror, Harmless Poisons, Blameless Sins, Look and Move On—10 novels by Mohammed Mrabet, all written in collaboration with and translated by Paul Bowles.
Five Eyes, short stories by Mohammed Mrabet, Mohammed Choukri, Larbi Layachi, Ahmed Yacoubi and Abdesalam Boulaich, and translated by Paul Bowles (Black Sparrow Press). An excellent introduction to Maghrebi fiction, distinguished by its fast narrative and plots, its violence and recurring theme of betrayal by friends and lovers.

European fiction
Under The Sheltering Sky, Paul Bowles (Granada), £1.95—set in the Algerian Sahara
Let It Come Down, Paul Bowles (Arena), £2.95
The Spider's House, Paul Bowles (Arena) £3.95—set in Fez during the struggle for Independence
Collected Stories, Paul Bowles (Black Sparrow Press), £9.00
Points in Time, Paul Bowles (Peter Owen), £6.95
The Forging of a Rebel, Arturo Barea (Flamingo), 3 vols. at £3.95 each—the second vol, *The Track* is set during the Riff war.
In the Lap of the Atlas, Richard Hughes (Chatto), £4.95—set in a fictional Telouet
The Process, Brian Gysin (Abacus), £3.50—set in sixties Tangier.
Enderby, Anthony Burgess (Penguin). £6.95—scenes from Tangier.

Memoirs
Second Son, David Herbert (1972)
All My Sins Remembered, Lord Churchill.
Tangier, a writer's notebook, Angus Stewart (1977)
The Wrong People, Robin Maugham (1970)
Without Stopping, Paul Bowles
Harem, David Edge

INDEX

Note: Page references in *italics* indicate maps; references in **bold** type indicate illustrations.

551